ZAGATSURVEY.

SO-AUU-055

2006

LOS ANGELES
SO. CALIFORNIA
RESTAURANTS

LA Editors: Brad A. Johnson
and Joshua Tompkins

Orange County Editor: Gretchen Kurz

Senior Consulting Editor:
Merrill Shindler

Editor: Randi Gollin

Published and distributed by
ZAGAT SURVEY, LLC
4 Columbus Circle
New York, New York 10019
Tel: 212 977 6000
E-mail: losangeles@zagat.com
Web site: www.zagat.com

Acknowledgments

We thank Kathy Aaronson and Thomas Mohler, Margot Dougherty, Richard Drapkin, Carolyn Heller, Merri Howard, Bob and Marilyn Johnson, Sarah Shindler, Steven Shukow, Alan Tivoli and William Tomicki. We are also grateful to our assistant editor, Emily Parsons, and editorial assistant, Jason Briker, as well as the following members of our staff: Catherine Bigwood, Reni Chin, Larry Cohn, Schuyler Frazier, Jeff Freier, Natalie Lebert, Mike Liao, Dave Makulec, Donna Marino, Robert Poole, Troy Segal, Robert Seixas, Thomas Sheehan, Joshua Siegel, Daniel Simmons, Carla Spartos, Erinn Stivala, Yoji Yamaguchi and Sharon Yates.

Contents

About This Survey 5

What's New 6

Ratings & Symbols 7

Most Popular 9

TOP RATINGS

Food: Cuisines, Features, Locations... 10

Decor: Outdoors, Romance,
Stargazing, Views 15

Service 16

Best Buys 17

RESTAURANT DIRECTORY

Names, Addresses, Phone Numbers,
Web Sites, Ratings and Reviews

• Los Angeles 19

• Orange County............... 249

• Palm Springs & Environs 292

• Santa Barbara & Environs........ 299

**INDEXES TO LOS ANGELES AND
OUTLYING AREAS (Orange County,
Palm Springs, Santa Barbara)**

	LA	OA
Cuisines	204	312
Locations	217	318
Special Features		
Breakfast..........................	232	324
Brunch............................	232	324
Business Dining	232	324
Child-Friendly.....................	233	324
Dancing...........................	235	325
Entertainment.....................	235	325
Garden Dining	236	–
Historic Places	237	325
Hotel Dining	237	326
Late Dining	238	326
Meet for a Drink	239	326
Noteworthy Newcomers	240	327
Offbeat	240	327
Outdoor Dining....................	–	327
People-Watching	241	328
Power Scenes.....................	241	328
Private Rooms	242	328
Romantic Places	243	328
Singles Scenes....................	244	329
Special Occasions	245	329
Trendy............................	245	329

Views   246   330
Visitors on Expense Account   246   330
Waterside   247   331
Winning Wine Lists.   247   331
Worth a Trip   248   331
Wine Chart.   332

About This Survey

Here are the results of our *2006 Los Angeles/So. California Restaurant Survey,* covering 1,968 restaurants as tested, and tasted, by 7,357 local restaurant-goers.

This marks the 26th year that Zagat Survey has reported on the shared experiences of diners like you. What started in 1979 as a hobby involving 200 of our friends rating NYC restaurants has come a long way. Today we have over 250,000 active surveyors and now cover entertaining, golf, hotels, resorts, spas, movies, music, nightlife, shopping and tourist attractions. All of these guides are based on consumer surveys. Our guides are also available on PDAs, cell phones and by subscription at zagat.com, where you can vote and shop as well.

By regularly surveying large numbers of avid customers, we hope to have achieved a uniquely current and reliable guide. This year's participants dined out an average of 3.7 times per week, meaning this *Survey* is based on roughly 1.4 million meals. Of these 7,300 plus surveyors, 47% are women, 53% men; the breakdown by age is 12% in their 20s; 29%, 30s; 21%, 40s; 21%, 50s; and 17%, 60s or above. Our editors have synopsized our surveyors' opinions, with their comments shown in quotation marks. We sincerely thank each of these people; this book is really "theirs."

We are especially grateful to our editors, Brad A. Johnson, food and travel editor for Modern Luxury publications and dining critic for *Angeleno*; Joshua Tompkins, a writer and former editor at *Los Angeles Magazine*; Gretchen Kurz, a journalist who covers the Orange County dining scene for various publications and KRLA radio; and Merrill Shindler, a CBS radio commentator and columnist, food writer, host of *Fine Living: Critics* and Zagat editor for 19 years.

To help guide our readers to the LA area's best meals and best buys, we have prepared a number of lists. See Los Angeles' Most Popular (page 9), Top Ratings (pages 10–16) and Best Buys (page 17). Top Listings for Orange County, Palm Springs and Santa Barbara can be found at the start of those areas' directories. In addition, we have provided 54 handy indexes.

To vote in any of our upcoming *Surveys*, just register at zagat.com. Each participant will receive a free copy of the resulting guide (or a comparable reward). Your comments and even criticisms of this guide are also solicited. There is always room for improvement with your help. Just contact us at losangeles@zagat.com.

New York, NY
October 4, 2005

Nina and Tim Zagat

What's New

Boldface names make the eternally hot LA restaurant scene go round, with established and emerging celeb-chefs vying for diners' attention. But while some of our surveyors may live a life straight out of HBO's *Entourage,* placing buzz above all else, most want great food too, especially since they say 55% of their meals are takeout or eaten out, with restaurant tabs averaging about $31.21 each (a 3.4% increase from last year).

Franc-ly Speaking: LA's love affair with France turned passionate, with the arrival of Brass.-Cap. in Santa Monica; Chameau, a Franco-Moroccan on Fairfax; Ortolan, the chic charmer from ex-L'Orangerie chef Christophe Emé and actress Jeri Ryan; and Tower Bar in the Argyle Hotel.

Prime Time: Never mind that Atkins filed for bankruptcy – Angelenos are riding high on new steakhouses including Boa, from the Katana–Sushi Roku team; Sterling, in the old Sunset Room; and the Lodge Steakhouse, partly owned by the Dolce Group (Dolce; Geisha House). Unique seafood is also luring hipsters, as witnessed by the rebirth of Il Grano; and Providence, which set up shop in the old Patina space.

Tapas Repasts: The gospel of small plates continues to spread, with Suzanne Goin's established trailblazer A.O.C. now this *Survey*'s Most Popular restaurant, and fledgling innovators like Mako and Orris expanding on the theme.

Ring in the New: Tim and Liza Goodell shuttered Aubergine in Newport Beach and opened two hot Hollywood properties, the Dakota steakhouse and tapas titan Meson G. While Wolfgang Puck's Granita in Malibu and Joachim Splichal's Pinot Hollywood folded, Puck's opening a steakhouse inside the Regent Beverly Wilshire and Splichal is replacing Pinot with a new concept restaurant.

The Next Big Thing: Chef Ben Ford (son of Harrison) plans to pull his Ford's Filling Station into Culver City. Mario Batali and Nancy Silverton's mozzarella concept, Osteria del Latte, will arrive in months to come, while Wilshire, from the O-Bar team, is slated to open in Santa Monica.

OC Boom: Though Aubergine closed, the rest of Orange County's culinary scene is thriving. David Wilhelm's Culinary Adventures continues to bring the Left Bank to OC – his latest Gallic homage, Rouge Brasserie, is set to open at press time. And Richard Mead of Sage opened Sage on the Coast in the dazzling new Crystal Cove Promenade.

Los Angeles, CA

Brad A. Johnson
Joshua Tompkins
Gretchen Kurz

Orange County, CA
October 4, 2005

subscribe to zagat.com

Ratings & Symbols

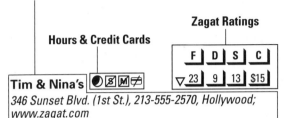

Name, Address, Phone Number & Web Site

Zagat Ratings

Hours & Credit Cards

F	D	S	C
▽ 23	9	13	$15

Tim & Nina's ◑ 🅢 🅜 ⌗

346 Sunset Blvd. (1st St.), 213-555-2570, Hollywood;
www.zagat.com

"Trend"-spotters hail this "high-concept" production on Sunset offering "fantastic" Asian-deli fare that includes "addictive pastrami-uni rolls" and "tantalizing tongue sushi" slathered in "to-die-for hijiki coleslaw"; decor that "hasn't changed since Cecil B. DeMille" was a regular and "reeeal New Yawk–style" service doesn't seem to deter "agents", "stars" and "working gals" hooked on the "delicious sake-celery soda-tinis."

Review, with surveyors' comments in quotes

Top Spots: Places with the highest overall ratings, popularity and importance are listed in BLOCK CAPITAL LETTERS.

Hours: ◑ serves after 11 PM
🅢 closed on Sunday
🅜 closed on Monday

Credit Cards: ⌗ no credit cards accepted

Ratings are on a scale of **0** to **30**. Cost **(C)** reflects our surveyors' estimate of the price of dinner with one drink and tip.

F	Food	D	Decor	S	Service	C	Cost
23		9		13		$15	

0–9 poor to fair   **20–25** very good to excellent
10–15 fair to good   **26–30** extraordinary to perfection
16–19 good to very good   ▽ low response/less reliable

For newcomers or survey write-ins listed without ratings, the price range is indicated as follows:

I	$25 and below	E	$41 to $65
M	$26 to $40	VE	$66 or more

Most Popular

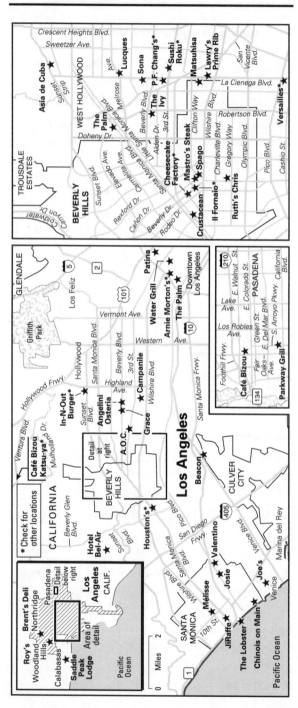

Crescent Heights Blvd.
Sweetzer Ave.

Lucques ★
Sona ★
P.F. Chang's* ★
Sushi Roku* ★
Matsuhisa ★
Lawry's Prime Rib ★

Asia de Cuba ★

WEST HOLLYWOOD

The Palm ★

The Ivy ★

Versailles* ★

Cheesecake Factory* ★
Mastro's Steak ★
Spago ★

Il Fornaio* ★
Crustacean ★
Ruth's Chris ★

TROUSDALE ESTATES

BEVERLY HILLS

GLENDALE

Griffith Park

Patina ★
Water Grill ★
Arnie Morton's* ★
The Palm ★

Downtown Los Angeles

PASADENA

Café Bizou ★
Parkway Grill ★

Campanile ★
Grace ★

In-N-Out Burger* ★
Angelini Osteria ★
A.O.C. ★

Café Bizou ★
Katsu-ya* ★

Los Angeles

Beacon ★

CULVER CITY

* Check for other locations

CALIFORNIA

Detail at right

BEVERLY HILLS

Houston's* ★

Hotel Bel-Air ★

Valentino ★
Josie ★
Joe's ★

Brent's Deli ★
Roy's ★

Mélisse ★

Saddle Peak Lodge ★

JiRaffe ★
The Lobster ★
Chinois on Main ★

Pacific Ocean

SANTA MONICA

Pacific Ocean

LA's Most Popular

Each of our surveyors has been asked to name his or her five favorite restaurants. The following list reflects their choices.

1. A.O.C.
2. Campanile
3. Café Bizou
4. Cheesecake Factory
5. Spago
6. Water Grill
7. Matsuhisa
8. Joe's
9. Mélisse
10. Ruth's Chris
11. P.F. Chang's
12. Angelini Osteria
13. JiRaffe
14. Patina
15. Houston's
16. Ivy
17. Mastro's Steak
18. Chinois on Main
19. Arnie Morton's
20. Crustacean*
21. Lucques
22. Hotel Bel-Air
23. In-N-Out Burger
24. Valentino
25. Josie
26. Lawry's Prime Rib
27. Saddle Peak
28. Asia de Cuba
29. Parkway Grill
30. Roy's*
31. Brent's Deli
32. Il Fornaio
33. Katsu-ya
34. Palm
35. Versailles
36. Sona
37. Grace
38. Sushi Roku
39. Beacon
40. Lobster

It's obvious that many of the restaurants on the above list are among the Los Angeles area's most expensive, but if popularity were calibrated to price, we suspect that a number of other restaurants would join the above ranks. Given the fact that both our surveyors and readers love to discover dining bargains, we have added a list of 80 Best Buys on page 17. These are restaurants that give real quality at extremely reasonable prices.

* Indicates a tie with restaurant above

Top Ratings

Excludes places with low voting or outside of greater LA.

Top Food

28 Mélisse
   Matsuhisa
   Katsu-ya
27 Brandywine
   Nobu Malibu
   Water Grill
   Sushi Sasabune
   Maison Akira
   Hamasaku
   Angelini Osteria
   Sona
   Derek's
   La Cachette
   Josie
   Brent's Deli
   Frenchy's Bistro
   Giorgio Baldi
   Joe's
26 Sweet Lady Jane
   Saddle Peak

   Shiro
   Campanile
   Asanebo
   Sushi Nozawa
   A.O.C.
   Chinois on Main
   Spago
   Capo
   Din Tai Fung
   Takao
   R23
   Belvedere
   Mori Sushi
   JiRaffe
   Orris
   Hump
   Yujean Kang's
   Tuscany
   Mastro's Steak
   Mako

By Cuisine

American (New)
27 Josie
26 Saddle Peak
   Belvedere
   Grace
25 Avenue

American (Traditional)
24 Grill on the Alley
   G. Garvin's
   Morton's
   Lasher's
   Clementine

Asian/Asian Fusion
26 Shiro
   Chinois on Main
   Orris
   Mako
25 Max

Barbecue
23 Dr. Hogly Wogly's
   Phillips BBQ
22 Lucille's BBQ
   Johnny Rebs'
21 Ribs USA

Californian
27 Derek's
   Joe's
26 Campanile
   Spago
   JiRaffe

Caribbean/Cuban
24 Asia de Cuba
22 Versailles
   Cha Cha Cha
21 Prado
   Bamboo

Chinese
26 Din Tai Fung
   Yujean Kang's
24 Sea Harbour
23 Ocean Star
   NBC Seafood

Coffee Shops/Diners
23 Uncle Bill's Pancake
21 Cora's Coffee
19 Pie 'N Burger
   Duke's Coffee
18 Kate Mantilini

Top Food

Continental
27 Brandywine
25 Dal Rae
   Mandevilla
24 Raymond
23 Fins

Delis
27 Brent's Deli
24 Langer's Deli
22 Johnnie's Pastrami
20 Barney Greengrass
   Nate 'n Al's

Desserts/Bakeries
26 Sweet Lady Jane
   Spago
20 Toast
   Misto Caffé
   Babalu

Dim Sum
24 Sea Harbor
23 Ocean Star
   NBC Seafood
22 Empress Pavilion
   Ocean Seafood

Eclectic
25 Chez Melange
24 Chaya Brasserie
   Depot
23 Chaya Venice
   Nook Bistro

French
28 Mélisse
27 Maison Akira
   Derek's
26 Patina
   Lucques

French (Bistro)
27 Frenchy's Bistro
26 Julienne
   Mistral
24 Pinot Bistro
   Mimosa

Greek
23 Papadakis Taverna
   Papa Cristo's
22 Taverna Tony
   Great Greek
21 Sofi

Hamburgers
24 In-N-Out Burger
23 Father's Office
22 Counter
   Tommy's
   Apple Pan

Indian
26 Addi's Tandoor
25 Bombay Cafe
22 Surya India
   Akbar
   Nawab of India

Italian
27 Angelini Osteria
   Giorgio Baldi
26 Capo
   Tuscany
   Valentino

Japanese
28 Matsuhisa
   Katsu-ya
27 Nobu Malibu
   Sushi Sasabune
   Hamasaku

Mediterranean
26 Campanile
   A.O.C.
25 Christine
24 Gardens
23 Little Door

Mexican
25 Lotería!
24 Tlapazola Grill
23 La Serenata Gourmet
22 Guelaguetza
   El Tepeyac

Middle Eastern
26 Sunnin
24 Zankou Chicken
23 Carousel
22 Carnival
   Shaherzad

Pizza
26 Spago
   Parkway Grill
24 Abbot's Pizza
   Village Pizzeria
   Casa Bianca

Top Food

Seafood
27 Water Grill
24 Sea Harbour
Il Grano
23 Malibu Seafood
Ocean Ave.

Small Plates
26 A.O.C.
Orris
Mako
23 Meson G
Father's Office

South American
24 Mario's Peruvian
23 Carlitos Gardel
21 Green Field Churr.
20 Café Brasil
19 El Pollo Inka

Southern/Cajun
23 Les Sisters
22 Lucille's BBQ
Harold & Belle's
Johnny Rebs'
Gumbo Pot

Steakhouses
26 Mastro's Steak
25 Arnie Morton's
Ruth's Chris
Arroyo Chop Hse.
Lawry's Prime Rib

Thai
24 Saladang
23 Palms Thai
21 Rambutan Thai
Talesai
Tuk Tuk Thai

Vegetarian/Health Food
21 Inn of Seventh Ray
20 Urth Caffé
19 A Votre Sante
Real Food Daily
Jack Sprat's

Vietnamese
24 Golden Deli
Crustacean
Michelia
21 Pho 79
Gingergrass

By Special Feature

Breakfast
25 Lotería!
23 Pacific Dining Car
22 Griddle Cafe
Lemon Moon Cafe
La Terza

Brunch
27 Joe's
26 Campanile
24 Ritz Huntington
Jer-ne
23 Röckenwagner

Business Dining
28 Mélisse
27 Water Grill
Derek's
La Cachette
Josie

Garden Dining
26 Saddle Peak
Spago
25 Hotel Bel-Air
Michael's
24 Bastide

Hotel Dining
26 Belvedere
Peninsula, BH
Diaghilev
Wyndham Bel Age
25 Hotel Bel-Air
Hotel Bel-Air
Chez Melange
Palos Verdes Inn
24 Gardens
Four Seasons

Late Dining
24 Casa Bianca
Katana
Jer-ne
23 Dan Tana's
Chaya Venice

Lunch
28 Matsuhisa
Katsu-ya
27 Brandywine
Water Grill
Sushi Sasabune

subscribe to zagat.com

Top Food

Newcomers/Rated

26 Orris
25 Avenue
24 Chameau
23 Meson G
22 La Terza

Other Major Arrivals

Dakota
Lodge Steak
Ortolan
Providence
Tower Bar

People-Watching

28 Katsu-ya
26 A.O.C.
Spago
Mastro's Steak
24 Grill on the Alley

Power Scenes

28 Matsuhisa
27 Water Grill
Hamasaku
Sona
La Cachette

Trendy

28 Katsu-ya
27 Nobu Malibu
Sona
Giorgio Baldi
26 R23

Winning Wine List

28 Mélisse
27 Water Grill
26 Campanile
A.O.C.
Valentino

Worth a Trip

27 Nobu Malibu
   Malibu
Frenchy's Bistro
   Long Beach
26 Saddle Peak
   Calabasas
Din Tai Fung
   Arcadia
Tuscany
   Westlake Village

By Location

Beverly Boulevard

27 Angelini Osteria
26 Grace
24 JAR
Mimosa
22 Pastis

Beverly Center/Cedars

25 Arnie Morton's
Locanda Veneta
24 Hirozen
Michelia
22 Akbar

Beverly Hills

26 Spago
Belvedere
Mastro's Steak
Mako
25 Ruth's Chris

Brentwood

26 Takao
25 Vincenti
24 Toscana
Divino
23 Pizzicotto

Chinatown

23 Yang Chow
22 Empress Pavilion
Ocean Seafood
21 Pho 79
Mandarin Deli

Downtown

27 Water Grill
26 Patina
25 Arnie Morton's
24 Langer's Deli
Noé

Fairfax

25 Lotería!
24 Chameau
23 Nyala Ethiopian
22 Gumbo Pot
21 California Chicken

Hollywood

23 Pace
Off Vine
Carousel
22 Griddle Cafe
Ammo

Top Food

La Brea
26 Campanile
22 Ca'Brea
   Sonora Cafe
20 Luna Park
   Pink's Chili Dogs

La Cienega Corridor
28 Matsuhisa
27 Sona
25 L'Orangerie
   Lawry's Prime Rib
23 Koi

Long Beach
27 Frenchy's Bistro
26 Sunnin
25 Christy's
24 555 East
   Lasher's

Malibu
27 Nobu Malibu
23 Malibu Seafood
22 Allegria
   Taverna Tony
   Guido's

Melrose
26 Sweet Lady Jane
   Lucques
25 Table 8
   Citrine
24 Bastide

Pasadena/South Pasadena
27 Maison Akira
   Derek's
26 Shiro
   Yujean Kang's
   Parkway Grill

San Fernando Valley
28 Katsu-ya
27 Brandywine
   Brent's Deli
26 Saddle Peak
   Asanebo

San Gabriel Valley
25 Dal Rae
24 Sea Harbour
   Golden Deli
23 Ocean Star
   NBC Seafood

Santa Monica
28 Mélisse
27 Josie
   Giorgio Baldi
26 Chinois on Main
   Capo

Silver Lake/Los Feliz
24 Blair's
23 Il Capriccio
   Farfalla Trattoria
22 Cobras & Matadors
   Cafe Stella

South Bay
26 Gina Lee's Bistro
   Addi's Tandoor
25 Avenue
   Chez Melange
   Fleming Prime Steak

Sunset Strip
24 Asia de Cuba
   Katana
23 Norman's
   Boa
22 Le Dome

Third Street
26 A.O.C.
24 G. Garvin's
23 Little Door
   Sushi Roku
22 La Terza

Venice
27 Joe's
24 Abbot's Pizza
23 Chaya Venice
22 Hama Sushi
21 Wabi-Sabi

West Hollywood
26 Diaghilev
25 Madeo
24 Palm
   Chaya Brasserie
23 Dan Tana's

West LA
27 Sushi Sasabune
   Hamasaku
26 Mori Sushi
   Orris
25 Bombay Cafe

Top Decor

28 Hotel Bel-Air
   Diaghilev
   Cicada
   L'Orangerie
   Belvedere
27 Inn of Seventh Ray
   Yamashiro
   Geoffrey's
   La Boheme
   Madison
   Saddle Peak
26 Crustacean
   Gardens
   Asia de Cuba
   O-Bar
   Oceanfront
   One Pico
   Il Cielo
   Koi
   Polo Lounge

   Ritz Huntington
   Bastide
   Mélisse
   Meson G
25 Little Door
   Katana
   Grace
   Thousand Cranes
   Michael's
   Spago
   Geisha House
   Norman's
   Vibrato
   Getty Center
   Chateau Marmont
   Sky Room*
   Bistro Gdn./Coldwater
   Dar Maghreb
   Tantra
   Firefly

Outdoors

Asia de Cuba
Bastide
blue on blue
Chateau Marmont
Hotel Bel-Air

Little Door
Noé
Polo Lounge
Saddle Peak
Whist

Romance

Chateau Marmont
Diaghilev
Gardens
Il Grano
L'Orangerie

Lucques
Patina
Saddle Peak
Sona
Valentino

Stargazing

Abbey
Geisha House
Grill on the Alley
Ivy
Katana

Koi
Mastro's Steak
Mr. Chow
Ortolan
Spago

Views

Asia de Cuba
Geoffrey's
Lobster
Moonshadows
Oceanfront

One Pico
Reel Inn
Tower Bar
Windows
Yamashiro

Top Service

28 Diaghilev
27 Belvedere
   Hotel Bel-Air
26 Mélisse
   Sona
   Brandywine
   Bastide
   L'Orangerie
   Gardens
25 Water Grill
   Papadakis Taverna
   Valentino
   Mistral
   Saddle Peak
   Derek's
   Parkway Grill
   Josie
   Lasher's
   Patina
   Michael's

   Grace
24 La Cachette
   Ritz Huntington
   Dal Rae
   Lawry's Prime Rib
   Noé
   Spago
   Cicada
   Thousand Cranes
   Morton's
   Leila's
   Mama D's
   Mako
   Frenchy's Bistro
   555 East
   Raymond
   JiRaffe
   Spumante
   Campanile
   Arnie Morton's

Best Buys

Top Bangs for the Buck

1. In-N-Out Burger
2. Tommy's
3. Noah's NY Bagels
4. Lamonica's NY Pizza
5. Astro Burger
6. Baja Fresh Mexican
7. Pink's Chili Dogs
8. Stand
9. Golden Deli
10. Poquito Más
11. Apple Pan
12. Jody Maroni's
13. Sandbag Sandwiches
14. Asahi Ramen
15. Village Pizzeria
16. Philippe the Original
17. Abbot's Pizza
18. Sharky's Mexican
19. Zankou Chicken
20. California Chicken
21. Uncle Bill's Pancake
22. Maxwell's Cafe
23. El Tepeyac
24. Barney's Hamburgers
25. Lotería!
26. Mulberry St. Pizzeria
27. Cafe 50's
28. Counter
29. La Salsa
30. Falafel King
31. Sunnin
32. Johnny Rockets
33. Martha's 22nd St.
34. Cha Cha Chicken
35. Sweet Lady Jane
36. Pho 79
37. Pho Café
38. Rae's
39. Johnnie's Pastrami
40. Feast from the East

Other Good Values

Alejo's
BCD Tofu
Beacon
Brent's Deli
Café Bizou
Casa Bianca
Clay Pit
Clementine
Cole's P.E. Buffet
Doughboys
El Pollo Inka
Gorikee
Griddle Cafe
Guelaguetza
Hide Sushi
Hop Li
Johnny Rebs'
La Bottega Marino
La Serenata/Garibaldi
Lemon Moon Cafe
Le Pain Quotidien
Le Petit Bistro
Lilly's French Cafe
Luna Park
Mandarette
Minibar
Monsieur Marcel
Newsroom Café
Nook Bistro
Orris
Pace
Pastis
Porta Via
Sawtelle Kitchen
Soot Bull Jeep
Spark Woodfire Grill
Standard
Taylor's Steak
Toast
Tuk Tuk Thai

Los Angeles
Restaurant Directory

Abbey, The ◗   17 | 23 | 15 | $24
*692 N. Robertson Blvd. (Santa Monica Blvd.), West Hollywood,
310-289-8410; www.abbeyfoodandbar.com*
"The experience is a religious one" vow disciples of this "delightful"
WeHo hot spot, a "gay Disneyland" that's "calm in the day and
jumping at night"; the "inventive" American cuisine is "surprisingly
good", "but the reason to go here is the scene", so "ask the
bartender to create something special", then "feast your eyes
on the crowd" and the "pretty boy" staff.

Abbot's Pizza   24 | 7 | 15 | $11
*1811 Pico Blvd. (18th St.), Santa Monica, 310-314-2777
1407 Abbot Kinney Blvd. (California Ave.), Venice, 310-396-7334*
Feels like that "little pizza joint you dream of finding" agree students
and wallet-watchers who delight in this Santa Monica–Venice
twosome's "delectable" pies, "generous slices" and air of "fun
trashiness"; in addition to "gourmet toppings", the "unique bagel
crust" "variations equally beguile", while "new combinations
surprise and satisfy"; still, the "sparse decor and sparser service"
make it "strictly take-home" for many.

ABC Seafood   20 | 10 | 14 | $21
205 Ord St. (New High St.), Chinatown, 213-680-2887
Bring a "large group or out-of-town guests" and "do the dim sum"
declare devotees of this "massive" Chinatown "standby" that
offers an "interesting assortment" of "seafood specialties" at a
"reasonable cost"; but the less-spellbound snap that it's "gone
downhill"– perhaps the "glory days are gone" for this "old dame."

Absolutely Phobulous 🈺   – | – | – | I
*350 N. La Cienega Blvd. (Beverly Blvd.), West Hollywood, 310-360-3930;
www.abpho.com*
Despite its cringe-worthy name, this minimalist cafe on La Cienega
offers affordable 'Vietnamese cuisine with a modern sensibility',
which translates into steaming bowls of pho that can be made low-
carb (fewer noodles, more protein), along with a wide assortment
of exotic rolls and savory crêpes.

Adagio Ⓜ   ▽ 23 | 15 | 23 | $34
*22841 Ventura Blvd. (Fallbrook Ave.), Woodland Hills,
818-225-0533*
The "always accommodating owner" "makes you feel like you've
come home for dinner" (he even "knows everyone by name") at
this "small, quaint, lovely" Northern Italian "neighborhood place"
in Woodland Hills; from the "excellent" osso buco to the "cooked-
to-order" pasta, "we've never had less than a great meal" reveal
loyalists, who also relish the "unrushed" tempo of the service.

Addi's Tandoor   26 | 18 | 21 | $24
*800 W. Torrance Blvd. (bet. PCH & Prospect Ave.), Redondo Beach,
310-540-1616; www.addistandoor.com*
"An intimate place to come for a joyous experience" exult
enthusiasts of this Redondo Beach "destination" specializing
in Indian dishes "full of flavor" from "gracious" owner Addi
DeCosta's Goan homeland; heat-seekers praise the "fiery, palate-
dissolving" sauces (the "responsive kitchen" can "spice to order")
while others tout the "delicious, authentic fare", including the
"extensive vegetarian" selection and "large array of breads."

Admiral Risty   22 | 19 | 21 | $38
31250 Palos Verdes Dr. W. (Hawthorne Blvd.), Rancho Palos Verdes, 310-377-0050; www.admiral-risty.com
"Truly a classic", this "long-established" surf 'n' turf "favorite" of the "posh" "PV crowd" lures locals with its "glorious view of the ocean", "lively bar scene" and "wonderful service"; don't expect anything "cutting-edge, just good old comfort food" and "delicious side dishes"; if a few find the menu "unimaginative", most maintain if "you come during sunset, you won't be disappointed."

Adobe Cantina   ▽ 17 | 17 | 17 | $20
29100 Agoura Rd. (Kanan Rd.), Agoura Hills, 818-991-3474
"Happy-hour heaven" agree amigos of this Agoura Hills cantina, giving a thumbs up to the "killer Cadillac margaritas", "tasty" guacamole and "plentiful" portions of "homestyle Mexican" food; grab a seat on one of the "pleasant patios" on a "warm summer's eve" and "relax with your friends"; if prickly sorts find the fare "unpredictable", adobe advocates attest it's "exactly what you'd expect from a casual place" like this.

Ago ●   22 | 21 | 20 | $49
8478 Melrose Ave. (La Cienega Blvd.), Los Angeles, 323-655-6333
"Be sure to drive your showiest car" to this "industry hot spot", co-owned by Robert De Niro, among other boldface names, where "LA's most beautiful people", "power players" and "looky-loos" "care about who's around" ("A- and B-list celebrity sightings") and "how they look eating" the "authentic, lovely" Tuscan-accented Italian fare; but the less-starry-eyed pout that "on the 'in' nights" the "huge" West "Holly–scene" "overshadows the food", which can be served with a "side of attitude."

Ahi Sushi   ▽ 21 | 15 | 18 | $30
12915 Ventura Blvd. (Coldwater Canyon Ave.), Studio City, 818-981-0277; www.ahisushi.com
"Another hit in the Valley" vow vaunters of this "well-kept sushi secret" in Studio City offering a "good variety of entrees" and "incredibly fresh fish", including its namesake tuna; still, the put-off pan the "small servings" and find it a tad "too expensive."

Aioli   19 | 20 | 19 | $32
1261 Cabrillo Ave. (Torrance Blvd.), Torrance, 310-320-9200
This "friendly", "relaxing" Torrance standby "full of businessmen" from nearby Honda and Toyota dealerships gets motors purring with its "delicious" Mediterranean dishes cooked with a "California flair" and even offers a "tapas bar for when you don't have time for the full adventure"; but others deride it as "wildly inconsistent" with "indifferent" service, harrumphing it's "not what it used to be."

Ajisen Ramen   ▽ 15 | 13 | 14 | $12
Hilton Plaza, 227 W. Valley Blvd. (S. Del Mar Ave.), San Gabriel, 626-281-8388
"Ramen, ramen and ramen – it's their specialty and they do it well" at this "tiny" San Gabriel offshoot of the ubiquitous Asian chain; the "creative, unique" noodles are their "main game", but they also serve up "satisfying curry and fried rice dishes", all delivered "quickly" by a "friendly" staff; still, it's not everybody's bowl of carbs – the less-enthused muse it's "found a way to entrance the masses with above average, but not spectacular, food."

Akbar Cuisine of India   22 | 15 | 19 | $24
1101 Aviation Blvd. (Prospect Ave.), Hermosa Beach, 310-937-3800
8514 W. Third St. (La Cienega Blvd.), Los Angeles, 310-652-7755
3115 Washington Blvd. (Yale Ave.), Marina del Rey, 310-574-0666
44 N. Fair Oaks Ave. (Union St.), Pasadena, 626-577-9916
2627 Wilshire Blvd. (26th St.), Santa Monica, 310-586-7469
www.akbarcuisineofindia.com
"Not dumbed down" for "American palates", this "cozy" chain serves "fragrant", "progressive" Indian dishes that may even "bring a sweat to your brow"; even more "mind-boggling", the "owner is dedicated to pairing the food" with an "impressive" wine list "instead of beer"; if a few tikka-ed-off feel the cuisine's "lost its original spice", insiders insist it turns nonbelievers into "converts."

Akwa   21 | 24 | 19 | $45
1413 Fifth St. (Santa Monica Blvd.), Santa Monica, 310-656-9688
There's "something for everybody" at this "great space" in SM serving "quality sushi" in a "Zen-like atmosphere downstairs" and "artfully displayed" New American–Asian fusion plus "desserts worth the extra spinning classes" upstairs, offset by a "happening" rooftop patio; still, foes huff it "can't make up its mind" what it wants to be and deem the service "scattered."

A La Tarte Bistrot ⓜ   ∇ 18 | 17 | 13 | $21
1037 Swarthmore Ave. (bet. Monument St. & Sunset Blvd.),
Pacific Palisades, 310-459-6635
"Sit on the sidewalk" on Sundays and watch the "farmer's market unfold" "outside the front door" of this "civilized" Parisian cafe in Pacific Palisades; it's "excellent for breakfast pastries" and "heavenly desserts" and "*très* convenient" for a weekday lunch of "delish quiche" and "standard light bistro fare"; if the tart-tongued snap service can be "snooty", *amis* shrug "they are very French, so you must behave."

Alcove   – | – | – | I
1929 Hillhurst Ave. (Franklin Ave.), Los Feliz, 323-644-0100
The destination of choice for the hipoisie of Los Feliz and Silver Lake, this mostly alfresco dining patio built around a California bungalow just down the hill from Griffith Park offers affordable old-fashioned American fare at lunch and dinner, but it's breakfast that draws the biggest crowds.

Alegria   21 | 20 | 20 | $28
115 Pine Ave. (bet. B'way & 1st St.), Long Beach, 562-436-3388;
www.alegriacocinalatina.com
Share "tasty towers of tapas" and "sinfully sipable sangria" at this Nuevo Latino restaurant/club in Long Beach done up with "festive" Dali-style murals; "it's a great place to do a little flamenco dancing" or indulge in "people-watching" at the "beautiful bar"; while it may be "loud", you can always bust a move to the music "if you want to get to know your date . . ."; N.B. not related to the Allegria in Malibu.

Alejo's   20 | 8 | 17 | $18
4002 Lincoln Blvd. (bet. Maxella Ave. & Washington Blvd.),
Marina del Rey, 310-822-0095
8343 Lincoln Blvd. (84th St.), Westchester, 310-670-6677
"Mamma mia! stop, look, inhale!" – no "worries about vampires" after a meal at this "bustling" duo known for its "garlicky" Italian

at "rock-bottom prices", "zero ambiance" and "great brown bag policy" at the Marina del Rey mini-mall location (Westchester serves wine and beer); "you can't go wrong with the spaghetti and meatballs", so "take the kids" or order takeout – either way, it's "worth the wait."

Alessio Ristorante Italiano
19 | 22 | 18 | $35

9725 Reseda Blvd. (Superior Ave.), Northridge, 818-709-8393
Platt Vlg., 6428 Platt Ave. (Victory Blvd.), West Hills, 818-710-0270
3731 E. Thousand Oaks Blvd. (Marmon Ave.), Westlake Village, 805-557-0565
www.alessiorestaurant.com

"Centered in the West San Fernando Valley and Ventura counties", this "beautiful" trio tempts locals with "nicely prepared and presented Italian" fare, including thin-crust pizza, all served by a "caring staff"; but disappointed diners declare that the "food and service don't measure up to the decor" and find the "music from the bar area overpowering", concluding it's "got great potential", "but it's not there yet."

Alessi Ristorante & Bar
▽ 20 | 18 | 21 | $32

6602 Melrose Ave. (Highland Ave.), Los Angeles, 323-935-1197

"They treat you like family" at this "stylish" "local neighborhood joint" on Melrose at Highland where "thin-crust pizzas are the specialty", the Italian fare is "great for a group (love the family platters)" and "prices are reasonable"; if a few feel "something is missing", others "go back often", particularly for lunch and the occasional wine tasting.

Allegria
22 | 18 | 19 | $32

22821 PCH (south of Malibu Pier), Malibu, 310-456-3132;
www.allegriamalibu.com

"Feels like you're coming home to the Tuscan villa you'd love to own" declare daydreamers who "cozy" up to this "comfortable" Italian "favorite"; diners relish the "star sightings" as much as the "out-of-this-world pasta", noting it's "our 'go-to' in Malibu"; but a handful harrumph the service "varies" from "attentive" to "spotty" and warn "forget about those booths at the front unless you got an Oscar last year."

All India Café
21 | 13 | 17 | $20

39 S. Fair Oaks Ave. (bet. Colorado Blvd. & Green St.), Pasadena, 626-440-0309
Santa Monica Plaza, 12113 Santa Monica Blvd. (Bundy Dr.), West LA, 310-442-5250
www.allindiacafe.com

With dishes "from different regions of India", this "perennial favorite" in Pasadena and West LA "goes beyond the usual", offering "real aficionados" "delicately spiced" "ethnic comfort food" with "bright, wonderful flavors"; if few deride the "erratic service" and "spartan room in need of warming up", devotees divulge that the "to-die-for chicken tikka" makes up for any lapses.

Amalfi
19 | 19 | 17 | $34

143 N. La Brea Ave. (bet. Beverly Blvd. & 1st St.), Los Angeles, 323-938-2504

A "pretty crowd" coasts over to this "romantic" yet "family-friendly" "funky Italian" on La Brea's Restaurant Row for "tasty fare in normal-sized portions, thank goodness"; with the "always excellent Acme Sketch Comedy Theatre next door (they're connected" via same ownership) it's also a "late-night hangout" for "post-show pizza and pasta cravings"; still, critics find the food "reliable, not exciting."

Ami   – | – | – | M |
1051 Broxton Ave. (Weyburn Ave.), Westwood, 310-209-1994
Situated on a tree-lined street in Westwood Village, this modern, two-floor sushi bar with an industrial interior and outdoor patio serves up an inexpensive menu of special rolls; the thought-provoking names may give you pause as they range from the exotic, like Albacore Jungle, to the disturbing, like Heart Attack Roll; good thing UCLA Med is down the street.

Amici   21 | 17 | 20 | $38 |
(aka Trattoria Amici)
Beverly Terrace Hotel, 469 N. Doheny Dr. (Santa Monica Blvd.), Beverly Hills, 310-858-0271
2538 San Vicente Blvd. (26th St.), Brentwood, 310-260-4900
www.tamici.com
"What's not to love about" this "charming" trattoria, a "hangout" for "Beverly Hills' middle-agers and nouveau agents" that's "small in room, but big in quality" and its newer Brentwood sibling, a suburban "oasis" with the feel of an "Italian mom's kitchen"; "sit under the stars" and "feast on endless bowls" of pasta served by a "caring" staff with "real Italian accents (or they are all good actors")"; still, the sound-sensitive suggest "go early" because it gets "very noisy on busy nights."

Ammo   22 | 18 | 18 | $33 |
1155 N. Highland Ave. (bet. Fountain Ave. & Santa Monica Blvd.), Hollywood, 323-871-2666; www.ammocafe.com
With "warm" oak panels, green booths and a "recently expanded interior, this innovative" Californian "wins points for always trying to up the ante" attest admirers who give this "hipster-gourmet" and its "well-informed staff" a round of applause; chef Amy Sweeney lures the "working Hollywood crowd" that "dominates at lunch" with "unique, fresh" "comfort fare" "prepared with passion" and "brown rice that's simplistic perfection."

Amori ⓜ   ▽ 24 | 21 | 26 | $37 |
110 E. Lemon Dr. (Myrtle Ave.), Monrovia, 626-358-1908
"What a find!" assert sleuthers who track down this "hidden gem in Monrovia" for "delicious" Californian cuisine with a "witty", "original French" and Asian "touch" created by ex Scampi/ex Shiro chef Pedro Simental; the "wonderful choices", "attentive service" and "small but sweet setting", including a patio and streetside seating, exalt the "exceptional" experience – it's a "true winner."

Angeli Caffe ⓜ   22 | 14 | 19 | $30 |
7274 Melrose Ave. (Poinsettia Pl.), Los Angeles, 323-936-9086
The "Woody Guthrie of LA Italian cooking", "inventive" Slow Food champion Evan Kleiman "delivers on" her "rustic, simple approach", "whipping up" "heavenly" pasta, "ethereal" gnocchi, "very flavorful tomato-rich dishes" and "addictive bread" ("carb heaven") at this "cozy" "off-the-radar" Melrose nook; but what really "keeps us coming back" to this "friendly" "stalwart" muse admirers are the "Thursday family-style dinner extravaganzas, a special treat" and a "fabulous value."

ANGELINI OSTERIA Ⓜ | 27 | 17 | 22 | $46 |
7313 Beverly Blvd. (Poinsettia Pl.), Los Angeles, 323-297-0070
At his "wildly popular" Beverly Boulevard osteria, "hospitable" chef-owner Gino Angelini of La Terza proffers a "fantastic" Italian "feast for the senses" that "puts you back in Rome"; dishes like the "perfectly prepared" lasagna are so "splendid" "you'll remember your meal long after you dine" – "if only mama's cooking was as good"; sure, it's a "sardinelike" scenario, but that just enhances the "noisy, alive" "authentic feel."

Angelique Cafe Ⓢ | 22 | 15 | 17 | $18 |
840 S. Spring St. (bet. 8th & 9th Sts.), Downtown, 213-623-8698;
www.angeliquecafe.com
"Lunch is the bomb" at this "bustling", "boho cool" Fashion District "find" where the "excellent salads" and "inexpensive" bistro standards allow you to "eat as the French do daily"; "tucked" on a Brie-shaped triangular "wedge" in the "middle of an oddball Downtown area", the "unique space" "transports you to the Left Bank", though sidewalk habitués confide the "roaring buses may bring you back."

Anna's | 16 | 14 | 18 | $23 |
10929 W. Pico Blvd. (bet. Veteran Ave. & Westwood Blvd.), West LA,
310-474-0102; www.annaitalian.com
"When the moon hits your eye like a big pizza pie, go to" this "worn but dependable" West LA bastion of "delightfully old-fashioned fare" that still sports a "red leather booth" look that "hasn't changed in years"; "you're talkin' red-sauce, family-style Italian", doled out by an "ancient staff right out of central casting"; but it's a different scene to cynics who consider the "room rather shopworn" and the "menu tired."

Antica Pizzeria | 19 | 15 | 17 | $22 |
Villa Marina Mktpl., 13455 Maxella Ave. (Lincoln Blvd.), Marina del Rey,
310-577-8182; www.anticapizzeria.net
"Once you get seated, you're in Italy" at this "sweet little" pizzeria that "provides an almost surreal respite from the busy" mini-mall downstairs; the "wonderfully thin" Neapolitan pies from a wood-burning oven are best enjoyed on the "open-air patio overlooking" Marina del Rey; if a few Anticagonists dismiss it as "a fast-food place with restaurant prices", most insist "it's the real thing."

Antonio's Ⓜ | ▽ 20 | 17 | 22 | $24 |
7470 Melrose Ave. (bet. Fairfax & La Brea Aves.), Los Angeles,
323-658-9060
"Gracious" owner Antonio Gutierrez and his son bring "great margaritas" and mariachis along with "consistently good old-fashioned hacienda fare" to the "wannabe trendy Melrose" scene at this "reliable Mexican choice" chockablock with "pics of the proprietor"; followers fall for the "festive atmosphere" and the "excellent" staff that "treats you like family" – no wonder it's "passed on to institution status."

A.O.C. | 26 | 22 | 23 | $50 |
8022 W. Third St. (Crescent Heights Blvd.), Los Angeles,
323-653-6359; www.aocwinebar.com
"Eat slowly and share everything" to "enjoy the abundance" of "unexpected" French, Cal and Med flavors, "executed with

perfection" at Suzanne Goin and Caroline Styne's "hip" Third Street "foodie heaven", rated this *Survey*'s Most Popular; from the "delicious" tapas to "esoteric yet sublime" vinos to the "informed staff", it's "impressive beyond belief", offering the "best grazing in town"; sure, it's "cramped", but that just "fuels the friendly feeding frenzy", and you can always "try to snag a seat" at the wine bar.

Apple Pan ● Ⓜ⇗   22 11 18 $11
10801 W. Pico Blvd. (Glendon Ave.), West LA, 310-475-3585
At this 58-year-old American "greasy spoon" West LA "shrine" in a *Leave It to Beaver*–style house", "Runyonesque characters" slap down "tasty" hickory burgers, "irresistible" fries and "wonderful" pies, with "no-nonsense" panache; "waiting for a spot" at the counter adds to the "time-capsule" "experience", but once seated don't dillydally, advise seasoned Wimpies, or it'll "earn you bad looks from folks" "looking over your shoulder."

ARNIE MORTON'S OF CHICAGO   25 22 24 $56
Le Méridien Hotel, 435 S. La Cienega Blvd. (bet. San Vicente & Wilshire Blvds.), West Hollywood, 310-246-1501
Pinnacle, 3400 W. Olive Ave. (Lima St.), Burbank, 818-238-0424
735 S. Figueroa St. (bet. 7th & 8th Sts.), Downtown, 213-553-4566
www.mortons.com
At this trio of "excellent", "noisy" "old boys' steakhouses" with "massive" portions of "melt-in-your-mouth meat" (you even "need a doggy bag for filet mignon"), a "knowledgeable" staff presides over a setting that exudes the "bonhomie of the '50s"; if some carp the show-and-tell "presentation is tiresome" ("I don't want to see my food paraded around like a holy relic"), most agree the "heart-stopping" fare requires a "healthy expense account."

Arroyo Chop House   25 24 22 $51
536 S. Arroyo Pkwy. (bet. California & Del Mar Blvds.), Pasadena, 626-577-7463
"A cattle baron would leave his ranch to eat a steak" at the Smith Brothers' "reliable" Pasadena chophouse and "sister to the always popular Parkway Grill" and Vibrato Grill, where the "excellent, well-seasoned" "costly" prime beef "can be cut with a fork" and service is "efficient'; it can be "noisy" when "busy", but most maintain the "attractive", "clubby" atmosphere that includes a "live pianist" makes for a "home away from home."

Art's Deli   19 11 17 $19
12224 Ventura Blvd. (bet. Laurelgrove & Vantage Aves.), Studio City, 818-762-1221
"The Humvees of sandwiches" – "sky-high" creations that it "would take a giant to wrap his lips around" – along with staples like stuffed cabbage are the draws at this Studio City deli that's been "family-owned and run" since 1957; a few contend it's "declined" and cite a "sterile" setting and "steep prices", but most of the "Hollywood power brokers" who frequent the joint positively appraise the "works of Art."

Asahi Ramen ⇗   21 8 18 $11
2027 Sawtelle Blvd. (bet. La Grange & Mississippi Aves.), West LA, 310-479-2231
"Lines out the door" are offset by "quick" service at this West LA "noodle king" where carb-cravers dig into "simple and delicious" "hits-the-spot" ramen in "bowls big enough to take a bath in" and

other "reliable" "bargain-priced" comfort food" like "tasty" gyoza; N.B. closed Thursdays.

Asakuma
22 | 16 | 19 | $30

141 S. Robertson Blvd. (bet. Charleville & Wilshire Blvds.), Beverly Hills, 310-659-1092
Hoyt Plaza, 2805 Abbot Kinney Blvd. (Washington Blvd.), Marina del Rey, 310-577-7999
11769 Santa Monica Blvd. (bet. Granville & Stoner Aves.), West LA, 310-473-8990
11701 Wilshire Blvd. (Barrington Ave.), West LA, 310-826-0013; www.asakuma.com

Whether eating in or carrying out, fans carry on about the "fresh and creative" sushi and "perfectly cooked" dishes like "awesome black cod" at this "popular" Japanese quartet around town; it "isn't hip" or "chic", nor is the "decor much to speak of", but service is "friendly" and "delivery is quick."

ASANEBO Ⓜ
26 | 14 | 21 | $52

11941 Ventura Blvd. (bet. Carpenter & Radford Aves.), Studio City, 818-760-3348

Supporters salute this chef-owned Studio City Japanese "hole-in-the-wall that's out of this world" as a "Matsuhisa of the Valley" where "excellent sushi" and "fantastic sashimi" are arranged with "Zen-like" artistry; it's "cramped" and "expensive", but that doesn't keep it from being "celebrity studded."

ASIA DE CUBA ●
24 | 26 | 20 | $54

Mondrian, 8440 Sunset Blvd. (bet. La Cienega Blvd. & Olive Dr.), West Hollywood, 323-848-6000; www.ianschragerhotels.com

This "hot", "hoity-toity" Caribbean–Asian fusion destination in Sunset Strip's Mondrian hotel is a "total sensual experience" thanks to "fantastic" mojitos, "excellent" cuisine, Philippe Starck's "sexy", "eye candy"–studded scene and "awesome" city views; "it doesn't get more LA than this", so "be prepared to wait even if you have a reservation – unless you're the agent of somebody's manager's sister's bodyguard."

Asian Noodles
∇ 21 | 14 | 12 | $19

643 N. Spring St. (Cesar Chavez Blvd.), Chinatown, 213-617-1083

With "excellent", "authentic" and "inexpensive" dishes like "crispy pata" and "heavenly calamari", this Filipino–Asian fusion in Chinatown offers "dishes you don't find elsewhere"; it's too bad "snail-paced service" spoils the experience for some noodlers.

Astra West Ⓢ
∇ 15 | 20 | 17 | $25

Pacific Design Ctr., 8687 Melrose Ave. (San Vincente Blvd.), West Hollywood, 310-652-3003; www.charliepalmer.com

"Breezy and light", Charlie Palmer's way-modern New American in the Pacific Design Center doubles as an events and "catering space" and as a "great place to meet friends during the business day" for a seasonal menu of "less-formal" lunchtime fare; but a "disappointed" handful harrumph "given its bloodlines, the food is surprisingly mediocre" and "overpriced" to boot.

Astro Burger ⊖
18 | 9 | 15 | $9

5601 Melrose Ave. (Gower St.), Los Angeles, 323-469-1924 ●
3421 W. Beverly Blvd. (Bradshawe St.), Montebello, 323-724-3995

(continued)

(continued)

Astro Burger
7475 Santa Monica Blvd. (bet. Fairfax & La Brea Aves.), West Hollywood, 323-874-8041 ◐

"If it's good enough for Hilary Swank on Oscar night, it's good enough for you" cheer customers who, like the *Million Dollar Baby,* order the "incredible" veggie burger when the "craving" hits at this "no-atmosphere" trio that "blows away" other "fast-food joints"; "if you still have a buzz from the bars and need some vitamin G (grease)", go for the "old-fashioned fries", a "basic" patty "and fixin's" – "what else do you need?"

Asuka   19 | 11 | 18 | $28 |
1266 Westwood Blvd. (Wilshire Blvd.), Westwood, 310-474-7412

Expect "freshness and variety" at this "solid", long-standing Westwood Japanese where the sushi is "simple, quick" and "good", and there's also a robata bar for grilled food; the decor is "shoddy" and it can be "noisy", but the "friendly staff" is kind to kids and the "price is right", which helps explain why it's been around since 1974.

Auld Dubliner Irish Pub & Restaurant   – | – | – | M |
The Pike at Rainbow Harbor, 71 S. Pine Ave. (Ocean Blvd.), Long Beach, 562-437-8300; www.aulddubliner.com

Enter the portals of this Dubliner pub and you may forget it's lodged in a new Long Beach shopping center because the setting looks like it was lifted whole from the auld sod, with wood-planked floors, brick walls and furniture imported from the Emerald Isle; it's a suitable setting for tall draughts of Guinness matched with Irish specialties like shepherd's pie.

Aunt Kizzy's Back Porch   20 | 14 | 16 | $20 |
Villa Marina Mktpl., 4325 Glencoe Ave. (Mindanao Way), Marina del Rey, 310-578-1005; www.auntkizzys.com

"Mississippi meets the Marina" at this temple of Southern cooking in Marina del Rey, where "ribs rule" and "you can hear your arteries closing with each tasty bite" of "kickin' fried chicken"; the "decor is nothing to write home about", but the "wall of celebrity photos is impressive", the atmosphere "relaxed" and the eats "inexpensive", so "if you go hungry, you'll leave happy."

Authentic Cafe Ⓜ   18 | 15 | 16 | $25 |
7605 Beverly Blvd. (Curson Ave.), Los Angeles, 323-939-4626

Since 1986, this "cute", chef-owned Fairfax Eclectic-Southwestern has been serving "reliable" fare like tortilla-crusted chicken breast and Chinese dumplings, most recently in a newly "expanded" space with a "hip bar area"; but skeptics sniff the place is "past its prime" and ask "what's authentic" about a "cultural mishmash of odd", "disappointing" dishes served by a "slow staff"?

Avenue Ⓜ   25 | 21 | 22 | $50 |
1141 Manhattan Ave. (Manhattan Beach Blvd.), Manhattan Beach, 310-802-1973; www.avenuemb.com

"Talented" chef/co-owner Christian Shaffer, the mastermind behind "sister" restaurant Chloe in nearby Playa del Rey, "scores again" with this "hot", "much-needed culinary mecca" in Manhattan Beach; the "superb", monthly changing New American menu, "professional" service and "casual yet sophisticated" atmosphere add up to a "great vibe" that's "as cool as South Bay dining gets."

A Votre Sante
19 | 13 | 18 | $20 |

13016 San Vicente Blvd. (26th St.), Brentwood, 310-451-1813
"Beautiful people in yoga clothes and running suits" crowd this tiny "New Wave Birkenstock haunt" in Brentwood, where "fresh" "healthy" vegetarian fare makes for "decent dinners and even better breakfasts"; while naysayers nix the nibbles as "bland" "rabbit food", most cite "large portions", "reasonable prices" and "star sightings" and ask "what's not to like?"

Axe Ⓜ
21 | 17 | 16 | $36 |

1009 Abbot Kinney Blvd. (B'way), Venice, 310-664-9787;
www.axerestaurant.com
Patrons whose "hipness quotient is off the charts" frequent this "enjoyably pretentious" Venice Californian (pronounced AH-shay – "don't get me started on the name") that's a showcase for "creative" "organic comfort food" and "service with attitude"; the "patio is gorgeous", but the "uncomfortable" wooden benches in the "painfully modern", "minimalist-as-a-yoga-studio" setting require "buns of steel" and lead some to sigh "I could have a similar experience eating an egg-white omelet in my bathroom."

Babalu
20 | 16 | 17 | $23 |

1002 Montana Ave. (10th St.), Santa Monica, 310-395-2500
In a "tropical setting", this "bustling", "perennial favorite" turns out "Californian cuisine with Caribbean flair", drumming up "gooey sandwiches", "refreshing", "light choices" and "truly dangerous desserts"; but a Desi-pointed few are left in limbo, citing "big line for little payoff" and a staff that runs "on island time."

Babita Mexicuisine Ⓜ
▽ 27 | 12 | 23 | $26 |

1823 S. San Gabriel Blvd. (Norwood Pl.), San Gabriel, 626-288-7265
"Forward the mail, I'm home" quip patrons who find this "tiny" Mexican marvel with an "inviting family atmosphere" "worth a trip" to a "lackluster" part of SG Valley; chef-owner Roberto Berrelleza "deals a hot hand of peppers, packing plenty of punch" into "joyous, delicious" dishes "not found" elsewhere, sending some guests straight to "sweat-induced nirvana"; settle in for the feast because the service, while "friendly", can be "extremely slow."

Baby Blues Bar-B-Q
▽ 21 | 10 | 16 | $19 |

444 Lincoln Blvd. (Sunset Ave.), Venice, 310-396-7675;
www.babybluesbarbq.com
Chase the "blues away" with "damn delicious" North "Carolina–style BBQ" at this "new, unpretentious Venice" smoke shack staffed by "charming" folk and done up with modern art; the siren "smell can torment you" declare diners who pile in for "luscious pulled pork", "tasty ribs" and "sides to die for"; if a smattering cite "sauce that's not up to par", most back this baby, adding it's "perfect for takeout" too.

Bacco Trattoria,
Marketplace & Wine Bar
▽ 20 | 19 | 22 | $28 |

3821 W. Riverside Dr. (N. Kenwood St.), Burbank, 818-845-8036
"Bursting with personality", this "swanky" Italian yearling with an "excellent wine list" and a deli to boot is one of the most "happening" "lunch spots in the 'Bank" for "studio types" and "residents" alike; while the "broad menu" is studded with regional specialties, for most chompers the "chopped salad is the way to

go"; but Bacco balkers bemoan "bland" dishes, concurring it's merely "decent for the price."

Back Home in Lahaina   18 ‖ 14 ‖ 17 ‖ $17 ‖
519 E. Carson St. (Grace Ave.), Carson, 310-835-4014
916 N. Sepulveda Blvd. (10th St.), Manhattan Beach, 310-374-0111
www.backhomeinlahaina.com
"Authentic down to the Spam", this "kitschy" Manhattan Beach "family spot", and its new Carson sidekick, is like a "one-hour vacation to the islands" insist the "homesick" who head here for "heaping portions" of "salty, tasty" Hawaiian "comfort food" like "must-try kalua pork" and loco moco; still, the "tiki environment" and "laid-back service" aren't everyone's cup of kava.

Back on the Beach   14 ‖ 19 ‖ 14 ‖ $17 ‖
445 PCH (California Blvd.), Santa Monica, 310-393-8282
"No shirt, no shoes, no problem" at this Santa Monica beachhead, where customers overlook the "adequate" American eats and "erratic service" for the simple joy of "wiggling their toes in the sand" while "taking in the rays" and "watching the Rollerbladers glide by"; sure, it's a "hole-in-the-wall", but it's a "nice way to spend a lazy Sunday morning" and "you can't beat the Pacific Ocean for decor."

Baja Fresh Mexican Grill   19 ‖ 10 ‖ 15 ‖ $10 ‖
475 N. Beverly Dr. (Little Santa Monica Blvd.), Beverly Hills, 310-858-6690
11690 San Vicente Blvd. (Barrington Ave.), Brentwood, 310-826-9166
Virgin Megastore Complex, 877 N. San Fernando Blvd. (Burbank Blvd.), Burbank, 818-841-4649
Los Altos Shopping Ctr., 2090 Bellflower Blvd. (bet. Abbeyfield St. & Britton Dr.), Long Beach, 562-596-9080
8495 W. Third St. (La Cienega Blvd.), Los Angeles, 310-659-9500
Villa Marina Mktpl., 13424 Maxella Ave. (Del Rey Ave.), Marina del Rey, 310-578-2252
899 E. Del Mar Blvd. (Lake Ave.), Pasadena, 626-792-0446
Bistro Ctr., 12930 Ventura Blvd. (Coldwater Canyon Ave.), Studio City, 818-995-4242
Westwood Vlg., 10916 Lindbrook Ave. (Westwood Blvd.), Westwood, 310-208-3317
Winnetka Sq., 19960 Ventura Blvd. (bet. Lubao & Penfield Aves.), Woodland Hills, 818-888-3976
www.bajafresh.com
Additional locations throughout Southern California
"Clean and bright" with an "accommodating" staff, this "In-N-Out of fresh Mexican chow" "does it right" with "cheap", "cooked-to-order" south-of-the-border "guilty pleasure" food offset by a "smorgasbord" of "zingy" salsa; but the "sterile" decor leaves others cold, and some customers complain the "quality seems to have slipped after going corporate" under Wendy's management.

Bamboo   21 ‖ 15 ‖ 19 ‖ $25 ‖
10835 Venice Blvd. (bet. Overland Ave. & Sepulveda Blvd.), Culver City, 310-287-0668; www.bambooretaurant.net
With "light-tasting", "unique Caribbean" cuisine that's also "well priced", "live music some nights" and a "helpful staff", this "funky but cool" "surprise" is a "real find on a nondescript stretch along Venice Boulevard"; sit outside on the "gardenlike patio" for the "best atmosphere", dive into the "fruity sangria" and soak up the

"tasty island-style sauces complementing the fresh fish, chicken and steak" dishes.

Bamboo Inn   23 | 17 | 19 | $22
14010 Ventura Blvd. (bet. Hazeltine & Woodman Aves.), Sherman Oaks, 818-788-0202; www.bamboocuisine.com
Shooting out some of the "finest Chinese food" "outside of Monterey Park", this "friendly", "eternally popular" "Far East favorite" in Sherman Oaks is "ideal for large groups", offering "generous portions" of "consistently good, fresh" fare that's "sure to please"; "it's always packed", so the "lines waiting for tables must agree" that a meal here is "memorable."

Bandera   21 | 20 | 20 | $32
11700 Wilshire Blvd. (Barrington Ave.), West LA, 310-477-3524; www.houstons.com
"Houston's clubby spin-off is more hip than its big brother chain" and it's "loved by adult singles" who head to West LA (and the Corona del Mar outpost) to "see and be seen, though you have to wait for the pleasure"; raise your martini and toast the "good jazz" in the "lively bar", then settle down for "spit-roasted" American-Southwestern fare that "makes all your troubles melt away."

Banzai Sushi   ▽ 23 | 17 | 19 | $31
23508 Calabasas Rd. (Valley Circle Blvd.), Calabasas, 818-222-5800; www.banzaisushi.com
"One of the better bait shops in the Valley" quip fish mongers who find the "special rolls too good to pass up" at this "friendly local" Japanese in Old Town Calabasas; the "great selection" and "dependable results" make it "one of the better sushi choices in the area", plus you may even catch a seat on the "outdoor patio in the summertime."

Barbara's at the Brewery Ⓢ   ▽ 16 | 14 | 14 | $18
Brewery Art Complex, 620 Moulton Ave. (Main St.), Downtown, 323-221-9204; www.barbarasatthebrewery.com
"More than a bit off the beaten track", owner Barbara West's "funky joint" Downtown in The Brewery, an artists-in-residence "loft/ studio collective", is "not the place to go for an elegant meal", but locals "love it" nonetheless; while the Eclectic-International fare is "good, not spectacular", the "cold Pabst on tap", "biggest wine list ever" and "bohemian-hideaway" "vibe" more than "make up for it."

Bar Celona   15 | 20 | 16 | $29
46 E. Colorado Blvd. (Raymond Ave.), Pasadena, 626-405-1000; www.sorrisopasadena.com
"You can now have a hip night on the town" in "Old Pas'" say fans aflutter over this "welcome addition", a "fun" Spanish "place to meet friends for drinks or a light snack before or after events"; but while the "high-style" "atmosphere is there", many gauchos gripe that the "timid tapas" doesn't "measure up" – "oh, how I wish they'd be a bit more authentic"; still, it "has potential" – "they may need more time to get into a groove."

Barefoot Bar & Grill   18 | 19 | 18 | $30
8722 W. Third St. (bet. George Burns Rd. & S. Robertson Blvd.), Los Angeles, 310-276-6223; www.barefootrestaurant.com
"Bring your picky friends" to this "offbeat", "delightful" Beverly Center destination "when everyone wants to eat different foods"

from "very good" sushi to "melt-in-your-mouth" Cal-Eclectic dishes; while some hand it to the "beautiful patio, a number one choice for delicious cocktails on a warm afternoon", others muse that the inside doesn't toe the line, noting that while it "carries a bit of faded elegance" it could "use some sprucing up."

Bar Marmont ◐   18 22 16 $36
8171 W. Sunset Blvd. (Havenhurst Dr.), West Hollywood, 323-650-0575
Never mind the "delicious burgers", fries and Cal-Eclectic offerings: this shabby-chic "supper club" next to the Chateau Marmont hotel is really for "watching – and being rejected by – the most beautiful people in LA" ("are you someone?") while sipping "nectar of the gods" cocktails and ogling the "to-die-for" (if somewhat "uppity") servers and the "groovy butterfly collection" on the ceiling; it's a "perpetual scene for both industryites and awkward first dates alike", so "sit back and enjoy the charm of old Hollywood."

Barney Greengrass   20 17 16 $30
Barneys New York, 9570 Wilshire Blvd., 5th fl. (Camden Dr.),
Beverly Hills, 310-777-5877
Known as "The Commissary" to Hollywood's "top 10-percenters", this "industry lunch" spot atop Barneys New York is the Beverly Hills bookend of the Manhattan deli, serving "gargantuan salads", "killer smoked fish and other "extravagantly priced Jewish soul food" to players and pretenders "wheeling and dealing"; "yeah it's trendy, sceney" and "overpriced", "but there isn't much that beats eating outside on a nice day" ("it's all about the terrace, baby").

Barney's Gourmet Hamburgers   21 12 16 $13
Brentwood Country Mart, 225 26th St. (San Vicente Blvd.),
Brentwood, 310-899-0133 ⊟
11660 San Vicente Blvd. (Barrington St.), Brentwood, 310-447-6000
www.barneyshamburgers.com
Serving "big, juicy burgers for when you want to be bad, and turkey, chicken and veggie patties for when you don't", these Brentwood satellites of the SF mini-chain coddle customers with "perfect curly fries" and "awesome shakes"; the "American classics" use "highbrow ingredients" and come "heaped with whatever you want on it", all served by "cute waitresses"; still, a few beef about the "sterile" space sniping "it's got no personality."

Barsac Brasserie ▣   21 19 21 $36
4212 Lankershim Blvd. (bet. Moorpark St. & Ventura Blvd.),
North Hollywood, 818-760-7081; www.barsac.com
The "exemplary hospitality" of chef James Saliba and owner Lisa Long and their "attentive" wait staff make this "comfy yet upscale" Cal-French "find" in North Hollywood a "bustling", "deal-making" "favorite" of more studio "suits than you can shake a stick at" during lunchtime; at night, the "airy" place "goes romantic", with canoodlers enjoying "delicious bistro fare" oftentimes prepared by a roster of visiting European chefs and "great martinis."

Basix Cafe   18 15 18 $21
8333 Santa Monica Blvd. (N. Flores St.), West Hollywood,
323-848-2460; www.basixcafe.com
Just as its name suggests, this Cal-Italian is a "sturdy" "WeHo basic" – "dependable but nothing amazing" and "better for breakfast than for dinner", welcoming theatergoers with plenty of "Boystown bonhomie" and ladling out some of the "best"

housemade soup; but service can vary from "excellent" to "absent-minded", and "you may get a makeover from the guys at the next table if you don't look hip enough."

BASTIDE 🔲Ⓜ   24 | 26 | 26 | $102
8475 Melrose Pl. (La Cienega Blvd.), Los Angeles, 323-651-5950
"Genius" new chef Ludovic Lefebvre's "creative" dishes enthrall Francophiles at this Provençal bastion on Melrose that's still hailed as a "flawless experience", from the "hunger-inducing menu", "phenomenal wine list" and "candlelit magic" of the "beautiful" dining room to service that's "immaculate down to the smallest detail"; but a handful huff that the no-corkage policy is a bottle-stopper, especially since wine "prices range from high to insane."

BCD Tofu House   20 | 10 | 13 | $14
11818 South St. (Pioneer Blvd.), Cerritos, 562-809-8098
1201 S. Los Angeles St. (12th St.), Downtown, 213-746-2525 ❶
869 S. Western Ave. (9th St.), Koreatown, 213-380-3807 ❶
3575 Wilshire Blvd. (Kingsley Ave.), Koreatown, 213-382-6677 ❶
18044 Saticoy St. (Rindley Ave.), Reseda, 818-342-3535 ❶
1731 Fullerton Rd. (Colima Rd.), Rowland Heights, 626-964-7073 ❶
1607 Sepulveda Blvd. (Western Ave.), Torrance, 310-534-3480 ❶
www.bcdtofu.com
Synergizing the "greatness" of a "hole-in-the-wall" with the "consistency" of a corporation, this "Korean Denny's" mini-chain (with branches in South Korea) fills bowls and bellies with "bubbling hot tofu" and other high-protein choices that "get the job done at 3 AM"; sure, service can be "rushed", but late hours at most branches compensate (some are "24-hour standbys") – it's the "perfect" "place to detox after hitting the clubs."

BEACON   23 | 18 | 20 | $34
Helms Bldg., 3280 Helms Ave. (Washington Blvd.), Culver City, 310-838-7500; www.beacon-la.com
A "neat little newcomer" to an area that until recently "hasn't had much to offer", Kazuto Matsusaka's "spartan, contemporary" Pan-Asian engine in Culver City's Helms Bakery complex "shines" with "imaginative" fusion fare; "small plates with flair rule" the "user-friendly menu", making for "great grazing", and while "portions are mini", "every morsel is delicious"; but disgruntled diners take a dim view, declaring the space "cramped" and huff that the "attentive" servers become "harried" during busy hours.

Beau Rivage   20 | 22 | 20 | $46
26025 PCH (Corral Canyon Rd.), Malibu, 310-456-5733; www.beaurivagerestaurant.com
A "grown-up's restaurant" in a town better known for slacker surfers, this "romantic" Med medallion "loaded with atmosphere" in Malibu employs "professional waiters, not actors playing waiters" and offers "nice live music" nightly to complete the "very civilized", "satisfying experience"; but the "uneven food" leaves a few afloat wondering why it's "just ok in a place that looks like it should be a knockout."

Beckham Grill   19 | 18 | 19 | $32
77 W. Walnut St. (Fair Oaks Ave.), Pasadena, 626-796-3399; www.beckhamgrill.com
"Heart-warmingly old-fashioned", this "Disneyland version of an English country inn" mollycoddles Pasadena traditionalists with

"very good" American steakhouse fare served by "friendly" staffers amid "warm ambiance"; still, some modernists maintain that it's getting "stale", saying the "decor's a little tired", "the service sometimes slips" and the "food is not exceptional"; N.B. no affiliation with that famous footballer.

Beechwood 🅂 Ⓜ   20 | 23 | 17 | $37 |
822 W. Washington Blvd. (Marr St.), Venice, 310-448-8884; www.beechwoodrestaurant.com
An "incredible remodel" "of the old Menemsha space" has resulted in this "welcome addition to Venice", whose "handsome" decor, "hip bar" and "refined" yet "earthy" New American fare "draw major crowds" of "resident beautiful people"; service is still "a bit spotty", but with "young chef-owners Brooke [Williamson] and Nick" Roberts "running it, how can it lose?"; P.S. "scene"-sters suggest you "stay in" the "attractive" lounge or "large outdoor area" (with a "fire pit to boot").

Bel-Air Bar & Grill   19 | 18 | 20 | $40 |
662 N. Sepulveda Blvd. (Moraga Ln.), Bel Air, 310-440-5544; www.belairbarandgrill.com
This "always-reliable" "hillside hideaway" in Bel-Air "near the Getty" is manned by a "caring" staff that serves "consistently delicious" Californian cuisine within a "contemporary but warm" space boasting a "comfy bar", "nice fireplace" and "charming", "covered year-round patio"; no wonder "locals" laud it as "a satisfying refuge in an area with little in the way of options" – even if its "location next to a gas station isn't ideal."

Belmont Brewing Co.   18 | 18 | 18 | $23 |
25 39th Pl. (bet. Allin & Midway Sts.), Long Beach, 562-433-3891; www.belmontbrewing.com
The obvious draw of this "working microbrewery" in "an ideal location" "overlooking the Queen Mary" "at the base of [Long Beach's] Belmont pier" is the "beautiful ocean view" from its "spacious heated patio", where first mates and first dates enjoy "amicable service" and "consistently good" American grub as they "sample" the "fine beers made on premises"; add in a "nice sunset" "over the Pacific" and "you're guaranteed a night to remember."

BELVEDERE, THE   26 | 28 | 27 | $66 |
The Peninsula Beverly Hills, 9882 Little Santa Monica Blvd. (Wilshire Blvd.), Beverly Hills, 310-788-2306; www.peninsula.com
"An elegant setting for stargazing" over "power breakfasts and lunches" or "outstanding dinners", this "prime spot" in the "beautiful" Peninsula Beverly Hills is a "true destination" that's "pricey but worth every penny"; give in to the "gorgeous setting", "magnificent service" from a "top-notch staff" and "exemplary" New American "cuisine fit for a king"; P.S. though every meal is a "near-perfect experience", the "lovely Sunday brunch", with its "endless champagne", is an especially "wonderful" "winner."

Benihana   19 | 17 | 19 | $32 |
38 N. La Cienega Blvd. (Wilshire Blvd.), Beverly Hills, 323-655-7311
Plaza at Puente Hills, 17877 Gale Ave. (Fullerton Rd.), City of Industry, 626-912-8784
16226 Ventura Blvd. (bet. Libbet & Woodley Aves.), Encino, 818-788-7121
3760 E. Inland Empire Blvd. (N. Haven Ave.), Ontario, 909-483-0937
1447 Fourth St. (B'way), Santa Monica, 310-260-1423

(continued)

Benihana

21327 Hawthorne Blvd. (Torrance Blvd.), Torrance, 310-316-7777
www.benihana.com
The "charismatic" "knife-wielding" chefs "are to Japanese food
what the Harlem Globetrotters are to basketball" at this "reliable
teppan-style" steakhouse chain that strikes supporters as "a sure
bet" for "a fun family dinner"; though some call it "a caricature of
itself" that's "lost its luster" and is "expensive for what you get",
more don't mind the "high cost" – after all, it's one-stop shopping
for "dinner and a show"; N.B. there's sushi, too.

Benny's BBQ   ▽ 15 | 4 | 12 | $15

4077 Lincoln Blvd. (bet. Maxella Ave. & Washington Blvd.),
Marina del Rey, 310-821-6939; www.bennysbbq.com
Some Marina del Rey-sidents looking to "satisfy that craving" for
"huge hunks of tangy meat" with "all the fixin's" followed by "good
sweet-potato pie" head to this "tiny place" (rather than "eating in",
most "take it to go"); "disappointed" denizens, though, declare that
the merely "acceptable" eats "just don't cut it."

Berri's Pizza Cafe   17 | 15 | 15 | $21

8412 W. Third St. (S. Orlando Ave.), Los Angeles, 323-852-0642 ◗
8415 Pershing Dr. (Manchester Ave.), Playa del Rey, 310-823-6658
Pie-sanos peg this pair as "oases in a barren landscape" for serving
"thin-crust pizza" "with a wide range of unusual toppings" as
well as "a diverse menu" of "solid" Ital-Med dishes; still, the
disappointed pan the "spotty service"; P.S. the Third Street branch
has "no liquor license" but is open "late at night – a rarity in LA."

Big Mama's Rib Shack Ⓜ   ▽ 16 | 12 | 14 | $19

1453 N. Lake Ave. (Rio Grande St.), Pasadena, 626-797-1792;
www.bigmamas-ribshack.com
Proponents give this Pasadena pig purveyor (sibling of the same-
named Vegas outfit) a messy thumbs-up for its "huge portions" of
"hearty soul food" and "accommodating service"; but critical
carnisseurs claim it's "nothing to write home about" and find
a "disconnect between the food and decor", beefing that the
"strangely" "classy" ambiance is "too formal" for a "BBQ joint."

Billingsley's   15 | 12 | 18 | $21

11326 W. Pico Blvd. (Sawtelle Blvd.), West LA, 310-477-1426
Though "loyal followers" of this "old-style steakhouse" "institution"
(owned by a son of *Leave It to Beaver*'s Barbara) were "sad to see"
the "unfortunate closure" of its Van Nuys outpost, they can still
get their "comfort-food" fix of "good", "inexpensive" American
"meat-and-potatoes" fare at its "survivor" of a sibling in West LA;
some youngsters may find it "stale", but "older locals" descend
"in droves" for the "early-bird special."

Bistro 45 Ⓜ   – | – | – | E

45 S. Mentor Ave. (bet. Colorado Blvd. & Green St.), Pasadena,
626-795-2478; www.bistro45.com
A fine-dining destination for 15 years running, Robert Simon's cozy,
candlelit Pasadena bistro continues to lure the special-occasion-
bound with a seasonally changing selection of Cal-French dishes,
all beautifully presented and matched with an encyclopedic wine
list; the romantic ambiance, historic art deco setting and soft
background jazz add to the celebratory feel.

BISTRO GARDEN AT COLDWATER, THE 21 | 25 | 22 | $47

12950 Ventura Blvd. (Coldwater Canyon Ave.), Studio City, 818-501-0202; www.bistrogarden.com

Boasting a "lovely" space with an "indoor-outdoor" feel, this "romantic bistro" keeps "Old Hollywood–style elegance" alive in Studio City thanks to an "excellent, experienced staff" that doles out "incredible chocolate soufflé" and other "traditional" French-Continental goodies to a mixed clientele of "elders" and "celebrities"; some sigh it "doesn't have the charisma" of the long-shuttered Beverly Hills original, but more find it "a joy" "for special occasions."

Bistro K ⊠ Ⓜ   ▽ 25 | 18 | 19 | $39

1000 Fremont Ave. (El Centro St.), South Pasadena, 626-799-5052; www.lqmanagementservices.com

"Creative" chef-owner Laurent Quenioux "continues to shine" with "exquisite" Eclectic fare incorporating European, Mexican and Asian influences at this "cozy" South Pasadena bistro with garden seating; "tables are tight", but the "warm service" and "fair prices" (plus "no-corkage BYO" policy) enhance its "exceptional-value" status, and it's also "a good place to stop before" a visit to the nearby Fremont Center, "but even better when you're not in a rush."

Bistro 767 ⊠ Ⓜ   ▽ 22 | 19 | 19 | $40

767 Deep Valley Dr. (bet. Drybank & Roxcove Drs.), Rolling Hills, 310-265-0882

Chef-owner "Deanna Kaiser is doing well" according to supporters of her "classy" two-year-old Rolling Hills-ide aerie (an especially "welcome addition" to the neighborhood "considering the lack of choices" nearby) where "excellent" Californian cuisine is ferried by a "helpful staff"; some say it's "on the pricey side" and the "service can vary", but all agree the "pleasant" patio is "perfect for a warm summer evening."

Bistro 31 ⊠   ▽ 20 | 15 | 16 | $23

Art Institute of Los Angeles, 2900 31st St. (Ocean Park Blvd.), Santa Monica, 310-314-6057

"Foodies may find their next favorite chef training" at the Art Institute's BYO "culinary-school" "classroom" in Santa Monica, where "everyone from cooks to waiters" are "eager" students; "you'll root for these kids to get it right, and they most often do", serving up "ambitious" Californian cuisine at "rock-bottom prices"; the "service can be clumsy", but it's still a "remarkable value" that has fans sighing "too bad it's only open" Monday–Wednesday "during school" and "closed off-semester."

Bistro Verdu Ⓜ   ▽ 21 | 15 | 18 | $31

3459 N. Verdugo Rd. (bet. Oceanview Blvd. & Sunview Dr.), Glendale, 818-541-1532

Many Glendale Francophiles are enamored with this "little neighborhood bistro" for the "excellent" fare on its "small but thorough" "seasonal menu" ("don't miss the $25 three-course prix fixe dinners on Wednesdays" and Sundays), and even those who feel its "reach" sometimes "falls short" note that the "hard"-working staff has "heart and talent"; P.S. though it "recently received a license" and now sports a "well-priced wine list", BYO-ers are "thankful" it "still has a reasonable corkage" fee.

BJ's   17 | 15 | 16 | $18

400 E. Huntington Dr. (Gateway Dr.), Arcadia, 626-462-1494
107 S. First St. (Olive St.), Burbank, 818-557-0881
11101 183rd St. (Rte. 605), Cerritos, 562-467-0850
5258 E. Second St. (La Verne St.), Long Beach, 562-439-8181
22920 Centerpoint Dr. (Fredrick St.), Moreno Valley, 951-571-9370
24320 Town Center Dr. (McBean Pkwy.), Valencia, 661-288-1299
Eastland Shopping Ctr., 2917 Eastland Center Dr. (Barranca St.),
West Covina, 626-858-0054
3955 E. Thousand Oaks Blvd. (Westlake Blvd.), Westlake Village,
805-497-9393
939 Broxton Ave. (bet. Leconte & Weyburn Aves.), Westwood,
310-209-7475 ●
6424 Canoga Ave. (Victory Blvd.), Woodland Hills, 818-340-1748
www.bjsbrewhouse.com
Additional locations throughout Southern California
A slice of surveyors swears that the "delectable deep-dish" at
these "solid chain" outposts is the "closest thing to real Chicago
pizza in LA" (with "out-of-control portions" of "all-American" eats
and "great, cheap" "house brews" sweetening the deal), though
hecklers bash the "typical bar food", "sporadic service" and "oh-
so-noisy" digs; still, all agree "you gotta love" that "decadent
pizookie", a "warm" and "wonderful dessert."

Blair's   24 | 18 | 21 | $40

2903 Rowena Ave. (bet. Glendale & Hyperion Blvds.), Silver Lake,
323-660-1882
"Silver Lake locals" "love" this "classy" sophomore, where they
peruse an "innovative" menu of "excellent" New American entrees
(including a "delicious" signature halibut) and "wonderful wine
list" while chatting with "friendly, knowledgeable servers" and
soaking up a "casual neighborhood feel"; the "tight seating" of its
"intimate" space strikes expansive sorts as "cramped", but it's
nevertheless labeled "a wonderful find"; P.S. "save room for
the unique desserts."

Bliss ●☒Ⓜ   ▽ 16 | 21 | 16 | $48

650 N. La Cienega Blvd. (Melrose Ave.), West Hollywood,
310-659-0999; www.blissla.com
"Unique decor" and "cool lighting" make for "slick" surroundings
at this big, bi-level "scene" on La Cienega with a "showy dining
room", "great lounges" and a "nice private VIP" space; some say
it's "unfairly overlooked" for its New American cuisine, but more
maintain "you don't go" to this "hopping nightclub" "masquerading
as a restaurant" for the merely "decent food" but "for the low-cut
jeans and tanned young bodies."

Blowfish Sushi To Die For   20 | 24 | 18 | $45

9229 Sunset Blvd. (Doheny Dr.), West Hollywood, 310-887-3848;
www.blowfishsushi.com
"Roll up in your H2" at this "trendy", "pricey" raw-fishery on Sunset
Strip co-owned by Julian Lennon, where the "hip industry" crowd
pays less attention to the "innovative" Japanese eats than to the
"wonderful anime decor", "great bathroom faucets", "thumpy
music", "excellent sake selection" and, natch, "star sightings";
though foodies may dismiss such fashionistas as "restaurant
lemmings", even they admit it's the "place to go if you like
your sushi creative."

Blue Bamboo   – | – | – | M

*359 N. La Cienega Blvd. (bet. Beverly Blvd. & Melrose Ave.),
West Hollywood, 310-854-0622; www.bluebamboo.cc*

Pioneers who've trekked to this La Cienega Thai report "hip
ambiance" and "good service", not to mention "delicious" Siamese
fare with "unique" twists – including "awesome curries" and some
of "the best chicken satay in town"; P.S. "if you can resist the deep-
fried yam chips, you have more strength of character than" most.

Blue Hen   ▽ 19 | 17 | 20 | $15

*1743 Colorado Blvd. (Argus Dr.), Eagle Rock, 323-982-9900;
www.eatatbluehen.com*

Pho fans "searching for a fresh" take on Vietnamese cuisine can
"find it in an unlikely location" – namely, this "strip-mall" tyro;
though its menu may be "limited, what's on it is good" thanks to
"organic ingredients" from "local farms"; in fact, supporters say
that "Eagle Rock may be the next Silver Lake if this" "great addition"
predicts "the future of its restaurant scene."

blue on blue   19 | 24 | 17 | $44

*Avalon Hotel, 9400 W. Olympic Blvd. (Cañon Dr.), Beverly Hills,
310-277-5221; www.avalon-hotel.com*

The "perfect place to impress a date", this "slick" watering hole at
the Avalon Hotel in Beverly Hills ("The Standard for the Westside")
keeps a "chichi crowd" happy with "great cocktails" that "rock";
the libations may outshine the "limited" Cal-American menu, but
the "fab" "clientele draped casually around the pool" or spending
a "romantic evening" in "cozy cabanas" contend that "anything
would taste good in this" ultra-"cool" "Miami in LA" setting.

Blue Pacific   ▽ 24 | 18 | 21 | $30

201 Hermosa Ave. (2nd St.), Hermosa Beach, 310-406-8986

Pacifists "cannot rave enough" about this "fun fusion restaurant",
a Hermosa Beach "gem" "that takes chances with its" Cal-Asian
menu; the "outstanding" sushi and "seafood" lure a surprisingly
"hip" clientele, and the "ridiculously low" prices (at least by LA
standards) ensure that the experience "will not leave you blue."

Bluewater Grill   19 | 17 | 18 | $31

*King Harbor Marina, 665 N. Harbor Dr. (Beryl St.), Redondo Beach,
310-318-3474; www.bluewatergrill.com*

"Bring out-of-town guests for a taste of the ocean" counsel
customers hooked on this "friendly" American seafood outpost
where the fish is "simply grilled", prices are "reasonable" and
in some locations, you can land a seat on the "lovely" patio
"overlooking the water"; while a handful crab the "preparations
have no flair", defenders retort if it "were any fresher you'd be
catching it yourself."

Blvd, The   – | – | – | M

*Regent Beverly Wilshire, 9500 Wilshire Blvd. (Rodeo Dr.), Beverly Hills,
310-275-5200; www.regenthotels.com*

This lush cafe inside the former Lobby Lounge of the Regent Beverly
Wilshire offers an Eclectic global menu, providing a relatively
casual alternative to the Wolfgang Puck steakhouse slated for the
hotel's more formal dining room; the sumptuous space has been
given a modernist-meets-art-deco update with an 18-ft. black onyx
bar and clear acrylic wine cellar.

Boa   23 | 24 | 21 | $57 |
(fka Balboa)
101 Santa Monica Blvd. (Ocean Ave.), Santa Monica, 310-899-4466 ◑
The Grafton Hotel, 8462 W. Sunset Blvd. (La Cienega Blvd.),
West Hollywood, 323-650-8383
www.innovativedining.com
From the Katana/"Sushi Roku crew", "finally, a Boa you would want
to curl up in" quip customers who slither over to this recently
renamed "sleek, loungey" steakhouse in the Grafton Hotel and its
SM offshoot for "perfectly marbled beef", "great Caesars" and a
"towering wine library"; this is "where the real money goes", and
no wonder, with a "hot bar scene" and a "to-die-for view of the
ocean"; still, a few fume it's "more style than substance."

Bob Morris' Paradise Cove Beach Cafe   15 | 19 | 16 | $28 |
28128 PCH (Paradise Cove Rd.), Malibu, 310-457-2503;
www.paradisecove.org
"Tourists" and "families" "on their way up the coast" stop at this
"bustling", "funky" Malibu haven to "hang out on the beach" and
eat "hearty" American seafood "with their toes in the sand"; if
wavemakers find the "disappointing" service and "mediocre"
eats far from paradise, the "fabulous" ocean view compensates,
in fact, "everything else is just in a supporting role."

boe restaurant   – | – | – | M |
The Crescent, 403 N. Crescent Dr. (Brighton Way), Beverly Hills,
310-247-0505
Go on, "enjoy the environment" enthuse a handful who slink
into The Crescent hotel's indoor/outdoor loungey dining room, a
sleek, streamlined candlelit retreat designed by boldfaced name
scenesetter Dodd Mitchell; relax over small plates of Eclectic-
Californian fare on the patio or nibble while downing signature
martinis from your perch on the white sofas near the fireplace.

Boiling Pot   ▽ 17 | 17 | 16 | $21 |
345 S. Lake Ave. (E. Del Mar Blvd.), Pasadena, 626-796-8870
Cook-it-yourselfers doff their toques to the creative shabu-shabu
theme at this Pasadena Japanese, a "fun" "concept" (and "favorite
with kids") with a "friendly" staff and "crisp, modern interior" that
just may be "the next in-thing"; but a handful huff that this "hot-pot"
spot's selection is "bare-bones" and "Americanized", adding "go
to an Asian neighborhood for the real thing."

Bombay Bite   ▽ 20 | 15 | 19 | $21 |
1051 Gayley Ave. (Le Conte Ave.), Westwood, 310-824-1046;
www.bombaybite.com
"When you don't want to think where to go for Indian food", this
"cozy" "gem" hits the spot, luring locals with "good tandoori" and
"excellent frankies" (curried veggies, chicken or beef wrapped in
a tortilla); although it may not be worth a special trip, it's "nice for
a tasty lunch" "right in the middle of Westwood Village"; N.B. there
are also intriguing Chinese-influenced menu items.

Bombay Cafe   25 | 16 | 19 | $27 |
12021 W. Pico Blvd. (Bundy Dr.), West LA, 310-473-3388;
www.bombaycafe-la.com
Some of "the most savory" Indian dishes you'll find "outside of
Bombay" come from this West LA kitchen known for its "addictive

lamb frankie" (no, it's not a "character from a bad *Godfather* movie"), "nuanced sauces" and "interesting" "street foods like samosas and *sev puri*"; pleased patrons precede the "inventive", "dependably delicious" offerings with "wowie" martinis, give kudos to the "knowledgeable" servers and sigh it would be near-"perfect if it wasn't for" the "deafening" decibel level.

Bombay Palace   21 | 20 | 20 | $34
8690 Wilshire Blvd. (bet. Hamel & Willaman Drs.), Beverly Hills, 310-659-9944
"If you like your curry hot", this "old faithful" in Beverly Hills is the place for "mouthwatering" Northern Indian food, including "standout" chicken "tikka masala" and an "excellent" lunch buffet; the space is especially "lovely", and though a minority mutters "over decorated" and "under" seasoned, most maintain that while "it may be far from Bollywood, this place is jolly good."

Bono's   22 | 22 | 21 | $38
4901 E. Second St. (St. Joseph Ave.), Long Beach, 562-434-9501; www.bonoslongbeach.com
"Another winner from Bono", this "sophisticated" Californian "perfectly located" on LB's "popular Belmont Shore" is "not nearly as stiff" as Christy's, her first self-named restaurant; the "light, airy" space with a waterfall and "wraparound patio" is "so inviting you want to chat your way from lunch to dinner" while the "excellent" food, "fun martinis" and a "friendly staff" make it a "great experience every time"; this Cherished owner has "learned well from her dad, Sonny, about putting together a class-act eatery."

Bora Bora Ⓜ   ▽ 21 | 19 | 22 | $34
3505 Highland Ave. (35th St.), Manhattan Beach, 310-545-6464
"In a small, intimate setting where the owner works hard to treat every guest like an old friend", this Cal-Polynesian "gem" in Manhattan Beach doesn't bora anybody with its "great" appetizers and "best ribs in the South Bay", which make for "sexy beachside dining" in a "quiet part of town"; "we drive here from the Valley" vouch South Sea-nsters, and "the drive says it all."

Border Grill   22 | 19 | 19 | $30
1445 Fourth St. (bet. B'way & Santa Monica Blvd.), Santa Monica, 310-451-1655; www.bordergrill.com
Although "the buzz has cooled off", this "primary-colored *zarzuela*" in Santa Monica with "a young, hot staff and delicious Mexican food" still packs in crowds lured by "killer margaritas", "addictive" quesadillas and other "fabulous" fare from those two "talented tamales" Susan Feniger and Mary Sue Milliken; gripers grumble about the "Toys R Us–meets–Tijuana" look and shout about the "mucho, mucho noise" ("loud, loud, loud!"), but even they agree that the "festive happy hour" "makes it all worthwhile."

Bourbon Street Shrimp Company   16 | 15 | 14 | $21
(fka Bourbon Street Shrimp & Grill)
10928 W. Pico Blvd. (Kelton Ave.), West LA, 310-474-0007
"A place to get your New Orleans fix", this "damn authentic" West LA gumbo house keeps Louisiana lovers coming back for the "feisty flavors" of po' boys and jambalaya, paired with "cheap" beer; despite the "raucous" atmosphere, though, some ragin' Cajuns hoot at the "slow" service and charge that even if many Angelenos simply "don't know better", it's a "poor imitation" of NO cuisine.

BRANDYWINE ⊠ 27 | 21 | 26 | $53
22757 Ventura Blvd. (Fallbrook Ave.), Woodland Hills, 818-225-9114
Locals laud this "lovely" Continental "classic" in Woodland Hills as a "flashback to another time", and just the ticket "for a special night of indulgence", thanks to "superb" offerings like "exquisite" lobster medallions and "incredibly fresh" vegetables; factor in "personal service" in an "intimate" space, and you have a "gourmet experience" "to impress a date or reignite a flame"; still, a handful find it "rather pricey for the neighborhood."

Brass.-Cap. – | – | – | M
100 W. Channel Rd. (PCH), Santa Monica, 310-454-4544
Chef-owner Bruce Marder (Capo) has turned the oceanfront space that was once home to the Beach House into this warm, casual French-Eclectic (the name is short for Brasserie Capo); the cuisine, made largely from organic ingredients, ranges from pissaladière and cassoulet to borscht and burgers.

Brasserie Les Voyous ◑ – | – | – | M
6541 Hollywood Blvd. (Whitley Ave.), Hollywood, 323-957-0167;
www.lesvoyous.com
"A welcome alternative to the Hollywood eateries nearby", this "bohemian" brasserie "enhanced by the owner's warm presence" attracts *amis* with its "unique versions of French" staples and a "nice patio with outdoor seating"; if faultfinders fret that the "service is lackadaisical and the food average", even they agree that the "groovy" photo-filled, red-walled setting "makes up for it."

Bravo Cucina 18 | 14 | 18 | $21
1319 Third St. Promenade (bet. Arizona Ave. & Santa Monica Blvd.),
Santa Monica, 310-394-0374
Bravo Pizzeria ◑
2400D Main St. (Hollister Ave.), Santa Monica, 310-392-7466
At this "people-watching spot" on SM's Third Street Promenade and its "perfect for the neighborhood Main Street pizzeria" sibling, locals dig into "enjoyable" pies and pastas delivered by a "capable" staff; but while fans find the food from the Lepore brothers of NYC's Ferrara's "tasty" enough to "meet the criteria" of transplants "looking for a" Little Italy "surrogate", naysayers retort it's "not primo by a long shot."

Breeze 20 | 20 | 19 | $40
Century Plaza Hotel & Spa, 2025 Ave. of the Stars (Constellation Ave.),
Century City, 310-277-2000; www.breezela.com
"Look! executives! everywhere!" – yes with big-shot lawyers and "suits" tucking into "solid" sushi and "light" Californian seafood on the "lovely" patio, this "expense-account" enclave at the Century Plaza Hotel is "becoming the place where a lot of Century City business is done"; but it's a good thing restaurants don't bill by the hour, though, because it can "take so long to eat here, you are hungry again" before you leave.

BRENT'S DELI & RESTAURANT 27 | 12 | 21 | $18
19565 Parthenia St. (bet. Corbin & Shirely Aves.), Northridge,
818-886-5679; www.brentsdeli.com
"Packed to the gills", this family-run "gold standard" of Jewish delis brings culinary fame to Northridge with "gargantuan" portions of "great" chopped liver and "to-die-for" blintzes; even East Coast

"transplants" moon over the "mouthwatering" meats, and endure "long" waits, the sometimes-"sassy" waitstaff and the "kitsch comfort" decor of this "hamish" "pastrami heaven" to eat at the "best delicatessen west of NYC."

Brentwood, The ●　　　　　　22 │ 20 │ 21 │ $45
148 S. Barrington Ave. (Sunset Blvd.), Brentwood, 310-476-3511
"Dark and clubby", this "neighborhood celebrity hangout" in Brentwood is "perfect" for everything from "Sunday dinner with the in-laws" to "impressing" "even the most finicky model or actress"; satisfy hankerings for New American "comfort food" with "unbelievable" steaks and "juicy" Kobe beef hamburgers, swill a "not too shabby" Cosmopolitan and soak up the "comfy, loungey" atmosphere; still, a few frown it's "expensive for what you get."

Brighton Coffee Shop　　　　17 │ 8 │ 16 │ $14
9600 Brighton Way (Camden Dr.), Beverly Hills, 310-276-7732
"A page out of city life from years gone by", this "retro" American "greasy spoon" in Beverly Hills is the "real deal for real people" (and "celebs", too, natch), who've been sidling up to the counter since 1930 for "no-nonsense" "favorites" like the "homemade" meatloaf sandwich or a "classic pancake-eggs-bacon" breakfast; though the decor isn't exactly Rodeo caliber, the staff is "friendly" and it sure "beats rushing off for fast food"; N.B. no dinner.

Broadway Deli ●　　　　　　15 │ 14 │ 14 │ $21
1457 Third St. Promenade (B'way), Santa Monica, 310-451-0616
An "epic menu" reveals there's "something for everyone" at this "bustling" Eclectic deli, an "ideal place for people-watching" on SM's Third Street Promenade that plays to SRO crowds with "breakfast that's a step above", "comfort food" and a "popular" wine bar; still, critics spurn the "inconsistent" service and contend this production doles out "big fat sandwiches at a big fat price."

Buca di Beppo　　　　　　　15 │ 17 │ 17 │ $22
505 W. Foothill Blvd. (Indian Hill Blvd.), Claremont, 909-399-3287
17500 Ventura Blvd. (Encino Ave.), Encino, 818-995-3288
80 W. Green St. (De Lacey Ave.), Pasadena, 626-792-7272
1670 S. PCH (Palos Verdes Blvd.), Redondo Beach, 310-540-3246
1442 Second St. (bet. B'way & Santa Monica Blvd.), Santa Monica, 310-587-2782
Universal CityWalk, 1000 Universal Studios Blvd. (off Frwy. 101), Universal City, 818-509-9463
www.bucadibeppo.com
"Take TGI Fridays and have your Uncle Vito run it" – that sums up this "family-style" Italian chain, where diners "don't count carbs" as they "wolf down" an "avalanche" of "satisfying" pastas and pizzas "larger than the average nine-year-old"; the "hyper" waiters and "campy" setting make it "fun for groups", "so bring the whole family"; but gripers pounce on the "industrial"-sized "mounds" of "mediocre" chow, concurring it "doesn't get better by piling it on."

Buddha's Belly　　　　　　20 │ 18 │ 20 │ $24
7475 Beverly Blvd. (Gardner St.), West Hollywood, 323-931-8588; www.bbfood.com
At this "trendy-as-yoga" "tour of the Pacific Rim" on Beverly Boulevard, "you can count on" a "friendly" greeting from co-owner Jonathan Chu and his staff before assuming the lotus position for the "delicious" Alaskan black cod and other "flavorful", "pantastic

Pan-Asian fare"; admirers muse that perhaps "even Buddha would be happy" ducking into this "funky" place for a "quick, casual bite."

Buffalo Club ☒   21 | 22 | 18 | $51

1520 Olympic Blvd. (bet. 14th & 16th Sts.), Santa Monica, 310-450-8600
Still a place to be seen – but not heard (it's so "loud" you "can't hear the waiter announcing the specials") – this "cool, speakeasylike" "Hollywood hangout" in industrial Santa Monica is where "actors, models and wannabes" pose on the "enchanted garden" patio or slither into "leather booths" to sup on "top-notch" steaks and "something-for-everyone" American fare; mere mortals, however, may feel buffaloed by the "arrogant" service and find the scene "way too full of itself."

Buffet City   ∇ 13 | 8 | 12 | $17

11819 Wilshire Blvd. (Granville Ave.), West LA, 310-312-0880; www.buffetcity.net
If you can get past the "plastic" environment and the "tacky" name, some surveyors say this "bargain" West LA smorgasbord is a metropolis of "well-prepared" sushi, dim sum, Mongolian barbecue and other Asian-influenced Eclectic fare; still, Jimmy No-Buffets disdain the grub, deeming it "weird" or just "not very interesting"; N.B. kids 2–10 pay their age multiplied by 80 cents.

Buggy Whip   17 | 15 | 18 | $33

7420 La Tijera Blvd. (74th St.), Westchester, 310-645-7131
"Still reliable", this recently refurbished, "old-school" Continental steakhouse in Westchester near LAX tends to "fly-in" travelers and "regulars" with "consistent" prime rib and salads with "classic Green Goddess dressing"; while most appreciate the "campy" "time-warp" feel, complete with "stately ladies in turbans" and a "weekend piano player", frequent criers "can't see the attraction" and snarl it's "hanging on to a fading glory."

Buona Sera   ∇ 20 | 16 | 16 | $39

247 Avenida del Norte (bet. Palos Verde Blvd. & PCH), Redondo Beach, 310-543-2277
At this Redondo Beach sophomore, the "great" homemade pasta, "must-try" thin-crust pizza and other "thoughtfully prepared" Italian offerings continue to impress South Bay guests; as at many "relative newcomers", however, the service can be "inconsistent", and dissenters declare that the eatery "would do well to" cut the "noise" and "drop the prices" – otherwise, *que sera sera.*

Burger Continental   15 | 10 | 14 | $17

535 S. Lake Ave. (California Blvd.), Pasadena, 626-792-6634; www.burgercontinental.com
An Eclectic menagerie ("where else can you watch belly dancers on a weekend afternoon?") masquerading as a burger joint, this "kooky" "Caltech hangout" serves up a "great" weekend brunch and an "ersatz" Med–Middle Eastern combo of "affordable" dishes; ironically, the hamburgers earn mixed reviews, and in-continentals argue this "faux casbah" "needs an extreme makeover."

Cabo Cantina   ∇ 12 | 15 | 13 | $16

8301 W. Sunset Blvd. (Sweetzer Ave.), West Hollywood, 323-822-7820
11829 Wilshire Blvd. (Barrington Ave.), West LA, 310-312-5840 ☾
Filled with a "young crowd" and "hot" waitresses, this "loud" West LA "college hangout" decorated with beer company ads feels "like

spring break in Cabo"; the "accent is on margaritas", in fact, "happy hour is so much fun" that the "just ok" Mexican grub is almost incidental and, for most, worth ordering "just to sober up"; N.B. the WeHo branch set in the former Le Petite Zinc site is unrated.

Ca'Brea
22 | 20 | 21 | $38

346-348 S. La Brea Ave. (bet. 3rd & 4th Sts.), Los Angeles, 323-938-2863; www.cabrearestaurant.com

"A real diamond in a Swarovski world" of "mediocre Italian" dining rooms, Antonio Tommasi's sparkler, a sibling of Ca' del Sole and Locanda Veneta on La Brea's Restaurant Row, sets itself apart "year after year" with "eye-catching" Northern Italian cuisine (the "pumpkin ravioli is a hands-down favorite") that manages to be both "traditional yet imaginative"; lunch can be a "power scene", while dinner is more "leisurely", and the "prompt" service simply adds shine to the "rustic vibe."

Ca' del Sole ●
22 | 22 | 21 | $36

4100 Cahuenga Blvd. (Lankershim Blvd.), North Hollywood, 818-985-4669; www.cadelsole.com

"You feel as if you're in a villa in Europe" when you dine at this "pleasant", "popular" Italian "hot spot" in North Hollywood, either for a "power lunch" (it's the "ancillary executive dining room" for neighborhood movie studio suits) or for a "leisurely", "romantic dinner"; cognoscenti who devour Venetian "delicacies" "between cell phone calls" claim that supping on the "lovely" "leafy" patio is "what LA eating is all about" – just "touch thumb to middle finger, kiss the tips and say *si*."

Cafe Atlantic
20 | 15 | 15 | $23

53 E. Union St. (Raymond Ave.), Pasadena, 626-796-7350

Offering "Xiomara quality without the Xiomara prices", Xiomara Ardolina's other Pasadena restaurant has developed a "cult following" with its "grand portions" of "wonderfully authentic" Cuban fare; this "cute", "offbeat" "little place" with a coffee bar and a domino table is "family-friendly", and while the "uneven" service "can be slow", try this for Fidel-ity: some amigos assert that the "succulently delicious" pork sandwich is "better than we had in Cuba."

CAFÉ BIZOU
22 | 19 | 20 | $30

91 N. Raymond Ave. (Holly St.), Pasadena, 626-792-9923
14016 Ventura Blvd. (bet. Costello & Murietta Aves.), Sherman Oaks, 818-788-3536
www.cafebizou.com

Serving "fine" Cal-French cuisine "at bargain prices" – "a formula that will allow them to take over the world" – these "perennially popular" bistros in Pasadena and Sherman Oaks captivate Angelenos with an "innovative menu that's always being tweaked"; it's constantly "crowded", and "deservedly" so, what with "$1 daily soups" and salads and "$2 corkage" ("yes – two"); N.B. Bizou Gardens (fka Café Bizou) in Santa Monica is separately owned.

Café Brasil
20 | 15 | 15 | $17

10831 Venice Blvd. (Westwood Blvd.), Palms, 310-837-8957; www.cafe-brasil.com

With its "quaint shabby-chic" decor and mostly outdoor setting, this counter-service Brazilian in Palms exudes a "bare-bones attitude", but there's nothing "minimal" about the food – not with the "tasty" grilled dishes, "wonderful" plantains and black beans on offer; it's an "inviting", "tropical" "neighborhood hangout" that can even be a Cariocan-style "date place", at least if you and your beloved like picnic tables; N.B. a Culver City branch is slated to open in late 2005.

Café Deco ⊠ Ⓜ — | — | — | I

850 S. Baldwin Ave. (Huntington Dr.), Arcadia, 626-294-9628
Peter Lee, co-owner of the Monterey Park Cantonese fave Ocean Star, broadens his horizons with this Hong Kong–style Arcadia Eclectic, a stylish spot with an outdoor patio and a menu that caroms from Mexican taquitos to Philly cheese steaks; desserts are just as diverse – and tastiest of all, prices are downright reasonable.

Cafe Del Rey 23 | 23 | 21 | $44

4451 Admiralty Way (bet. Lincoln Blvd. & Via Marina), Marina del Rey, 310-823-6395; www.cafedelreymarina.com
"The beacon of the Marina del Rey restaurant scene", this culinary lighthouse "overlooking millions of dollars' worth of yachts" is "a first pick for special occasions" or to "take out-of-town guests", thanks to its "breathtaking" sunset views and "inspired" "Pacific Rim–influenced" Cal-French creations; each dish is "artfully placed on lovely plates", and if a few carp that it's rather "costly", the "wonderful atmosphere" still shines "inside and out."

Cafe des Artistes 19 | 22 | 19 | $38

1534 N. McCadden Pl. (Sunset Blvd.), Hollywood, 323-469-7300; www.cafedesartistes.info
With a "charming" setting in a "delightful", "rustic" "bungalow", a "wonderful" staff and the "best tarte flambé this side of Alsace", this French bistro "hidden in Hollywood" is where "celebs" and "bohemians" lap up chef-owner Jean-Pierre Bosc's "excellent", "authentic" fare; while the "gorgeous" back patio is perfect for a "romantic evening for two", starving artists know that the "lunch specials" are the real "bargains."

Café D'Marco Ⓜ — | — | — | M

709 N. PCH (Irena Ave.), Redondo Beach, 310-937-1400; www.cafedmarco.com
Never mind the "nondescript aging" South Bay strip-mall locale, "we go back time and again" vow beach folk who duck into this airy "gem" with yellow-dappled walls to dine on Italian classics and "wonderful" dishes with a Californian flair; "great service" seals the deal, with diners noting "we're never disappointed."

Cafe 50's 15 | 17 | 17 | $13

4609 Van Nuys Blvd. (Hortense St.), Sherman Oaks, 818-906-1955 ●
838 Lincoln Blvd. (Lake St.), Venice, 310-399-1955 ⊟
11623 Santa Monica Blvd. (bet. Barry & Federal Aves.), West LA, 310-479-1955 ●
www.cafe50s.com
Thanks to "jukeboxes at the tables" and vintage newspapers on the walls, this trio of "retro" "all-American" individually owned diners has some surveyors donning "poodle skirts" and sock-hopping "back to the future" for "dependable" breakfasts and "out-of-this-world milkshakes"; while pajama night is "super fun" (wear PJs and eat free at the West LA branch on the last Wednesday of the month), some oldsters pooh-pooh the "iffy" service and "corny kitsch."

Café 14 🅼   ∇ 25 16 23 $38
30315 Canwood St. (Reyes Adobe Rd.), Agoura Hills, 818-991-9560
Serving up "home cooking" "in an unpretentious but gracious fashion", this "perfect bistro" "tucked into a strip mall" in Agoura Hills "aims to please" with a "reasonable" wine list and "delicious" Californian-Continental cuisine cooked up by husband-and-wife chef-owners Neal Kramer and Claudine Bernard-Kramer; satisfied locals insist it "would be twice the price in Santa Monica" and "don't mind keeping this" "find" to themselves.

Café Med ◗   18 16 17 $31
8615 Sunset Blvd. (Sunset Plaza Dr.), West Hollywood, 310-652-0445
"Very LA without being too Hollywood", this Sunset Strip Italian is "a favorite" place for "Sunset people-watching" on the outside patio while enjoying "delicious (if predictable) choices from the "huge" "reasonably priced" menu; some Med-lers maintain that the food can't keep up with the "eye candy", however, and quip "you're right in the middle of lots of out-of-work actors", so "be sure to wear appropriate designer shades."

Cafe Montana   20 17 18 $29
1534 Montana Ave. (16th St.), Santa Monica, 310-829-3990
At this "glass-walled" "anchor" of Santa Monica's Montana Avenue, "a convenient neighborhood" bistro where you're likely to "spot celebs", stargazers tolerate the "high-density" "fishbowl" seating and "higher than desirable" noise level for the "fresh" "chic Californian food", particularly during the "great Sunday brunch scene"; still, a few find it "nothing special" and decry the staff as "airheads with attitude."

Café Mundial   ∇ 23 20 20 $33
514 S. Myrtle Ave. (Colorado Blvd.), Monrovia, 626-303-2233;
www.cafemundial.net
A surprisingly "hip eatery" in Monrovia, this worldly Cal-Med titillates SG Valley denizens with "consistently good" fare that ranges from filet mignon to seafood and finishes with the signature chocolate soufflé; the well-executed menu may be "nothing exciting", but regulars report that owner Travis Ensling "is always happy to see us"; N.B. check out the monthly wine dinners.

Cafe Pacific   ∇ 23 26 23 $40
Trump National Golf Club, 1 Ocean Trails Dr. (Palos Verdes Dr. S.),
Rancho Palos Verdes, 310-303-3260; www.trumpgolf.com
At the Trump National Golf Club (fka Ocean Trails), linksters yell 'fork!' to try the Californian cuisine, which some say "has improved under The Donald's watch"; though visitors also laud the "elegant" look and "beautiful" setting with its "gorgeous ocean views", they "hope nothing about the restaurant ever resembles Trump's hair"; N.B. a post-*Survey* revamp may impact the Decor score.

Café Pierre   23 20 21 $40
317 Manhattan Beach Blvd. (bet. Highland Ave. & Morningside Dr.),
Manhattan Beach, 310-545-5252; www.cafepierre.com
"Always a winner", this "solid" French bistro serves up classics "that never go out of vogue"; despite dissenters who are "*très désolés*" about the "shoulder-to-shoulder" seating, service is quite "knowledgeable", with *amis* asserting that "the owner even watches your facial expressions and is eager to fix anything."

Cafe Pinot   23 ⎮ 22 ⎮ 22 ⎮ $44 ⎮
*700 W. Fifth St. (Flower St.), Downtown, 213-239-6500;
www.patinagroup.com*
Diners headed for "the theater or symphony" seek out this
"civilized" Downtown "oasis", Joachim Splichal's haven of
"divine" Cal-French cuisine served in a "spectacular" "alfresco"
setting "with a view of the library"; if a few find the "preparation
too precious" – "more style than substance" and whine about "lax
service", Pinot-ponents proclaim a meal here "always brightens
your day"; N.B. corkage is free, as is the Disney Hall shuttle.

Café Santorini   22 ⎮ 20 ⎮ 19 ⎮ $30 ⎮
*64 W. Union St. (bet. De Lacey & Fair Oaks Aves.), Pasadena,
626-564-4200; www.cafesantorini.com*
The "magnificent" aromas wafting from this "romantic" "brick-
walled" retreat lure passing pedestrians in to "enjoy a glass of
wine with assortment of" meze or to sup on "artfully crafted"
Mediterranean fare; if you "sit outside" on the "magical" balcony
"on a warm evening", you may mistake this "charming" "standby"
"in the heart of Old Pasadena" for the home island of owners Panos
and Vasken Haytayan.

Cafe Stella ⌧ Ⓜ   22 ⎮ 21 ⎮ 17 ⎮ $38 ⎮
*3932 Sunset Blvd. (bet. Hyperion & Sanborn Aves.), Silver Lake,
323-666-0265*
Beckoning to wannabe expatriates like a "little French island on
the sea of Silver Lake", this "romantic" al-ley fresco bistro with
a "funky-cool European vibe" curbs Left Bank longings with
"authentic" Francophone classics; "order wine immediately",
then "sit back and relax", and you may feel less Galled by the
"slightly snooty" service and "overpriced" menu that has some
visiteurs wondering "what's with the Westside" rates?

Cafe Sushi ❶   ▽ 21 ⎮ 11 ⎮ 15 ⎮ $33 ⎮
8459 Beverly Blvd. (N. La Cienega Blvd.), Los Angeles, 323-651-4020
"What it lacks in decor" "it makes up for in quality sushi", insist
afishionados of this long-standing "neighborhood" Japanese
eatery in Fairfax that serves some of "the freshest" fin fare around
(it's definitely "not gefilte"); prices are "fair", service is "attentive"
and scenesters report "lots of star sightings" too.

Cafe Tartine Ⓜ   ▽ 16 ⎮ 13 ⎮ 15 ⎮ $19 ⎮
7385 Beverly Blvd. (Martel Ave.), West Hollywood, 323-938-1300
With its "great" breads (flown in from France), this Beverly
Boulevard "French bistro dropped in the middle of LA" is "good
for a hipster brunch" or other light meal (open-faced sandwiches
and tartines are the specialties) or to sip and graze in the new wine
bar; some habitués find the "minimalist" interior "a little cold" and
the service rather too "blasé" – *malheureusement,* the food can
be "erratic" as well.

Café Tu Tu Tango   18 ⎮ 20 ⎮ 16 ⎮ $23 ⎮
*Universal CityWalk, 1000 Universal Studios Blvd. (off Frwy. 101),
Universal City, 818-766-4222; www.cafetututango.com*
In an atmosphere that "makes the Hard Rock Cafe seem serene",
this art-filled duo in Universal City Walk and OC (branches of a
Miami chainlet) feels like "a big party" with painters "at work" and
"Hawaiian hula dancers" taking a spin; the tapas are "perfect for

noshing and chatting", and "hanging out" here is undeniably "fun", but the artistically disinclined find the Eclectic food "inconsistent" and the setting "too noisy."

Cafe Veneto 🅱   18 | 19 | 19 | $29
8636 W. Third St. (Willaman Dr.), West Hollywood, 310-273-3605
"To sample Italian tapas and wine with good friends", head for this "fun" Beverly Center area spot that "transports you back to an osteria in Italy"; while some surveyors say it doesn't size up against its more formal sister, Locanda Veneta, next door, bargain-hunters whisper that the "reasonable" prices are actually a "great deal" in comparison; besides, the dessert pizzas here are so "terrific" they "haunt" you.

Caffe Delfini   23 | 17 | 20 | $37
147 W. Channel Rd. (PCH), Santa Monica, 310-459-8823; www.caffedelfini.com
"Evoking memories of a seaside Italian bistro", this Santa Monica trattoria has been imprinting its own recollections for years with its "fresh pastas" and other "simple and flavorful" fare; "the sound of the waves in the background" is soothing, as is the "gracious" service, and even though some grumble that the space is "way too small", others insist it simply "makes for great eavesdropping."

Caffe Latte   17 | 10 | 15 | $15
6254 Wilshire Blvd. (Crescent Heights Blvd.), Los Angeles, 323-936-5213
"Go for the breakfasts, stay for the coffee" – particularly the "namesake lattes" – at this Miracle Mile stalwart, where the java beans are roasted on the premises and diners pile in for "tasty" muffins and other "decent" morning eats; later in the day, the menu runs to "simple" New American fare, and the "friendly staff" adds to its reputation as a "reliable" (if "tiny") "joint."

Caffe Pinguini Ⓜ   22 | 19 | 19 | $36
6935 Pacific Ave. (Culver Blvd.), Playa del Rey, 310-306-0117; www.caffepinguini.com
"Steps from the beach but very secluded", this "small but authentic" Northern Italian hideout in Playa del Rey rewards finders with a "gorgeous candlelit interior", a "lovely patio" and cuisine that is "fantastic" (at least "90 percent of the time"); add the "personal attention" from the doting servers, and that's why "locals love" this "neighborhood place."

Caioti Pizza Cafe   21 | 11 | 15 | $18
4346 Tujunga Ave. (Moorpark St.), Studio City, 818-761-3588; www.caiotipizzacafe.com
Credit chef-owner Ed LaDou, the godfather of California designer pizza, for the "delectable" Cal-Italian cuisine at this "great little" BYO "dive" in Studio City where "the menu is creative" and the pies are "sublime"; though the atmosphere and service make beatniks "feel part of the neighborhood", neat-nicks say the place would be "more inviting" if the "decor improved."

California Chicken Cafe   21 | 9 | 15 | $11
15601 Ventura Blvd. (bet. Haskell Ave. & Sepulveda Blvd.), Encino, 818-789-8056
6805 Melrose Ave. (bet. Mansfield Ave. & Orange Dr.), Los Angeles, 323-935-5877

(continued)
California Chicken Cafe
University Plaza, 18445 Nordhoff St. (Reseda Blvd.), Northridge, 818-700-9977 ⊠
2401 Wilshire Blvd. (24th St.), Santa Monica, 310-453-0477
2005 Westwood Blvd. (bet. Olympic & Santa Monica Blvds.), West LA, 310-446-1933
www.californiachickencafe.com
"Worshipers" grovel at the "righteous rotisserie" of this fiendishly popular mini-chain, braving a "madhouse atmosphere" for the "best Chinese chicken salad in town" and for other "low-fat, low-priced" poultry and American sides that are ideal "for takeout after a long day at the office" or "for people who don't want to cook"; there's "absolutely no decor" and the lines can be "long", so "call in your order ahead of time" to get in and out faster.

California Pizza Kitchen   18 | 14 | 17 | $19 |
Beverly Ctr., 121 N. La Cienega Blvd. (bet. Beverly Blvd. & 3rd St.), West Hollywood, 310-854-6555
207 S. Beverly Dr. (bet. Olympic & Wilshire Blvds.), Beverly Hills, 310-275-1101
Media City Ctr., 601 N. San Fernando Blvd. (Burbank Blvd.), Burbank, 818-972-2589
Wells Fargo Ctr., 330 S. Hope St. (bet. 3rd & 4th Sts.), Downtown, 213-626-2616
Hollywood & Highland Complex, 6801 Hollywood Blvd. (Highland Blvd.), Hollywood, 323-460-2080
Manhattan Village Mall, 3280 N. Sepulveda Blvd. (Rosecrans Ave.), Manhattan Beach, 310-796-1233
Plaza Las Fuentes, 99 N. Los Robles Ave. (Union St.), Pasadena, 626-585-9020
210 Wilshire Blvd. (bet. 2nd & 3rd Sts.), Santa Monica, 310-393-9335
12265 Ventura Blvd. (Laurel Grove St.), Studio City, 818-505-6437
Westwood Vlg., 1001 Broxton Ave. (Weyburn Ave.), Westwood, 310-209-9197
www.cpk.com
Additional locations throughout Southern California
The "default choice" for some, a "reasonably priced" "fallback" for others, this seemingly "ubiquitous" chain does "imaginative" pizzas and "quick salads for on-the-go people" dished up by a "friendly" crew; while many snobs who wouldn't so much as give CPK CPR disdain the "dated" "noisy setting" and "assembly-line food", those who venture in often confess that, even though they "feel like franchise foodies", "the formula works."

California Wok   17 | 7 | 16 | $15 |
12004 Wilshire Blvd. (Bundy Dr.), Brentwood, 310-479-0552
Encino Vlg., 16656 Ventura Blvd. (bet. Balboa Blvd. & Hayvenhurst Ave.), Encino, 818-386-0561
Cienega Plaza, 8250 W. Third St. (La Cienega Blvd.), Los Angeles, 310-360-9218
www.california-wok.com
"They must cook the food in a time machine, it's so fast" at this outfit (with a new location in Costa Mesa) serving "healthy" and "cheap" Chinese chow; power wokkers single out the "inexpensive lunch specials", speedy delivery and "light, fresh" cooking style (no MSG, low oil on request), and aren't fazed by the decidedly "undistinguished" decor.

Camilo's Ⓜ   22 | 21 | 21 | $29
2128 Colorado Blvd. (Caspar Ave.), Eagle Rock, 323-478-2644
While some fans flock to this "comfortable" Eagle Rock refuge for "delightful" Californian-style lunches or dinners, most come for "delicious" breakfast and brunch favorites served by "hospitable" staffers; it may "not be worth a drive across town, but if you're in the area, it's worth a try", since this "straight-ahead, no-fuss" experience "has put" this community "on the dining map."

CAMPANILE   26 | 24 | 24 | $51
624 S. La Brea Ave. (bet. W. 6th St. & Wilshire Blvd.), Los Angeles, 323-938-1447; www.campanilerestaurant.com
"First choice" for even the pickiest palates, this "gourmand's institution" on La Brea turns out "terrific" Cal-Med "food that only gets better", thanks to "flawless" chef-owner Mark Peel who's "always at the helm", and his "ever-so-attentive" staff; with a "delightful" "architectural space" built by Charlie Chaplin, the experience is "worth every Benjamin" declare disciples, who predict that you'll remember your meal here "for the next 20 years"; N.B. co-founder Nancy Silverton is no longer involved.

Canal Club   16 | 18 | 17 | $29
2025 Pacific Ave. (N. Venice Blvd.), Venice, 310-823-3878
Such a "bizarrely broad" menu – from carne asada to "first-rate sushi" to chocolate volcano cakes – would spell disaster for most eateries, but club kids insist the "mix 'n' match" approach "works" at this Venice Eclectic; perhaps that's because food isn't the priority for most beachcombers who flip-flop into the "dark, sexy" space for "strong margaritas" or "cool, crisp" mojitos during "one of the finest-value happy hours" "in town."

C & O Trattoria   19 | 16 | 18 | $21
31 Washington Blvd. (Pacific Ave.), Marina del Rey, 310-823-9491
3016 Washington Blvd. (Thatcher Ave.), Marina del Rey, 310-301-7278
www.cotrattoria.com
"Dino, vino, and a cappuccino" could be the motto of these MdR Italian "houses o' carbs" where the staff sings "Dean Martin's 'That's Amore'" and the "family-style bowls of pasta and Chianti a-flowing" "never disappoint"; "sit outside" and drool like a pasta fazool over the "never-ending supply of garlic rolls" and "delight" in the fact that it's "still crazy" "fun" and the "best bargain" around; but, a few whine it's "average" and "not worth the long wait."

Canter's ◑   17 | 9 | 14 | $17
419 N. Fairfax Ave. (bet. Beverly Blvd. & Melrose Ave.), Los Angeles, 323-651-2030; www.cantersdeli.com
"Perfect pastrami and corned beef sandwiches", "grumpy" "100-year-old" servers, "throwback" decor – yep, this "kitschy-cool" all-night deli with a menu "longer than the Torah" has been the commissary of the Fairfax district for decades; while most mavens like being able to get "matzo balls 24 hours a day" and insist the Canter-ankerous service is "part of the charm", kvetches chant that this "institution" is "living off its reputation."

CAPO Ⓢ Ⓜ   26 | 24 | 23 | $71
1810 Ocean Ave. (Pico Blvd.), Santa Monica, 310-394-5550
"Sell your first son into slavery" if you must, but don't miss chef/co-owner Bruce Marder's "exquisite" Italian masterpieces at this

Santa Monica *ne plus ultra* where "cool art" and a wood-burning fireplace set the scene for regular "celebrity sightings"; sure the "extensive wine list" created by partner Steve Wallace of Wally's Wine Shop fame is "stellar", and "more exorbitant than Westside real estate", but for most, it's "worth every extravagant dollar" – "if you're signing that two-picture deal and the studio is paying."

Caribbean Bistro   ▽ 17 7 15 $18
(aka Tropical Caribbean)
526 S. Lake Ave. (California Blvd.), Pasadena, 626-795-0675
Sure it's "a bit of a hole-in-the-wall, but this family-styled restaurant" in Pasadena decorated with bamboo and mirrors delivers an "authentic taste of the Carribean" "with a great kick" at "super affordable" prices; the "menu is different than most" and the staff makes you "feel at home" – no wonder boosters consider it a "find."

Carlitos Gardel   23 19 21 $37
7963 Melrose Ave. (bet. Crescent Heights Blvd. & Fairfax Ave.), Los Angeles, 323-655-0891; www.carlitosgardel.com
"Argentine royalty seems to eat" at this "family-run" "carnivore's" heaven on Melrose, and if it's good enough for them, it more than suffices for average Joses, who soak up the "fantastic" atmosphere (complete with live music) while digging into the "huge" steaks and "luscious garlic fries"; jet-setters acknowledge that it's "not quite like being in" Buenos Aires, but it may be "closer than anywhere else in LA."

Carmine's Italian Restaurant   18 14 17 $20
311 E. Live Oak Ave. (bet. 3rd & 4th Aves.), Arcadia, 626-445-4726
424 Fair Oaks Ave. (bet. Columbia St. & Frwy. 110), South Pasadena, 626-799-2266
"The place for pizza and partying", the South Pasadena branch of this Italian pair is "fun but loud", while the Arcadia location is more "family-friendly"; either way, you get "generous portions" of "satisfying" and "affordable" (if "not particularly inspired") "home-cooked" fare; service is "quick" enough, too, so bring "the kids."

Carney's Express   – – – I
12601 Ventura Blvd. (Whitsett Ave.), Studio City, 818-761-8300
8351 W. Sunset Blvd. (Sweetzer Ave.), West Hollywood, 323-654-8300 ●
www.carneytrain.com
Picture a concession stand inside a vintage railroad car and you get the gist of this pair of Pullmans in Studio City and on the Strip, where the hustling counter staff hands out fast-food American eats in little cardboard boxes; Carney-vores indulge in cheeseburgers and chili dogs on the split-wood patio, and the late-night Sunset location even serves beer and wine.

Carnival   22 8 14 $17
4356 Woodman Ave. (bet. Moorpark St. & Ventura Blvd.), Sherman Oaks, 818-784-3469; www.carnivalrest.com
Urging not to "judge a restaurant by its cover", thrill-seekers cheer "hurrah" as they rush to this "cheap and cheerful" joint in Sherman Oaks for the "enormous" portions of "wonderful" Lebanese "soul food", particularly the "outstanding appetizers" and "kebabs"; the service can "border on surly" (at least until "they get to know you"), but the "fantastic" flavors will "linger with you for days."

Carousel ⓜ   23 | 14 | 18 | $24 |

304 N. Brand Blvd. (California Ave.), Glendale, 818-246-7775
High Plaza, 5112 Hollywood Blvd. (Normandie Ave.), Hollywood,
323-660-8060

"Make a meal of the meze" or savor some of the "best kebabs on the planet" at this Felix and Oscar–like pair of Middle Eastern–Armenian faves (the Glendale location "features entertainment and grand decor", while the Hollywood branch "is only about the food"); in either setting, the service is "efficient" and the portions may be "intimidating", so "bring an extra stomach."

Casa Bianca ⏺ⓈⓂ⇗   24 | 11 | 16 | $17 |

1650 Colorado Blvd. (Vincent Ave.), Eagle Rock, 323-256-9617

"Heavenly" pizza after a "horrendous" wait – that's the refrain from visitors to this insanely "popular" Eagle Rock Italian that has been "impressing New York snobs" and loyal locals for more than 50 years; "forget the rest" of the "old-style" menu, ignore the "stuffy" dining room that "could use sprucing up" and just focus on some of the "best" pies "in Southern California."

Casablanca   19 | 19 | 20 | $22 |

220 Lincoln Blvd. (Rose Ave.), Venice, 310-392-5751

"First, wrap your head around the idea of a Mexican restaurant with a *Casablanca* theme" ("the movie, not the city", that is), then "wrap your mouth around" the "unbelievable" handmade tortillas and signature calamari steaks at this Venice "old standard"; you can "lounge" in the "huge booths" with a "delish" margarita and listen to the guitarist, too, but a few critics contend that the Bogart-and-Bergman concept seems increasingly "corny" as time goes by.

Casa Vega ⏺   17 | 16 | 17 | $21 |

13301 Ventura Blvd. (Fulton Ave.), Sherman Oaks, 818-788-4868

Drinking "awesome" margaritas in the "cramped bar" "is a contact sport" at this "crowded" Sherman Oaks cornerstone; still, it's the kind of "fun hangout" "you'd want in your neighborhood" (complete with "some celeb sightings"), and the Mexican standards are "decent enough" – not that you can see your food in the "incredibly dark" interior, but it's a boon to anyone "having an affair."

Casbah Cafe   ▽ 14 | 20 | 15 | $14 |

3900 W. Sunset Blvd. (Hyperion Blvd.), Silver Lake, 323-664-7000

If he weren't wooing coquettes in Algiers, movie gangster Pépé le Moko might stop by this "shabby-chic" French-Moroccan BYO cafe/boutique in Silver Lake for a "great" latte or espresso or trinkets to aid his next conquest; he might even nibble a "tasty" sandwich, but he'd soon tire of the "too cool to smile" staff at this "bizarre bazaar" and whisper 'come wiss me to zumplace less expenzeev' to the nearest mademoiselle.

Cassell's Ⓢ⇗   18 | 5 | 11 | $11 |

3266 W. Sixth St. (Vermont Ave.), Koreatown, 213-387-5502

"Whenever they need a burger fix", carnivores head for this Koreatown "institution" for a "legendary" "made-to-order" hamburger paired with an "array of condiments", including "homemade mayonnaise", and "tasty potato salad"; however, patty-panners contend that this onetime "landmark" is "just a memory of its former glory" and is "coasting on sentimental value"; N.B. lunch only.

Castaway   15 | 21 | 17 | $30
1250 E. Harvard Rd. (Sunset Canyon Dr.), Burbank, 818-848-6691;
www.castawayrestaurant.com
With its "sweeping", "scenic" Valley vistas, this Burbank hilltop
bastion is a "romantic place for an anniversary", a "holiday brunch"
or just "relaxing with a drink" around "the fire pits" "on the patio";
although Tom Hanks' marooned movie character would gladly sink
his teeth into the Cal-Continental food, many find it "mediocre" and
advise "go for the atmosphere, stay for the, um, atmosphere."

Cayenne Café   – | – | – | I
7169 Beverly Blvd. (N. La Brea Ave.), West Hollywood,
323-857-1252; www.cayennecafe.net
On weekend nights, visitors feel *très* sheik at this comfy Beverly
Boulevard Mediterranean-Moroccan BYO, puffing hookahs, dining
on dishes like chicken pomegranate and watching the belly dancers
in full-sway; breakfast is also an exotic affair, with eggs paired with
fava beans or merguez sausage, while lunch leans toward the
Middle East with falafel and hummus options.

Celestino ☒   24 | 19 | 22 | $38
141 S. Lake Ave. (bet. Cordova & Green Sts.), Pasadena, 626-795-4006
"In a town with too many imposters", this "authentic" Pasadena
trattoria gives diners a "sophisticated" take on Tuscan traditions
with "divine" "homemade pastas" and other "Italian comfort food";
the staff is filled with "pros" ("they know their wines", too), there's
a "cute patio" and the interior manages to feel both "classy and
homey", so if a few celestial snipers complain about the "price-
value" ratio, admirers insist that the Drago brothers are "the best
thing to come to LA since the sun."

Cézanne   ▽ 21 | 24 | 24 | $47
Le Merigot Hotel, 1740 Ocean Ave. (bet. Colorado Ave. & Pico Blvd.),
Santa Monica, 310-395-9700; www.lemerigothotel.com
Though the notion of a "quiet" yet well-regarded restaurant "steps
from" the Santa Monica shore seems like an oxymoron, this
"sleeper" run by a "courteous staff" in Le Merigot Hotel proves
otherwise, serving "beautifully presented" Cal-French fare in a
"classy" setting; perhaps the food is a bit "pricey for what you
get", but pleased patrons paint it "a hidden gem" and appreciate
the "free wine" tastings Fridays and Saturdays.

Chaba   ▽ 21 | 19 | 18 | $26
525 S. PCH (Ruby St.), Redondo Beach, 310-540-8441
South Bay denizens feeling fit to be Thai-ed might tuck into the
"inventive" cuisine at this Redondo Beach number, where the
"broad menu offers something for everyone"; surveyors say it's
both "fun" "for the family" (there's "a gong the kids can smack")
and home to an "active bar scene", despite a few purists who
protest that the fusion-style fare is "not very authentic."

Cha Cha Cha   22 | 20 | 19 | $25
656 N. Virgil Ave. (Melrose Ave.), Silver Lake, 323-664-7723
7953 Santa Monica Blvd. (Fairfax Ave.), West Hollywood, 323-848-7700
www.theoriginalchachacha.com
Nothing says "festive" like this "funkadelic" Caribbean duo that
keeps revelers on their toes with the "happiest of happy hours" and
some of the "best jerk chicken anywhere"; whether you two-step

into the Silver Lake original or the West Hollywood branch, the "congenial" staff and "voodoo-esque" decor keep things "sizzling"; sure a few party-poopers "aren't thrilled" with the food, but "one sangria and you'll be cha-cha-cha-ing all over the place."

Cha Cha Cha Encino Ⓜ   18 19 17 $26
17499 Ventura Blvd. (bet. Balboa Blvd. & White Oak Ave.), Encino, 818-789-3600; www.chachachaencino.com
With a "huge drink menu" that's "longer than the food" list, this "colorful" crib in Encino (separately owned from the original Cha Cha Cha) hydrates happy humans with "delish" martinis and "tasty mojitos", which accompany "generous" portions of "reliable" Californian-Caribbean fare; "take a large group" or a couple of pals, 'cause everything "tastes better in this festive" and "fun" space.

Cha Cha Chicken   19 13 15 $13
1906 Ocean Ave. (Pico Blvd.), Santa Monica, 310-581-1684; www.chachachicken.com
Scantily clad beach roamers "feel like they're on vacation" when they belly up to the order window at this "quirky" SM "shack" for "to-die-for" jerk chicken, fried plantains ("a must") and other "inexpensive" "finger lickin'" Caribbean treats; "prompt" service is "perfect for lunch on the run" and whether you "get it to go" or chow down on "the colorful patio", it'll "put some zing in your life."

Chadaka   – – – I
310 N. San Fernando Blvd. (Magnolia Blvd.), Burbank, 818-848-8520; www.chadaka.com
It's as if you're dining inside a polished bamboo box at this starkly elegant Burbank Siamese, the latest creation from the Tuk Tuk Thai and Rambutan Thai team; the stylish offerings include an extensive martini list and a modern menu with charbroiled options galore.

Chameau Ⓜ   24 20 22 $37
339 N. Fairfax Ave. (Beverly Blvd.), Los Angeles, 323-951-0039; www.chameaurestaurant.com
Devotees would "walk a mile" for this Fairfax Avenue "find" (whose name is French for 'camel') that was "transplanted from Silver Lake" to this "ultramod" space; the "inventive" Franco-Moroccan fare, including a "divine" duck b'steeya, feels "straight from chichi nouvelle Marrakesh" – it's "wildly exciting" – and the staff is "the nicest", too, so "believe the hype" and "hump" on down.

Chan Dara   21 18 18 $25
310 N. Larchmont Blvd. (Beverly Blvd.), Hancock Park, 323-467-1052
1511 N. Cahuenga Blvd. (Sunset Blvd.), Hollywood, 323-464-8585
11940 W. Pico Blvd. (Bundy Dr.), West LA, 310-479-4461; www.chandarawestla.com
The "hip crowd" that frequents this "sexy" Siamese outfit lauds the "cover-girl waitresses" – they're as "hot as the spicy noodles" – and considers the "creative" Thai food "a real delight"; but others hedge it's "not really exotic or imaginative" and sound off that the "eye-candy staff" can be rather "lackadaisical."

Chao Krung   ▽ 21 17 22 $16
111 N. Fairfax Ave. (W. 3rd St.), Los Angeles, 323-932-9482; www.chaokrung.com
Even refined diners "lick the plates clean" at this "unassuming" Fairfax Thai temple that's been catering to locals (and "stars" from

the nearby CBS studios) since the '70s; plop down in the "peaceful setting", amid carved woodwork and glow-in-the-dark paintings, for "delicious and reasonably priced" dishes served by a staff that "makes you feel at home"; P.S. it's "veggie-friendly" too.

Chart House   19 | 21 | 19 | $37

18412 PCH (Topanga Canyon Rd.), Malibu, 310-454-9321
13950 Panay Way (Via Marina St.), Marina del Rey, 310-822-4144
231 Yacht Club Way (bet. Harbor Dr. & Herondo St.), Redondo Beach,
310-372-3464
www.chart-house.com
"Still the place to go for romantic sunsets and frilly drinks", or to dine with your "three-generation family", this coastal surf 'n' turf chain earns more kudos for the "unparalleled" ocean views than for the "consistent" if "uninspired" food; diners strain to see past the "freshmen" staff and declare the "stuffy" interiors "a bit outdated", but admit the "beautiful" vistas alone can be worth a visit.

CHATEAU MARMONT   21 | 25 | 20 | $48

Chateau Marmont, 8221 W. Sunset Blvd. (Marmont Ln.), West Hollywood,
323-656-1010
"Beyond private", with only "A-list stars" and "the ghosts of old Hollywood" for company, this "discreet" spot at the famed Sunset Strip hotel caters primarily to overnight guests, but it's still "great for seducing your next love"; it's so picturesque, in fact, that many surveyors don't even mention the "delicious" Cal-French food or the "excellent service" – perhaps such details matter little when "heaven might just look like these" "enchanting gardens."

Chaya Brasserie   24 | 23 | 21 | $45

8741 Alden Dr. (bet. Beverly Blvd. & 3rd St.), West Hollywood,
310-859-8833; www.thechaya.com
"Consistently wonderful for more than 20 years", this "old standby" in West Hollywood serves "dreamy" Asian-Eclectic dishes paired with "fun cocktails" (like raspberry or litchi martinis) to diners more concerned with "creative" cuisine than a "roaring scene"; while the room is "a tad too noisy", the "friendly" staff and the "very LA stargazing" make this a "still hot" "place where you don't have to wait a month to get in."

Chaya Venice ◗   23 | 21 | 20 | $42

110 Navy St. (Main St.), Venice, 310-396-1179;
www.thechaya.com
A "sassy after-work spot" where you can "bring a date or steal someone else's" while plundering the "happening" "sushi happy hour" (it's "as crowded as the Tokyo subway"), this Asian-Eclectic "staple" set in a "gorgeous" Venice space is just as "hopping" as its WeHo doppelganger; service is "on the ball" and the menu is "unique", so never mind that some call it "P.F. Chang's on steroids" – most have nothing but praise for this "classic California scene."

Checkers Downtown   22 | 24 | 23 | $50

Hilton Checkers, 535 S. Grand Ave. (bet. 5th & 6th Sts.),
Downtown, 213-624-0000; www.checkershotel.com
Exuding "old-school formality filtered through a California lens", this "tranquil" Downtown dandy at the Hilton Checkers gets a crown for a "civilized" breakfast meeting, "leisurely" biz lunch or pre-concert dinner of "sophisticated" Cal cuisine served by a "top-notch" staff; if you can double-jump the doubters who dub the food "uninspired",

a complimentary limo will be waiting to whisk you to the Disney Hall or Dorothy Chandler – or, heaven forbid, "you can walk."

Cheebo   19 | 15 | 16 | $22

7533 W. Sunset Blvd. (Sierra Bonita Ave.), Hollywood, 323-850-7070; www.cheebo.com

Like a "cool coffee shop", this orange-walled Hollywood "hipster hangout" with "retro" decor and celeb sightings "delights all the senses" with "perfect" pizzas served by the slab and other "tasty victuals" that range from Italian dishes to a pulled pork and manchego sandwich that "elicits audible moans"; still, you might want to BYO snacks, since service is "slow, slow, slow."

CHEESECAKE FACTORY   20 | 18 | 18 | $24

364 N. Beverly Dr. (Brighton Way), Beverly Hills, 310-278-7270
11647 San Vicente Blvd. (bet. Barrington Ave. & Wilshire Blvd.), Brentwood, 310-826-7111
4142 Via Marina St. (Admiralty Way), Marina del Rey, 310-306-3344
2 W. Colorado Blvd. (Fair Oaks Ave.), Pasadena, 626-584-6000
605 N. Harbor Dr. (190th St.), Redondo Beach, 310-376-0466
Sherman Oaks Galleria, 15301 Ventura Blvd. (Sepulveda Blvd.), Sherman Oaks, 818-906-0700
Thousand Oaks Mall, 442 W. Hillcrest Dr. (Lynn Rd.), Thousand Oaks, 805-371-9705
Warner Center Trillium, 6324 Canoga Ave. (Victory Blvd.), Woodland Hills, 818-883-9900
www.thecheesecakefactory.com

Even die-hard chain-haters confess to periodic "gorge-athons" at this "solid" American, where the menu "goes on for miles" and the "gargantuan portions" could "feed a small army"; sure, it's a good "value", but the tradeoff lies in the "hit-or-miss" service, the "noisy" atmosphere (it's "always a mob scene") and the "painful" wait for a table – a "purgatory" that can last "two or three eternities."

Cheng Du   19 | 12 | 16 | $15

(fka Chung King)
11538 W. Pico Blvd. (bet. Federal Ave. & Gateway Blvd.), West LA, 310-477-4917

"The reliable Chinese place that every neighborhood should have" boast boosters of this "casual, friendly" West LA staple; "lightning-fast delivery with a smile" and "economical" prices are its strong suit, so set your sights on fare that's "not great, but fresh tasting, filling, cheap" and "well seasoned."

Chez Jay   19 | 14 | 18 | $30

1657 Ocean Ave. (Colorado Ave.), Santa Monica, 310-395-1741; www.chezjays.com

A "fall from a cliff" amid mere dives, this "funky" SM "sea shanty" is "frozen in time" – Sinatra time – and still hooks "screenwriters", "execs" and "surfers" with "delicious" steaks and "drinks as strong as the space is dark"; "throw your peanut shells on the floor with abandon" (the "wonderful" staff doesn't mind), and "if you're lucky", owner Jay Fiondella "will regale you" with Rat Pack tales.

Chez Melange   25 | 16 | 24 | $40

Palos Verdes Inn, 1716 S. PCH (bet. Palos Verdes Blvd. & Prospect Ave.), Redondo Beach, 310-540-1222; www.chezmelange.com

Chef Robert Bell is a "genius at combining flavors", concocting a "true mélange" of Eclectic dishes at this Redondo Beach icon where there's "always something new to enchant" loyal diners; add the "reasonably priced" wine list and "top-notch" service (directed by co-owner Michael Franks), and though it looks "like a glorified Denny's", it's "still one of the best restaurants in the South Bay"; P.S. the "unsung" breakfasts are "fantastic", too.

Chez Mimi Ⓜ   22 | 24 | 21 | $41

246 26th St. (San Vicente Blvd.), Santa Monica, 310-393-0558; www.chezmimirestaurant.com
Working her *magique* in a "lovingly restored old house" full of "nooks and crannies", chef-owner (and "bundle of joy") Mimi Hebert has created a "great escape" in Santa Monica; with "smiling" servers delivering "generous" portions of "rich and hearty" country French "comfort food", dining at this "most comfortable of special-occasion restaurants" (particularly in the "enchanting garden") is "almost like being in the south of France."

Chi Dynasty   20 | 14 | 20 | $25

2112 Hillhurst Ave. (bet. Ambrose Ave. & Los Feliz Blvd.), Los Feliz, 323-667-3388
"It's all about the" food, from the "outstanding" "Chinese chicken salad" to the "consistently well-prepared" dishes, according to the Chi-nese fans who've been packing this Los Feliz "staple for more than" two decades; it's a "convivial" "neighborhood" eatery that benefits from the "above and beyond" service from "waiters who always remember you"; P.S. a recent face-lift may quell qualms about the "run-down-looking" interior.

Chili John's Ⓢ Ⓜ ⇄   ▽ 23 | 8 | 21 | $10

2018 W. Burbank Blvd. (Keystone St.), Burbank, 818-846-3611
"Chili is the claim to fame" at this "Burbank institution" that's been slogging "huge bowls" of the stuff – which many consider "the best in LA" – across its horseshoe-shaped counter since 1946; "don't dress" up (this "tell-it-like-it-is family-run operation" is basically an American "diner"), and if the service isn't perfect, have patience: "the staff warms up to you after multiple visits"; N.B. closed July and August.

China Beach Bistro   ▽ 16 | 8 | 18 | $14

2024 Pacific Ave. (Venice Blvd.), Venice, 310-823-4646
"There's not much atmosphere" at this BYO "joint" in Venice, but buff boardwalkers bring their own ambiance as they inhale "good, cheap" Vietnamese fare (including vegetarian options) on the "small patio" "just one block from the beach"; become a regular and you might score an autograph from "totally cool" actress-owner Hiep Thi Le, a veteran of *Cruel Intentions* and other films.

Chin Chin   16 | 13 | 15 | $21

206 S. Beverly Dr. (Gregory Way), Beverly Hills, 310-248-5252
11740 San Vicente Blvd. (bet. Barrington & Montana Aves.), Brentwood, 310-826-2525
Villa Marina Mktpl., 13455 Maxella Ave. (Lincoln Blvd.), Marina del Rey, 310-823-9999
12215 Ventura Blvd. (Laurel Canyon Blvd.), Studio City, 818-985-9090
Sunset Plaza, 8618 W. Sunset Blvd. (Sunset Plaza Dr.), West Hollywood, 310-652-1818
www.chinchin.com
"Deserving credit for the Chinese chicken salad copied by 237 other restaurants", this Sino-Cal mini-chain is worshipped by "trim types"

who pop in for some "reliable" chow "after spin class"; purists pan the "Americanized" fare (it's "dim sum for dummies"), "slow service" and "cafeteria feel", but if you stick to the "wholesome" "fast food", you might avoid growing a double chin-chin.

CHINOIS ON MAIN   26 | 20 | 22 | $55

2709 Main St. (bet. Ashland Ave. & Ocean Park Blvd.), Santa Monica, 310-392-9025; www.wolfgangpuck.com

The "original gem of the Wolfgang Puck empire", SM's two-decade-old "epicurean's delight" – the "granddaddy of French-Asian dining" – "continues to shine" through its "transcendent" cuisine that "will never go out of style"; even if a few pucker at the "intolerable" noise level in the packed-"like-sardines" space – and declare the whole experience is "not all it's cracked up to be" – supporters swear it's "where to go for your last meal."

Chloe ⊠ Ⓜ   24 | 19 | 22 | $48

333 Culver Blvd. (Vista del Mar), Playa del Rey, 310-305-4505; www.chloerestaurant.com

"Tucked away" in a "nondescript building" near LAX, this "shoebox-sized" New American–Cal "home run" brings a "Rey of sunshine to Playa" with "creative" fare from a menu that changes monthly; the staffers "clearly love their jobs", and the "luscious" "food makes up for the cramped quarters", though some surveyors caution that you'd better "bring a high credit limit."

Chocolat   – | – | – | M

8155 Melrose Ave. (Crescent Heights Blvd.), Los Angeles, 323-651-2111

What used to be the Melrose Avenue branch of the Moustache Café is now under new ownership with a new name, but it's still a close culinary relative of its well-known forebear, offering a new version of the original French bistro menu expanded with Continental dishes, though the signature chocolate soufflé remains.

Cholada   ▽ 23 | 10 | 20 | $20

18763 PCH (Topanga Beach Dr.), Malibu, 310-317-0025

"Ignore the shabby surroundings" and "the traffic noise from the PCH" and concentrate on the "amazing views from all the tables" at this "old beach shack", an "unlikely setting" that serves up "shockingly good" Thai fare; this "funky" spot with a "friendly staff" is a "best buy" for "cheap eats in Malibu", so fans only "wish it were larger", 'cuz sometimes the "wait is long."

Christine   25 | 19 | 23 | $39

Hillside Vlg., 24530 Hawthorne Blvd. (Via Valmonte), Torrance, 310-373-1952; www.restaurantchristine.com

With a "creative" menu that "beckons for multiple visits", and "congenial" service from the "knowledgeable foodie staff", "true gourmet" chef-owner Christine Brown "packs them in year after year" at this South Bay "rarity" for "delicious" Pacific Rim–Med fare; the "imaginative" dishes take advantage of "the freshest seasonal produce", so admirers' only objection is that the "cozy" space in a Torrance mini-mall could be "a little bigger."

Christy's   25 | 23 | 22 | $41

3937 E. Broadway (Termino Ave.), Long Beach, 562-433-7133; www.christyslongbeach.com

A "must"-visit "favorite" in LB's Belmont Heights area, this first restaurant from Christy Bono (Sonny's daughter) puts guests in the right mood with "wonderful" martinis or something from the "great wine" list before indulging them with the "signature" rigatoni con carne or other "sophisticated" Italian fare; despite the eatery's "popularity", the "impeccable" service and "ornately decorated" space with an indoor waterfall make you feel "relaxed."

Ciao Trattoria 🖾

| 21 | 21 | 21 | $33 |

815 W. Seventh St. (bet. Figueroa & Flower Sts.), Downtown, 213-624-2244; www.ciaotrattoria.com
A "staple" "for those attending events" at the Staples Center or the Downtown theaters, this Italian "sleeper", where owner Harry Hagani "makes everyone feel welcome", is a pre-concert fave, thanks to its "heavenly" garlic rolls and "tasty pastas"; it's tucked into an "architecturally significant" space, but a few hecklers who "say ciao" contend that, convenience aside, "there are better choices all around."

CICADA 🖾

| 24 | 28 | 24 | $50 |

617 S. Olive St. (bet. 6th & 7th Sts.), Downtown, 213-488-9488; www.cicadarestaurant.com
Whether you're orchestrating a "business meeting" or "a marriage proposal", this "ritzy" "oasis of elegance" that "glows" in the landmark Oviatt building elicits "well-deserved oohs and aahs"; the "unobtrusive" service and "exquisite" Cal-Italian cuisine make you "feel like you're rich and famous", and guests' sole gripe is that they eventually have to "leave" this "lavish" art deco "palace" "and reenter the real world."

Cinch

| 16 | 24 | 16 | $42 |

1519 Wilshire Blvd. (16th St.), Santa Monica, 310-395-4139; www.cinchrestaurant.com
In this Santa Monica hot spot, "impeccably designed" by Dodd Mitchell, "young, loud crowds" abound, particularly around the "fabulous" upstairs bar teeming with "beautiful people trying to be noticed"; but while the scene is a cinch, the French-Asian fare isn't always a walk in the park: supporters tout it as "tantalizing", but others who "suffocate" in the "Hollywood"-style "attitude" whine it's "all style, no substance"; N.B. a post-*Survey* chef change may impact the Food rating.

Cinespace 🖾 🅜

| ▽ 18 | 22 | 18 | $31 |

6356 Hollywood Blvd. (bet. Cahuenga Blvd. & Ivar Ave.), Hollywood, 323-817-3456; www.cine-space.com
Taking "dinner and a movie to a whole new level", this "soaring" Hollywood space allows diners to watch classic and indie films (Thursday–Saturday only) while they munch "tasty" New American cuisine brought by black-clad servers who "move like ninjas"; critics carp that the merely "decent" food "doesn't live up" to its potential, but it's nevertheless an awesome "first date spot", since "you won't have to talk much."

Citrine

| 25 | 24 | 24 | $55 |

8360 Melrose Ave. (Kings Rd.), Los Angeles, 323-655-1690; www.citrinerestaurant.com
Chef Kevin Meehan "has raised the bar" at this New French sophomore on Melrose, where the "stellar" cuisine "finally" "lives up to" the "classy", cosmopolitan Michael Berman–designed setting; "you must" "try the seared foie gras", but the "gracious" and "knowledgeable" servers can guide you to any number of

"fabulous" menu selections; the wine list is "solid", too, so most respondents report that it's "worth saving up for" this "real find."

City Kitchen ⊠　　　　　　　　　　－ ｜ － ｜ － ｜ I
950 S. Flower St. (Olympic Blvd.), Downtown, 213-614-1442
As the revitalization of Downtown picks up steam, this popular catering company expands into the world of sit-down dining with a casual New American cafe that fits the laid-back lifestyle of local homesteaders; look for updated but affordable American fare served indoors as well as out.

Ciudad　　　　　　　　　　　　21 ｜ 20 ｜ 20 ｜ $36
Union Bank Plaza, 445 S. Figueroa St. (5th St.), Downtown,
213-486-5171; www.ciudad-la.com
"Where scene meets cuisine", this Downtown "foodie fiesta" – sibling to SM's Border Grill – keeps up a "party atmosphere", thanks to the "sexy" servers, the "famous mojitos" served during the *muy caliente* happy hour and one of the "best rum selections in town"; the "fantastic" Nuevo Latino fare prepared "with passion" satisfies most city dwellers, though a frustrated few recommend learning "sign language to communicate" through the "unbearable" noise.

Clafoutis ●　　　　　　　　　　17 ｜ 17 ｜ 16 ｜ $30
Sunset Plaza, 8630 W. Sunset Blvd. (Sunset Plaza Dr.), West Hollywood,
310-659-5233
You might "feel like you're waiting for your screen test" amid all the "models and handsome" "Euro" types "hanging out" at this Sunset Strip French bistro where the kitchen generates "more buzz than sizzle"; the fare is "adequate", particularly at "breakfast or brunch", but let's face it: you're really here for the "hysterical people-watching", which compensates for the "overwhelming" din and the "slinky waitresses not interested in" service.

Claim Jumper Restaurant　　　　　18 ｜ 17 ｜ 18 ｜ $22
18061 Gale Ave. (Fullerton Rd.), City of Industry, 626-964-1157
Marketplace Shopping Ctr., 6501 E. PCH (2nd St.), Long Beach,
562-431-1321
820 W. Huntington Dr. (Frwy. 210), Monrovia, 626-359-0463
Northridge Mall, 9429 Tampa Ave. (Plummer St.), Northridge,
818-718-2882
Torrance Crossroads, 24301 Crenshaw Blvd. (Lomita Blvd.),
Torrance, 310-517-1874
25740 N. The Old Rd. (McBean Pkwy.), Valencia, 661-254-2628
www.claimjumper.com
Additional locations throughout Southern California
From the "humongous" steaks to the "ultrarich mother lode cake", this "cowboy-themed" "glutton's paradise" hauls out "heaps of chow" that will "feed an army" of miners; some forty-not-ers say this all-American mini-chain sacrifices "quality" for "quantity" and flap their wings about the "sizable wait" for a table, but at least some old prospectors claim that the "courteous" servers know "the customer is gold."

Clay Pit　　　　　　　　　　　　22 ｜ 16 ｜ 20 ｜ $26
145 S. Barrington Ave. (Sunset Blvd.), Brentwood, 310-476-4700;
www.theclaypitinc.com
"To indulge all their naan needs", "Indian food lovers" dig into the "delicious" "traditional" fare at this "Brentwood gem" where everything is "cooked with keen attention to detail"; beyond the

"white tablecloths" – and the "numerous star sightings" – the setting is "nothing special", but enthusiasts extol the "solicitous" service and insist the $10.25 "lunch buffet is a real treat."

Clementine ⊠   24 | 12 | 16 | $16
1751 Ensley Ave. (Santa Monica Blvd.), Century City, 310-552-1080; www.clementineonline.com
It's "hard to get a seat" – and "even harder to get a parking space" – but that doesn't deter local office workers and "ladies who lunch" from seeking out the "fresh" American "home cooking" at this "unassuming" Century City cafe, where the "shiny young" staff dishes out "out-of-this-world" sandwiches and baked goods, including the "best peanut butter cookies known to man."

Cliff's Edge ◑   20 | 23 | 18 | $36
3626 Sunset Blvd. (Edgecliffe Dr.), Silver Lake, 323-666-6116
Social climbers rave about the "enchanting" back patio at this "smart, sleek" Italian bistro in Silver Lake, whose "bamboo and luscious foliage" (love that big ficus tree) make it "perfect on a balmy night"; alas, the Cliff notes left by the "fashionable" hedge on the "inconsistent" small-plate cuisine and call service a "comedy of errors", though it's still considered a "cool place to hang."

Cobra Lily ⊠   20 | 17 | 16 | $29
8442 Wilshire Blvd. (Hamilton Dr.), Beverly Hills, 323-651-5051
When you want to "taste lots of different things", slither over to this "trendy" yet "friendly" Beverly Hills pad, a "dark", "cool tapas scene" serving up a "nice variety" of Spanish small plates "perfect" "for noshing" with "killer sangria"; the "laid-back staff" helps make it an "easy place to hang out" in – "as long as you don't want to talk much, as the music's a little loud."

Cobras & Matadors   22 | 17 | 18 | $31
4655 Hollywood Blvd. (Vermont Ave.), Los Feliz, 323-669-3922
7615 W. Beverly Blvd. (bet. Fairfax & La Brea Aves.), West Hollywood, 323-932-6178
With "a laundry list of tapas that'll blow your taste buds away", these "terrific" Spaniards in Los Feliz and on Beverly serve up "big flavors on small plates"; reviewers are bullish about the "sexy" (if "ultranoisy") atmosphere that's "fun for a group", although they wave a red cape about the "spotty" service; N.B. at the BYO WeHo location, you can bring in wine from the store next door.

Cole's P.E. Buffet ⊠   ▽ 17 | 13 | 16 | $12
Pacific Electric Bldg., 118 E. Sixth St. (bet. Los Angeles & Main Sts.), Downtown, 213-622-4090; www.colespebuffet.com
Nothing like "stepping into a Raymond Chandler novel for lunch" swear fans of this "seedy yet cool" Downtowner that's been slicing up "classic French dip" sandwiches since 1908 (reportedly invented here); while most wax nostalgic about the "old-timey" atmosphere, "cheap" American chow and "great" beer selection, a handful quiver it's "kinda scary", though perhaps they may reevaluate now that it has a new owner, nightclub impresario Marc Smith.

Continental, The ◑⊠   – | – | – | M
8400 Wilshire Blvd. (Gale Dr.), Beverly Hills, 323-782-9717; www.continentalbar.homestead.com
Though no longer owned by founders Matt Damon and Ben Affleck, this mildly swanky corner club in Beverly Hills still draws industry

bigwigs as much for the happy hour as the Cal-Continental cuisine; weekly themes like half-price Mondays and all-you-can-eat sushi Tuesdays bring in even more hungry movers and shakers.

Coral Tree Café   19 | 17 | 14 | $17
11645 San Vicente Blvd. (Darlington Ave.), Brentwood, 310-979-8733; www.coraltreecafe.net
Proving "healthy comfort food" is not an oxymoron, this counter-service Cal-Ital "hangout" packs in Brentwood's "beautiful people" for "great java" "and eggs in the morning", "innovative salads" and panini "later on"; however "awesome" and warm the "roaring fire pit" is, though, respondents conversely report "less than friendly" service from the "cooler than cool" staff, and cynics charge that "organic is just another way to say 'overpriced.'"

Cora's Coffee Shoppe   21 | 12 | 17 | $20
1802 Ocean Ave. (Pico Blvd.), Santa Monica, 310-451-9562
If you "can't afford" its sister restaurant next door, this "itsy-bitsy" SM coffee shop will cater to your Capo cravings with "to-die-for" omelets and "huge" orange-blueberry pancakes; there's "no frills and no view" (and "little service" either), but it's still a "popular" place to linger over a "lazy lunch" or "sit outside, read the paper and start your morning right"; N.B. dinner is served May–July only.

Counter, The   22 | 16 | 17 | $15
2901 Ocean Park Blvd. (29th St.), Santa Monica, 310-399-8383; www.thecounterburger.com
"It's easy to go overboard" "building your own" "gourmet burger" at this "kid-friendly" SM diner, what with the "astonishing" number of "irresistible" toppings and the "excellent" "onion strings and fries"; give into the "greasy, gooey mess" of "pure" carnivore "heaven" ("great veggie" patties, too), and never mind that "you pay a steep price for the privilege" and that service is "a bit slow."

Courtyard, The ◐   ▽ 19 | 19 | 23 | $36
8543 Santa Monica Blvd. (La Cienega Blvd.), West Hollywood, 310-358-0301; www.dinecourtyard.com
This new WeHo addition to LA's already crowded small-plate market "takes you back to Spain" with "authentic tortilla española" and other "tasty" tapas dished out by a "super-friendly" staff; early adopters concede that it's "still getting its legs" – "nothing stands out" yet – but it's already a "great place for outdoor dining."

Coyote Cantina   24 | 20 | 23 | $23
King Harbor Ctr., 531 N. PCH (190th St.), Redondo Beach, 310-376-1066; www.coyotecantina.net
"Heavy lines" form on weekends at this longtime "local fave" in an "unassuming" Redondo Beach strip mall, where the "potent" margaritas and "amazing tequila selection" (more than 60 labels) prep wily patrons for the "innovative" Southwestern dishes; prices are "fair" and the staff is "engaging", and though some vets bark that the "vibe has changed" under the new ownership, you're still guaranteed a "howling good time."

Cozymel's   16 | 17 | 17 | $23
2171 Rosecrans Ave. (Continental Way), El Segundo, 310-606-5464; www.cozymels.com
Travelers to this "colorful", "tropical-looking" El Segundo spot meet for "great margaritas" "after work" or "take the office" crew at

lunchtime for "fresh", "plentiful portions" of "spicy" Mexican toted to table by a "young, attractive staff"; but other journeymen and women find it better for "drinks and appetizers", because the "very average formulaic fare" is "nothing to write home about."

Crazy Fish | 18 | 7 | 12 | $26 |

9105 W. Olympic Blvd. (Doheny Dr.), Beverly Hills, 310-550-8547
You'd have to be a lunatic not to appreciate the "huge" maki rolls at this "always slammed" Beverly Hills sushi center, where the decor isn't "the prettiest", the waits can be "unbearable" and nobody raves about the service; still, for "fresh fish" at "very reasonable prices", it's worth checking yourself into this Japanese institution.

Crescendo at Fred Segal | ▽ 18 | 12 | 14 | $21 |

Fred Segal Store, 500 Broadway (5th St.), Santa Monica, 310-395-5699
"If you're hungry while shopping" in the "hipster" "bazaar that is Fred Segal" in Santa Monica, stop into this adjoining "very casual" cafe for a "quick bite" to "rest up" between dashes to the "posh" "collection of stores"; it's a "solid pick if you want Italian" and "surprisingly" "healthy and tasty" to boot.

Crocodile Café | 15 | 14 | 15 | $21 |

626 N. Central Ave. (Doran St.), Glendale, 818-241-1114
140 S. Lake Ave. (Cordova St.), Pasadena, 626-449-9900
www.crocodilecafe.com
Though this "once booming" "casual" Californian chain has been "whittled down" to two LA-area locations, the "ample" portions of "designer food at diner prices" still please diehards; it may be a "solid" "family destination", but gator-baiters gnash at the "uninspired" menu and the "inexperienced" servers, rumbling that the whole operation "needs rejuvenation."

CRUSTACEAN 🈺 | 24 | 26 | 21 | $55 |

9646 Little Santa Monica Blvd. (Bedford Dr.), Beverly Hills, 310-205-8990; www.secretkitchen.com
"Beautiful people" flock to this "see-and-be-seen" Beverly Hills "loud beehive" for the "brilliant" Vietnamese-inspired Euro-Asian cuisine; regulars recommend the "amazing garlic noodles", the "divine crab" or anything "from the secret kitchen menu" – they're all a fine match for the "enchanting" setting with a "glass-tiled floor revealing" koi "swimming" "underfoot"; still, a smattering of cynics snipe it's an "overpriced refuge for the star-struck."

C2 Cafe & Kitchen 🈺 | ▽ 16 | 10 | 14 | $20 |

2039 Century Park E. (Olympic Blvd.), Century City, 310-551-1600; www.patinagroup.com
With "numerous choices", outdoor seating, and the option of table service or cafeteria dining, this Cal-French member of Joachim Splichal's archipelago is handy "for a biz lunch" in Century City; but foes find the "froufrou food" "disappointing, object to the "noise" from the adjacent construction site and snap they're "holding office workers hostage"; N.B. no dinner and closed weekends.

Cuban Bistro Ⓜ | ▽ 18 | 17 | 18 | $26 |

28 W. Main St. (Garfield Ave.), Alhambra, 626-308-3350; www.cubanbistro.com
Offering live music on weekends, the "best first-date restaurant in Alhambra" has Latin lovers "dancing in the aisles" after sampling the "delicious" Cuban fare (there's "real garlic happening here"); in

this "comfy setting" "for young and old alike", the "great" service and all-glass bar provide extra motivation to get up and salsa.

Cucina Paradiso   − | − | − | M
3387 Motor Ave. (National Blvd.), Palms, 310-839-2500
This well-respected Italian closed in Redondo Beach several years ago only to reopen in a warm, old-fashioned space in an industrial building on a nondescript block halfway between the Fox and Sony lots in Palms; the well-priced menu of upscale dishes makes it unique in this pizza-and-pasta part of town.

Cynthia's   20 | 14 | 14 | $39
8370 W. Third St. (La Cienega Blvd.), Los Angeles, 323-658-7851;
www.cynthias-restaurant.com
For "comfort food at its best" with a side of "attitude", this Third Street American garners mixed reactions from diners, most of whom praise the "deservedly famous fried chicken" and "mind-blowing" blackberry cobbler; however, "infamous" owner Cynthia Hirst "rules" her "raucous" restaurant "with an iron fist" − she's a "hoot" or "impossible", depending on your tastes − and the "treat-for-the-eye" servers seem "unconcerned" either way.

Daily Grill   18 | 16 | 18 | $27
Brentwood Gardens, 11677 San Vicente Blvd. (Barrington Ave.),
Brentwood, 310-442-0044
Burbank Hilton, 2500 Hollywood Way (Thornton Ave.), Burbank,
818-840-6464
2121 Rosecrans Ave. (Continental Way), El Segundo, 310-524-0700
LA Int'l Airport, 280 World Way (Tom Bradley Terminal), LAX, 310-215-5180
Beverly Connection, 100 N. La Cienega Blvd. (bet. Beverly Blvd. &
3rd St.), Los Angeles, 310-659-3100
Laurel Promenade, 12050 Ventura Blvd. (Laurel Canyon Blvd.),
Studio City, 818-769-6336
Universal CityWalk, 1000 Universal Studios Blvd. (off Frwy. 101),
Universal City, 818-760-4448
www.dailygrill.com
Serving "everyday" American "home cooking" with "style", this quotidian chain, spun off from The Grill on the Alley, gets credit for "excellent chicken pot pie" and other "quality comfort food" doled out in "substantial" portions and at "fair prices"; never mind the daily growls about the "boring" menu or the "variable" service, most vets deem it "a favorite that never disappoints."

Dakota ☻   − | − | − | E
Hollywood Roosevelt, 7000 Hollywood Blvd. (N. Orange Dr.),
Hollywood, 323-769-8888; www.dakota-restaurant.com
Celebrated restaurateurs Tim and Liza Goodell (Meson G, Troquet) stake a claim in retro-modern American steakhouse turf with this newcomer designed by hot property Dodd Mitchell in stone, dark wood and black leather and set next to the historic Hollywood Roosevelt's lobby (site of the first Academy Awards presentation); Jeff Armstrong mans the stove, turning out meat, fish and poultry dishes galore with penty of luscious sides.

DAL RAE   25 | 20 | 24 | $48
9023 E. Washington Blvd. (Rosemead Blvd.), Pico Rivera,
562-949-2444; www.dalrae.com
The "race track meets the Rat Pack" at this Pico Rivera "cholesterol heaven", a "family tradition since the 1950s" that still "seems frozen

in time"; the "classic" Continental fare is "wonderful", especially the items that the "seasoned staff" "prepares tableside", so whether you think this place is "old school", "old boy" or just old hat, it's a "prize" in a "gastronomically challenged" part of town.

Damon's Steakhouse   17 | 18 | 19 | $25
317 N. Brand Blvd. (bet. California Ave. & Lexington Dr.), Glendale, 818-507-1510
"Convenient to the Alex Theater" in Glendale, this "South Seas retro fantasy" is a spectacle in itself, a "kitschy" "Tahitian time warp" with "good steaks" and "potent mai tais that send you to tiki heaven"; what's really been keeping customers coming back to this "old-fashioned" steakhouse (since 1937), though, are the "bargain" prices and the "ancient waitresses who call you 'hon.'"

D'Amore's Pizza Connection   22 | 7 | 17 | $13
7137 Winnetka Ave. (Sherman Way), Canoga Park, 818-348-5900
15928 Ventura Blvd. (bet. Haskell & Woodley Aves.), Encino, 818-907-9100
22601 PCH (Cross Creek Rd.), Malibu, 310-317-4500
12910 Magnolia Blvd. (Coldwater Canyon Ave.), Sherman Oaks, 818-505-1111
14519 Ventura Blvd. (Van Nuys Blvd.), Sherman Oaks, 818-905-3377
Skyline Shopping Ctr., 2869 Thousand Oaks Blvd. (Skyline Dr.), Thousand Oaks, 805-496-0030
1077 Broxton Ave. (Kinross Ave.), Westwood, 310-209-1212
"Maybe bringing in water from Boston" for the dough "really does make a difference" speculate supporters of the "delicious" "thin-crust" pies with "tangy sauce" and "fresh ingredients" wheeled out at this chain, where you should "get it delivered or pick it up" (the decor is basically "lousy"); though detractors dub it "overrated", most muse "what more could you want" than East Coast "pizza served by California girls"?

Dan Tana's ●   23 | 18 | 21 | $49
9071 Santa Monica Blvd. (Doheny Dr.), West Hollywood, 310-275-9444
Legend has it that "Frank Sinatra ate" at this West Hollywood "landmark", a "throwback to the '60s" that knockaround guys still *salute* as one of the better "old-school Italian places in town"; both "stars" and schlubs settled into the "red leather booths" for "thick, mouthwatering" steaks and "fantastic" pastas served by a "kitschy" "cast of characters", but "you may have to wait if walk-in celebs jump to the head of the line."

Da Pasquale ☒   20 | 13 | 19 | $29
9749 Little Santa Monica Blvd. (bet. Linden & Roxbury Drs.), Beverly Hills, 310-859-3884
When chef/co-owner Anna Morra "is at the stove, all is well with the world", praise patrons of this "swell" Italian "family affair", a "carbfest" where the "lovingly prepared" pasta and "wonderful" bread are "testaments to consistency"; loyalists also laud the "cheerful" service at this "homey" trattoria and appreciate being able to dine in Beverly Hills "without mortgaging your house"; N.B. now has a full bar.

DAR MAGHREB   20 | 25 | 21 | $44
7651 Sunset Blvd. (bet. Fairfax & La Brea Aves.), Hollywood, 323-876-7651; www.darmaghrebrestaurant.com
Evoking "an *Arabian Nights'* fantasy" complete with "authentic" belly dancers, this "Moroccan oasis" is an "exotic destination" "to

take a crowd" (or "adventurous out-of-towners") for "flavorful" food served "with flair"; though a few left-foots dismiss it as a "hokey" Hollywood "theme park", other voyagers avow it's "all about sitting on pillows, having drinks and eating with your hands."

De Lacey's Club 41   18 19 20 $31

41 S. De Lacey St. (bet. Colorado Blvd. & Green St.), Pasadena, 626-795-4141; www.delaceysclub41.com

"Chicago gangster meets little old lady from Pasadena" at this "step-back-in-time" steakhouse, where the "reliable" staff and "clubby" atmosphere with "plenty of wood and leather" (the bar was built in 1906) set the tone for "solid" "comfort food"; some claim it serves merely "ok" eats "for an ok price", but the joint still hops on weekend evenings when "'70s and '80s bands play."

Delmonico's Lobster House   22 20 21 $42

16358 Ventura Blvd. (Hayvenhurst Ave.), Encino, 818-986-0777; www.delmonicoslobsterhouse.com

Unrelated to the Seafood Grille of the same name, this Encino port o' call reels 'em in with "numerous lobster preparations" and plenty of other "consistent" "fresh" fish choices; the "intimate" booths and "personalized" service give this house a surprisingly "upscale" feel, and though some penny-pinching crabs call the tariffs "too expensive", others assert that the "ample" portions justify "a bit of a splurge."

Delmonico's Seafood Grille   19 17 19 $36

9320 W. Pico Blvd. (bet. Beverly & Doheny Drs.), Los Angeles, 310-550-7737
Paseo Colorado, 260 E. Colorado Blvd. (Garfield Ave.), Pasadena, 626-844-7000
www.delmonicos.com

"If it swims, you'll find it" at this "tried and true" pair of sole food specialists in Pasadena and on Pico, where the "quiet" rooms with their "comfy booths" let diners focus on the "classic" shellfish, steaks and pastas; to faithful fisherfolk, it's "just all-around good eating", but some anglers aver that the "tired decor" is casting about for "a redo" and call the whole cruise "nothing special."

Delphi Greek Cuisine ⊠   20 12 19 $22

1383 Westwood Blvd. (Wilshire Blvd.), Westwood, 310-478-2900

"A great neighborhood restaurant" lies in your future if you visit this "intimate", "family-run" taverna in Westwood where the "welcoming" atmosphere and "knightly" service almost upstage the "excellent" "traditional Greek fare"; although some philistines call it "fast, serviceable, but otherwise unremarkable", most patrons predict that it's a "terrific value – as long as you don't care about the decor."

Depot, The ⊠   24 22 22 $38

1250 Cabrillo Ave. (Torrance Blvd.), Torrance, 310-787-7501; www.depotrestaurant.com

Auto execs and "all those who love" "innovative" food board the chew-chew train for this "terrific" "destination" housed in an Old Torrance railroad station, an "always packed" whistle-stop thanks to the "superb" Eclectic cuisine from "gracious" chef-owner Michael Shafer's "creative" kitchen; the "outstanding" service and free valet parking help make this "gem of the South Bay" just the ticket for everything from "business lunches" to "special events."

Derby, The ▽ 22 | 21 | 22 | $39

233 E. Huntington Dr. (bet. Gateway Dr. & 2nd Ave.), Arcadia,
626-447-2430; www.thederbyarcadia.com

"Filled with horse racing history", this "old-style" steakhouse –
once owned by jockey George Woolf – is an "ol' stomping ground"
for Arcadia natives, particularly "after the races" at Santa Anita; the
"awesome" servers trot over with "great steaks", and while some
bookies wager that this "throwback" is "better for people-watching
than eating", odds are that "Seabiscuit would have loved" it.

DEREK'S ⓈⓂ 27 | 22 | 25 | $54

181 E. Glenarm St. (Marengo Ave.), Pasadena, 626-799-5252;
www.dereks.com

"Great host" Derek Dickenson titillates "serious food lovers"
with "innovative" "top-tier" Cal-French cuisine full of "beautiful,
balanced flavors" and paired with "outstanding" wines at his
"homey", "romantic" bistro set in an "unlikely location" "in a
Pasadena strip mall"; "sit near" the "inviting fireplace" and indulge
in "quiet conversation" – it's a "classy adult dining experience",
enhanced all the more by the "tremendously knowledgeable staff";
N.B. wear a jacket and leave the kids at home.

Devon, Restaurant Ⓜ ▽ 24 | 19 | 22 | $49

109 E. Lemon Ave. (Myrtle Ave.), Monrovia, 626-305-0013;
www.restaurantdevon.net

"Come for the game dishes" and the "dynamic wine list" and bring
bundles of "money" advise diners who find this "real gem" "off
the beaten path" in Old Town Monrovia "capable of putting out
darn good", "creative" Cal-French fare; it's "one of our favorites",
still the close-mouthed prefer to "keep it secret" – if this place got
any busier, "the wait would be unbearable."

DIAGHILEV ⓈⓂ 26 | 28 | 28 | $72

Wyndham Bel Age, 1020 N. San Vicente Blvd. (Sunset Blvd.),
West Hollywood, 310-854-1111; www.wyndham.com

The "beyond great" staff always "at your beck and call" has been
voted No. 1 for Service in this *Survey* five years running at this
"celebrated celebration restaurant", a "romantic" "gem" at
WeHo's Wyndam Bel Age that wows guests with "excellent"
Russian-French cuisine, "awesome" caviar and "homemade
flavored vodkas"; sure, this "crème de la crème" of "fantasy
evenings" is "astronomically expensive", but how often do "you
feel like a king, queen or czar"?; P.S. "perfect maitre d'" Dimitri
Dimitrov has moved on to Tower Bar.

Dino's Italian Inn ▽ 15 | 14 | 18 | $20

2055 E. Colorado Blvd. (bet. Allen Ave. & Sierra Madre Blvd.),
Pasadena, 626-449-8823

"They'll feed you like an Italian grandmother" would at this "retro"
Pasadena "institution", complete with "red booths" and "comfort
food" "drowning in sauce"; it feels as if "some waiters have
been there 40 years" – this "classic" dates back to 1939 – and it's a
"bargain" to boot, but critics deem this Dino-saur a "throwback."

DIN TAI FUNG 26 | 13 | 16 | $17

1108 S. Baldwin Ave. (Duarte Rd.), Arcadia, 626-574-7068

"You no longer have to go to Taiwan" for "the best dumplings" "in
the world", now that these "delicate" "bursts of sublime flavor" are

available at this "legendary" San Gabriel Valley "experience" (the Arcadia affiliate of a Taipei-based eatery); even when it's "crowded beyond belief", it runs "like a well-oiled machine", so nobody seems to mind that the decor is "not much to speak of", and vets will assure you the "simply delicious" Chinese food is "worth the hideous wait."

Dish   17 | 14 | 15 | $21
734 Foothill Blvd. (Commonwealth St.), La Cañada Flintridge, 818-790-5355; www.dishbreakfastlunchanddinner.com
"Breakfast is where it's at" insist enthusiasts for this "cutesy" and "funky" American cafe in La Cañada Flintridge where you could "take your mother, grandmother and the kids" (dads and granddads, too); plate-cleaners also praise the "simple" "homestyle cooking" at lunch and dinner, as well as the "friendly" vibe, but protestors pan the "plain"-Jane setting and "unexciting" food.

Divino   24 | 19 | 23 | $38
11714 Barrington Ct. (Sunset Blvd.), Brentwood, 310-472-0886
"Exemplary host" and owner Goran Milic "tirelessly works the room" at this "real find" in a Brentwood mini-mall, while his brother, chef Davor, cooks "like Mama Italiana – who went to finishing school"; the result, from the "sumptuous pastas" to the "intimate" and "relaxing" setting, adds up to a *divino* experience; P.S. if it's a little "too noisy" and "crowded", "ask for a table on the terrace."

Dolce Enoteca e Ristorante   17 | 23 | 18 | $46
8284 Melrose Ave. (Sweetzer Ave.), Hollywood, 323-852-7174; www.dolceenoteca.com
"Beautiful people", "beautiful space" sums up the Dolce Group's "ultrahip" Melrose Avenue Northern Italian with a "gorgeous" Dodd Mitchell–designed interior; "bring friends" to soak up the "cool vibe", since it's all about "the scene" (not the "forgettable" cuisine), but trendies caution that these days the celeb sightings are "down to C-list" with "more tourists than stars."

Dominick's ●   21 | 22 | 20 | $40
8715 Beverly Blvd. (San Vicente Blvd.), West Hollywood, 310-652-2335; www.dominicksrestaurant.com
"Everything old is new again" at this Beverly Boulevard bastion, remodeled and revived by "hospitable" restaurateur Warner Ebbink with "mouthwatering" wood-fired "grilled dishes" and "old-fashioned Italian standbys" from chef Brandon Boudet; "dine under the moon with friends" beside the "roaring fireplace" on the "lovely patio" or settle into the "soothing" "cool Manhattan bistro"-like setting for a "light meal or a full-on feast."

Dona Rosa ●   14 | 13 | 13 | $13
577 S. Arroyo Pkwy. (California Blvd.), Pasadena, 626-449-2999; www.dona-rosa.com
Eager to venture "a step above typical Mexican takeout", diners line up at the window for "yummy" burritos and an "awesome selection of *pan dulce*" at this Pasadena taqueria and bakery open from dawn till midnight; despite the "cheap" prices, those with a less rosy view suggest bypassing the "average" fare and "so-so" service and head for sister restaurant "El Cholo down the street."

Doug Arango's ⊠   20 | 20 | 21 | $48
8826 Melrose Ave. (Robertson Blvd.), West Hollywood, 310-278-3684;
www.dougarangos.com
Designing men and women (even Bill Gates) "indulge" in the "well-prepared" Cal-Italian fare at this Palm Desert–to–Melrose Avenue transplant and "decorator's hangout", set in a villalike space near the Pacific Design Center; the "warm" and "attentive" staff makes "everyone feel welcome", from the "beautiful people to the beautiful people-watchers", but gripers grouse that the "not terribly exciting menu" appeals largely to "an older crowd."

Doughboys ●   22 | 13 | 15 | $16
8136 W. Third St. (Crescent Heights Blvd.), Los Angeles, 323-651-4202;
www.doughboys.net
Braving often "hellish" waits, dough nuts flock to this "hipsterish" yet "comfy" Third Street American cafe for "hearty breakfasts", "stellar sandwiches" and "the most decadent dessert counter around"; hungry clock-watchers are irked by the "erratic" service but all is eventually forgiven thanks to "enormous" portions, the "phenomenal red velvet cake" and (of course) "good, chewy bread"; N.B. open until midnight daily.

Down Town Kabob   – | – | – | I
2515 Artesia Blvd. (Prospect Ave.), Redondo Beach, 310-370-9515
This lively, brightly lit South Bay Persian grill serves more than 30 inexpensive kebab combinations built around meat, fish or veggies, with feed-the-whole-family deals for the budget-conscious; while takeout is the main thrust, the skewers can also be consumed in the spare but comfortable dining room.

Drago   24 | 20 | 23 | $48
2628 Wilshire Blvd. (26th St.), Santa Monica, 310-828-1585;
www.celestinodrago.com
"A standby that has endured for good reason", chef-owner Celestino Drago's "trustworthy", "celebrity-laden" Santa Monica home base "passes the ultimate test of an Italian restaurant with flying colors", offering "outstanding pasta" and "savory" dishes that "soar" above "expectations", all "professionally" served; true, you sit so "close together" "it's impossible to ignore the conversation at the next table", but all in all, it remains a "buzz"-worthy "classy place" that "never disappoints."

Dragon   ▽ 13 | 19 | 16 | $24
22 Pier Ave. (Beach Dr.), Hermosa Beach, 310-372-4462;
www.dragonbar.net
Reviewers are split on whether this New American–Asian fusion sophomore on the Hermosa Beach pier should sink or swim: some tip the scales to praise the "great" sushi, the "cool" setting that's at least "trying to be upscale" and the "gorgeous" staff, while slayers scoff at the "below average" food and the "spring break in Daytona Beach" scene – your call.

Dr. Hogly Wogly's BBQ   23 | 7 | 18 | $19
8136 Sepulveda Blvd. (Roscoe Blvd.), Van Nuys, 818-780-6701
"Belly up" to this "no-frills" SF Valley "open pit" barbecue shack (which launched back in the '60s at Lyndon Johnson's suggestion), where supporters stage "incredible pig-outs" on the "heavenly brisket", "excellent ribs" and "baked beans to die for"; while

paying no mind to the "humble interior", some pignitaries snort that it's not worth "all the praise", but most are in "hog heaven" at this "taste of Texas in Van Nuys."

Duke's Coffee Shop   19 | 10 | 17 | $14

8909 Sunset Blvd. (San Vicente Blvd.), West Hollywood, 310-652-3100

"Please don't talk loudly at breakfast" plead regulars at this "funky hipster joint" and "landmark" "hangover haven" on the Sunset Strip, 'cause "the rest of us are still recovering from the night before"; while "sharing a table is part of the charm" ("even for a dive, it's a dive"), the "huge portions" of "basic" American "comfort food" make "rock 'n' rollers" young and old revere this duke of WeHo – "long may it reign."

Duke's Malibu/Huntington Beach   18 | 21 | 18 | $30

21150 PCH (Las Flores Canyon Rd.), Malibu, 310-317-0777;
www.hulapie.com

"Location, location, location" – say that twice and you'll sum up this oceanfront pair in Malibu and Huntington Beach where the decor is "a big picture window" "with waves crashing below"; the "fresh" fish and other Pacific Rim fare is "not bad" (the hula pie is a "best bet"), so if it's "not quite Hawaii", you can still "drink mai tais" and "pretend" – at least "if you can actually get" the "lackluster" staff "to serve you one."

Du-par's   14 | 9 | 14 | $14

Farmer's Mkt., 6333 W. Third St. (Fairfax Ave.), Los Angeles, 323-933-8446
Studio City Plaza, 12036 Ventura Blvd. (Laurel Canyon Blvd.),
Studio City, 818-766-4437 ●
Best Western Thousand Oaks Inn, 75 W. Thousand Oaks Blvd.
(bet. Frwy. 101 & Moorpark Rd.), Thousand Oaks, 805-373-8785
www.dupars.com

Beloved first for "great pancakes", second for "delicious" pies" and third for the "no-nonsense, old-time servers", this American outfit takes its lumps for its "rickety booths" and "tattered decor" – "this is your father's Oldsmobile of a diner"; while Par-tisans consider it "an institution", cynics snort "if you don't have nostalgic memories, don't bother"; N.B. the original Fairfax location, now under new ownership and closed for revnovation, is slated to reopen November 2005.

Ebizo's Skewer   ▽ 18 | 14 | 17 | $23

229 Manhattan Beach Blvd. (Highland Ave.), Manhattan Beach,
310-802-0765

You can cook your own "fresh, healthy, and delicious" hot pot at this Japanese shabu-shabu joint, whose "comfortable, modern" setting and "hospitable owner" make it a "nice alternative to" the area's "sports bars and chain restaurants"; it's a "great value" that "won't skewer your wallet", but skeptics take jabs at the "spotty service" and moan "sadly enough, this is about as exotic as Manhattan Beach can get."

Edendale Grill   17 | 23 | 19 | $36

2838 Rowena Ave. (bet. Auburn & Rokeby Sts.), Silver Lake,
323-666-2000; www.edendalegrill.com

Everyone loves the "gorgeous" bar and the "lively" vibe at this "part neighborhood joint, part swanky fine dining" spot in Silver Lake with a "unique" interior that pays "homage to silent movies that were shot" nearby; sadly, the rest of this 1924 "converted firehouse" sets off alarms, from the "cranky" servers to the "upscale" American "comfort food" that's "consistently inconsistent."

El Cholo
`18` `18` `18` `$22`

LA Int'l Airport, 209 World Way (Terminal 5), LAX, 310-417-1910
1121 S. Western Ave. (bet. Olympic & Pico Blvds.), Los Angeles, 323-734-2773
958 S. Fair Oaks Ave. (bet. California Blvd. & Glenarm St.), Pasadena, 626-441-4353
1025 Wilshire Blvd. (11th St.), Santa Monica, 310-899-1106
www.elcholo.com

A "landmark" to some, a place simply "famous for being famous" to others, this "venerable" chainlet starts diners off with "bulletproof margaritas" and finishes 'em off with "huge portions" of the "amazing" signature green corn tamales and other "*muy bueno*" Mexican dishes; if el grouchos guffaw that the grub's "too gringo" and complain about service that's "*el slow-o*", most maintain that this "party central" is "always a good time."

El Coyote Cafe
`12` `14` `16` `$18`

7312 Beverly Blvd. (bet. Fairfax & La Brea Aves.), Los Angeles, 323-939-2255; www.elcoyotecafe.com

The parking lot backs up onto Beverly Boulevard on weekend nights at this "boisterous" Fairfax "crowd-pleaser" that "hasn't changed in decades", with revelers more interested in the "legendary margaritas" than the "nothing-to-howl"-about Mexican "basics"; many growl that the "dirt cheap" food in this "cheesy setting" is merely "mediocre", but if you "drink enough, you'll forget about that and keep coming back."

Electric Lotus ●
`20` `22` `17` `$25`

1870 N. Vermont Ave. (Franklin Ave.), Los Feliz, 323-953-0040; www.electriclotus.com

Hailed as "the hippest place for Indian food in LA", this "new-age" Los Feliz "favorite" attracts a "bohemian clientele" to its "dark, mysterious" space with "a DJ spinning" "progressive music" and "screens showing Bollywood movies"; while the "tasty" but "not electrifying" food's "lack of authenticity" misses the mark for some lotus-eaters, most agree that the "wildly outlandish decor" and "lively" vibe make for an "exotic date" destination.

El Inka House Ⓜ
`19` `12` `16` `$15`

1938 E. Road 66 (Lone Hill Ave.), Glendora, 626-963-1044

El Pollo Inka
Gateway Plaza, 1425 W. Artesia Blvd. (Normandie Ave.), Gardena, 310-516-7378
1100 PCH (Aviation Blvd.), Hermosa Beach, 310-372-1433
Lawndale Plaza, 15400 Hawthorne Blvd. (154th St.), Lawndale, 310-676-6665
23705 Hawthorne Blvd. (bet. Lomita Blvd. & PCH), Torrance, 310-373-0062
www.elpolloinka.com

Sure, the Pollo is gone from the Glendora branch's moniker, but like the rest of this Peruvian outfit, it still serves up "juicy, delicious rotisserie chickens" "full of flavor", with "incredibly flavorful" chimichurri "sauce that's the bomb"; sure the "decor is a bit funky", perhaps even reminiscent of an "Incan cave", but it may be one of the "cheapest sit-down meals in town."

El Tepeyac ⊅   22 | 8 | 18 | $13
*812 N. Evergreen Ave. (bet. Cesar E. Chavez & Wabash Aves.),
East LA, 323-267-8668*
1965 Potrero Grande Dr. (Arroyo Dr.), Monterey Park, 626-573-4607 Ⓜ
"Bring an empty stomach" to these East LA–Monterrey Park
"holes-in-the-wall" (named for the hill in Mexico where the Virgin
Mary supposedly appeared in 1531), since the meal of choice
among the "down-home Mexican" dishes is a "gargantuan burrito";
fans also adore "incredibly friendly" owner Manuel Rojas and his
staff that "treats everyone like family."

El Torito   15 | 15 | 16 | $19
4012 W. Riverside Dr. (Pass Ave.), Burbank, 818-848-4501 ◗
16817 Ventura Blvd. (Balboa Ave.), Encino, 818-784-5925
*11855 S. Hawthorne Blvd. (bet. 118th & 119th Sts.), Hawthorne,
310-679-0233*
6605 PCH (bet. 2nd St. & Westminster Ave.), Long Beach, 562-594-6917
13715 Fiji Way (Lincoln Blvd.), Marina del Rey, 310-823-8941
*8855 Tampa Ave. (bet. Nordhoff & Parthenia Sts.), Northridge,
818-349-1607*
3333 Foothill Blvd. (Madre St.), Pasadena, 626-351-8995
*100G Fisherman's Wharf (S. Catalina Ave.), Redondo Beach,
310-376-0547*
18568 Ventura Blvd. (Reseda Blvd.), Tarzana, 818-343-7027
449 Moorpark Rd. (Thousand Oaks Blvd.), Thousand Oaks, 805-497-3952
www.eltorito.com
Additional locations throughout Southern California
Carving a niche with "cold, salty margaritas", "guacamole made
tableside" and a "lively bar scene", this "friendly" chain "keeps
the fiesta going" with an "extended happy hour" on weeknights;
opinions on the food range from "fairly good" to "*el terribilo*", still,
the Mexican "regional specialties make for a nice change."

El Torito Grill   18 | 16 | 17 | $23
9595 Wilshire Blvd. (Camden Dr.), Beverly Hills, 310-550-1599
21321 Hawthorne Blvd. (Torrance Blvd.), Torrance, 310-543-1896
www.eltorito.com
"Even though it's a chain" (with OC offshoots), these "slightly
upscale Mexican" cousins of El Torito have guests giddy over the
"sizzling fajitas" and "delicious standbys"; though some matadors
see red over the "Americanized" chow and "fast-foody decor",
regulars respect the "extensive tequila bar" and hail the "hand-
rolled" "piping-hot tortillas" as a "real treat."

EM Bistro Ⓢ Ⓜ   22 | 21 | 21 | $49
8256 Beverly Blvd. (Sweetzer Ave.), Los Angeles, 323-658-6004
The "serene" atmosphere and "sophisticated" "retro" design
at this Beverly Boulevard bistro make it a "place for a long talk
with friends", while enjoying "sublime short ribs" and other "solid"
American specialties; with co-owner Charles Nuzzo "always ready
to go the extra mile", you can't help but "feel at home"; N.B. live
jazz Wednesday–Saturday evenings.

Empress Harbor   19 | 14 | 12 | $21
*Atlantic Plaza, 111 N. Atlantic Blvd. (Garvey Ave.), Monterey Park,
626-300-8833; www.empressharbor.com*
"If it looks interesting, try it" – or "bring someone who reads
Chinese" – at this Monterey Park bastion, offering "carefully

prepared" dim sum, "fresh seafood" and other "quality Cantonese fare" from a "large, varied" menu; though it's a "huge place", "it fills up quickly", so loyal subjects suggest "get there by 10 AM" on weekends "to avoid the crowds."

Empress Pavilion   22 | 14 | 14 | $20

Bamboo Plaza, 988 N. Hill St. (Bernard St.), Chinatown, 213-617-9898
"One hundred million Chinese can't be wrong – at least that's what it looks like on a Sunday morning" when this "cavernous" Chinatown "banquet hall" is "crowded" with patrons waiting for some of the "best dim sum"; "little old ladies" "wheeling" around "steam carts" "add to the charm" of this "lively" scene, but heed the royal credo: "come early to avoid long waits" on weekends.

Encounter   16 | 23 | 16 | $32

LA Int'l Airport, 209 World Way (bet. Terminals 1, 2 & 6), LAX, 310-215-5151; www.encounterrestaurant.com
Dining at this "jet-set-meets-*The Jetsons*" eatery, with an "out-of-this-world location" inside LAX's iconic, arachnid-shaped center building, is "like waiting out a layover on the Starship Enterprise" avow voyagers who dig the "groovy bar" and the "*Austin Powers*"–like setting; despite the admittedly "average" Californian food and "slow" service, it's still the "best place" to "prep for a red-eye."

Engine Co. No. 28   20 | 21 | 21 | $36

644 S. Figueroa St. (bet. 7th St. & Wilshire Blvd.), Downtown, 213-624-6996; www.engineco.com
"Firemen truly know how to eat" if their grub is anything like the "unfussy" American chow at this circa-1912 fire station Downtown; the "handsome" "landmark setting" sets the "backdrop" for "professionally" served lunches and pre-concert dinners, and while it's "not exciting", it's still "far too popular, so prepare to wait."

Enoteca Drago   22 | 21 | 20 | $44

410 N. Cañon Dr. (Brighton Way), Beverly Hills, 310-786-8236; www.celestinodrago.com
"The wines are the stars" at Celestino Drago's "lively" Beverly Hills spot where "a knowledgeable staff helps you make sense of the vast" "winning list"; "it's all about discovering new" vinos and "food combos", so "sip and savor" each glass with "small plates delightful to behold and taste"; if a few whine about the "ear-splitting noise", insiders retreat "upstairs – it's a little quieter" with a "more exclusive" feel.

Enterprise Fish Co.   17 | 16 | 17 | $29

174 Kinney St. (Main St.), Santa Monica, 310-392-8366; www.enterprisefishco.com
Employing a "no-frills formula" of "fresh seafood straight up", this "family-friendly fish house" in Santa Monica (with a branch in Santa Barbara) reels in locals and tourists with its weekday lobster and crab "bargains" and "extensive menu" of fin fare; if some seadogs assail the "barely passable" service and an "assembly-line feel", most laud it as "dependable" and "reasonably priced."

E's Wine Bar ●Ⓜ   ▽ 17 | 21 | 18 | $25

115 E. Colorado Blvd. (Arroyo Pkwy.), Pasadena, 626-793-6544; www.eswinebar.com
"Chic" and "trendy", this "fun" Old Town Pasadena "change"-of-pace place draws admirers with "innovative", "beautifully

presented" Cal-Italian dishes and a "good" vino selection, including "flights of wine"; but even those e-clined to "hang out" at the "excellent bar" with the "noisy" "pretty people" and "Gen-X" crowd reveal that the "restaurant seems to be an afterthought"; N.B. live jazz on weekends.

Eurochow M   18 | 24 | 18 | $44

1099 Westwood Blvd. (Kinross Ave.), Westwood, 310-209-0066;
www.eurochow.com

Gleaming with "stunning glass staircases" and centered around a 25-ft. obelisk, this "high-powered" Westwood spin-off of Mr. Chow boasts an "arty" "all-white" interior that is "so crazy"-"cool", you may want to "dress in black to blend in", and has "lovely food" so "skillfully prepared" in separate Chinese and Italian kitchens it's "sure to impress a date"; but other chowhounds deride the "tiny portions" and "snobbish attitude", snarling it "feels like something out of a Steve Martin movie."

Fabiolus Café   20 | 16 | 20 | $22

6270 Sunset Blvd. (bet. Gower & Vine Sts.), Hollywood, 323-467-2882
5255 Melrose Ave. (Van Ness Ave.), Los Angeles, 323-464-5857 ⊠
www.fabiolus.com

"Paramount's other commissary" on Melrose and its Sunset sibling (good for "pre-theater dining") still dish out "piping-hot pastas" and other "reliably good" Italian fare ferried to table by a "friendly" staff; the surroundings seem a tad "lacking" to a few, nevertheless for most the "upbeat" vibe makes these trattorias pretty *fabuloso*"; N.B. the Hollywood branch has a 200-plus bottle wine selection, but its sister is BYO.

Fab's Italian Kitchen   16 | 11 | 17 | $20

4336 Van Nuys Blvd. (Ventura Blvd.), Sherman Oaks, 818-995-2933

"When you don't feel like cooking", stop into this "comfortable" "family-owned" Sherman Oaks "neighborhood" trattoria for some "simple Italian" fare; "upgrading the decor would make it a slam dunk", and some say the rather "mediocre" cuisine – not fab in any respect – could use some work as well, but at least you get "a whole lotta food for da money."

Factor's Famous Deli   17 | 11 | 17 | $18

9420 W. Pico Blvd. (Beverly Dr.), Los Angeles, 310-278-9175

The sandwiches are "huge", the servers "chatty" and the atmosphere "congenial" at this "old-fashioned" circa-1948 deli in Pico's glatt gulch, where locals scarf down "typical Jewish favorites" just "like mama" "used to make"; if cynics carp it's merely "decent" and "not worth a trip across town", most noshers note "you'll plotz" over the "great chopped salads" and "delicious matzo ball soup."

Falafel King   18 | 6 | 12 | $10

The Promenade, 1315 Third St. Promenade (bet. Arizona Ave. & Santa Monica Blvd.), Santa Monica, 310-587-2551
1059 Broxton Ave. (bet. Kinross & Weyburn Aves.), Westwood, 310-208-4444

As "awesome" as the falafel is, the "special sauces" "are the real lure" at this toothsome twosome in Westwood and Santa Monica where you "feel like you're in Tel Aviv"; just grin and bear the "surly help behind the counter" and the "zero atmosphere", because the "cheap", "quick", "tasty" Middle Eastern food is even "worth putting up with the obnoxious undergrads" who still *schwarma* in "after graduation."

Farfalla Trattoria   23 | 17 | 18 | $29

1978 Hillhurst Ave. (Finley Ave.), Los Feliz, 323-661-7365; www.farfallatrattoria.com

Drawing an "eclectic Los Feliz crowd" and "freeway and overpass" commuters, this Italian "stalwart" satisfies with "fabulous pasta" and pizza cooked in a wood-burning oven; the staff "is nicer than it needs to be", even when the "rustic" "brick-walled" space is "crowded", so just note the lovers' lament: it's a "romantic" setting "for a date, but not to propose" – she might not hear you over the "incredible din."

Farm of Beverly Hills   19 | 16 | 17 | $27

439 N. Beverly Dr. (bet. Brighton Way & Santa Monica Blvd.), Beverly Hills, 310-273-5578
The Grove at Farmer's Mkt., 189 The Grove Dr. (bet. Fairfax Ave. & 3rd St.), Los Angeles, 323-525-1699
www.thefarmofbeverlyhills.com

"More of a breakfast, brunch or lunch spot" (though it serves evening meals as well), this "unpretentious" Californian–New American near Rodeo Drive with a Grove satellite, which now takes reservations, ease shoppers' remorse with "yuppie blue-plate specials", featuring "fresh ingredients", "lots of vegetarian options" and "killer brownies"; service is "pleasant" enough, if sometimes "spotty", but the "stargazing" is always a sure thing.

Far Niente   24 | 18 | 23 | $33

204½ N. Brand Blvd. (Wilson Ave.), Glendale, 818-242-3835

"Simple but worth remembering", this Glendale Northern Italian is no do-nothing when it comes to food – witness the "fantastic" bread, "excellent" fish, "wonderful" pastas and "plethora of specials" "so numerous that" some don't "bother looking at the menu"; though it's "always busy", fans feel it "deserves more recognition than it gets", especially when you consider the "attentive service" and the "reasonable prices."

Fat Fish   21 | 19 | 18 | $34

616 N. Robertson Blvd. (bet. Melrose Ave. & Santa Monica Blvd.), West Hollywood, 310-659-3882; www.fatfishla.com

"Chill-out music" and "cosmic" decor help make this Asian fusion on Robertson Boulevard "a popular spot to take a hottie" or "to hang out" "with friends"; explore the "phenomenal" sake selection or sip "great martinis", while nibbling "novelty" maki "twice the size of normal sushi" made with the "finest ingredients"; while cynics carp that the concoctions seem "contrived", afishionados quip "who wouldn't like a Fat Ass roll?"

Father's Office   23 | 13 | 10 | $19

1018 Montana Ave. (bet. 10th & 11th Sts.), Santa Monica, 310-393-2337; www.fathersoffice.com

Chef-owner Sang Yoon has borrowed "God's recipe for the perfect" patty at this Santa Monica bar, which "rages like a frat house" with "yuppies" savoring the "incredible" beer selection, "excellent tapas" and "orgasmic burgers" (have "it their way" – "they're not joking about the no-substitutions" rule); service is "almost laughably rude", and some daddy-o's despair the "first come, first served" seating where "the most aggressive win."

Fatty's & Co. Ⓜ   ▽ 22 | 18 | 13 | $18
1627 Colorado Blvd. (Vincent Ave.), Eagle Rock, 323-254-8804
Tasting the "imaginative food" made "with top-notch ingredients", "you might not even notice it's vegetarian" weigh in meat-loathers and -lovers alike who laud this Eagle Rock eatery's "original menu" and "wonderfully ironic" name; set in a "funky" "converted garage", it's "fast becoming a local hangout" – now "if only they could get it together with the service."

Feast from the East Ⓢ   20 | 6 | 14 | $11
1949 Westwood Blvd. (bet. Olympic & Santa Monica Blvds.), West LA, 310-475-0400; www.feasteast.com
The "ever-popular Chinese chicken salad" may be the "best west of the Pecos" at this West LA Asian "landmark" "joint"; "forget the rest of the menu" – it's "average at best" – and there's absolutely "no atmosphere" in this "stark" space, so just "stand in line to order, then take" your feast to go.

Figaro Bistrot ●   19 | 21 | 15 | $30
1802 N. Vermont Ave. (bet. Franklin Ave. & Hollywood Blvd.), Los Feliz, 323-662-1587
A "glam Los Feliz crowd hangs out" at this "fin-de-siècle"-style Parisian bistro "beautifully decorated" with "communal booths and a mirrored interior"; though it's served with a "big dose of attitude", the "simple French fare" (especially the "*magnifique* breakfasts" and "awesome pastries") pleases Francophiles, as does the "great star-watching"; still, disbelievers figaro that the food "should be better for" the "inflated prices."

Fins   23 | 19 | 21 | $36
23504 Calabasas Rd. (Mulholland Dr.), Calabasas, 818-223-3467
Westlake Plaza, 982-8 S. Westlake Blvd. (bet. Agoura & Townsgate Rds.), Westlake Village, 805-494-8163
www.finsinc.com
Fish fans flip for the "consistently fine" seafood at this pair of West Valley Continentals, where the macadamia-crusted halibut "is a favorite" that "keeps 'em coming back"; both the "friendly" service and the "sophisticated" yet "casual" atmosphere set the right tone, particularly at the Calabasas branch, where you can "get a table on the patio and hear the frogs croak"; N.B. the Westlake location has reopened after a fire.

FIREFLY ●Ⓢ   20 | 25 | 18 | $39
11720 Ventura Blvd. (Colfax Ave.), Studio City, 818-762-1833
With an "ethereal" interior that's a "cross between London library" and *Arabian Nights,* this "celeb"-studded Studio City "people-watching bonanza" exudes such a "chic" vibe it's like a "Westside hangout in the Valley"; "once you settle" by the "roaring fireplace" on the patio, "you'll want to stay" for "great drinks" and "surprisingly good" French–New American fare and "talk all night"; still, a few fly by, bemoaning the "hipper-than-thou" attitude.

Firefly Bistro Ⓜ   20 | 19 | 19 | $33
1009 El Centro St. (Meridian Ave.), South Pasadena, 626-441-2443; www.eatatfirefly.com
Housed in a "lovely" tent with a "laid-back ambiance" that seems "far away from LA's artifice", this "sophisticated" South Pasadena "sleeper" awakens palates with a "clever" New American menu

of "creative seasonal cooking"; while the staff earns points for "impeccable" service, and the space is undeniably "romantic", a few low-lights "wish the food were as unique as the setting."

Fish Grill   – | – | – | I
7226 Beverly Blvd. (Alta Vista Blvd.), West Hollywood, 323-937-7162
In a bright indoor-outdoor space with wood shavings on the floor and condiments in little silver buckets, this Beverly Boulevard kosher seafooder sears up snapper, whitefish and salmon and baits them with sides like baked potatoes and cucumber salad; a second location is slated to open in Brentwood in fall 2005.

555 EAST   24 | 22 | 24 | $47
555 E. Ocean Blvd. (Linden St.), Long Beach, 562-437-0626; www.555east.com
For a "damn fine piece of meat", "palate-pleasing" side dishes and a "top-notch wine list", all served by a "very personable staff", carnivores canter over to this "old-school, East Coast–type" steakhouse in Downtown Long Beach; the "comfortable atmosphere", complete with "lots of wood, brass and leather", an "action-packed bar" and booth seating, makes it "worth the trip", especially for "corporate entertaining."

Five Sixty-One   ∇ 22 | 18 | 21 | $36
Southern CA School of Culinary Arts, 561 E. Green St. (Madison Ave.), Pasadena, 626-405-1561
"To experience fine dining at half the price", try the "beautifully crafted tasting menus" and other "adventurous" Cal-European selections at this "gourmet" Pasadena bistro run by students from the California School of Culinary Arts; though the results can be "uneven", and service earns grades of "attentive while tentative" – "hey, they're learning" – it's "always interesting to see the young chefs at work."

Flavor of India   21 | 15 | 18 | $22
9045 Santa Monica Blvd. (Doheny Dr.), West Hollywood, 310-274-1715; www.theflavorofindia.com
A convenient "place to eat before a show at the Troubadour", this WeHo Indian eatery entertains with "huge portions" of "yummy, rich" cuisine served in a "surprisingly cozy", "garden setting" full of imported art and furnishings; regulars report that "everything is well prepared", and the "funky Bollywood dance music makes the courtyard a hoot."

Fleming's Prime Steakhouse & Wine Bar   25 | 23 | 23 | $53
2301 Rosecrans Ave. (Douglas St.), El Segundo, 310-643-6911; www.flemingssteakhouse.com
"Hobnob with the well-heeled crowd" at these "bulletproof" steakhouses in Newport and El Segundo that more than "live up to a carnivore's expectations"; "clubby" surroundings, "super" "cuts of beef", "terrific" sides and an "extensive wine list that isn't too elitist" make for "memorable meals", backed by "silky smooth service" and a "very active bar scene."

Flora Kitchen   18 | 17 | 16 | $20
460 S. La Brea Ave. (6th St.), Los Angeles, 323-931-9900; www.florakitchen.com
Dine "amid over-the-top flowers and under-the-radar stars" at this cafe connected to a florist that makes "a quick shopping

break for La Brea fashion hounds" and others seeking "fresh, straightforward" Cal-Med fare; it's "a cool spot for breakfast" (the waffles are "awesome") and "a lovely concept" overall, but since the blooms are so fragrant, some surveyors "just wish the service didn't stink."

Fogo de Chão　　　　　　　　　　– | – | – | E
133 N. La Cienega Blvd. (Clifton Way), Beverly Hills, 310-289-7755; www.fogodechao.com
Somewhere, Dr. Atkins must be smiling – this Brazilian churrascaria chain stretches from São Paulo to Chicago and now to a massive, modern gaucho farmhouse in the middle of La Cienega's Restaurant Row; carnivores pile on the protein with unlimited portions of spit-roasted meat, and sidle up to the buffet, too, all for one fixed price.

Fonz's　　　　　　　　　　22 | 18 | 22 | $39
1017 Manhattan Ave. (bet. 10th Pl. & 11th St.), Manhattan Beach, 310-376-1536; www.fonzs.com
Heeeeey, the bar is "hopping with locals" at this "pretty casual" Manhattan Beach surf 'n' turfer, which brings back "happy" days with a "personable staff" serving up "great steaks" and seafood; sure, some feel stifled by "grown-up frat boys" and "yuppies" "crowding" the dining room, but most find it a "fun scene" and "love" to "take a walk to the beach" after dinner.

Foodies: An American Grill ⊠　　▽ 20 | 10 | 21 | $21
11701 Wilshire Blvd. (Barrington Ave.), West LA, 310-473-8272; www.foodiescatering.com
Stuck "near a cluster of office buildings" in a West LA strip mall with a "nothing-special" atmosphere that "feels like a mess hall", this American sophomore "makes up" for it "big time" with "inventive food and great value" across the "diverse menu"; the staff "tries to please", and the "fantastic hot pretzels" "alone are worth a trip" for foodies and mere mortals alike.

Food Studio　　　　　　　　　　– | – | – | M
1611 Catalina Ave. (Ave. I), Redondo Beach, 310-543-4379
This surfside Californian in Redondo Beach offers two dining options in the space that used to house Cucina Paradiso: up front, there's a comfortable wood-paneled bar with a casual, moderately priced menu and to the rear, a spacious dining room offering more ambitious fare.

Formosa Cafe ●　　　　　　　　13 | 18 | 15 | $25
7156 Santa Monica Blvd. (La Brea Ave.), Hollywood, 323-850-9050
Like a "piece of movie history wrapped up in a fortune cookie", this "Old Hollywood personified" "landmark" is "a fun way to step back in time to Bugsy Siegal's era" ("think *LA Confidential* meets *Swingers*") courtesy of "golden-age photos and red vinyl booths"; the Pan-Asian food is "mediocre at best", so "just go for" the "kick-ass drinks", and if you have enough of them, you may even "see Marilyn Monroe's ghost."

Four Oaks Ⓜ　　　　　　　　　22 | 23 | 22 | $53
2181 N. Beverly Glen Blvd. (Beverly Glen Pl.), Bel Air, 310-470-2265; www.fouroaksrestaurant.com
"Hard to find and hard to forget" vow vaunters who venture "into the woods" of Bel Air to this "century-old former brothel and railroad station", now a "romantic hideaway" beloved for its

"magical woodland scenery" and "wonderful special-occasion" French–New American cuisine; but a handful feel that the fare "isn't up to its former standards" and declare it "doesn't match the view by a long shot"; N.B. a recent change of chefs may impact the Food rating.

410 Boyd ⊠   18 | 16 | 18 | $26
410 Boyd St. (San Pedro St.), Downtown, 213-617-2491
"Still the boho eatery" of the "local Artists District", this "edgy, cool" "hangout" "on the fringes of Little Tokyo" lures the creative clan and "younger Downtown professionals" with its "eclectic" Californian cuisine, "changing exhibits" and "film noir" vibe; intrepid sorts revel in its "offbeat" location, but lost souls wail it's in the "middle of nowhere"; N.B. there's now an outdoor patio too.

Frankie & Johnnie's   ∇ 20 | 12 | 17 | $22
9533 Santa Monica Blvd. (N. Beverly Dr.), Beverly Hills, 310-860-1155
8947 W. Sunset Blvd. (Hilldale Ave.), West Hollywood, 310-275-7770 ◗
Dishing out thin-crust pizza that's "as close as you get to NYC", this Beverly Hills–WeHo duo brings the East Coast to the West Coast; if a few toss it off as a wannabe that "doesn't quite" make the Gotham cut, for most it fills the bill as a "good spot for a quick lunch", "takeout for a group" or a late-night bite (the Sunset branch is open till 2 AM).

Frascati   ∇ 21 | 21 | 20 | $34
1800 S. PCH (Vista Del Parque), Redondo Beach, 310-698-6700; www.frascatiristorante.com
Chef-owner Enrico Glaudo "makes a point of remembering you" at this Northern Italian "gem", a "great alternative to Redondo Beach's chain restaurants" where "thin, crisp" pizzas and "enormous" portions of pasta are bolstered by a "terrific" wine list; while sensitive types tut "it can get way too noisy", others find it a "warm, inviting" "fun experience" with a "gorgeous" patio, adding where else can you get "Westside food at South Bay prices"?

Fred 62 ◗   16 | 15 | 14 | $17
1850 N. Vermont Ave. (Russell Ave.), Los Feliz, 323-667-0062; www.fred62.com
"Pierced and tattooed customers" saunter into this "fun, funky" all-night Los Feliz "hipster coffee shop with attitude" for "greasy spoon choices" and "modern healthier fare", including "many choices for vegetarians"; the "headache" service is "slow, slow, slow" and "you pay extra for the ambiance", but few care as "anything at 2 AM tastes good", and "comfort food" "from Fred 62 just tastes better."

FRENCHY'S BISTRO Ⓜ   27 | 16 | 24 | $42
4137 E. Anaheim St. (bet. Termino & Ximeno Aves.), Long Beach, 562-494-8787; www.frenchysbistro.com
"Don't let the drab exterior" or "off-the-beaten-path" neighborhood "put you off" because this "charming little" French "bistro is among the best tables in town" – in fact, "everything changes once you're inside" with "Parisian husband-and-wife" team Andre and Valerie Angles offering "seriously good, seriously authentic" Gallic cuisine, "carefully selected wines" and live music on weekends; if a few whiners "wish it would move", others realize a "nicer location" would mean "higher prices."

Fresco Ristorante ☒   ▽ 25 | 20 | 24 | $41

514 S. Brand Blvd. (Colorado St.), Glendale, 818-247-5541;
www.frescoristorante.com

This "great find" on Glendale's "auto row" keeps things rolling
with a Venetian-style setting, "knowledgeable staff" and "very
continental" Italian fare that "tends toward the rich end of the
spectrum" at "refreshingly moderate" prices"; but while it's an
"outstanding" outing for most, a few find the "dated interior
and unlikely location on the boulevard of car" dealerships a
"drawback"; N.B. new ownership may impact the ratings.

Friars of Beverly Hills, The ☒   – | – | – | E

9900 Little Santa Monica Blvd. (Charleville Blvd.), Beverly Hills,
310-553-0850; www.thefriarsbh.com

Following a multimillion-dollar renovation, this once-dowdy
fortysomething private club in Beverly Hills opens its second-
floor doors to the public, offering American fare from chef Robert
Van Houton (ex Gardens on Glendon) that's no joking matter; ascend
the spiral staircase (paging Loretta Young) to reach the modern,
revamped dining room, and relax over a rib-eye or salmon pizza;
sure, there's grilled fare, but most of the roasts take place onstage.

Fritto Misto   21 | 12 | 19 | $21

316 Pier Ave. (Monterey Blvd.), Hermosa Beach, 310-318-6098
601 Colorado Ave. (6th St.), Santa Monica, 310-458-2829

"Huge portions" of "build-your-own pastas", a "surprisingly good
wine selection" and "responsive service" are just a few reasons
why "in a low-carb universe", "locals" "come back" to these
"wonderful neighborhood Italian" joints in Santa Monica and
Hermosa Beach; sure, the decor is "bare-bones" and the place is
"always crowded", but "you're guaranteed" "high-end food at
midrange prices" and a "BYO option", so "what's not to like?"

Fromin's Restaurant & Deli   14 | 10 | 17 | $16

17615 Ventura Blvd. (bet. Encino & White Oak Aves.), Encino,
818-990-6346
1832 Wilshire Blvd. (19th St.), Santa Monica, 310-829-5443

"Like comfortable shoes, it's always a pleasure to slip into" this
deuce of Jewish delis in Santa Monica and Encino that may no
longer be related but still serve "wholesome, filling, fattening"
favorites like "flu-curing matzo ball soup" to the "older set"; still,
doubting Thomases sniff it's "way past its prime" so "don't expect
the best and you won't be disappointed"; N.B. recent renovations
at both locations may impact the above Decor score.

Fukui Sushi   ▽ 18 | 8 | 14 | $21

2645 Lincoln Ave. (Ocean Park), Santa Monica, 310-452-9835

The fish is either "unbelievably delicious" or just "average" and
"worthy of its low price" tussle surveyors about this "bizarre sushi
shop converted from a mom-and-pop coffee shop" in Santa
Monica; sure, the atmosphere may be "severely lacking", but "who
can't love a place with this name?"

Fu-Shing   21 | 12 | 18 | $20

2960 E. Colorado Blvd. (El Nido Ave.), Pasadena, 626-792-8898;
www.fu-shing.com

Tanking "live lobster at reasonable prices", this "very authentic"
Pasadena Chinese also sizzles up "ample" portions of "solid"

Szechuan items "served family-style"; "courteous and speedy" staffers "cater to large parties in a gracious fashion", leading some patrons to find it "hard to believe this excellent place is not in Monterrey Park."

Gaetano's Ristorante Ⓜ ▽ 21 20 19 $45
23536 Calabasas Rd. (Calabasas Park Rd.), Calabasas, 818-223-9600
A "neighborhood favorite with staying power", "friendly service" and a "charming garden with tiny white lights", this "special" Calabasas trattoria under "new ownership" proves you don't "need to leave the Valley to get" "wonderful" Northern Italian cuisine; still, detractors snipe "it's over the hill" and a "pricey" "disappointment."

Galletto ▽ 21 16 18 $32
Westlake Plaza, 982 S. Westlake Blvd. (Townsgate Rd.), Westlake Village, 805-449-4300
"Give yourself over to the boisterous" atmosphere at this Westlake Village Brazilian-Italian "standby", where the staff "greets you like family", the risotto is "creamy, gooey and just right", and the live music "kicks it up a notch"; "don't go when you're in a rush" because the "sexy waitresses" can be "slow", but do go if you're looking for an "enjoyable" "place on a Friday or Saturday" night.

Galley, The 18 17 20 $33
2442 Main St. (bet. Ocean Park & Pico Blvds.), Santa Monica, 310-452-1934
The "oldest continually operating restaurant in Santa Monica", this "kitschy" "beach dive bar" "hasn't lost it": the atmosphere is still pure "Captain Nemo", the service is "shipshape" and the surf 'n' turf fare is good enough even for the pickiest "steak snobs", who share the place with a "nice mix of regulars and tourists" while guzzling "stiff drinks" and having a "blast from the past."

GARDENS 24 26 26 $54
Four Seasons Hotel, 300 S. Doheny Dr. (Burton Way), Beverly Hills, 310-273-2222; www.fourseasons.com
With "elegant, excellent" Cal-Med cuisine, "one of the loveliest rooms in the city" and "great celeb sightings", this "spoil-yourself" restaurant at the Four Seasons in Beverly Hills lavishes "personal attention" on guests in an "intimate, quiet" atmosphere; the "exceptional" Sunday buffet brunch is one of the "best around", but if it's too steep for you, "try the bar menu for an economical meal of high quality."

Gardens on Glendon 20 21 19 $36
1139 Glendon Ave. (Lindbrook Dr.), Westwood, 310-824-1818; www.gardensonglendon.com
"Innovatively prepared" "contemporary" Californian "comfort" fare like "show-stopping guacamole" prepared "tableside" and "gourmet burgers" makes this Westwooder a "reliable" pre- or post-"theater" choice and a lunchtime "favorite"; "friendly" service and a "calming atmosphere" add to its appeal for "family gatherings or meetings" – as long as the "in-laws" pick up the check as it can be a "bit pricey" for a "neighborhood" "hangout."

Gate of India ▽ 21 13 14 $21
115 Santa Monica Blvd. (Ocean Ave.), Santa Monica, 310-656-1664
Opinions diverge on this "hole-in-the-wall" Santa Monica Indian with "tacky" decor, where loyalists maintain the "food remains

excellent" while others claim the place "used to be terrific" but "a change of owners has sunk this ship"; either way, most agree that the "staff needs to adopt a friendlier attitude", adding, "prepare to be assertive" "if you want any service."

Gaucho Grill   18 | 15 | 17 | $23

11754 San Vicente Blvd. (Gorham Ave.), Brentwood, 310-447-7898
121 W. Colorado Blvd. (bet. De Lacey & Pasadena Aves.), Pasadena, 626-683-3580
1251 Third St. Promenade (3rd St.), Santa Monica, 310-394-4966
12050 Ventura Blvd. (Laurel Canyon Blvd.), Studio City, 818-508-1030
7980 Sunset Blvd. (Laurel Ave.), West Hollywood, 323-656-4152
6435 Canoga Ave. (Victory Blvd.), Woodland Hills, 818-992-6416
"Big portions", "free refills" and "the right blend of spices" make this "friendly" "meat-anchored" Argentine steakhouse chain "Atkins heaven" – unless you "pig out on warm bread" and the "best chimichurri sauce" while waiting for your "tasty" entree; if grouchos gripe it's a "tourist trap", gauchos are giddy about grub that's "certainly not gourmet, but definitely worth the price."

GEISHA HOUSE ●☑   21 | 25 | 21 | $47

6633 Hollywood Blvd. (Cherokee Ave.), Hollywood, 323-460-6300; www.geishahousehollywood.com
Dishing out "better" Japanese "food and less attitude than you'd expect from such a trendoid joint" with a "celeb-spotting" "scene, scene, scene" that's "off the charts", the Dolce Group's "sexy nightspot" with a "killer menu" is "full of somebodies, but even nobodies get attention" while they sample the "excellent" sushi and "expensive" sake; still, some find the "Hollywood crowd" and "decor too hip and cool" . . . "for the moment", anyway.

Genghis Cohen   20 | 14 | 17 | $24

740 N. Fairfax Ave. (Melrose Ave.), Los Angeles, 323-653-0640; www.genghiscohen.com
Baffled by the "typically enigmatic LA" name, diners "can't find the Cohen part" at this Fairfax "staple", which isn't kosher but simply a "New Yorky" Chinese with an "edgy nightclub atmosphere"; Mongols, moguls and "industry wannabes" enjoy "crackerjack shrimp" and the "best Szechuan green beans" before stepping into the "cozy" "churchlike performing space" to hear "up-and-comers play" and rejoice that it "fills a void you never knew" existed.

Gennaro's Ristorante ☑   ▽ 23 | 20 | 23 | $41

1109 N. Brand Blvd. (Dryden St.), Glendale, 818-243-6231
"The housemade pastas are fabulous" at this venerable Glendale Italian, now under new ownership; the food remains "impeccable" and the staff is still "terrific" gush loyalists who also laud this "romantic" "standby" for its "old-world style."

GEOFFREY'S   22 | 27 | 22 | $49

27400 PCH (¼ mi. north of Latigo Canyon), Malibu, 310-457-1519; www.gmalibu.com
"Pricey", but with a "priceless" ocean view from the "incredible cliffside seating", this open-air Malibu "institution" is "perfect" for wowing "out-of-towners"; the vistas are so "breathtaking" they "almost make you forget you're there to eat, but don't" – the Californian seafood is "delicious" ("do brunch"), plus service is "attentive", and the "fire pit is beautiful" for a drink "under the stars, like in the movies – and you might see some movie stars" too.

George's Greek Café   ▽ 16 | 11 | 17 | $13

735 S. Figueroa St. (7th St.), Downtown, 213-624-6542 Ⓢ
318 Pine Ave. (bet. 3rd & 4th Sts.), Long Beach, 562-437-1184
A handful of surveyors are split over this Downtown–Long Beach
"addition to the eating scene"; fans put it on a pedestal praising
the "good Greek staples" "convenient for lunch on the run" but
others are myth-stified by the "very disappointing", "tasteless"
chow and find the setting less than "relaxing."

GETTY CENTER,   23 | 25 | 22 | $41
RESTAURANT AT THE Ⓜ

The Getty Ctr., 1200 Getty Center Dr. (Frwy. 405), Brentwood,
310-440-6810; www.getty.edu
Gastronomes "go to" Getty just "to go to lunch" at this "light, airy"
"treat" that brings together – "how cultured is this! – art and fine
gourmet dining in one spot"; it "takes full advantage of its setting"
with "shockingly good" panoramic ocean and city views, so "feast
the eyes, then the palate" on "outstanding Californian cuisine";
"if all museum restaurants were this good, America would be a
nation of museum-goers."

G. Garvin's Ⓢ   24 | 20 | 20 | $50

8420 W. Third St. (bet. Croft & Orlando Aves.), Los Angeles, 323-655-3888
"Marvelously memorable" ribs and other "mind-numbingly tasty",
"soul-inspired" American dishes from chef-owner Gerry Garvin
make this Third Street number a "great place" for "elegant down-
home cooking"; it's a "delight overall", with a "friendly" staff that
"steers you right" and an "intimate setting" that works for a "date
or a family meal"; still, a few gripers grouse about "tiny portions
for big bucks" and "very slow service."

Gigi Brasserie   – | – | – | M

Sofitel Los Angeles, 8555 Beverly Blvd. (N. La Cienega Blvd.), Los Angeles,
310-358-3979; www.sofitel.com
The few surveyors who've discovered this French brasserie in
the Sofitel declare it's "not a compromise as hotel dining" can
sometimes be; the "staff is uniformly excellent" while the
"interesting" food is "nicely presented"; even so, some "can't
quite put my palate on what's missing", adding "eat at the bar –
it has better ambiance."

Gina Lee's Bistro Ⓜ   26 | 15 | 23 | $34

Riviera Plaza, 211 Palos Verdes Blvd. (bet. Catalina Ave. & PCH),
Redondo Beach, 310-375-4462
An "incongruous strip-mall setting" "belies the sophisticated"
Cal–Pac-Rim cuisine at this Redondo Beach bistro, where diners
are, like, "totally wowed by every bite" of the catfish and "ever-
changing" bento boxes; owners Scott and Gina Lee "keep the
kitchen on its toes" and oversee the "outstanding" staff – and
despite the "terrible acoustics" the results are "amazing all the
way around"; N.B. a recent refurb may impact the Decor score.

Gingergrass   21 | 15 | 18 | $21

2396 Glendale Blvd. (Brier Ave.), Silver Lake, 323-644-1600;
www.gingergrass.com
"Even the same stuff you see on every menu is bursting with flavor"
at this "bare-bones" Silver Lake haunt where local "hipsters"
are "becoming addicts" of chef Mako Antonishek's "ultrafresh"

Vietnamese fare; some gingerly suggest prices are "a bit high", but it's still "as close as LA gets to lunch in Ho Chi Minh City"; N.B. check out 'Mako Mondays' for family-style prix fixe meals.

GIORGIO BALDI Ⓜ　　　　　27 | 17 | 21 | $60

114 W. Channel Rd. (PCH), Santa Monica, 310-573-1660; www.giorgiobaldi.com

"Don't let the stars distract you from the" "delicious authentic food" at this namesake chef-owner's "perfect beachy" Italian; the "crowded", "noisy" Santa Monica digs are filled with "show-biz" types savoring a "stellar wine list" and pasta so "sublime" "you almost cry when finished"; but service turns some surveyors snarky: it's "great if you're famous", but it can be "too cool for mere mortals"; P.S. DIYers "buy the house sauce" en route "out the door."

Girasole Ⓢ Ⓜ　　　　　24 | 17 | 22 | $28

225½ N. Larchmont Blvd. (bet. Beverly Blvd. & 3rd St.), Hancock Park, 323-464-6978

This "charming" "family-run" "jewel of Larchmont" Boulevard may be "tiny", but with "mama in the kitchen", only a total claustrophobe would want to miss the "knockout", "home-cooked" Italian that "never disappoints"; the BYO policy (and "no corkage fee") dictates you "bring that special bottle you've been saving", making this pint-sized contender "by far" one of the "best" in the neighborhood.

Gladstone's Malibu　　　　15 | 17 | 15 | $33

17300 PCH (Sunset Blvd.), Pacific Palisades, 310-573-0212; www.gladstones.com

"Big portions", "friendly servers" (and seagulls) and a "raffish" setting make this "busy, bawdy seaside fish house" in Pacific Palisades the "perfect beach experience", especially for soaking up the "breathtaking ocean view"; but mad-stones label it a "tourist trap", advising "never mind the food"– come here to "eat peanuts, drink your margarita and watch the waves."

Gladstone's Universal　　　15 | 15 | 15 | $30

Universal CityWalk, 1000 Universal Studios Blvd. (Cahuenga Blvd.), Universal City, 818-622-3474; www.citywalkhollywood.com

Some Universal CityWalkers count on this literally shipshape seafooder (unrelated to the Pacific Palisades bastion of the same name) for a "pretty good meal" before a show delivered "quickly" by an "upbeat" staff; but others deride it as an "overpriced" "bland experience", though it sure "beats fishing for yourself any day."

Golden Deli ⬧　　　　　　24 | 8 | 15 | $10

Las Tunas Plaza, 815 W. Las Tunas Dr. (Mission Dr.), San Gabriel, 626-308-0803

"Don't be fooled by the decor" at this "cramped" San Gabriel Vietnamese: the "the long lines should clue you in" to its popularity, attributed to "awesome" egg rolls, an "amazing variety of drinks" and the "best pho in the Valley"; "since the prices can't be beat", "your wallet will thank you as well."

Gordon Biersch　　　　　15 | 16 | 16 | $23

145 S. San Fernando Blvd. (Angeleno Ave.), Burbank, 818-569-5240
41 Hugus Alley (off Colorado Blvd.), Pasadena, 626-449-0052
www.gordonbiersch.com

"Loud or lively, depending on how you look at it", these "friendly" microbrewery chain links in Burbank and Pasadena are "great for beers with might"; "hang with friends" and "watch the game" while quaffing pints and inhaling "pub-style" American food, including some of the "best damned garlic fries on the planet"; still, for many it's "all about" the brewskis, not the "forgettable foodskis."

Gorikee Ⓜ   ▽ 24 | 11 | 21 | $24
Warner Plaza Shopping Ctr., 21799 Ventura Blvd. (Canoga Ave.), Woodland Hills, 818-932-9149; www.gorikee.com
The "imaginative" Californian cooking of former Chaya Brasserie chef Atsuhiro Esuji "more than makes up for the dreary strip-mall setting" at this "fabulous" Woodland Hills discovery; early adopters rave as much about the "lovely staff" and "bargain prices" as they do about the "delicious dishes" that "make you beg for more."

Gozar   ▽ 19 | 20 | 17 | $30
8948 Santa Monica Blvd. (N. Robertson Blvd.), West Hollywood, 310-855-7560
"Everything else has failed" in the space this new Spanish spot occupies, so fans of the "inventive" tapas fare hope for longer life this time, citing the "flirtacious waiters" and "hot scenery" as reasons to return and "dish WeHo gossip" while enjoying "pungent" small plates; but detractors declare "don't Go-zar" – "the cruz'n's great" but "the food ain't."

GRACE Ⓜ   26 | 25 | 25 | $58
7360 Beverly Blvd. (Fuller Ave.), Los Angeles, 323-934-4400; www.gracerestaurant.com
Still "excellent in every way", this Beverly Boulevard standout from chef-owner and "talented fella" Neal Fraser is a "lovely experience" thanks to "adventurous" New American cuisine, "stellar service" (even if you're not "Ashton or Leo") and Michael Berman's "soothing, contemporary" interior; if a few are put off by presentation that's "too fussy" and atmosphere that's "a tad sceney", for most this "smashing" place remains an "icon."

Grand Lux Cafe   19 | 20 | 18 | $25
Beverly Ctr., 121 N. La Cienega Blvd. (3rd St.), West Hollywood, 310-855-1122; www.grandluxcafe.com
"Give yourself an extra 30 minutes to read the menu" at this "massive" yet "quasi-upscale" chainlet link, a Cheesecake Factory "offshoot" in Beverly Center serving "monstrous" portions of New American fare and "desserts worth every calorie" in an "over-the-top" setting that makes you "feel like a Venetian prince"; like the Factory, it doesn't take reservations, so "be prepared to wait."

Great Greek   22 | 16 | 20 | $27
13362 Ventura Blvd. (bet. Dixie Canyon & Nagle Aves.), Sherman Oaks, 818-905-5250
"Opa!" "be prepared for noise" "and to be stuffed" at this "lively" Hellenic "experience" in Sherman Oaks with "festive" live music and "friendly" "dancing waiters" and patrons; "go with a crowd and share all" the "addictive appetizers" like "terrific taramasalata" and skip the "middling entrees" – "you are going to have fun!" – and you may even "feel like you've had a Greek mini-vacation."

Greek Island   – | – | – | I
4511 Sepulveda Blvd. (Ventura Blvd.), Sherman Oaks, 818-501-7255
Joining other ethnic eateries on a multicultural Sherman Oaks block, this Greek stands out with an affordable menu of Hellenic

classics served in a bright, blue-and-white space with tall windows; for a change of pace, try the grilled halloumi cheese with tomatoes and onions, one of the pita wraps on offer.

Greenblatt's Deli & Fine Wines ◑　19 | 12 | 17 | $21

8017 Sunset Blvd. (Laurel Ave.), Hollywood, 323-656-0606

"The pastrami king meets the wine cellar" – "yes it's a strange mix", but it works at this Sunset Boulevard "benchmark" that's "true to its mission" serving "classic deli" sandwiches "on rye" with "top-notch" vintages from the "fab" on-premises vino store; it's a "great hangout" with "retro-charm", especially "if you miss New York" – just be ready for "New York prices."

Green Field Churrascaria　　21 | 18 | 20 | $30

5305 E. PCH (Anaheim St.), Long Beach, 562-597-0906

381 N. Azusa Ave. (Workman Ave.), West Covina, 626-966-2300

www.greenfieldchurrascaria.com

"Go with a group of carnivores" to these Brazilian BBQ "protein palaces" in Long Beach and West Covina and "come prepared" to "unbuckle your belts" because the "circulating" "parade of waiters" keeps "bringing on" the "delicious meat" "until you beg them to stop"; just save a little room to graze on soup and salad from the "buffet with bling" suggest experienced beef eaters.

Green Patio Cafe　　　　　　– | – | – | I

24002 Vista Montana (PCH), Torrance, 310-378-0229

This hard-to-find Cal-Italian in an easy-to-miss South Bay mini-mall has two casual outdoor seating areas buttressing its warm, retro dining room; the reasonably priced menu (including what may be the only tilapia piccata in town) attracts locals from the nearby hills.

Greta Tunisian　　　　　　– | – | – | M

7168 Melrose Ave. (La Brea Ave.), Los Angeles, 323-954-0755

It may be shocking to find a kosher restaurant on Melrose, let alone a kosher Tunisian, but once you compose yourself you'll find this plain-Jane dining room offers a moderately priced menu tempering the tastes of North Africa with flavors right out of the Californian cuisine playbook, including phyllo pastry filled with tuna and capers.

Griddle Cafe, The　　　　22 | 12 | 15 | $15

7916 Sunset Blvd. (Fairfax Ave.), Hollywood, 323-874-0377;

www.thegriddlecafe.com

"Hungry" "hipsters" brook "indifferent service" and "ridiculous" waits at this "popular" Hollywood breakfast-lunch hangout, where the "epic" pancakes with "toppings only Willy Wonka could rival" and other American fare come in "King Kong"–size portions; while scoffers pout about the "poseurs", most agree it's "affordable" "fun", and besides, the "French-press coffee is the bomb"; N.B. a second location is in the works.

Grill on Hollywood, The　　19 | 18 | 20 | $40

Hollywood & Highland Complex, 6801 Hollywood Blvd. (Highland Ave.), Hollywood, 323-856-5530; www.thegrill.com

"Hollywood's outpost of the venerable" Grill on the Alley "doesn't hold a candle to the original", but then again it "isn't nearly as busy" either; the "huge portions" of American fare like "solid steaks and salads" and "Sunday brunch with champagne" are "always reliable", plus it's "open late for dinner after a Friday night movie here in Tinseltown."

Grill on the Alley, The   24 | 21 | 23 | $52
(aka The Grill)
9560 Dayton Way (Wilshire Blvd.), Beverly Hills, 310-276-0615;
www.thegrill.com
Serving up "down-to-earth", yet "gourmet" American food and
"hard-to-pass-up martinis" to an "abundance of agents" and
"power brokers", this "clubby" Beverly Hills "standby" still gets
nods for "excellent" steaks, "off-the-hook" burgers" and "hearty"
"comfort food", all served "professionally"; the "great old-style"
setting makes you "feel like a player", especially at "lunch, when
everyone who's anyone is here" – but "forget the [green leather]
booths", because they're "for the real" heavy "hitters."

Grub   ▽ 22 | 16 | 19 | $15
911 N. Seward St. (bet. Melrose Ave. & Santa Monica Blvd.),
Hollywood, 323-461-3663; www.grub-la.com
"Step onto the porch" of this 1920s bungalow "hidden in a
residential area near the Hollywood studios" and "step into
another era where butter isn't banned, abundance is good" and you
BYO wine; thanks to its "offbeat menu" of "consistently delicious"
American grub, this "homey" locale with "outstanding" service
has earned a reputation as an "oasis of flavor", so for anyone
suffering from "lunch doldrums", it's "like a little bit of sunshine."

Guelaguetza   22 | 10 | 17 | $16
3337½ W. Eighth St. (Irolo St.), Koreatown, 213-427-0601
3014 W. Olympic Blvd. (S. Normandie Ave.), Koreatown, 213-427-0608
11127 Palms Blvd. (Sepulveda Blvd.), Palms, 310-837-1153
"Mole heaven" sigh admirers taken with "real deal" sauces and
"lip-smacking Oaxacan specialties" at this "authentic", "friendly"
"find" in Palms and separately owned Koreatown branches;
groupies gladly ignore the "downtrodden", "luncheonette" setting
to try the "souped-up horchata" and dishes "bursting with
flavors", adding while "there are other" Mexican "places on the
Westside, there's nothing like this."

Guido's   22 | 20 | 23 | $36
3874 Cross Creek Rd. (PCH), Malibu, 310-456-1979;
www.guidosmalibu.com
11980 Santa Monica Blvd. (Bundy Dr.), West LA, 310-820-6649
Evoking a "1950s supper club" with its kinda "cozy, kinda
romantic" atmosphere, these two stalwarts in West LA and
Malibu may seem "worn down" "on the outside", but inside
awaits "fabulous" pasta and other "reliable" Northern Italian
fare, plus the "wonderful" tableside Caesar salad made by
"super-polite waiters"; as the "older crowd" explains, "you feel
classy eating here."

Gulfstream   20 | 19 | 20 | $33
Century City Shopping & Mktpl., 10250 Santa Monica Blvd.
(Century Park W.), Century City, 310-553-3636; www.houstons.com
"They have the right formula" at these "always happening",
"stylishly chic" "Houston's offshoots" in Century City (and
Newport Beach) assert admirers hooked on the "incredibly
fresh" American offerings, particularly "simply prepared"
seafood, capped with "crisp" service; come nightfall, the OC
branch is a "big hangout" thanks to "great patios" and "fun
outside fire pits" for "dining, cocktailing" and "people-watching."

Gumbo Pot
22 | 7 | 15 | $13

Farmer's Mkt., 6333 W. Third St. (Fairfax Ave.), Los Angeles, 323-933-0358; www.thegumbopotla.com
A menu full of "wonderful Cajun treats" makes this Farmer's Market walk-up on Fairfax "perfect for chowing down" on "to-die-for po' boys", "piping hot seafood gumbo" and "incredible" collard greens and cornbread; bayou bushwhackers muse it's "as close to NOLA as you're going to get in LA" – "where else can you get alligator" tail?

Gyu-Kaku
21 | 17 | 18 | $27

163 N. La Cienega Blvd. (Clifton Way), Beverly Hills, 310-659-5760
14457 Ventura Blvd. (bet. Beverly Glen & Van Nuys Blvds.), Sherman Oaks, 818-501-5400
Cross Road Plaza, 24631 Crenshaw Blvd. (Sky Park Dr.), Torrance, 310-325-1437
10925 W. Pico Blvd. (bet. Kelton & Midvale Aves.), West LA, 310-234-8641
www.gyu-kaku.com
It's "almost like camping" when you have "fun with fire" at these "cramped" DIY Japanese BBQ offshoots of an Asian chain where "you grill your own" "skillfully marinated meats", veggies and s'mores on a tableside hibachi while the "friendly" staff hovers nearby; the "waits can be long" and "teeny-weeny portions" mean "the bill can add up", but for most, it's a "tasty" "alternative."

Halie, Restaurant Ⓜ
21 | 21 | 18 | $46

Cheesewright Bldg., 1030 E. Green St. (Catalina Ave.), Pasadena, 626-440-7067; www.restauranthalie.com
Lodged in Pasadena's "splendid", historic Cheeseworth Building where "Albert Einstein" had an office, this "beautifully appointed" "minimalist" Californian from Restaurant Devon's owners makes a "serious date place" with rooms full of "character", including a "huge fireplace"; if a few feel "the food isn't what it used to be" now that "chef Claude Beltran has left", others suggest seeking out the "secret wine bar, off the lobby" – the vino "list rocks" and it's "more fun."

Hal's Bar & Grill
21 | 20 | 19 | $36

1349 Abbot Kinney Blvd. (bet. Main St. & Venice Blvd.), Venice, 310-396-3105; www.halsbarandgrill.com
This "vintage Venice watering hole" overseen by "hands-on" owners is a "happening" "place where everybody knows your name and remembers your order" (go for the "steak frites, which doesn't get any better", and a "well-made martini"); enjoy your "wonderful" New American food in an "arty atmosphere" that "channels SoHo" while being serenaded by live jazz Sundays and Mondays and "ignore the loud chatter from the attached bar."

HAMASAKU Ⓩ
27 | 18 | 23 | $49

11043 Santa Monica Blvd. (Sepulveda Blvd.), West LA, 310-479-7636; www.hamasakula.com
"Oh, my! I've died and gone to sushi heaven" sigh Japanese junkies enamored by this West LA destination, where "you're sure to see one celebrity or another" – and pay "insane" prices for some of the "most creative rolls in town" along with "great cuts of fish"; it helps that owner Toshi Kihara "makes it an incredible, personal experience" even for the non-famous, but "don't bother without reservations."

Hama Sushi　　22　12　18　$33
213 Windward Circle (Main St.), Venice, 310-396-8783
Offering beachcombers a place to have "sushi in flip-flops", this
Venice "hang" lacks "froufrou" decor but compensates with a
"dependably fun" atmosphere where "crazy chefs" "yell" greetings
and make "great" rolls and servers "pour premium sake from
bamboo flutes"; but the more fin-nicky frown it's "so-so" and quip
it's a "better place for hearing loss than for wasabi."

Hamburger Hamlet　　15　14　16　$19
*Topa Old Country Shopping Ctr., 11648 San Vicente Blvd.
(bet. Montana Ave. & Wilshire Blvd.), Brentwood, 310-826-3558
6914 Hollywood Blvd. (N. Highland Ave.), Hollywood, 323-467-6106
214 S. Lake Ave. (bet. E. Colorado & E. Del Mar Blvds.), Pasadena,
626-449-8520
4419 Van Nuys Blvd. (Ventura Blvd.), Sherman Oaks, 818-784-1183
27430 The Old Rd. (Magic Mountain Pkwy.), Valencia, 661-253-0888
9201 Sunset Blvd. (N. Doheny Dr.), West Hollywood, 310-278-4924 ◐
2927 Sepulveda Blvd. (National Blvd.), West LA, 310-478-1546
www.hamburgerhamlet.com*
Rising "a notch above coffee shops" with a "huge" menu and
"mainstream service", this "no-frills" mini-chain doles out "classic"
"chargrilled" burgers and American "comfort food" at "fair prices";
sure, it can be fun to go "where it's still 1978" and you can "relax
in big leather" booths, but detractors declare it's a "dinosaur" that's
"lost its mojo" and is a "sad vestige of a once-great institution."

Hamburger Mary's ◑　　–　–　–　M
*8288 Santa Monica Blvd. (Sweetzer Ave.), Hollywood,
323-654-3800; www.hamburgermarysweho.com*
Urged to 'eat, drink and be Mary', visitors to this gay-friendly
WeHo American chain link choose from a litany of meaty options,
including the $30 hamburger – a one-pound colossus of Kobe
beef – one of the few expensive items on a modestly priced menu
that also features pizza, steak and sandwiches; festivities include
celebrity bingo on Wednesdays and an open mike on Thursdays.

Hanoi Cafe　　▽　16　16　17　$15
2002 Sawtelle Blvd. (Olympic Blvd.), West LA, 310-477-4885
Fans give props to this West LA strip-mall Vietnamese, fondly
ruminating on the "delicious pho" and "authentic", "exotic"
dishes ferried to the table by "friendly and helpful" staffers;
nevertheless, the put-off are a little Hanoied by the "diluted"
ethnic fare and the "rather slow" kitchen.

HanWoori　　–　–　–　M
9711 Reseda Blvd. (Lassen St.), Northridge, 818-717-0234
Set inside a San Fernando Valley shopping mall, this unexpectedly
elegant Korean steak and seafooder offers a baronial palace–style
setting for do-it-yourself tabletop cooking involving both grilling
and a version of shabu-shabu; expect a glorious excess of small
dishes, including kimchi, with whatever entree you order.

Harbor Drive　　–　–　–　M
*655 N. Harbor Dr. (Beryl St.), Redondo Beach, 310-379-2900;
www.harbor-drive.com*
This spacious waterfront New American is low-lit and romantic,
with a commanding view of the boats floating by, so it's no wonder

it's a soothing destination for South Bay yups looking to dine on surf 'n' turf; a massive bar serving trendy libations like cucumber mojitos also makes it a popular pre-party pit stop.

Hard Rock Cafe   13 | 20 | 15 | $22
Beverly Ctr., 8600 Beverly Blvd. (San Vicente Blvd.), West Hollywood, 310-276-7605
Universal CityWalk, 1000 Universal Studios Blvd. (off Frwy. 101), Universal City, 818-622-7625
www.hardrock.com
"Not bad for burgers and fries", but otherwise these "deafeningly loud", "cheesy all-American" "tourist trap" chain offshoots in the Beverly Center and Universal City trade on "rock 'n' roll nostalgia", "a theme whose time has come and gone"; hipsters huff the "mall-quality food" is suitable "for teens only" and hiss "service is hit-or-miss"; in short, "ho-hum."

Harold & Belle's   22 | 14 | 18 | $32
2920 W. Jefferson Blvd. (bet. Arlington Ave. & Crenshaw Blvd.), Los Angeles, 323-735-3376
Choose your favorite "N'Awlins food" at this Mid-City "treasure", where the "friendly staff" doles out "great" shrimp Creole and other "wonderful Southern" "treats" in "quantities massive" enough for "leftovers"; "forget about watching calories or cholesterol" and overlook the "dicey" neighborhood – just shut your eyes and imagine "you're down in the French Quarter."

Hayakawa ⓜ   ▽ 26 | 15 | 24 | $37
750 Terrado Plaza (bet. Citrus & Workman Aves.), Covina, 626-332-8288
"Matsuhisa-like food" and "excellent sushi" for a lot less yen lure acolytes to this "ever-mysterious", "quiet" Japanese situated in an "out-of-the-way" Covina mini-mall; "call in advance to let them know you'll be ordering" the "wonderful omakase dinners" "left up to the chef's discretion" – they're "always a treat and make you feel lucky to have such a place."

Heroes Bar & Grill ◑   19 | 16 | 16 | $17
131 N. Yale Ave. (bet. 1st & 2nd Sts.), Claremont, 909-621-6712
"College kids" and "boys out for a night on the town" crowd this brew "lovers' dream" of a sports bar in Claremont (and the SoCo district) for an "unsurpassed selection of beers" and American "pub grub" in the "largest portions ever seen"; it's a "true" local hang, so kick back with your free "peanuts", "throw your shells" on the sawdust-covered floor and "watch the game."

Hide Sushi ⓜ⌦   24 | 9 | 17 | $26
2040 Sawtelle Blvd. (bet. La Grange & Mississippi Aves.), West LA, 310-477-7242
"Come early or bring a book" because "the wait can be long" at this "zero-ambiance" West LA Japanese, where the "generous", "affordable" portions of "fantastic" "working man's sushi" and the "efficient" staff make patrons overlook the "unbelievable din" and "draconian cash-only policy"; "if you're fed up with the trendy roll places", queue up – "you won't go away hungry."

Hirosuke   25 | 14 | 21 | $34
Plaza de Oro, 17237 Ventura Blvd. (Louise Ave.), Encino, 818-788-7548
"Competition is fierce" on a boulevard crammed to the gills with sushi options, but this "busy, noisy" "well-kept secret" in Encino

("Westsiders, stay away!") lures Valley afishionados with "phenomenally fresh" fin fare that "practically swims on your plate" and "special service"; it's "so good it'll make you forget about the lack of ambiance", plus "you can get anything you want and anything you can imagine."

Hirozen ☒ 24 | 10 | 21 | $31 |

8385 Beverly Blvd. (Orlando Ave.), West Hollywood, 323-653-0470; www.hirozen.com
Having "sushi anywhere else is a letdown" after experiencing the "wonder, majesty and elegance" of this "under-the-radar" "hole-in-the-wall" on Beverly, with "delectable morsels" and "note-perfect omakase"; sure, the decor is "lacking character" and the "tiny" space gets "jammed", but the "menu is far more authentic than the glitzier competition" (read: it's "not annoyingly trendy").

Hollywood & Vine ☻ 19 | 21 | 19 | $33 |

6263 Hollywood Blvd. (Vine St.), Hollywood, 323-464-2345; www.hollywoodandvine.net
"Doubles the pleasure of theater in Hollywood" muse show-goers who duck into this "excellent" new late-night American before heading to the "Pantages" Theatre or to swizzle a few "well-made cocktails" post-curtain; it can be a "ghost town during the day", but it's "not too crowded at night", when its "cushy booths" and "convivial atmosphere" set the tone for diners to explore a "limited" but "inventive" menu.

Hollywood Canteen ☒ ▽ 17 | 19 | 16 | $29 |

1006 N. Seward St. (Romaine St.), Hollywood, 323-465-0961
"Like a secret too good to be true", this "old-style Hollywood diner" (and "after-hours club") is where wannabes can "rub shoulders with producers and directors" while eating "standard American fare" in "tufted booths" or "chilling" on the patio in Bette Davis' Airstream trailer; it's "outstanding for lunch", but it's the "cool shark tank" and "fabulous '40s decor" that keep loyalists coming back; N.B. new ownership may impact the ratings.

Hop Li 20 | 13 | 16 | $20 |

855 S. Baldwin Ave. (Huntington Dr.), Arcadia, 626-445-3188
526 Alpine St. (Yale St.), Chinatown, 213-680-3939
4730 Lincoln Blvd. (Mindanao Way), Marina del Rey, 310-305-3700
10974 W. Pico Blvd. (Westwood Blvd.), West LA, 310-441-3708
The "closest thing to Chinese food" "outside of Monterey Park", this "genuine sleeper" outfit doles out "plentiful portions" of "solid", "traditional favorites"; on a Friday or Saturday night the wait "can be atrocious" warn regulars, but the "authentic" fare is "worth it" – just "witness the number of Chinese eating there."

Hop Woo 19 | 8 | 14 | $16 |

1 W. Main St. (Garfield Ave.), Alhambra, 626-289-7938
845 N. Broadway (bet. Alpine & College Sts.), Chinatown, 213-617-3038; www.hopwoo.com ☻
11110 W. Olympic Blvd. (S. Sepulveda Blvd.), West LA, 310-575-3668; www.hopwoo.com
"You're not going for the ambiance", you're going for the "fresh, delicious" "authentic Cantonese cooking" (and the "late-night hours" in Chinatown) agree advocates of this chow-main trio; but the vexed vent it's woofully "average" Chinese and only warrants a "take-out" "stop" if "you're in a hurry or no one cooks at home."

HOTEL BEL-AIR RESTAURANT   25 | 28 | 27 | $67
Hotel Bel-Air, 701 Stone Canyon Rd. (Sunset Blvd.), Bel Air, 310-472-1211; www.hotelbelair.com
"Heaven on earth" is how hedonists hail this haute "hideaway" in the Hotel Bel-Air, a "breathtaking" oasis that "wows" the "rich" and "famous" with its "sublimely romantic" setting, rated No. 1 for Decor in this *Survey*, "delightful garden patio", "superlative service" from a "pampering" staff and "exceptional" Cal-French fare; be warned, though, that this "top-of-the-line" experience comes at a "top price", and "try not to stare at the starlet at the next table"; P.S. word is that "Nancy Reagan loves this place."

Hot Oven ⊠   – | – | – | I
9705 Santa Monica Blvd. (Roxbury Dr.), Beverly Hills, 310-777-0040
Budget-conscious customers looking "to load up on delicious, simple Italian fare" with a California "twist" warm up to this "casual" "gem" in Beverly Hills that's just right for "quiet conversation"; while cold turkeys find the space "cramped", they may reevaluate now that it's doubled in size.

House of Blues   15 | 21 | 15 | $30
8430 Sunset Blvd. (Olive Dr.), West Hollywood, 323-848-5100; www.hob.com
"Soul"-seekers praise the "large portions" of "hearty" Southern BBQ at this "off-the-hook" tin-roofed Sunset Strip chainster that pays "tribute to the unsung blues legends", but it's the Sunday "gospel brunch that reigns supreme"; still, others bewail it's a "real shame such a cool spot can't catch its food up to its level of hip."

House of Ribs   ▽ 16 | 11 | 15 | $23
11701 Wilshire Blvd. (Barrington Ave.), West LA, 310-914-9009
"Plan to be messy" at this "no-atmosphere" American, whose "friendly" service and "melt-in-your-mouth" ribs lead some pork rangers to deem it the "white-collar BBQ of the Westside"; but foes find it a total rib-off, sniping it's "nothing to write home about."

HOUSTON'S   21 | 20 | 20 | $31
Century City Shopping & Mktpl., 10250 Santa Monica Blvd. (Century Park W.), Century City, 310-557-1285
Bristol Farms, 1550A Rosecrans Ave. (bet. Aviation & Sepulveda Blvds.), Manhattan Beach, 310-643-7211
320 S. Arroyo Pkwy. (Del Mar Blvd.), Pasadena, 626-577-6001
202 Wilshire Blvd. (2nd St.), Santa Monica, 310-576-7558
www.houstons.com
This "dark, intimate", "popular" outfit with "consistent" American eats, "enthusiastic service" and "wonderful electricity" "makes a chain feel like a real dining experience"; the "winning formula": offer "limited items" like "fall-off-the-bone ribs", "do them well" and add "new" features like the sushi bar at Santa Monica; sure, waits can be "atrocious", but reservations are taken for larger parties.

Hugo's   21 | 13 | 18 | $21
12851 Riverside Dr. (Coldwater Canyon Ave.), Studio City, 818-761-8985
8401 Santa Monica Blvd. (bet. Kings Rd. & Orlando Ave.), West Hollywood, 323-654-3993
www.hugosrestaurant.com
"When you can't face yet another egg" head to this WeHo–Studio City Cal–New American "joint" with a "cheerful" "coffee shop

atmosphere"; the "healthy and hearty" all-day breakfast is the "most divine way to start the day" – just ask the "eclectic" mix of "celebs", "industry clientele" and "earth mamas and papas"; P.S. it's also a "lunchtime favorite", "great in a pinch for dinner", plus the "tea selection rivals most wine lists."

HUMP, THE   26 | 22 | 23 | $54
Santa Monica Airport, 3221 Donald Douglas Loop S. (Airport Ave.), Santa Monica, 310-313-0977; www.typhoon.biz
Named after the aviation slang term for the Himalayas, this "exotic" Japanese at the Santa Monica Airport is a first-class ride owing to "luscious" sushi and "beautifully presented" "innovative fare"; "you can't beat the view overlooking" the runway and the decor makes you "think of *Casablanca*", but prices at Rick's Café Américain probably weren't as "sky-high", so play it "cool" and "don't order the specials before asking the cost."

Hungry Cat, The ●   – | – | – | M
1535 N. Vine St. (Sunset Blvd.), Hollywood, 323-462-2155; www.thehungrycat.com
Felix would lick his whiskers at this seafooder from husband-and-wife team David Lentz (ex Opaline) and Suzanne Goin (Lucques, AOC); tucked in the back of an upscale Hollywood mall, the minimalist room with high ceilings, an open kitchen and patio offers a similarly stripped-down slate of raw bar, salads, chowders and traditional faves like crab cakes and lobster rolls.

Hu's Szechwan   21 | 5 | 17 | $16
10450 National Blvd. (bet. Motor & Overland Aves.), Palms, 310-837-0252
There's no reason to boo Hu, as in chef-owner Chung Ming Hu, at this "ancient neighborhood" Chinese BYO, a Palms "dump" serving "to-die-for" broccoli beef and Szechuan dumplings so "excellent" that fans "have dreams about them"; "kind" service helps make it the "best corner joint in the area" say diners who don't want "glamour", "just very good and plentiful food."

Hwang Jae Korean BBQ/Denno Sushi   – | – | – | M
22640 Golden Springs Dr. (Grand Ave.), Diamond Bar, 909-861-9030
Drive east of the Asian community clustered in Rowland Heights to get to this two-in-one affair, comprised of a sprawling Korean BBQ restaurant with private rooms and a sushi bar specializing in exotic rolls; variety-seekers can also order both cuisines at once.

i Cugini   21 | 21 | 20 | $37
1501 Ocean Ave. (B'way), Santa Monica, 310-451-4595; www.icugini.com
It's the "awesome Sunday brunch" with live jazz that's the highlight of this Santa Monica Italian "favorite" (whose name means "the cousins"), which benefits from "inspired" cuisine, "attentive servers", a "romantic patio" and "just enough beautiful people to appeal to your senses"; if a few consider cussin' the "Disney" decor and "inconsistent" fare, for most the "Ocean Avenue setting" "near the beach" makes it "worth it."

Il Boccaccio   ∇ 24 | 15 | 21 | $35
39 Pier Ave. (bet. Hermosa Ave. & The Strand), Hermosa Beach, 310-701-0211; www.ilboccaccio.com
The "authentic fare" at this Hermosa Beach Northern Italian on the Promenade is credited to the "flawless execution of quality ingredients" and accented by "attentive service"; while loyalists

laud the "inviting interior" and "nice patio", others bemoan digs that "could be more attractive", but even they admit the location "about 15 steps from the sand is a huge bonus."

Il Buco 22 | 16 | 22 | $31
107 N. Robertson Blvd. (Wilshire Blvd.), Beverly Hills, 310-657-1345
"Always good and often very good", with "great bread", "to-die-for" ravioli and a "moderately priced" wine list, this "small, cozy, comfy" "neighborhood Italian" by the Drago family fits the bill for anyone seeking the "perfect little trattoria" in Beverly Hills; but the less-impressed shrug "only if you are attending something close by."

Il Capriccio on Vermont 23 | 15 | 21 | $27
1757 N. Vermont Ave. (bet. Kingswell & Melbourne Aves.), Los Feliz, 323-662-5900
"A little slice of Italy in Los Feliz", "on a charming street" no less, draws a "loyal", "eclectic crowd" that comes to "mangia" the "homey" "trattoria dishes" in a "low-key atmosphere" that's "cute for date night" and "comfortable" for a "tasty" plate of "neighborhood pasta"; add in "amiable service" from "charming owners and servers" and it's "easy" to see why it's the "perfect Italian" "joint" round the corner.

IL CIELO ⊠ 20 | 26 | 22 | $49
9018 Burton Way (bet. Almont & Wetherly Drs.), Beverly Hills, 310-276-9990; www.ilcielo.com
Italian "food for romance" sigh lovebirds, but for most it's the "amazing atmosphere" that sets the *Under the Tuscan Sun*–like backdrop for "wow"-worthy "first dates", "private affairs" or "that special night out"; the "gorgeous garden patio" "filled with twinkling lights" "transports you to another world", so overlook the "never quite up to snuff" portions and "high prices", and fall under the spell of this "beautiful" "Italian villa" in Beverly Hills.

IL FORNAIO 20 | 19 | 19 | $31
301 N. Beverly Dr. (Dayton Way), Beverly Hills, 310-550-8330
Gateway Shopping Ctr., 1800 Rosecrans Ave. (bet. S. Sepulveda Blvd. & Village Dr.), Manhattan Beach, 310-725-9555
One Colorado, 24 W. Union St. (Fair Oaks Ave.), Pasadena, 626-683-9797
1551 Ocean Ave. (Colorado Ave.), Santa Monica, 310-451-7800
www.ilfornaio.com
With "rotating chefs" who "visit Italy" and monthly passport dinners that feature "exciting" regional menus, this "bustling" Italian has converted countless chain-foes; while the "creative" daily specials and "divine" pasta "always satisfy", for most carbo-loaders the "amazing" "bread alone is worth the prices."

Il Forno 21 | 16 | 21 | $28
2450 Colorado Ave. (bet. Cloverfield Blvd. & 26th St.), Santa Monica, 310-449-9244 ⊠
2901 Ocean Park Blvd. (29th St.), Santa Monica, 310-450-1241
www.ilfornocaffe.com
This *vero Italiano* "quasi-cafe" in Santa Monica and its cafeteria-style satellite on Colorado Avenue have concocted a "fairly flawless dining experience" laud loyalists, who admit the atmosphere "isn't too special" but adore the "sweet little wine list", "dependable", "artistically presented" fare and "best bruschetta in town"; with a "family-friendly" staff holding down the Forno, you can't help but "feel right at home."

Il Grano ⧄ | 24 | 19 | 22 | $46 |

11359 Santa Monica Blvd. (bet. Corinth & Purdue Aves.), West LA, 310-477-7886

"For raw fish the way it's supposed to be served", "forget sushi – try the crudo platter" at this "elite" West LA destination where "charming" chef-owner Sal Marino's "forward-thinking" Italian cuisine is characterized by "fabulous" fish and "innovative, market-fresh" organic ingredients; supporters praise the "fancier" new decor after a recent remodel and adore the "attentive" service, which helps ease the sting of "high prices."

Il Moro ⧄ | 22 | 20 | 21 | $38 |

11400 W. Olympic Blvd. (Purdue Ave.), West LA, 310-575-3530; www.ilmoro.com

Offering "serenity" in an "unlikely setting" "off the beaten path in an office complex" on Olympic Boulevard, this "comfortably stylish" West LA Italian woos admirers with an "enchanting" "patio for alfresco dining"; it's "all-around delightful", with "incredible" pasta, "excellent salads" and "great wines" all shepherded by a "pleasant staff" that "bends over backwards to make you happy."

Il Pastaio | 25 | 16 | 20 | $37 |

400 N. Cañon Dr. (Brighton Way), Beverly Hills, 310-205-5444; www.giacominodrago.com

"Fabulous Sicilian waiters" wriggle between "elbow-to-elbow" diners at this Beverly Hills trattoria that's "packed to the gills" with "good" reason: chef-owner "Giacomino Drago's unparalleled risotto and heavenly pastas are second to none"; "every town should have" a "great local haunt" "like this: food available at the bar", a "cool patio" and a "staff that treats you like family"; sure you can "expect to age while waiting for your table" (no reservations), but for most, it's so "worth it."

Il Sole | 23 | 19 | 20 | $50 |

8741 Sunset Blvd. (Sherbourne Dr.), West Hollywood, 310-657-1182

A ray of "Little Italy on Sunset", this "busy" "stargazer central" in WeHo keeps looky-loos coming back as much for the "great celeb spotting" as for the "fabulous", "truly authentic" Italian; "chic" yet "rustic", it makes you "feel like you're in Tuscany", a "tiny" Tuscany, that is, so you "must reserve"; but a few lost soles lament that "what was once the best secret" is now "overpriced and attitudinal."

Il Tiramisu Ristorante Ⓜ | – | – | – | M |

13705 Ventura Blvd. (Woodman Ave.), Sherman Oaks, 818-986-2640; www.il-tiramisu.com

Yes, this casually comfortable father-and-son owned San Fernando Valley Italian trattoria with a terra-cotta floor and clean-lined design does serve its own tempting version of the namesake *dolci,* but it also turns out moderately priced Northern Italian dishes that run the gamut from *zuppe* to *pesce* to pasta; monthly wine dinners paired with special dishes sweeten the offerings.

Il Tramezzino | ∇ 20 | 13 | 14 | $17 |

454 N. Cañon Dr. (Santa Monica Blvd.), Beverly Hills, 310-273-0501
13031 Ventura Blvd. (Coldwater Canyon Ave.), Studio City, 818-784-2244
www.iltram.com

Fans of Italian are "glad" this Beverly Hills "favorite was brought to the Valley" to enrich a new neighborhood with "wholesome, tasty, filling food" like the "signature chicken sandwich", truly "a blessing in disguise"; if you're looking for a "nice place to meet a friend for lunch", "don't venture past", it's a "real find"; still, disbelievers berate the "small" portions and "slow" service.

India's Oven | 21 | 12 | 17 | $21

7231 Beverly Blvd. (bet. Alta Vista Blvd. & Formosa Ave.), Los Angeles, 323-936-1000; www.indiasovenla.com
11645 Wilshire Blvd. (bet. Barrington & Barry Aves.), West LA, 310-207-5522

Owned separately, this "tasty" Fairfax–West LA duo comes through with "polite service" and "generous portions" of Indian cuisine boasting "well-blended and calibrated flavors"; hungry mahatmas love the "great combo dinners on big silver plates", adding, "if you say spicy, they will make it spicy"; but naysayers nix the "no surprises" fare and find the "diner decor" "only suitable for those blinded by the cumin."

India's Tandoori | 18 | 11 | 16 | $20

Burbank Vlg., 142 N. San Fernando Blvd. (E. Olive Ave.), Burbank, 818-846-7500
5947 W. Pico Blvd. (S. Point View St.), Los Angeles, 323-936-2050
Windsor Ctr., 19006 Ventura Blvd. (Donna Ave.), Tarzana, 818-342-9100; www.indiastandooricuisine.com
11819 Wilshire Blvd., Ste. 206 (bet. Granville & S. Westgate Aves.), West LA, 310-268-9100; www.indiastandoori.com

With "very tasty Vindaloo" and other "dependable Indian" dishes, these separately owned outlets have opened the Bombay doors to Westside and Valley fans who "go for the lunch buffet" and "some of the best naan in town"; still, fuss buckets bridle at "uninspired" fare and dis the "plain-Jane-all-around" setting.

Indo Cafe | ▽ 23 | 15 | 19 | $17

10428½ National Blvd. (Motor Ave.), Palms, 310-815-1290

"Lovely owner Farida" Tio "makes you feel welcome" at this "family-run" Palms BYO, whose "authentic, spicy and delicious" Indonesian fare keeps gastronomes intrigued with "fresh, complex flavors"; surrounded by "exotic paintings", diners receive "lots of help negotiating the foreign menu" from the "knowledgeable staff" and seal the deal with one of the "wacky tropical dessert drinks."

INN OF THE SEVENTH RAY | 21 | 27 | 21 | $39

128 Old Topanga Canyon Rd. (4 mi. north of PCH), Topanga, 310-455-1311; www.innoftheseventhray.com

"Tranquil" and "romantic to the extreme", this "heavenly" Topanga sanctuary and former church "could bring out the hippie in anyone" with a "beautiful wooded setting" filled with "fountains and fairy lights", "service as calm as the atmosphere" and a "sophisticated" vegan-vegetarian skewed menu of "earthy" Californian fare; loyalists over the moon about the "rainbow of colors and flavors" assert they "could make a shoe taste good", and while it's "far from civilization, it's worth the drive."

IN-N-OUT BURGER ● ⊅ | 24 | 11 | 19 | $7

13425 Washington Blvd. (Centinela Ave.), Culver City
7009 Sunset Blvd. (Orange Dr.), Hollywood
5864 Lankershim Blvd. (Burbank Blvd.), North Hollywood
4444 Van Nuys Blvd. (Moorpark St.), Sherman Oaks
3640 Cahuenga Blvd. (Lankershim Blvd.), Studio City

(continued)

IN-N-OUT BURGER

7930 Van Nuys Blvd. (Blythe St.), Van Nuys
9149 S. Sepulveda Blvd. (La Tijera Blvd.), Westchester
9245 W. Venice Blvd. (Canfield Ave.), West LA
922 Gayley Ave. (Le Conte Ave.), Westwood
19920 Ventura Blvd. (Winnetka Ave.), Woodland Hills
www.in-n-out.com
Additional locations throughout Southern California
Both a "standard" and a "standout", this "SoCal institution" has been grilling up "cheap", "juicy", "thick" hamburgers made with "brutally fresh" ingredients since 1948 and remains the No.1 Bang-for-the-Buck "favorite" in this *Survey*; accompanied by "excellent" fries and "real ice-cream shakes", they're "served with a smile" by "eager" staffers and word is "it's worth braving the long drive-through lines" for a "double-double animal style" ("double-double joy-joy") – it "should be the official state food of California."

Iroha ●   24 | 18 | 21 | $36

12953 Ventura Blvd. (Coldwater Canyon Ave.), Studio City, 818-990-9559
"Recently expanded", this "funky" Japanese "tucked-away" in Studio City and graced with "B-list celeb sightings" slices up "spot-on" raw fish; the atmosphere is "relaxing", and the "cute hut"-like "decor and backyard feel make you think you're in Big Sur"; if a handful huff it "doesn't always cut it in this sushi red zone" and find service "friendly but not quick", most retort, "for the price, it can't be beat."

Islands   16 | 16 | 16 | $15

350 S. Beverly Dr. (Olympic Blvd.), Beverly Hills, 310-556-1624
101 E. Orange Grove Ave. (N. 1st St.), Burbank, 818-566-7744
15927 Ventura Blvd. (Gloria Ave.), Encino, 818-385-1200
117 W. Broadway (Orange St.), Glendale, 818-545-3555
3200 Sepulveda Blvd. (bet. 30th & 33rd Sts.), Manhattan Beach, 310-546-4456
404 Washington Blvd. (Via Dolce), Marina del Rey, 310-822-3939
3533 E. Foothill Blvd. (Rosemead Blvd.), Pasadena, 626-351-6543
2647 PCH (Crenshaw Blvd.), Torrance, 310-530-5383
10948 W. Pico Blvd. (Veteran Ave.), West LA, 310-474-1144
23397 Mulholland Dr. (Calabasas Rd.), Woodland Hills, 818-225-9839
www.islandsrestaurants.com
Additional locations throughout Southern California
Despite "Polynesian" decor and "extreme-surfing and -skiing videos played on a continuous loop", this beefy chain serves a "typical American menu of "bountiful burgers", "tasty tacos" and "endless" soda in a "family-friendly" atmosphere; the servers are "cute" but their performance is "hit-or-miss" say scoffers, who recommend "checking into a gym" after a "decadent" meal here.

Ita-Cho 🚫Ⓜ   22 | 12 | 18 | $32

7311 Beverly Blvd. (bet. Fuller Ave. & Poinsettia Pl.), Los Angeles, 323-938-9009
"The fish is fresh and the crowd is too" at this "friendly" Beverly Boulevard Japanese joint, where the sushi-fatigued come for "interesting" and "affordable" tapas-style dining with "sparkling sashimi", "unique, hard-to-find sides" and other "wonderful" dishes; "no reservations" can translate into "intolerable waits", but "major star sightings" help pass the time.

IVY, THE　　　　　　　　　　　　23 | 23 | 21 | $53
*113 N. Robertson Blvd. (bet. Beverly Blvd. & 3rd St.), West Hollywood,
310-274-8303*
"Bring the gold card", "snag a seat on the front patio" and "smile
for the photogs camped out across the street" at this "major celeb
hangout" on Robertson Boulevard with "superb service"; "believe
the hype": the "comfy" "cottage" is "darling", the New American
dishes like "fried chicken are out of this world" and, of course, the
"people-watching never disappoints"; if the jaded jeer it's a "stuffy
power lunch-aroo" magnet with "attitude", "expense-account"-ers
shrug this is "star-grazing at its best."

Ivy at the Shore ◐　　　　　　　21 | – | 20 | $53
*1535 Ocean Ave. (bet. B'way & Colorado Ave.), Santa Monica,
310-393-3113*
"More relaxed", with a "beachlike vibe" and "less Hollywood
hoopla" than its famous "big brother" on Robertson, this "staple
celeb spot" near the SM Pier is nonetheless a "happening place
where even the unhip feel hip"; Ivy leaguers head to its new digs
(next door to its former home) for "simple" New American food
done beautifully" and "fantastic gimlets"; if detractors deem it an
"overpriced icon on the ocean", for most it's a "quintessential
LA experience"; N.B. the move took place post-*Survey.*

Jaan　　　　　　　　　　　▽ 22 | 22 | 22 | $65
*Raffles L'Ermitage Hotel, 9291 Burton Way (bet. Foothill Rd. &
Maple Dr.), Beverly Hills, 310-278-3344; www.jaanrestaurant.com*
Thanks to a "superb" Californian tasting menu with an Indonesian
twist, "excellent" service and "upscale decor", including a
fireplace in the cocktail-perfect library, a meal at Raffles L'Ermitage
Hotel's "minimal, yet elegant" "best-kept secret" is "a beautiful"
Beverly Hills "experience"; "love the privacy" assert undercover
types who also find the "atmosphere so soothing" and "quiet" you
feel like "you should only whisper."

Jack 'n Jill's　　　　　　　　　– | – | – | I
*342 N. Beverly Dr. (bet. Brighton & Dayton Ways), Beverly Hills,
310-247-4500*
Amid the boutiques on upscale Beverly Drive sits this down-home
American with shopper-friendly fare, including a country-fried
steak for breakfast (in Beverly Hills?), replaced as the day goes
by with burgers, sandwiches and (naturally) lots of salads.

Jackson's Village Bistro　　　　22 | 16 | 22 | $30
*517 Pier Ave. (bet. Bard St. & Cypress Ave.), Hermosa Beach,
310-376-6714*
Bestowing Cal–New American "upscale comfort food with some
excitement on the edges" this "great neighborhood bistro" and
"pearl of Hermosa Beach" sparkles with a "short but interesting"
wine list, "genuinely friendly" service and a "comfy atmosphere";
a few village people say recent "changes in the kitchen have hurt",
but for most it's still the local "jewel."

Jack Sprat's Grille　　　　　　19 | 12 | 17 | $21
*10668 W. Pico Blvd. (Overland Ave.), West LA, 310-837-6662;
www.jackspratsgrille.com*
Weight watchers en-wraptured by "healthy eats" that "don't taste
like low-fat food" "love" that you get "wonderful" complimentary

"pretzels as a starter instead of bread" at this "lovely" West LA Californian; but it's the "unbeatable air-baked fries", "wide array of salads" and "tasty wraps" that make it so "memorable" for others; but what stands out for detractors is the "noise" level now that it's "become an industry hangout."

Jacopo's | 17 | 8 | 13 | $17 |

490 N. Beverly Dr. (Little Santa Monica Blvd.), Beverly Hills, 310-858-6446
15415 Sunset Blvd. (Via de la Paz), Pacific Palisades, 310-454-8494
8166 W. Sunset Blvd. (N. Crescent Heights Blvd.), West Hollywood, 323-650-8128
11676 W. Olympic Blvd. (Barrington Ave.), West LA, 310-477-2111
www.jacopos.com
Turning out "thin, crispy-crust" "pizza for the fussy New Yorker" in "specialty" varieties that "do not disappoint", along with pasta and salads, this "friendly" Westside Italian mini-chain is "reliable" for "carryout after a day at the beach"; but that doesn't mean jake to critics who pronounce the pies "overpriced" and the "ambiance lacking everything", concluding, "t'ain't what it used to be."

James' Beach | 18 | 18 | 18 | $34 |

60 N. Venice Blvd. (Pacific Ave.), Venice, 310-823-5396
Thanks to the "neighborhood secret Sunday brunch" on the "tropical" outdoor patio and the "happening" "bar scene", this "friendly" Craftsman "beachside getaway" is where "half of Venice met their partners"; it's so "laid-back" – who cares that the "heavenly" mojitos are better than the "American standards"; but a few gripe it's a "pickup joint", prompting party boys to quip "got to go back when my wife is out of town."

Jan's ◗ | ▽ 14 | 8 | 15 | $16 |

8424 Beverly Blvd. (Croft Ave.), West Hollywood, 323-651-2866
"You gotta love" the "extensive menu", "reasonable prices" and "large portions" at this "no-nonsense" WeHo "blue-hair standby" diner that's "great if you're in a rush near Cedars"; if bashers blast the "atmosphere is lousy" and the servers "bored out of their minds", the sanguine see it as proof that "the coffee shop lives – this one just hasn't gotten hip yet"; N.B. open until 2 AM daily.

Japon Bistro | ▽ 20 | 16 | 20 | $27 |

927 E. Colorado Blvd. (Lake Ave.), Pasadena, 626-744-1751;
www.japonbistro.com
If you enjoy Nippon at the bottle, "try the sake flight" at this Pasadena Japanese, where the tasting menu, "delicious" sushi and "beautiful" fusion dishes stem from "fresh ingredients"; fence-sitters maintain the quality is "inconsistent, ranging from mediocre to masterpiece", but owner "Clarence [Wong] is a charmer" and the "top-rate" service is "warm and friendly."

JAR | 24 | 21 | 22 | $51 |

8225 Beverly Blvd. (Harper Ave.), West Hollywood, 323-655-6566;
www.thejar.com
At this "truly cool" Beverly Boulevard New American, "foodies congregate and cruise each other" between bites of "perfect pot roast" and other "miraculous" "comfort food" from chef/co-owner Suzanne Tracht; the recently redesigned, "minimalist yet elegant" "mid-century modern" setting is "wonderful for a special dinner" with "gracious" service to boot; if a few find the "high prices" jarring, the payoff is that "portions are often big enough to split."

Javan   21 | 17 | 17 | $22
11500 Santa Monica Blvd. (Butler Ave.), West LA, 310-207-5555;
www.javanrestaurant.com
Before or after a show at the Royal Theater, a "diverse" crowd
flows into this "friendly" "Persian palace" in West LA to sup on
"delicious lamb chops", "nicely grilled" kebabs and "fragrant
rice" enhanced by "spices and fruit"; if a few find the "flavors
disappointingly mild", for most it's a "fun way to mix things up."

Jer-ne ●   24 | 25 | 23 | $55
Ritz-Carlton, 4375 Admiralty Way (off Lincoln Blvd.), Marina del Rey,
310-574-4333; www.ritzcarlton.com
Chef Troy Thompson's "imaginative" Asian fusion fare, featuring
entrees cooked tableside on hot river rocks, keeps pace with the
"professional" service and "incredible view of the Marina" from
the "lovely" patio of the Westside Ritz-Carlton; it's "one of the
great brunch destinations in LA" suggest those who make the
sojourn, but it can be "terribly expensive", so "bring your wallet
and hopefully somebody else's too."

Jinky's   21 | 12 | 16 | $15
1447 Second St. (B'way), Santa Monica, 310-917-3311
14120 Ventura Blvd. (Hazeltine Ave.), Sherman Oaks, 818-981-2250
www.jinkys.com
"Breakfast nirvana", and "don't forget lunch too", yes, this "always
mobbed" SM–Sherman Oaks daytime duo with "crusty service" still
"rocks" for Southwestern-American eats attest admirers who
find the pancakes and "French toast beyond reproach", the "chili
selection incredible" and the omelets "eggs-ellent" – and "almost
as big as the line to get in"; if skeptics sniff it's "definitely not worth
waiting" for, nevertheless most grab some java and queue up.

JIRAFFE   26 | 22 | 24 | $49
502 Santa Monica Blvd. (5th St.), Santa Monica, 310-917-6671;
www.jirafferestaurant.com
Chef-owner Raphael Lunetta's "exquisite" Californian cuisine
made with "fresh, seasonal ingredients" attains "understated
perfection" at this "perennial favorite" with "staying power" in
Santa Monica; "sophisticated without being stuffy", it "feels like a
slice" of "NYC" "on the left coast" with "extremely cordial service";
if rubberneckers find the noise level "overbearing", others suggest
it's "quieter" upstairs and just right for "that special occasion like
selling your script"; P.S. the prix fixe "Monday night bistro dinners
are a delicious bargain."

Jitlada Ⓜ   ▽ 23 | 11 | 17 | $21
5233½ W. Sunset Blvd. (bet. Harvard Blvd. & Kingsley Dr.),
East Hollywood, 323-667-9809
"Worth the adventure" insist the intrepid who brave the "sketchy"
neighborhood surrounding this East Hollywood Thai and a lack
of "atmosphere" for "zippy", "spicy" fare "served with pride" at
prices "that can't be beat"; it's "definitely not for the garlic sensitive,
so don't expect to get close to anyone for a few days."

JJ Steak House Ⓜ   22 | 22 | 23 | $49
88 W. Colorado Blvd. (De Lacey Ave.), Pasadena, 626-844-8889
Dig the "dignified, old-school setting" and "beautiful patio"
overlooking Colorado Boulevard, "exemplary" service and, oh, the

"great steak" declare diners who flock to this "romantic getaway" in Old Town Pasadena; but bashers beef that it's "a bit too dark", the "pricey sirloin" "a bit too dry" and the servers "pompous" to boot.

Joan's on Third
— | — | — | I

8350 W. Third St. (bet. Fairfax Ave. & La Cienega Blvd.), West Hollywood, 323-655-2285
Hammer Museum, 10899 Wilshire Blvd. (Westwood Blvd.), Westwood, 310-443-7037 Ⓜ
www.joansonthird.com

What began as a family-owned catering firm and take-out deli on Third Street has since morphed into a de facto American restaurant with counter service and plans to triple its space, plus a Hammer Museum offshoot for alfresco dining; customers demolish carefully constructed salads, sandwiches and sweets galore, accompanied by wine and beer at the new Westwood branch.

Jody Maroni's Sausage Kingdom
20 | 6 | 13 | $9

Westfield Shoppingtown, 10250 Santa Monica Blvd. (Century Park W.), Century City, 310-556-0899
Howard Hughes Ctr., 6081 Center Dr. (Sepulveda Blvd.), Culver City, 310-348-0007
LA Int'l Airport, 201 World Way (Terminals 3 & 6), LAX, 310-646-8056
Universal CityWalk, 1000 Universal Studios Blvd. (off Frwy. 101), Universal City, 818-622-5639
2011 Ocean Front Walk (20th Ave.), Venice, 310-822-5639 ⊅
www.jodymaroni.com

"One of a kind, despite multiple locations", these walk-up wiener wonderlands teem with "great chili cheese dogs" and other "delicious, hot, dripping" sausages filled with "the stuff dreams are made of"; fans relish the "super-friendly" service and "various flavors" concocted from poultry, pork or beef; sure, some barkers growl it's "overpriced" and "not what it used to be", but others frankly feel it's a "must-try."

JOE'S Ⓜ
27 | 21 | 23 | $48

1023 Abbot Kinney Blvd. (bet. Main St. & Westminster Ave.), Venice, 310-399-5811; www.joesrestaurant.com

"Eat at Joe's", as in Joe Miller's, and "you won't be disappointed" intone fans of this "crowded" Venice "gem", where the "genius" chef-owner "works the room" – actually a "mad labyrinth" of recently refurbished rooms, plus a "neat" patio – and "makes you feel like he cooked" the "magnificently executed" Cal–New French cuisine "just for you"; if a few have "no clue why it's so beloved", no sleuthing is necessary for loyalists who deem the prix fixe lunch "dollar for dollar, bite for bite, the best value in the city."

Joe's Crab Shack
14 | 14 | 15 | $24

1420 S. Azusa Ave. (Colima Rd.), City of Industry, 626-839-4116
6550 Marina Dr. (Studebaker Rd.), Long Beach, 562-594-6551
230 Portofino Way (Harbor Dr.), Redondo Beach, 310-406-1999
www.joescrabshack.com

A "partylike" "Chuck E. Cheese" offering "fried fish", this "festive" "family-friendly" outfit with offshoots "right on the water" has "kids clamoring to return", if only to watch the staff "dance and make fools of themselves" while seafaring grown-ups "sail into" the "fresh" crabs; if some squids find the food "average" and the atmosphere "too corny", at least "you can get in and out in a hurry."

Johnnie's New York Pizzeria　　19 | 11 | 15 | $15

Fox Apts., 10251 Santa Monica Blvd. (bet. Ave. of the Stars &
Beverly Glen Blvd.), Century City, 310-553-1188
Museum Park Sq., 5757 Wilshire Blvd. (Courtyard Pl.), Los Angeles,
323-904-4880
22333 PCH (bet. Carbon Canyon Rd. & Malibu Pier), Malibu, 310-456-1717
Hoyt Plaza, 2805 Abbot Kinney Blvd. (Washington Blvd.), Marina
del Rey, 310-821-1224
"They must import" the H^{2}0 muse admirers of this Italian outfit, and
they're not far off: the wet stuff is specially filtered to match New
York's tap supply to make pizza that "blows Mulberry Street", well,
"out of the water"; other "affordable" faves include "fresh" "puffy
rolls" and "wonderful salads", all perhaps best consumed at home
because there's "no atmosphere" and the staff can be "rude."

Johnnie's Pastrami　●🌱　　22 | 8 | 16 | $13

4017 S. Sepulveda Blvd. (bet. Washington Blvd. & Washington Pl.),
Culver City, 310-397-6654
Craving the "perfect" "late-night repast", night-owls brave the
"diner atmosphere" and "no-frills" service from "waitresses
as old" as this 1952 "classic" to get their hands on the "primo
pastrami" at this Culver City kosher deli "staple"; kudos also to the
"table jukeboxes that work", and the "enjoyable Paleolithic fire
pits" on the patios; N.B. open until 3:30 AM Fridays and Saturdays.

Johnny Rebs'　　　　　　22 | 18 | 21 | $20

16639 Bellflower Blvd. (bet. Alondra & Flower Sts.), Bellflower,
562-866-6455
4663 Long Beach Blvd. (bet. 46th & 47th Sts.), Long Beach, 562-423-7327
www.johnnyrebs.com
With "peanut shells on the floor and BBQ on your shirt", saucy fans
give a greasy thumbs-up to the "great ribs", hushpuppies and
Southern "country" standards "worth whistling about" at these
"bare-bones" Bellflower, Long Beach (and Orange) "roadhouses";
the "warm staff" and "casual atmosphere" twang of "Texas", and
the "grub is "bodacious" enough to satisfy "homesick hillbillies."

Johnny Rockets　　　　　16 | 14 | 16 | $12

474 N. Beverly Dr. (Little Santa Monica Blvd.), Beverly Hills, 310-271-2222
Media City Ctr., 201 E. Magnolia Blvd. (3rd St.), Burbank, 818-845-7055
Century City Shopping Ctr., 10250 Santa Monica Blvd. (Century Park W.),
Century City, 310-788-9020
Howard Hughes Ctr., 6081 Center Dr. (Sepulveda Blvd.), Culver City,
310-670-7555
16901 Ventura Blvd. (Balboa Blvd.), Encino, 818-981-5900
Hollywood & Highland Complex, 6801 Hollywood Blvd. (Highland Ave.),
Hollywood, 323-465-4456
Pine Ct., 245 Pine Ave. (bet. B'way & 3rd St.), Long Beach, 562-983-1332
Farmer's Mkt., 6333 W. Third St. (Fairfax Ave.), Los Angeles, 323-937-2093
7507 Melrose Ave. (Gardner St.), Los Angeles, 323-651-3361
Manhattan Mktpl., 1550-C Rosecrans Ave. (Sepulveda Blvd.),
Manhattan Beach, 310-536-9464
www.johnnyrockets.com
Additional locations throughout Southern California
Tolerate the white-capped "teenyboppers" at this "sparkly",
"kitschy" "blast-from-the-past" and you'll get a "nice sloppy"
burger (or "veggie patty") and a "smiley face made of ketchup" for
your fries; the "tiny tabletop jukeboxes" are nifty, but the "'50s

theme can get tiresome": some sodajerks deem the "idealized all-American atmosphere" a "Disney-fied version of the Apple Pan."

John O'Groats   21 | 13 | 18 | $17
10516 W. Pico Blvd. (½ block west of Beverly Glen Blvd.), Rancho Park, 310-204-0692
The pancakes are a "gift from God" at this daytime-only Rancho Park American "landmark", a "real family business for families" where a "feisty" staff also delivers "crunchy fried chicken", "rib-sticking meatloaf" and "biscuits to die for" to a "Hollywood"– "blue hair" mix; while there's "always a line" for the "awesome breakfast" (their "specialty"), "free coffee mitigates" the weekend wait.

Jones Hollywood ◐   19 | 20 | 15 | $29
7205 Santa Monica Blvd. (Formosa Ave.), West Hollywood, 323-850-1727; www.committedinc.com
After almost 12 years, WeHo's "dark" "hipster hangout" "has transcended time and remains an excellent place to dine" on "fresh, healthy" Italian-American fare and ogle "stars"; "keeping up with the Joneses is not cool, but Jones is", so, hey, "rock 'n' roll", baby: soak up the "fabulous bar scene", "sip your martini" and "rub elbows with Hollywood types."

Joseph's Cafe   ▽ 18 | 15 | 17 | $28
1775 N. Ivar Ave. (Yucca St.), Hollywood, 323-462-8697; www.josephscafe.com
It may "bear no resemblance" to its former spartan self, but this "hip Hollywood Greek"-Med turned "club after dark" is still a "neighborhood restaurant" at "heart" offering food "fit for the gods at prices mortals can afford"; but nostalgists "liked it better when the old men sat at the counter smoking" – now it's just another "celeb hangout"; N.B. a recent refurb may impact the Decor score.

JOSIE RESTAURANT   27 | 23 | 25 | $55
2424 Pico Blvd. (25th St.), Santa Monica, 310-581-9888; www.josierestaurant.com
"Gastronomic delight", "culinary bliss" – surveyors run out of supper-latives to describe chef Josie Le Balch's "flawless" French-accented New American cuisine at this Santa Monica "gem"; enthusiasts "embrace" the "imaginative but comforting" dishes, including "earthy truffle fries" and the "best game in town", cradled by "seamless" service in a "classy" setting, with "soft lighting and a glowing fireplace"; if a few whine the "excellent wine list" is "pricey", most reveal "as you leave, you're already planning your return."

Joss   – | – | – | M
9255 W. Sunset Blvd. (N. Sierra Dr.), West Hollywood, 310-276-1886
"Romantic" lighting, an elegantly industrial ambiance and "smooth, soft service" set the stage for a relaxing meal at this WeHo Chinese "gem"; insiders deem the creative variations on "high-end" Cantonese classics "delicious", the all-day "dim sum fantastic" and the prodigious 280-bottle wine list a "delight."

JR's BBQ 🗷   19 | 8 | 19 | $16
3055 S. La Cienega Blvd. (Blackwelder St.), Culver City, 310-837-6838; www.jrs-bbq.com
"Stay on Mama Jeannie's good side" or she'll dish you up "a side of attitude" with some "incredible" "Dixie" BBQ at this Culver City

BYO pork park, where the rib meat is "tender and smoky" and the brisket "solid"; some cowboys gathered round the horseshoe-shaped counter shoot down the "bargain" 'cue as "nothing to write home about", but even they advise "don't pass on the 'Sock It to Me' cake."

JR Seafood   20 11 14 $21
11901 Santa Monica Blvd. (Amacost Ave.), West LA, 310-268-2463
The "mac daddy of Westside Chinese", this stand-in for Monterey Park tempers "huge lobsters", shrimp dishes and other "fresh" *fruits de mer* with "surly" service and "no-frills" decor; explorers find the "best food is off the menu", so "go with someone who speaks the language."

Juliano's Raw   16 15 14 $29
609 Broadway (6th St.), Santa Monica, 310-587-1552;
www.planetraw.com
An "original" place to broach the "unusual tastes" of uncooked edibles, this Santa Monica spot offers "high-quality, small portions" of "healthy" raw vegan fare, all "beautifully presented"; if doubters declare it's the "most expensive greenery we've ever eaten", wondering how can it "take forever to 'prepare' the food", troopers rationalize it may be "more concept than real meal", but "like Disneyland, you have to go at least once."

Julienne ⊠   26 22 21 $24
2649 Mission St. (bet. El Molino & Los Robles Aves.), San Marino,
626-441-2299; www.juliennetogo.com
"San Marino moms" "mix with gourmet-seeking gamines" at this "quaint" sidewalk cafe with "warm" service, "charming decor" and "spectacular" French bistro fare; "why eat lunch" or breakfast "at home when you can go here" for "wonderful" soups, scones and pastries "to make you swoon"; "don't mind the wait – you can pass the time in the little" gourmet market perusing the "perfectly packaged food."

Junior's   17 10 15 $19
2379 Westwood Blvd. (W. Pico Blvd.), West LA, 310-475-5771
Don't let the "salty" servers get under your skin as you devour "big portions" of "wonderful whitefish", a "winner of a Reuben" and other Jewish "comfort food" at this "old standby" across from the Westside Pavilion; but the disgruntled gripe it's "overpriced" "pedestrian deli fare" and lament this place is "living on its history which is all in the past."

Kaiten   – – – M
1456 Third Street Promenade (Broadway), Santa Monica,
310-451-8080; www.eatkaiten.com
Not just a revolving sushi bar, but 'the first magnetic runway sushi bar', this intensely lit Third Street Promenade hot spot looks like a club in *Lost In Translation*; the chefs work behind a 'catwalk', from which you can grab special rolls like the Napoleon Dynamite.

Kamiyama ⊠   ▽ 25 8 22 $25
2408 Lomita Blvd. (Pennsylvania Ave.), Lomita, 310-257-1363;
www.kamiyamasushi.com
"Never has a visit been a disappointment" agree admirers who pop into this recently expanded Lomita Japanese, where the "friendly" chefs hand out "superb rolls", "healthy salads" and other "fresh,

delicious" fish; the only decision is whether to "belly up to the sushi bar" or stop off for takeout "on the way home"; N.B. the Manhattan Beach branch closed, but plans are underway for a new location.

Kanpai Japanese Sushi Bar & Grill – – – M
8325 Lincoln Blvd. (83rd St.), Westchester, 310-338-7223
For a "lower-cost Koi-like experience" that's "very trendy for Westchester", this "tiny" "neighborhood treat" "is the place to be" believe boosters who make a beeline for "excellent", "authentic" sushi; no surprise, it gets busy (despite the 14-seat bar), so "get there early or make reservations"; N.B. the changing omakase menu is available daily.

KATANA ◗ 24 25 19 $49
8439 W. Sunset Blvd. (bet. La Cienega Blvd. & Sweetzer Ave.), West Hollywood, 323-650-8585; www.katanarobata.com
"Come for the food, stay for the gossip" at this "gorgeous" Dodd Mitchell–designed "agents' watering hole", a Japanese "creation from the owners of Boa and Sushi Roku" swarming with "beautiful people"; "chill out" on the "incredible patio" and "watch the Sunset Strip chaos" and "celeb-packed scene" while dining on "innovative sushi" and "robata grill offerings"; but cynics snipe it's so "tragically hip" "you'll leave hungry, drunk or broke" "before slithering across the road to Sky Bar."

Kate Mantilini 18 18 18 $33
9101 Wilshire Blvd. (Doheny Dr.), Beverly Hills, 310-278-3699 ◗
5921 Owensmouth Ave. (bet. Califa St. & Oxnard Ave.), Woodland Hills, 818-348-1095
Dishing out American "comfort food" "like mama makes" at "uncomfortable prices", this "upscale coffee shop" in Beverly Hills and its young Woodland Hills branch placate diner-loving diners with "large" portions", a "chic" setting, "spot-on service and late-night hours" that "make it a New York transplant's dream"; nonetheless, the less-impressed mouth off about "marginal food, snobby service" and deem it "Denny's for the William Morris set."

KATSU-YA 28 14 20 $37
16542 Ventura Blvd. (Hayvenhurst Ave.), Encino, 818-788-2396
11680 Ventura Blvd. (Colfax Ave.), Studio City, 818-985-6976
Cloaked in a mini-mall and packed with "starlets", this "noisy" Encino "heaven" and Studio City "industry fave" serve sushi that's "as good as sushi gets"; "don't go without a reservation", but do "order everything from the specials board", and be ready to "tolerate the crowds"; finally, eat your "sublime", "extremely fresh" fish quickly because "they're always rushing to get you out."

Kay 'n Dave's 18 13 18 $18
15246 Sunset Blvd. (bet. Monument St. & Swarthmore Ave.), Pacific Palisades, 310-459-8118
10543 W. Pico Blvd. (bet. Patricia & Prosser Aves.), Rancho Park, 310-446-8808
262 26th St. (San Vicente Blvd.), Santa Monica, 310-260-1355
"The high-chair set" babbles its approval of this "family favorite" Mexican trio as parents sample "great tamales" and "mammoth burritos"and the staff "hangs the kids' artwork on the walls"; while a couple of cranks decry the "noisy" din and "weird cafeteria-style ambiance", most eat up the "star sightings", and their canine companions dig the "dog-friendly outdoor seating."

Kendall's Brasserie   17 | 20 | 17 | $41

Dorothy Chandler Pavilion, 135 N. Grand Ave. (bet. 1st & Temple Sts.),
Downtown, 213-972-7322; www.patinagroup.com

Munching Mozarts agree that Joachim Splichal's "relaxed yet
elegant" French brasserie on the ground floor of the Music Center
(and across from Disney Hall) is "wonderful for dinner before
or after the opera or Philharmonic"; but others harp it's all about
"location, location, location" – "you want to like" the fare, but
it's "very inconsistent" and merely satisfies a "captive audience"
"when it should be a standout."

Khoury's   16 | 16 | 17 | $31

110 Marina Dr. (bet. PCH & 2nd St.), Long Beach, 562-598-6800;
www.khourys.net

"If you love lobster", check out the all-you-can-eat crustacean-
filled buffet weekend nights at this LB Continental "at the end of
the pier"; the regular menu features "tons of seafood" too, but
the highlight is the "wonderful view" of the marina and wafting
"ocean breezes"; however, critics carp the "muddle" of food
"defines ordinary cooking" and kvetch that quarters are "tight",
so just go "for a glass of wine and watch the sailboats" luff by.

Kikuchi ⓈⓂ   ▽ 25 | 14 | 25 | $47

(fka Bistro 21)
Cienega Ctr., 846 N. La Cienega Blvd. (bet. Waring & Willoughby Aves.),
West Hollywood, 310-967-0021

Formerly known as Bistro 21 and now named after its "super chef"-
owner Koh Kikuchi, this "quiet, unassuming" WeHo Japanese lures
locals and "serious visiting foodies" to an "unlikely mini-mall"
setting with a "pared-down menu" that's still "unsurpassed" for its
"elegance"; service is "warm and dedicated", while the "sensibility
is France via" Asia, and the results are "excellent in every way."

Killer Shrimp   21 | 10 | 15 | $20

523 Washington Blvd. (Via Marina), Marina del Rey, 310-578-2293
4000 Colfax Ave. (Ventura Blvd.), Studio City, 818-508-1570

The "no-brainer" menu at this Marina del Rey–Studio City duo lists
"three items: shrimp, shrimp and shrimp", which means visitors
"de-shell" the crustaceans, "dip the bread" in the "tasty" sauce
and indulge in "messy, spicy, finger-lickin' good fun" with "Cajun
heat" that "hurts so good but won't kill"; still, cynics sputter "what's
the big deal? you can try this at home."

Kinara Café Ⓜ   ▽ 22 | 23 | 17 | $30

656 N. Robertson Blvd. (bet. Melrose Ave. & Santa Monica Blvd.),
West Hollywood, 310-657-9188; www.kinaraspa.com

Co-owner Christine Splichal, wife of Pinot impresario Joaquin, is
doing her own thing with "fresh, natural" health food at this "oasis"
tucked inside a WeHo spa, where the "serene" setting on the
"beautiful" patio makes you "forget you are paying a fortune"; it's
"a great place to have a light meal before being pampered" so
"relax" and dig into the "simple", "tasty" offerings.

Kincaid's   21 | 23 | 20 | $38

Redondo Beach Pier, 500 Fisherman's Wharf (Torrance Blvd.),
Redondo Beach, 310-318-6080; www.kincaids.com

"Ask for window seating" and "feast your eyes" on the "180 degree
ocean view" from this "cheery" Redondo Beach surf 'n' turf chain

link "on the Redondo Beach pier", truly an "ideal place to watch the sunset"; sure, there are "selections for every palate", from "fresh, inventive fish" and "second-to-none prime rib" to "great cocktails", but they "can't compete" with the "fabulous" vistas.

King's Fish House/King Crab Lounge 21 19 20 $30
The Commons, 4798 Commons Way (Calabasas Rd.), Calabasas, 818-225-1979
100 W. Broadway (Pine Ave.), Long Beach, 562-432-7463
www.kingsfishhouse.com
Whether you go for the "dark wood and white tablecloths" of the main room or the "casual, inviting" lounge, you'll be rewarded with "straight at ya" seafood "and plenty of it" at this "bustling" outfit in Calabasas and Long Beach; the "oyster selection sings", the "fish is always reliable" and "who can complain about" sides like "homemade mac 'n' cheese"; but pouters find it "acceptable, never outstanding" and "too noisy" to boot.

Kings Road Cafe 18 12 16 $17
8361 Beverly Blvd. (Kings Rd.), West Hollywood, 323-655-9044;
www.kingsroadcafe.com
"Stars and babes abound" at this "funky" Beverly Boulevard American BYO, a "total scene" where "breakfast is king" ("who shacked up with whom? come Saturday morning to see!"), the hand-pressed coffee is like a "meal-in-a-cup" and the "salads are palpitation inducing"; "hang for hours" as you scope the "industry crowd" in its most "disheveled" state: "no makeup", just their "best ripped denim and Stanley Kowalski"-esque T-shirts.

Kitchen, The ● 20 12 17 $22
4348 Fountain Ave. (Hoover St.), Silver Lake, 323-664-3663
"Don't let the facade fool you, the cooking is top-notch" at this "happenin'" Silver Lake "joint" where "hipsters" reach their "comfort zone, prairie-style" with "Midwestern"-sized portions of "eclectic" American fare and the "cool staff acts like everyone has a ring though their nose"; it tastes like "mom's food without mom, and you don't have to clear the table afterwards", but you do have to squeeze into "cramped" quarters.

KOI 23 26 19 $56
730 N. La Cienega Blvd. (bet. Melrose & Willoughby Aves.),
West Hollywood, 310-659-9449; www.koirestaurant.com
"Paris Hilton is a regular" at this "sexy, sleek" Japanese "celebrity haven" on La Cienega done up with bamboo and waterfalls, but don't let that stop you from checking out this "quintessential LA scene"; dine on "pricey" "sushi so fresh you want to slap it" and "outstanding Kobe beef", then "stay for a drink by the outdoor fireplace" and indulge in people-watching amid "starlets, moguls and wannabes"; but bashers balk at the "pretentious atmosphere" filled with "gold diggers in miniskirts."

Kokomo Cafe 18 11 15 $17
Farmer's Mkt., 6333 W. Third St. (Fairfax Ave.), Los Angeles,
323-933-0773; www.kokomocafe.com
A "Hollywood crowd" "talks deal points over toast points", "great AM coffee cake" and the "best BLT ever" at this "cool-looking" Old Farmer's Market diner, where the "simple" "tasty" Cal-Southern fare "always delivers"; while a handful find it hampered by "inconsistent" service ("pack a weekend bag, you're gonna be

there a while"), most shrug "where else can you get fried catfish and eggs for breakfast?"

Koo Koo Roo   15 | 9 | 13 | $11

262 S. Beverly Dr. (bet. Charleville Blvd. & Gregory Way), Beverly Hills, 310-274-3121
445 S. Figueroa St. (5th St.), Downtown, 213-629-1246 ⊠
255 S. Grand Ave. (3rd St.), Downtown, 213-620-1800
301 N. Larchmont Blvd. (Beverly Blvd.), Hancock Park, 323-962-1500
5779 Wilshire Blvd. (bet. Courtyard Pl. & Curson Ave.), Los Angeles, 323-954-7200
Manhattan Village Mall, 3294 N. Sepulveda Blvd. (Rosecrans Ave.), Manhattan Beach, 310-546-4500
Villa Marina Mktpl., 4325 Glencoe Ave. (bet. Maxella Ave. & Mindanao Way), Marina del Rey, 310-305-8100
238 S. Lake Ave. (bet. Cordova St. & E. Del Mar Blvd.), Pasadena, 626-683-9600
8520 Santa Monica Blvd. (La Cienega Blvd.), West Hollywood, 310-657-3300
11066 Santa Monica Blvd. (Sepulveda Blvd.), West LA, 310-473-5858
www.kookooroo.com
Additional locations throughout Southern California
"All chains should be this good" crow customers who give this American outfit Koo-dos for its "moist, yet crisp" "rotisserie chicken", "low-fat skinless" birds and a "tasty, fresh variety of sides"; if a few cluck about "tiny portions" and compare the decor to a "bad disco", most flock for a "quick bite" at "affordable prices."

Koutoubia Ⓜ   ▽ 23 | 23 | 22 | $35

2116 Westwood Blvd. (bet. Mississippi Ave. & W. Olympic Blvd.), Westwood, 310-475-0729; www.koutoubiarestaurant.com
"Great" host-owner Michael Ohayon "always has something special waiting" for you at this "lovely" Westwood Moroccan that's "fun for a group meal"; the "wonderful" couscous, "magnificent fish" and other "exquisite" dishes are served in a "traditional" or "modern room" and the vibe is far from "hokey" – in fact, it's a "unique experience", complete with "entertaining belly dancers."

Kung Pao Bistro   19 | 12 | 18 | $19

15025 Ventura Blvd. (bet. Kester & Noble Aves.), Sherman Oaks, 818-788-1689
11838 Ventura Blvd. (bet. Colfax Ave. & Laurel Canyon Blvd.), Studio City, 818-766-8686; www.kpbistro.com
Fan Fair Mall, 7853 Santa Monica Blvd. (Fairfax Ave.), West Hollywood, 323-848-9888; www.kpbistro.com
Whipping up "healthy versions of old favorites" like "awesome orange chicken", this "solid" Chinese trio (the Sherman Oaks site is separately owned) also boasts a "satisfying" "vegetarian menu with mock meats"; when you can't be there in person to enjoy the "nice" outdoor seating, "you can always count on fast delivery."

La Boca del Conga Room ⊠Ⓜ   ▽ 14 | 16 | 14 | $33

5364 Wilshire Blvd. (2 blocks west of La Brea Ave.), Los Angeles, 323-938-1696; www.congaroom.com
This "sexy" white-on-white eatery with vibrant lighting downstairs from the Conga Room on the Miracle Mile is better known for its celebrity investors Jennifer Lopez and Jimmy Smits than for its "mediocre" Nuevo Latino food; still, all is forgiven once the plates

are cleared because "the real fun begins after dinner" when the music starts and the salsa lessons kick in.

LA BOHEME
23 | 27 | 23 | $48

8400 Santa Monica Blvd. (N. Orlando Ave.), West Hollywood, 323-848-2360; www.global-dining.com
The "red velvet" accents, "magnificent chandeliers" and "glowing" fireplaces at this WeHo "favorite" (and older sibling of Monsoon) with "top-notch service" "may make you think you've walked into an old bordello" – or *The Phantom of the Opera*" set; "each bite is better than the last", plus the "high-drama" decor (including a "lovely patio") "has improved drastically" following a refurb – this must be "where Lestat takes his dates" for "Gothic gastronomy", make that "fine" Californian cuisine, when he floats into town.

La Bottega Marino
21 | 13 | 17 | $20

Larchmont Vlg., 203 N. Larchmont Blvd. (bet. Beverly Blvd. & W. 1st St.), Hancock Park, 323-962-1325
11363 Santa Monica Blvd. (Purdue Ave.), West LA, 310-477-7777
Owner Sal Marino "makes everyone feel like family" at these "everyday Italian" cafes in Larchmont and West LA that "exceed expectations", serving some of the "the best thin-crust pizzas" and "tasty pasta" dishes "at prices that won't make you go back to the ATM"; it "feels like one of those little finds" affirm *amici*, plus you can also get "delicious takeout" and "Euro groceries" for dining *en casa*.

La Bruschetta Ristorante
22 | 18 | 23 | $36

1621 Westwood Blvd. (bet. Massachusetts & Ohio Aves.), Westwood, 310-477-1052; www.labruschettaristorante.com
There's "nothing nouvelle" about the "satisfying" Italian fare at this "welcoming" Westwood "haunt" where "everyone is greeted as a regular" and every meal starts with a "treat of free bruschetta"; after over 20 years, "the pastas still sparkle", plus you can "talk (and hear!) over a leisurely meal" – no wonder it's a "civilized choice for families visiting their UCLA students."

LA CACHETTE
27 | 25 | 24 | $58

10506 Little Santa Monica Blvd. (Thayer Ave.), Century City, 310-470-4992; www.lacachetterestaurant.com
"Expect graciousness at every turn" at this "delicious bit of France" in Century City attest *amis* who agree that "brilliant" chef-owner Jean Francois Meteigner is "doing brilliant things" with "modern French" fare at this recently refurbished "hideaway" "for grown-ups"; join the "great mix of blue-haired ladies" and "high-powered" "sunglass-wearing Hollywood producers" and you'll be rewarded with "creative cuisine" lavished with "Gallic flavor" yet "light" enough "for the California palate."

la di da ◗ ☒
▽ 15 | 16 | 19 | $36

8840 Beverly Blvd. (Clark Dr.), West Hollywood, 310-492-0880; www.ladidarest.com
"Have a drink" on the "great" outside deck of this "friendly" yearling on top of Beverly Boulevard's Antiquarian Guild in WeHo's design district, then admire the "nice ambiance" within, enhanced by the works of local talent; but the Hawaiian-accented New American dishes strike another note: supporters appreciate the "artistically arranged" plates while dissenters deem the menu "poorly conceived."

La Dijonaise Café et Boulangerie   20 | 15 | 15 | $21

Helms Bldg., 8703 Washington Blvd. (Helms Ave.), Culver City,
310-287-2770; www.ladijonaise.com

"A genuine bistro experience in the happening Helms Bakery"
complex, this "bright, bustling" "solid neighborhood standby"
makes you "feel like you're on the streets of Paris"; "they care
and it shows", "never failing to deliver" "croissants to die for",
plus "homey", "affordable French" fare for lunch and dinner; oui,
the service can be "the slowest this side of the Seine", but *amis*
agree it just adds to the "European" vibe.

La Dolce Vita ●🖬   19 | 19 | 21 | $52

9785 Little Santa Monica Blvd. (Wilshire Blvd.), Beverly Hills,
310-278-1845; www.ladolcevitabeverlyhills.com

It feels like "not much has changed" since "Sinatra used to hang
here" but now that new owners have restored this "intimate"
Beverly Hills "throwback" with "red-leather booths", it's "back
in vogue" and teeming with "Hollywood" players, "old-money
regulars" and "Rat Pack ghosts"; the "traditional" Italian food is
"good", but rarely "great" but never mind, they make "everyone
feel important, even when there's a star dining 10 feet away."

L.A. Farm 🖬   21 | 22 | 21 | $39

3000 W. Olympic Blvd. (bet. Centinela Ave. & Stewart St.), Santa Monica,
310-449-4000; www.lafarm.com

A Santa Monica magnet for the "industry crowd" (think "power
by day, romance by night"), this Californian charmer could be
mistaken for a country villa were it not located in a "corporate"
office "complex"; despite this "unlikely" venue, you can sit "under
the canopy" in the "exotic garden" and feast on "delightful" fare
served up by an "efficient" crew; overall, though, a few former
farmers feel that the "celebs are A-list, but the food gets a B+."

La Finestra 🅼   ▽ 21 | 15 | 20 | $30

19647 Ventura Blvd. (bet. Corbin & Shirley Aves.), Tarzana, 818-342-2824

The "passionate owners" "greet you with a hug" at this "small but
cozy" Italian that resembles a "Tuscan villa" in Tarzana; the "rustic"
"housemade pastas and thin-crust pizzas" are "consistently good"
and "reasonably priced" – little wonder why this "pleasant" place
is a local "favorite."

La Fondue Restaurant & Bar   16 | 13 | 17 | $37

13359 Ventura Blvd. (bet. Dixie Canyon & Fulton Aves.), Sherman Oaks,
818-788-8680

"Reliving your youth" is "fun, fun, fun" at this "grungy" "old-world
restaurant" in Sherman Oaks where the point of the prix fixe "cook-
it-yourself" meal is to "fondue everything"; still, it's "such a sinful
indulgence" "that you only want to do once in a very great while",
plus dunkers declare you might "walk away hungry" and "smelling
like a barnyard"; sweet talkers suggest "go just for the chocolate."

LA Food Show   16 | 17 | 18 | $25

Manhattan Village Mall, 3212 N. Sepulveda Blvd. (Rosecrans Ave.),
Manhattan Beach, 310-546-5575; www.cpk.com

With a "broad" selection of "creative" American eats, "colorful
martinis" and a "grown-up" vibe that's still family-"friendly", this
"not too showy" California Pizza Kitchen "spin-off" makes a "nice
stop before a movie" at Manhattan Village Mall; but grumblers surf

by this "jack of all trades" Show, dubbing it "CPK on steroids" with a "menu that casts too wide a net" and "balloon-clutching kids and shopping-pooped parents that take away from the luster."

La Frite   20   16   18 $26
15013 Ventura Blvd. (Lemona Ave.), Sherman Oaks, 818-990-1791
22616 Ventura Blvd. (bet. Ponce & Sale Aves.), Woodland Hills, 818-225-1331
"After we ate, I thought I could speak French" quip patrons who tout the "tasty salads, crêpes", "light, perfect soufflés" and daily Gallic specials as well as the service "without attitude" at this "quaint" "grande dame of Sherman Oaks dining" and its Woodland Hills *soeur*, but it's all Greek to others who find the fare a bit "pedestrian" and feel the "menu could use some updating."

Lake Spring Shanghai   ∇ 21   10   15 $23
219 E. Garvey Ave. (Lincoln Ave.), Monterey Park, 626-280-3571
"Adventurous" chowhounds looking for an "intro" to "authentic Shanghainese" cuisine seek out the house special "pork pump", a "quivering mass of" "melt-in-your-mouth" porcine goodness served family-style at this nondescript dining hall in Monterey Park; there's "not much" in the way of "atmosphere" or service here, but the well-regarded Chinese food is "always worth the trip."

La Korea Korean B.B.Q.   ∇ 19   9   17 $11
Farmer's Mkt., 6333 W. Third St. (Fairfax Ave.), Los Angeles, 323-936-3930; www.lakoreabbq.com
Pull up a chair "on the patio" at this "friendly" "no-frills" "Korean food stall" in the Fairfax Farmer's Market and join the "adventurous shoppers" for "steaming bowls" of bibimbop and "tasty" "barbecue beef short ribs"; if a handful would "rather drive to K-town", loyalists counter this "institution" is "just as authentic."

La Loggia   20   19   23 $37
11814 Ventura Blvd. (bet. Colfax Ave. & Laurel Canyon Blvd.), Studio City, 818-985-9222
"Music biz" insiders and Studio City "locals" are "treated like family" at this "unpretentious" "home in the Valley" serving "consistently fresh" Italian specialties like "interesting risottos"; followers that lodge complaints about "overcrowding" may have more legroom following a recent expansion (including a new tapas lounge), plus the "always charming and lively" Tuscan-style patio is open year-round.

La Luna   21   19   20 $33
113 N. Larchmont Blvd. (bet. Beverly Blvd. & 1st St.), Hancock Park, 323-962-2130; www.ristorantelaluna.com
One of the "only upscale places right on Larchmont", this "classic" "hangout" is the "go-to spot" for "can't-be-missed appetizers" and "delicious", "authentic" Italian dishes muse admirers who are also over the moon about the "nightly specials"; frequenters find the "cozy" digs "quite romantic", though a few advise "ask for a table in the back" because "the front room is always too noisy."

Lamonica's NY Pizza   22   9   14 $9
518 W. Sixth St. (bet. Grand Ave. & Olive St.), Downtown, 213-614-1100
1066 Gayley Ave. (Kinross St.), Westwood, 310-208-8671
The "honest-to-god New York–style pizza" at this Downtown and Westwood duo "takes you all the way to Times Square in a single

bite", according to NY transplants homesick for "greasy" "thin-crust" pies; it's "authentic down to the rude service and grubby decor" (a rather "feeble attempt" to re-create a Big Apple subway stop), but it's more "affordable" than a "3,000 mile plane trip."

Langer's Deli 🏵   24 | 8 | 18 | $16
704 S. Alvarado St. (7th St.), Downtown, 213-483-8050
"Guaranteed to bring out the Yiddish in everyone", the "world-class" "hand-cut" "pastrami on rye", paired "with old-fashioned cream soda", "rivals" "any Jewish deli in New York", declare the diehards who regularly make the "trek" to this LA "landmark"; "the wait staff knows its stuff" and "it'll deliver curbside" "if you call ahead" ("you can take the Red Line", too), an advantage in this "sketchy" Downtown neighborhood; N.B. they close at 4 PM.

La Paella 🏵   22 | 19 | 20 | $36
476 S. San Vicente Blvd. (bet. La Cienega & Wilshire Blvds.), West Hollywood, 323-951-0745; www.usalapaella.com
"Lots of tasty little dishes", an *authentico* lineup of "show-stopping paellas" and pitchers of "sangria that never run dry" – yes the "Spanish really know how to eat" and drink declare devotees who "get their fix" at this "lovely" WeHo "find" that "feels like a cottage in Barcelona"; if a handful pan the fare as "average", for most it's "a nice alternative" to "the hipper tapas joints."

La Parisienne   ▽ 23 | 19 | 23 | $41
1101 E. Huntington Dr. (bet. Buena Vista & Mountain Aves.), Monrovia, 626-357-3359; www.laparisiennerestaurant.net
"Seduced" by the "old-school charm", complete with "candles and flowers", die-hard romantics "go out of their way to visit" this Monrovia standby, the older sibling of Marla's, for some of "the best French food east of Downtown"; "yes, they experiment with nouvelle touches" *amis* aver, "but not enough to ruin the overall classical approach"; still, a Galled few feel it "misses the mark."

La Pergola   23 | 21 | 22 | $35
15005 Ventura Blvd. (Lemona Ave.), Sherman Oaks, 818-905-8402
"Perfect for a romantic date", this "Italian treasure" in Sherman Oaks coddles customers with its "very authentic" "Tuscan villa" setting and "unfussy" dishes made "from the freshest ingredients", including herbs and vegetables "obtained daily" from the "friendly" "owner's own garden"; "don't be afraid to try something new" – you're sure to find the preparations "light", "original and delicious."

La Piazza   ▽ 15 | 19 | 14 | $30
The Grove at Farmer's Mkt., 189 The Grove Dr. (bet. Fairfax Ave. & 3rd St.), Los Angeles, 323-933-5050
"Don't expect a very daring menu" at this Italian "find" in the "convenient" Grove at Farmer's Market, but do expect "simple, satisfying pasta and pizza" as well as an "unbeatable" "people-watching" "scene in front of the stunning", "melodic fountain"; while "service can be lukewarm at times", a "glass of wine" on the "popular" "patio" "isn't such a bad" way to soothe your spirits.

La Rive Gauche   ▽ 19 | 19 | 20 | $41
320 Tejon Pl. (Via Corta), Palos Verdes Estates, 310-378-0267
"Worth the trip for special occasions" assert nostalgists besotted by the "romantic" French country ambiance, "memorable" Gallic fare and "unparalleled wine list" at this hideaway near the Palos

Verdes Estates country club; but a handful no longer bank on this "tired" standby, pouting it's "pretentious and expensive."

L'Artiste Patisserie
| – | – | – | I |

17312A Ventura Blvd. (Louise Ave.), Encino, 818-386-0061
The latest in a mini-wave of casual Gallic cafes, this cozy Encino eatery offers an all-day alternative to mall grub; offerings include brioche French toast and a Parmesan-Brie chicken melt, plus plenty of salads to cheer the hearts of ladies-who-lunch lightly.

La Salsa
| 16 | 9 | 13 | $10 |

9631 Little Santa Monica Blvd. (bet. Bedford & Camden Drs.), Beverly Hills, 310-276-2373 🗷
11740 San Vicente Blvd. (Gorham Ave.), Brentwood, 310-826-7337
601 W. Fifth St. (Grand Ave.), Downtown, 213-623-6390 🗷
Ontario Mills Mall, 1 Mills Circle (4th St.), Ontario, 909-476-1313
2790 Manhattan Beach Blvd. (bet. Gibson Pl. & Inglewood Ave.), Redondo Beach, 310-793-9444
1401 Third St. Promenade (Santa Monica Blvd.), Santa Monica, 310-587-0755
Sherman Oaks Fashion Sq., 14006 Riverside Dr. (Woodman Ave.), Sherman Oaks, 818-789-8587
12048 Ventura Blvd. (bet. Laurel Canyon Blvd. & Ventura Pl.), Studio City, 818-760-0797
11901 Santa Monica Blvd. (Amacost Ave.), West LA, 310-473-7880
www.lasalsa.com
"Can't beat" this "relatively healthy Mexican" chain "for lunch on the run" assert fleet-footed fans who find it also "satisfies a certain craving" "for the late rush home after work"; the salsas are "zippy", the fish-and-veggie tacos are "killer" and "flautas are killer" and "service is courteous"; if hotheads huff that "newcomers have surpassed it for quick" meals, even they concede it's "ok in a pinch."

La Scala 🗷
| 21 | 18 | 20 | $37 |

434 N. Cañon Dr. (bet. Brighton Way & Little Santa Monica Blvd.), Beverly Hills, 310-275-0579
It's all about "the best chopped salad in LA" (and always has been) at this "old-school" "Beverly Hills treasure", where the Northern "Italian standards" include "incredible veal" and pasta; the staff is "well trained" (if sometimes "a bit sassy"), and the "clubby" setting still feels "glamorous", at least to the lunch bunch, but some scenesters call this "classic" "yesterday's news."

La Scala Presto 🗷
| 20 | 14 | 17 | $25 |

11740 San Vicente Blvd. (Barrington Ave.), Brentwood, 310-826-6100
"Why bother ordering anything else but the chopped salad" at this "casual" Brentwood "spin-off" of the Beverly Hills Italian original – lettuce lovers reveal owner Gigi "Leon's famous" leafy greens are "even better here"; but there's plenty more "semi-casual dinner" fare in store, from "authentic pizza" to "divine" pasta, all served in an "intimate" setting.

La Serenata de Garibaldi
| 22 | 17 | 19 | $29 |

1842 E. First St. (bet. Boyle Ave. & State St.), Boyle Heights, 323-265-2887
1416 Fourth St. (bet. B'way & Santa Monica Blvd.), Santa Monica, 310-656-7017
www.laserenataonline.com
"When you're bored with the combination plate at your usual Mexican joint", "spoil your taste buds" with "delicious seafood"

and "imaginative sauces" at these "peachy" "little pueblos" that recall "a hacienda in Mexico"; though the Santa Monica location is usually "not crowded", amigos assert it's "worth the drive to the original" in Boyle Heights where the fare is *muy bueno.*"

La Serenata Gourmet   23 | 14 | 18 | $24

10924 W. Pico Blvd. (Westwood Blvd.), West LA, 310-441-9667
"Awesome seafood" and "lip-smacking salsas" draw fans to this West LA Mexican, where the "authentic" "regional cuisine" "defies the stereotype" of "the usual stuff" you find around town; in spite of its name, this "downscale location" is "not fancy", and the service can be rather "indifferent", but the "fresh" and "tasty" dishes are "certainly worth a try."

LASHER'S Ⓜ   24 | 24 | 25 | $39

3441 E. Broadway (bet. Newport & Redondo Aves.), Long Beach, 562-433-0153; www.lashersrestaurant.com
"You might think you're entering a friend's house as you walk" into this "classic Craftsman" bungalow in Long Beach, and when "the owner greets you at the door", "that's not far from the truth"; "the wait staff is equally friendly and helpful" as it serves up the "divine" American "meat and potatoes" fare (including an "awesome cranberry meatloaf"), though a few lash out that this "upscale comfort food" is "a little pricey."

La Sosta Enoteca   – | – | – | M

2700 Manhattan Ave. (27th St.), Hermosa Beach, 310-318-1556
This South Bay Italian features large windows that open to catch the ocean breeze, well-worn wood floors and pleasant outdoor seating; a similarly casual menu is built around a large selection of cured meats and Italian cheeses, sliced to order while you watch, along with Venetian dishes like *bigoi in salsa* – spaghetti tossed with Mediterranean anchovies.

La Terza   22 | 19 | 19 | $53

8384 W. Third St. (Orlando Ave.), West Hollywood, 323-782-8384
"Name-brand chef" Gino Angelini of Angelini Osteria has done it again in this "modern" Third Street location, serving "inventive" Italian cuisine straight from the wood-burning oven to a "look-at-me" WeHo crowd; the rotisserie "duck is a triumph", and for dessert only "two words" matter: "ricotta fritters (one "taste, you're hooked for life"), so don't mind the "staff that takes itself too seriously" and that the space is rather "minimalist."

La Vecchia Cucina   21 | 17 | 19 | $31

2654 Main St. (bet. Hill St. & Ocean Park Blvd.), Santa Monica, 310-399-7979; www.lavecchiacucina.com
"Rub elbows with all the right people" at this "airy" Italian on SM's Main Street, a "neighborly" "hangout" where the menu includes "options to suit everyone's tastes"; "it may not win any awards for interior design" and "the noise level can get high", but the food is "consistent", the staff is "accommodating" and "the price is right"; P.S. there's live jazz at "the excellent Sunday brunch."

La Velvet Margarita Cantina ◗   ▽ 15 | 24 | 15 | $28

1612 N. Cahuenga Blvd. (½ block south of Hollywood Blvd.), Hollywood, 323-469-2000; www.velvetmargarita.com
"It's like being in a Robert Rodriguez movie" at this "funky" Mexican cantina, with its "Day of the Dead meets Elvis" decor that's "strictly

for vampires" (or Hollywood club kids); thanks to the "delish" margaritas, "the bar scene is" "fun for a group" (at least "if no one is a foodie"), but service is "slow" and even the "simplest dishes don't stack up"; N.B. open till 4 AM weekends.

LAWRY'S THE PRIME RIB   25 | 21 | 24 | $45

100 N. La Cienega Blvd. (bet. Beverly Blvd. & W. 3rd St.), Beverly Hills, 310-652-2827; www.lawrysonline.com

"Busloads of tourists" and "football players" converge on this La Cienega "landmark" for "good old-fashioned prime rib dinners" served "with all the fixin's"; this "beloved institution" is "a favorite for celebrating special occasions" too, and the "top-notch staff" obliges with "entertaining service, from the spinning salad bowls to the tableside carving"; sure, a few snipe that it is "a relic", but the faithful affirm "quality never goes out of style."

Le Chêne   ▽ 23 | 19 | 21 | $40

12625 Sierra Hwy. (Sierra Vallejo Rd.), Saugus, 661-251-4315; www.lechene.com

"For a relaxing meal" of "delectable" French fare that "brings your senses alive" "in the absolute middle of Timbuktu", it's "worth a Sunday drive" to this "charming" "hidden treasure" in Saugus that feels like a "rustic stagecoach stop"; choose from a "daily menu handwritten on a chalkboard" accompanied by a "wine list from heaven", soak up the "spectacular views" from the "beautiful back patio" and don't forget to "leave a breadcrumb trail to find your way home."

Le Dome 🅂🅼   22 | 22 | 23 | $59

8720 Sunset Blvd. (La Cienega Blvd.), West Hollywood, 310-659-6919; www.ledomerestaurant.com

We're "glad they're back", insist admirers of this long-standing WeHo "power-meal scene" that's been given "a face-lift with style"; chef Sam Marvin revamped the menu with "amazing" French-Med fare, while designer Dodd Mitchell's Tuscan-inspired decor feels "glamorous" (if too "Goth" for some); if traditionalists sniff that it's "not what the old Le Dome was", for most it remains a "solid upper-crust restaurant."

LEILA'S 🅼   25 | 18 | 24 | $40

Oak Park Plaza, 706 Lindero Canyon Rd. (Kanan Rd.), Oak Park, 818-707-6939; www.leilasrestaurant.com

Reviewers wonder what this "strip-mall" "jewel" with a staff that "wants to make your experience special" is doing in "the culinary hinterlands" of the Conejo Valley; whatever the answer, the "inspired" Californian "cooking executed perfectly" in a "relaxing setting" makes it a "joy for the gourmet-challenged" area; an "unexpectedly good" vino list and live jazz in the wine bar cement its status as "everything a restaurant should be."

Le Marmiton   19 | 14 | 17 | $27

1327 Montana Ave. (14th St.), Santa Monica, 310-393-7716

"Santa Monica needs more cafes like this" "very pleasant" "true neighborhood" spot that's been dishing out "lovely" French bistro fare in a "handy location" for 30 years; *amis* agree that the "casual atmosphere is perfect for Sunday brunch", "expecially if you can snag a spot on the sidewalk to people-watch" on "see-and-be-seen Montana Avenue" while the "adjoining patisserie is a bonus" for the picnic-bound.

Lemon Moon Café ⊠   22 | 16 | 16 | $16
Westside Media Ctr., 12200 W. Olympic Blvd. (S. Bundy Dr.), West LA,
310-442-9191; www.lemonmoon.com
The "incredible" chefs from Melisse and JiRaffe "team up" and
"hit the moon" at the "coolest cafeteria you'll ever find" winning
accolades for their "super delicious" breakfasts and "creative"
Cal-Med "lunch treats"; sure, it's "sorta self serve", but it's still a
"refreshing place" "for a bite with the girls or a casual" noontime
"date" over "divine salads and sandwiches" on the "sunny patio"
and a "godsend" for Westside Media Center worker bees; the only
sour note: "it's not open weekends" or for dinner.

Le Pain Quotidien   19 | 17 | 15 | $18
9630 Little Santa Monica Blvd. (bet. Bedford & Camden Drs.),
Beverly Hills, 310-859-1100
11702 Barrington Ct. (bet. Barrington Ave. & Sunset Blvd.),
Brentwood, 310-476-0969
8607 Melrose Ave. (Westbourne Dr.), Los Angeles, 310-854-3700
www.lepainquotidien.com
"Just what I 'knead' when I blow off the good Dr. Atkins": "crusty
baguettes" and "expertly crafted" croissants and pastries "that
remind me of Paris" concur carbo-loaders who rise to the occasion
at this Belgian bakery chain; "saddle up a seat at the communal
table" and "kick back" with a "bowl" of java and "fresh", "organic
sandwiches" and "listen in on the latest LA drama."

Le Petit Bistro   21 | 17 | 18 | $32
13360 Ventura Blvd. (Fulton Ave.), Sherman Oaks, 818-501-7999
631 N. La Cienega Blvd. (Melrose Ave.), West Hollywood, 310-289-9797
There's nothing like "excellent" "steak frites" and a "glass of red
wine" "to make you feel like you're in Paris" insist *amis* of these
bistro "favorites" in Sherman Oaks and on La Cienega; but while
most enjoy the "great Gallic energy" "*sans* pretension" and
"satisfying" fare, a few find the service "rude" and the digs too
"congested"; N.B. the Wilshire branch aka Le Petit Zinc closed.

Le Petit Cafe ⊠   22 | 15 | 21 | $30
2842 Colorado Ave. (bet. Stewart & Yale Sts.), Santa Monica,
310-829-6792; www.lepetitcafe.info
"*C'est une petite* surprise! a cute French" "charmer" "plunked
down" in a "somewhat secluded spot" in "SM's corporate
corridor" – no wonder it's frequented by the "Lions Gate and MTV
crowd" that huddles over "hearty standards" like bouillabaisse;
oui, it's a "come-back-to-again-and-again bistro" "where monsieur
cooks and mademoiselle serves" "with just enough attitude to make
you feel like you're in France"; if a few would rather "bluescreen
out the background", for most it feels "warm and fuzzy."

Le Petit Four   18 | 17 | 18 | $31
Sunset Plaza, 8654 W. Sunset Blvd. (Sunset Plaza Dr.), West Hollywood,
310-652-3863; www.lepetitfour.com
Brush up on your language skills so you can eavesdrop on the
"very international crowd" that packs this sidewalk cafe, a
"Sunset Plaza classic, especially if you are into the Euro scene"
and "unparalleled people-watching" on the Strip; sure, the "tables
are close together", but the staff is "accommodating" and "it's
so nice to sit alfresco, sipping wine, eating" French bistro food,
"looking at the beautiful people . . . not bad, not bad at all."

Le Petit Greek ⊠   21 | 16 | 20 | $27 |
*127 N. Larchmont Blvd. (bet. Beverly Blvd. & 1st St.), Hancock Park,
323-464-5160*
"Try the sampler serving of appetizers – they're Greek to me" – and
so are "delicious" offerings like "exceptional lamb" and "super
salads" at this "lively", "friendly not so petite" Hellenic taverna
on Larchmont where insiders try to sit "curbside" "to watch the
neighborhood go by"; if a few grouch that it's Mediterranean "for
the uninitiated", even they admit it's a "charming way to spend
some time dipping a warm pita" and "sipping Retsina."

Le Petit Jacques   ▽ 21 | 15 | 20 | $29 |
*13456 Ventura Blvd. (Sunnyslope Ave.), Sherman Oaks,
818-789-3575; www.lepetitjacques.com*
There's always room for "another Bizou clone" agree *amis* of this
"welcome addition to the Valley food scene", an all-day French
bistro with "lots of promise" and a BYO policy, which makes it a
"winner" for euro-counters; while the "warm staff" "couldn't try
harder to please", a few cold shoulder the "geriatric ambiance"
in need of "some pizzazz."

Le Saigon Ⓜ⌀   19 | 10 | 16 | $13 |
*11611 Santa Monica Blvd. (bet. Barry & Federal Aves.), West LA,
310-312-2929; www.lesaigoncuisine.com*
"Good thing they just expanded, since this teeny-tiny Vietnamese
eatery was always jammed" with "a line out the door"; while noodle
houses "in Westminster may be superior", it's still "pho so good"
and one of the phew spots in West LA to satisfy "a craving" for
"cheap, filling" fare phull "of flavor"; N.B. the Decor rating may
not reflect the recent growth spurt.

Les Sisters Southern Kitchen Ⓜ   23 | 9 | 20 | $19 |
21818 Devonshire St. (Jordan Ave.), Chatsworth, 818-998-0755
You can almost "smell the moss dripping from the trees in the
bayou" at this Chatsworth soul-food shack that cooks some of
the "best" Southern victuals "this side of the Mississippi" –
unless "you've got your own mama making you down-home fried
chicken"; aesthetes might be "put off" by the "no-frills decor",
"but that would be a bad move because there's too much to eat –
and it's too good to stop."

Lilly's French Cafe & Wine Bar   20 | 19 | 17 | $36 |
*1031 Abbot Kinney Blvd. (bet. Main St. & Westminster Ave.),
Venice, 310-314-0004*
"Take a good Parisian bistro, plunk it down in Abbot Kinney, add a
funky beach vibe" and modern artwork, and you get this "slice" of
"France in Venice"; "smell the flowers" from your "idyllic" perch
on the "breezy patio" and order the $10 weekday lunch special
that's *magnifique,* which is French for 'you'll want to come
back'" – "what more could you want on a nice summer day?"

Lincoln ◗   19 | 20 | 17 | $55 |
*2460 Wilshire Blvd. (25th St.), Santa Monica, 310-828-3304;
www.thelincoln.cc*
Squeeze past the "gauntlet of bare flesh at the bar" at this way-
"cool", way-"noisy" SM steakhouse designed by Kelly Wearstler in
a "Goth" palette of "inky" colors and settle into the "giant suede
chairs" under the "deer-antler chandeliers" for "big chunks" of

beef with "killer side dishes"; it's "so dark you can't see your food, but it sure tastes good."

Literati Café
18 | 17 | 14 | $14

12081 Wilshire Blvd. (S. Bundy Dr.), West LA, 310-231-7484;
www.literaticafe.com

Literati II ☒
12081 Wilshire Blvd. (S. Bundy Dr.), West LA, 310-479-3400;
www.literati2.com

"Bring your laptop" and "watch unemployed screenwriters spend their last few bucks" as they over-caffeinate on "delicious coffee" at this West LA "self-serve" cafe with a "bohemian" "collegiate" vibe; "local literati" appreciate the "surprisingly varied menu" of "light" Eclectic-Californian choices and desserts and may find the photo-filled digs more "lovely" now that it's expanded next door with Literati II, the more sophisticated, unrated offshoot.

LITTLE DOOR, THE
23 | 25 | 21 | $50

8164 W. Third St. (bet. Crescent Heights Blvd. & La Jolla Ave.),
Los Angeles, 323-951-1210; www.thelittledoor.com

"You feel like you've left LA for more exotic locales" "when you enter the little door" and into the "beautiful outdoor patio lit by twinkling lights" and fountains at this Third Street "oasis"; the "incredible" Mediterranean food, "stylish service" and ambiance can "turn a cynic into a hopeless romantic", and since "there's no signage" at this "private paradise", "you know it must be cool" – "just make sure you're hip enough to fit in and rich enough to hang."

LOBSTER, THE
23 | 24 | 20 | $49

1602 Ocean Ave. (Santa Monica Pier), Santa Monica, 310-458-9294;
www.thelobster.com

"The location is the real seller" at this New American seafooder agree Angelenos who bring "out-of-towners" to this "mainstay" overlooking the Santa Monica Pier, to take in "breathtaking" Pacific sunsets, even if they do "pay" for the privilege; if a few crab it's "noisy", for most the "swinging bar scene" and "impeccably fresh" "lobsters as big as your head" more than compensate.

Local Place, The
– | – | – | I

18605 S. Western Ave. (I-405), Torrance, 310-523-3233

With its floor-to-ceiling windows and open kitchen, this casual American-Hawaiian cafe feels more like California than Maui; fittingly, the food roams from the islands to the mainland, including, diet be damned, Spam scramble and kalua pork.

Locanda del Lago
20 | 18 | 18 | $36

231 Arizona Ave. (3rd St. Promenade), Santa Monica,
310-451-3525; www.lagosantamonica.com

"A respite" from the "chaos" of the Third Street Promenade, this Northern Italian trattoria rises "above expectations for a prime tourist spot", turning out "perfectly crafted pastas" and a "great" lunchtime buffet; locals go loco for the "people-watching"–perfect patio, opining it's a "destination all its own."

Locanda Veneta
25 | 18 | 22 | $44

8638 W. Third St. (bet. Robertson & San Vicente Blvds.), Los Angeles,
310-274-1893

"It's worth a trip to the hospital", to the Cedars Sinai vicinity, that is, to dine at this "small" piece of "heaven" next to sibling Cafe Veneto, which sweeps surveyors off their feet with "exquisite" Venetian dishes, including "gnocchi that floats on the plate" served by an "accommodating" staff; "you practically sit on your neighbor's lap, but then again . . . all the better to taste their food."

Lodge Steakhouse ⦿   – | – | – | E |
14 N. La Cienega Blvd. (Wilshire Blvd.), Beverly Hills, 310-854-0024
Designer Dodd Mitchell strikes again at this postmodern brick, glass and timber La Cienega steakhouse, the latest meatery that, given its neighbors Arnie Morton's, Lawry's and Fogo de Chão, is helping to turn 'Restaurant Row' into 'Steak Street'; with owners from Dolce Group and Hollywood Canteen behind this sizzling new hot spot, the scene is way-trendy with prime cuts accompanied by über-*courant* martinis.

Loft, The   18 | 15 | 17 | $15 |
20157 Pioneer Blvd. (Del Amo Blvd.), Cerritos, 562-402-3538 Ⓜ
23305 Hawthorne Blvd. (Lomita Blvd.), Torrance, 310-375-4051
www.loft.d2g.com
It's "love at first bite" – this "popular" trio (with a Huntington Beach branch) serves an "addictive" "taste" of the islands that "blows your hair back" with its "Hawaiian-warrior sized portions" of "luau"-worthy fare from Spam creations to "crazy-good fried chicken"; it's "not quite" as "authentic" as what's across the Pacific, but the "homesick" hail it as "not too shabby" either.

Lola's ⦿   17 | 18 | 17 | $29 |
945 N. Fairfax Ave. (bet. Romaine St. & Willoughby Ave.), West Hollywood, 213-736-5652; www.lolasla.com
"Everyone can find something to eat" from the "reasonably priced", "consistent" New American menu, but for most, this WeHo watering hole is all about the "hip bar scene" and the multipage "mind-boggling martini selection", "each one equally delicious"; still, Lola lollers suggest it's "great for a quick bite" and there are always "pretty people to view" while supping "late" into the night.

L'Opera   23 | 24 | 22 | $45 |
101 Pine Ave. (1st St.), Long Beach, 562-491-0066; www.lopera.com
"Still a class act in Downtown Long Beach", this "impress-a-client-type" Northern Italian is a "thoroughly lovely dining experience", with a "well-trained staff" and "phone-book-size" "wine list to back it up"; however, if you're looking for a quiet spot", note that "conversation can be impossible" ("on any given day, someone is celebrating something"), so retreat to a "table by the window" or give into its "fun" "operatic tendencies."

L'ORANGERIE Ⓢ Ⓜ   25 | 28 | 26 | $84 |
903 N. La Cienega Blvd. (Willoughby Ave.), West Hollywood, 310-652-9770; www.lorangerie.com
"Old Hollywood glamour" lives on at this "timeless", "tip-top" special-occasion spot on La Cienega that's "magnificent, every step of the way, and terribly romantic" too (rumor has it "Brad and Jennifer spent one of their last nights together here"), with a "sublime", "fresh flower"–bedecked setting, "outstanding" French food and "service a king would be proud of"; "dress up", "go early, have a glass of champagne in the lounge and listen to the piano" and presto, "you feel like you're in Paris."

Los Balcones del Peru   – | – | – | M

1360 N. Vine St. (Leland Way), Hollywood, 323-871-9600

This relaxed Peruvian cafe is a sea of South American calm and
cuisine in the midst of Hollywood's honky-tonk hullabaloo; the
affordable menu features a half-dozen seviche and Andean dishes
not often found this side of the Panama Canal – pour on the green
sauce and dream of Machu Picchu.

Lotería! Grill   25 | 9 | 13 | $12

Farmer's Mkt., 6333 W. Third St. (Fairfax Ave.), Los Angeles,
323-930-2211; www.loteriagrill.com

"A semblance of authenticity in a Mex-epicurean world" can be
found at this "real deal" taqueria that's "worth crossing a desert
for", or at least the Farmer's Market; belly up to the "monster line"
and you'll be rewarded with "cheap", "delish" tacos and agua
frescas, served "without fanfare" but "soooo much flavor"; "holy"
"mole", "we've been in Mexico and still dreamed of Lotería –
it's that good."

Louise's Trattoria   15 | 14 | 16 | $22

264 26th St. (Minerva St.), Brentwood, 310-451-5001
232 N. Larchmont Blvd. (Beverly Blvd.), Hancock Park, 323-962-9510
7505 Melrose Ave. (Gardner St.), Los Angeles, 323-651-3880
10645 W. Pico Blvd. (bet. Manning & Overland Aves.), Los Angeles,
310-475-6084
4500 Los Feliz Blvd. (Hillhurst Ave.), Los Feliz, 323-667-0777
2-8 E. Colorado Blvd. (Fair Oaks Ave.), Pasadena, 626-568-3030
1008 Montana Ave. (10th St.), Santa Monica, 310-394-8888
12050 Ventura Blvd. (Laurel Canyon Blvd.), Studio City, 818-762-2662
North Ranch Mall, 3825 E. Thousand Oaks Blvd. (Westlake Blvd.),
Westlake Village, 805-373-6060
www.louises.com

"If you still eat carbs", then "load up" at this "no-muss no-fuss"
Cal-Italian chain that "serves its purpose" with "huge portions"
of "assembly line" spaghets, pizzas and focaccia so "good" you
don't know whether to "eat it or propose to it"; if a few killjoys snap
it's for "takeout only when you want to watch *The Sopranos* with
their pasta dishes", most assert it's "better than you think."

Luce ⓩ   – | – | – | E

(fka Avenue)

301 N. Cañon Dr. (Dayton Way), Beverly Hills, 310-275-2900

"Cool atmosphere, cool location, good food" and an extensive wine
list inherited from former occupant Avenue lure a few surveyors to
this modern candlelit Californian in Beverly Hills with two patios;
but a flurry of chefs passing through the revolving door faster
than Christmas shoppers at Macy's prompts a few to let loose it's
"very quiet" and "empty."

Lucille's Smokehouse Bar-B-Que   22 | 18 | 19 | $24

7411 Carson St. (Nectar Ave.), Long Beach, 562-938-7427
4828 E. Second St. (St. Joseph Ave.), Long Beach,
562-434-7427
Del Amo Fashion Ctr., 21420 Hawthorne Blvd. (Del Amo Circle Blvd.),
Torrance, 310-370-7427
www.lucillesbbq.com

Strap on a "bib" and "grab the Wet Naps" because you're about
to get "messy" devouring "finger licking good BBQ" ribs and "damn

fine biscuits" at this "wacky Southern roadhouse" outfit; if a few find the food "just ok" and the "kitsched up" staff in "down-home" "checkered shirts" a "bit heavy handed", they're outnumbered by "satisfied" throngs – and "there are always lines to prove it."

LUCQUES 26 | 23 | 23 | $56

8474 Melrose Ave. (La Cienega Blvd.), Los Angeles, 323-655-6277; www.lucques.com

"There's a genius in the kitchen" attest acolytes who bound over to Suzanne Goin's WeHo "culinary experience" for "flawless" Cal-French "creations" and "wine discoveries" served in a "serene" setting with a "lovely patio" and fireplace; you may not "recognize three-quarters" of the "bedazzling seasonal ingredients", but "go with the flow", because the "interesting combinations" work "beautifully", while the "above-average celeb-spotting", with "below-average 'tude make it" a "damn-the-cost extravagance"; P.S. the "Sunday prix fixe dinner barely leaves a dent in your wallet."

Luna Park 20 | 19 | 19 | $29

672 S. La Brea Ave. (Wilshire Blvd.), Los Angeles, 323-934-2110; www.lunaparkla.com

"Not ordering the goat cheese fondue is a fon-don't" at this "sceney" American on La Brea, an offshoot of the San Francisco bistro, where "young professionals" and "hipsters" "come for the gazing and stay for the grazing"; it's a "fun party" "hangout for modern comfort food", "incredible desserts" and "killer mojitos" festooned with "little plastic animals", and if you're "cool enough" you may even "secure a curtain-lined booth."

Lunaria ●⊠Ⓜ 17 | 18 | 17 | $40

10351 Santa Monica Blvd. (Beverly Glen Blvd.), Century City, 310-282-8870; www.lunariajazzscene.com

Lover's of "jazz and steak tartare" turn to this "old-fashioned supper club" in a Century City office building for French-Italian cuisine, Saturday evening "murder mystery dinners" and "a little night music"; but it "hits a sour note" for a few scenesters who snipe the "staid" setting "could use some pizzazz" and lament that it "fails to boast the luster of the past."

Luxe Cafe Rodeo – | – | – | E

Luxe Hotel Rodeo Dr., 360 N. Rodeo Dr. (bet. Santa Monica & Wilshire Blvds.), Beverly Hills, 310-273-0300; www.luxehotels.com

It's hard to imagine a restaurant any tinier than this lovely oasis tucked into the boutique Luxe Hotel in Beverly Hills; settle into a cushy banquette and dive into chef RaShon Smith's inventive Californian fare (including utterly addictive truffled French fries) or dine alfresco on Rodeo Drive and watch the well-heeled crowd bop from one exclusive boutique to another.

Madeo 25 | 20 | 24 | $54

8897 Beverly Blvd. (bet. Doheny Dr. & Robertson Blvd.), West Hollywood, 310-859-4903

WeHo's "heavy hitters" make for "fascinating people-watching" at this Northern Italian "stalwart" that "fits like an old slipper"; with a basement location "tucked away from the hustle and bustle", a staff with "adorable accents" and "high-quality fare" admirers muse it's "just like being in NYC"; if a few find the attitude "haughty", most are mad for "the owners who service every table with humor and knowledge."

MADISON, THE 🚫   22 | 27 | 22 | $50
102 Pine Ave. (1st St.), Long Beach, 562-628-8866;
www.themadisonrestaurant.com

"When you're in trouble with the wife", "spiffy up" and take her
out for "Châteaubriand and martinis" along with "live jazz and
swing" at this "romantic" seafooder-and-steakhouse in a "fantastic
converted bank lobby" with a "speakeasy feel" that recalls "Long
Beach's golden days"; but while it may be a "sight to behold", a few
feel the "hit-or-miss" food "doesn't always rise to the occasion."

Madre's Ⓜ   11 | 18 | 14 | $38
897 Granite Dr. (Lake Ave.), Pasadena, 626-744-0900;
www.madresrestaurant.com

J. Lo's "sexy" Pasadena "homage to the cooking of Puerto Rico" is
a "visual achievement" that "any self-respecting girlie girl would
cherish"; but perhaps the superstar should "stick to movies"
because, even for "Jennifer fans", the food is so "disappointing"
"it should be called Bennifer's – it's that big a bust" – while the
"clueless" staff should focus on serving the "sublime mojitos."

Maggiano's Little Italy   19 | 19 | 19 | $27
The Grove at Farmer's Mkt., 189 The Grove Dr. (bet. Fairfax Ave. &
3rd St.), Los Angeles, 323-965-9665
The Promenade at Woodland Hills, 6100 N. Topanga Canyon Blvd.
(bet. Erwin & Oxnard Sts.), Woodland Hills, 818-887-3777
www.maggianos.com

"So what if it's part of a chain", these "celebratory" spots "have
a winning formula", so "bring a gang" and an "appetite" to these
"gregarious" purveyors of "shockingly good" Italian; "gluttony
isn't a sin here", plus it's "cheap as heck, especially if you split"
the "family style" portions; but naysayers nix the "Americanized"
dishes, concurring "quantity does not equal quality."

Magic Carpet   ▽ 23 | 12 | 18 | $20
8566 W. Pico Blvd. (La Cienega Blvd.), Los Angeles, 310-652-8507
For a "full-on cultural experience" fly on over to this Pico Boulevard
Middle Eastern non-dairy kosher restaurant serving "huge
portions" of "home cooking just like your Yemenite mother used to
make", including "fabulous *mellawach*", a "fried Israeli pizza" that's
a "treat"; though the decor may be "simple", the "wonderful hosts"
make you "feel like family" and everything is "mm-mm-good."

MAISON AKIRA Ⓜ   27 | 21 | 24 | $51
713 E. Green St. (bet. El Molino & Oak Knoll Aves.), Pasadena,
626-796-9501; www.maisonakira.com

You might "feel like you're eating dishes from the *Iron Chef*" when
you dine at this "intimate", "posh" Franco-Japanese "destination"
near the Pasadena Playhouse Theatre where "it's so quiet, you can
hear a pin drop" and the "accommodating staff" "never makes you
feel rushed"; "lunchtime bento boxes are a bargain", but expect to
"fork over a wad of cash" for "very impressive" "big nights" out.

Ma'kai   ▽ 11 | 22 | 13 | $37
(fka Kai)
101 Broadway (Ocean Ave.), Santa Monica, 310-434-1511;
www.makailounge.com

"Come for the cool surroundings" at this "21st-century tiki" lounge
in Santa Monica with "outdoor seating that's fun on a perfect LA

night", a "great DJ" and "wall-to-wall hipsters on weekends"; the Pan-Asian tapas, however, is "underwhelming to say the least", so stick with the cocktails – thankfully the "ridiculously snotty" servers are "quick with the drinks" "even when the bar is mobbed."

MAKO ☒
26 | 19 | 24 | $48

225 S. Beverly Dr. (Charleville Blvd.), Beverly Hills, 310-288-8338; www.makorestaurant.com

At this "Beverly Hills favorite" with a "minimalist sushi bar–like storefront", "friendly" chef/co-owner Makoto 'Mako' Tanaka (ex Chinois on Main) "arouses the senses" and "introduces you to a whole new world" of Asian cooking; loyalists "look forward" to devouring the "delicate" dishes spiked with "exquisite flavors" and accompanied by a "terrific wine list" but caution that it can be "pricey if you're not prepared for a small plates adventure."

Malibu Seafood
23 | 12 | 14 | $17

25653 PCH (1½ mi. north of Malibu Canyon Rd.), Malibu, 310-456-3430; www.malibufishandseafood.com

"The fish swim right up to the kitchen" begging to be turned into the "best" "no-frills" fin fare around at this "seafood shack with an outdoor seating tent"; "grab" your "Malibu comfort food" at the window, "plant your butt at a picnic table" alongside "surfers and Pepperdine brats" and "count the dolphins" in the distance.

Malo
18 | 17 | 15 | $26

4326 Sunset Blvd. (Fountain Ave.), Silver Lake, 323-664-1011; www.malorestaurant.com

Silverlake has no shortage of casual taco cafes, but nothing like Steve Arroyo's "eccentric" Mexican cantina with "red velvet wallpaper and goats' heads on the wall" and *muy bueno* fare; but cynics snarl it's a "hipster hangout" for "margarita-guzzling" "twentysomethings who think a burrito on a ceramic plate equals fine dining" and wonder "why service is so *malo* ('bad' in Spanish)."

MAMA D'S
24 | 13 | 24 | $21

1125 Manhattan Ave. (Manhattan Beach Blvd.), Manhattan Beach, 310-546-1492

A no-reservations, "beachy" "hole-in-the-wall' with "the friendliest service in Manhattan Beach", this "red-sauce and pizza" place is "exactly what an old-fashioned family Italian restaurant should be"; the "fresh-baked bread makes the entire town smell fantastic", so "follow your nose" and "feast" while you wait – but save room for the "tasty" pasta, "gnocchi that rocks your world" and "free chocolate chip cookies" ("please, Mama, can I have another?").

Mama Voula
▽ 20 | 10 | 20 | $16

11923 Santa Monica Blvd. (Brockton Ave.), West LA, 310-478-9464

"Life revolves around gyros at Mama's house", a "colorful sliver of Santorini" in a Westside strip mall; acolytes agree it's all about the "authentic" Greek comfort food like "carefully prepared" lamb souvlaki and "delicious moussaka" and confide that while "the staff won't exactly spoil you" "at least it's friendly."

Mandaloun
▽ 20 | 17 | 17 | $31

141 S. Maryland St. (Harvard St.), Glendale, 818-507-1900; www.mandalounusa.com

"Bring a big lively crowd" and "release your inner belly dancer" at this "Vegas-style" Lebanese "party palace" in Glendale; "pace yourself" as the "platters of unusual meze" are "enormous", the "kebabs grilled-to-perfection" and "the fresh pita bread" "is as good as anything you'd get back home in the Mid East"; P.S. for a "beautiful, elegant experience you'll long remember, sit outside in the evening" on the terrace.

Mandarette　　　　　　　20 | 13 | 17 | $26

8386 Beverly Blvd. (bet. N. Kings Rd. & N. Orlando Ave.), West Hollywood, 323-655-6115; www.mandarette.com

"It's fun to watch celebrities try to slip in unnoticed through the kitchen door" at this "ersatz" "strip mall without the strip mall", a "dependable" WeHo "gathering place for swapping" Mandarin "chow" where the "homemade ginger ale is worth a visit alone"; it may have some of "the best overpriced Chinese food on the Westside" but it's "not at all authentic" – "when they say 'spicy', they mean if you were raised on nothing but water and matzo."

Mandarin Deli　　　　　　21 | 9 | 14 | $13

727 N. Broadway (bet. Alpine & Ord Sts.), Chinatown, 213-623-6054 ⊟
701 W. Garvey Ave. (Atlantic Blvd.), Monterey Park, 626-570-9795 ⊟
9305 Reseda Blvd. (Prairie St.), Northridge, 818-993-0122

"Don't expect any fancy decorations" at this "hole-in-the-wall" Asian "oasis", but then again, "who cares about decor" when the "potstickers ooze juiciness" and the scallion pancakes and "steamed dumplings are to beg for"; "if you want cheap, fast and authentic" Asian, "this is one of the city's great bargains."

Mandevilla　　　　　　　25 | 22 | 23 | $33

951 S. Westlake Blvd. (Hampshire Rd.), Westlake Village, 805-497-8482; www.mandevillarestaurant.com

"Take someone special" for "just a casual meal" to this "lovely", "hard to find" "little oasis" with a "personable staff" "in the rear of a Westlake Village parking lot"; lunch on the heated, covered "patio is superb", plus the Continental "menu is so eclectic you can return again and again and not get bored", though for a handful the "best part is the great, reasonably priced wine list."

Mäni's Bakery & Café　　　18 | 10 | 15 | $15

519 S. Fairfax Ave. (bet. 3rd St. & Wilshire Blvd.), Los Angeles, 323-938-8800
2507 Main St. (Ocean Park Blvd.), Santa Monica, 310-396-7700
www.manisbakery.com

"Laid-back" Westside "hipsters" "can't get enough" of this "comfortable neighborhood joint" that's "good for a late-night, low-guilt binge" on "naturally sweetened", "delicious low-fat desserts" and "great for sugar-free/lactose-free vegans", while "big portions and creative" vegetarian dishes make it the "perfect" "brunch alternative"; still, granolaphobes "wonder what the fuss is about" – "maybe it's an acquired taste."

Manna　　　　　　　▽ 21 | 11 | 13 | $22

3377 W. Olympic Blvd. (bet. Gramercy Ave. & St. Andrews Pl.), Koreatown, 323-733-8516

It's "well worth the long line" for the "all-you-can-eat Korean BBQ" served at this "no frills whatsoever" "tentlike setting" in Koreatown so "bring as many friends as you can" to share the "raucous" "experience"; the "well-prepared" shabu-shabu is also "not to be missed", and "don't forget to save room for the rice porridge at the end."

Maple Drive ⌧

24 | 22 | 22 | $52

345 N. Maple Dr. (Alden Dr.), Beverly Hills, 310-274-9800;
www.mapledriverestaurant.com

"Frequent chef changes" make it "a gamble", but most surveyers "praise the reincarnation" of this "very refined" "hot spot" that's "just like the fancy Beverly Hills restaurants you see in the movies"; by day, it's an "outstanding" "power lunch" spot offering "very fresh, unique" Euro-accented New American fare, and by night, it's "simply the only place to hear a great jazz trio"; in short, it's "one of the few hype places worth the hype."

Marcello Tuscany Room

∇ 23 | 24 | 23 | $34

470 W. Seventh St. (S. Pacific Ave.), San Pedro, 310-519-7100

For a "little bit" of Tuscany "in the heart of the LA harbor area", set sail for this "stunningly beautiful space" with an "elaborate" dining room reminiscent of a ballroom; the "traditional", "old-world" fare runs the gamut from osso buco to tiramisu and "never disappoints" – and may be "the best Italian in San Pedro."

Maria's Italian Kitchen

17 | 13 | 17 | $20

29035 Thousand Oaks Blvd. (Kanan Rd.), Agoura Hills, 818-865-8999
11723 Barrington Ct. (Sunset Blvd.), Brentwood, 310-476-6112
16608 Ventura Blvd. (Rubio Ave.), Encino, 818-783-2920
9161 Reseda Blvd. (Nordhoff St.), Northridge, 818-341-5114
Hastings Ranch Shopping Ctr., 3537 E. Foothill Blvd.
(bet. Rosemead Blvd. & Sierra Madre Villa Ave.), Pasadena,
626-351-2080
13353 Ventura Blvd. (bet. Dixie Canyon & Fulton Aves.), Sherman Oaks,
818-906-0783
23460 Cinema Dr. (Valencia Blvd.), Valencia, 661-287-3773
10761 Pico Blvd. (bet. Oberland Ave. & Westwood Blvd.), West LA,
310-441-3663
El Camino Shopping Ctr., 23331 Mulholland Dr. (Calabasas Rd.),
Woodland Hills, 818-225-0586
www.mariasitaliankitchen.com

"There's a reason Maria's is everywhere" declare "devoted" diners who hop over to this "happy-feeling", "reliable" "spaghetti-and-meatballs chain" with a "nifty '60s"-style decor for "flavorful", "plentiful" portions of "homey Italian" food and "cheap house wine"; while it's "nothing to go nuts over, if you need a quick bite with the family you won't go wrong."

Marino ⌧

∇ 23 | 16 | 24 | $41

6001 Melrose Ave. (Wilcox Ave.), Hollywood, 323-466-8812

"Hollywood just wouldn't be the same" and "Paramount execs would starve" if not for this Brooklyn-style Italian "throwback" that's "so old-school" it "feels like a *Saturday Night Live* skit", in fact, "Frank Sinatra should be at the next table"; the "impeccable" staff "treats you like a king", or at least "like a member of the family", "but the food is the reason to go" – "is it possible for pizza to get better than this?"

Mario's Peruvian

24 | 5 | 12 | $14

5786 Melrose Ave. (Vine St.), East Hollywood, 323-466-4181

"Bummer you have to fight for a table" but "there's no way around the long wait" because "the secret has gotten out" that this brightly lit "hole-in-the-wall" in East Hollywood serves "unbelievably good", "outrageously cheap" Peruvian seafood; the "seviche transport you to Machu Picchu" but the "spotty service" and "low-rent strip-mall location" "bring you back down to sea level."

Marix Tex Mex Café
| 17 | 14 | 17 | $24 |

118 Entrada Dr. (PCH), Santa Monica, 310-459-8596
1108 N. Flores St. (Santa Monica Blvd.), West Hollywood, 323-656-8800
www.marixtexmex.com

"It's a party all the time" at these "lively" Mexican cantinas where "buff boys" go to "get an enchilada with a side of beefcake"; fans of the Santa Monica branch wonder if that "salty tang in the air" is from the ocean breeze or the "lethal margaritas that never stop flowing", musing "who goes here for food?", while the "WeHo crowd" snipes that their "popular" "hot spot" was probably "better before Hollywood discovered it."

Market City Caffe
| 17 | 18 | 16 | $22 |

Santa Anita Fashion Park, 400 S. Baldwin Ave. (W. Huntington Dr.), Arcadia, 626-462-0218
164 E. Palm Ave. (San Fernando Blvd.), Burbank, 818-840-7036
www.marketcitycaffe.com

"The ambiance is what makes" this Cal-Italian outfit "happen" muse marketeers who enjoy the "great urban experience of sitting outside" on the "lovely patio" while enjoying "Sunday brunch with chamber music"; the "to-die-for antipasto buffet", wood-fired pizzas and "great dishes with enough garlic to chase away vampires" further cement its status as a "family favorite."

Mark's Restaurant
| 16 | 18 | 16 | $36 |

861 N. La Cienega Blvd. (Waring Ave.), West Hollywood, 310-652-5252; www.marksrestaurant.com

The "new" "totally hands-on chef" at the "gayest restaurant within the Boystown" radius gets mixed reviews for his Californian cuisine, ranging from "innovative" to downright "disappointing"; but it's unanimous that the "hottie waiters are fun to look" at, even if a few frown that they can be "way too pretentious"; still, "half-priced Mondays" are a bargain, and "hey, at least the drinks are strong" and "the owner may give you a hug even if he doesn't know you."

Marla's
| – | – | – | M |

39 W. Main St. (Garfield Ave.), Alhambra, 626-282-9300

Following in the footsteps of its Monrovia sibling, La Parisienne, this Alhambra newcomer serves up classic French food of the garlicky snails and Dover sole variety paired with an extensive wine list; the sophisticated white-tablecloth setting is done up with mirrors and artwork from local talent plus a sidewalk patio.

Marmalade Café
| 18 | 18 | 17 | $23 |

The Commons, 4783 Commons Way (Calabasas Rd.), Calabasas, 818-225-9092
3894 Cross Creek Rd. (PCH), Malibu, 310-317-4242
Ave. of the Peninsula Mall, 550 Deep Valley Dr. (Crossfield Dr.), Rolling Hills, 310-544-6700
710 Montana Ave. (7th St.), Santa Monica, 310-395-9196
14910 Ventura Blvd. (Kester Ave.), Sherman Oaks, 818-905-8872
Promenade at Westlake, 140 Promenade Way (Thousand Oaks Blvd.), Westlake Village, 805-370-1331
www.marmaladecafe.com

"Ladies who lunch talk about how delightful their salads are" at this "crowded" Cal-American "country-kitsch" chain serving "mammoth portions" of "familiar" "coffee-shop" dishes and "gorgeous desserts"; still, critics cavil the "menu tries too hard to cover all the bases."

Marouch   ▽ | 25 | 15 | 19 | $26 |

4905 Santa Monica Blvd. (N. Edgemont St.), East Hollywood, 323-662-9325; www.marouchrestaurant.com

"Go with friends and have an eating orgy", consuming "lusty" "Lebanese food with some Armenian notes" at this meze master in "an obscure corner of East Hollywood"; "service is slow" but "gracious", and the food's "tangy flavors" distract from the somewhat "tacky decor" and "odd little strip-mall" location.

Marrakesh   ▽ | 19 | 23 | 21 | $38 |

13003 Ventura Blvd. (Coldwater Canyon Ave.), Studio City, 818-788-6354; www.marrakeshrestaurant.com

"Be prepared to eat with your fingers" at this Moroccan prix fixe "party den" in Studio City, featuring a "realistic North African setting", nightly belly dancers and "tons of food"; it's "good for large parties" or "a colorful date", even if cynics say it's more "for the entertainment" "experience" than the merely "consistent" eats.

Marston's Ⓜ | 23 | 16 | 19 | $20 |

151 E. Walnut St. (bet. N. Marengo & N. Raymond Aves.), Pasadena, 626-796-2459; www.marstonsrestaurant.com

Occupying a "charming little" bungalow (complete with "laid-back front porch"), this Pasadena American is such a "great weekend wake-up joint" that, if you don't "get there early, you will wait awhile"; most willingly brave the lines for "the best macadamia nut pancakes this side of Oahu" and other "old-fashioned, fattening breakfast fare"; but if you hate queues, "it's much easier to get in on a weekday" or for dinner.

Martha's 22nd St. Grill | 23 | 16 | 19 | $16 |

25 22nd St. (Hermosa Ave.), Hermosa Beach, 310-376-7786

"Bring your sun block and shades" and join the "fabulous beachy" "surfer/lawyer crowd" waiting for "fun-in-the-sun brunches", "the widest selection of eggs Benedict" and "not exactly gourmet", but always "tasty", sandwiches at this "bare-bones" American "sidewalk cafe" just off Hermosa Beach's Rollerblading bikini trail, "about 10 feet from the sand."

Mason Jar Cafe | – | – | – | M |

8928 Santa Monica Blvd. (San Vicente Blvd.), West Hollywood, 310-659-9111

Crab cakes, guiltless fried chicken and other Californian fare take a somewhat healthful turn, or at least that's the intent, at this quaint WeHo newcomer hoping to get in touch with the good-fat-versus-bad-fat, gym-bod mentality of Boystown; rotating artwork and sidewalk seating add to its neighborhood appeal.

Massimo   ▽ | 22 | 19 | 21 | $45 |

9513 Little Santa Monica Blvd. (bet. Camden & Rodeo Drs.), Beverly Hills, 310-273-7588; www.massimobh.com

After a day of intensive retail therapy on Rodeo Drive, the "humble", "hearty" Tuscan cooking of chef-owner Massimo Ormani – aka "Italy's gift to Beverly Hills" – is just what the doctor ordered; the "sincere" fare is "served with care", and while a visit is "a bit pricey", it's "pleasurable" nonetheless.

MASTRO'S STEAKHOUSE   26 | 23 | 22 | $65
*246 N. Cañon Dr. (bet. Clifton & Dayton Ways), Beverly Hills,
310-888-8782; www.mastrossteakhouse.com*
"Now, *this* is a steakhouse" cry carnivores who crave the
"gargantuan portions" of meat "served sizzling" ("the only thing
hotter than the plates are the gorgeous" customers at the bar),
"shrimp the size of lobster tails" and "stiff drinks" at this "big-time"
Beverly Hills venue with a "lush", "Old Hollywood atmosphere";
but "the noise level is about the same as a rock concert" and
you'll have "wait for your table, unless you're an A-lister or the
manager's life coach"; P.S. "if you're single, eat upstairs – that's
where the action is."

Matisse   ∇ 21 | 20 | 22 | $46
*Ayres Hotel, 14400 Hindry Ave. (W. Rosecrans Ave.), Hawthorne,
310-536-0805; www.matisserestaurant.net*
"Exquisitely presented dishes in a room dripping with elegance" –
even the "attentive staff's" uniforms are "beautiful" – sums up
the scene at this Hawthorne newcomer; with its pseudo-stone
walls and tapestrylike rugs, the "palatial setting takes you
back centuries" as you dine on "creative" French-American fare,
and you can "watch the street performers" from the terrace, too.

MATSUHISA   28 | 16 | 23 | $74
*129 N. La Cienega Blvd. (bet. Clifton Way & Wilshire Blvd.),
Beverly Hills, 310-659-9639; www.nobumatsuhisa.com*
You're "almost certain to see a celebrity" at this "unassuming"
Beverly Hills Japanese on La Cienega "where the worldwide Nobu
empire began" back in 1987; most are awed by the "inspired"
"edible art" produced by this "temple of sushi" and cooked fare
(the much-"copied" "miso cod still rocks"), but "the secret is
knowing what to order", so either "go with someone [savvy] or let
the staff direct the show"; otherwise, "you'll be horrified" by the
seemingly "overhyped" eats at "insanely expensive" prices.

Matteo's 🅼   19 | 18 | 20 | $42
2321 Westwood Blvd. (bet. Olympic & Pico Blvds.), West LA, 310-475-4521
"Step into the past" (1963, to be precise) at this "old-school",
"Hoboken-style" "red-leather booth establishment" in West LA,
complete with "tuxedoed waiters", "dim lights" and "heavy-duty
Italian" dishes that are "pleasant", "but nothing to challenge the
palate"; it's the kind of place where, "if they know you, they're
terrific to you" – but if "you're not a regular, forget about it."

Matteo's Hoboken 🅂   19 | 11 | 18 | $20
2323 Westwood Blvd. (bet. Olympic & Pico Blvds.), West LA, 310-474-1109
"As the name says, this little piece of Hoboken" – a "casual",
"lighter" offshoot of Matteo's next door – offers "homestyle Italian
food" "for a reasonable price" and in a "stark atmosphere";
however, the "simple" eats can be "spotty" – "you need to know
what not to order" – and "you have to dine early, as they close the
kitchen around 8 PM" on weeknights.

Matterhorn Chef 🅼   ∇ 19 | 21 | 22 | $29
*13726 Oxnard St. (Woodman Ave.), Van Nuys, 818-781-4330;
www.matterhornchef.com*
The "chef-owner takes an interest in his patrons' satisfaction" – he
actually "comes out and greets you" at this chalet "in the center

of the San Fernando Valley"; serving "huge" amounts of "Swiss and German cuisine, with some Italian in there too", it's "definitely different from anything else in LA" – especially when the accordion players arrive on weekends.

Maurya

| – | – | – | M |

151 S. Doheny Dr. (Wilshire Blvd.), Beverly Hills, 310-786-7858;
www.mauryabeverlyhills.com

In the space next to the Writers' Guild Theater, this opulent Indian newcomer shines with dark-wood decor, low lighting and a vivid orange-and-blue color scheme; the kitchen shrugs off the usual curry-and-chutney combos in favor of such sophisticated yet affordable northern and western specialties as mustard-flavored prawns, spinach and corn samosas and a mint-flavored bread called *pudina paratha*.

Maximilians ⊠ Ⓜ

| – | – | – | M |

11330 Weddington St. (Tujunga Ave.), North Hollywood,
818-980-6294

A wholly unexpected restaurant on a semi-industrial street across from a local park, this SF Valley Continental surprises with its warm, candlelit interior, pleasant outdoor patio, open display kitchen and serious menu of moderately priced dishes.

Max Restaurant

| 25 | 18 | 20 | $39 |

13355 Ventura Blvd. (bet. Dixie Canyon & Fulton Aves.), Sherman Oaks,
818-784-2915; www.maxrestaurant.com

"Thank God there's a place like this in the Valley" sigh supporters of this "sophisticated" Sherman Oaks Asian fusion destination whose "eclectic" menu mixes bento boxes and braised beef ribs; the "confines are somewhat cramped" and though "professional", "the service is often curt"; the "extremely creative" "food is worth the unpleasantries, though."

Maxwell's Cafe

| 19 | 13 | 18 | $13 |

13329 Washington Blvd. (Walgrove Ave.), Venice, 310-306-7829

It "isn't open for dinner, but it doesn't need to be – the breakfast will last you 24 hours" avow Venetians who "wake up craving" the "can't-miss garbage omelets" at this American "hole-in-the-wall" that "maintains an unpretentious attitude despite decades of pretentious customers"; "if you want a table on weekends", however, better rise with the roosters, or else "brace yourself for a long wait."

Mazzarino's

| 18 | 12 | 18 | $21 |

12920½ Riverside Dr. (Coldwater Canyon Ave.), Sherman Oaks,
818-788-5050

"Even if the decor does leave something to be desired", we "love it as did our gramps" say Sherman Oaks folks about this 1947 Southern Italian, a "homey", "old-fashioned" "red-sauce" standby, complete with red-and-white tablecloths; it's a "good place to get your pizza fix" or "satisfying" basics in a "friendly atmosphere."

M Cafe de Chaya

| – | – | – | M |

7119 Melrose Ave. (La Brea Ave.), Los Angeles, 323-525-0588;
www.mcafedechaya.com

The Chaya chain (Chaya Brasserie and Chaya Venice) takes a radical turn toward the realm of contemporary macrobiotic cuisine with this casual cafe designed by a team featuring a feng shui master; the healthy, guilt-free food features myriad faux-meat dishes (the seafood is real), drinks like roasted twig tea and pastries made with no eggs, no dairy, no refined sugar.

McCormick & Schmick's   19 | 19 | 19 | $35
Two Rodeo, 206 N. Rodeo Dr. (Wilshire Blvd.), Beverly Hills, 310-859-0434
Library Tower, 633 W. Fifth St. (bet. 4th & Hope Sts.), Downtown, 213-629-1929
2101 Rosecrans Ave. (Nash St.), El Segundo, 310-416-1123
111 N. Los Robles Ave. (Union St.), Pasadena, 626-405-0064 ●
www.mccormickandschmicks.com
"A chain, but a nice chain" sums up the sentiment about this "consistent" string of seafooders, known for its "great variety of fresh fish" (harpooned, alas, by "uninventive preparations") that's "cordially served" amid "classy", if "institutional", "dark-wood decor"; and even those who deem it "decidedly mediocre" "can't help but be happy" during happy hour, with its "unbelievably cheap" drinks and eats.

McGrath's Fish House   ∇ 17 | 18 | 19 | $23
400 S. Baldwin Ave. (Huntington Dr.), Arcadia, 626-574-7800;
www.mcgrathsfishhouse.com
This Arcadia branch of a West Coast chain offers up a "large selection" of "seafood with a Pacific Northwest touch" (e.g. alder-planked salmon) at "incredibly reasonable prices" in a woody, "pleasant setting"; however, the hostile hiss "the fare is just average" and "service isn't always that friendly."

McKenna's on the Bay   21 | 23 | 19 | $38
190 Marina Dr. (PCH), Long Beach, 562-342-9411;
www.mckennasonthebay.com
Blessed with a "lovely location on the Bay" ("it's the perfect spot to take land-locked out-of-towners"), this Long Beach venue attracts a "boisterous crowd" of "over-30 singles"; but "man does not live by view alone", and while many praise the surf 'n' turf menu – the "individual seafood steam kettles are a must-try" – malcontents mutter there's "more atmosphere than quality food" here.

Mediterraneo   ∇ 20 | 18 | 18 | $25
73 Pier Ave. (Hermosa Ave.), Hermosa Beach, 310-318-2666
"Unique for the South Bay", "this busy cafe" in Hermosa Beach is a "fun place" to grab some "wonderful sangria" and "graze" on "delicious" Mediterranean food and "innovative tapas" while "watching the beachgoers from the outdoor patio"; if the "service is slow", at least the "wine flights are a nice" distraction.

MÉLISSE ⌧ Ⓜ   28 | 26 | 26 | $78
1104 Wilshire Blvd. (11th St.), Santa Monica, 310-395-0881;
www.melisse.com
"Dress your best" – you're about to "embark on a fabulous journey" to "nirvana" when you visit this "swanky" Santa Monica destination, rated No. 1 for Food in this *Survey* for its "brilliant" French–New American fare; chef-owner Josiah Citrin's near-"perfect" creations (tip: "the tasting menu with wine pairings is the way to go") are "the culinary equivalent of the Louvre" – "this isn't food, it's art" – and what's more, they're "deftly" presented by a "formal", but "superlative" staff; it's a "memorable splurge", so "save up for the pleasure of eating here."

Mel's Drive-In ◗   15   16   16 $16
1650 N. Highland Ave. (Hollywood Blvd.), Hollywood, 323-465-2111
14846 Ventura Blvd. (Kester Ave.), Sherman Oaks, 818-990-6357
8585 Sunset Blvd. (La Cienega Blvd.), West Hollywood, 310-854-7200
www.melsdrive-in.com
"Everything's good – enough" at this '50s "retro" coffee-shop chain "frequented by both locals and late-night partiers" "listening to their favorite [jukebox] oldies" while "chomping on burgers and slurping down shakes"; but critics cavil the "service can be lukewarm, just like the food" – and there's nothing nostalgic about the "pricey" tabs.

MESON G   23   26   22 $56
6703 Melrose Ave. (Highland Ave.), Los Angeles, 323-525-1415;
www.mesongrestaurant.com
Superstar restaurateurs Tim and Liza Goodell (Dakota, Troquet) grace LA with "one of the best-looking new restaurants" – a kind of giant Hermès package neatly wrapped in orange ribbon; already, a "pretty crowd" is flocking to Melrose to "enjoy an evening of delicious small plates" that put a New American "spin on Med-style tapas"; at times the kitchen and "accommodating" staff may suffer some "beginners' jitters", but overall, this is a "great addition to the hot-spot" roster.

Mexicali ◗   15   16   15 $21
12161 Ventura Blvd. (Laurel Canyon Blvd.), Studio City, 818-985-1744
"Expect to shout to your companions" because you "can't have a conversation below yelling level" at this Studio City Mexican that's always a "late-night zoo"; it may feel like "a fraternity party, but sometimes that's what you want": a "too dark" "hangout" with "hot waiters" where you can imbibe a "vast assortment of tequilas"; natch, the "food is hit-or-miss, so bring on the chips and salsa."

Mexico City   17   15   15 $22
2121 Hillhurst Ave. (Avocado St.), Los Feliz, 323-661-7227
Los Feliz "locals rave" about this "friendly" Mexican that offers "family dining for hip people" amid a vaguely "Day-of-the-Dead decor" with "personality"; but while City folk champion the homemade dishes and "proudly potent margaritas", foes wince at the "tequila-induced noise problem" and "inefficient service."

Miceli's   17   19   20 $23
1646 N. Las Palmas St. (Hollywood Blvd.), Hollywood, 323-466-3438
3655 Cahuenga Blvd. W. (Regal Pl.), Universal City, 323-851-3345
www.micelis1949.com
"No Californian cuisine here, just good ol'-fashioned Eye-talian" quip customers who hightail it to this "busy" Hollywood–Studio City duo for "red-sauce" dishes and "pretty good pizza"; "time stands still here" with a decor "so camp, it looks like a theme park, complete "with hanging Chianti bottles" and "checkered tablecloths", while "singing waiters" add to the "novelty"; but bashers pooh-pooh the "shtick" and snipe it offers "few surprises."

MICHAEL'S ✉   25   25   25 $59
1147 Third St. (bet. California Ave. & Wilshire Blvd.), Santa Monica,
310-451-0843; www.michaelssantamonica.com
After over 25 years, the "enduring elder statesman" of Californian cuisine (and older sibling of the Manhattan counterpart) "hasn't lost

its edge", delivering "pricey", "divine" dishes in a "romantic setting" under the watchful eye of owner Michael McCarty whose "attention to detail and pursuit of the freshest ingredients remains the gold standard"; acolytes agree you should "always eat" on "enchanting garden" "patio, as this bit of Eden" provides an "oasis of calm, beauty and fine dining" in the "frenetic craziness that is Santa Monica."

Michelia ⊠   24 20 23 $35
8738 W. Third St. (S. George Burns Rd.), Los Angeles,
310-276-8288; www.micheliabistro.com
"A little different, a lot delicious" declare diners who happen upon "friendly", "gracious" chef/co-owner Kimmy Tang's "nouvelle" Vietnamese cafe tucked away near Cedars-Sinai; it's a "feast for the senses", so "enjoy the tranquility" of a "pretty waterfall fountain" near the entrance, a "festive" patio and "adventurous" "food cooked to perfection."

Michel Richard   - - - M
310 S. Robertson Blvd. (bet. 3rd St. & Burton Way), Beverly Hills,
310-275-5707; www.maisonrichard.com
It's been years since culinary icon Michel Richard left his bakery-cum-cafe on busy Robertson near Cedars-Sinai to open Citronelle in Washington, DC, but an ably trained staff still upholds his legacy, feeding fans flaky croissants, fine pastries and French brasserie fare; sit at the outdoor cafe and watch stylesetters set drop buckets of greens at the tony boutiques or just set your sights on the celebrity-filled Ivy nearby.

Michi ⊠   19 18 17 $41
903 Manhattan Ave. (9th St.), Manhattan Beach, 310-376-0613
In addition to "mouthwatering", "interesting" Asian fusion fare, this "stark", "modern", "noisy" Manhattan Beach nightspot now also boasts a sushi bar packed with "lip-smacking" choices – "if you have the money to spend"; but what it's "best known for is its" "hopping" "late-night bar scene" and "extensive martini list" that "caters to the young successful nightlife crowd", the "beautiful people" and the "divorcée pack" reluctant to "admit their age."

Milky Way   ▽ 19 14 22 $23
9108 W. Pico Blvd. (Doheny Dr.), Los Angeles, 310-859-0004
"You don't have to keep kosher to love it" at this "homey" "nice spin on a dairy" restaurant on the Westside run by "Steven Spielberg's mom" who "schmoozes" "every table", offering "lots of haimish choices" from "blintzes to Mexican dishes" to "satisfying vegetarian" and Californian fare; "it's like eating at bubbe's house" and "fun in a weird kind of way" – oy, "what a joy."

Mimi's Cafe   17 17 17 $18
2925 Los Feliz Blvd. (bet. Revere & Seneca Aves.), Atwater Village,
323-668-1715
12727 Towne Center Dr. (Bloomfield Ave.), Cerritos, 562-809-0510
19710 Nordhoff Pl. (Corbin Ave.), Chatsworth, 818-717-8334
17919 Gale Ave. (S. Azusa Ave.), City of Industry, 626-912-3350
8455 Firestone Blvd. (Brookshire Ave.), Downey, 562-862-2828
6670 E. PCH (N. Studebaker Rd.), Long Beach, 562-596-0831
500 Huntington Dr. (S. Mayflower Ave.), Monrovia, 626-359-9191
24201 W. Magic Mountain Pkwy. (Valencia Blvd.), Santa Clarita,
661-255-5520

(continued)

Mimi's Cafe

25343 S. Crenshaw Blvd. (Airport Dr.), Torrance, 310-326-4477
15436 E. Whittier Blvd. (Santa Gertrudes Ave.), Whittier, 562-947-0339
www.mimiscafe.com
Additional locations throughout Southern California

Scattered throughout Southern California, this chain of all-day coffee shops with "efficient service" feels like the "Hallmark card of restaurants" turning out American comfort food in "cutesy", "faux-French" surroundings; if a few deride it as a "senior magnet", for most it's a "wholesome family"-"friendly" option and at the very least, "good in a pinch."

Mimosa 🅢 Ⓜ   24 | 18 | 22 | $43

8009 Beverly Blvd. (bet. N. Edinburgh & N. Laurel Aves.), Los Angeles,
323-655-8895; www.mimosarestaurant.com

"Fantastique chef"-owner "Jean Pierre Bosc does great things" with "satisfying", "superb", yet "simple dishes like cassoulet" boasting "complex flavors" at his "little find" on Beverly that feels like "France, without all the frills"; "charming" and "intimate", it's the "perfect place to take your sweetheart on Valentine's Day" for "timeless bistro fare" "at its best."

Minibar ●   ▽ 23 | 23 | 21 | $38

3413 Cahuenga Blvd. W. (bet. Barham & Universal Studios Blvds.),
Universal City, 323-882-6965; www.minibarlounge.com

Breathing fresh life into the "quirky", "no-man's land" of Cahuenga Pass, this "snazzy" Eclectic tapas bar with "exceedingly hip servers" is a "great location for people who work" but don't live in the Valley; but while the "small plates are delicious" and "exotic", especially for a "hot spot" that "cranks out cocktails", the cost of those "little orders" "sneaks up on you", just like items nabbed from a hotel minibar.

Mio Babbo's   ▽ 19 | 17 | 23 | $20
(fka Di Stefano)

1076 Gayley Ave. (bet. Kinross & Weyburn Aves.), Westwood,
310-208-5117; www.miobabbos.com

"The name changed from Di Stefano, but at least they didn't change the familiar tasty, reasonable" "classic Italian fare" at this "wonderfully quiet" (so "rare in LA") "neighborhood" "standby" "where you can actually carry on a conversation"; "small and cozy", it's the "ideal place" to eat a plate of "great spaghetti and meatballs" "prior to catching a movie in Westwood."

Mi Piace   20 | 18 | 17 | $29

801 N. San Fernando Blvd. (Burbank Blvd.), Burbank, 818-843-1111
The Commons, 4799 Commons Way (Calabasas Rd.), Calabasas,
818-591-8822
25 E. Colorado Blvd. (bet. Fair Oaks & Raymond Aves.), Pasadena,
626-795-3131 ●

"Europe meets Pasadena", Burbank and Calabasas at this always "evolving", "perennially popular" Cal-Italian "neighborhood favorite" that lures "families and groups" with a "hearty and uncomplicated" yet "perfunctory" menu and a "noisy", "bustling", "stylish" setting; regulars reveal that "reservations are a must for dinner, but expect to find yourself waiting in the bar", and most grumble that "service is lacking."

Mirabelle ❶   20 | 20 | 19 | $38

8768 W. Sunset Blvd. (bet. Horn Ave. & N. Sherbourne Dr.),
West Hollywood, 310-659-6022; www.mirabellehollywood.com
"Delightful" and "comfortable", this "family-run" "favorite" feels
like a "welcome throwback", providing a "unique experience" with
an open-air patio bar that "offers a better atmosphere than the
dining room" and a "great" perch for "people-watching on Sunset
Strip", plus "fresh, tasty" Cal-Eclectic fare; it's "always packed",
and if a few toss it off as a "has-been", for most, it's still "one big
party scene" — "who even notices the celebrities?"

Mi Ranchito Family Mexican   ▽ 18 | 16 | 16 | $17

12223 Washington Blvd. (Centinela Ave.), Culver City, 310-398-8611
Hold onto your sombrero because "the margaritas are generous" at
this "relaxed" "hole-in-the-wall" Mexican in Culver City where the
"satisfying traditional seafood" is "Veracruz-style all the way"; the
decor is the "definition of kitsch" and feels like an open "treasure
chest" with tchotchkes, "toys" and "stuff" covering "the walls and
even the ceilings" "making it an interesting place for first dates."

Mishima   20 | 13 | 18 | $16

8474 W. Third St. (La Cienega Blvd.), Los Angeles, 323-782-0181
East Gate Plaza, 21605 S. Western Ave. (W. 216th St.), Torrance,
310-320-2089
www.mishima.com
"When you're on the run" and "crave a bowl of chewy", "delicious
soba or udon" noodles, drop into this "modern, casual" pair of
"fun", "quickie" Japanese Third Street–Torrance cafes suggest
slurpers; even with "shallow pockets" you get a "truckload of food"
made from the "freshest ingredients" and "unadulterated for the
American palate" — "what a deal": "I'm hooked."

Mission 261   21 | 19 | 16 | $25

261 S. Mission Dr. (W. B'way), San Gabriel, 626-588-1666
"Situated incongruously" in a "beautiful hacienda" in the "heart
of SG's Mission District", this "opulent Hong Kong–style" "jewel"
is "capable of high achievements", "outshining the competition"
with "unique", "expensive" "high-end dim sum" you order from a
menu, along with "Cantonese offerings" like BBQ pig; but those
who "prefer looking" and choosing dishes "miss the carts and the
noise" — that's the "fun part" — and find it "overpriced" to boot.

Misto Caffé & Bakery   20 | 13 | 19 | $20

Hillside Vlg., 24558 Hawthorne Blvd. (bet. Newton St. & Via Valmonte),
Torrance, 310-375-3608; www.mistocaffe.com
For "creative" Californian fare, "locals" head to this "casual",
"cute cafe hidden" in the Hillside Village shopping center; "sit
outside on the patio" and enjoy a "relaxing weekend" brunch
or "catch up with friends" over "excellent salads" and "tasty,
creative dishes" — and "don't forget to visit the bakery" for "delicate
pasteries and fresh-baked bread"; P.S. those who find the setting
"very plain" may reevaluate now that it's been renovated.

MISTRAL ☒   26 | 23 | 25 | $45

13422 Ventura Blvd. (bet. Dixie Canyon & Greenbush Aves.),
Sherman Oaks, 818-981-6650; www.mistralrestaurant.com
"Charming host-owner" Henri Abergel and his "top-of-the-line",
"orchestrated" staff "make you feel like their favorite relative" at

this "cozy little" French "bistro on the Boulevard" of Sherman Oaks that would "fit in quite nicely on the Left Bank"; the "gracious atmosphere", "especially good steaks" and "divine dishes" "work just as well for a romantic dinner or business" get-together as they do for a "more formal evening out" – little wonder it's usually "crowded" and "hard to book."

Mix Restaurant ●Ⓓ Ⓜ   20 | 21 | 20 | $54
1114 N. Crescent Heights Blvd. (Santa Monica Blvd.), West Hollywood, 323-650-4649; www.mixfreely.com
"Who would think that sitting near one of the busiest intersections in town would be enjoyable", but for many, it is, especially those "relaxing" on this "Old-Hollywood-type bungalow's" "unique" wraparound porch built around living trees; it's an "incredibly pleasant outdoor-indoor dining experience" enhanced by the "restrained elegance" of set designer Christopher Lawrence's interiors and "hard-to-categorize" Californian cuisine; but pouters are put off by "portions fit for an anorexic", concluding we "didn't mix with Mix."

Miyagi's ●   16 | 17 | 15 | $32
8225 Sunset Blvd. (Crescent Heights Blvd.), West Hollywood, 323-650-3524
"The Big Kahuna" of Japanese restaurants with seven sushi and five cocktail bars, this karaoke "party hub" "in the shadow of the Chateau Marmont" has "fun written all over it" – if you're part of the "frat boy-and-sorority-sister" posse; "you don't come here" for the "ok food", "you come here for the scene", so catch the wave of "happy hour", but remember, the "action usually gets started later" when it "transforms into a club."

Modo Mio Cucina Rustica Italiana ⓈⓂ — | — | — | E
15200 Sunset Blvd. (La Cruz Dr.), Pacific Palisades, 310-459-0979; www.modomiocucinarustica.com
'Modo Mio' translates to 'my way' in Italian, and that's the path owner Gian Franco Bertolino takes at this Pacific Palisades trattoria (and its offshoot in the new Crystal Cove Promenade); first-rate, natural ingredients are used to create specialties like housemade pastas, gnocchi, lasagna and veal chops, all served in a warm, rustic setting (enhanced by a waterfall and peekaboo views of the coastline at the Newport Beach newbie).

Moishe's ⋫   ▽ 22 | 6 | 14 | $11
Farmer's Mkt., 6333 W. Third St. (Fairfax Ave.), Los Angeles, 323-936-4998
Falafel, "hummus, tabouli, oh my!", yes the Middle Eastern eats at this "Farmer's Market fixture from the old days" are "addictive" agree acolytes who "keep coming back", bellying up to a take-out counter in the food court for "consistently tasty", "cheap" chow; who cares that "there's no decor" – "you can tell by the line that many agree" it's a "find" and one of the "best values" around.

Momoyama   ▽ 21 | 23 | 17 | $35
1810 S. PCH (bet. Palos Verdes Blvd. & Prospect Ave.), Redondo Beach, 310-540-8211
Drink in the waterfall, bridge, star-lit ceiling and "roomy interior" and "pretend you're in an [Asian] tea garden" at South Bay's "best-kept secret" with a "pleasant staff" and mostly Japanese team of chefs; the "deep menu" goes well beyond "delicious sushi and

appetizers", boasting "many unusual offerings", making it a "good" choice "for entertaining" and "neighborhood" meals.

Monsieur Marcel   21 | 17 | 17 | $22 |
Farmer's Mkt., 6333 W. Third St. (Fairfax Ave.), Los Angeles, 323-939-7792; www.mrmarcel.com

"Really charming" and "unassuming", this open-air bistro/market "far from the madding crowd" at the Fairfax Farmer's Market feels like a "Parisian oasis"; "go in a group and taste everything" on the "excellent", "varied" French-Med menu, "delivered *sans* attitude", "then shop between courses" for "fantastic cheese and olives" or just "kick it with a glass of wine and watch the passing scene" – add a "taste of wonderful fondue" and you're "in heaven, a very rich heaven."

Monsoon Cafe   18 | 23 | 17 | $27 |
1212 Third St. Promenade (bet. Arizona Ave. & Wilshire Blvd.), Santa Monica, 310-576-9996; www.global-dining.com

"Feels like you're in Manila or Bangkok" agree globe-trotters who blow into La Boheme's sibling, a "spectacular"-looking Pan-Asian on the Third Street Promenade, to "nosh and people-watch"; the "eclectic menu" "wraps up regional favorites", making it a "treat" for "fun dates", plus "happy hour is dynamite"; but stormy types snipe that while the "gorillas feeding in the bamboo forest" decor is "worth a trip", the fare is "underwhelming."

Monte Alban ◗   ▽ 23 | 13 | 19 | $18 |
11927 Santa Monica Blvd. (bet. Armacost & Brockton Aves.), West LA, 310-444-7736

"One of the hidden treasures" in West LA, this "cheerful" "mini-mall Oaxacan" boasting "colorful murals" could be called the "house of mole" muse admirers who "never knew there were so many kinds"; "it's as authentic as you can get" with "delicious" Mexican specialties like "transcendental tamales" and clayudas (homemade tortillas) "epic in size and flavor", plus it's a "great value" to boot.

Monty's Steakhouse   21 | 16 | 20 | $43 |
592 S. Fair Oaks Ave. (California Blvd.), Pasadena, 626-792-7776
5371 Topanga Canyon Blvd. (Ventura Blvd.), Woodland Hills, 818-716-9736

If you're looking "to go retro" with "cavemen portions" of "red meat", head for this duo of "old-school steakhouses", the 1946 original in Pasadena and its younger sib in Woodland Hills; in either location, there's "no froufrou" here – just "tender steaks" and "iceberg lettuce salads", "comfy leather booths" and "reliable" service; better hurry, though: these "classic" "local hangouts" may be "the last of the breed."

Moonshadows   18 | 22 | 16 | $38 |
20356 PCH (Big Rock Dr.), Malibu, 310-456-3010; www.moonshadowsmalibu.com

"Catch the dolphins dancing while you" "drink the night away under the stars" at this "killer oceanfront location" above the Malibu surf, and in this "romantic setting" with such "spectacular views", "the rest really does not matter"; that's fortunate, perhaps, since the New American fare is fairly "mediocre" and you often "feel like the wait staff is doing you a favor by taking your order."

Morels First Floor Bistro   16 | 18 | 16 | $27

The Grove at Farmer's Mkt., 189 The Grove Dr. (bet. Fairfax Ave. & 3rd St.), Los Angeles, 323-965-9595

Shoppers stop into this "simple" "typical French bistro" amid "the hustle and bustle of the Grove" at the Fairfax Farmer's Market "for the fondue", "a glass of wine" and chocolate soufflé; the "array of cheeses from around the world" is worthwhile, too, and you can't beat "the people-watching", particularly "on the patio on a sunny day", but beware the otherwise "unimpressive" (and "expensive") cuisine and the "disaffected service."

Morels French Steakhouse Ⓜ   17 | 20 | 17 | $44

The Grove at Farmer's Mkt., 189 The Grove Dr. (bet. Fairfax Ave. & 3rd St.), Los Angeles, 323-965-9595

Upstairs from the First Floor Bistro in the Grove at the Fairfax Farmer's Market, this "beautiful room" houses a "well-done" French steakhouse; regulars recommend sitting on "the balcony" and sampling the "tasty" beef and "great frites" (inside, the "densely packed" tables can be "noisy"), but forlorn Francophones bemoan that it's "just another mall restaurant" offering "make-believe everything", with "inept service" in a pseudo-Gallic setting.

MORI SUSHI Ⓢ   26 | 18 | 21 | $62

11500 W. Pico Blvd. (Gateway Blvd.), West LA, 310-479-3939

"Indulge in the" "transcendental omakase" at this "sublime" West LA Japanese and let "perfectionist" master chef Mori Onodera concoct an "astounding" array of "fresh and delicate" raw-fish creations, "which he serves on ceramic plates he also makes"; even in this "minimalist" setting, worshipers at the shrine of Mori-san (he's "our hero") swear it's "worth the splurge" to dine at "one of the best sushi bars in" the city.

MORTON'S Ⓢ   24 | 21 | 24 | $58

8764 Melrose Ave. (N. Robertson Blvd.), West Hollywood, 310-276-5205

"When you die in Hollywood and go to heaven" – or if you score an invite to the annual Oscar party here – you can join "lots of show biz folk" at this Robertson Cal-American "classic" that's managed to "sustain the quality over so many years"; it's "still one of the best" choices "for business lunches and dinners", since "the staff is responsive and professional", though some sigh that the service is "lovely" only "if you're someone."

Mort's Deli   13 | 8 | 13 | $16

1035 Swarthmore Ave. (W. Sunset Blvd.), Pacific Palisades, 310-454-5511

"If you're sick and don't have a grandma", the "reliable" matzo ball soup at this "homey" "cafeteria-style deli" – a "Palisades institution" with "a good heart" – may be "the best cure" available; otherwise, "take the kids" or join "the locals" when you need to "satisfy those corned beef cravings"; it's a real "part of the" "community", so most partisans are willing to overlook the "tired" setting and just "ok food."

Mo's   17 | 13 | 17 | $19

4301 Riverside Dr. (bet. N. Rose & N. Valley Sts.), Burbank, 818-845-3009; www.eatatmos.com

"Load up on all the fixings" at this "gourmet" "build-a-burger joint" in Burbank that's "a busy studio lunch place by day" ("you never know who you might see at the next table") and "a mellow neighborhood hangout by night"; the "staff is friendly", and the "no-surprises menu" includes "lots of other American favorites", but dissenters dismiss "many dishes" as "simply boring."

Moun of Tunis
▽ 19 | 20 | 20 | $33

7445½ W. Sunset Blvd. (bet. Fairfax & La Brea Aves.), Hollywood, 323-874-3333; www.mounoftunisrestaurant.com

At this "kitschy" Hollywood "harem tent", you're "completely immersed in a" "festive" "dining experience that transports you" to North Africa; bring "a group" to share in the "celebration", as you "sit comfortably on cushions and eat" "simple", "plentiful" Tunisian fare "with your hands", and the "sexy belly dancers" help make this "a fun evening out."

Moustache Café
19 | 17 | 17 | $30

1071 Glendon Ave. (bet. Kinross & Weyburn Aves.), Westwood, 310-208-6633

"Take an old boyfriend" or "the mistress" to this "quaint" Westwood bistro that's a "reliable standby" for "intimate conversation" and "French comfort food" "served by aspiring actors"; this "classy" little joint "always impresses the freshmen", and while the cuisine may "lack sparkle" and the "setting has seen better days", "memories of" such "inconsistencies" "perish, once you" taste the "heavenly" "chocolate soufflé"; N.B. the Melrose location is now Chocolat.

Mr. Cecil's California Ribs
20 | 11 | 15 | $23

13625 Ventura Blvd. (Woodman Ave.), Sherman Oaks, 818-905-8400
12244 W. Pico Blvd. (Bundy Blvd.), West LA, 310-442-1550

"Thank God Mr. Cecil came to town" chorus customers of these "barbecue heavens" in West LA and Sherman Oaks, where the signature ribs are "smoky and fall-off-the-bone delicious"; it may be "a tad expensive" for "down-home" joints "that serve on paper plates", but most simply suggest "don't wear white" when you pray at the altar of this "completely delicious way to make a mess."

Mr. Chow ●
22 | 21 | 20 | $62

344 N. Camden Dr. (bet. Brighton Way & Wilshire Blvd.), Beverly Hills, 310-278-9911; www.mrchow.com

"Chock-full of big-fish celebs and their feeder-fish entourages", this "cool", "modern" Beverly Hills "hangout" dishes up "savory" Chinese chow "with a side of stars"; "wear your trendiest duds" and prepare for the staff's "nose-in-the-air attitude" – it's "hard to get in unless you know someone (or are someone)" – though the unimpressed don't understand "all the fuss" for "faux" Beijing-style fare at "sky-high prices."

Mulberry Street Pizzeria
23 | 10 | 16 | $13

347 N. Cañon Dr. (bet. Brighton & Dayton Ways), Beverly Hills, 310-247-8998
240 S. Beverly Dr. (bet. Charleville Blvd. & Gregory Way), Beverly Hills, 310-247-8100
17040 Ventura Blvd. (Oak Park Ave.), Encino, 818-906-8881

For "a little slice of home" served with "free copies of the NY Post", migrants from Manhattan maintain that the bites of "super-thin"-crusted "heaven" from these "no-frills" Italian joints are "straight from the streets of New York City"; this is "real pizza at down-to-earth prices", and not that we're complaining, but the "gigantic" whole pies don't even "fit in most refrigerators."

Musha   22   16   19 $26 ◑
424 Wilshire Blvd. (bet. 4th & 5th Sts.), Santa Monica, 310-576-6330
1725 W. Carson St. (W. Western Ave.), Torrance, 310-787-7344
"Lively" and "energetic" "like an authentic Tokyo pub", this pair of
"funky Japanese *izakayas*" in Santa Monica and Torrance earns
"mad props" for their "addictive", "reasonably priced" "small
plates" ("sized so that you can try various dishes"), paired with a
"good sake selection"; with "tables so close" together "in this
friendly place", "folks often end up exchanging recommendations"
for what to eat, and the "exceedingly nice" staff looks after you, too.

Musso & Frank Grill 🅂 Ⓜ   18   19   20 $38
6667 Hollywood Blvd. (Highland Ave.), Hollywood, 323-467-7788
While the "career staff" may be "grumpy", they "care about their
customers" at this "historic Hollywood" "comfort food museum"
where "you feel as if Humphrey Bogart or Orson Welles could step
through the door" at any moment; from the extensive Traditional
American menu (it's "like reading *War and Peace*"), regulars
recommend "ordering a proper martini and anything grilled", and
though it's undoubtedly a "tourist trap", "nostalgics" urge "time
traveling" to this circa-1919 "icon" "at least once."

Nadpob Thai Cafe 🅂 Ⓜ   –   –   –   I
4321 W. Sunset Blvd. (Vermont Ave.), Silver Lake, 323-666-9000
Tucked away in an oft-overlooked Silver Lake strip mall, this
casual, no-frills Thai newcomer is slowly drawing customers with
a fairly typical straightforward menu; traditionalists choose from
classic dishes like chicken larb and pad Thai.

Naked Sushi   –   –   –   M
18 Washington Blvd. (Pacific Ave.), Marina del Rey, 310-827-6209;
www.nakedsushi.com
No, this isn't one of those places where they serve Japanese fin
fare on the body of a young woman; instead it's a casual sushi bar
in Marina del Rey, near the beach, with outdoor tables that allow
diners to chow down while tattooed Rollerbladers skim by in string
bikinis; along with the usual suspects, there are oddities like the
Acid Drops Roll and the Bar Mitzvah Roll.

Nak Won Korean ◑   ▽ 19   12   15 $16
3879 Wilshire Blvd. (Western Ave.), Koreatown, 213-388-8889
"Satisfy your cravings" for kalbi and kimchi at this 24-hour
Koreatown barbecue joint that's "a popular late-night" destination
"after clubbing"; you don't need a translator, because you can
"order from pictures on the wall", and if you've got the munchies,
you'll be pleased that the "typical homestyle fare at affordable
prices" "comes out" of the kitchen "very quickly."

Napa Valley Grille   20   22   20 $39
1100 Glendon Ave. (Lindbrook Dr.), Westwood, 310-824-3322;
www.napavalleygrille.com
With grapevine upholstery and plenty of polished wood, the "lovely
surroundings" "recall Northern California" at this Westwood link
of an "upper-class chain" that, perhaps predictably, offers an
"outstanding wine list, with a huge by-the-glass selection"; the
"seasonal" Cal cuisine and "competent service" are pluses, too,
so if some say it feels too "corporate", it's "a safe bet" "to impress
a date – or her parents."

Natalee Thai
19 | 16 | 16 | $20 |

998 S. Robertson Blvd. (Olympic Blvd.), Beverly Hills, 310-855-9380
10101 Venice Blvd. (Clarington Ave.), Palms, 310-202-7003
www.nataleethai.com

"It's not Bangkok, but" the "decent" "Americanized Thai" fare, "complete with Korean barbecue and sushi", keeps this Siamese duo in Beverly Hills and Palms "always jumpin'"; maybe because of the "crowds", "service could be faster", and if the "futuristic" interior adds to both the "nontraditional" feel and the "deafening noise level", at least "no one can hear your kids cry."

Nate 'n Al's
20 | 9 | 16 | $21 |

414 N. Beverly Dr. (bet. Brighton Way & Little Santa Monica Blvd.), Beverly Hills, 310-274-0101

"If your name is 'hon', the" "snappy" "waitresses know you" at this "legendary" Beverly Hills deli that's been dishing out "Jewish soul food" to "studio people" and "Milton Berle wannabes" "since the beginning of time" (or at least since 1945); "wait in line, have your pastrami and see the celebs" – you could do worse "for an informal nosh" – but critics kvetch that this joint is "past its prime."

Native Foods
▽ 22 | 17 | 16 | $15 |

1110½ Gayley Ave. (Wilshire Blvd.), Westwood, 310-209-1055;
www.nativefoods.com

Whole food disciples insist "you don't need to wear Birkenstocks to enjoy" the "fabulous" "100%" vegan victuals covering a "wide range of possibilities" so "terrific", "non-vegetarians won't miss the meat" at this SoCal outfit (including Costa Mesa's only eatery sheltered in a yurt) fittingly located at The Camp, a faux-rustic retail complex; the sting of "slow service" is forgotten in the face of "very cheap, but very good", "healthy, healthy, healthy" organic dishes.

Nawab of India
22 | 15 | 19 | $26 |

1621 Wilshire Blvd. (bet. 16th & 17th Sts.), Santa Monica,
310-829-1106; www.nawabindia.com

"Flavor a-go-go" – that's the verdict on the "mouthwatering vegetarian selections", "moist tandoori chicken" and "smooth, silky" curries at this "classic Indian" in Santa Monica that's a "wonderful" choice for South Asian fare; "the lunch buffet is an amazing bargain" as is the "great champagne brunch", though some nattering nawabs nitpick about the "nothing-special decor."

Naya Restaurant Moderne Ⓜ
▽ 23 | 21 | 19 | $52 |

49 E. Colorado Blvd. (Raymond Ave.), Pasadena, 626-793-4712;
www.nayadining.com

Pasadena patrons "could hardly believe their luck" when this "comet streaked across" the Old Town "scene", bringing "creative" New American fare to a community that "needs it"; though this "hip place" remains a "welcome addition", some surveyors wish the "service matched the quality of the food", and the post-*Survey* departure of "gifted chef" Scooter Kanfer – Ray Luna is now the top toque – leaves guests guessing about its future direction.

NBC Seafood
23 | 12 | 14 | $21 |

404 S. Atlantic Blvd. (bet. Harding & Newmark Aves.), Monterey Park,
626-282-2323

At this "popular" "dim sum palace" in Monterey Park, regulars recommend "arriving early to avoid long waits", particularly on weekends when it's more crowded than a Hong Kong bus stop at rush hour; the "barnlike atmosphere" is "devoid of decor", and the service isn't "much to speak of", but the "classic Cantonese" cuisine emphasizing "high-quality seafood" is "rewarding."

Neptune's Net   18 | 10 | 9 | $18

42505 PCH (2 mi. north of Leo Carillo Bch.), Malibu, 310-457-3095; www.neptunesnet.itgo.com

"With Harleys galore" parked out front, this "seafood shack" "across the highway from the ocean" reels in "bikers, surfers and yuppies" alike with "cold beer", "fresh crab" and "fried fish"; "you're overdressed unless your jeans are tattered and your Birkies are worn out", the better to go with the "paper plates", but those hooked on this Malibu "dive" just say "party on, dude."

New Concept   ▽ 22 | 16 | 13 | $22

700 S. Atlantic Blvd. (El Portal Pl.), Monterey Park, 626-282-6800

A "contender for the best dim sum in the San Gabriel Valley", this Monterey Park newcomer "distills" the traditional tea lunch "into an art form", serving "interesting dishes you won't find elsewhere", and since "it's cooked to order, rather than served by a cart", the "quality is tops"; the "staff tries to help" novices, and the rest of the "sophisticated Chinese" fare is earning kudos as well.

New Flavors   – | – | – | I

4135 S. Centinela Ave. (Washington Blvd.), Mar Vista, 310-390-7849

"My mouth waters" for the "delightfully presented" Chinese-Hawaiian fare sigh admirers who seek out new flavors at this plain-Jane Asian on a Culver City strip near the Sony studio; the low-cost, mixed menu of BBQ pork, chicken, short ribs and loco moco is a "plus for a neighborhood" mired in Mexican offerings.

New Moon   ▽ 19 | 14 | 16 | $23

2138 Verdugo Blvd. (Clifton Pl.), Montrose, 818-249-4868

"Great Chinese chicken salad" is a signature dish at this Montrose newcomer that serves a mix of classic and contemporary Sino selections; early reports indicate that "these folks know what they're doing" in this "modern" space, and though they're "still working out the kinks", their foodie pedigree is evident from the TV in the bar that's always tuned to the Food Network.

Newsroom Café   19 | 13 | 15 | $19

120 N. Robertson Blvd. (bet. Alden Dr. & W. Beverly Blvd.), West Hollywood, 310-652-4444
530 Wilshire Blvd. (bet. 5th & 6th Sts.), Santa Monica, 310-319-9100

Periodical perusers sing the praises of these "health-conscious" cafes on Robertson and in Santa Monica where it's "socially acceptable to read at the table" while wolfing down "sprouty" "vegan options"; as witnessed by the "screenwriters, wannabe actors" and "celeb overflow", you don't have to "sacrifice taste or the cool factor" to eat "natural"; but some reviewers feel "the magazine rack has better selections."

Nick & Stef's Steakhouse   23 | 21 | 21 | $50

Wells Fargo Ctr., 330 S. Hope St. (bet. 3rd & 4th Sts.), Downtown, 213-680-0330; www.patinagroup.com

A "dreamy mix of modern design and hearty food" coo carnivores who canter over for "great patio dining against the skyline" or a pre-"Disney Concert Hall date" to The Patina Group's "woodsy" "big-bucks steakhouse" Downtown; "start with a real Caesar salad" made tableside, then mooove on to "excellent beef" "dry-aged" like a "scene from *Rocky*" "in their lockers" and "interesting sides"; P.S. the "best deal is the happy-hour menu in the bar."

Nicola's Kitchen   18 11 17 $20
French Quarter, 20969 Ventura Blvd. (bet. Canoga & De Soto Aves.), Woodland Hills, 818-883-9477; www.nicolaskitchen.com
Whether you "take grandma or a date", you'll be "pleasantly surprised" by this" "perfect hangout" in Woodland Hills that doubles as a "sweet sandwich shop" and a "reliable" "favorite" for "wonderful Italian cuisine", the "ultimate chopped salad" and "addictive focaccia"; sure, the "decor's very simple, almost cafeterialike", but you get "unusual" "good food for the money."

Nic's ⊠   22 21 20 $42
453 N. Cañon Dr. (Little Santa Monica Blvd.), Beverly Hills, 310-550-5707; www.nicsbeverlyhills.com
"Gentle, magnanimous" chef-owner Larry Nicola "works the room with poise and panache" at his "modern, stylish" New American restaurant and "happening bar" "where the bohemian chic" Beverly Hills set gathers for "creative yet familiar" fare and "world-class martinis" ("oh my"); yes, it can get a "bit cramped" and the "terrific live music on weekends" can get "almost too loud", but "something just feels right about the place."

Nikko Sushi   – – – M
8457 Santa Monica Blvd. (Holloway Dr.), West Hollywood, 323-654-6200
"Large portions of all the good stuff!" fawn fin finatics who make waves to this "great little gem" in West Hollywood for "wonderful sushi rolls that go a little beyond the norm" made with "succulent pieces of quality fish"; add in a "friendly staff", nightly happy hours and lunchtime bento boxes and you get a lot for your nikkos.

Nine Thirty   ▽ 19 25 18 $51
W Hotel, 930 Hilgard Ave. (bet. La Conte & Weyburn Aves.), Westwood, 310-443-8211; www.ninethirtyw.com
This "trendy" Westwood "hot spot" blessed with the "incredible W Hotel wow factor" is slowly building up a foodie following with farm-fresh New American cuisine that works for "business or pleasure"; the "excellent Asian"-inspired setting is "almost as beautiful as the people who dine there" and if early-comers pronounce it "too sceney", even they admit "maybe it's gotten better"; N.B. a recent chef change may impact the Food rating.

Nirvana ☾   ▽ 16 23 15 $41
8689 Wilshire Blvd. (bet. N. Hamel & N. Willaman Drs.), Beverly Hills, 310-657-5040; www.nirvanabeverlyhills.com
"With *Kama Sutra*" scenes on "every wall and candlelight on every table", "exotic" "beds to eat" "interesting" Tandoori-focused Indian on, "not too mention aquarium walkways", this "hangout for the nouveau-boho Bev Hills" crowd is one of the most provocative "hot" spots; it's "hard to find" so look for the carved wooden Buddha door and the stream of Mercedes idling on Wilshire.

Nishimura ⊠   ▽ 27 23 22 $69
8684 Melrose Ave. (N. San Vicente Blvd.), West Hollywood, 310-659-4770
Still "remarkably undiscovered", this "hidden delight" with an "understated interior" in the West Hollywood design district offers

an "exquisite respite from the norm", achieving "Zen perfection" with "sublime" worth-the-"splurge" sushi and sashimi that excels in "flavor and presentation"; chef-owner "Shiro Nishimura is a true master chef and amiable to boot", while his "staff is gracious and helpful", making this "serene" "rarefied experience" a "treat for all five senses."

Nizam | 22 | 15 | 20 | $22 |

10871 W. Pico Blvd. (Westwood Blvd.), West LA, 310-470-1441

"Come for a nice, quiet dinner" or "bargain"-priced "high-quality lunch buffet" beckon boosters of this "old standby for top-notch Indian" on the Westside where the "always present" host-owner "makes sure that everyone is happy" and the "simple food" is "delicious"; if a handful lament "there's not much to distinguish" it, for most it's "pleasant" and "dependable."

Noah's New York Bagels | 17 | 10 | 14 | $8 |

11911 San Vicente Blvd. (Montana Ave.), Brentwood, 310-472-5651
250 N. Larchmont Blvd. (Beverly Blvd.), Hancock Park, 323-466-2924
330 Manhattan Beach Blvd. (Morningside Dr.), Manhattan Beach, 310-937-2206
Marina del Rey Shopping Ctr., 546-548 Washington Blvd. (Via Marina), Marina del Rey, 310-574-1155
895 Silver Spur Rd. (Crenshaw Blvd.), Palos Verdes Estates, 310-541-7824
Hastings Ranch Shopping Ctr., 3711 E. Foothill Blvd. (Rosemead Blvd.), Pasadena, 626-351-0352
605 S. Lake Ave. (E. California Blvd.), Pasadena, 626-449-6415
1426 Montana Ave. (14th St.), Santa Monica, 310-587-9103
14622 Ventura Blvd. (Van Nuys Blvd.), Sherman Oaks, 818-907-9570
10910 Lindbrook Dr. (bet. Gayley Ave. & Westwood Blvd.), Westwood, 310-209-8177
www.noahs.com

"Killer bagels generous on the schmear" and as "fresh as the staff" lure "carbo" loaders to this "always packed" chain; "they know how to roll" one, and the "coffee is surprisingly good", making it a "weekend tradition" and "worth driving past" competitors to get to; but kvetchers carp "oy – they bear no resemblance to the NY" "real deal" – only in a "craving" "emergency."

NOBU MALIBU | 27 | 20 | 23 | $66 |

3835 Cross Creek Rd. (PCH), Malibu, 310-317-9140;
www.nobumatsuhisa.com

It may be "Malibu-casual, but an extraordinary dining" experience still awaits at this "unbelievably inviting", "lively scene" that "has Nobu magic" aplenty; follow the "knowledgeable" "servers' advice" and order "astonishing" dishes along with the "perfect sushi" – "every bite is worth every dollar" – then "star gaze" as you "graze" (there are so many "celebs" it's "distracting"); if a few find the "drive a drawback" and the "decor nondescript", most "would go every night" if they could.

NOÉ Ⓜ | 24 | 24 | 24 | $56 |

Omni Los Angeles Hotel, 251 S. Olive St. (2nd St.), Downtown, 213-356-4100; www.omnilosangeles.com

"Delightful and so peaceful", this "elegant" "grown-up choice" for "fine dining" Downtown with a skyline backdrop is an "excellent place to get in the right mindset for high culture nearby"; the "wonderfully creative" New American fare reveals a "superbly"

deft "Asian influence" – the "only thing better than the food is the
presentation and phenomenal service"; if a few say noe way to
the "overreaching" "odd pairings", for most it's an "exquisite"
"pre-theater and lengthy dinner" "experience"; N.B. the patio
is cigar friendly.

Nonya 22 24 20 $32

61 N. Raymond Ave. (Union St.), Pasadena, 626-583-8398;
www.nonyarestaurant.com
Offering "grazers" "a great fresh take on Southeast Asian cooking",
this "true find in Old Town Pasadena" blends flavors of Singapore,
Malaysia, Indonesia and India in a "Zen-like", "seductive"
setting with "high ceilings", "cushioned benches" and a koi pond;
it's a "tranquil" choice for a "romantic rendezvous" replete with
"satisfying food" and "exotic cocktails", and if it occasionally draws
the "bright young things", it's "worth the hubbub."

Nook Bistro 🗷 23 18 22 $28

11628 Santa Monica Blvd. (Barry Ave.), West LA, 310-207-5160;
www.nookbistro.com
Though its "hidden" location "in the back" of a West LA mini-mall
makes it "hard to find, everyone does", because the "inspired"
American-Eclectic "homestyle fare" with "lovely twists" "tastes
superior to mom's cooking" and "prices are realistic"; the "menu
options (small plates and large) allow you to indulge as much (or
as little) as you want" and it's all served with "no pretense" by a
"smart, sexy" staff.

NORMAN'S 🗷Ⓜ 23 25 24 $63

8570 W. Sunset Blvd. (bet. La Cienega Blvd. & Sunset Plaza Dr.),
West Hollywood, 310-657-2400; www.normans.com
Combining "succulent" "ingredients from the Caribbean, Mexico
and South America, chef Norman Van Aken of Miami fame"
conjures up "often startling but successful" New World "creations"
"so unique, they're not for everyone" at his "stylish", "spacious,
contemporary" "jewel"; add in "top-notch service" and you've got
"elegance on the Strip" that's "worth the splurge"; but bashers
find it "stuffy" for Sunset and dis the fare as "dramatically
overpriced" "pseudo-Cuban."

Norton Simon Museum Garden Café ▽ 11 16 11 $14

411 W. Colorado Blvd. (Orange Grove Blvd.), Pasadena,
626-449-6840; www.nortonsimon.org
"A wonderful place to chill between rounds at the museum" sez
Simonites who "relax in the outdoor patio in the sculpture garden"
of the Norton Simon grounds in Pasadena with "interesting"
American fare; but balkers believe that while you can't "beat
the surroundings", the menu is somewhat "limited" and the
food "typical" concession fare.

Noura Cafe 17 16 12 $17

8479 Melrose Ave. (La Cienega Blvd.), West Hollywood,
323-651-4581
Amateur astrologers "love being able to look up at the night sky"
out on the "open-air" patio "while munching on delicious", "healthy
and fresh tasting" Middle Eastern fare at this "groovy", "hip
place"; they "rock a pita like no one", plus it's an "incredible
bargain for high-rent" WeHo, making it a "fun" "hangout" for "a
group on a budget."

Nyala Ethiopian ◐   23 | 16 | 18 | $18
1076 S. Fairfax Ave. (bet. W. Olympic Blvd. & Whitworth Dr.),
Los Angeles, 323-936-5918; www.nyala-la.com
A "fun and delicious excuse to eat with your hands" exult
enthusiasts who find this South Fairfax Ethiopian a "good intro"
to this style of African cuisine; it's a "great change from the
usual", so scoop up the "vast piles of terrific" chow with a "sheet
of injera bread that covers the entire table" – and bring your
"vegetarian girlfriend" or boyfriend to share the "exotic feast."

Oasis ◐   ∇ 18 | 25 | 17 | $31
611 N. La Brea Ave. (Melrose Ave.), Los Angeles, 323-939-8900;
www.oasislosangeles.com
"A festive night out" declare kasbah habitués, delighting in the
"divine" "decor that makes you feel like a genie in a bottle",
"happening bar scene" and "excellent appetizers" at this
"Moroccan hideaway" on La Brea that's "ideal for an intimate
meal before a show"; but desert-ers dis the "sketchy service" and
"bland entrees", suggesting "skip the food, just go for the drinks."

O-BAR ◐   18 | 26 | 19 | $39
8279 Santa Monica Blvd. (N. Sweetzer Ave.), West Hollywood,
323-822-3300; www.obarrestaurant.com
"Sleek and sexy, with a friendly" "staff of hot, hot men" "to boot",
this "open, airy, interesting" hangout boasting "romantic" draped
booths offers a "mixed" but "primarily gay" crowd plenty of
"spectacular scenery", plus the "clever" American creations "ain't
bad either"; but O my, others find the "gorgeous space can't
disguise the mediocre food", suggesting "sit and have a drink" and
just soak up "amazing atmosphere."

Ocean & Vine   – | – | – | M
Loews Santa Monica Beach Hotel, 1700 Ocean Ave. (Pico Blvd.),
Santa Monica, 310-576-3180; www.oceanandvine.com
Residing in the Loews Santa Monica Beach Hotel space that used
to house Lavande, this stylish New American boasts an oceanfront
setting, with a bar that overlooks the water, a fire pit and indoor-
outdoor dining areas offering dazzling views of the SM Pier; the
fairly priced menu features a solid lineup, including muscovy duck
breast with grits and steamed Prince Edward Island mussels.

Ocean Ave. Seafood   23 | 20 | 21 | $42
1401 Ocean Ave. (Santa Monica Blvd.), Santa Monica,
310-394-5669; www.oceanave.com
"Truly a fish phenomenon" affirm fin-atics who flip for SM's
"comfortable" little "brother of Water Grill", a "must for out-of-
town guests" with a "lovely" "view of the Pacific" and "pleasant"
glassed-in "alfresco dining area"; choose from a "menu that goes
on forever" and you'll be rewarded with "satisfying" seafood that's
"as fresh as it gets unless you own a boat and reel"; if a few feel
"the decor lacks a personality", for most it's a "reliable" "standby."

OCEANFRONT   23 | 26 | 21 | $53
Hotel Casa Del Mar, 1910 Ocean Way (Pico Blvd.), Santa Monica,
310-581-7714; www.hotelcasadelmar.com
"Impress a business contact" at this "elegant, atmospheric" glass-
walled Californian set in the storied "wonderful old" Hotel Casa Del
Mar with the "pretty Pacific all around"; it's such a "high spot in

Santa Monica" ("may be the best combination of view and food in town"), you might be tempted to "get a room"; P.S. check out the "action at the adjacent bar."

Ocean Seafood 22 | 13 | 15 | $22
750 N. Hill St. (bet. Alpine & Ord Sts.), Chinatown, 213-687-3088; www.oceansf.com
"If Hong Kong seems too far", make waves for this "gigantic" Chinatown "dim sum palace" "in a tiny shopping center" offering oceans of "tasty" "choices"; "expect" a "long wait" because it's "hyper-crowded on weekends", "but once seated, you're soon satisfied, full of the freshest seafood found anywhere"; "service can be erratic" and the ambiance could "use an interior designer", but for most it's a "favorite, year after year."

Ocean Star 23 | 15 | 14 | $21
145 N. Atlantic Blvd. (bet. Emerson & Garvey Aves.), Monterey Park, 626-308-2128
Try to sit near the kitchen for "first pickings" from the pushcarts that emerge "steaming and bulging" with baskets full of "fantastic", "very traditional", "can't-be-beat" dumplings and chicken feet at this "Yankee-Stadium-sized" "opulent but industrial" Chinese dim sum standby in Monterey Park; "discerning food lovers" are "constantly annoyed by the deafening noise" that sounds like "a 747 landing in the dining room", but will "brave the long waits" and "indifferent service" for a "virtual trip to Hong Kong and back."

Odyssey ∇ 18 | 22 | 19 | $29
15600 Odyssey Dr. (Rinaldi St.), Granada Hills, 818-366-6444
"Ask to sit by the window" and the Continental seafood buffet "will taste even better" insist insiders who particularly prefer Granada Hills' "moderately priced" Victorian-style "old favorite" with crystal chandeliers "early in the week when there's no mad rush"; if the just "ok food" isn't always a Homer run and in "need of reinvention", who cares – it's "worth going just for the breathtaking view of the Valley."

Off Vine 23 | 22 | 23 | $36
6263 Leland Way (Vine St.), Hollywood, 323-962-1900; www.offvine.com
When you "want to escape the scene" this "little" Hollywood Arts and Crafts "hideaway" behind "beautiful bougainvillea" "feels like a special find"; with "creative" Cal-American fare, an "enchanting outdoor patio" and service that'll get you "to the theater on time", it comes "highly recommended."

Ogamdo – | – | – | M
842 S. La Brea Ave. (bet. 8th & 9th Sts.), Los Angeles, 323-936-1500
A surreal dining experience, this affordable Chinese-Korean just south of Hollywood is set inside a red-brick building dating back 112 years and decorated with ancient railroad and nautical artifacts; waiters dress in Laotian sailor suits, and if you need service, you press a button and a loud bell rings – a trick not found at Spago.

Old Spaghetti Factory, The 14 | 17 | 16 | $17
5939 Sunset Blvd. (Tamarind Ave.), Hollywood, 323-469-7149; www.osf.com
"Kitschy", and "lively", these offshoots of a national chain set in converted vintage buildings provide "garish fun" "that will surely make the kids happy" as they "carbo load" on "supercheap" "all-

inclusive" Italian meals that "even include spumoni"; so what if the "pedestrian pasta" is "nothing to rave about", "interminable waits" prove these "theme" joints with "prices too good to resist" "get the job done" "when you have many mouths to feed."

Ole! Tapas Bar
▽ 16 | 20 | 16 | $32

13251 Ventura Blvd. (bet. Coldwater Canyon & Woodman Aves.), Studio City, 818-986-3190; www.oletapasbar.com

A "young, hip newcomer to the Valley", this Studio City Spanish tapas bar has the kind of "trendy ambiance" that makes for an exciting "nightlife scene" with cozy booths, murals and "soon-to-be-legendary sangria"; even though it's "more about the drinks" than the "so-so food" or the "blasé service", patient patrons posit they're "still learning" at this "good addition to the 'hood."

Omelette Parlor
– | – | – | I

2732 Main St. (Ocean Park Blvd.), Santa Monica, 310-399-7892

This American breakfast and lunch counter in Santa Monica a stone's throw from the beach not only lives up to its name with "tasty" "large omelets", it also cracks a few eggs for "especially good waffles", and lures locals with sandwiches and salads, all served in a countrified setting or on the "nice patio courtyard."

Omino Sushi
▽ 26 | 13 | 21 | $27

20957 Devonshire St. (De Soto Ave.), Chatsworth, 818-709-8822; www.ominosushi.com

Let's "keep it a secret" beg boosters of this "terrific" sushi bar in Chatsworth that "looks like a hole-in-the-wall but really isn't" given the "superb", "super fresh" fare and "always friendly service"; the often "crowded" space and "very loyal following" probably mean the word's already gotten out.

O-Nami
18 | 13 | 13 | $24

1925 W. Carson St. (Cabrillo Ave.), Torrance, 310-787-1632
West Covina Plaza, 1526 Plaza Dr. (Vincent Ave.), West Covina, 626-962-8110
www.o-nami.com

Belt-busters befriend this "all-you-can-eat" "gigantic buffet" Japanese outfit that "has it all – sashimi, sushi, salads, lobster, hot dishes, desserts" – and is a "great deal for lunch" (less so for dinner); sure, it's all "kinda mass produced" and you'll need "to wait", but if you're with a group "there's something for everyone."

ONE PICO
23 | 26 | 23 | $53

Shutters on the Beach, 1 Pico Blvd. (Ocean Ave.), Santa Monica, 310-587-1717; www.shuttersonthebeach.com

"Request a coveted table by the window" at this "elegant" oceanside New American in the Shutters on the Beach hotel to fully enjoy the "dreamy setting" and "gorgeous" "unobstructed sunset views" of Santa Monica Bay (and occasional celebrities); best for a "romantic" date, Sunday brunch or "when someone else is paying", it offers "creatively prepared" fare and "smooth service"; just a few are put off by "attitude."

Opus Bar & Grill ◗
– | – | – | E

Western Theatre Bldg., 3760 Wilshire Blvd. (Western Ave.), Los Angeles, 213-738-1600

Finally there's an upscale Koreatown option with the arrival of this new Californian steakhouse with a hefty wine list in Mid-Wilshire's

Western Theatre Building; with high ceilings, a sleek bar, an outdoor patio and a room decked out with custom-built leather love seats and massive chandeliers, it brings some high-style to mesquite-grilled fare.

Original Pantry Bakery ⊅　15 | 9 | 15 | $15
875 S. Figueroa St. (9th St.), Downtown, 213-627-6879; www.pantrycafe.com
"They get you in, feed you, then get you the hell out" of this "throwback" greasy-spoon bakery and breakfast/lunch counter catching the overflow of its "landmark" 24-hour sibling next door; legions of loyalists laud the "big and greasy ham and eggs", "fluffy", "dinner-plate sized" pancakes and other "splash and dash, good ol' food", but the unimpressed just "laugh at all the people waiting in line" and go to Denny's.

Original Pantry Cafe ●⊅　15 | 9 | 16 | $15
877 S. Figueroa St. (9th St.), Downtown, 213-972-9279; www.pantrycafe.com
Former Mayor Richard Riordan's 24-hour "cheap" and "fun" "classic" coffee shop draws "long lines" for "blue-plate specials" of American comfort food served by "waiters who've been there since Moses was in high school"; "breakfast is the ticket" – it's so "popular among" "Downtown politicos and the after-hours crowd" it spawned the Bakery next door; but anti-Pantry-raiders pout it's advisable only "when everything else is closed."

ORRIS ⊠　26 | 15 | 22 | $33
2006 Sawtelle Blvd. (La Grange Ave.), West LA, 310-268-2212; www.orrisrestaurant.com
"Brave" chef Hideo Yamashiro "takes center stage in an open kitchen", combining French-Asian flavors in "novel" ways at his simple izakaya (Japanese pub), smack in the epicenter of Asian pop culture on the Westside's bustling Sawtelle Boulevard; it's an "enjoyable performance", with "delicious, creative" small plates crafted from "well-chosen ingredients that make every dish taste fresh" – and "leave you wanting much more."

Orso　20 | 21 | 20 | $41
8706 W. Third St. (bet. S. Hamel Rd. & S. Willamen Dr.), Los Angeles, 310-274-7144
With roots in New York, this "dark, intimate" "low-key" Italian charmer near the Beverly Center draws an "old-Hollywood crowd", "stargazers" and couples looking for "romance" beneath the gigantic trees on the "lovely", "roomy" backyard candlelit patio; advocates agree this is where to find "never heavy" pastas and the "thinnest ever Margherita pizza", and some even go so far as to say this is "the only place you'll ever want to eat liver and onions."

Ortolan ⊠　▽ 26 | 22 | 21 | $68
8338 W. Third St. (bet. Orlando & Sweetzer Aves.), West Hollywood, 323-653-3300; www.ortolanrestaurant.com
"Just what this town needed" coo acolytes whose "hearts are aflutter" over Third Street's long-awaited "chic" newcomer from star chef Christophe Emé (ex L'Orangerie) and blonde bombshell actress Jeri Ryan; the "attentive staff" tends to "beautiful people" who bask in the glow radiated by "more chandeliers than Liberace's house" and linger over "brilliantly flavored" platefuls of modern French fare – oh, what "a fabulous experience."

Osteria Latini   23 | 17 | 21 | $39
11712 San Vicente Blvd. (Barrington Ave.), Brentwood,
310-826-9222; www.osterialatini.com
Brentwood certainly doesn't suffer a shortage of "quaint" Italian restaurants, but this "cramped", "warm, friendly", "simple bistro-style" destination "definitely stands out from the crowd" with a staff that "pampers you until you couldn't possibly think of anything else you might want" and "inventive" fare; still, the list of 25 "daily specials is very impressive" by some accounts, but a few find it an "overly ambitious number with uneven results."

Osteria Nonni   ▽ 19 | 11 | 18 | $27
3219 Glendale Blvd. (Glenfeliz Blvd.), Atwater Village, 323-666-7133
An Atwater Village "trattoria worth saying tra-la-la about", this "handy neighborhood" spot lures a "regular crowd" that sings the praises of a "can't-miss menu of basic Italian fare" at "reasonable prices" and "solid service"; if a few find the "pasta hit-or-miss", most find it o-so-"enjoyable", adding to "eat here is to love it."

Outback Steakhouse   18 | 15 | 18 | $25
166 E. Huntington Dr. (2nd Ave.), Arcadia, 626-447-6435
Empire Ctr., 1761 N. Victory Pl. (W. Empire Ave.), Burbank, 818-567-2717
1418 Azusa Ave. (Frwy. 60), City of Industry, 626-810-6765
1476 N. Azusa Ave. (Arrow Hwy.), Covina, 626-812-0488
5305 Clark Ave. (Candlewood St.), Lakewood, 562-634-0353
18711 Devonshire St. (Reseda Blvd.), Northridge, 818-366-2341
137 E. Thousand Oaks Blvd. (Moorpark Rd.), Thousand Oaks, 805-381-1590
Del Amo Fashion Ctr., 21880 Hawthorne Blvd. (bet. Carson St. & Sepulveda Blvd.), Torrance, 310-793-5555
25261 N. The Old Rd. (I-5), Valencia, 661-287-9630
www.outback.com
Additional locations throughout Southern California
"No need to go Down Under for" a "tasty steak" and a "to-die-for bloomin' onion" because "tha' food's alright" at this "upbeat" Aussie-themed chain with "pleasant service" and "stereotypical 'roo' decor; "it's nothing fancy", so "don't expect haute cuisine", but do expect "consistent quality" and "honest value for your money"; if a few harrumph "this gimmick is as worn out as Crocodile Dundee", for most it's "corny" "family" "fun"

Outlaws Bar & Grill   ▽ 18 | 14 | 15 | $20
230 Culver Blvd. (Vista del Mar), Playa del Rey, 310-822-4040
For some "the jury's still out" as to whether the new owners have "improved" this popular Playa del Rey American "hangout", but for most it remains a "kitschy but fun" "dive" with a "beachy cowpoke" vibe "filled with neighborhood characters"; "quiet your inner carnivore" with "massive", "juicy burgers" and "quench your thirst" with the "top-notch beer selection", all delivered by a "take-no-prisoners staff."

Pace   23 | 22 | 21 | $37
2100 Laurel Canyon Blvd. (Kirkwood Dr.), Hollywood,
323-654-8583; www.peaceinthecanyon.com
"Totally LA in the best hippie way", this "cozy Canyon hideaway" "tucked in the hills" delights locals with "always delicious" Italian and "pleasing pizzas" made from organic ingredients; the "quaint" setting, done up with "funky art" and a "romantic patio", feels like

an "escape from the spiff of Beverly Hills", making it a particularly "lovely" "date" destination.

Pacific Dining Car ◑   23 | 20 | 23 | $51 |
1310 W. Sixth St. (bet. Valencia & Witmer Sts.), Downtown, 213-483-6000
2700 Wilshire Blvd. (Princeton St.), Santa Monica, 310-453-4000
www.pacificdiningcar.com
"Make your rich uncle take you" to this "expense-account-class" American chophouse duo popular with "movers and shakers", serving "perfect pancakes" at breakfast as well as "superb steaks" "in the middle of the night" (the Downtown original is open 24/7, while the SM branch closes at 2 AM); the service is "wonderful", and "in a city constantly looking for the hot, new place", many find the "civilized", "old-school" setting a "refreshing" change.

Pacifico's   18 | 14 | 18 | $21 |
9341 Culver Blvd. (Washington Blvd.), Culver City, 310-559-3474;
www.pacificos.net
"Not your typical Mexican", this Culver City "seafood carnival" specializes in "fresh" *mariscos* with a "south-of-the-border flair", including the signature whole huachinango (red snapper), served by "friendly waiters" in a "beach" setting with "indoor picnic tables" and an "open fire pit on the patio"; critics question the "above-average prices" for "so-so" fare that's "not consistent" and *muy* "casual" decor.

Paco's Tacos   19 | 12 | 16 | $16 |
4141 S. Centinela Ave. (bet. Culver & Washington Blvds.), Mar Vista, 310-391-9616
6212 W. Manchester Ave. (bet. La Tijera & Sepulveda Blvds.), Westchester, 310-645-8692
www.pacoscantina.com
A "popular family destination", this Mexican duo serves up "huge portions" of "handmade, fresh tortillas" and other "traditional Cali-Mex" dishes in "colorful", "kitschy" digs that can "seem fun after a pitcher of margaritas"; the "service is crisp and so are the chips", but some skeptics "don't understand" "why anyone would stand in line for an hour" to get in.

Padri   22 | 20 | 19 | $32 |
29008 Agoura Rd. (bet. Cornell & Kanan Rds.), Agoura Hills, 818-865-3700; www.padrirestaurant.net
The "atmosphere and menu are strictly for grown-ups" at this "rustic" "Tuscan farmhouse" in Agoura Hills that offers "elegant" Northern Italian "comfort food", "good martinis" and "gracious" (if sometimes "slow") service in a "warm", "inviting" setting; if you "want to burn off calories after dinner", the dance scene is pretty happening", with DJs spinning on weekends, and the "outdoor bar is a blast."

Paladar   20 | 20 | 16 | $32 |
1651 Wilcox Ave. (bet. Hollywood Blvd. & Selma Ave.), Hollywood, 323-465-7500; www.paladar.cc
At this Hollywood Cuban, a "young, trendy crowd" is "havana good time" over "fantastic mojitos" and "contemporary" island fare served in a "handsome space" located next to sister lounge Nacional; an "overpriced" menu and "inattentive service" lead to charges that it's "too hip for its own good", and clubbers complain that "having dinner here doesn't help you get into the club."

Palermo   18 15 20 $19
1858 N. Vermont Ave. (bet. Franklin Ave. & Hollywood Blvd.), Los Feliz, 323-663-1178

"Tony, Tony, Tony" is not the vibe but the "wonderful host who puts everyone at ease" at this "friendly, low-key" Italian that caters to the "hip and hungry" of Los Feliz (as well as a regular contingent of "hot cops") with "reliable" "down-home" red-sauce fare; the "tacky" digs are "so out, they're in" and a "friendly" staff contributes to the "bustling, happy atmosphere."

PALM, THE   24 19 22 $55
1100 S. Flower St. (11th St.), Downtown, 213-763-4600
9001 Santa Monica Blvd. (bet. Doheny Dr. & Robertson Blvd.), West Hollywood, 310-550-8811
www.thepalm.com

It's always a "power scene" at these outposts of the national chophouse chain in Downtown and West Hollywood, where "LA's power hitters" and the "expense-account crowd" gather over "monster lobsters", "super steaks" and "perfectly concocted martinis"; the "serious" staff "doesn't mess around", and while some find the decor "dated" and "awkward", others "love the caricatures" of celebrities gracing the walls.

Palmeri   21 20 20 $41
11650 San Vicente Blvd. (Barrington Ave.), Brentwood, 310-442-8446

A "nice addition to the Brentwood area", this "high-end" Sicilian newcomer impresses with "nicely presented" "imaginative selections" on a daily-changing menu, including pizzas "with a delectable crunch" from a wood-burning oven; the service can be "a bit hectic" as the staff "gets their sea legs", and with the "tables so close together", the "noise level can be too much" for some.

Palms Thai ●   23 – 19 $16
5900 Hollywood Blvd. (Bronson St.), East Hollywood, 323-462-5073;
www.palmsthai.com

Fans lament this newly relocated East Hollywood Thai has turned into "hipsterville with a hard-to-bear wait", but the "long lines" are "worth it" for an "adventurous" menu that includes "toad and wild boar"; the staff's "zeal to turn tables can be a turnoff", but all's forgiven when the "killer" "Elvis impersonator" comes on; P.S. "when you ask for it spicy, they bring the heat."

Palomino   18 19 18 $34
10877 Wilshire Blvd. (Glendon Ave.), Westwood, 310-208-1960;
www.palomino.com

A "stylish" establishment, with a "unique, creative" Euro-Med menu, "friendly" staff and a "jumping bar scene" that draws an "attractive" clientele – "who would guess this is a chain" offshoot posit pros of this Westwood spot; detractors deem the cuisine "uninspired" and the service "spotty", but most insist it's a "place you can rely on" for a "nicer night out without breaking the bank."

Panda Inn   20 16 18 $23
111 E. Wilson Ave. (bet. Brand Blvd. & Maryland Ave.), Glendale, 818-502-1234
Centrelake Plaza, 3223 E. Centrelake Dr. (Guasti Rd.), Ontario, 909-390-2888

(continued)

(continued)

Panda Inn
3488 E. Foothill Blvd. (Rosemead Blvd.), Pasadena, 626-793-7300
www.pandainn.com
Sinophiles who prefer to "get away from the crowds in Chinatown or Monterey Park" "come back over and over again" to this triad for "creative", "dependable" Chinese at "reasonable prices", served in "clean", "elegant" surroundings; critics, though, feel the "food is becoming more like [fast-food sibling] Express", "except more expensive", and the service is "slipping" as well; P.S. the Pasadena location has an "amazing" Sunday buffet.

Pane e Vino　　　　　　　　20 | 19 | 19 | $34
8265 Beverly Blvd. (Sweetzer Ave.), Los Angeles, 323-651-4600;
www.panevinola.com
"Don't sit inside if you can help it" counsel cognoscenti at this trio of "affordable" Italians boasting "lovely garden patios" that are "perfect for a romantic date"; "always solid", "authentic regional dishes" and a "relaxing", "intimate" setting make it "as reliable and comfortable as going to the house of a dear friend who cooks well."

Panzanella　　　　　　　　23 | 22 | 21 | $42
14928 Ventura Blvd. (bet. Sepulveda & Van Nuys Blvds.), Sherman Oaks,
818-784-4400; www.giacominodrago.com
The "innovative, fresh" Northern Italian cuisine and "fine pairings of wine" from an "amazing" list "easily match the Drago family standard" at their "upscale" Sherman Oaks production; it's "a bit on the pricey side", and while some find the service "inconsistent" and feel the decor "could be better", others deem it a "worthy restaurant in a worthy location."

Papa Cristo's Ⓜ　　　　　23 | 10 | 16 | $16
2771 W. Pico Blvd. (Normandie Ave.), Los Angeles, 323-737-2970;
www.papacristo.com
There are "no pretenses" or "frills" to this Greek restaurant/market on a "sketchy" stretch of Pico in Mid-City, just "authentic" Hellenic fare ("unbelievable" lamb, "excellent chicken") and a "friendly" atmosphere; though the "cramped" room "feels like a hospital cafeteria", "you haven't lived until you've been there for family night" on Thursdays – "seven courses of bliss and belly dancing."

PAPADAKIS TAVERNA　　　23 | 18 | 25 | $41
301 W. Sixth St. (Centre St.), San Pedro, 310-548-1186;
www.papadakistaverna.com
There is "never a dull moment or a disappointing dish" at this Greek in downtown San Pedro that's "really dinner and a show – and both are excellent"; it's "noisy as all getout" and "you have to be in the mood for singing, crashing plates and dancing", but fans insist it's "one of the most fun evenings you can have."

Parker's Lighthouse　　　18 | 21 | 18 | $31
435 Shoreline Village Dr. (E. Shoreline Dr.), Long Beach, 562-432-6500;
www.parkerslighthouse.com
Yes, the "view is the draw" of this waterfront Long Beach seafooder housed in a "converted lighthouse overlooking the Queen Mary" and the bay; while some locals would leave it to the "convention crowd" and "tourists", others are "pleasantly surprised" by fin fare that's "reliable, if somewhat lacking in innovation", "nice ambiance" and a "civilized bar."

PARKWAY GRILL   26 | 24 | 25 | $46 |

510 S. Arroyo Pkwy. (bet. California & Del Mar Blvds.), Pasadena, 626-795-1001

A "Pasadena institution", the Smith Brothers' first restaurant is "still their best" and with new chef David Tarrin in the kitchen, it's "headed toward cool once again", offering "inventive" pizzas and Californian cuisine that's "creative but not overdone" in a "comfortable" space that is "elegance defined" with a "beautiful bar area"; "attentive, knowledgeable" service is another reason why it's many surveyors' "favorite for special occasions."

Pastina 🛇   22 | 17 | 21 | $33 |

2260 Westwood Blvd. (bet. Olympic & Pico Blvds.), West LA, 310-441-4655

"The chef cooks his mother's Neapolitan recipes" including "the best eggplant Parmesan" and the "friendly staff" delivers them with "lots of smiles" at this "casual" Westside neighborhood Southern Italian "beloved by the over-50 crowd"; "it's mobbed on Fridays and Saturdays", but "great for a Monday night" say those who "go at least twice a month."

Pastis   22 | 19 | 19 | $39 |

8114 Beverly Blvd. (Crescent Heights Blvd.), Los Angeles, 323-655-8822

"Excellent dishes" dominate the menu of this "charming", "little" French bistro on Beverly Boulevard, from "delicious sautéed frogs' legs" to its signature lavender crème brûlée; "very helpful" service is "without attitude", creating the perfect setting "for a casual meal, romantic date or serious business dinner"; P.S. the "once-a-month wine-tasting dinners are always worth it."

PATINA   26 | 25 | 25 | $70 |

Walt Disney Concert Hall, 141 S. Grand Ave. (2nd St.), Downtown, 213-972-3331; www.patinagroup.com

Chef-owner "Joachim Splichal is a master", and moving his Cal-French flagship from sleepy Melrose to the Walt Disney Concert Hall Downtown was a "brilliant move" say fans smitten by Hagy Belzberg's "sexy", yet "elegant" design, the "innovative" seasonal tasting menus (don't miss the decadent cheese and caviar carts) and the "flawless service"; if you can snag one of the "impossible reservations" and "you have money to burn, this is the place to light it on fire."

Patinette Cafe at MOCA   17 | 14 | 12 | $19 |

Museum of Contemporary Art, 250 S. Grand Ave. (bet. 2nd & 3rd Sts.), Downtown, 213-626-1178; www.patinagroup.com

For a "quick bite" during a break from touring the Museum of Contemporary Art, head to Joachim Splichal's Continental-French self-service eatery, set on a patio under a glass and metal canopy; "imaginative" salads and sandwiches, "reasonable prices" and "competent" service make it "convenient when you're in a hurry."

Patrick's Roadhouse   17 | 16 | 15 | $18 |

106 Entrada Dr. (PCH), Santa Monica, 310-459-4544

A "funky place for breakfast" and the "best burgers" around, this "classic LA" "relic" across from the beach in Santa Monica has "attracted celebs and power players" "for more than 30 years"; some scoff that it's "like a shrine to [Arnold] Schwarzenegger" (his mom's Austrian farmer's omelet is on the menu) and snarl about the "old" "diner" digs, but others just find it "real" "zany" fun."

Pat's   21   16   21 $33
9233 W. Pico Blvd. (Glenville Dr.), Beverlywood, 310-205-8705
"Bring your yarmulke" and keep it kosher at this Cal-Italian in
Beverlywood where the "variety of creative choices" and "well-
trained, culturally sensitive staff" win praise; given its "pretty"
setting and "excellent quality for the price", it's the place to "take
your observant parents" "for special occasions."

Paul's Cafe   20   18   20 $29
18588 Ventura Blvd. (Mecca Ave.), Tarzana, 818-343-8588
"Consistently good" Cal-French fare coupled with "moderate
prices invite repeat visits" to this Tarzana "favorite", a "poor man's
Café Bizou" offering a "cozy ambiance" just right "for dates",
especially "on a cold rainy Valley night", or a "Saturday evening
with friends"; but a few feel "it seems to have lost its luster" since
it changed hands – "sometimes it's good, and sometimes it's not."

Pearl ●⊠Ⓜ   ▽ 18   20   16 $37
*665 N. Robertson Blvd. (bet. Melrose Ave. & Santa Monica Blvd.),
West Hollywood, 310-358-9191; www.pearl90069.com*
"Heard it was just a club, but the food's surprisingly great" ("cookie
plate is heaven") attest those who party down to this WeHo New
American to "eat, drink, then dance"; but others toss it off as an "LA
scene" that "unjustly thinks very highly of itself."

Pearl Dragon   18   20   16 $31
*15229 Sunset Blvd. (bet. Monument St. & Swarthmore Ave.),
Pacific Palisades, 310-459-9790; www.thepearldragon.com*
Even if this weren't "the only sushi restaurant with a full bar in the
Palisades" ("excellent martinis") it would still be "crowded" with
trendies from the surrounding affluent hilltops because of its
"creative" Pan-Asian tapas, "pickup scene" and "slick decor";
though most feel "the area needs more places like this", a few
frown on the "slow service" and "hit-or-miss" menu.

Pecorino   20   19   21 $46
11604 San Vicente Blvd. (Mayfield Ave.), Brentwood, 310-571-3800
This "Cal-Italian" Brentwood newcomer (in the San Vicente
storefront space of the former Zax) "has potential" say early fans of
its "warm service" and "solid" "adventurous menu" that includes
"barely-out-of-the-water fish" and "fantastic wines"; though
"growing pains" include "long waits" and "noisy", "crowded"
conditions, most find it definitely "worth a second try."

Pedals   21   22   21 $31
*Shutters on the Beach, 1 Pico Blvd. (Ocean Ave.), Santa Monica,
310-587-1707; www.shuttersonthebeach.com*
Offering an "incredible" oceanside location, this "informal" Cal-
Italian in SM's Shutters on the Beach reminds locals "why they
live in Southern California" and "wows out-of-towners" as well;
brunch on "lemon ricotta pancakes and salads that are amazing"
and then "stroll along the sand later for exercise", just "get there
early, since they don't take reservations" at this "pricey" spot.

Pei Wei Asian Diner   16   13   14 $15
*3455 E. Foothill Blvd. (bet. N. Rosemead Blvd. & Sierra Madre Villa Ave.),
Pasadena, 626-325-9020
Valencia Crossroads, 24250 Valencia Blvd. (McBean Pkwy.),
Santa Clarita, 661-600-0132*

(continued)

Pei Wei Asian Diner

2777 PCH (bet. Crenshaw Blvd. & Rolling Hills Way), Torrance, 310-517-9366
www.peiwei.com

Though "not authentic", this rampant Pan-Asian chain and "inexpensive" "son of P.F. Chang's" "will do in a pinch", pleasing the population with a "huge" (not a pee-wee) "variety of dishes prepared your way" "on the spot"; it's a "new breed of quasi-fast-food" eating, with "mix 'n' match" noodles and stir-fries delivered in "clean, not fancy" digs; if detractors dub it "pseudo Chinese", for most it's a "welcome sight", especially when "traveling with kids."

Penang Malaysian Cuisine – | – | – | M

971 S. Glendora Ave. (Valley Blvd.), West Covina, 626-338-6138
Spreading the gospel of Malaysian cooking to West Covina, this offshoot of a NYC chainlet is luring locals with a plethora of spicy, adventurous dishes that integrate the exotic flavors of China and India; the unique setting transports you to the East, while satays, sambals and other dishes inspired by faraway lands seal the deal.

Peninsula Grille, The ∇ 22 | 27 | 24 | $48

Trump International Golf Club, 1 Ocean Trails Dr. (Palos Verdes Dr. S.), Rancho Palos Verdes, 310-303-3260; www.trumpinternational.com
The "spectacular setting overlooking the ocean" in Rancho Palos Verdes and the "Trump-i-fied" decor have diners gushing over this American in the Trump International Golf Club (fka Ocean Trails), where the "food is good, but the view seals the deal" ("go before sunset"); "pampering service" and "creative plates" please most, but you'll have to "break the piggy bank" to fill the Donald's coffers.

Pentimento ∇ 18 | 15 | 16 | $26

LA County Museum of Art, 5905 Wilshire Blvd. (Fairfax Ave.), Los Angeles, 323-857-4761; www.patinagroup.com
"Convenience" and a "pleasant" setting make the Patina Group's full-service cafe at LACMA an "enjoyable" respite for museum-goers; though protestors paint the Cal-Med provisions as "pretty ordinary", most maintain the fare's "better than average", right down to the pastries; N.B. now open for afternoon tea (2 PM–5 PM).

Peppone 23 | 18 | 23 | $56

11628 Barrington Ct. (Sunset Blvd.), Brentwood, 310-476-7379; www.peppone.com
"It hasn't changed a bit" say fans of this circa-1975 "old-school" Brentwood Italian where regulars "don't mind overpaying" to "treat themselves" to "fabulous" food including "awesome filet mignon meatballs", "superb" wines and "attentive" service; though the atmosphere may be "testosterone"-charged, the red-leather booths and wood paneling help keep things "cozy."

Pete's Café & Bar ● 18 | 18 | 16 | $26

400 S. Main St. (W. 4th St.), Downtown, 213-617-1000; www.petescafe.com
Hip hounds sniff out this "trendy", high-ceilinged outpost set in a turn-of-the-century building in Downtown's Historic District; fans "root for" the "upscale" New American "comfort food" (especially the obligatory, "to-die-for" Maytag fries and "best burgers in town") and wish, for Pete's sake, that the area "had more spots like this"; critics confess, though, that service is "variable."

Petrelli's Steakhouse 17 | 14 | 18 | $29
5615 S. Sepulveda Blvd. (Jefferson Blvd.), Culver City, 310-397-1438;
www.georgepetrellisteaks.com
Get "a decent hunk of meat for a small chunk of change" at this
"dependable" Culver City Italian steakhouse still going strong after
nearly 75 years; though foes scold it for "substandard" food,
loyalists laud this "old-timer" as a "good choice."

Petrossian Paris ⊠ – | – | – | E
321 N. Robertson (W. Beverly Blvd.), West Hollywood, 310-271-0576;
www.petrossian.com
Like "heaven on a mother of pearl spoon", this 20-seat French cafe,
a "secret hideaway" on Robertson Boulevard, serves caviar,
smoked fish and duck confit in a casual, yet elegant setting; do
note that prices are "in line with the Petrossian name."

P.F. CHANG'S CHINA BISTRO 20 | 19 | 18 | $26
Beverly Ctr., 121 N. La Cienega Blvd. (bet. Beverly Blvd. & 3rd St.),
West Hollywood, 310-854-6467
2041 E. Rosecrans Ave. (Nash St.), El Segundo, 310-607-9062
Paseo Colorado, 260 E. Colorado Blvd. (Garfield Ave.), Pasadena,
626-356-9760
326 Wilshire Blvd. (4th St.), Santa Monica, 310-395-1912
Sherman Oaks Galleria, 15301 Ventura Blvd. (Sepulveda Blvd.),
Sherman Oaks, 818-784-1694
The Promenade at Woodland Hills, 21821 Oxnard St.
(Topanga Canyon Blvd.), Woodland Hills, 818-340-0491
www.pfchangs.com
It may "not be authentic", but it's a "great formula" that works
attest "hordes of faithful" fans that "keep coming back" to this
"lively", "cool"-looking "champ of the Chinese chains"; "after an
endless wait, treat yourself" to "worth-the-trip lettuce wraps" and
"delicious" dishes with "just the right spices"; "don't know what the
fuss is all about" pout the put-off, who insist it "tastes corporate."

Philippe the Original ⊉ 21 | 12 | 15 | $11
1001 N. Alameda St. (Ord St.), Chinatown, 213-628-3781;
www.philippes.com
Head to the edge of Chinatown and enter this century-old
"institution", where you'll stand shoulder to shoulder with "cops,
Dodgers fans, stockbrokers and hippies" to consume the "best
French dip sandwiches" washed down with the equally admired
(and famed) 10-cent coffees; the sawdust-strewn floor enhances
the "original" experience; P.S. the wine list is "pretty decent" too.

Phillips Bar-B-Que 23 | 3 | 13 | $14
1517 Centinela Ave. (Beach Ave.), Inglewood, 310-412-7135 ⊠
4307 Leimert Blvd. (43rd St.), Leimert Park, 323-292-7613 ⊠
2619 Crenshaw Blvd. (W. Adams Blvd.), Los Angeles, 323-731-4772 Ⓜ
The "genuine article", this no-frills BBQ take-out trio offers
"superb" ribs, chicken and brisket that "compete with the best in
the country"; addicts advise new 'cue-comers to beware: the food
is so "good", once you have it, "you really gotta have it."

Pho Café ●⊉ 20 | 13 | 16 | $14
2841 W. Sunset Blvd. (Silver Lake Blvd.), Silver Lake, 213-413-0888
Thrifty hipsters converge at this Silver Lake Vietnamese whose
kitchen cranks out "tasty" soups and other "flavorful" fare ferried

by a "cranky staff"; the "mod" setting, though, may be "minimalist to a fault", and the "cool" clientele may wish to wear sunglasses to deal with "harsh lighting" better suited to "performing surgery."

Pho 79
21 | 6 | 13 | $11

29 S. Garfield Ave. (Main St.), Alhambra, 626-289-0239
727 N. Broadway (bet. Alpine & Ord Sts.), Chinatown, 213-625-7026

Pho-get about the "nonexistent" decor and pay a visit to these Vietnamese noodle houses priding themselves on "incredible soups" and other "delicious" goodies offered at "dirt-cheap" prices; slurp lovers keep focused on the fare and try not to get too steamed over the "inhospitable" (albeit "fast") service.

Piatti
20 | 20 | 18 | $30

101 S. Westlake Blvd. (Thousand Oaks Blvd.), Thousand Oaks, 805-371-5600; www.piatti.com

"Good" Italian food and a "comfortable" rustic setting make this Thousands Oaks chainster "an easy choice" for fans; if cynics sneer at a menu that "lacks variety", many find happiness in "desserts that alone are worth the trip" and the DIY pizzas (for children under 10).

Picanha Churrascaria
18 | 13 | 18 | $34

269 E. Palm Ave. (bet. San Fernando Blvd. & 3rd St.), Burbank, 818-972-2100; www.picanharestaurant.com

"Those tired of spa food" will surely score at these Brazilian "meat" meccas in Burbank and Palm Desert, where the never-ending protein supply is enhanced by the surreal sight of "waiters who dress like gauchos" and wield "really sharp knives"; if some find the "amount of food overwhelming" and the quality "pedestrian", many carnivores consider them "a delight."

Piccolo
▽ 26 | 15 | 24 | $45

(fka Piccolo Cipriani)
5 Dudley Ave. (Speedway), Venice, 310-314-3222;
www.piccolovenice.com

A day at the beach isn't complete without a trip to this Venice Italian that "transcends" its "so-small" space with "heavenly" dishes such as beet-filled ravioli tossed with poppy seeds; chef Antonio Muré (from Valentino, Las Vegas) and front man Stefano De Lorenzo (ex Il Moro) "seem to be having a blast" and "make you feel like a regular on your first visit"; N.B. reservations required.

Piccolo Paradiso
22 | 18 | 21 | $41

150 S. Beverly Dr. (Wilshire Blvd.), Beverly Hills, 310-271-0030;
www.giacominodrago.com

It might "taste like mama's in the kitchen", but it's really Giacomino Drago behind the burners cooking "paradisiacal pastas" and other "absolutely delicious" Italian fare at his "charming" Beverly Hills trattoria; it's "a little quieter" than bursting-at-the-scenes sibling Il Pastaio, so you can count on a "relaxing" meal made more "delightful" by the "friendly staff."

Pie 'N Burger
19 | 9 | 17 | $13

913 E. California Blvd. (bet. S. Lake & S. Mentor Aves.), Pasadena, 626-795-1123; www.pienburger.com

For a "good" 'n' "greasy" fix, sample a slice of "yesteryear" in the form of "mighty-fine", "hard-on-the-arteries" burgers and "unmatched pies" at this 1963 "national treasure" in Pasadena;

though the "name says it all", extra credit goes to the "best milkshakes" around and fries that "deserve to be acknowledged"; P.S. "bless this hole-in-the-wall, and may it never depart."

Pig, The　　　　　　　　　| 17 | 9 | 15 | $17 |
612 N. La Brea Ave. (Melrose Ave.), Los Angeles, 323-935-1116; www.thepigcatering.com
"Happy little piggies" trot over to this La Brea BBQ stop for "the best pulled-pork sandwiches" and "messiest" "Memphis-style ribs" in the city; while fans give the "small" joint points for "superb sides", 'cuenoisseurs criticize the "so-so" chow.

Pig 'n Whistle　　　　　　| 16 | 17 | 16 | $26 |
6714 Hollywood Blvd. (bet. Highland & Las Palmas Aves.), Hollywood, 323-463-0000; www.pignwhistle.com
Once a playground for stars from Hollywood's Golden Age, this "lovingly restored" landmark next to the Egyptian features a "beautiful" space complete with an "amazing" carved wood cathedral ceiling and "solid" Continental food; if the fare's "marginal" to some, others suggest to "stick with the fish 'n' chips" and grab "a pint."

Pink's Famous Chili Dogs ●⇷　| 20 | 6 | 13 | $9 |
709 N. La Brea Ave. (Melrose Ave.), Los Angeles, 323-931-4223; www.pinkshollywood.com
It doesn't matter if you drive a pickup truck or "arrive in a limo", "everyone waits in line" at the "elder statesman" of hot dog joints on La Brea for "the best dawgs in the universe" including a chili version as fiery as a "flame thrower"; the wieners have long served as restoratives to "post-bar hoppers" at 2 AM, and if you encounter "gastric backlash" from one of the "cholesterol bombs", remember that legions of the faithful think it's "well worth it."

Pinot Bistro　　　　　　　| 24 | 22 | 22 | $44 |
12969 Ventura Blvd. (Coldwater Canyon Ave.), Studio City, 818-990-0500; www.patinagroup.com
Joachim Splichal's "all-around" winner of a French bistro in Studio City maintains its reputation with its "fantastic" fare, "gracious" service and "comfortable", yet "elegant" setting; it "never disappoints" fans who deem it the "best in the Valley" for a consistently "wonderful" experience; P.S. children under eight-years-old dine for free, and the no corkage fee is "a big plus."

Pistachio Grill　　　　　　| – | – | – | I |
8560 Wilshire Blvd. (bet. La Cienega Blvd. & Stanley Rd.), Beverly Hills, 310-854-1020
This "unassuming" BYO yearling near the Beverly Hills border in the Wilshire corridor "slays the competition" with "delicious" Persian-Iranian fare and a pistachio hummus that's an "absolute must"; prices will "make you feel guilty for paying so little."

Pizza Rustica ●　　　　　| – | – | – | I |
231 N. Beverly Dr. (Wilshire Blvd.), Beverly Hills, 310-550-7499; www.pizza-rustica.com
Beverly Hills' gourmet pizzeria has roots not in New York or Chicago, but Miami's South Beach, with pies served whole or by the square slice, in variations both traditional (pizza Margherita; pizza con pepperoni) and exotic (baby greens and chicken breast; chocolate and ice cream); we'd say 'only in LA' – if that were actually the case.

Pizzicotto   23 | 16 | 19 | $28

*11758 San Vicente Blvd. (bet. Gorham & Montana Aves.),
Brentwood, 310-442-7188*

You'll think you're in "Little Italy in NYC" at this "charming"
Brentwood Italian where patrons sit "elbow to elbow" to feast on
"phenomenal pastas", "wonderful pizza" and other standards
from The Boot in a "cozy" (i.e. there's "no room between you and
the next table") setting; indeed, the "amazing" food (that "feels like
a grandma poured her soul into it") justifies the "wait" for a table.

POLO LOUNGE ◗   20 | 26 | 23 | $53

*Beverly Hills Hotel, 9641 Sunset Blvd. (bet. Beverly & Crescent Drs.),
Beverly Hills, 310-276-2251; www.thebeverlyhillshotel.com*

Certifiably "swank and sophisticated", yet "low-key enough to be
unpretentious", this "legend" in the Beverly Hills Hotel serves as
a second home to its "glamorous" clientele and as an ideal venue
for those keen on "stargazing"; the "really good" Continental food
is complemented by a "swell wine list", and visitors should know
that "a trip to LA isn't complete without sipping a martini" here.

Pomodoro Cucina Italiana   18 | 14 | 17 | $19

*201 E. Magnolia Blvd. (San Fernando Blvd.), Burbank, 818-559-1300
7100 Santa Monica Blvd. (La Brea Ave.), Hollywood, 323-969-8000
401 Manhattan Beach Blvd. (Morningside Dr.), Manhattan Beach,
310-545-5401
14622 Ventura Blvd. (Vesper Ave.), Sherman Oaks, 818-501-7400
21600 Victory Blvd. (bet. Canoga & Owensmouth Aves.),
Woodland Hills, 818-340-2400
www.pastapomodoro.com*

Thanks to "excellent value", "fresh ingredients" and a "casual
atmosphere", it's no mystery that locations of this Bay Area Italian
chain keep popping up like daisies in the Southland; if the fare's
"nothing special" to some, others opine that the offerings are "a
cut above the typical red-sauce" spots.

Poquito Más   22 | 10 | 16 | $11

*2635 W. Olive Ave. (Buena Vista St.), Burbank, 818-563-2252
10651 Magnolia Blvd. (Cartwright Ave.), North Hollywood, 818-994-8226
3701 Cahuenga Blvd. W. (bet. Barham & Lankershim Blvds.),
Studio City, 818-760-8226 ◗
Rolling Hills Plaza, 2625 PCH (Crenshaw Blvd.), Torrance, 310-325-1001
Valencia Town Ctr., 24405 Town Center Dr. (McBean Pkwy.),
Valencia, 661-255-7555
8555 Sunset Blvd. (Londonderry Pl.), West Hollywood, 310-652-7008
2215 Westwood Blvd. (Olympic Blvd.), West LA, 310-474-1998
21049 Ventura Blvd. (Paralta Ave.), Woodland Hills, 818-887-2007
www.poquitomas.com*

"Don't count on getting a seat", but don't let that deter you from
getting in line at these "popular", ubiquitous Valley-based Baja-
style taco stands, where the "incredible" tortillas, ahi tacos "that
rule" and "killer salsas" add up to the "ultimate" in Mexican "fast
food"; FYI, "if you think you can find something else this cheap
and tasty", then "head to Mexico."

Porta Via   ▽ 23 | 15 | 21 | $29

424 N. Canon Dr. (Santa Monica Blvd.), Beverly Hills, 310-274-6534

Beverly Hill locals "love" this 30-seat "neighborhood" cafe noted
for its "outstanding" Californian victuals served throughout the

day; fans go for the "wonderful breakfasts" and "delightful lunches" and add that the "caring" staff treats you "like family."

Porterhouse Bistro
21 | 18 | 21 | $44

8635 Wilshire Blvd. (bet. La Cienega & Robertson Blvds.), Beverly Hills, 310-659-1099; www.porterhousebistro.com

Naturally, "they do porterhouses right" at this "low-key" "no-attitude" Beverly Hills steakhouse "alternative" to the bigger guns, serving up a "prix fixe menu that can't be topped"; but while meat mavens swear by the "good value" "tender, tasty monumental steaks", bashers beef "the old saying holds true that you get what you pay for": "portions are tiny" and the "staff inexperienced."

Posh on Pico
– | – | – | I

5542 W. Pico Blvd. (Sierra Bonita Ave.), Los Angeles, 323-931-4338; www.poshonpico.com

Decorated with chandeliers and colorful tropical art, this new Latin-American bakery/cafe in the restaurant-deficient stretch of Pico in Mid-Wilshire features breakfast treats including banana pancakes and traditional Mexican sweet breads, and for lunch and dinner, a Latina burger flavored with Hispanic slight-of-hand.

Prado
21 | 17 | 21 | $30

244 N. Larchmont Blvd. (bet. Beverly Blvd. & 1st St.), Hancock Park, 323-467-3871

"A cut above the expected", this "tiny gem" on Larchmont owned by the "friendly" Prado family (who also run Cha Cha Cha) "sets the gold standard" with "zing"-packed "Caribbean delights"; the "special atmosphere", including "colorful ceiling frescos", "lovely" murals and non-matching chairs, adds a "wonderfully eclectic" element to the "charming" equation – it's "like taking a trip across the Americas in one dinner."

Prego
20 | 19 | 20 | $39

362 N. Camden Dr. (bet. Brighton Way & Wilshire Blvd.), Beverly Hills, 310-277-7346; www.spectrumfoods.com

"Local businessmen" and "power shoppers from Rodeo Drive" "stop to chow" "divine" wood-fired pizzas and Italian fare while "relaxing" in the outdoor patio at this "busy" duo in Beverly Hills and Irvine; if a handful find the food "uneven", ranging from "on a good day, the best" to "dependable, if not inspired", most retort there's "no need to reinvent what's already good."

Primitivo Wine Bistro
21 | 19 | 19 | $35

1025 Abbot Kinney Blvd. (bet. Main St. & Westminster Ave.), Venice, 310-396-5353; www.primitivowinebistro.com

"Come for the wine, stay for the wine" – and pair it with a "delicious assortment" of Med tapas at this "crazy cool" "killer of a place" on Abbot Kinney; the "pacing is perfect", the "energy great" and the "food not an afterthought" – just "learn to love thy neighbor because the seating can be too close for comfort"; still, for most it's "worth it" for a "night on the town" with the "beautiful people."

Prizzi's Piazza
∇ 23 | 18 | 17 | $29

5923 Franklin Ave. (bet. Bronson Ave. & Gower St.), Hollywood, 323-467-0168; www.prizzispiazza.com

For "surprisingly good" pizza and breadsticks loaded "with enough garlic to kill a vampire" swoop down to this "nice" "neighborhood" Italian "in the heart of Hollywood" that's "popular with the

Beachwood Canyon crowd"; still, the put-off pronounce "the staff surly", "which means it doesn't always feel welcoming."

Providence   ∇ 25 | 25 | 27 | $92
5955 Melrose Ave. (Cole Ave.), Los Angeles, 323-460-4170; www.providencela.com
Chef/co-owner Michael Cimarusti is "the anointed Neptune of California" – he's even "surpassed" the "high bar he set for himself at the Water Grill" at this "outstanding" new seafooder in the "spiffed up" former Patina space near Paramount Studios where frontman/partner Donato Poto (ex Bastide) also oversees the "superb service"; early-comers enthuse it's the "best fish-centered menu in LA" – we "didn't know that it could be fixed in so many creative ways" – plus the "wine pairings are astounding."

P6 Restaurant & Lounge ☻   ∇ 17 | 24 | 17 | $35
2809 Agoura Rd. (Westlake Blvd.), Westlake Village, 805-778-0123; www.p6lounge.com
The nightlife scene in "sleepy Westlake Village" just got a lot hotter with the addition of this "trendy" "up and comer" that "brings a little bit of Hollywood" to the Conejo Valley with modern American cooking and DJs who mix it up on weekends; but not everyone is so sure this is quite what the neighborhood needed, whining it's "oh, so very trendy, dahling", and ends up coming off as "silly" and "overdone."

Radhika's   19 | 15 | 16 | $22
140 Shoppers Ln. (Cordova St.), Pasadena, 626-744-0904
For "appropriately spicy" Indian, shoppers pop into this Pasadena standby and advise "come early" for the best selection from the "excellent-value" all-you-can-eat lunch buffet; but a few gripe that service is "friendly but slow" and find the fare a "disappointment."

Rae's ⊭   15 | 10 | 17 | $12
2901 Pico Blvd. (29th St.), Santa Monica, 310-828-7937
It's "hard to spend more than $10" at SM's "blast from the past" "greasy spoon" that serves "biscuits and gravy" "just like mom used to make" and "has appeared in so many commercials and films" thanks to its "nostalgia-in-the-flesh" "charm"; "nothing's changed since 1958", except perhaps the "local hipsters" who join the early-risers "waiting for a table on weekends."

Rae's ⊠   – | – | – | M
522 S. PCH (Beryl St.), Redondo Beach, 310-543-5100; www.raesrestaurant.com
Formerly known as Bella Blu, this friendly, cheery Redondo Beach Italian in a tiny storefront with an outdoor patio on PCH follows a New York–style Little Italy script, but adds a California flair to classics like fettuccine Bolognese, osso buco and tiramisu; an interesting cocktail list and monthly wine dinners enhance its local allure; N.B. unrelated to the same-name Santa Monica diner.

Ragin' Cajun Cafe   21 | 18 | 19 | $20
422 Pier Ave. (PCH), Hermosa Beach, 310-376-7878; www.ragincajun.com
If you're looking for "a loud, crazy" Cajun "place to get the party started", head to this "festive" little "slice" of the Big Easy in Hermosa Beach where the "decor is a kick", the house-brand "beer cold and refreshing" and the "jambalaya can't be beat" for

a "taste of the bayou"; if a handful "bam!" back it's "authentic" so long as "you're not from Louisiana", for most it's "gumbolicious."

Rambutan Thai　　　21 | 21 | 17 | $23

*2835 W. Sunset Blvd. (Silver Lake Blvd.), Silver Lake,
213-273-8424; www.rambutanthai.com*
"If a local strip-mall joint can be both cool and spicy, this is it" attest admirers of this "dark, stylish", "sexy" Silver Lake "neighborhood salvation" that shakes up "creative soju cocktails" and offers an "excellent twist on gourmet Thai"; but while the "consistently appealing" fare feels like "comfort food of the new millennium", a handful harrumph what's up with the "chilly service"?

RAYMOND, THE M　　　24 | 25 | 24 | $44

*1250 S. Fair Oaks Ave. (Columbia St.), Pasadena, 626-441-3136;
www.theraymond.com*
"A step back in time with all the innovations of today", this former caretaker's cottage–turned–"cozy retreat" "has been rejuvenated" under new ownership with a "charming, elegant" Matthew White–designed interior and three "intimate" patios, yet still "reminds us of the days when a roadside stop would reveal a marvelous adventure"; "when you want to splurge" on "delicious" Cal-Continental "gourmet" fare, it's the "quintessential Pasadena dining experience" and the "perfect place for a romantic date."

Real Food Daily　　　19 | 13 | 17 | $21

*242 S. Beverly Dr. (bet. Charleville Blvd. & Gregory Way), Beverly Hills,
310-858-0880*
514 Santa Monica Blvd. (bet. 5th & 6th Sts.), Santa Monica, 310-451-7544
*414 N. La Cienega Blvd. (bet. Beverly Blvd. & Melrose Ave.),
West Hollywood, 310-289-9910*
www.realfood.com
This "nouveau hippie" trio with a "simple, bright" ambiance and organic, "insanely healthy" fare "might not be everyone's cup of chai", but it's "great for vegans, and those who love them"; "who knew that" soy products "masquerading as meat could taste so" "tantalizing" – "for once, you can indulge and feel good about it"; still, a few throw a tempeh tantrum tsking it's "highly uninventive" and "slightly" too "pricey."

Reata Grill　　　16 | 19 | 18 | $29

*Promenade at Woodland Hills, 6100 Topanga Canyon Blvd.
(Oxnard St.), Woodland Hills, 818-347-2090; www.reata.net*
Truly "a Promenade sleeper" for straight outta Texas chow "done rustic style", this Southwestern saloon-style chain offshoot rounds up families with "big appetites" for "cowboy-sized portions" at "reasonable" prices; but "disappointed" gauchos grouch the "food lacks verve"; N.B. celeb-chef Grady Spears who was involved in the defunct Beverly Hills branch has moved onto other pastures.

Reddi Chick BBQ 🗷⇗　　　▽ 22 | 7 | 17 | $10

*Brentwood Country Mart, 225 26th St. (San Vicente Blvd.),
Brentwood, 310-393-5238*
Get in line and "gawk at the celebs" hiding beneath their baseball caps at this take-out BBQ "institution" in the Brentwood Country Mart; get ready for some "unbelievably good", "addicting" spit-roasted chicken and "wonderful fries" flavored with secret "patented seasonings", but brace yourself for virtually "no service" and "be prepared to fight for extra ketchup."

Red Moon Cafe ⊠   ▽ 16 | 9 | 16 | $17

Westdale Shopping Ctr., 11267 National Blvd. (Sawtelle Blvd.), West LA, 310-477-3177

Just off the 405, this "hard to spot" West LA "hole-in-the-wall" in a "plain-Jane mini-mall storefront" serves up a Pan-Asian "mixture" with the focus on "surprisingly good" Vietnamese fare; but it's a once-in-a-blue moon stop for others who frown the "food has no character" and the "utter lack of decor" makes it "feel more like a take-out joint."

Reed's   23 | 18 | 22 | $35

Manhattan Village Mall, 2640 N. Sepulveda Blvd. (bet. Marine & Rosecrans Aves.), Manhattan Beach, 310-546-3299; www.reedsrestaurant.com

Set in a "nondescript" site "next door to Ralph's", South Bay's "sweet, sweet hideaway" for "excellent" Cal-French cuisine "proves strip-mall and fine dining aren't mutually exclusive"; with "attentive service" and the "tinkling of a piano" Thursday–Saturday, it "fills the need for a special-occasion destination in this beach neighborhood"; still, a few proponents pout "please, please find a place worthy of your cooking."

Reel Inn   20 | 13 | 14 | $21

18661 PCH (Topanga Canyon Rd.), Malibu, 310-456-8221

"Don't be scared off by the communal bench seating" and "slow service" at this "funky" Malibu "beach shack" because this "real deal" "summer hangout" is a "shrine" for worshipers that like their "plentiful" plates of fish "fresh and basic"; slip into your "shorts and sandals", "get on line and choose, then return to your communal table – if this is your thing, you're home."

Ribs USA   21 | 9 | 17 | $18

2711 W. Olive Ave. (bet. Buena Vista & Florence Sts.), Burbank, 818-841-8872; www.ribsusa.com

"Abandon your sense of fashion, and undo the top button on your pants" because the baby-back ribs are "finger lickin' good" ("sorry, Colonel") and the "collard greens are done right" at this circa-1968 Burbank BBQ joint; "while waiting for your food", "munch on peanuts and throw the shells" on the sawdust floor ("as it should be"), but if that's not your idea of decor (it "blows" report a vocal few), "get it to go."

Rio Carnaval Ⓜ   – | – | – | M

29601 S. Western Ave. (Summerland St.), Rancho Palos Verdes, 310-241-0001

There's a samba floor show on Fridays and a Rio de Janeiro–style party every night at this new all-you-can-eat Brazilian churrascaria at the front of a motel on the border of Rancho Palos Verdes and San Pedro; the dark, nighclubbish-looking space sets the scene for an eating orgy, with grilled meats delivered by the skewerful and a hot/cold buffet to boot.

RITZ-CARLTON HUNTINGTON Ⓜ   24 | 26 | 24 | $55

Ritz-Carlton Huntington Hotel & Spa, 1401 S. Oak Knoll Ave. (Huntington Dr.), Pasadena, 626-568-3900; www.ritzcarlton.com

"Service is an art" at this "absolutely beautiful", "stately", recently revamped Pasadena institution "built for romance" where you will "be pampered" and "treated like royalty" in typical Ritz-Carlton fashion; the "amazing" chef, Craig Strong, always "dreams up great menus, especially his tasting menu", and "exceeds expectations" with "deliciously satisfying" European-influenced New American fare; P.S. the Sunday brunch "simply doesn't get any better" – and it's served in The Terrace restaurant.

Rive Gauche Cafe Ⓜ   21 | 24 | 22 | $34 |
14106 Ventura Blvd. (Hazeltine Ave.), Sherman Oaks, 818-990-3573
"The French decor may be a bit too frilly for most men" but never mind, this "comfortable old friend" in the Valley serves "real bistro food" accompanied by an "extraordinary wine list" in a "cozy farmhouse" atmosphere; the "charming patio" and "lovely" courtyard make you "feel like you're in Carmel", and what's more, "you don't have to shout to your dinner companion to be heard."

Robin's Woodfire BBQ & Grill Ⓜ   19 | 16 | 16 | $19 |
395 N. Rosemead Blvd. (Foothill Blvd.), Pasadena, 626-351-8885; www.robinsbbq.com
For "real deal" 'cue, make tracks to this "fun" memorabilia-filled smoky roadhouse next door to the Pacific Hastings Theater in Pasadena where the pitmaster gets it right and serves "large" platters of "unexpectedly fine" ribs and links ("love that garbage-can combo" served on lids); if a few find "service uneven" and the food "disappointing", for most it's a "gastronomic" BBQ bonanza.

Rocca   24 | 18 | 21 | $42 |
1432A Fourth St. (bet. B'way & Santa Monica Blvd.), Santa Monica, 310-395-6765; www.roccarestaurant.com
If you're looking for a "great date place" that's "different from the usual", this SM "real contender" for "foodie heaven" offers an "adventurous", "original", "sophisticated" roster of "rustic" homestyle dishes from every region of Italy; the "small" "portions are just right" and the "menu always surprises", except on "very special" "pig heaven" Tuesdays; if a few find the "ambiance lacking", supporters deem the "simple setting" a "bit of a relief."

Röckenwagner   23 | 19 | 21 | $46 |
The Edgemar Ctr., 2435 Main St. (bet. Ocean Park & Pico Blvds.), Santa Monica, 310-399-6504; www.rockenwagner.com
After two decades, chef/co-owner "Hans Röckenwagner has still got the magic" and "always has something playful" on the "seasonal" menu at this Austrian in Santa Monica, a "great place for a lingering conversation" that toes the line between "fancy" and "casual"; "every plate looks like it should be photographed", and if you stumble in during "white asparagus season", "you'll savor every bite" – nonetheless, "nothing beats" the "lovely Sunday brunch."

Rock 'N Fish   21 | 18 | 18 | $31 |
120 Manhattan Beach Blvd. (bet. Manhattan Ave. & Manhattan Bch.), Manhattan Beach, 310-379-9900; www.rocknfishmb.com
You can smell the ocean but you can't see it from this "noisy", "see-and-be-seen", "ultrafriendly" Manhattan Beach surf 'n' turf "hangout" with high-ceilings, French chandeliers and a patio with retractable roof; it "continues to please locals and visitors alike" with "can't-miss appetizers" like the "oak-grilled artichokes" that impart "smoky goodness", plus "excellent fish" and dry-aged steak and even the signature "grog that may turn you into a sailor."

Roll 'n Rye Deli   17 | 10 | 17 | $18

Studio Village Shopping Ctr., 10990 W. Jefferson Blvd. (Machado Rd.), Culver City, 310-390-3497

Maybe you "wouldn't expect to find such a good deli" in this "neck of Culver City", but catchers of the Rye confirm this 1960s throwback offers Jewish "comfort food" and "hefty" pastrami sandwiches, along with "great matzo ball soup" for those "sick" days; still, kvetchers shrug "it'll do in a pinch", but it's "overpriced."

Romano's Macaroni Grill   17 | 17 | 18 | $22

12875 Towne Center Dr. (bet. Bloomfield Ave. & 183rd St.), Cerritos, 562-916-7722
2321 Rosecrans Ave. (Aviation Blvd.), El Segundo, 310-643-0812
945 W. Huntington Dr. (5th Ave.), Monrovia, 626-256-7969
19400 Plummer St. (Tampa Ave.), Northridge, 818-725-2620
25720 N. The Old Rd. (McBean Pkwy.), Santa Clarita, 661-284-1850
Promenade Shopping Ctr., 4000 E. Thousand Oaks Blvd. (Westlake Blvd.), Thousand Oaks, 805-370-1133
25352 S. Crenshaw Blvd. (Airport Dr.), Torrance, 310-534-1001
www.macaronigrill.com

They don't take reservations and there's "always a long wait" at this "crowded" Italian chain that draws Mac daddies and the family; it "feels a bit like Las Vegas" with "roving opera singer" waiters "serenading you as you gobble down the goodies" and drink jug wine served "on the honor system", so "relax" and "enjoy"; if foes find the fare just "mediocre", even they admit "kids love it."

Roscoe's House of Chicken 'n Waffles 21 | 9 | 16 | $15

1514 N. Gower St. (bet. Hollywood & Sunset Blvds.), Hollywood, 323-466-7453 ●
730 E. Broadway (bet. Alamitos & Atlantic Aves.), Long Beach, 562-437-8355
106 W. Manchester Ave. (Main St.), Los Angeles, 323-752-6211
5006 W. Pico Blvd. (La Brea Ave.), Los Angeles, 323-934-4405 ●
830 N. Lake Ave. (bet. Mountain St. & Orange Grove Blvd.), Pasadena, 626-791-4890

You'll "drool every time you drive by" this "definitive soul food joint" because it's "the one and only place to get your waffle on", topped with the "biggest, plumpest, juiciest ever" Southern fried chicken (and perhaps a bite of mac 'n' cheese that "will make you daydream for weeks"); nevermind the "gruff service", "wait that'll kill ya" and "clogged arteries" because you can't "tamper with a legend."

Rose Cafe   19 | 17 | 17 | $22

220 Rose Ave. (Main St.), Venice, 310-399-0711; www.rosecafe.com

"Favored by creative types", this "funky", "bohemian" Venice coffeehouse near – but not at – the beach is "unbeatable for breakfast" and "the perfect place to discuss your script over a lunch" of "good healthy" Californian food; but for most it's "best for weekend brunch" – "if you can get a table on the patio" it feels like a "garden escape from LA" with a "Zen setting."

Rosti   16 | 12 | 16 | $21

233 S. Beverly Dr. (bet. Olympic & Wilshire Blvds.), Beverly Hills, 310-275-3285
Encino Mktpl., 16403 Ventura Blvd. (Hayvenhurst Ave.), Encino, 818-995-7179

(continued)

(continued)
Rosti

931 Montana Ave. (10th St.), Santa Monica, 310-393-3236
Promenade at Westlake, 160 Promenade Way (Thousand Oaks Blvd.),
Westlake Village, 805-370-1939
www.rostituscankitchen.com
"Comfort food to the max" affirm fans who flock to this "casual"
Italian chain for "super" rosemary chicken and roasted potatoes
straight from the wood-burning ovens; supporters praise the
"handy" Tuscan takeout that's "better than fast food", still, the
less-impressed roast it as "nothing to rave about."

Royal Star Seafood   18 | 12 | 15 | $23

3001 Wilshire Blvd. (Stanford St.), Santa Monica, 310-828-8812
"Good and plenty", "this one's a keeper" proclaim proponents of
this Hong Kong–style SM seafooder, a "bare-bones" place that's
probably the "closest thing to Chinatown on the Westside"; but
scores "shocked to discover it stopped serving dim sum" sigh
that was the "reason to eat" here – now it's "nothing special."

Roy's   24 | 22 | 22 | $45

6363 Topanga Canyon Blvd. (Victory Blvd.), Woodland Hills,
818-888-4801; www.roysrestaurant.com
"Mahalo!" sigh worshipers thankful for the "little bit of paradise"
found at Roy Yamaguchi's "festive" Hawaii Regional chain;
this "change-of-pace islander never fails to intrigue" with "highly
creative fare", "seafood prepared in a myriad of ways" and "old
standbys" served with "aloha spirit" in a "beautiful" setting; if a few
grumble that "the rep is better than the food", for most it's a "relief
from other me-too spots that lack" this "celeb chef's" "originality."

R23 ⌧   26 | 22 | 22 | $46

923 E. Second St. (bet. Alameda St. & Santa Fe Ave.), Little Tokyo,
213-687-7178; www.r23.com
Feel like a "true Angeleno" and seek out Little Tokyo's "back alley"
"warehouse district hideaway" for "inventive" Japanese creations
and "achingly fresh" sushi "served in a grand fashion on long
carved boards"; sitting on the "edge of civilization" in an "art-
gallery"–type setting that's "hip and elegant" replete with "über-
cool" Frank Gehry–designed cardboard chairs makes you want
to "discuss *Blade Runner*" – or just "power lunch" over an
"incredible meal" "with your most important clients."

Ruby's   15 | 16 | 17 | $14

LA Int'l Airport, 209 World Way (Terminal 6), LAX, 310-646-2480
Villa Marina Mktpl., 13455 Maxella Ave. (Lincoln Blvd.), Marina del Rey,
310-574-7829
245 N. Harbor Dr. (Beryl St.), Redondo Beach, 310-376-7829
Ave. of the Peninsula Mall, 550 Deep Valley Dr. (Crossfield Dr.),
Rolling Hills, 310-544-7829
Whittwood Mall, 10109 Whittwood Ln. (Whittier Blvd.), Whittier,
562-947-7829
The Promenade at Woodland Hills, 6100 Topanga Canyon Blvd.
(Oxnard Blvd.), Woodland Hills, 818-340-7829
www.rubys.com
Additional locations throughout Southern California
These ubiquitous "retro '50s-style" red-and-white diners are
"bright and cheery", "just like the ones in the movies" muse

celluloid fans who wax poetic about the "nostalgic", "familiar" American menu stuffed with "good burgers", "creamy shakes" and "cherry Cokes"; but detractors gripe it's "just standard chain fair", but even so, hey, "it's fun for the kids."

Russell's Burgers   18 | 12 | 15 | $14

30 N. Fair Oaks Ave. (bet. Colorado Blvd. & Union St.), Pasadena, 626-578-1404

"Nostalgia plays a large role" in the appeal of this "great local joint" in Old Town Pasadena, "a respite from look-alike chains"; "when you need good old-fashioned" American "comfort food", rustle up a "sloppy", "messy" half-pound burger, "fabulous hash browns" and "mile-high lemon meringue pie", "served with a smile" in a "warm", "dinerlike" atmosphere.

RUTH'S CHRIS STEAK HOUSE   25 | 21 | 23 | $54

224 S. Beverly Dr. (bet. Olympic & Wilshire Blvds.), Beverly Hills, 310-859-8744; www.ruthschris.com

"Year after year", this "clubby", "reliable" "old-school" Beverly Hills steakhouse chainster with a "talented staff" serves "consistently perfect" "tender, juicy" "sizzling hunks of beef" "drenched in butter"; "try to heed your greed – you'll be tempted to order all the sides, but try to refrain" because the "protein" is "filling" and it gets "pricey"; still, it's "splurge"-worthy, in fact, "hands down and forks up" it's among the "best of the chains"– you "cannot mess with a classic."

SADDLE PEAK LODGE Ⓜ   26 | 27 | 25 | $58

419 Cold Canyon Rd. (Piuma Rd.), Calabasas, 818-222-3888; www.saddlepeaklodge.com

Whether you park yourself "by the fireplace and wallow in rustic elegance" or sit "outside and listen to the brook", you're in for an "epicurean escape" at this "hunting lodge"–themed New American steakhouse, a "wilderness retreat" set in a former Pony Express station in Calabasas; while the menu is more streamlined under chef Mark Murillo, it's "still the place to go" "if you're game for game, have the bucks" and lust for farm-raised "meats you only see on *Animal Planet*"; it's all served by a "superb staff" with a "terrific wine list to boot."

Saddle Ranch Chop House ◑   17 | 20 | 17 | $25

1000 Universal Studios Blvd. (off Frwy. 101), Universal City, 818-760-9670
8371 Sunset Blvd. (bet. Crescent Heights & La Cienega Blvds.), West Hollywood, 323-656-2007
www.srrestaurants.com

"Yee haw!" never mind the "tourists" and "tequila-shot" crowd, this "kitschy", "wannabe honky-tonk" duo in Universal City and Sunset Strip may be the only place in town to get a "decent", "real Southern-style chicken-fried steak", plus, "surprise", the "brunch is a fantastic way to start your morning-after"; at any rate, please "ride the mechanical bull" before you eat.

Sagebrush Cantina   13 | 15 | 13 | $21

23527 Calabasas Rd. (El Canon Ave.), Calabasas, 818-222-6062

"Popular with the biker set and Calabasas locals", this "fun, funky, lively" Southwestern-Mexican "roadhouse on steroids" with a "huge patio" is "great for hanging with friends"; "do people really come here for food?" – well, some tip their Stetsons to the "enormous" weekend brunch, otherwise, most relegate it to

"gringo-style" grub that "tastes good after a few visits to the bar"
for a "stiff drink."

Sai Sai 🈯　　　21　20　19　$39
*Millennium Biltmore Hotel, 501 S. Olive St. (5th St.), Downtown,
213-624-1100; www.thebiltmore.com*
"The Japanese food with a spicy" Latino "twist" is "stunningly
good" agree adventurers who head to this "elegant" restaurant
in the Millennium Biltmore Hotel "before the theater" for "top-
quality" "special rolls from the sushi chef" and "savory" cooked
dishes, served by a "kimono"-robed "staff that takes care of your
every need"; but others sai it's expensive with smallish portions."

Saketini　　　▽　20　15　17　$33
150 S. Barrington Ave. (Sunset Blvd.), Brentwood, 310-440-5553
Blink and you could miss this "tiny" "oddly shaped" "Brentwood
sleeper" that serves "tasty" "nouveau" Asian fusion fare including
"delicious hot dishes", "creative" rolls and, yes, "great sake"; if
some sock it to the "inconsistent" service, deriding the "airhead"
staff, others shrug there's "room for improvement, so I'd go back."

Saladang　　　24　19　19　$24
*363 S. Fair Oaks Ave. (bet. California & Del Mar Blvds.), Pasadena,
626-793-8123*
*383 S. Fair Oaks Ave. (bet. California & Del Mar Blvds.), Pasadena,
626-793-5200*
These Pasadena siblings "knock your socks off" with some of
"the best" Siamese food outside of LA's "Thai Town"; "get there
early, or prepare to wait on the line" at the original, which serves
"reliably excellent" traditional fare in "an industrial, noisy setting";
Saladang Song next door is more "chic and modern" with an
"arty flair", "tranquil garden", the "speediest" "eye-candy staff"
and an "inventive" menu geared toward the "trendy" set.

Salt Creek Grille　　　20　20　18　$32
*Valencia Town Ctr., 24415 Town Center Dr. (McBean Pkwy.),
Valencia, 661-222-9999; www.saltcreekgrille.com*
"Perfect for an upscale, relaxed meal", these "Craftsman-style-
themed" American steakhouses pack in a "lively crowd" with
"fall-off-the-bone ribs" and a "rocking bar"; Dana Point is a "great
ocean-close choice with a wonderful fire ring" where you can "sip
your drink while waiting for your table", while Valencia is a
"fun" "Friday night gathering place" for "great jazz"; nevertheless,
detractors deem the fare "forgettable" and the staff "snotty."

Samba　　　▽　19　15　18　$32
*207 N. Harbor Dr. (Beryl St.), Redondo Beach, 310-374-3411;
www.sambaredondo.com*
"If you like a little meat with your meat" and "plenty" of "skewers
to pick from", you'll "enjoy" this "noisy" all-you-can-eat Brazilian
churrascaria in Redondo Beach, the "ultimate Atkins blow-out
restaurant" that's especially "fun" "if you go with a big group";
yes, the buffet can be "skimpy, but so are the dancers' outfits" –
and "who wouldn't like the samba girls?" – they're "hot hot hot!"

Sam's Ⓜ⇄　　　–　–　–　M
108 W. Channel Rd. (PCH), Santa Monica, 310-230-9100
Cozy and comfortable with a retro-Gallic feel enhanced by olive-
green-colored walls and cherry-wood accents, this welcoming

artist-designed bistro in Santa Monica Canyon's little Restaurant Row draws diners with an ambitious menu of Cal-Med creations and a well-rounded wine list; owner Sam Elias is usually on hand to make you feel welcome in this home away from home.

Sandbag's Gourmet Sandwiches   19 | 9 | 16 | $10
9497 Santa Monica Blvd. (Rodeo Dr.), Beverly Hills, 310-786-7878
11640 San Vicente Blvd. (Wilshire Blvd.), Brentwood, 310-207-4888
818 Wilshire Blvd. (bet. Figueroa & Flower Sts.), Downtown, 213-228-1920 ⑤
138 S. Brand Blvd. (bet. B'way & Colorado St.), Glendale, 818-241-0740
6404 Wilshire Blvd. (San Vicente Blvd.), Los Angeles, 323-655-4250 ⑤
9255 Sunset Blvd. (W. Sunset Blvd.), West Hollywood, 310-888-0112 ⑤
1134 Westwood Blvd. (Wilshire Blvd.), Westwood, 310-208-1133 ⑤
www.sandbaggs.com
"If you want" a "tasty sandwich" that's "original and made how you like it", "you've come to the right place" assert admirers of this "cute" chainlet that wraps up "every order" "with a chocolate chip cookie treat"; but it's not everyone's "brown bag" – gripers grouch that "for the price, you're better off making it yourself."

San Gennaro Cafe   16 | 14 | 18 | $24
140 S. Barrington Pl. (Sunset Blvd.), Brentwood, 310-476-9696
9543 Culver Blvd. (Washington Blvd.), Culver City, 310-836-0400
www.sangennarocafe.com
"Ten dollar wines by the bottle" and "homey Italian" dishes "make for happy diners" at this "lively", "welcoming" "neighborhood asset"; "casual" "Brentwood is home to the after-school crowd" while the supper-club-style Culver City site has "kitschy" Sinatra tributes and a "nightly piano player", and if a few quip the "live entertainment's" "covered in cheese", even they admit "somehow it works – pass the cheese, please."

Sapori   ▽ 22 | 22 | 24 | $35
13723 Fiji Way (Lincoln Blvd.), Marina del Rey, 310-821-1740;
www.sapori-mdr.com
Truly an "outstanding find", this "real delight" within the underappreciated harbor walk in Marina del Rey's Fisherman's Village lures those in-the-know with "thoughtfully prepared" traditional Italian fare and a "small, quaint" setting; the "caring owner" is "always on hand to offer suggestions from the excellent wine list", so enjoy the "hospitality" as you sit on the patio and "watch the sailboats march back into the harbor at sunset."

Sawtelle Kitchen ⑤   20 | 14 | 17 | $22
2024 Sawtelle Blvd. (bet. La Grange & Mississippi Aves.), West LA, 310-445-9288
There "aren't enough seats", so diehards would rather not put the word out about this "funky but fun", "cramped" "no-reservations" Sawtelle "secret" with a "caring staff"; "delicious" Asian fusion "comfort food" with a French-Italian "twist" is the lure, and whether you go for the "killer meatloaf" or the "one-dish wonder lamb shank", this is "fare you won't find anywhere else."

Scampi Ⓜ   ▽ 23 | 15 | 21 | $36
40 N. Mentor St. (bet. Colorado Blvd. & Union St.), Pasadena, 626-568-4959; www.scampirestaurant.com
You "would never guess by the looks of it that the food is top-notch" confide customers who congregate at this "quaint", "tiny but

comfortable" Pasadena "hole-in-the-wall" "in an obscure location" for "terrific" Cal-French cooking that flaunts Asian ingredients; if a few feel it "hasn't quite hit its stride", for most it's "always a delight", though adding a "can of nice color paint and lighting would perk the place up."

Schatzi on Main   15 | 15 | 16 | $36

3110 Main St. (bet. Marine & Navy Sts.), Santa Monica, 310-399-4800; www.schatzi-on-main.com

The "plentiful star-watching" and lively happy hour at "one of the few cigar-friendly places left in California" make Arnold Schwarzenegger's shrine to himself in Santa Monica "fun fun fun", plus the strudel-and-schnitzel-centric Austrian-European food is "solid and hardy", just like the "Governator himself"; but critics' total recall consists of "subpar dishes" and "no atmosphere."

Schwab's ●   16 | 18 | 16 | $24

Sunset & Vine Bldg., 1521 Vine St. (Sunset Blvd.), Hollywood, 323-462-4300; www.schwabsrestaurant.com

The "location is great" "before a movie at the Arclight" agree once-option-starved show-goers who seek out American "comfort food" at this "swanky", "cool throwback" to the long-defunct legendary diner where Lana Turner was discovered; but this "modern twist on Hollywood history" is too "schmancy" for disbelievers who snipe "this ain't the real place, so don't be fooled", and while the "the food is better than at the original" it still "needs breaking in."

Sea Empress   21 | 13 | 15 | $21

Pacific Sq., 1636 W. Redondo Beach Blvd. (bet. Normandie & Western Aves.), Gardena, 310-538-6868

It may be "in need of a face-lift", but this "typically humongous" South Bay Chinese dining hall still provides a "quick fix for authentic" specialties and "tasty dim sum" when "you don't want to travel to Monterey Park"; "cart service is fun, and good to the wallet", plus the "servers watch your tables like hawks, making sure your teapots are always full."

Sea Harbour   24 | 16 | 16 | $25

3939 N. Rosemead Blvd. (Valley Blvd.), Rosemead, 626-288-3939
Ranch Market 99, 1015 S. Nogales St. (Gale Ave.), Rowland Heights, 626-965-2020

Navigating the "exotic", "innovative" menu of fin fare is "easier if you speak Chinese" – and many diners do at this massive airport-hangarlike duo in Rowland Heights and Rosemead where the "exemplary" dim sum is "made to order" and the Cantonese seafood dishes "set a new standard"; "it's obvious the chefs put effort into creating" the "wide selection", all "brought to your table piping hot."

Seashell   20 | 17 | 21 | $36

19723 Ventura Blvd. (Corbin Ave.), Woodland Hills, 818-884-6500

A "staple" with the "early-bird special" crowd, this "always busy", "quaint" "old-school" Woodland Hills Continental seafooder with "accommodating" service is "still plugging along", pleasing plenty of patrons with "rich", "solid" "artistically prepared" dishes; if a handful huff it "feels like you're in a time warp", for most it's a "safe choice" with "a lot of charm."

Second City Bistro   23 | 22 | 22 | $33
223 Richmond St. (Grand Ave.), El Segundo, 310-322-6085;
www.secondcitybistro.com
Downtown El Segundo "really needed" a "grown-up" steak and
chops place like this "unexpectedly cosmopolitan" "hideaway"
agree admirers who also give kudos to the "good looking" refurb
that rendered this historic bricks-and-beams building "posh in a
rustic way"; "we're addicted" to the "innovative" New American
fare – "every dish is like a piece of art" – coupled with "friendly"
service, it makes for a "lovely evening."

Señor Fred ◑   17 | 19 | 17 | $27
13730 Ventura Blvd. (Woodman Ave.), Sherman Oaks,
818-789-3200; www.senorfred.com
Decked out like a "dark" "den of iniquity" with "plush booths",
this "sexy" Sherman Oaks sibling of Max is a "trendy" "hot spot"
offering "creative" takes on Mexican cuisine as well as "fruity
margaritas" and "amazing sangria"; to cynics underwhelmed by
the "froufrou" fare, it's little more than a "noisy" "pickup joint for
twentysomethings" with "expensive" "bar food."

Seoul Jung   ▽ 21 | 22 | 22 | $38
Wilshire Grand, 930 Wilshire Blvd. (Figueroa St.), Downtown,
213-688-7880; www.wilshiregrand.com
If you "don't have time to venture to K-town", fans tout this
"upscale" Downtown Korean in the Wilshire Grand for tabletop
BBQ that "delivers flavor", a "beautiful" space that includes "great
private rooms for entertaining VIPs" and "reliable" service; a few
feel the "portions could be bigger", as it is on the "pricey" side.

17th Street Cafe   19 | 15 | 19 | $25
1610 Montana Ave. (bet. 16th & 17th Sts.), Santa Monica, 310-453-2771
"Popular" for its "huge", "lovely salads", "fresh" New American
dishes and "deadly-to-a-diet muffins", this "cheery" neighborhood
cafe is the "quintessential brunch stop" for shoppers drawn to
Montana Avenue's upscale "in" boutiques and a "home away from
home" for a "leisurely lunch or dinner"; but beware "the clan" of
"stroller moms, who will mow you down while waiting for a table."

Shabu Shabu House Ⓜ   23 | 8 | 15 | $20
127 Japanese Village Plaza Mall (bet. Central Ave. & San Pedro St.),
Little Tokyo, 213-680-3890
There's "always a line" at this "one-dish wonder" in Little Tokyo,
sometimes "before it even opens", but the "fabulous" shabu-shabu
is "worth waiting for" "more than an hour"; the "high-quality meats
and veggies" you boil and then dip in sauces that "rock" also "make
you forget" the "non-decor" and "assembly-line" atmosphere.

Shack, The   18 | 10 | 14 | $14
185 Culver Blvd. (Vista del Mar), Playa del Rey, 310-823-6222
2518 Wilshire Blvd. (26th St.), Santa Monica, 310-449-1171
Perhaps it's "not for gourmets", but the signature Shackburger (a
"burger with a hot link") is "cholesterol heaven" for cronies of this
American duo of "dive bars extraordinaire" in Playa del Rey and
Santa Monica, which also serve "terrific cheese steaks"; the
"surfer" setting has a "strong Philly" accent and it's a "fun place
to watch a ball game" on TV, but "don't go on Sundays during
football season unless you are an Eagles fan."

Shaherzad   22 | 14 | 15 | $22
1422 Westwood Blvd. (bet. Santa Monica & Wilshire Blvds.), Westwood, 310-470-9131
"Gigantic portions" of "savory" Persian fare, "served with a touch of elegance", make this Westwood spot an "unbeatable value" and all but ensure that you'll "leave with leftovers", especially if you can't "avoid filling up" on the "excellent flatbread" "hot from the oven"; it "gets quite crowded" but fans insist it's "worth the wait."

Shane ●Ⓜ   ▽ 18 | 19 | 17 | $27
2424 Main St. (bet. Ocean Park & Pico Blvds.), Santa Monica, 310-396-4122; www.shanerestaurant.com
A "hip" new "place to be seen" in Santa Monica, this "trendy" Eclectic-Filipino spot is a "magnet" for "singles", boasting a "fantastic happy hour" and "spirited bar scene", especially on weekends when "DJs pump out house music"; fans praise the "great sides and apps", but most find the fare "uninteresting" and feel the staff "struggles" when it comes to service.

Shanghai Grill   – | – | – | I
9383 Wilshire Blvd. (Canon Dr.), Beverly Hills, 310-275-4845
In the heart of Beverly Hills, this classic yet simple Chinese standby pleases patrons with standard fare ranging from tangerine shrimp and kung pao chicken to Mongolian beef.

Sharky's Mexican Grill   18 | 11 | 15 | $11
435 N. Beverly Dr. (bet. Brighton Way & Santa Monica Blvd.), Beverly Hills, 310-858-0202
Burbank Empire Ctr., 1791 N. Victory Pl. (Empire Ave.), Burbank, 818-840-9080
Creekside Village Shopping Ctr., 26527 Agoura Rd. (Las Virgenes Rd.), Calabasas, 818-880-0885
1716 N. Cahuenga Blvd. (Hollywood Blvd.), Hollywood, 323-461-7881
51 The Paseo (Pine Ave.), Long Beach, 562-435-2700
841 Cordova St. (Lake Ave.), Pasadena, 626-568-3500
13238 Burbank Blvd. (Fulton Ave.), Sherman Oaks, 818-785-2533
2410 Sycamore Dr. (Cochran St.), Simi Valley, 805-522-2270
5511 Reseda Blvd. (Ventura Blvd.), Tarzana, 818-881-8760
111 S. Westlake Blvd. (Thousand Oaks Blvd.), Westlake Village, 805-370-3701
www.sharkys.com
Additional locations throughout Southern California
"This is what good Baja-style Mexican food is all about" say fans of this growing chain that appeals to a "hip crowd" as well as "fire fighters and police" with "killer fish tacos" and other "healthy" "fresh Mex" dishes "prepared simply and well"; a few find it a bit "pricey" for what it is, though the "service is nice for a fast-food restaurant" and helps excuse "mediocre" decor.

Shige   ▽ 23 | 19 | 18 | $33
(fka Shabu Two)
401 Santa Monica Blvd. (4th St.), Santa Monica, 310-576-7011
For "inventive" Japanese cuisine, including "excellent quality sushi", "fresh sashimi" and "creative dishes", shoot over to this "simple and elegant" "little secret" in Santa Monica just off the Third Street Promenade; the lunch prix fixe is a "fantastic buy" and the rest of the menu is "well priced"; P.S. former Matsuhisa chef Shigenori Fujimoto recently left, which may impact the Food rating.

Shima M   – – – M
1432 Abbot Kinney Blvd. (California Ave.), Venice, 310-314-0882
It's "like eating in Tokyo" at this "tiny", "low-key" newcomer tucked
in amid the bars on Abbot Kinney, serving "refined", "beautifully
presented" Japanese, including "very fine" brown-rice sushi and
"handmade" tofu, in a "minimalist" space with a "cozy" mezzanine;
its "attention to detail" makes this spot "worth watching."

SHIRO M   26 18 24 $44
1505 Mission St. (Fair Oaks Ave.), South Pasadena, 626-799-4774;
www.restaurantshiro.com
Definitely a "delight, year in and year out", this "perennial favorite"
in South Pasadena is "worth the trip" for "lovely presentations"
of "inventive" seafood-centric Asian fusion cuisine "done with
finesse", including the "amazing" fried catfish in ponzu sauce; a
"wonderful" staff makes you "feel welcome" and the setting is an
"oasis of relaxation", making it a "great date place", especially
"if you want to impress a foodie."

Sir Winston's   ▽ 24 23 24 $52
Queen Mary, 1126 Queen's Hwy. (south of Frwy. 710), Long Beach,
562-435-3511; www.queenmary.com
A "unique dining experience" awaits at this Continental blessed
with a "phenomenal location aboard the Queen Mary" in Long
Beach Harbor, where you can relive the "trans-Atlantic passage"
while tucking into "serious" fare; the "staff and ambiance make
you feel special" amid "sophisticated" art deco surroundings,
although critics charge it's "not up to" the "price tag."

Sisley Italian Kitchen   18 16 18 $24
15300 Ventura Blvd. (Sepulveda Blvd.), Sherman Oaks, 818-905-8444
The Oaks Mall, 446 W. Hillcrest Dr. (bet. Lynn Rd. & McCloud Ave.),
Thousand Oaks, 805-777-7511
Valencia Town Ctr., 24201 Valencia Blvd. (McBean Pkwy.),
Valencia, 661-287-4444
Westside Pavilion, 10800 W. Pico Blvd. (bet. Overland Ave. &
Westwood Blvd.), West LA, 310-446-3030
www.sisleykitchen.com
A mall "oasis", this "family-owned" Italian chain is a "handy"
option for "large portions" of "dependable" fare and a "nice array
of desserts"; "fast" service makes up for the "noisy atmosphere"
and while it's "nothing spectacular", "you could do a lot worse."

SKY ROOM, THE ⊠   23 25 22 $50
The Historic Breakers Bldg., 40 S. Locust Ave. (Ocean Blvd.), Long Beach,
562-983-2703; www.theskyroom.com
"Every evening is a special occasion" at this "classy place" atop
the Historic Breakers Building (now a senior living center), where
an attendant "in tux and top hat" leads you to the elevator that takes
you to the "high-class art deco" room with "truly spectacular"
views; "big-band dancing", "wonderful" New American fare and
"formal" service all contribute to make it a "romantic destination"
that's "expensive, but worth every penny."

Smitty's Grill   21 20 20 $33
110 S. Lake Ave. (bet. Cordova & E. Green Sts.), Pasadena, 626-792-9999
"Another beauty from the Smith Brothers" (Arroyo Chop House,
Parkway Grill), this Pasadena American offers a "roadhouse-

style menu" of "classic comfort food", including "skillet cornbread so good it should be illegal", and "friendly" service in a "dark, clubby" setting; a "wild bar" scene can make things "noisy" at night, though the "patio provides a safe haven" from the din.

Smoke House   19 17 21 $32
4420 Lakeside Dr. (Barham Blvd.), Burbank, 818-845-3731
"As much a museum as a restaurant", this steakhouse "standard" (circa 1946) in Burbank takes you "back to the days of the Rat Pack" with its "old-school charm" and "red vinyl booths"; the "incomparable" garlic bread highlights a "reliable", albeit "unremarkable", menu, and though critics dismiss it as a "faded star", others are "glad it's still here."

Sofi   21 22 20 $30
8030¾ W. Third St. (bet. Crescent Heights Blvd. & Fairfax Ave.), Los Angeles, 323-651-0346
The "flower-strewn courtyard" is a "perfect escape" and the "cozy" interior is like "someone's Mediterranean house" at this Third Street Greek; "delicious meze and entrees" are served by a "friendly" staff, and while critics find the fare "uneven", insiders insist it's "underappreciated."

Soleil Westwood Ⓜ   21 16 22 $29
1386 Westwood Blvd. (Rochester Ave.), Westwood, 310-441-5384; www.soleilwestwood.com
At this "bright spot in Westwood", chef-owner Luc Alarie "makes everyone feel at home" and his "friendly" staff showers diners with "lots of personal attention"; "wonderful", "reasonably priced" French-Canadian cuisine is served in "comfortable, sweet" surroundings with a "charming", "seductive" atmosphere – just the "place to impress a date."

SolyAzul Ⓜ   ▽ 16 19 18 $23
20 E. Colorado Blvd. (Fair Oaks Ave.), Pasadena, 626-796-0919; www.solyazul.com
"Just enough off the beaten path" to be "overlooked", this Mexican "tucked away in Old Pasadena" is an "eye-opener" with its "elegant", "chic" interior and "modern" "sophisticated menu" of "fresh" fare that's more than "just tacos and burritos"; a few cynics sniff that the *cocina* "looks prettier than it tastes."

SONA ⓈⓂ   27 23 26 $77
401 N. La Cienega Blvd. (bet. Beverly Blvd. & Melrose Ave.), West Hollywood, 310-659-7708; www.sonarestaurant.com
"Simply the best husband-wife team cooking and baking in LA", David and Michelle Myers are "visionaries" who "always take risks" in their freestyle approach to modern French cuisine, adding "subtle twists" and "unexpected ingredients" that result in an "astonishingly good" "dining experience" on La Cienega; the "staff bends over backwards" to assure that you have a "memorable culinary adventure", and the 1,300-selection wine list "boggles the mind" – just "make sure you're sitting down when you get the bill."

Sonora Cafe Ⓜ   22 21 20 $37
180 S. La Brea Ave. (bet. Beverly Blvd. & 3rd St.), Los Angeles, 323-857-1800; www.sonoracafe.com
"We forget how good the food is until we go again" to this "enchanting", "upscale sibling of El Cholo" on La Brea; it's LA's

"only real outlet for Southwestern cuisine" with "sublime duck tacos" and a "kick-ass bar" that pours "potent margaritas" – "take out-of-towners and watch their eyes grow big"; but cynics shrug it's a "snore-a" stuck in a "cuisine routine": "wake up call – it's not the 1980s anymore."

Soot Bull Jeep   25 | 7 | 14 | $24 |

3136 Eighth St. (Catalina St.), Koreatown, 213-387-3865
"The soot grows thicker" as the years tick by at this Korean BBQ "dive" in K-town; it's an "absolute must" given the "delicious", "aromatic" bulgoki and kalbi that you "cook on your own" at your table's charcoal grills, but do "expect a long wait" and "dress accordingly", as in "your worst clothes", since countless critics confirm that "you'll reek of smoke" "for days."

Sor Tino   19 | 16 | 18 | $34 |

908 S. Barrington Ave. (San Vicente Blvd.), Brentwood, 310-442-8466
Acolytes of Ago agree that this "pleasant" Brentwood relative is "worth the money" for Italian standards including "top-notch" gnocchi, "great pizzas" from the wood-burning oven and for its "pleasant" atmosphere; less sympathetic sorts scold it for "underwhelming food" and walk away "disappointed."

Souplantation   16 | 11 | 12 | $12 |

2131 W. Commonwealth Ave. (bet. Date & Palm Aves.), Alhambra, 626-458-1173
301 E. Huntington Dr. (bet. Gateway Dr. & 2nd Ave.), Arcadia, 626-446-4248
11911 San Vicente Blvd. (Montana Ave.), Brentwood, 310-476-7080
375 W. Ventura Blvd. (S. Las Posas Rd.), Camarillo, 805-389-3500
Puente Hills Mall, 17411 Colima Rd. (Asuza Ave.), City of Industry, 626-810-5756
4720 Candlewood St. (Faculty Ave.), Lakewood, 562-531-6778
Beverly Connection, 8491 W. Third St. (La Cienega Blvd.), Los Angeles, 323-655-0381
Villa Marina Mktpl., 13455 Maxella Ave. (Lincoln Blvd.), Marina del Rey, 310-305-7669
19801 Rinaldi St. (Corbin Ave.), Northridge, 818-363-3027
201 S. Lake Ave. (bet. Cordova St. & Del Mar Blvd.), Pasadena, 626-577-4798
www.souplantation.com
Additional locations throughout Southern California
A throwback to the days of Jazzercise, this successful self-serve American chain has turned the mundane idea of the salad bar into an "extreme" sport by offering an "overwhelming array" of goods – "excellent soups", "great" breads and pastas, and "yummy desserts"; granted, it's "totally un-hip", but at least it can be "fun" to play the "health"-nut or the "glutton" as you see fit.

South Street   ▽ 21 | 12 | 15 | $11 |

117 N. Victory Blvd. (Olive St.), Burbank, 818-563-2211
1010 Broxton Ave. (Weyburn Ave.), Westwood, 310-443-9895
www.southstreetcheesesteak.com
"Cancel the trip to Philly" and get your hands around the "best cheese steaks in the West" at these Burbank and Westwood Village favorites; aficionados avow that what you get is the "real deal" that's "on par" with the stuff from Philadelphia, but first you may have to "get the cell-phone-chatting college kids at the counter" to make you one.

SPAGO
26 | 25 | 24 | $66

176 N. Cañon Dr. (Wilshire Blvd.), Beverly Hills, 310-385-0880; www.wolfgangpuck.com

Wolfgang Puck's "incomparable" Beverly Hills flagship "lives up to its impossible reputation" and provides a refresher course on what a "premier dining" establishment can be; it's still the "center of the universe" for foodies who treat themselves to Lee Hefter's "unforgettable" Californian cuisine (including the "ever-famous pizza") and Sherry Yard's "incredible desserts" served by a staff "that treats you like a star" in a "celeb"-filled room; so, while the tabs may be "sky high", it remains "unforgettable."

Spanish Kitchen, The ◑
16 | 20 | 16 | $33

826 N. La Cienega Blvd. (bet. Melrose Pl. & Santa Monica Blvd.), Los Angeles, 310-659-4794; www.thespanishkitchen.com

Singles swing into this Mexican on La Cienega to toss down "great sangrias" while soaking up the "pickup scene" in a "splendid" south-of-the-border setting; the "dull" chow and staff "attitude", however, mean some "don't want to waste their time or money."

Spark Woodfire Grill
19 | 18 | 18 | $29

9575 W. Pico Blvd. (Beverly Dr.), Los Angeles, 310-277-0133
11801 Ventura Blvd. (bet. Carpenter & Colfax Aves.), Studio City, 818-623-8883
www.sparkwoodfiregrill.com

This Italian triad is a "real surprise" considering the "hearty fare" that arrives in "heaping portions"; though it's "standard" to some, backers say it's "great" for a "reliable" pizza; P.S. there's a "lovely view" of the Pacific at the Huntington Beach locale.

Spazio ◑
∇ 23 | 22 | 22 | $36

14755 Ventura Blvd. (bet. Cedros & Willis Aves.), Sherman Oaks, 818-728-8400; www.spazio.la

"Come for the food" and "stay for the great [nightly] live jazz" at this Sherman Oaks French-Italian showcasing a "delicious" lineup that includes "exceptional pasta" "cooked to perfection"; the "supper club" ambiance and "lively" bar makes it feel "special."

Spin Rotisserie Chicken
∇ 18 | 9 | 19 | $11

3216 Washington Blvd. (Lincoln Blvd.), Marina del Rey, 310-823-7299; www.spinchicken.com

Poultry partisans praise this Marina del Rey rotisserie specialist offering "quality" American fare with "tasty sides" like "creamed spinach better than grandma's" served by a "friendly staff"; it's "good and cheap – just the way I like my [chicken] breasts."

SPUMANTE ⊠
22 | 17 | 24 | $30

12650 Ventura Blvd. (bet. Coldwater Canyon & Whitsett Aves.), Studio City, 818-980-0734

So "welcoming" it's "like going to a friend's house for dinner", this Studio City Italian is a "winner" serving "excellent" Cal-accented Italian food that comes with a "reasonable" price tag; happy habitués hail a "romantic patio" that's "perfect for a relaxed meal."

Stand, The
18 | 15 | 16 | $11

17000 Ventura Blvd. (Genesta Ave.), Encino, 818-788-2700; www.thestandlink.com

Franks be to this Encino hot dog eatery for providing a "super selection" of "great", "gourmet" wieners; the "guilty pleasures" don't stop there, though, since you can wash everything down with beer and wine (served in "plastic cups"), and end with a "heavenly cobbler"; P.S. it's "kid friendly" to boot.

Standard, The ❶   15 | 22 | 15 | $31
The Standard, 550 S. Flower St. (6th St.), Downtown, 213-892-8080
The Standard, 8300 Sunset Blvd. (Sweetzer Ave.), West Hollywood, 323-650-9090
www.standardhotel.com
These "ultracool" coffee shops in Andre Balazs' "ultratrendy" hotels provide "perfect" perches for prime "people-watching" (especially at Downtown's "fab" rooftop bar) amid "retro", "lemon-yellow" decor; the Eclectic "comfort" fare splits surveyors – it's either "surprisingly good" or "standard" issue, and the staff's "only concerned about tomorrow's audition."

Stanley's   19 | 16 | 18 | $22
13817 Ventura Blvd. (bet. Mammoth & Matilija Aves.), Sherman Oaks, 818-986-4623; www.stanleys83.com
At this 20-plus-year-old "standby" in Sherman Oaks there's "something for everyone", from "delicious salads" (the Chinese chicken version "can't be beat") to "good" soups and seafood on an "affordable" Cal-American menu; the "charming patio" enhances the "pleasant" vibe.

Sterling Steakhouse ⊠ Ⓜ   – | – | – | E
1429 Ivar Ave. (Sunset Blvd.), Hollywood, 323-463-0008
Bringing a touch of class to Hollywood, this grand steakhouse serves prime meats with sauces galore in the space that once housed the hyper-trendy Sunset Room; there's also an outdoor patio built around a blazing fireplace, a wine cellar for private dinner parties and an imposing turn-of-the-century oak bar where hipsters gather for classic cocktails and an encyclopedic array of whiskeys.

Stevie's Creole Cafe   ▽ 21 | 13 | 13 | $28
16911 Ventura Blvd. (Balboa Blvd.), Encino, 818-528-3500
3403 Crenshaw Blvd. (W. Jefferson Blvd.), Los Angeles, 323-734-6975 ⊅
They may be far from New Orleans, but these Cajun joints whip up the "best gumbo you can find" and other "very good" items in portions "generous" enough to inspire a post-meal "nap"; rabble-rousers reveal that the Encino branch is "very, very busy on nights with music", which may account for "slow service", while Mid-City is mostly for takeout that "hits the spot."

Stinking Rose, The   17 | 18 | 17 | $31
55 N. La Cienega Blvd. (Wilshire Blvd.), Beverly Hills, 310-652-7673; www.thestinkingrose.com
"Bring a truck full of mints" to this "gimmicky" house of garlic on La Cienega that adds the stinking rose to everything; no item on the Italian menu is spared, not the "40-clove chicken", not the "succulent prime rib", not even the ice cream; while fans "love" the fare, opponents opine otherwise, and find it "unappetizing."

Suishaya   – | – | – | M
Hong Kong Plaza, 1017 S. Glendora Ave. (Valley Blvd.), West Covina, 626-480-8080
This spacious scarlet-hued sushi bar in the Hong Kong Plaza attempts to cover all bases with a menu of special rolls, as well as a wide variety of noodle dishes, rice bowls and house specialties

like salmon tartare with salmon caviar; for the undecided, there are three-roll combinations that easily feed two.

Sunnin
26 | 4 | 18 | $13

5110 E. Second St. (bet. Granada & Nieto Aves.), Long Beach, 562-433-9000
1779 Westwood Blvd. (Santa Monica Blvd.), Westwood, 310-477-2358
www.sunnin.com

A bona fide "dive", this five-table Westwood and its LB offshoot produces Lebanese food "so good it should be illegal", featuring "fabulous mezes", "tantalizing chicken kebabs" and "to-die-for hummus served by a "friendly" staff; the line of fans extends "out the door", but it's no surprise since this "jewel" is the "best of its kind outside Lebanon."

Surya India
22 | 17 | 22 | $31

8048 W. Third St. (Crescent Heights Blvd.), Los Angeles, 323-653-5151

You'll surya-ly savor a "mouthwatering" meal at this Third Street Northern Indian offering "awesome" fare that is "on the healthy side" in a "minimalist" setting; part of the appeal, for many, is the "personable servers" who are happy to help "navigate the menu."

Sushi & Kushi Imai
– | – | – | M

8300 Wilshire Blvd. (San Vicente Blvd.), Beverly Hills, 323-655-2253; www.sushiandkushiimai.com

Located in a mini-mall south of the Beverly Center, this industrial-looking Japanese is named after Takeo Imai, the chef who reputedly introduced sushi to LA; the eatery specializes in kushiyaki (meats and veggies grilled on skewers) along with Edo-style sushi (fish over warm rice) often made tableside at its 'sushi wagon', an homage to the ancient pushcarts where the dish originated.

Sushi Masu Ⓜ
▽ 24 | 14 | 23 | $37

1911 Westwood Blvd. (bet. Olympic & Santa Monica Blvds.), West LA, 310-446-4368

You could drive by a million times and never notice this West LA "sleeper" of a sushi bar, where the chef-owner manages to create "heavenly" Cal-accented Japanese fare worthy of an "artist" while "entertaining his guests"; given the "pretty-good prices", the "nothing-fancy" digs seem like an afterthought.

Sushi Mon
20 | 13 | 14 | $27

8562 W. Third St. (Holt Ave.), West Hollywood, 310-246-9230

"Fresh sushi" and "tasty rolls" bait backers to this Japanese eatery near the Beverly Center; if the "hilariously inconsistent service" sends some swimming away, others think the fare's good for the mon-ey (it's "surprisingly inexpensive"), and add that the place is "close to Cedars-Sinai if you're looking to date a doctor."

SUSHI NOZAWA Ⓩ
26 | 6 | 14 | $52

11288 Ventura Blvd. (Main St.), Studio City, 818-508-7017

A fixture to legions of fans, this "zero-decor" Japanese in Studio City humbles those who've tasted its "sublime", "superlative" sushi that's guaranteed to "ruin your enjoyment of the fare at the competitors"; the fish is so "undeniably exceptional" that even "celebs" "follow the rules" and "don't talk back" to "master" chef Kazunori Nozawa, whose "his-way-or-the-highway" attitude means you may feel "like you're spending an intimate evening with Mussolini"; N.B. closed weekends.

SUSHI ROKU   23 | 22 | 19 | $43

8445 W. Third St. (bet. Croft Ave. & La Cienega Blvd.), Los Angeles, 323-655-6767 ◗

One Colorado, 33 Miller Alley (Colorado Blvd.), Pasadena, 626-683-3000

1401 Ocean Ave. (Santa Monica Blvd.), Santa Monica, 310-458-4771 ◗

www.sushiroku.com

Schools of scenesters swim to these "beautiful", "buzzy" Japanese mainstays, where the "too-cool-for-school" crowds of "Hollywood A-listers and wannabes" tuck into "fabulous", "innovative" sushi; if some float around complaints about price (aka "Sushi Broke-You") and the staff ("uppity"), the trio still inspires fans who "can't live without them."

SUSHI SASABUNE ⊠   27 | 7 | 18 | $56

11300 Nebraska Ave. (Sawtelle Blvd.), West LA, 310-268-8380

"Go with the flow" and put yourself "at the mercy of the chef" at this West LA Japanese, where even patrons who object to "omakase" on principle bow down before "transcendental", "bliss-inducing" sushi that's packed with "fascinating flavors and textures"; it's a "unique experience", and most take a tip from devotees who forget about the "shabby decor" and sit back and eat up till either their stomachs or "pocketbooks call it quits"; N.B. closed weekends.

Sushi Sushi ⊠   ▽ 27 | 16 | 20 | $44

326½ S. Beverly Dr. (bet. Gregory Way & Olympic Blvd.), Beverly Hills, 310-277-1165

The few who know about LA's "best-kept secret" say it may look "plain", but this Beverly Hills Japanese creates "melt-in-your-mouth", "traditional sushi" that's "second to none"; though the "efficient service" can "slow down at busy times", the majority is "willing to wait."

Sushi Wasabi   – | – | – | M

1200 PCH (Pier Ave.), Hermosa Beach, 310-318-2781

With graffiti adorning the walls, this South Bay shopping-mall newcomer is going for a look that's as spicy as its name; choose from over 60 types of sushi rolls, and for those who prefer to walk on the mild side, there are staples like teriyaki and udon noodles.

Susina Bakery   – | – | – | I

7122 Beverly Blvd. (La Brea Ave.), Los Angeles, 323-934-7900; www.susinabakery.com

Formerly known as Sugar Plum, this "charming" bakery off La Brea is a "favorite for breakfast, lunch" and "sweet" treats; it's "impossible to resist" the "scrumptious" cakes and pastries, but it's also "lovely" for a "quick sit-down" over light American fare including "good soups, salads, quiches, sandwiches" and panini.

SWEET LADY JANE ◗⊠   26 | 14 | 17 | $16

8360 Melrose Ave. (bet. N. Kings Rd. & N. Orlando Ave.), Los Angeles, 323-653-7145; www.sweetladyjane.com

Sweets lady Jane Lockhart's "fabulous" "desserterie" on Melrose purveys "dreamy", "designer" baked goods – cakes, pies, pastries and other confections that rise to "perfection" – to patrons crammed into "small", "cute" quarters; the sandwiches are "surprisingly good" to boot, and more than a few romantics suggest it's "perfect for a date."

Swingers ☻　　　　　　16 | 17 | 16 | $16
Beverly Laurel Motor Hotel, 8020 Beverly Blvd. (Laurel Ave.), Los Angeles, 323-653-5858
802 Broadway (Lincoln Blvd.), Santa Monica, 310-393-9793
www.committedinc.com
"Actors in waiting", "hipsters" and "hungover rock stars" chow down on tuna melts and turkey burgers into the wee hours at these "retro" Americans in Fairfax and Santa Monica, where the "great breakfast" items, "fantastic milkshakes" and other diner-style fare arrive via "hot waitresses" clad in fishnet stockings; note all the "pretty people."

Table 8 ⊠　　　　　　25 | 22 | 22 | $54
7661 Melrose Ave. (bet. Spaulding & Stanley Aves.), Los Angeles, 323-782-8258; www.table8la.com
Govind Armstrong's "chic", "first-class" Californian beneath a tattoo parlor on Melrose features "sublime" cuisine fit for "foodies", a "relaxing" setting and an "unobtrusive" staff that "treats civilians like kings"; it's still "trendy", and fans agree that it's an example of "what restaurants must be like in heaven."

Taiko　　　　　　21 | 16 | 18 | $24
Brentwood Gardens, 11677 San Vicente Blvd. (Barrington Ave.), Brentwood, 310-207-7782
2041 Rosecrans Ave. (Sepulveda Blvd.), El Segundo, 310-647-3100
These "laid-back", "spartan" Japanese cafes feature a "wide variety" of "tasty fare" offered at "reasonable prices"; though they're considered "some of the better sushi places" in SoCal, the troika "set the standard" when it comes to udon and soba "delicious enough to please discerning experts"; P.S. the lunchtime bento box meal is a "super deal."

Taix French Restaurant　　　　17 | 15 | 21 | $27
1911 Sunset Blvd. (½ block east of Alvarado St.), Echo Park, 213-484-1265; www.taixfrench.com
Some "younger Angelenos" might feel out of place at this family-run Echo Park 1927 "institution" that "doesn't get any more old-school", with "saucy", "soup to nuts" French dinners, a "reasonable wine list" and "personable service", while others have discovered its "Dresdenesque""antiquated charm", making it a "hangout for the multicultural highlife" with "live music in the bar"; nevertheless, your visiting "great aunt" would "feel at home" at this "time warp."

TAKAO　　　　　　26 | 11 | 21 | $50
11656 San Vicente Blvd. (bet. Barrington & Darlington Aves.), Brentwood, 310-207-8636
"Rubbing elbows with celebrities" is unavoidable at this "jam-packed" "limited-seating" Japanese "favorite" in Brentwood where the "inventive, melt-in-your-mouth sea goodies shine under the careful tutelage of chef"-owner Takao Izumida (ex Matsuhisa); it's "not much for atmosphere", but service is "heartwarmingly friendly" and "the food is very special": "you will be astonished by the quality of the exotic omakase offerings", the "gold-plated sushi", the "impressive sake list" and the "high tabs."

Talesai　　　　　　21 | 17 | 19 | $31
9198 Olympic Blvd. (Oakhurst Dr.), Beverly Hills, 310-271-9345; www.cafetalesai.com

(continued)

Talesai
*11744 Ventura Blvd. (bet. Colfax Ave. & Laurel Canyon Blvd.),
Studio City, 818-753-1001
9043 Sunset Blvd. (Doheny Dr.), West Hollywood, 310-275-9724;
www.talesai.com*
"Sophisticated", "edgy", "arty" – yes, the ambiance varies from
one location to the third, but this Thai trio takes the same "light,
flavorful" approach to its "upscale" fare so "delectable" it can
make you into a "curry convert"; "very rarely are there any leftovers
to take home – we eat everything we order" – and "if the owners
are there, put yourself in their hands" and prepare to "be dazzled."

Talia's
▽ 23 | 23 | 21 | $42
1148 Manhattan Ave. (12th St.), Manhattan Beach, 310-545-6884
After a 15-month hiatus and a "beautiful renovation", this "friendly"
"new edition" of the Manhattan Beach date place "is even better
than the old"; "impeccable service", a location "just a short
distance off the ocean" and a "romantic yet hip ambiance" with
a Venetian chandelier and "sexy, low-lit" onyx bar set the scene
for "robust" Italian food that "hits the right notes"; sure, it's a "little
cramped, but worth it."

Tamarin 🅜
▽ 21 | 18 | 17 | $30
*Beverly Palm Plaza, 9162 Olympic Blvd. (bet. Oakhurst & Palm Drs.),
Beverly Hills, 310-777-0360; www.tamarindining.com*
"Don't let the strip-mall location fool you" because "serene beauty"
awaits at this "hidden Indian gem" in Beverly Hills with waterfalls,
plants, mirrors and Buddhas create a "blissful" ambiance and the
"charming chef-owner" has a "masterful touch", turning out a
"perfect hybrid of classic" and "unusual, intricate dishes"; but
critics carp that the "uneven service" is "sometimes problematic."

Tama Sushi
▽ 26 | 20 | 22 | $35
*11920 Ventura Blvd. (bet. Carpenter Ave. & Laurel Canyon Blvd.),
Studio City, 818-760-4585*
"Great value" and "really nice chefs" prompt patrons to "tell the
tourists to go next door" so they "can keep this" "elegant", "low-
key" Japanese "treasure" to themselves; "if price and fish quality
are critical to you", expect some of the "best and freshest on the
Boulevard", plus "outstanding appetizers and cooked dishes" – it
feels like "undiscovered sushi gold" on "Studio City's sushi row."

Tamayo ⓢ
▽ 20 | 22 | 20 | $34
*5300 E. Olympic Blvd. (bet. Amalia & S. Hillview Aves.), East LA,
323-260-4700*
Bravehearts who venture into East LA are rewarded with a
multiregional Mexican "feast" "at its finest" at this "well-hidden"
"oasis in a neighborhood known more for fast-food franchises";
the "spectacular setting" in a high-ceilinged mission-style space
with "extraordinary artwork" has a "church"-like feel, making it
an "interesting" "date" destination.

Tam O'Shanter Inn
21 | 22 | 21 | $33
*2980 Los Feliz Blvd. (Boyce Ave.), Atwater Village, 323-664-0228;
www.lawrysonline.com*
"There is something very comforting about the Tam" – "no wonder"
Lawry's older sibling has "thrived" in Atwater Village since 1922;
with a "kitschy but charming" "jolly ole England tavern" setting and

"waitstaff in Scottish garb", this "period piece" "beckons you back for more of the same" "lovely" "old tyme" American fayre, particularly "melt-in-your-mouth prime rib"; "come at Christmas time for the carolers" – it "really puts us in the holiday mood!"

Tangerine ◐   – – – E

8788 W. Sunset Blvd. (Halloway St.), West Hollywood, 310-360-0274
Inspired by hot spots of another era, everything's coming up retro at this tangerine-tinged Sunset Boulevard steakhouse, from the old-fashioned cocktails to the photos reminiscent of the Brown Derby to the newly introduced piano bar; even the fare, ranging from filet mignon to Eclectic offerings, is inspired by supper-club menus past.

Tanino   21 22 20 $38

1043 Westwood Blvd. (bet. Kinross & Weyburn Aves.), Westwood, 310-208-0444; www.tanino.com
For the "perfect meal before" a show at the Geffen Playhouse, head to this "tiny, appealing" Southern Italian Westwood Village "gem", "another Drago brother hit" named for chef-owner Tanino; the Renaissance-style "vintage 1920s space" is "as casual or formal as you want it to be", the "staff seeks to please" and the "Sicilian-based cooking is an indulgent pleasure"; but a few find the fare "doesn't quite live up to" the "beautiful setting."

TANTRA   21 25 18 $33

3705 W. Sunset Blvd. (bet. Edgecliffe Dr. & Lucille Ave.), Silver Lake, 323-663-8268
The "richly colored" dining room is a "great date hideaway", but the "sassy" "Indian-style *Sex and the City*" lounge area is the "real" "party scene", drawing Silver Lake "hipsters" with "Bollywood flicks" flashing silently on screens and "pounding" "trance music"; the "tiny bites" offer "daring" "twists" on subcontinental "staples" with "creative cocktails" "to match", and if critics carp about "pricey" tabs, for most the "groovy decor" is "worth the trip."

Taste   – – – M

8454 Melrose Ave. (La Cienega Blvd.), West Hollywood, 323-852-6888; www.ilovetaste.com
Set on Melrose in a converted bungalow, this homey WeHo newcomer offers diners a taste of the affordable life; watch the fashionistas flit from shop to shop on designer row from your perch on the patio or chill in the modern, leather-walled dining rooms, all the while sipping an intriguingly flavored lemonade or iced tea with innovative New American nibbles and entrees.

Taste Chicago   ▽ 20 9 18 $11

603 N. Hollywood Way (Verdugo Ave.), Burbank, 818-563-2800; www.tastechicago.biz
"Bravo to Joe Mantegna's" wife, Arlene, for "bringing Chicago flavors" to Burbank cheer boosters; "Eli's cheesecake", "Vienna" hot dogs, "decent" deep-dish pizza and "authentic Italian beef" sandwiches soothe the "homesick" blues for Midwestern transplants, who always "look for an excuse to pull off the 134 for a dose" of Windy City cooking at this "unpretentious little joint."

Tasty Kitchen   – – – M

1324 W. Artesia Blvd. (S. Normandie Ave.), Gardena, 310-515-2251
Owned by veterans of several nearby Cantonese restaurants, this brightly lit Chinese strip-mall spot in Gardena offers locals all-day

dining options aplenty, but it's particularly "crowded at lunch"; the expansive menu boasts a bounty of "solid, authentic" dishes, including an assortment of seafood pulled straight from the tank.

Taverna Tony
22 | 19 | 21 | $35

Malibu Country Mart, 23410 Civic Center Way (Cross Creek Rd.), Malibu, 310-317-9667; www.tavernatony.com

"Drink some ouzo and get up and dance" at this "lively" Greek eatery in Malibu showcasing "sublime" belly dancing (Fridays and Saturdays), "wonderful", "filling" fare including "delicious appetizers" and "friendly service"; the "noise" level on the terrace isn't nearly as "hard to endure", and the bar is the place to be "on weekends when it turns into a 'meat market' for singles."

Taylor's Steak House
21 | 17 | 20 | $33

3361 W. Eighth St. (bet. Normandie & Western Aves.), Koreatown, 213-382-8449
901 Foothill Blvd. (Angeles Crest Hwy.), La Cañada Flintridge, 818-790-7668
www.taylorssteakhouse.com

This 1953 "old-school" K-town stalwart and its suburban offspring win over meat-eaters' hearts by offering "consistently good" steaks on a "reasonably priced" surf 'n' turf lineup that delights "budget-conscious" carnivores; the "dark" decor replete with "leather chairs" transports you to "time warpville", albeit "for the good."

Tempest ⊠Ⓜ
▽ 27 | 23 | 25 | $34

Country Hills, 2933 Rolling Hills Rd. (Crenshaw Blvd.), Torrance, 310-891-0148

The word's out on this "up and coming" Torrance newcomer where the kitchen turns out "delicious" Californian fare ferried by a staff "that cares"; the "serene" setting negates the strip-mall locale, and helps make the newcomer "an excellent addition to the area."

Tempo
18 | 14 | 15 | $21

16610 Ventura Blvd. (bet. Balboa Blvd. & Hayvenhurst Ave.), Encino, 818-905-5855; www.tempobarandgrill.com

There's an up-tempo vibe at this Encino Middle Eastern where fans "love the live music" as much as the "tasty" food; its "nondescript" Encino digs may not inspire many fantasies and service can be "slow", but it's still a "wonderful" bet for a "taste of Tel Aviv."

Tengu
21 | 21 | 17 | $41

10853 Lindbrook Dr. (Glendon Ave.), Westwood, 310-209-0071; www.tengu.cc

"Hip" and "trendy" are written all over this Japanese-Asian in Westwood serving "fresh", "pretty-out-there" sushi to "beautiful" patrons sipping "exotic drinks" and "great sakes"; some say, however, it's "overpriced", and also warn that once the DJ starts "to crank it up", you'll have to prick up your ears "if you want to hear your dinner partner", as its gets "very loud."

Tenmasa ⊠
– | – | – | M

9016 W. Sunset Blvd. (bet. N. Doheny Dr. & Hammond St.), West Hollywood, 310-275-7808

A staple on the funky western end of the Sunset Strip for over 25 years, this bare-bones sushi bar serves up a Japanese menu of cooked favorites and sushi specialties that never changes; items like spider rolls, and tempura and chicken teriyaki still receive attention from tourists and loyalists alike.

Teru Sushi   21 | 19 | 21 | $36
11940 Ventura Blvd. (bet. Carpenter & Radford Aves.), Studio City, 818-763-6201; www.terusushi.com

A Valley "institution" dating to 1979, this Japanese "pioneer" in Studio City produces "reliably good" raw fare that keeps regulars "satisfied"; the "comfortable booths" and "large sushi bar" make it "wonderful for a quick bite or longer visit", and given the "friendly" floor crew and "tolerable prices", many say it "deserves respect."

Tesoro Trattoria ⌧   19 | 18 | 20 | $33
California Plaza, 300 S. Grand Ave. (3rd St.), Downtown, 213-680-0000; www.tesorotrattoria.com

"Hard to find but worth the trouble", this "pleasing" alternative to the "fancier places" near the Music Center feeds fans "pretty good" Italian food priced "reasonably"; since it's a "convenient" pre-theater option, the "fast staff" will get you "out the door in time for a show."

Thai Dishes   18 | 11 | 17 | $17
9901 Washington Blvd. (Hughes Ave.), Culver City, 310-559-0987
150 S. Sepulveda Blvd. (El Segundo Blvd.), El Segundo, 310-416-1080 ⌧
11934 Aviation Blvd. (W. 119th St.), Inglewood, 310-643-6199 ⌧
6234 W. Manchester Ave. (Sepulveda Blvd.), LAX, 310-342-0046
22333 PCH (bet. Carbon Canyon Rd. & Malibu Pier), Malibu, 310-456-6592
1015 N. Sepulveda Blvd. (Manhattan Beach Blvd.), Manhattan Beach, 310-546-4147
239 E. Colorado Blvd. (bet. Garfield & Marengo Sts.), Pasadena, 626-304-9975
111 Santa Monica Blvd. (bet. Ocean Ave. & 2nd St.), Santa Monica, 310-394-6189
1910 Wilshire Blvd. (bet. 19th & 20th Sts.), Santa Monica, 310-828-5634
23328 Valencia Blvd. (Bouquet Canyon Rd.), Valencia, 661-253-3663
Additional locations throughout Southern California

En-thai-ced enthusiasts "keep coming back" to this "reliable" Thai chain for "consistently good" fare including "solid" standards such as pad Thai; though negativists knock the fare as "uninspiring", others opine it's fine for a "cheap", "fast" meal; P.S. home-delivery devotees deem it "great for takeout."

THOUSAND CRANES, A   23 | 25 | 24 | $50
The New Otani, 120 S. Los Angeles St. (bet. 1st & 2nd Sts.), Little Tokyo, 213-253-9255; www.newotani.com

"If you want to impress someone", this "jewel" in Little Tokyo's New Otani hotel "does the trick" with a "peaceful" setting and "delicious", "authentic" Japanese cuisine featuring "excellent sushi" and "great tempura"; a stroll through the "beautiful rooftop garden" is a must, while the "meticulous service" and "spectacular Sunday brunch" make it a "special experience."

310 Lounge & Bistro ◑   17 | 20 | 18 | $44
3321 Pico Blvd. (Santa Monica Frwy.), Santa Monica, 310-453-5001; www.310lounge.com

"Feels like you're in a '40s movie", yes, even "Bogart and Bacall would approve" of this "chill" SM "spot" with its "sleek, sexy", "loungelike atmosphere" and "satisfying" New American fare; like "frosting on a very nice cake", jazz "sets the mood" for "ordering a martini" – "who can ask for more?"; apparently detractors who snipe that it's "lost its edge" "since the new chef arrived."

Tibet Nepal House
∇ 21 | 16 | 18 | $20

36 E. Holly St. (N. Fair Oaks Ave.), Pasadena, 626-585-9955;
www.tibetnepalhouse.com
The trek to Tibet begins in Old Town Pasadena, where one of the area's "best-kept secrets" offers "tasty", "interesting" Nepalese cuisine with a bonus of a "great lunch deal"; the "unobtrusive service" and "serene", if "somewhat dark" atmosphere may put you in a "meditative state."

Tlapazola Grill M
24 | 13 | 21 | $27

11676 Gateway Blvd. (Barrington Ave.), West LA, 310-477-1577
A "treasure worth discovering", this strip-mall "surprise" in West LA serves "seriously good" Mexican "so authentic you should be required to bring a passport to get in"; while the Oaxacan cooking "amazes", the "killer" margaritas and "warm" service keep fans "pleased"; one thing's certain: "it beats going to Mexico."

Toast
20 | 16 | 17 | $17

8221 W. Third St. (Harper Ave.), Los Angeles, 323-655-5018
"Spend more time waiting for a table than sitting at one" at this "crazy-packed" Third Street bakery/cafe, where the "terrific" American fare includes "great omelets and sandwiches", and "dangerously amazing desserts"; it's home of the "hottest weekend breakfast in town" and "brunch-central" for "babes", "scene" seekers and stealers, but "good luck with the service" ("can I get a fork? hello?").

Todai
13 | 11 | 12 | $24

Westfield Mall, 400 S. Baldwin Ave. (Huntington Dr.), Arcadia,
626-445-6155
Beverly Ctr., 8612 Beverly Blvd. (bet. La Cienega & San Vicente Blvds.),
West Hollywood, 310-659-1375
Cerritos Mall, 18425 Gridley Rd. (bet. 183rd Rd. & South St.),
Cerritos, 562-467-1668
Puente Hills Mall, 1600 S. Azusa Ave. (Colima Rd.), City of Industry,
626-913-8530
Glendale Galleria, 50 W. Broadway (Orange St.), Glendale,
818-247-8499
Studio City Plaza, 11239 Ventura Blvd. (bet. Tujunga & Vineland Aves.),
Studio City, 818-762-8311
20401 Ventura Blvd. (bet. De Soto & Winnetka Aves.), Woodland Hills,
818-883-8082
www.todai.com
They "may not attain the height of Japanese cuisine", say fans, but these sushi-serving, all-you-can-eat chain spots are there when you "need to replace all the carbs after a marathon"; detractors, however, deride the "bulk-over-quality" philosophy and caution to "leave your taste buds at home, as they won't survive the food."

Tokio ● ✉ M
∇ 19 | 21 | 15 | $37

1640 N. Cahuenga Blvd. (bet. Hollywood Blvd. & Selma Ave.),
Hollywood, 323-464-2065; www.tokiola.com
Pretty things swing to this "hip" Hollywood Japanese eatery/lounge sporting a "beautiful" setting (complete with rock garden) and featuring "not-too-shabby sushi", drinks and Wednesday-night karaoke; P.S. if you need to stretch your legs, be sure to "reserve the tatami table."

Tommy's ◐⇗ | 22 | 6 | 15 | $7 |

2575 W. Beverly Blvd. (bet. Coronado St. & Rampart Blvd.),
Downtown, 213-389-9060; www.originaltommys.com
For the "greasiest, sloppiest, best treat at 3 AM", "do right by
yourself" and visit this 24/7 no-seat Downtown "legend" serving
"amazing", "quintessential" chili burgers, and dogs and fries that
provide "great" backup; just don't forget words from the wise
who say "beware brother, beware" the "orange stains on your
fingers for days", "stinky car" and inevitable "heartburn."

Tongdang Thai Kitchen   ∇ | 20 | 17 | 21 | $18 |

Brentwood Gardens, 11677 San Vicente Blvd. (Barrington Ave.),
Brentwood, 310-820-3200
932 Huntington Dr. (S. Oak Knoll Ave.), San Marino, 626-300-1010
www.tongdang.com
Adoring acolytes "wish they lived closer" to this "lovely" Thai
twosome in Brentwood and San Marino; the "attentive" staff
presents "good" goodies including "terrific tofu dishes" and
"yummy soups" that, given the quality, are an "amazing value."

Tony P's Dockside Grill | 16 | 17 | 17 | $23 |

4445 Admiralty Way (bet. Bali Way & Via Marina), Marina del Rey,
310-823-4534; www.tonyps.com
"Sit on the patio", "watch the boats come in" and enjoy the "great
view" of the Marina del Rey harbor from your "plastic-chair"
perch at this American sports bar; "have a beer" and "catch a
game" on one of the "thousand TVs", but don't expect too much
from the "nothing-special" chow.

Tony Roma's | 16 | 13 | 15 | $22 |

68 W. Main St. (1st St.), Alhambra, 626-300-6656
333 E. Huntington Dr. (2nd St.), Arcadia, 626-445-3595
50 N. La Cienega Blvd. (Wilshire Blvd.), Beverly Hills, 310-659-7427
220 N. San Fernando Rd. (Orange Grove Ave.), Burbank, 818-557-7427
1901 Daily Dr. (Carmen Ave.), Camarillo, 805-987-4939
20720 Avalon Blvd. (E. Dominguez St.), Carson, 310-329-5723
16575 Ventura Blvd. (Hayvenhurst Ave.), Encino, 818-461-8400
126 N. Maryland Ave. (Wilson Ave.), Glendale, 818-244-7427
9335 Monte Vista Ave. (Frwy. 10), Montclair, 909-626-3391
3550 Porsche Way (Inland Empire Blvd.), Ontario, 909-484-8444
246 S. Lake Ave. (bet. Cordova St. & Del Mar Blvd.), Pasadena,
626-405-0612
www.tonyromas.com
Additional locations throughout Southern California
"Go for the babyback ribs and never look back" after ordering the
signature dish at this "family-friendly" BBQ chain offering "ample
portions" of food at "a good value"; though supporters swear the
fare's "tasty", critics cue up and counter it's "nothing special."

Torafuku | 23 | 21 | 21 | $39 |

10914 W. Pico Blvd. (Westwood Blvd.), West LA, 310-470-0014;
www.torafuku-usa.com
An American outpost of a trio in Tokyo, this West LA Japanese
delivers "high-caliber" fare featuring its much-heralded rice
that's "worth the hype", "excellent sushi" and the "best rolls";
"adventurous" eaters find "so many fabulous things to choose
from", and the "professional staff" helps make dining here
"enjoyable in all respects."

Toscana   24 | 17 | 21 | $47
11633 San Vicente Blvd. (Darlington Ave.), Brentwood, 310-820-2448
"Anyone who's anyone" goes to Brentwood's "granddaddy of Italians" serving "outstanding" Tuscan standards to a "packed", "noisy" house where "you're sure to see some stars"; the welcome is so "warm" (don't be surprised if "they hug you on the way out") that you may forget about the "pricey tabs."

Tower Bar ⊠   – | – | – | E
Argyle Hotel, 8358 Sunset Blvd. (bet. Crescent Heights & La Cienega Blvds.), West Hollywood, 323-848-6677
This swanky boîte at the art deco Argyle Hotel on the Sunset Strip has lured legendary maitre d' Dimitri Dimitrov (ex Diaghilev) to oversee one of the hottest new scenes in West Hollywood where Piero Morovich (ex Ammo) creates French bistro classics; the crowd is posh, and the supper-club setting retro-yet-thoroughly modern, with commanding views of the city.

Towne   17 | 20 | 15 | $39
1142 Manhattan Ave. (Manhattan Beach Blvd.), Manhattan Beach, 310-545-5405
As "trendy as it gets in the neighborhood", this "upscale" New American in "casual Manhattan Beach" beckons "beautiful people" with its "hip", "deafening bar scene" and "clubby ambiance"; though some find the food "good", others go to town on it ("average") and on service ("inconsistent").

Trader Vic's   17 | 23 | 19 | $47
The Beverly Hilton, 9876 Wilshire Blvd. (Santa Monica Blvd.), Beverly Hills, 310-276-6345; www.tradervics.com
"Mai tais are a must" at the Beverly Hilton's "old-school" "throwback", a "good substitute for a tropical vacation" that "originated" the fruity "umbrella drink" and kicked off the "'50s-style" "Polynesian" "tiki" trend; if a handful claim it's "holding its own" with "still titillating pupu" platters, most muse the "sun has set on this once-happening place" so "go for" the "over-the-top decor" and "kitschy cocktails, but beware" the "mediocre food."

Tra Di Noi   21 | 19 | 20 | $39
Malibu Country Mart, 3835 Cross Creek Rd. (PCH), Malibu, 310-456-0169
Feel like you're "in" with the multimillionaire "Malibu crowd" at this "homey" "Country Mart neighborhood" Italian "treasure" "peppered with celebs"; "come to watch the stars, but stay to enjoy" the "excellent food", from "delicious pizza" to "creative" specials, served by a "professional" staff; the "delightful" "outdoor patio is the place to be in the summer", but then again, "you want to sit here on spring and fall nights" too.

Trastevere   18 | 17 | 17 | $29
Hollywood & Highland Complex, 6801 Hollywood Blvd. (Highland Ave.), Hollywood, 323-962-3261
1360 Third St. Promenade (Santa Monica Blvd.), Santa Monica, 310-319-1985
www.trastevereristorante.com
These "pleasant", "upscale" Italians in the Hollywood & Highland mall and the Third Street Promenade are a welcome sight for weary shoppers lured by "surprisingly good", "interesting pastas" and the mirage of "an open-air cafe" in "Rome"; but detractors deride

it as "a fluff and flash" "tourist trap" with "mediocre food" that doesn't "match the fun locations."

Traxx 🗵
21 | 22 | 19 | $39

Union Station, 800 N. Alameda St. (bet. Cesar Chavez Ave. & Frwy. 101), Downtown, 213-625-1999; www.traxxrestaurant.com

The "age of elegance" lives on at this "noir fantasy" inside Union Station, "one of LA's most beautiful" historical buildings where the art deco–Spanish colonial architecture "harkens back to the days when train stations were the heart of the city"; the "movie-set"-like ambiance coupled with Tara Thomas' "well-executed" New American fare make it "great for a business lunch" Downtown, while "romantics" "enjoy" dining on the "lovely back patio."

Tre Venezie 🅼
26 | 21 | 23 | $52

119 W. Green St. (bet. De Lacey & Pasadena Aves.), Pasadena, 626-795-4455

"So inventive, and yes so true to Venice" – "there's passion in the kitchen" of this "charming little" "hideaway" in Old Town Pasadena; the masterminds behind this "truly intimate dining experience" hail from Northern Italy, apparent in the "authentic", "thoughtfully prepared" "fabulous cuisine" that's so "much more interesting" than "traditional Italian food", and it's all served by a "wonderful staff"; *si*, "it'll cost ya" a pretty "lire", but "it's worth it" for a "rare treat."

Trinity
– | – | – | M

San Gabriel Hilton, 225 W. Valley Blvd. (Del Mar Ave.), San Gabriel, 626-270-2700; www.hilton.com

This new restaurant at the San Gabriel Hilton is one of the area's most elegant, serving a mix of Asian fusion and Continental favorites along with a well-priced weekend seafood buffet.

Trio Mediterranean Grill
▽ 18 | 13 | 18 | $23

Peninsula Ctr., 46B Peninsula Ctr. (Hawthorne Blvd.), Rolling Hills, 310-265-5577; www.triogrill.com

It's "great" to have a "little bistro" with a "pleasant family atmosphere" in the neighborhood nod Rolling Hills regulars who convene at this "crowded", "good value" strip-maller for "imaginative" Mediterranean dishes; if a few frown that the "chairs are not made for long stays" and find the food doesn't match the "ambition", for most it's a "local gem."

Tsuji No Hana 🅼
22 | 13 | 20 | $29

4714 Lincoln Blvd. (Mindanao Way), Marina del Rey, 310-827-1433

Ever "since word got out, it's been hard to get into" this "favorite" Japanese hangout in a "nondescript" Marina del Rey strip mall; little wonder it has a "loyal following": the "owner makes you feel welcome" and you get "huge portions of tempura, sashimi and sushi at surprisingly low prices" with "fine sakes" to boot.

Tsukiji 🗵
▽ 26 | 18 | 22 | $35

1745 W. Redondo Beach Blvd. (Western Ave.), Gardena, 310-323-4077

"Close your eyes and you'll swear you're in Tokyo" at this "extremely authentic" sushi bar in Gardena where "Japanese businessmen" do deals over "masterful" "high-quality" eel and the "biggest, juiciest, plumpest, tastiest shrimp" ever; take a seat at one of the "elegant tatami tables" then "sit back and wait for your taste buds to explode."

Tufaan ∇ 23 | 18 | 20 | $22
4523 Sepulveda Blvd. (Ventura Blvd.), Sherman Oaks, 818-986-8555
"Not too many people seem to know" about this "friendly" Sherman Oaks Indian that puts a "nice" "nouvelle spin" on northern Indian kebabs and serves "very good" southern and coastal "mix 'n' match curries" that are "not like the rest"; insiders proclaim the neighborhood "is lucky to have" this "peaceful" "romantic" "pish-posh" spot, musing it "should be more popular."

Tuk Tuk Thai 21 | 15 | 18 | $20
8875 W. Pico Blvd. (bet. Doheny Dr. & Robertson Blvd.), Los Angeles, 310-860-1872; www.tuktukla.com
"We can tuk tuk a lot in our tummies and still have leftovers to take home" quip proponents of this "cute", "friendly", "loud" Thai cafe that "overflows with charm"; Westsiders are "hooked" on the "large portions" and "low prices" of "always fresh" fare, maintaining it's a "cut above standard neighborhood" choices and the "perfect take-out" option.

Tulipano Ⓜ ∇ 24 | 13 | 23 | $29
530 S. Citrus Ave. (Gladstone St.), Azusa, 626-967-6670
How this "little charmer" ended up "in a little-known spot in Azusa" may be a mystery, but "don't let the strip-mall location" or "1980s decor" "keep you away" because the Italian fare is "surprisingly excellent"; the "warm, friendly" owner greets everyone with "humor and a handshake" and the "kitchen is accommodating" making this "friendly" spot "worth the trek."

Tung Lai Shun ∇ 23 | 13 | 15 | $18
San Gabriel Sq., 140 W. Valley Blvd. (Del Mar Ave.), San Gabriel, 626-288-6588
"It's often very busy" at San Gabriel's "great place for dumplings" because word is out about the "vibrant flavors", also evident in the "handmade Shanghai noodles" and very popular lamb; but while the food is "interesting", don't come looking for pork or booze, because this "Islamic-style Chinese" follows halal dietary rules.

TUSCANY IL RISTORANTE Ⓢ 26 | 22 | 24 | $44
Westlake Plaza, 968 S. Westlake Blvd. (Townsgate Rd.), Westlake Village, 805-495-2768; www.tuscanyrestaurant.net
"A grown-ups' restaurant for West Valley people who don't want to trek to the Westside", this "excellent", "elegant" "longtime favorite" strip-maller serves some of the "best" "classic Italian" around with a "good wine selection and excellent appetizers to complement the main dishes"; as befits the "scrumptious" fare, "service is impeccable", and if a few find it a tad too "stuffy", for most it remains a "first-class option."

2117 Ⓜ 24 | 13 | 19 | $34
2117 Sawtelle Blvd. (bet. Mississippi Ave. & Olympic Blvd.), West LA, 310-477-1617
"The decor isn't anything special", but the Asian-European fusion "food will pleasantly surprise you" insist insiders who find "heaven in a strip mall" at this "quiet" "hideaway" on Sawtelle's Little Tokyo with "well-intentioned service"; the "wonderful" "prix fixe is a steal" and the "tasty entrees" boast "interesting flavor combos", all making it "worth the effort to find."

22nd St. Landing
▽ 19 | 17 | 18 | $29

141 W. 22nd St. (Harbor Blvd.), San Pedro, 310-548-4400

"If you like water and boats", set sail for this "relaxed" "fisherman's restaurant", a "local hangout" offering an "excellent view" of San Pedro's Cabrillo Marina and "fresh", "reliable seafood" served by an "attentive" staff; but it's less dock-worthy for a few faultfinders who find the "food good, but nothing memorable."

26 Beach Restaurant
20 | 17 | 18 | $23

3100 Washington Blvd. (Yale Ave.), Marina del Rey, 310-823-7526

"Kick back" with a "big bite after Rollerblading at the beach" at this "popular", "lighthearted" American in Marina del Rey with "thoughtful" servers and an "adorable English" tea garden; "you get lots for your buck", from "huge burgers" to "gigantic salads" with an "ample" side of people-watching; if a few feel it "lost its magic when it moved" from Venice, most maintain it's a "great neighborhood spot."

Twin Palms
16 | 21 | 17 | $36

101 W. Green St. (De Lacey Ave.), Pasadena, 626-577-2567;
www.twin-palms.com

"Fun" live bands contribute to the "great energy" of the "bustling" "singles scene" on this "cool" "tented patio", a true "urban oasis" in Pasadena set on a courtyard beneath twin palm trees; but while a few find the "awesome ambiance" in sync with the "beautiful food", most feel this once-pioneering New American "needs an infusion of inspiration", advising "stick to lunch" or the "affordable" Sunday jazz "brunch buffet."

Typhoon
22 | 21 | 19 | $34

Santa Monica Airport, 3221 Donald Douglas Loop S. (Airport Ave.), Santa Monica, 310-390-6565; www.typhoon.biz

Oh, go ahead, try the "worms", or at least the "crickets" – ok, so maybe the "squeamish" can't handle the "mind-blowing" "fresh insect dishes", but this "cool" Pan-Asian sibling to The Hump downstairs is still a "great place to experiment with exotic dishes"; "out-of-town guests may wonder why you're taking them back to" Santa Monica Airport, but "once they eat" the "spicy Mongolian beef" while "watching the planes", "they know why."

Ulysses Voyage
▽ 17 | 15 | 18 | $26

Farmer's Mkt., 6333 W. Third St. (Fairfax Ave.), Los Angeles, 323-939-9728; www.ulyssesvoyage.com

"A solid Greek option", this "charming" "surprise in the Farmer's Market" offers "fresh, well-prepared" meze made from recipes from the owner's mother, the matriarch behind Mama Voula and served by "flirty" waiters; "bring a friend so you can try all of the garlicky, flavorful dips" while sitting on the "delightful outdoor" patio or duck "inside by the fire, a very romantic" spot.

Uncle Bill's Pancake House
23 | 12 | 19 | $14

1305 Highland Ave. (13th St.), Manhattan Beach, 310-545-5177

"Get there early" or "bring the newspaper to endure the weekend wait" with the "masses of hungry humanity" who swarm this "crazy crowded" "old coffee shop" with "gruff service" and a "great view of the ocean" hoping to devour those "golden crispy waffles" and the "best pancakes in the South Bay"; flapjack junkies muse maybe "it's better to go during the week if you're playing hooky."

Urasawa
▽ 27 | 25 | 25 | $229

218 N. Rodeo Dr. (Wilshire Blvd.), Beverly Hills, 310-247-8939
Although the $250 prix fixe "seems inconceivable", a "magnificent" Japanese kaiseki "experience" awaits at this Rodeo Drive destination (in the former Ginza Sushiko space) with "unbelievably attentive service" that's even "better" now that it's run by "predecessor" Masayoshi Takayama's former assistant; sit at the "beautiful" tiny bar while chef-owner Hiroyuki Urasawa prepares "awesome sushi" and "tiny delectable plates that throw your palate for a loop"; "you salivate each time you go" – in fact, "words quickly become inadequate"; N.B. reservations required.

Urth Caffé
20 | 15 | 15 | $16

267 S. Beverly Dr. (Gregory Way), Beverly Hills, 310-205-9311
8565 Melrose Ave. (bet. La Cienega & San Vicente Blvds.), Los Angeles, 310-659-0628
2327 Main St. (bet. Ocean Park & Pico Blvds.), Santa Monica, 310-314-7040 ●
Start your "morning ritual" at this "packed" cafe trio with one of the "best lattes this side of Rome" made from "organic coffee", then move onto "healthy" American "sandwiches in a league of their own" and "vegan pastries that weigh as much as a small child"; "don't be intimidated by paparazzi on the street" – they're there to shoot the "celebs" soaking up the "sunshine on the patio."

Uzbekistan ●
▽ 19 | 13 | 16 | $25

7077 Sunset Blvd. (La Brea Ave.), Hollywood, 323-464-3663
"Get ready for something different" at this "weird", "welcoming' Uzbek supper club in a "Hollywood strip mall" where "old Russian women" pound back "shots of vodka" while "regulars" and "expats" tuck into "hearty" "feasts" reminiscent of the food served in its namesake "former Soviet Central Asian Republic"; P.S. the live Eastern European "entertainment is a major plus."

U-Zen
22 | 15 | 21 | $29

11951 Santa Monica Blvd. (Brockton St.), West LA, 310-477-1390
West LA's "quintessential neighborhood" spot has "a *Cheers* kind of coziness" with a "friendly staff that treats you like family" and "smiley chefs" that prepare "well-crafted sushi"; "so long as you don't mind vinyl booths and little atmosphere", "why go anywhere else" for Japanese at "very gentle prices"?

VALENTINO ⊠
26 | 23 | 25 | $65

3115 Pico Blvd. (bet. 31st & 32nd Sts.), Santa Monica, 310-829-4313;
www.welovewine.com
After over 30 years, "consummate host"-owner "Piero Selvaggio still deserves his reputation as an innovator" offering "world-class Italian" cuisine at SM's "chic", "ultimate date spot"; the "truly memorable experience" begins "the instant you walk in the door" and continues with "so many beautiful moments", from dining on "superb" dishes to choosing a bottle from the "extraordinary wine list" comparable to "Webster's dictionary"; if a few feel it's "coasting on past reputation", for most it "never disappoints."

Vegan Glory
– | – | – | I

8393 Beverly Blvd. (Orlando Ave.), Los Angeles, 323-653-4900
Aiming to please even the strictest of vegetarians, this simple vegan Beverly Boulevard storefront cafe with a sun-soaked dining room

and open kitchen uses a variety of meat substitutes and tofu to create a wide variety of Thai standards.

Venice Cantina

▽ 18 | 19 | 16 | $22

23 Windward Ave. (Pacific Ave.), Venice, 310-399-8420

A "favorite hangout" with a "cool vibe" near the beach in Venice for anyone who likes "watching sports on TV" and "drinking tasty margaritas", this "uniquely decorated" tequila-soaked sibling to Paladar and Lincoln offers "an interesting take on Mexican food"; but while a few applaud "service sans attitude", others hiss "beware the inexperienced staff."

vermont

21 | 22 | 20 | $40

1714 N. Vermont Ave. (Prospect Ave.), Los Feliz, 323-661-6163; www.vermontrestaurantonline.com

"Trendy but not overbearingly so", this "funky fresh" "class act in Los Feliz" with a "sleek, hip bar" serves up "delicious" New American for the "beautiful", "metrosexual" "late-night" crowd; you "can't miss" with the "well-prepared fare", "excellent drinks" and "buzzing, friendly atmosphere" – all of which make this "eclectic neighborhood restaurant" "enchanting" for a "date" or to "close a deal."

VERSAILLES

22 | 9 | 17 | $17

17410 Ventura Blvd. (bet. Louise & White Oak Aves.), Encino, 818-906-0756
1415 S. La Cienega Blvd. (Pico Blvd.), Los Angeles, 310-289-0392
1000 N. Sepulveda Blvd. (10th St.), Manhattan Beach, 310-937-6829
10319 Venice Blvd. (Motor Ave.), Palms, 310-558-3168
Universal CityWalk, 1000 Universal Studios Blvd. (off Frwy. 101), Universal City, 818-505-0093

"Get your mojo" on at these "popular" Cuban "comfort food" shacks where the "humble" "divey" digs are "tolerable" because the "sangria is cheap" and the "outstanding garlic chicken" among the "best this side of Havana"; you "can't beat the prices – they're lower than in Castro's" island – or the "fast service."

Vert

21 | 19 | 18 | $40

Hollywood & Highland Complex, 6801 Hollywood Blvd. (Highland Ave.), Hollywood, 323-491-1300; www.wolfgangpuck.com

"Interesting" French brasserie fare from a wood-burning oven, a "cool" setting and proximity to the "Kodak Theater" draw diners to Wolfgang's "oasis"; but others put-off by its location in the "Felliniesque collection of shops known as Hollywood & Highland" opine "it promises more than it delivers – it's not Puck's finest."

Via Veneto

25 | 19 | 20 | $52

3009 Main St. (bet. Marine St. & Pier Ave.), Santa Monica, 310-399-1843

If you don't mind "rubbing elbows" with strangers at the next table, you might find this "cozy" "family-run" Italian staffed with "witty waiters" "incredibly romantic" and even the "perfect date destination" on Santa Monica's Main Street; it's a "superb dining experience every time"– but maybe save it for the third date because "wow, is it expensive."

Vibe

– | – | – | M

The Belamar Hotel, 3501 Sepulveda Blvd. (Rosecrans Ave.), Manhattan Beach, 310-750-0300; www.thebelamar.com

On the second floor of the recently remodeled (and renamed) Belamar Hotel, this second-floor Californian sports a minimalist, industrial look, and a menu filled with cocktail-friendly food like duck confit egg rolls; not surprisingly, the bar looks larger than the restaurant, suggesting that the goal is martini scene first, designer food second.

VIBRATO GRILL & JAZZ   21   25   22 $56
2930 Beverly Glen Circle (Mulholland Dr.), Bel Air, 310-474-9400;
www.vibratogrilljazz.com
"What a perfect marriage" – the "guys from Pasadena" (aka Arroyo Chop House–Parkway Grill owners the Smith Brothers) "join forces" with music legend Herb Alpert at this "sophisticated" Bel Air "supper club revived" for contemporary times with a "modern", "jaw-dropping" decor, a "wonderful vibe" and an "impressive" American steakhouse menu; enjoy the "rare experience" of a "fun evening out" complete with "spectacular jazz" and "incredible acoustics" "well suited" for conversation.

Village Pizzeria   24   13   18 $13
131 N. Larchmont Blvd. (bet. Beverly Blvd. & 1st St.), Hancock Park,
323-465-5566; www.villagepizzeria.net
"Anyone who says there's better pizza than this is lying" taunt supporters of this "friendly" Larchmont Village "neighborhood" pie "nirvana" frequented by Hancock Park "celebs" and loyalists alike; the "excellent" offerings "satisfy those who want thin crust and no cheese" and "those who want thick crust with the works" – and it's even a "favorite" of "East Coast transplants jonesing" for a "great" slice.

Villa Piacere   20   23   18 $34
22160 Ventura Blvd. (bet. Shoup Ave. & Topanga Canyon Blvd.),
Woodland Hills, 818-704-1185; www.villapiacere.com
Everyone in the Valley wants to have a "great Sunday brunch" or "lovely" "summer evening" meal on the "lush patio" in the "heavenly" garden at this "cozy" Italian, a "hidden piece of paradise in Woodland Hills"; Villa people opine it's got "all the ingredients to make me a repeat customer", from a "warm, inviting atmosphere" to "solidly good food" and service; still, a few find the fare and service "inconsistent."

Villa Sorriso   18   21   17 $32
168 W. Colorado Blvd. (Pasadena Ave.), Pasadena, 626-793-8008;
www.sorrisopasadena.com
Now that its settled into "cool" "digs" near its "original" site, there's "more buzz" about this "popular" sophomore that "almost makes you forget that you're on a busy corner in Old Town Pasadena"; the "trendy Italian offerings" become a "treat" when eaten in the "lovely courtyard" while the "terrific upstairs lounge" makes it a "destination for singles and couples"; still, for most it's more about the "overall scene than the food."

Vincenti 🏠   25   23   23 $55
11930 San Vicente Blvd. (Montana Ave.), Brentwood, 310-207-0127
Amid the "overwhelming tide of Brentwood Italian restaurants" is "one of the classiest", "presided over by Maureen" Vincenti, an "owner who truly cares" and "sets the tone" for an "all-around marvelous" experience enhanced by "unobtrusive service"; only the "freshest, finest ingredients" are used to prepare the "excellent food" – this is the stuff dreams are made of" – making it "worthy of a return visit – again, and again and again!"

Vineyard Terrace   ▽ 18 | 16 | 18 | $38
Restaurant & Wine Bar
11266 Ventura Blvd. (Vineland Ave.), Studio City, 818-506-9463;
www.vineyardterracerestaurant.com
"Though it's still getting its legs, this "friendly" Studio City yearling
boasting a menu inspired by the California wine country is "one to
keep an eye on", with an "interesting" vino list that "complements"
the "solid food"; but others suggest you "forego the inconsistent
entrees" and "stick to the flights" and "happy-hour appetizers."

Violet Ⓜ   22 | 18 | 21 | $36
3221 Pico Blvd. (32nd St.), Santa Monica, 310-453-9113
At this Santa Monica yearling, a "creative young chef" puts
"original twists" on Cal-Med "comfort food" like "brilliant" mac 'n'
cheese, offering a "palette of color and taste" in "human-sized"
portions; but while the "knowledgeable staff enhances your
dining experience", a few sing the blues about the "tiny menu"
and portions – "when they say small plates, they mean it" – and
"wish it wasn't so noisy" "on weekends."

V.I.P. Harbor Seafood   21 | 13 | 15 | $23
11701 Wilshire Blvd. (Barrington Ave.), West LA, 310-979-3377
One of the "only choices" on the Westside for "dimply sumlicious"
"authentic dim sum" and seafood "fresh from the tank", this
standby sprawled across the second floor of a strip mall serves
"Chinese as it should be"; never mind that it "has all the ambiance
of a third-rate hotel ballroom", because "the cooks rival those in
Monterey Park", well, almost.

Vitello's   16 | 16 | 18 | $25
4349 Tujunga Ave. (Moorpark St.), Studio City, 818-769-0905;
www.vitellosrestaurant.com
Though now under new ownership, there's no denying "Robert
Blake" made this "midpriced" "red-sauce" Studio City Italian
"joint" famous, and although the "question of 'did he or didn't
he?'" was settled by a jury, the question remains as to whether
the "old-world charm" and "dependable" dishes warrant more
than a looky-loo; still, loyalists declare "forget the controversy" –
"it's a lotta fun when you go to the opera lounge."

Vito   22 | 20 | 21 | $36
2807 Ocean Park Blvd. (28th St.), Santa Monica, 310-450-4999;
www.vitorestaurant.com
"Ask for a special dining card" and reap the rewards at this
"reliable", "intimate", "crowded" and "clubby" "real New York–
style Italian" with "attentive waiters" who "still wear tuxes"; with
it's "heavy-handed" "charm", "old Italian feel" and "Caesars
prepared tableside", this hidden Santa Monica gem is "almost
the last" of its kind.

Vittorio Ⓜ   18 | 12 | 18 | $22
16646 Marquez Ave. (Sunset Blvd.), Pacific Palisades, 310-459-9316
By virtue of its Pacific Palisades location, you're bound to see a
few "celebrity" faces at this "real trattoria", a "neighborhood
treasure" that's "good for when mamma doesn't want to boil a
pot" of water; but while some "can never get enough of the little
garlic rolls" and "pretty good pasta", many can do without the
"surprisingly unfriendly staff" at this "family place."

Vivoli Café & Trattoria
▽ 26 | 15 | 24 | $29

7994 Sunset Blvd. (Laurel Ave.), West Hollywood, 323-656-5050;
www.vivolicafe.com

It's hard to believe there are any "neighborhood secrets" left on
Sunset Boulevard, but that's how surveyors describe this "cozy,
comfy little" Italian "find in a hole-in-the-wall" strip-mall location; "it
is such a delight", with "simple but great tasting food", "charming
service" and a "host who remembers regulars."

Wa ●Ⓜ
▽ 27 | 11 | 22 | $52

La Cienega Plaza, 1106 N. La Cienega Blvd. (Holloway Dr.),
West Hollywood, 310-854-7285

"Although the location on the second floor" of a strip center on La
Cienega "is a dump", there's really "only one word to say about"
this Japanese fusion "hangout": it's "exceptional" thanks to the
"three talented chefs", all former disciples of Nobu Matsuhisa;
while the "sushi is spectacular", it's easy to get "distracted" by the
other "incredibly creative dishes" that spur "recurring dreams."

Wabi-Sabi
21 | 19 | 18 | $39

1635 Abbot Kinney Blvd. (Venice Blvd.), Venice, 310-314-2229

"Off the charts", "fresh sashimi" and sushi "coupled with star
sightings, make for fun nights out" at this "trendy Abbot Kinney"
Asian fusion "standby" with "hip, Zen architecture"; the "vibe" is
so "good" there's even a "bustling" feel "on Sunday nights"; but
others shrug "Wabi-Sabi" does just an "ok jobby", dismissing the
"overpriced" fare as "pretty standard."

Wahib's Middle East
▽ 19 | 12 | 18 | $18

910 E. Main St. (bet. Garfield Ave. & Mission Dr.), Alhambra,
626-576-1048; www.wahibsmiddleeast.com

When the craving hits for "delicious Middle Eastern food" and
a "smorgasbord" of "good meze" acolytes descend on this
Alhambra standby; it's a "great value" with "consistent", "generous
portions" and a "helpful" staff; still, a few former habitués huff it
"used to be much better."

Wahoo Shabu Shabu
– | – | – | M

111 N. Atlantic Blvd. (W. Garvey Ave.), Monterey Park, 626-293-8322

Wahoo, this modern Monterey Park Japanese done up with
contemporary lighting and flat-screen TVs serves some of the
most upscale shabu-shabu in town; it's "great" fun to swish-swish
your meat, veggies or seafood in a bubbling hot pot on a "cold
night"; there's a bevy of appetizers to complete the experience.

Warszawa Ⓜ
23 | 18 | 21 | $32

1414 Lincoln Blvd. (Santa Monica Blvd.), Santa Monica, 310-393-8831

Maybe it's neither "chic" nor "trendy", but this "warmly lit" old
house in Santa Monica is a "treasure" for "authentic Polish
cuisine"; "it's hard not to be charmed by the artful" Eastern
European "theater and circus posters adorning the walls", or the
"comfort food" like "perfect" duck and "plates of steaming pierogi"
washed down with "shots of vodka."

WATER GRILL
27 | 24 | 25 | $58

544 S. Grand Ave. (bet. 5th & 6th Sts.), Downtown, 213-891-0900;
www.watergrill.com

"If the fish were any fresher, it would be on the end of your rod
and reel" proclaim patrons of this "clubby", "classy" "splurge"-

worthy Downtown seafooder that's "perfect for that special occasion", "pre-theater treat" or "power business dinner"; if a few feel that new chef David LeFevre (ex Charlie Trotter's in Chicago) "needs time to catch up", most "enjoy every morsel" of the "exotic, flavorful fin fare, exquisitely presented by a down-to-earth staff", and "worth the dent to your wallet."

Whale & Ale, The   ▽ 18 | 21 | 18 | $21
327 W. Seventh St. (bet. Centre & Mesa Sts.), San Pedro, 310-832-0363; www.whaleandale.com
"If you miss the coziness of a traditional pub, you needn't travel to London" as this "great British" hangout in San Pedro has "eerily" "authentic" atmosphere and "better food" too, particularly "distinctive fish 'n' chips"; the "lively" across-the-pond feel comes "complete with dartboards and live music regularly"; still, a few shrug "it's trying" to be the real thing, but "doesn't quite make it."

Wharo Korean BBQ   ▽ 18 | 16 | 19 | $31
4029 Lincoln Blvd. (Washington Blvd.), Marina del Rey, 310-578-7114
It's "a convenient place to get your Korean" BBQ "food fix if you live on the Westside" agree advocates who deem the "fare interesting" and "tasty" and find it "fun to cook at your own table"; sure, "K-town has better, but this is pretty darn good" – and while it may not be a "place to linger", hopefully "you won't leave smelling like a Weber grill."

Whisper Lounge, The   18 | 22 | 20 | $30
The Grove at Farmer's Mkt., 189 The Grove Dr. (bet. Fairfax Ave. & 3rd St.), Los Angeles, 323-931-0202; www.thewhisperlounge.com
A "hip" Fairfax "oasis in the Vegas-y Grove", this "sexy", "relaxing" supper-club refuge straight out of *Casablanca* with a "cabana-style patio" "lends sophistication to any happy hour or dinner"; American dishes like "mac 'n' cheese give new meaning" to comfort food, plus the "appetizers knock your socks off"; but for most the "fabulous scene" is best for a "late-night drink when you're tired of the usual haunts."

Whist   20 | 24 | 19 | $57
Viceroy Santa Monica, 1819 Ocean Ave. (Pico Blvd.), Santa Monica, 310-451-8711; www.viceroysantamonica.com
Designer Kelly Wearstler's "spectacular" interiors and "lovely", palm tree–lined, poolside patio with "white leather chairs" and "enclosed" cabanas are "too fabulous for words", making this Viceroy Santa Monica hotel setting a "beautiful place" for "guests, foodies and hipsters" to dine on "delicious" French fare; acolytes insist the food's "returned to form" under ex–Saddle Peak Lodge chef Warren Schwartz, nevertheless, for many it "comes second to the cool" decor.

White Lotus ⊠ Ⓜ   18 | 22 | 15 | $43
1743 N. Cahuenga Blvd. (Hollywood Blvd.), Hollywood, 323-463-0060; www.whitelotushollywood.com
"Surprisingly good" Asian-Eclectic "food and service given what an 'in' crowd they cater to" muse lotus-eaters of this "intriguing" Hollywood "hangout with plenty of buzz"; but others agree it's really the "eye candy" and "chill atmosphere" that "turn you on" – you go for the "scene" and "to gain easy entry into the club" next door, "not because you want an excellent meal."

Wildflour Pizza　　　　　　　　　– | – | – | I

2807 Main St. (bet. Ashland Ave. & Hill St.), Santa Monica,
310-392-3300

A "true" down-market "pizza joint", this "fantastic" find on a
nondescript stretch of Main Street in Santa Monica has been
turning out East Coast–style pies with "mouthwatering toppings"
and "meaty crusts" and healthy options for over three decades;
enjoy your slice on the back patio by the banana trees or get
it to go.

Windows ☒　　　　　　　　19 | 25 | 20 | $47

SBC Bldg., 1150 S. Olive St., 32nd fl. (bet. 11th & 12th Sts.), Downtown,
213-746-1554

"You can see forever" thanks to the "unbeatable" "360-degree
view" "from 32 floors up" the SBC Tower at this Downtown
Californian where Lakers lovers head for "surprisingly good" "pre-
game meals"; but the less starry-eyed declare it "needs a vision
to capitalize on its great potential" because the food is just "so-
so", the "service sleepy" and the decor vaguely reminiscent of a
"hotel convention room."

Wine Bistro ☒　　　　　　　21 | 20 | 21 | $38

11915 Ventura Blvd. (Laurel Canyon Blvd.), Studio City,
818-766-6233; www.winebistro.net

"Intimate" and "cozy", this French spot on the Boulevard in
Studio City is just what a "bistro should be": it's "crowded with
followers" and "friendly" with a "raging local scene at the bar",
"but not too boisterous"; with the owner now manning the stove,
some find the fare "delightful" ("you can't beat that prix fixe"),
but others anticipating a "culinary treat" lament it's "somewhat
of a let down."

Wokcano Cafe　　　　　　　16 | 14 | 15 | $22

Century Club, 10131 Constellation Blvd. (Ave. of the Stars),
Century City, 310-551-6688
913 S. Figueroa St. (bet. 9th St. & Olympic Blvd.), Downtown,
213-892-8999
8408 W. Third St. (S. Orlando Ave.), Los Angeles,
323-653-1998 ●
33 S. Fair Oaks Ave. (bet. W. Colorado Blvd. & W. Green St.),
Pasadena, 626-578-1818 ●
www.wokcanocafe.com

"Ideal for party people who need to nosh on sushi or other Asian
finger foods" agree evening-owls who head to these "late-late-
night hot spots" for a "nice mixture" of "basic", "tasty" Chinese-
Japanese; it's "nothing fancy" but portions are "more than
adequate", the selection "extensive" and the "service quick."

Wolfgang Puck Cafe　　　　　17 | 15 | 17 | $24

Ontario Mills Mall, 1 Mills Circle (bet. Franklin & Ontario Mills Aves.),
Ontario, 909-987-2299
Universal CityWalk, 1000 Universal Studios Blvd. (off Frwy. 101),
Universal City, 818-985-9653
www.wolfgangpuck.com

"You can't go wrong pucking around" these "crazy-colored cafes"
serving pizzas and Californian food with "new-age flair" that's
"certainly not Spago" level, "but adequate for a quick meal"; still,
most cry "boo-hoo", the "recipes are tired" and "like any other

F D S C

run-of-the-mill" dwindling chain, it's "probably no longer "what Wolfie had in mind."

Wood Ranch BBQ & Grill
20 | 16 | 18 | $24

Whizins Plaza, 5050 Cornell Rd. (Roadside Dr.), Agoura Hills, 818-597-8900
Westfield Shoppingtown Santa Anita, 400 S. Baldwin Ave. (W. Huntington Dr.), Arcadia, 626-447-4745
1101 Daily Dr. (Lantana St.), Camarillo, 805-482-1202
The Grove at Farmer's Mkt., 189 The Grove Dr. (bet. Fairfax Ave. & 3rd St.), Los Angeles, 323-937-6800
540 New Los Angeles Ave. (bet. Science Dr. & Spring Rd.), Moorpark, 805-523-7253
Northridge Mall, 9301 Tampa Ave. (bet. Nordhoff & Plummer Sts.), Northridge, 818-886-6464
Valencia Mktpl., 25580 N. The Old Rd. (Lyons Ave.), Valencia, 661-222-9494
www.woodranch.com

"Get here early to beat the crush" because it's always "crowded" at this "friendly" American BBQ chain, a "nice informal family place" that plies "regulars" with "*Flintstones*-sized beef ribs" and "moist tri-tip", "done right" with "all the fattening sides" you "crave"; sure, "waiting can be a hassle" but "reasonably priced food", "roomy booths" and an "accommodating staff" help compensate.

Woody's Bar-B-Que
▽ 23 | 8 | 14 | $14

3446 W. Slauson Ave. (Crenshaw Blvd.), Downtown, 323-294-9443

Stay in the car and "keep a low profile" because nobody travels to this Downtown "hole-in-the-wall joint" "for the atmosphere" ("it's all takeout"), but everybody gets a craving now and then for "real slow-cooked barbecue" "with a killer sauce"; simply put, it's the kind of "sticks to your ribs" 'cue others "aspire to, but can't achieve."

Woo Lae Oak
22 | 21 | 19 | $39

170 N. La Cienega Blvd. (Clifton Way), Beverly Hills, 310-652-4187; www.woolaeoak.org

When "you're in the mood to cook your own food" on virtually "smokeless tabletop" grills yet don't feel like dressing down, "you can't go wrong" at this "lovely", "upscale Korean barbecue" destination on La Cienega; if a handful hiss "you're better off going to K-town", for most it's a "great date/family/fun eatery" with "enough options to keep" pros and "novices" "happy."

Woomi Sushi
– | – | – | M

400 S. Baldwin Ave. (Huntington Dr.), Arcadia, 626-462-0703; www.woomisushi.com

Loud music, booming chefs and waiters feverishly ferrying oversized boats of raw fish through a brightly colored room set the scene at this Japanese newcomer in a San Gabriel Valley mall; the sushi roll–obsessed can choose from over 40 varieties, along with a few cooked items.

Xi'an
21 | 17 | 17 | $29

362 N. Cañon Dr. (bet. Brighton & Dayton Ways), Beverly Hills, 310-275-3345; www.xian90210.com

Reviewers are fairly united in their praise for the "healthy twist" on "delicious Chinese" cuisine at this Beverly Hills "favorite" with a "hip" architecturally interesting setting and "real waiters" ferrying

198   subscribe to zagat.com the "fresh food", "not actors biding their time"; but quibblers carp it's "nice, not fabulous", sniping "it's too damn noisy."

Xiomara   23 | 21 | 21 | $40

6101 Melrose Ave. (Seward St.), Hollywood, 323-461-0601
69 N. Raymond Ave. (bet. Colorado Blvd. & Walnut St.), Pasadena,
626-796-2520
www.xiomararestaurant.com

"Enjoy an evening in Havana" "minus the cigar smoke" while "expanding your palate" at Xiomara Ardolina's "haven of pre-Castro charm" in Hollywood and Old Town Pasadena that delivers "memorable" Nuevo Latino cuisine with a strong Cuban accent; if a few find service "attentive", most wail it's "absentminded at best", nevertheless, once you "knock" back what may be the "best mojitos in town" "nothing else matters."

XO Wine Bistro Ⓜ   – | – | – | M

1209 Highland Ave. (12th St.), Manhattan Beach, 310-545-3509;
www.xowinebistro.com

A sister venture of Bacchus wine shop nearby, this Downtown Manhattan Beach cafe by the pier offers over 50 wines by the glass and to match, Cal-Eclectic dishes that range from crab cakes to wild mushroom crêpes and a chipotle flavored tri-tip; the woodsy, warm setting is just right for a casual meal, whether you're dressed in shorts and flip-flops or workday regalia.

Yabu   23 | 16 | 20 | $28

521 N. La Cienega Blvd. (Melrose Ave.), West Hollywood, 310-854-0400
11820 W. Pico Blvd. (bet. Barrington Ave. & Bundy Dr.), West LA,
310-473-9757

"You don't need to speak Japanese to appreciate the chef's creativity" at these "secret hideaways" on the Westside that feel like "authentic Tokyo neighborhood restaurants" and serve a "little taste" of the Far East "in every bite"; "steaming" "perfect housemade soba" and udon noodles, "delectable sushi" and an "unpretentious vibe" all add up to a "wonderful meal."

YAMASHIRO   18 | 27 | 20 | $42

1999 N. Sycamore Ave. (Franklin Ave.), Hollywood, 323-466-5125;
www.yamashirorestaurant.com

For the most "mesmerizing", "spectacular night view" of Tinseltown's twinkling cityscape, head to this "unforgettable" Hollywood hilltop, home of a "magical" 90-year-old Japanese mansion with "memorable decor", "fabulous pagodas" and "delightful gardens"; if vision-questers sigh it's all about the "amazing" "location", not the "ok food", defenders declare the "delightful change of menu" to Cal-Asian under chef Jason Park has "greatly improved" "this elder establishment."

Yang Chow   23 | 11 | 17 | $21

6443 Topanga Canyon Blvd. (Victory Blvd.), Canoga Park,
818-347-2610
819 N. Broadway (bet. Alpine & College Sts.), Chinatown, 213-625-0811
3777 E. Colorado Blvd. (Rosemead Blvd.), Pasadena, 626-432-6868
www.yangchow.com

Home of the "amazing slippery shrimp" and other attractions, this Sino trio gives fans reason to "make pilgrimages from all corners of the city" to sample the "bizarrely named", "to-die-for" signature dish and "addictive spicy won ton soup" served by a "quick staff";

even conservative carpers who consider the fare "Americanized" stress it's the "best Americanized Chinese food" they've had.

Yard House ●   19 17 17 $25

401 Shoreline Village Dr. (Shoreline Dr.), Long Beach, 562-628-0455
Paseo Colorado, 330 E. Colorado Blvd. (bet. Fair Oaks &
N. Los Robles Aves.), Pasadena, 626-577-9273
www.yardhouse.com

"Come for the beer and stay for the beer" at these "cavernous" Americans in LB and Pasadena, where the 150-plus brew list is accompanied by a "surprisingly solid array" of victuals, "too-loud" music and suds-guzzling sports fans checking out a game in the bar area; P.S. they're "heaven" for singles who "need liquid courage" to help make a love match.

Yen Sushi & Sake Bar   –   –   –   M

4905 E. Second St. (bet. Argonne & St. Joseph Aves.), Long Beach,
562-434-5757
12930 Ventura Blvd. (Coldwater Canyon Ave.), Studio City, 818-907-6400
For some of the "finest sushi" around, head to this "cute" duo in Long Beach and Studio City advise afishionados hooked on the "satisfying" rolls; when you have a yen for cooked Japanese specialties, tuck into "excellent tempura" and "tasty udon" dishes, and don't forget to check out the "endless sake bar."

Ye Olde King's Head   17 18 18 $22

116 Santa Monica Blvd. (bet. Ocean Ave. & 2nd St.), Santa Monica,
310-451-1402; www.yeoldekingshead.com
Take a queue from "expats" and get your arse over to Santa Monica's "authentic" British pub, where "homesick Brits" and Anglophiles stoutly defend the "perfect fish 'n' chips", "good shepherd's pie" and the like, all washed down with a "pint"; it's "not the most beautiful place", but at least you can "play darts."

Yi Cuisine   22 24 20 $45

7910 W. Third St. (Fairfax Ave.), Los Angeles, 323-658-8028;
www.yicuisine.com
A "Sunset"-"WeHo" crowd gravitates to this "beautiful", "modern" "Zen-inspired retreat" at Third and Fairfax for "ambitious", "inventive" Filipino–Pan-Asian "small and mid-sized plates" "made for sharing", served by a "pleasant" staff in a "cool, hip" atmosphere; while some feel the "menu has too many options", with "uneven" results, others insist it's "worth checking out."

YUJEAN KANG'S   26 18 22 $36

67 N. Raymond Ave. (bet. Holly & Union Sts.), Pasadena, 626-585-0855
"Chinese food will never be the same" for some after experiencing "superb" chef Yujean Kang's "highly inventive" yet "authentic" "nouveau" Middle Kingdom cuisine at this "high-end" Old Pasadena establishment; "beautifully prepared" dishes are served by a "polite" and "efficient" staff at an "unhurried" pace, and though some find the "blandly upscale" room a bit "boring", this "old reliable" is "well worth a drive from any part of LA."

Yu Restaurant & Lounge   ▽ 19 23 18 $40

1323 Montana Ave. (14th St.), Santa Monica, 310-395-4727;
www.yurestaurants.com
Santa Monica "locals looking for a trendy dining spot" agree that this "hip" newcomer is a "welcome addition to weary Montana

Avenue", where "inventive", "pricey" Pan-Asian small plates are served amid "exotic" surroundings full of "dark wood, old leather and Buddhas"; "mechanical" service and "loud", "pounding music" make some "uncomfortable", while others contemplate the "teeny bar" and wonder "where exactly is the lounge?"

Zankou Chicken ⌐

24 | 4 | 12 | $10

5065 W. Sunset Blvd. (Normandie Ave.), East Hollywood, 323-665-7845 ●
1415 E. Colorado Blvd. (Verdugo Rd.), Glendale, 818-244-1937
1296 E. Colorado Blvd. (Hill Ave.), Pasadena, 626-405-1502
5658 Sepulveda Blvd. (Burbank Blvd.), Van Nuys, 818-781-0615
1716 S. Sepulveda Blvd. (Santa Monica Blvd.), West LA, 310-444-0550
www.zankouchicken.com

"Superlatives fail" surveyors trying to describe the "unbelievably savory" rotisserie chicken and "addictive garlic sauce" at this legendary Armenian chain that also wins raves for "top-notch falafel", "wonderful hummus" and schwarma that's a "cure for the doldrums"; it all comes "fast" and "ridiculously cheap", and devotees are undeterred by "depressing" decor or "surly" service.

Zazou ⊠

22 | 20 | 21 | $37

1810 S. Catalina Ave. (bet. Ave. I & Vista Del Mar), Redondo Beach, 310-540-4884; www.ezazou.com

A "South Bay gem", this "intimate" Redondo Beach sibling of Café Pierre offers "comforting", "beautifully presented" Mediterranean fare in a "romantic" "beach setting", as well as a "lively bar" scene; the staff is "knowledgeable" but service can be "uneven", and claustrophobes cavil that the "tables are too close together" in the otherwise "cute" and "welcoming" room.

Zeidler's Café Ⓜ

17 | 14 | 15 | $21

Skirball Cultural Ctr., 2701 N. Sepulveda Blvd. (Mulholland Dr.), Brentwood, 310-440-4515; www.skirball.org

"Generous portions" of "tasty kosher" Californian fare and "friendly" service make this "pleasant cafe" in Brentwood's Skirball Cultural Center a "perfect place for lunch before viewing an exhibition" or to "relax and unwind after a visit"; to some cynics, though, it's still "museum food."

Zeke's Smokehouse

19 | 12 | 17 | $20

2209 Honolulu Ave. (Verdugo Blvd.), Montrose, 818-957-7045
West Hollywood Gateway Ctr., 7100 Santa Monica Blvd. (Formosa Ave.), West Hollywood, 323-850-9353
www.zekessmokehouse.com

Leonard Schwartz and Michael Rosen bring a "fine-dining approach" to regional BBQ at their "high-end" smokehouses in Montrose and WeHo, and while the fare may not be "exactly traditional", to cuennoisseurs it's still "damn good"; the service is "hospitable" and the atmosphere "casual and friendly", but the "decor needs work" and frugal foes fume that it's "overpriced."

Zen Grill

20 | 18 | 18 | $24

9111 W. Olympic Blvd. (Doheny Dr.), Beverly Hills, 310-278-7773
8432 W. Third St. (bet. La Cienega Blvd. & Orlando Ave.), Los Angeles, 323-655-9991

This Westside Pan-Asian pair gives "equal love to tofu- and meat-eaters" with "awesome unusual dishes" that "aren't exactly authentic" but a "great value" nonetheless; "marvelous" interiors add to the "hip" ambiance, but sometimes the "noise overwhelms the food" and the "über-trendy" Third Street location is often "crowded" with "twentysomething wannabes."

Zip Fusion

| – | – | – | M |

744 E. 3rd St., Downtown, 213-680-3770 ⓈⓂ
11301 W. Olympic Blvd. (Sawtelle Blvd.), West LA, 310-575-3636;
www.zipfusion.com ◗

For hyper-modern, alt-rock sushi, zip over to this duo Downtown and hidden in the Olympic Collection and experience signature dishes like the Alba-Cado (albacore tartare wrapped in an avocado to look like an apple); while the food is made in an open kitchen instead of at a sushi bar, you can still sidle up to a stool for wild-and-wacky cocktails and high-end sakes.

Zita Trattoria & Bar Ⓢ

| 17 | 16 | 17 | $29 |

TCW Bldg., 865 S. Figueroa St. (W. Olympic Blvd.), Downtown, 213-488-0400; www.zitala.com

A "nice escape from the hot dogs at the Staples Center", this "quiet", "hard-to-find" Italian in the courtyard of the TCW Building offers "solid" fare and a "reasonable wine list" in a "pleasant" space with a "great outdoor patio"; the service is "efficient" (albeit a "little haughty"), but, not surprisingly, it "gets very busy on Laker nights."

Zucca Ristorante

| 22 | 24 | 22 | $44 |

801 Tower, 801 S. Figueroa St. (8th St.), Downtown, 213-614-7800; www.patinagroup.com

One of the "best of the Patina spin-offs", this "classy, elegant" Italian ristorante boasts one of the "prettiest spaces Downtown", with "posh" Venetian chandeliers, "beautiful" murals and an outdoor sculpture garden; "solid" cuisine, "excellent wines by the glass" and "attentive" service in a "tony" setting make it a "great pre-Staples" destination.

Los Angeles Indexes

CUISINES
LOCATIONS
SPECIAL FEATURES

CUISINES

American (New)
Akwa
Astra West
Avenue
Beechwood
Belvedere
Blair's
Bliss
blue on blue
Brentwood
Caffe Latte
Chloe
Cinespace
City Kitchen
Dragon
EM Bistro
Farm/Beverly Hills
Firefly
Firefly Bistro
Four Oaks
Grace
Grand Lux Cafe
Hal's B&G
Harbor Drive
Hugo's
Ivy
Ivy at the Shore
Jackson's Village
JAR
Josie
la di da
Lobster
Lola's
Maple Drive
Mélisse
Moonshadows
Naya
Nic's
Nine Thirty
Noé
Nook Bistro
O-Bar
Ocean & Vine
One Pico
Pearl
Pete's Café
P6 Rest./Lounge
Ritz Huntington
Saddle Peak
Second City Bistro
17th St. Cafe
Sky Room
Taste
310 Lounge
Towne
Traxx
Twin Palms
vermont

American (Traditional)
Abbey
Admiral Risty
Alcove
Apple Pan
Back on the Beach
Bandera
Beckham Grill
Belmont Brewing
Billingsley's
BJ's
Bluewater Grill
Bob Morris'
Brighton Coffee
Buffalo Club
Cafe 50's
California Chicken
Carney's Express
Cheesecake Factory
Chili John's
Claim Jumper
Clementine
Cole's P.E. Buffet
Cynthia's
Daily Grill
Dakota
De Lacey's
Dish
Doughboys
Du-par's
Edendale Grill
Engine Co. 28
Foodies
Friars
G. Garvin's
Gordon Biersch
Griddle Cafe
Grill on Hollywood
Grill on the Alley
Grub
Gulfstream
Hamburger Hamlet
Hamburger Mary's
Hard Rock
Heroes B&G
Hollywood & Vine
Hollywood Canteen
Houston's
Islands

Jack 'n Jill's
James' Beach
Jinky's
Joan's on Third
Johnny Rockets
John O'Groats
Jones Hollywood
Kate Mantilini
Kings Road
Kitchen
Koo Koo Roo
LA Food Show
Lasher's
Local Place
Luna Park
Marmalade Café
Marston's
Martha's 22nd St.
Matisse
Maxwell's Cafe
McKenna's
Mimi's Cafe
Morton's
Mo's
Musso & Frank
Norton Simon Café
Off Vine
Omelette Parlor
Original Pantry Cafe
Outlaws B&G
Pacific Dining Car
Peninsula Grille
Ruby's
Russell's Burgers
Salt Creek
Schwab's
Shack
Smitty's Grill
Souplantation
Spin Rotisserie
Stanley's
Susina Bakery
Swingers
Tam O'Shanter
Toast
Tony P's Dockside
26 Beach
Urth Caffé
Vibrato
Whisper Lounge
Wood Ranch BBQ
Yard House

Argentinean

Carlitos Gardel
Gaucho Grill

Armenian

Zankou Chicken

Asian

Blue Pacific
Chaya Brasserie
Chaya Venice
Chinois on Main
Feast from the East
Mako
Orris
2117
White Lotus
Yamashiro

Asian Fusion

Akwa
Asia de Cuba
Asian Noodles
Cinch
Crustacean
Dragon
Fat Fish
Jer-ne
Max
Michi
Saketini
Sawtelle Kitchen
Shiro
Tengu
Trinity
Wabi-Sabi

Austrian

Röckenwagner
Schatzi on Main

Bakeries

Dona Rosa
Le Pain Quotidien
Mäni's Bakery
Misto Caffé
Original Pantry Bakery
Posh on Pico
Susina Bakery
Sweet Lady Jane
Toast

Barbecue

Baby Blues BBQ
Benny's BBQ
Dr. Hogly Wogly's
House of Ribs
Johnny Rebs'
JR's BBQ
Lucille's BBQ
Mr. Cecil's Ribs
Phillips BBQ
Pig

Reddi Chick BBQ
Ribs USA
Robin's Woodfire BBQ
Tony Roma's
Wood Ranch BBQ
Woody's BBQ
Zeke's Smokehouse

Belgian
Le Pain Quotidien

Brazilian
Café Brasil
Fogo de Chão
Galletto
Green Field Churr.
Picanha Churrascaria
Rio Carnaval
Samba

Cajun
Bourbon St. Shrimp
Gumbo Pot
Ragin' Cajun
Stevie's Creole

Californian
Ammo
Amori
Axe
Babalu
Barefoot B&G
Bar Marmont
Barsac Brasserie
Basix Cafe
Bel-Air B&G
Bistro 45
Bistro 767
Bistro 31
blue on blue
Blue Pacific
boe
Bono's
Bora Bora
Breeze
Café Bizou
Cafe Del Rey
Café D'Marco
Café 14
Cafe Montana
Café Mundial
Cafe Pacific
Cafe Pinot
Caioti Pizza
Camilo's
Campanile
Castaway
Cézanne
Cha Cha Cha Encino

Chateau Marmont
Checkers
Chloe
Cicada
Cliff's Edge
Continental
Coral Tree
Crocodile Café
C2 Cafe
Derek's
Devon
Doug Arango's
Encounter
E's Wine Bar
Farm/Beverly Hills
Five Sixty-One
Flora Kitchen
Food Studio
410 Boyd
Gardens
Gardens on Glendon
Geoffrey's
Getty Center
Gina Lee's Bistro
Gorikee
Green Patio Cafe
Halie
Hotel Bel-Air
Hugo's
Inn of Seventh Ray
Jaan
Jackson's Village
Jack Sprat's
JiRaffe
Joe's
Kokomo Cafe
La Boheme
L.A. Farm
Leila's
Lemon Moon Cafe
Literati
Louise's Trattoria
Luce
Lucques
Luxe Cafe Rodeo
Market City
Mark's
Marmalade Café
Mason Jar Cafe
Michael's
Milky Way
Mi Piace
Mirabelle
Misto Caffé
Mix
Morton's
Napa Valley

Oceanfront
Off Vine
Opus B&G
Paco's Tacos
Parkway Grill
Patina
Pat's
Paul's Cafe
Pecorino
Pedals
Pentimento
Porta Via
Raymond
Reed's
Röckenwagner
Rose Cafe
Sam's
Scampi
Shiro
Spago
Stanley's
Table 8
Tempest
Vibe
Vineyard Terrace
Violet
Whist
Windows
Wolfgang Puck
XO Wine Bistro
Yamashiro
Zeidler's

Canadian
Soleil Westwood

Caribbean
Asia de Cuba
Bamboo
Caribbean Bistro
Cha Cha Cha
Cha Cha Cha Encino
Cha Cha Chicken
Prado

Cheese Steaks
South Street

Chinese
(* dim sum specialist)
ABC Seafood*
Bamboo Inn
California Wok
Cheng Du
Chi Dynasty
Chin Chin*
Din Tai Fung
Empress Harbor*

Empress Pavilion*
Eurochow
Fu-Shing
Genghis Cohen
Hop Li
Hop Woo
Hu's Szechwan
Joss*
JR Seafood
Kung Pao
Lake Spring Shanghai
Mandarette
Mandarin Deli
Mission 261*
Mr. Chow
NBC Seafood*
New Concept*
New Flavors
New Moon
Ocean Seafood*
Ocean Star*
Ogamdo
Panda Inn
P.F. Chang's
Royal Star Seafood
Sea Empress*
Sea Harbour*
Shanghai Grill
Tasty Kitchen
Tung Lai Shun
V.I.P. Harbor*
Wokcano Cafe
Xi'an
Yang Chow
Yujean Kang's

Coffee Shops/Diners
Brighton Coffee
Cafe 50's
Cora's Coffee
Duke's Coffee
Du-par's
Fred 62
Jan's
Johnny Rockets
Kate Mantilini
Mel's Drive-In
Mimi's Cafe
Original Pantry Bakery
Original Pantry Cafe
Patrick's
Pie 'N Burger
Rae's
Ruby's
Standard
Swingers
Uncle Bill's Pancake

Continental
Bistro Gdn./Coldwater
Brandywine
Buggy Whip
Café 14
Castaway
Chocolat
Continental
Dal Rae
Fins
Khoury's
Mandevilla
Maximilians
Odyssey
Patinette Cafe/MOCA
Pig 'n Whistle
Polo Lounge
Raymond
Seashell
Sir Winston's
Trinity

Cuban
Cafe Atlantic
Cuban Bistro
Paladar
Versailles

Delis
Art's Deli
Barney Greengrass
Brent's Deli
Broadway Deli
Canter's
Factor's Deli
Fromin's
Greenblatt's Deli
Johnnie's Pastrami
Junior's
Langer's Deli
Mort's Deli
Nate 'n Al's
Roll 'n Rye Deli

Dessert
Babalu
Cheesecake Factory
Michel Richard
Spago
Susina Bakery
Sweet Lady Jane

Eclectic
Authentic Cafe
Barbara's/Brewery
Barefoot B&G
Bar Marmont

Bistro K
Blvd
boe
Brass.-Cap.
Broadway Deli
Buffet City
Burger Continental
Café Deco
Café Tu Tu Tango
Canal Club
Chaya Brasserie
Chaya Venice
Chez Melange
Depot
Literati
Minibar
Mirabelle
Nook Bistro
Shane
Standard
Tangerine
White Lotus
XO Wine Bistro

English
Whale & Ale
Ye Olde King's Head

Ethiopian
Nyala Ethiopian

European
Five Sixty-One
Palomino
2117

Filipino
Asian Noodles
Shane
Yi Cuisine

Fondue
La Fondue

French
A.O.C.
Barsac Brasserie
Bistro Gdn./Coldwater
Cafe Del Rey
Cafe Pinot
Casbah Cafe
Cézanne
Chameau
Chateau Marmont
Chez Mimi
Chinois on Main
C2 Cafe
Derek's
Devon
Diaghilev

Firefly
Four Oaks
Hotel Bel-Air
La Frite
La Parisienne
La Rive Gauche
L'Artiste Patisserie
Le Chêne
Le Dome
L'Orangerie
Lucques
Lunaria
Maison Akira
Marla's
Matisse
Mélisse
Morels French Steak
Orris
Patina
Patinette Cafe/MOCA
Paul's Cafe
Petrossian
Reed's
Scampi
Soleil Westwood
Spazio
Taix French

French (Bistro)
A La Tarte
Angelique Cafe
Bistro 45
Bistro Verdu
Café Bizou
Cafe des Artistes
Café Pierre
Cafe Stella
Cafe Tartine
Chocolat
Clafoutis
Figaro Bistrot
Frenchy's Bistro
Julienne
La Dijonaise
Le Marmiton
Le Petit Bistro
Le Petit Cafe
Le Petit Four
Le Petit Jacques
Lilly's French Cafe
Mimosa
Mistral
Monsieur Marcel
Morels First Floor
Moustache Café
Pastis
Pinot Bistro

Rive Gauche
Tower Bar
Wine Bistro

French (Brasserie)
Brass.-Cap.
Brasserie Les Voyous
Gigi Brasserie
Kendall's Brasserie
Michel Richard
Vert

French (New)
Bastide
Citrine
Joe's
La Cachette
Ortolan
Sona

German
Matterhorn Chef

Greek
Delphi Greek
George's Greek
Great Greek
Greek Island
Joseph's Cafe
Le Petit Greek
Mama Voula
Papa Cristo's
Papadakis Taverna
Sofi
Taverna Tony
Ulysses Voyage

Hamburgers
Apple Pan
Astro Burger
Barney's Hamburgers
Burger Continental
Cassell's
Counter
Father's Office
Hamburger Hamlet
Hamburger Mary's
In-N-Out Burger
Islands
Johnny Rockets
Mel's Drive-In
Mo's
Outlaws B&G
Pie 'N Burger
Ruby's
Russell's Burgers
Shack
Tommy's
26 Beach

Hawaiian
Back Home/Lahaina
Local Place
Loft
New Flavors

Hawaii Regional
Roy's

Health Food
A Votre Sante
Jack Sprat's
Juliano's Raw
Kinara Café
M Cafe de Chaya
Newsroom Café
Real Food Daily
Urth Caffé

Hot Dogs
Jody Maroni's
Pink's Chili Dogs
Stand
Tommy's

Indian
Addi's Tandoor
Akbar
All India Café
Bombay Bite
Bombay Cafe
Bombay Palace
Clay Pit
Electric Lotus
Flavor of India
Gate of India
India's Oven
India's Tandoori
Maurya
Nawab of India
Nirvana
Nizam
Radhika's
Surya India
Tamarin
Tantra
Tufaan

Indonesian
Indo Cafe

Irish
Auld Dubliner

Italian
(N=Northern; S=Southern)
Adagio (N)
Ago
Alejo's
Alessio
Alessi
Allegria
Amalfi
Amici
Angeli Caffe
Angelini Osteria
Anna's
Antica Pizzeria
Bacco Trattoria
Basix Cafe
Berri's Pizza
Bravo
Buca di Beppo
Buona Sera
Ca'Brea (N)
Ca' del Sole (N)
Café D'Marco
Café Med
Cafe Veneto
Caffe Delfini
Caffe Pinguini (N)
Caioti Pizza
C & O Trattoria
Capo
Carmine's
Casa Bianca
Celestino (N)
Cheebo
Christy's
Ciao Trattoria
Cicada
Cliff's Edge
Coral Tree
Crescendo/Fred Segal
Cucina Paradiso
Dan Tana's
Da Pasquale
Dino's Italian
Divino
Dolce Enoteca (N)
Dominick's
Doug Arango's
Drago
Enoteca Drago
E's Wine Bar
Eurochow
Fabiolus Café
Fab's Italian
Farfalla Trattoria
Far Niente (N)
Frascati (N)
Fresco
Fritto Misto
Gaetano's (N)
Galletto

Gennaro's
Giorgio Baldi
Girasole
Green Patio Cafe
Guido's (N)
Hot Oven
i Cugini
Il Boccaccio (N)
Il Buco
Il Capriccio
Il Cielo
Il Fornaio
Il Forno
Il Grano
Il Moro
Il Pastaio
Il Sole
Il Tiramisu (N)
Il Tramezzino
Jacopo's
Jones Hollywood
La Bottega Marino
La Bruschetta
La Dolce Vita
La Finestra
La Loggia
La Luna
La Pergola
La Piazza
La Scala (N)
La Scala Presto
La Sosta Enoteca
La Terza
La Vecchia
Locanda del Lago (N)
Locanda Veneta (N)
L'Opera (N)
Louise's Trattoria
Lunaria
Madeo (N)
Maggiano's
Mama D's
Marcello Tuscany Rm. (N)
Maria's Italian
Marino
Market City
Massimo (N)
Matteo's
Matteo's Hoboken
Mazzarino's (S)
Miceli's
Mio Babbo's
Mi Piace
Modo Mio Cucina (N)
Mulberry St. Pizzeria

Nicola's Kitchen
Old Spaghetti Factory
Orso
Osteria Latini
Osteria Nonni
Pace
Padri (N)
Palermo
Palmeri (S)
Pane e Vino
Panzanella (N)
Pastina (S)
Pat's
Pecorino
Pedals
Peppone
Petrelli's Steak
Piatti
Piccolo
Piccolo Paradiso
Pizzicotto
Pomodoro
Prego
Prizzi's Piazza
Rae's
Rocca
Romano's Macaroni
Rosti (N)
San Gennaro
Sapori
Sisley Italian
Sor Tino
Spark Woodfire Grill
Spazio
Spumante
Stinking Rose
Talia's
Tanino (S)
Taste Chicago
Tesoro Trattoria
Toscana (N)
Tra Di Noi
Trastevere
Tre Venezie (N)
Tulipano
Tuscany
Valentino
Via Veneto
Villa Piacere
Villa Sorriso
Vincenti
Vitello's
Vito
Vittorio
Vivoli Café
Zita Trattoria
Zucca

Japanese
(* sushi specialist)
Ahi Sushi*
Ajisen Ramen
Akwa*
Ami*
Asahi Ramen
Asakuma*
Asanebo*
Asuka*
Banzai Sushi*
Benihana*
Blowfish Sushi*
Boiling Pot
Cafe Sushi*
Crazy Fish*
Ebizo's Skewer
Fukui Sushi*
Geisha House*
Gyu-Kaku
Hamasaku*
Hama Sushi*
Hayakawa*
Hide Sushi*
Hirosuke*
Hirozen*
Hump*
Hwang Jae BBQ*
Iroha*
Ita-Cho
Japon Bistro*
Kaiten*
Kamiyama*
Kanpai Japanese B&G*
Katana*
Katsu-ya*
Kikuchi
Koi*
Maison Akira
Matsuhisa*
Mishima
Miyagi's*
Momoyama*
Mori Sushi*
Musha
Naked Sushi*
Nikko Sushi*
Nishimura*
Nobu Malibu*
Omino Sushi*
O-Nami*
Pearl Dragon*
R23*
Sai Sai*
Shabu Shabu
Shige
Shima
Suishaya*
Sushi & Kushi*
Sushi Masu*
Sushi Mon*
Sushi Nozawa*
Sushi Roku*
Sushi Sasabune*
Sushi Sushi*
Sushi Wasabi*
Taiko*
Takao*
Tama Sushi*
Tengu*
Tenmasa*
Teru Sushi*
Thousand Cranes*
Todai*
Tokio*
Torafuku*
Tsuji No Hana*
Tsukiji*
Urasawa*
U-Zen*
Wa*
Wabi-Sabi*
Wahoo Shabu Shabu
Wokcano Cafe
Woomi Sushi*
Yabu*
Yen Sushi & Sake*
Zip Fusion*

Korean
(* barbecue specialist)
BCD Tofu
HanWoori*
Hwang Jae BBQ*
La Korea BBQ*
Manna*
Nak Won*
Ogamdo
Seoul Jung*
Soot Bull Jeep*
Wharo*
Woo Lae Oak*

Kosher
Fish Grill
Greta Tunisian
Johnnie's Pastrami
Magic Carpet
Milky Way
Pat's
Zeidler's

Lebanese
Carnival
Marouch
Sunnin

Malaysian
Penang

Mediterranean
Aioli
A.O.C.
Beau Rivage
Berri's Pizza
Café Mundial
Café Santorini
Campanile
Cayenne Café
Christine
Flora Kitchen
Gardens
Joseph's Cafe
Le Dome
Lemon Moon Cafe
Little Door
Mediterraneo
Meson G
Monsieur Marcel
Palomino
Pentimento
Primitivo
Sam's
Taverna Tony
Trio Med.
Violet
Zazou

Mexican
Adobe Cantina
Antonio's
Babita
Baja Fresh Mexican
Border Grill
Cabo Cantina
Casablanca
Casa Vega
Cozymel's
Dona Rosa
El Cholo
El Coyote
El Tepeyac
El Torito
El Torito Grill
Guelaguetza
Kay 'n Dave's
La Salsa
La Serenata/Garibaldi

La Serenata Gourmet
La Velvet Margarita
Lotería!
Malo
Marix Tex Mex
Mexicali
Mexico City
Mi Ranchito
Monte Alban
Pacifico's
Paco's Tacos
Poquito Más
Sagebrush Cantina
Señor Fred
Sharky's Mexican
SolyAzul
Spanish Kitchen
Tamayo
Tlapazola Grill
Venice Cantina

Middle Eastern
Carousel
Falafel King
Magic Carpet
Mandaloun
Moishe's
Noura Cafe
Tempo
Wahib's Mid-East

Moroccan
Casbah Cafe
Cayenne Café
Chameau
Dar Maghreb
Koutoubia
Marrakesh
Oasis

Nepalese
Tibet Nepal

New World
Norman's

Noodle Shops
Ajisen Ramen
Asahi Ramen
Mishima
Pho Café
Pho 79

Nuevo Latino
Alegria
Ciudad
La Boca del Conga
Xiomara

Pacific Rim
Christine
Duke's
Gina Lee's Bistro

Pan-Asian
Beacon
Buddha's Belly
Formosa Cafe
Ma'kai
Monsoon Cafe
Pearl Dragon
Pei Wei Diner
Red Moon Cafe
Typhoon
Yi Cuisine
Yu Rest./Lounge
Zen Grill

Pan-Latin
Posh on Pico

Persian/Iranian
Down Town Kabob
Javan
Pistachio Grill
Shaherzad

Peruvian
El Pollo Inka
Los Balcones del Peru
Mario's Peruvian

Pizza
Abbot's Pizza
Alessi
Antica Pizzeria
Berri's Pizza
BJ's
Caioti Pizza
California Pizza Kitchen
Casa Bianca
Cheebo
D'Amore's Pizza
Frankie & Johnnie's
Jacopo's
Johnnie's NY
La Bottega Marino
Lamonica's NY Pizza
Mulberry St. Pizzeria
Pace
Parkway Grill
Pizza Rustica
Prizzi's Piazza
Spago
Spark Woodfire Grill
Village Pizzeria

Wildflour Pizza
Wolfgang Puck

Polish
Warszawa

Polynesian
Bora Bora
Trader Vic's

Pub Food
Auld Dubliner
Gordon Biersch
Heroes B&G
Whale & Ale
Ye Olde King's Head

Puerto Rican
Madre's

Russian
Diaghilev

Sandwiches
Art's Deli
Barney Greengrass
Brent's Deli
Canter's
Factor's Deli
Greenblatt's Deli
Johnnie's Pastrami
Junior's
Langer's Deli
Mort's Deli
Nate 'n Al's
Nicola's Kitchen
Noah's NY Bagels
Philippe the Original
Roll 'n Rye Deli
Sandbag Sandwiches

Seafood
ABC Seafood
Bluewater Grill
Bob Morris'
Breeze
Chart House
Delmonico's Lobster
Delmonico's Seafood
Duke's
Enterprise Fish
Fins
Fish Grill
Fonz's
Galley
Geoffrey's
Gladstone's Malibu
Gladstone's Universal
Gulfstream
Hungry Cat

Il Grano
Joe's Crab
JR Seafood
Killer Shrimp
Kincaid's
King's Fish Hse.
Lobster
Madison
Malibu Seafood
Mario's Peruvian
McCormick/Schmick
McGrath's Fish Hse.
McKenna's
NBC Seafood
Neptune's Net
Ocean Ave.
Ocean Seafood
Odyssey
Pacifico's
Parker's Lighthouse
Providence
Reel Inn
Rock 'N Fish
Royal Star Seafood
Sea Harbour
Seashell
22nd St. Landing
V.I.P. Harbor
Water Grill

Small Plates
Aioli
A.O.C.
boe
Café Tu Tu Tango
Cafe Veneto
Cliff's Edge
Enoteca Drago
Father's Office
Ita-Cho
Ma'kai
Mako
Mediterraneo
Minibar
Musha
Orris
Pearl Dragon
Primitivo
Violet
Yi Cuisine
Yu Rest./Lounge

Soul Food
Big Mama's Rib
Roscoe's

Southeast Asian
Nonya

Southern
Aunt Kizzy's
Baby Blues BBQ
Harold & Belle's
House of Blues
Johnny Rebs'
Kokomo Cafe
Les Sisters
Lucille's BBQ
Roscoe's

Southwestern
Authentic Cafe
Bandera
Coyote Cantina
Jinky's
Reata Grill
Sagebrush Cantina
Sonora Cafe

Spanish
(* tapas specialist)
Bar Celona*
Cobra Lily*
Cobras & Matadors*
Courtyard*
Gozar*
La Paella*
Meson G*
Ole!*

Steakhouses
Arnie Morton's
Arroyo Chop Hse.
Beckham Grill
Benihana
Billingsley's
Boa
Buggy Whip
Carlitos Gardel
Chart House
Chez Jay
Dakota
Damon's Steak
De Lacey's
Derby
555 East
Fleming Prime Steak
Fonz's
Galley
Gaucho Grill
JJ Steak
Kincaid's
Lawry's Prime Rib
Lincoln
Lodge Steak
Madison
Mastro's Steak

McKenna's
Monty's Steak
Morels French Steak
Nick & Stef's Steak
Opus B&G
Outback Steak
Pacific Dining Car
Palm
Petrelli's Steak
Porterhouse Bistro
Rock 'N Fish
Ruth's Chris
Saddle Ranch Chop
Salt Creek
Smoke House
Sterling Steak
Tangerine
Taylor's Steak
Vibrato

Swiss
Matterhorn Chef

Thai
Blue Bamboo
Chaba
Chadaka
Chan Dara
Chao Krung
Cholada
Jitlada
Nadpob
Natalee
Palms Thai
Rambutan Thai
Saladang
Talesai
Thai Dishes
Tongdang Thai

Tuk Tuk Thai
Vegan Glory

Tibetan
Tibet Nepal

Tunisian
Greta Tunisian
Moun of Tunis

Uzbeki
Uzbekistan

Vegetarian
(* vegan)
A Votre Sante
Fatty's & Co.
Inn of Seventh Ray*
Juliano's Raw*
Mäni's Bakery*
Native Foods*
Newsroom Café*
Real Food Daily*
Urth Caffé*
Vegan Glory*

Vietnamese
Absolutely Phobulous
Blue Hen
China Beach Bistro
Crustacean
Gingergrass
Golden Deli
Hanoi Cafe
Le Saigon
Michelia
Pho Café
Pho 79
Red Moon Cafe

LOCATIONS

LA CENTRAL

Atwater Village
Mimi's Cafe
Osteria Nonni
Tam O'Shanter

Beverly Blvd.
(bet. La Brea & La Cienega)
Angelini Osteria
Buddha's Belly
Cafe Tartine
Cobras & Matadors
El Coyote
EM Bistro
Grace
Ita-Cho
JAR
Kings Road
Mimosa
Pane e Vino
Pastis
Swingers

Beverly Center/Cedars
Akbar
Arnie Morton's
Baja Fresh Mexican
Barefoot B&G
Cafe Sushi
Cafe Veneto
California Pizza Kitchen
Daily Grill
Gigi Brasserie
Grand Lux Cafe
Hard Rock
Hirozen
Locanda Veneta
Michelia
Orso
P.F. Chang's
Souplantation
Sushi Mon
Todai

Beverlywood/
Pico-Robertson
Delmonico's Seafood
Factor's Deli
Louise's Trattoria
Magic Carpet
Mäni's Bakery
Milky Way
Pat's
Spark Woodfire Grill

Tuk Tuk Thai

Chinatown
ABC Seafood
Asian Noodles
Empress Pavilion
Hop Li
Hop Woo
Mandarin Deli
Ocean Seafood
Philippe the Original
Pho 79
Yang Chow

Downtown
Angelique Cafe
Arnie Morton's
Barbara's/Brewery
BCD Tofu
Cafe Pinot
California Pizza Kitchen
Checkers
Ciao Trattoria
Cicada
City Kitchen
Ciudad
Cole's P.E. Buffet
Engine Co. 28
410 Boyd
George's Greek
Kendall's Brasserie
Koo Koo Roo
Lamonica's NY Pizza
Langer's Deli
La Salsa
McCormick/Schmick
Nick & Stef's Steak
Noé
Original Pantry Bakery
Original Pantry Cafe
Pacific Dining Car
Palm
Patina
Patinette Cafe/MOCA
Pete's Café
Sai Sai
Sandbag Sandwiches
Seoul Jung
Standard
Tesoro Trattoria
Tommy's
Traxx
Water Grill

Windows
Wokcano Cafe
Woody's BBQ
Zip Fusion
Zita Trattoria
Zucca

Echo Park/Silver Lake

Blair's
Cafe Stella
Casbah Cafe
Cha Cha Cha
Cliff's Edge
Edendale Grill
Gingergrass
Kitchen
Malo
Nadpob
Pho Café
Rambutan Thai
Taix French
Tantra

Fairfax

Authentic Cafe
California Chicken
Canter's
Chameau
Chao Krung
Du-par's
Farm/Beverly Hills
Genghis Cohen
Gumbo Pot
India's Oven
Johnny Rockets
Kokomo Cafe
La Korea BBQ
La Piazza
Lotería!
Maggiano's
M Cafe de Chaya
Moishe's
Monsieur Marcel
Morels First Floor
Morels French Steak
Nyala Ethiopian
Ulysses Voyage
Vegan Glory
Whisper Lounge
Wokcano Cafe
Wood Ranch BBQ

Hancock Park/ Larchmont Village

Chan Dara
Girasole
Koo Koo Roo
La Bottega Marino

La Luna
Le Petit Greek
Louise's Trattoria
Noah's NY Bagels
Prado
Village Pizzeria

Hollywood

Ammo
Brasserie Les Voyous
Cafe des Artistes
California Pizza Kitchen
Carousel
Chan Dara
Cheebo
Cinespace
Dakota
Dar Maghreb
Fabiolus Café
Formosa Cafe
Geisha House
Greenblatt's Deli
Griddle Cafe
Grill on Hollywood
Grub
Hamburger Hamlet
Hamburger Mary's
Hollywood & Vine
Hollywood Canteen
Hungry Cat
In-N-Out Burger
Jitlada
Johnny Rockets
Joseph's Cafe
La Velvet Margarita
Los Balcones del Peru
Marino
Mario's Peruvian
Marouch
Mel's Drive-In
Miceli's
Moun of Tunis
Musso & Frank
Off Vine
Old Spaghetti Factory
Pace
Paladar
Palms Thai
Pig 'n Whistle
Pomodoro
Prizzi's Piazza
Roscoe's
Schwab's
Sharky's Mexican
Sterling Steak
Tokio
Trastevere

Uzbekistan
Vert
White Lotus
Yamashiro
Zankou Chicken

Koreatown
BCD Tofu
Cassell's
Guelaguetza
Manna
Nak Won
Soot Bull Jeep
Taylor's Steak

La Brea
Amalfi
Ca'Brea
Campanile
Flora Kitchen
Luna Park
Oasis
Pig
Pink's Chili Dogs
Sonora Cafe
Susina Bakery

La Cienega Corridor
Absolutely Phobulous
Benihana
Bliss
Blue Bamboo
Fogo de Chão
Gyu-Kaku
Koi
Lawry's Prime Rib
Le Petit Bistro
L'Orangerie
Matsuhisa
Real Food Daily
Sona
Spanish Kitchen
Stinking Rose
Wa
Woo Lae Oak

Leimert Park
Phillips BBQ

Little Tokyo
R23
Shabu Shabu
Thousand Cranes
2117

Los Feliz
Alcove
Chi Dynasty
Cobras & Matadors
Electric Lotus

Farfalla Trattoria
Figaro Bistrot
Fred 62
Il Capriccio
Louise's Trattoria
Mexico City
Palermo
vermont

Melrose
Ago
Alessi
Angeli Caffe
Antonio's
Astro Burger
Bastide
Carlitos Gardel
Chocolat
Citrine
Dolce Enoteca
Fabiolus Café
Greta Tunisian
Johnny Rockets
Le Pain Quotidien
Louise's Trattoria
Lucques
Meson G
Providence
Sweet Lady Jane
Table 8
Urth Caffé
Xiomara

Mid-City
El Cholo
Harold & Belle's
India's Tandoori
Koo Koo Roo
Papa Cristo's
Phillips BBQ
Roscoe's
Stevie's Creole
Versailles

Mid-Wilshire
Ogamdo
Opus B&G
Posh on Pico
Sandbag Sandwiches

Miracle Mile
Caffe Latte
Johnnie's NY
La Boca del Conga
Pentimento

Robertson Corridor
Dominick's
Doug Arango's

Fat Fish
Il Cielo
Ivy
Morton's
Newsroom Café
Petrossian

Sunset Strip

Asia de Cuba
Bar Marmont
Blowfish Sushi
Boa
Cabo Cantina
Café Med
Carney's Express
Chateau Marmont
Chin Chin
Clafoutis
Duke's Coffee
House of Blues
Katana
Le Dome
Le Petit Four
Mel's Drive-In
Mirabelle
Miyagi's
Norman's
Saddle Ranch Chop
Standard
Tangerine
Tenmasa
Tower Bar
Vivoli Café

Third Street

(bet. La Brea & La Cienega)
A.O.C.
Berri's Pizza
California Wok
Cynthia's
Doughboys
G. Garvin's
Joan's on Third
La Terza
Little Door
Mishima
Ortolan
Sofi
Surya India
Sushi Roku
Toast

Yi Cuisine
Zen Grill

West Hollywood

Abbey
Astra West
Astro Burger
Basix Cafe
Cayenne Café
Cha Cha Cha
Chaya Brasserie
Courtyard
Dan Tana's
Diaghilev
Fish Grill
Flavor of India
Frankie & Johnnie's
Gaucho Grill
Gozar
Hamburger Hamlet
Hugo's
Il Sole
Jacopo's
Jan's
Jones Hollywood
Joss
Kikuchi
Kinara Café
Koo Koo Roo
Kung Pao
La Boheme
la di da
La Paella
Lola's
Madeo
Mandarette
Marix Tex Mex
Mark's
Mason Jar Cafe
Mix
Nikko Sushi
Nishimura
Noura Cafe
O-Bar
Palm
Pearl
Poquito Más
Sandbag Sandwiches
Talesai
Taste
Yabu
Zeke's Smokehouse

LA EAST

Boyle Heights

La Serenata/Garibaldi

East LA

El Tepeyac
Tamayo

LA SOUTH

Bellflower
Johnny Rebs'

Carson
Back Home/Lahaina
Tony Roma's

Cerritos
BCD Tofu
BJ's
Loft
Mimi's Cafe
Romano's Macaroni
Todai

Hawthorne
El Torito
Matisse

Lakewood
Outback Steak
Souplantation

Lawndale
El Pollo Inka

Lomita
Kamiyama

**Palos Verdes Peninsula/
Rolling Hills**
Admiral Risty
Bistro 767
Cafe Pacific
La Rive Gauche
Marmalade Café
Noah's NY Bagels
Peninsula Grille
Rio Carnaval
Ruby's
Trio Med.

LA WEST

Bel Air
Bel-Air B&G
Four Oaks
Hotel Bel-Air
Vibrato

Beverly Hills
Amici
Asakuma
Baja Fresh Mexican
Barney Greengrass
Belvedere
blue on blue
Blvd
boe
Bombay Palace
Brighton Coffee
California Pizza Kitchen
Cheesecake Factory
Chin Chin
Cobra Lily
Continental
Crazy Fish
Crustacean
Da Pasquale
El Torito Grill
Enoteca Drago
Farm/Beverly Hills
Frankie & Johnnie's
Friars
Gardens
Grill on the Alley
Hot Oven

Il Buco
Il Fornaio
Il Pastaio
Il Tramezzino
Islands
Jaan
Jack 'n Jill's
Jacopo's
Johnny Rockets
Kate Mantilini
Koo Koo Roo
La Dolce Vita
La Salsa
La Scala
Le Pain Quotidien
Lodge Steak
Luce
Luxe Cafe Rodeo
Mako
Maple Drive
Massimo
Mastro's Steak
Maurya
McCormick/Schmick
Michel Richard
Mr. Chow
Mulberry St. Pizzeria
Natalee
Nate 'n Al's
Nic's
Nirvana
Piccolo Paradiso
Pistachio Grill

Pizza Rustica
Polo Lounge
Porta Via
Porterhouse Bistro
Prego
Real Food Daily
Rosti
Ruth's Chris
Sandbag Sandwiches
Shanghai Grill
Sharky's Mexican
Spago
Sushi & Kushi
Sushi Sushi
Talesai
Tamarin
Tony Roma's
Trader Vic's
Urasawa
Urth Caffé
Xi'an
Zen Grill

Brentwood

Amici
A Votre Sante
Baja Fresh Mexican
Barney's Hamburgers
Brentwood
California Wok
Cheesecake Factory
Chin Chin
Clay Pit
Coral Tree
Daily Grill
Divino
Gaucho Grill
Getty Center
Hamburger Hamlet
La Salsa
La Scala Presto
Le Pain Quotidien
Louise's Trattoria
Maria's Italian
Noah's NY Bagels
Osteria Latini
Palmeri
Pecorino
Peppone
Pizzicotto
Reddi Chick BBQ
Saketini
Sandbag Sandwiches
San Gennaro
Sor Tino

Souplantation
Taiko
Takao
Tongdang Thai
Toscana
Vincenti
Zeidler's

Century City

Breeze
Clementine
C2 Cafe
Gulfstream
Houston's
Jody Maroni's
Johnnie's NY
Johnny Rockets
La Cachette
Lunaria
Wokcano Cafe

Culver City

Bamboo
Beacon
In-N-Out Burger
Jody Maroni's
Johnnie's Pastrami
Johnny Rockets
JR's BBQ
La Dijonaise
Mi Ranchito
New Flavors
Pacifico's
Petrelli's Steak
Roll 'n Rye Deli
San Gennaro
Thai Dishes

Malibu

Allegria
Beau Rivage
Bob Morris'
Chart House
Cholada
D'Amore's Pizza
Duke's
Geoffrey's
Guido's
Johnnie's NY
Malibu Seafood
Marmalade Café
Moonshadows
Neptune's Net
Nobu Malibu
Reel Inn
Taverna Tony
Thai Dishes
Tra Di Noi

Marina del Rey
Akbar
Alejo's
Antica Pizzeria
Asakuma
Aunt Kizzy's
Baja Fresh Mexican
Benny's BBQ
Cafe Del Rey
C & O Trattoria
Chart House
Cheesecake Factory
Chin Chin
El Torito
Hop Li
Islands
Jer-ne
Johnnie's NY
Killer Shrimp
Koo Koo Roo
Naked Sushi
Noah's NY Bagels
Ruby's
Sapori
Souplantation
Spin Rotisserie
Tony P's Dockside
Tsuji No Hana
26 Beach
Wharo

Mar Vista
Paco's Tacos

Pacific Palisades
A La Tarte
Gladstone's Malibu
Jacopo's
Kay 'n Dave's
Modo Mio Cucina
Mort's Deli
Pearl Dragon
Vittorio

Palms
Café Brasil
Cucina Paradiso
Guelaguetza
Hu's Szechwan
Indo Cafe
Natalee
Versailles

Playa del Rey
Berri's Pizza
Caffe Pinguini
Chloe

Outlaws B&G
Shack

Rancho Park
John O'Groats
Kay 'n Dave's

Santa Monica
Abbot's Pizza
Akbar
Akwa
Babalu
Back on the Beach
Benihana
Bistro 31
Boa
Border Grill
Brass.-Cap.
Bravo
Broadway Deli
Buca di Beppo
Buffalo Club
Cafe Montana
Caffe Delfini
California Chicken
California Pizza Kitchen
Capo
Cézanne
Cha Cha Chicken
Chez Jay
Chez Mimi
Chinois on Main
Cinch
Cora's Coffee
Counter
Crescendo/Fred Segal
Drago
El Cholo
Enterprise Fish
Falafel King
Father's Office
Fritto Misto
Fromin's
Fukui Sushi
Galley
Gate of India
Gaucho Grill
Giorgio Baldi
Houston's
Hump
i Cugini
Il Fornaio
Il Forno
Ivy at the Shore
Jinky's
JiRaffe
Josie
Juliano's Raw

Kaiten
Kay 'n Dave's
L.A. Farm
La Salsa
La Serenata/Garibaldi
La Vecchia
Le Marmiton
Le Petit Cafe
Lincoln
Lobster
Locanda del Lago
Louise's Trattoria
Ma'kai
Mäni's Bakery
Marix Tex Mex
Marmalade Café
Mélisse
Michael's
Monsoon Cafe
Musha
Nawab of India
Newsroom Café
Noah's NY Bagels
Ocean & Vine
Ocean Ave.
Oceanfront
Omelette Parlor
One Pico
Pacific Dining Car
Patrick's
Pedals
P.F. Chang's
Rae's
Real Food Daily
Rocca
Röckenwagner
Rosti
Royal Star Seafood
Sam's
Schatzi on Main
17th St. Cafe
Shack
Shane
Shige
Sushi Roku
Swingers
Thai Dishes
310 Lounge
Trastevere
Typhoon
Urth Caffé
Valentino
Via Veneto
Violet
Vito
Warszawa
Whist

Wildflour Pizza
Ye Olde King's Head
Yu Rest./Lounge

Topanga
Inn of Seventh Ray

Venice
Abbot's Pizza
Axe
Baby Blues BBQ
Beechwood
Cafe 50's
Canal Club
Casablanca
Chaya Venice
China Beach Bistro
Hal's B&G
Hama Sushi
James' Beach
Jody Maroni's
Joe's
Lilly's French Cafe
Maxwell's Cafe
Piccolo
Primitivo
Rose Cafe
Shima
Venice Cantina
Wabi-Sabi

West LA
All India Café
Anna's
Apple Pan
Asahi Ramen
Asakuma
Bandera
Billingsley's
Bombay Cafe
Bourbon St. Shrimp
Buffet City
Cabo Cantina
Cafe 50's
California Chicken
Chan Dara
Cheng Du
Feast from the East
Foodies
Guido's
Gyu-Kaku
Hamasaku
Hamburger Hamlet
Hanoi Cafe
Hide Sushi
Hop Li
Hop Woo
House of Ribs

Il Grano
Il Moro
India's Oven
India's Tandoori
In-N-Out Burger
Islands
Jack Sprat's
Jacopo's
Javan
JR Seafood
Junior's
Koo Koo Roo
La Bottega Marino
La Salsa
La Serenata Gourmet
Lemon Moon Cafe
Le Saigon
Literati
Mama Voula
Maria's Italian
Matteo's
Matteo's Hoboken
Monte Alban
Mori Sushi
Mr. Cecil's Ribs
Nizam
Nook Bistro
Orris
Pastina
Poquito Más
Red Moon Cafe
Sawtelle Kitchen
Sisley Italian
Sushi Masu
Sushi Sasabune
Tlapazola Grill
Torafuku

U-Zen
V.I.P. Harbor
Yabu
Zankou Chicken
Zip Fusion

Westwood
Ami
Asuka
Baja Fresh Mexican
BJ's
Bombay Bite
California Pizza Kitchen
D'Amore's Pizza
Delphi Greek
Eurochow
Falafel King
Gardens on Glendon
In-N-Out Burger
Joan's on Third
Koutoubia
La Bruschetta
Lamonica's NY Pizza
Mio Babbo's
Moustache Café
Napa Valley
Native Foods
Nine Thirty
Noah's NY Bagels
Palomino
Sandbag Sandwiches
Shaherzad
Soleil Westwood
South Street
Sunnin
Tanino
Tengu

SOUTH BAY

Downey
Mimi's Cafe

El Segundo
Cozymel's
Daily Grill
Fleming Prime Steak
McCormick/Schmick
P.F. Chang's
Romano's Macaroni
Second City Bistro
Taiko
Thai Dishes

Gardena
El Pollo Inka
Sea Empress

Tasty Kitchen
Tsukiji

Hermosa Beach
Akbar
Blue Pacific
Dragon
El Pollo Inka
Fritto Misto
Il Boccaccio
Jackson's Village
La Sosta Enoteca
Martha's 22nd St.
Mediterraneo
Ragin' Cajun
Sushi Wasabi

Inglewood
Phillips BBQ
Thai Dishes

LAX
Daily Grill
El Cholo
Encounter
Jody Maroni's
Ruby's
Thai Dishes

Long Beach
Alegria
Auld Dubliner
Baja Fresh Mexican
Belmont Brewing
BJ's
Bono's
Christy's
Claim Jumper
El Torito
555 East
Frenchy's Bistro
George's Greek
Green Field Churr.
Joe's Crab
Johnny Rebs'
Johnny Rockets
Khoury's
King's Fish Hse.
Lasher's
L'Opera
Lucille's BBQ
Madison
McKenna's
Mimi's Cafe
Parker's Lighthouse
Roscoe's
Sharky's Mexican
Sir Winston's
Sky Room
Sunnin
Yard House
Yen Sushi & Sake

Manhattan Beach
Avenue
Back Home/Lahaina
Bora Bora
Café Pierre
California Pizza Kitchen
Ebizo's Skewer
Fonz's
Houston's
Il Fornaio
Islands
Johnny Rockets

Koo Koo Roo
LA Food Show
Mama D's
Michi
Noah's NY Bagels
Pomodoro
Reed's
Rock 'N Fish
Talia's
Thai Dishes
Towne
Uncle Bill's Pancake
Versailles
Vibe
XO Wine Bistro

Redondo Beach
Addi's Tandoor
Bluewater Grill
Buca di Beppo
Buona Sera
Café D'Marco
Chaba
Chart House
Cheesecake Factory
Chez Melange
Coyote Cantina
Down Town Kabob
El Torito
Food Studio
Frascati
Gina Lee's Bistro
Harbor Drive
Joe's Crab
Kincaid's
La Salsa
Momoyama
Rae's
Ruby's
Samba
Zazou

San Pedro
Marcello Tuscany Rm.
Papadakis Taverna
22nd St. Landing
Whale & Ale

Torrance
Aioli
BCD Tofu
Benihana
Christine
Claim Jumper
Depot
El Pollo Inka
El Torito Grill
Green Patio Cafe
Gyu-Kaku

Islands
Jody Maroni's
Local Place
Loft
Lucille's BBQ
Mimi's Cafe
Mishima
Misto Caffé
Musha
O-Nami
Outback Steak

Pei Wei Diner
Poquito Más
Romano's Macaroni
Tempest

Westchester
Alejo's
Buggy Whip
In-N-Out Burger
Kanpai Japanese B&G
Paco's Tacos

INLAND EMPIRE

Moreno Valley
BJ's

Ontario
Benihana
La Salsa

Panda Inn
Tony Roma's
Wolfgang Puck

PASADENA & ENVIRONS

Arcadia
BJ's
Café Deco
Carmine's
Derby
Din Tai Fung
Hop Li
Market City
McGrath's Fish Hse.
Outback Steak
Souplantation
Todai
Tony Roma's
Wood Ranch BBQ
Woomi Sushi

Eagle Rock
Blue Hen
Camilo's
Casa Bianca
Fatty's & Co.

La Cañada Flintridge
Dish
Taylor's Steak

Monrovia
Amori
Café Mundial
Claim Jumper
Devon
La Parisienne
Mimi's Cafe
Romano's Macaroni

Montrose
New Moon
Zeke's Smokehouse

Pasadena
Akbar
All India Café
Arroyo Chop Hse.
Baja Fresh Mexican
Bar Celona
Beckham Grill
Big Mama's Rib
Bistro 45
Boiling Pot
Buca di Beppo
Burger Continental
Cafe Atlantic
Café Bizou
Café Santorini
California Pizza Kitchen
Caribbean Bistro
Celestino
Cheesecake Factory
Crocodile Café
De Lacey's
Delmonico's Seafood
Derek's
Dino's Italian
Dona Rosa
El Cholo
El Torito
E's Wine Bar
Five Sixty-One
Fu-Shing
Gaucho Grill
Gordon Biersch
Halie
Hamburger Hamlet
Houston's
Il Fornaio

Islands
Japon Bistro
JJ Steak
Koo Koo Roo
Louise's Trattoria
Madre's
Maison Akira
Maria's Italian
Marston's
McCormick/Schmick
Mi Piace
Monty's Steak
Naya
Noah's NY Bagels
Nonya
Norton Simon Café
Panda Inn
Parkway Grill
Pei Wei Diner
P.F. Chang's
Pie 'N Burger
Radhika's
Raymond
Ritz Huntington
Robin's Woodfire BBQ
Roscoe's
Russell's Burgers
Saladang

Scampi
Sharky's Mexican
Smitty's Grill
SolyAzul
Souplantation
Sushi Roku
Thai Dishes
Tibet Nepal
Tony Roma's
Tre Venezie
Twin Palms
Villa Sorriso
Wokcano Cafe
Xiomara
Yang Chow
Yard House
Yujean Kang's
Zankou Chicken

San Marino
Julienne
Tongdang Thai

South Pasadena
Bistro K
Carmine's
Firefly Bistro
Shiro

SAN FERNANDO VALLEY & BURBANK

Burbank
Arnie Morton's
Bacco Trattoria
Baja Fresh Mexican
BJ's
California Pizza Kitchen
Castaway
Chadaka
Chili John's
Daily Grill
El Torito
Gordon Biersch
India's Tandoori
Islands
Johnny Rockets
Market City
Mi Piace
Mo's
Outback Steak
Picanha Churrascaria
Pomodoro
Poquito Más
Ribs USA
Sharky's Mexican
Smoke House
South Street

Taste Chicago
Tony Roma's

Calabasas
Banzai Sushi
Fins
Gaetano's
King's Fish Hse.
Marmalade Café
Mi Piace
Saddle Peak
Sagebrush Cantina
Sharky's Mexican

Canoga Park
D'Amore's Pizza
Yang Chow

Chatsworth
Les Sisters
Mimi's Cafe
Omino Sushi

Encino
Benihana
Buca di Beppo
California Chicken
California Wok
Cha Cha Cha Encino

D'Amore's Pizza
Delmonico's Lobster
El Torito
Fromin's
Hirosuke
Islands
Johnny Rockets
Katsu-ya
L'Artiste Patisserie
Maria's Italian
Mulberry St. Pizzeria
Rosti
Stand
Stevie's Creole
Tempo
Tony Roma's
Versailles

Glendale
Bistro Verdu
Carousel
Crocodile Café
Damon's Steak
Far Niente
Fresco
Gennaro's
Islands
Mandaloun
Panda Inn
Sandbag Sandwiches
Todai
Tony Roma's
Zankou Chicken

Granada Hills
Odyssey

North Hollywood
Barsac Brasserie
Ca' del Sole
In-N-Out Burger
Maximilians
Poquito Más

Northridge
Alessio
Brent's Deli
California Chicken
Claim Jumper
El Torito
HanWoori
Mandarin Deli
Maria's Italian
Outback Steak
Romano's Macaroni
Souplantation
Wood Ranch BBQ

Reseda
BCD Tofu

Sherman Oaks
Bamboo Inn
Café Bizou
Cafe 50's
Carnival
Casa Vega
Cheesecake Factory
D'Amore's Pizza
Fab's Italian
Great Greek
Greek Island
Gyu-Kaku
Hamburger Hamlet
Il Tiramisu
In-N-Out Burger
Jinky's
Kung Pao
La Fondue
La Frite
La Pergola
La Salsa
Le Petit Bistro
Le Petit Jacques
Maria's Italian
Marmalade Café
Max
Mazzarino's
Mel's Drive-In
Mistral
Mr. Cecil's Ribs
Noah's NY Bagels
Panzanella
P.F. Chang's
Pomodoro
Rive Gauche
Señor Fred
Sharky's Mexican
Sisley Italian
Spazio
Stanley's
Tufaan

Simi Valley
Sharky's Mexican

Studio City
Ahi Sushi
Art's Deli
Asanebo
Baja Fresh Mexican
Bistro Gdn./Coldwater
Caioti Pizza
California Pizza Kitchen
Carney's Express
Chin Chin
Daily Grill
Du-par's
Firefly

Gaucho Grill
Hugo's
Il Tramezzino
In-N-Out Burger
Iroha
Katsu-ya
Killer Shrimp
Kung Pao
La Loggia
La Salsa
Louise's Trattoria
Marrakesh
Mexicali
Ole!
Pinot Bistro
Poquito Más
Spark Woodfire Grill
Spumante
Sushi Nozawa
Talesai
Tama Sushi
Teru Sushi
Todai
Vineyard Terrace
Vitello's
Wine Bistro
Yen Sushi & Sake

Tarzana
El Torito
India's Tandoori
La Finestra
Paul's Cafe
Sharky's Mexican

Universal City
Buca di Beppo
Café Tu Tu Tango
Daily Grill
Gladstone's Universal
Hard Rock

Jody Maroni's
Miceli's
Minibar
Saddle Ranch Chop
Versailles
Wolfgang Puck

Van Nuys
Dr. Hogly Wogly's
In-N-Out Burger
Matterhorn Chef
Zankou Chicken

West Hills
Alessio

Woodland Hills
Adagio
Baja Fresh Mexican
BJ's
Brandywine
Cheesecake Factory
Gaucho Grill
Gorikee
In-N-Out Burger
Islands
Kate Mantilini
La Frite
Maggiano's
Maria's Italian
Monty's Steak
Nicola's Kitchen
P.F. Chang's
Pomodoro
Poquito Más
Reata Grill
Roy's
Ruby's
Seashell
Todai
Villa Piacere

SAN GABRIEL VALLEY

Alhambra
Cuban Bistro
Hop Woo
Marla's
Pho 79
Souplantation
Tony Roma's
Wahib's Mid-East

Azusa
Tulipano

City of Industry
Benihana
Claim Jumper

Joe's Crab
Mimi's Cafe
Outback Steak
Souplantation
Todai

Claremont
Buca di Beppo
Heroes B&G

Covina/West Covina
BJ's
Green Field Churr.
Hayakawa
O-Nami

Outback Steak
Penang
Suishaya

Diamond Bar
Hwang Jae BBQ

Glendora
El Pollo Inka

Montclair
Tony Roma's

Montebello
Astro Burger

Monterey Park
El Tepeyac
Empress Harbor
Lake Spring Shanghai
Mandarin Deli
NBC Seafood
New Concept
Ocean Star
Wahoo Shabu Shabu

Pico Rivera
Dal Rae

Rosemead
Sea Harbour

Rowland Heights
BCD Tofu
Sea Harbour

San Gabriel
Ajisen Ramen
Babita
Golden Deli
Mission 261
Trinity
Tung Lai Shun

Whittier
Mimi's Cafe
Ruby's

CONEJO VALLEY/SIMI VALLEY & ENVIRONS

Agoura Hills/Oak Park
Adobe Cantina
Café 14
Leila's
Maria's Italian
Padri
Wood Ranch BBQ

Camarillo
Souplantation
Tony Roma's
Wood Ranch BBQ

Moorpark
Wood Ranch BBQ

Thousand Oaks
Cheesecake Factory
D'Amore's Pizza
Du-par's
El Torito
Outback Steak
Piatti
Romano's Macaroni
Sisley Italian

Westlake Village
Alessio
BJ's
Fins
Galletto
Louise's Trattoria
Mandevilla
Marmalade Café
P6 Rest./Lounge
Rosti
Sharky's Mexican
Tuscany

SANTA CLARITA VALLEY & ENVIRONS

Santa Clarita
Mimi's Cafe
Pei Wei Diner
Romano's Macaroni

Saugus
Le Chêne

Valencia
BJ's
Claim Jumper
Hamburger Hamlet
Maria's Italian
Outback Steak
Poquito Más
Salt Creek
Sisley Italian
Thai Dishes
Wood Ranch BBQ

SPECIAL FEATURES

(Indexes list the best in each category. Multi-location restaurants' features may vary by branch.)

Breakfast

(See also Hotel Dining)
Abbey
Brighton Coffee
Cora's Coffee
Fred 62
Griddle Cafe
Grub
Joan's on Third
Kate Mantilini
La Bottega Marino
La Terza
Lemon Moon Cafe
Le Pain Quotidien
Literati
Lotería!
Mäni's Bakery
Marmalade Café
Mel's Drive-In
Mimi's Cafe
Newsroom Café
Original Pantry Bakery
Pacific Dining Car
Patrick's
Philippe the Original
Porta Via
Posh on Pico
Roscoe's
Ruby's
Schwab's
Susina Bakery
Sweet Lady Jane
Swingers
Toast
Urth Caffé
Wolfgang Puck

Brunch

ABC Seafood
Belvedere
Campanile
Firefly Bistro
Hotel Bel-Air
Jer-ne
Joe's
Lilly's French Cafe
Massimo
McCormick/Schmick
Morels First Floor
Napa Valley

Newsroom Café
Nine Thirty
Ocean Ave.
Oceanfront
Ocean Seafood
One Pico
Polo Lounge
Raymond
Ritz Huntington
Röckenwagner
Saddle Peak
Spanish Kitchen
Twin Palms
Whist
Xiomara
Yi Cuisine

Business Dining

Ago
Arnie Morton's
Arroyo Chop Hse.
Avenue
Barney Greengrass
Beechwood
Belvedere
Benihana
Bistro 45
Blvd
Breeze
Buffalo Club
Cafe Del Rey
Campanile
Celestino
Checkers
Cicada
Crustacean
Dakota
Dan Tana's
Derek's
Doug Arango's
Drago
555 East
Five Sixty-One
Fogo de Chão
Food Studio
Gardens
Grace
Grill on Hollywood
Grill on the Alley
Harbor Drive
Il Grano

Il Moro
Jaan
JAR
Josie
Joss
Kincaid's
La Cachette
La Finestra
La Sosta Enoteca
Lunaria
Madeo
Maple Drive
McCormick/Schmick
Mélisse
Meson G
Michael's
Mistral
Mix
Nick & Stef's Steak
Nic's
Nonya
Ocean & Vine
One Pico
Opus B&G
Ortolan
Patina
Peppone
Pinot Bistro
Polo Lounge
Porterhouse Bistro
Providence
Ritz Huntington
Ruth's Chris
Spago
Sterling Steak
Taylor's Steak
Thousand Cranes
Valentino
Vert
Vincenti
Water Grill
Windows
Yujean Kang's
Zucca

Child-Friendly

(Alternatives to the usual
fast-food places; * children's
menu available)
Abbot's Pizza
Amici
Angeli Caffe
Anna's
Asian Noodles*
Astro Burger
Asuka
Back on the Beach*

Bandera*
Barney's Hamburgers*
Benihana*
Benny's BBQ
Big Mama's Rib*
BJ's*
Bluewater Grill*
Boa
Bob Morris'*
Bravo*
Brighton Coffee
Buca di Beppo
Burger Continental*
Cafe 50's*
Café Med
Café Mundial
Café Tu Tu Tango*
Caffe Delfini
Caffe Pinguini
California Chicken*
California Pizza Kitchen*
California Wok
C & O Trattoria*
Carmine's*
Carnival*
Carousel
Casa Bianca
Casablanca
Casa Vega*
Chaba
Cha Cha Cha
Cha Cha Cha Encino*
Cha Cha Chicken
Chart House*
Cheebo
Cheesecake Factory
Chi Dynasty
Chili John's*
Claim Jumper*
Clay Pit
Clementine*
Coral Tree*
Counter*
Coyote Cantina*
Cozymel's*
Crocodile Café*
Daily Grill*
D'Amore's Pizza
Da Pasquale
Delphi Greek
Dino's Italian*
Dish*
Dona Rosa*
Duke's*
El Coyote*
El Tepeyac*
El Torito*

El Torito Grill*
Enterprise Fish*
Fabiolus Café
Fab's Italian*
Farfalla Trattoria
Fat Fish
Feast from the East
Foodies*
Frankie & Johnnie's
Fritto Misto*
Fromin's*
Gaucho Grill
Gladstone's Malibu*
Gladstone's Universal*
Great Greek*
Green Field Churr.
Guelaguetza*
Gulfstream*
Hamburger Hamlet*
Harold & Belle's
Hop Li
Hop Woo
Hot Oven
Indo Cafe
Islands*
Jackson's Village
Jacopo's*
Jinky's*
Jitlada
Jody Maroni's*
Joe's Crab*
Johnnie's Pastrami*
Johnny Rockets*
John O'Groats*
Kay 'n Dave's*
Koo Koo Roo*
Kung Pao
La Dijonaise
La Finestra
Langer's Deli
La Salsa*
Le Petit Cafe
Le Petit Greek*
Les Sisters*
Lotería!*
Louise's Trattoria*
Lucille's BBQ*
Magic Carpet
Mama D's*
Mama Voula
Mandarin Deli
Mäni's Bakery
Maria's Italian*
Mario's Peruvian
Marston's
Martha's 22nd St.*
Maxwell's Cafe*

Miceli's*
Mimosa
Mi Piace*
Mi Ranchito*
Mishima*
Misto Caffé*
Moishe's
Mort's Deli*
Mo's*
Mulberry St. Pizzeria
NBC Seafood
Nicola's Kitchen
O-Nami
Outback Steak*
Outlaws B&G*
Pacifico's
Paco's Tacos*
Padri*
Palms Thai
Panda Inn
Pastina
P.F. Chang's
Piatti*
Pie 'N Burger*
Pistachio Grill
Pizzicotto
Poquito Más*
Rae's*
Ragin' Cajun*
Ribs USA*
Robin's Woodfire BBQ*
Rock 'N Fish*
Romano's Macaroni*
Rosti*
Ruby's*
Russell's Burgers*
Samba
17th St. Cafe*
Shack*
Sharky's Mexican*
Sisley Italian*
Smoke House*
SolyAzul*
Souplantation*
South Street
Stanley's
Stinking Rose
Swingers*
Taste Chicago
Thai Dishes
Tibet Nepal
Todai
Tommy's*
Tony P's Dockside*
Tony Roma's*
Tufaan
Tung Lai Shun

22nd St. Landing*
26 Beach*
Ulysses Voyage
Uncle Bill's Pancake*
U-Zen
Versailles*
Village Pizzeria
Vittorio
Vivoli Café
Wokcano Cafe
Wood Ranch BBQ*
Yabu*
Zankou Chicken
Zeke's Smokehouse*

Dancing

Alegria
Alessio
Buffalo Club
Café Tu Tu Tango
Carmine's
Cinespace
Cuban Bistro
Dal Rae
El Pollo Inka
Friars
Great Greek
Joseph's Cafe
Khoury's
La Boca del Conga
Lunaria
Madison
Mastro's Steak
Matterhorn Chef
Minibar
Monsoon Cafe
Padri
Paladar
Pearl
P6 Rest./Lounge
Saddle Ranch Chop
Samba
San Gennaro
Sky Room
Smoke House
SolyAzul
Stevie's Creole
Taverna Tony
Tokio
Villa Sorriso
White Lotus
Zita Trattoria

Entertainment

(Call for days and times of performances)
Addi's Tandoor (sitar)
Alegria (Latin)
Alessio (varies)
Amalfi (comedy/jazz)
Antonio's (mariachi)
Arroyo Chop Hse. (piano)
Auld Dubliner (Irish)
Baby Blues BBQ (blues)
Bandera (jazz)
Benihana (chefs)
Bistro Gdn./Coldwater (piano)
Border Grill (Mexican)
Brandywine (guitar)
Buffalo Club (bands/DJ)
Buggy Whip (piano)
Cafe Del Rey (piano)
Cafe des Artistes (DJ)
Cafe Stella (DJs)
Café Tu Tu Tango (varies)
Canal Club (DJ)
C & O Trattoria (vocals)
Canter's (varies)
Carlitos Gardel (varies)
Carmine's (bands/karaoke)
Carousel (varies)
Casablanca (Latin guitar)
Cayenne Café (belly dancing)
Cézanne (piano)
Cinespace (DJ)
Ciudad (Latin)
Courtyard (guitar)
Crustacean (jazz/piano)
Cuban Bistro (Latin)
Dal Rae (piano)
Dar Maghreb (belly dancing)
De Lacey's (rock)
Dragon (DJ)
Duke's (varies)
El Cholo (mariachi)
Electric Lotus (DJ)
El Pollo Inka (varies)
EM Bistro (jazz)
E's Wine Bar (jazz)
Fins (jazz/piano)
Frenchy's Bistro (guitar/piano)
Galletto (bands)
Geisha House (DJ)
Genghis Cohen (varies)
Gorikee (bands)
Great Greek (Greek)
Hal's B&G (jazz)
Hamburger Mary's (varies)
Hard Rock (varies)
House of Blues (varies)
Javan (piano)
Jer-ne (flamenco/jazz)
Joseph's Cafe (varies)
Khoury's (bands)
Koutoubia (belly dancing)

La Boca del Conga (varies)
La Boheme (DJ)
La Velvet Margarita (mariachi)
L'Opera (opera singer)
L'Orangerie (piano)
Lucille's BBQ (blues)
Lunaria (jazz/swing)
Madison (jazz/swing)
Maggiano's (piano)
Ma'kai (DJ)
Mandaloun (varies)
Maple Drive (jazz)
Market City (strings)
Marouch (belly dancing)
Marrakesh (belly dancing)
Mastro's Steak (piano/vocals)
Moonshadows (DJ)
Morels French Steak (jazz band)
Moun of Tunis (belly dancing)
Nic's (beatnik/R&B)
Oceanfront (jazz band/piano)
One Pico (bass/piano)
Padri (varies)
Palms Thai (vocals)
Papa Cristo's (varies)
Papadakis Taverna (varies)
Parker's Lighthouse (jazz)
Parkway Grill (jazz/piano)
Pig 'n Whistle (varies)
Polo Lounge (piano)
P6 Rest./Lounge (DJ)
Rio Carnaval (samba)
Ritz Huntington (guitar)
Romano's Macaroni (opera)
Saddle Ranch Chop (bull riding)
Sir Winston's (piano)
Sky Room (varies)
Spanish Kitchen (mariachi)
Sterling Steak (jazz)
Taix French (bands)
Tokio (DJ/karaoke)
Twin Palms (bands/jazz)
Vibrato (jazz)
Villa Sorriso (DJ)
Whisper Lounge (piano)
White Lotus (DJ)

Garden Dining

Abbey
Alcove
Allegria
Asia de Cuba
Bamboo
Bastide
Beechwood
Belvedere

Bistro K
blue on blue
Bravo
Buffalo Club
Café Bizou
Cafe des Artistes
Cafe Stella
Celestino
Chateau Marmont
Chez Mimi
Ciudad
Cliff's Edge
Dominick's
Edendale Grill
Fins
Firefly Bistro
Four Oaks
Gardens
Geoffrey's
Gladstone's Malibu
Hotel Bel-Air
Il Cielo
Inn of Seventh Ray
Ivy
Jer-ne
Katana
Kinara Café
Koi
La Boheme
L.A. Farm
Le Chêne
Lemon Moon Cafe
Little Door
Lobster
Malo
Marmalade Café
Maximilians
Michael's
Moishe's
Moonshadows
Newsroom Café
Nine Thirty
Noé
Norman's
Norton Simon Café
Off Vine
Opus B&G
Pace
Pane e Vino
Polo Lounge
Primitivo
Raymond
Saddle Peak
Sapori
Schatzi on Main
Spago
Stand

Tra Di Noi
Traxx
26 Beach
Twin Palms
Whist
Yamashiro
Yi Cuisine

Historic Places

(Year opened; * building)
1889 Four Oaks*
1900 Raymond*
1900 Saddle Peak*
1906 Pete's Café*
1908 Cole's P.E. Buffet
1908 Off Vine*
1908 Philippe the Original
1910 Via Veneto*
1910 Warszawa*
1912 Engine Co. 28*
1912 Polo Lounge*
1916 Madison*
1919 Musso & Frank*
1920 La Paella*
1920 Lasher's*
1921 Pacific Dining Car
1922 Derby*
1922 Second City Bistro*
1922 Tam O'Shanter
1923 Farfalla Trattoria*
1923 Grub*
1923 Lobster
1924 Canter's
1924 Edendale Grill*
1924 Original Pantry Cafe
1925 Palm*
1926 Greenblatt's Deli
1927 Benihana*
1927 El Cholo
1927 Pig 'n Whistle*
1927 Taix French
1928 Cafe Stella*
1928 Ciao Trattoria*
1929 Campanile*
1929 Chateau Marmont*
1929 Eurochow*
1929 Halie*
1929 Tanino*
1929 Tower Bar*
1930 Brighton Coffee
1931 El Coyote
1931 Petrelli's Steak
1932 Fatty's & Co.*
1934 Galley*
1936 Sir Winston's*
1937 Damon's Steak
1937 Traxx*

1938 Cassell's
1938 Du-par's
1938 Lawry's Prime Rib
1938 Paul's Cafe*
1939 Formosa Cafe
1939 Pink's Chili Dogs
1940 Il Cielo*
1942 Mr. Cecil's Ribs*
1945 Dominick's
1945 Nate 'n Al's
1946 Billingsley's
1946 Bob Morris'*
1946 Chili John's
1946 Monty's Steak
1946 Smoke House
1946 Tommy's*
1947 Apple Pan
1947 Hotel Bel-Air
1947 Langer's Deli
1947 Mazzarino's
1948 Factor's Deli
1948 Papa Cristo's
1948 Reddi Chick BBQ
1949 Dino's Italian
1949 Miceli's
1950 Hamburger Hamlet
1950 Neptune's Net
1950 Uncle Bill's Pancake
1952 Buggy Whip
1952 Cafe 50's*
1952 Johnnie's Pastrami
1953 Father's Office
1953 Taylor's Steak
1954 El Torito
1955 Casa Bianca
1955 El Tepeyac
1955 Trader Vic's
1955 Vineyard Terrace*
1956 La Scala

Hotel Dining

Argyle Hotel
    Tower Bar
Avalon Hotel
    blue on blue
Ayres Hotel
    Matisse
Bel-Air, Hotel
    Hotel Bel-Air
Belamar Hotel
    Vibe
Best Western
    Du-par's
Beverly Hills Hotel
    Polo Lounge
Beverly Hilton
    Trader Vic's

Beverly Laurel Motor Hotel
  Swingers
Beverly Terrace Hotel
  Amici
Burbank Hilton
  Daily Grill
Casa Del Mar, Hotel
  Oceanfront
Century Plaza Hotel & Spa
  Breeze
Chateau Marmont
  Chateau Marmont
Crescent
  boe
Four Seasons Hotel
  Gardens
Grafton Hotel
  Boa
Hilton Checkers
  Checkers
Hilton Plaza
  Ajisen Ramen
Hollywood Roosevelt
  Dakota
Le Méridien Hotel
  Arnie Morton's
Le Merigot Hotel
  Cézanne
Loews Santa Monica Beach
  Ocean & Vine
Luxe Hotel Rodeo Dr.
  Luxe Cafe Rodeo
Millennium Biltmore Hotel
  Sai Sai
Mondrian
  Asia de Cuba
New Otani
  Thousand Cranes
Omni Los Angeles Hotel
  Noé
Palos Verdes Inn
  Chez Melange
Peninsula Beverly Hills
  Belvedere
Raffles L'Ermitage Hotel
  Jaan
Regent Beverly Wilshire
  Blvd
Ritz-Carlton Huntington
  Ritz Huntington
Ritz-Carlton Marina del Rey
  Jer-ne
San Gabriel Hilton
  Trinity
Shutters on the Beach
  One Pico
  Pedals

Sofitel Los Angeles
  Gigi Brasserie
Standard
  Standard
Viceroy Santa Monica
  Whist
W Hotel
  Nine Thirty
Wilshire Grand
  Seoul Jung
Wyndham Bel Age
  Diaghilev

Late Dining

(Weekday closing hour)
Abbey (2 AM)
Apple Pan (12 AM)
Astro Burger (varies)
Bar Marmont (1:30 AM)
BCD Tofu (varies)
Berri's Pizza (varies)
BJ's (varies)
Brasserie Les Voyous (12 AM)
Bravo (varies)
Brentwood (varies)
Broadway Deli (12 AM)
Cabo Cantina (12 AM)
Cafe 50's (varies)
Cafe Sushi (12 AM)
Canter's (24 hrs.)
Carney's Express (varies)
Casa Bianca (12 AM)
Casa Vega (1 AM)
Chaya Venice (varies)
Clafoutis (12 AM)
Cliff's Edge (12 AM)
Continental (12 AM)
Courtyard (1 AM)
Dakota (12 AM)
Dan Tana's (1 AM)
Dominick's (12:45 AM)
Dona Rosa (12 AM)
Doughboys (12 AM)
Du-par's (varies)
Electric Lotus (12 AM)
El Torito (varies)
Figaro Bistrot (12 AM)
Firefly (12 AM)
Frankie & Johnnie's (varies)
Fred 62 (24 hrs.)
Geisha House (12 AM)
Greenblatt's Deli (1:30 AM)
Hamburger Hamlet (varies)
Hamburger Mary's (12 AM)
Heroes B&G (varies)
Hollywood & Vine (3 AM)
Hop Li (varies)

Hop Woo (varies)
Hungry Cat (12 AM)
In-N-Out Burger (1 AM)
Ivy at the Shore (12 AM)
Jan's (2 AM)
Jer-ne (12 AM)
Johnnie's Pastrami (varies)
Jones Hollywood (1:30 AM)
Katana (12 AM)
Kate Mantilini (varies)
Kitchen (12 AM)
la di da (12 AM)
La Dolce Vita (12 AM)
Lamonica's NY Pizza (varies)
La Velvet Margarita (2 AM)
Lola's (2 AM)
Lunaria (1:30 AM)
Mel's Drive-In (varies)
Mexicali (1 AM)
Minibar (2 AM)
Mi Piace (varies)
Mirabelle (12:30 AM)
Mix (12 AM)
Miyagi's (2 AM)
Monte Alban (12 AM)
Nak Won (24 hrs.)
Nirvana (2 AM)
O-Bar (1 AM)
Opus B&G (12 AM)
Original Pantry Cafe (24 hrs.)
Pacific Dining Car (varies)
Palms Thai (12 AM)
Pearl (2 AM)
Pete's Café (varies)
Pho Café (12 AM)
Pink's Chili Dogs (2 AM)
Pizza Rustica (12 AM)
Polo Lounge (2 AM)
Poquito Más (varies)
P6 Rest./Lounge (12 AM)
Roscoe's (varies)
Saddle Ranch Chop (varies)
Schwab's (12 AM)
Shane (2 AM)
Spanish Kitchen (varies)
Standard (24 hrs.)
Swingers (varies)
Tangerine (12 AM)
Tommy's (24 hrs.)
Uzbekistan (12 AM)
Wokcano Cafe (varies)
Yard House (varies)
Zankou Chicken (varies)
Zip Fusion (12 AM)

Meet for a Drink

Abbey
Adobe Cantina
Ago
Akwa
Arnie Morton's
Arroyo Chop Hse.
Asia de Cuba
Beechwood
Benihana
Bistro 45
BJ's
Bliss
Blowfish Sushi
Boa
boe
Bono's
Brass.-Cap.
Breeze
Brentwood
Cabo Cantina
Ca'Brea
Ca' del Sole
Café Mundial
Cafe Pinot
Campanile
Canal Club
Casa Vega
Castaway
Chocolat
Cobra Lily
Cozymel's
Crustacean
Cuban Bistro
Dakota
Dominick's
Doug Arango's
Drago
Edendale Grill
EM Bistro
E's Wine Bar
Father's Office
Fogo de Chão
Food Studio
Formosa Cafe
Geisha House
Grace
Grill on Hollywood
Hal's B&G
Harbor Drive
Hollywood & Vine
Hotel Bel-Air
Hungry Cat
Jaan
James' Beach
JAR
Joe's
Kate Mantilini
Kincaid's
La Sosta Enoteca

La Velvet Margarita
Little Door
Lobster
L'Orangerie
Madre's
Mastro's Steak
Mediterraneo
Meson G
Michi
Monsoon Cafe
Moonshadows
Napa Valley
Nick & Stef's Steak
Nic's
Nine Thirty
Nonya
Norman's
O-Bar
Ocean & Vine
Ocean Ave.
Oceanfront
Ole!
Opus B&G
Paladar
Palm
Palomino
Parkway Grill
Pig 'n Whistle
Pinot Bistro
Primitivo
Providence
Rock 'N Fish
Sonora Cafe
Spanish Kitchen
Sterling Steak
Table 8
Taste
310 Lounge
Tower Bar
Traxx
Trinity
Twin Palms
Typhoon
Vert
Vibe
Water Grill
Whale & Ale
Whist
White Lotus
Windows
Yi Cuisine
Zucca

Noteworthy Newcomers

Ahi Sushi
Auld Dubliner
Avenue

Baby Blues BBQ
Beechwood
Blue Bamboo
Brass.-Cap.
Brasserie Les Voyous
Café D'Marco
Café 14
Chameau
Cliff's Edge
Dakota
E's Wine Bar
Geisha House
George's Greek
Gorikee
Gozar
Hanoi Cafe
House of Ribs
La Terza
Ma'kai
Meson G
New Concept
Nine Thirty
Opus B&G
Orris
Ortolan
Pecorino
Providence
Rio Carnaval
Schwab's
Sor Tino
Sterling Steak
310 Lounge
Tower Bar
Violet
Woomi Sushi
Yu Rest./Lounge

Offbeat

Authentic Cafe
A Votre Sante
Babita
Back Home/Lahaina
Back on the Beach
Barbara's/Brewery
BCD Tofu
Benihana
Bistro 31
Blue Pacific
Buca di Beppo
Burger Continental
Café Brasil
Cafe Stella
Caioti Pizza
Canal Club
C & O Trattoria
Canter's
Cha Cha Chicken

Los Angeles – Special Features

Chameau
Cheebo
Chez Jay
Cholada
Damon's Steak
Duke's Coffee
Ebizo's Skewer
Edendale Grill
Encounter
Formosa Cafe
Fred 62
Galley
Grub
Guelaguetza
Gumbo Pot
Hollywood Canteen
Javan
JR's BBQ
Loft
Lotería!
Magic Carpet
Mama Voula
Manna
Monsoon Cafe
Moun of Tunis
Mr. Cecil's Ribs
Neptune's Net
Pacifico's
Palms Thai
Papadakis Taverna
Patrick's
Philippe the Original
Piccolo
Pig
Rae's
Roscoe's
Saladang
Sawtelle Kitchen
Stinking Rose
Swingers
Tibet Nepal
Tlapazola Grill
Tommy's
Uzbekistan
Versailles

Bono's
Buffalo Club
Cabo Cantina
Canter's
Chaya Brasserie
Chaya Venice
Chocolat
Cinch
Crustacean
Dakota
Dolce Enoteca
Formosa Cafe
Fred 62
Geisha House
Gozar
Grill on the Alley
Hungry Cat
Ivy
Jones Hollywood
Katana
Kate Mantilini
Katsu-ya
Koi
La Boheme
Little Door
Lola's
Madre's
Ma'kai
Maple Drive
Mastro's Steak
M Cafe de Chaya
Morels First Floor
Morton's
Mr. Chow
Nate 'n Al's
Nine Thirty
Norman's
O-Bar
Ortolan
Palm
Spago
Standard
Sterling Steak
Sushi Roku
Yi Cuisine

People-Watching

Abbey
Akwa
Alcove
A.O.C.
Asia de Cuba
Barney Greengrass
Beechwood
Blowfish Sushi
Blvd
Boa

Power Scenes

Ago
A.O.C.
Barney Greengrass
Bastide
Belvedere
Blvd
Buffalo Club
Dakota
Dominick's
Grace

Grill on the Alley
Hamasaku
Hotel Bel-Air
La Cachette
Le Dome
Locanda Veneta
Maple Drive
Mastro's Steak
Matsuhisa
Meson G
Morton's
Nick & Stef's Steak
Norman's
Ortolan
Palm
Patina
Providence
Sona
Spago
Sterling Steak
Toscana
Valentino
Water Grill

Private Rooms

(Restaurants charge less at off times; call for capacity)

Abbey
Admiral Risty
Aioli
Antonio's
A.O.C.
Arnie Morton's
Arroyo Chop Hse.
Back on the Beach
Banzai Sushi
Bar Celona
Barefoot B&G
Bar Marmont
Beau Rivage
Beckham Grill
Belvedere
Bistro Gdn./Coldwater
BJ's
Bliss
Bluewater Grill
Boa
boe
Brass.-Cap.
Bravo
Buca di Beppo
Buffalo Club
Buggy Whip
Buona Sera
Ca'Brea
Ca' del Sole
Café Bizou

Cafe Del Rey
Cafe Pinot
Café Santorini
Campanile
Canal Club
C & O Trattoria
Carmine's
Carnival
Castaway
Cézanne
Chart House
Checkers
Chez Jay
Chez Melange
Chez Mimi
Christine
Cicada
Cinch
Courtyard
Cucina Paradiso
Dal Rae
Dar Maghreb
De Lacey's
Depot
Derby
Derek's
Devon
Dino's Italian
Divino
Dolce Enoteca
Drago
Duke's
El Cholo
El Torito
Enoteca Drago
Fleming Prime Steak
Four Oaks
Galley
Gaucho Grill
Geisha House
G. Garvin's
Gigi Brasserie
Giorgio Baldi
Gladstone's Malibu
Gordon Biersch
Grace
Halie
Hal's B&G
Hollywood & Vine
House of Blues
Il Cielo
Il Fornaio
Il Moro
Il Sole
Inn of Seventh Ray
James' Beach
JiRaffe

Joe's Crab
John O'Groats
Jones Hollywood
Joss
Katana
Kate Mantilini
Kendall's Brasserie
Khoury's
King's Fish Hse.
Koi
La Cachette
La Terza
La Velvet Margarita
Lawry's Prime Rib
Le Dome
Little Door
Lola's
L'Opera
L'Orangerie
Madison
Maggiano's
Mandaloun
Maple Drive
Marino
Marla's
Massimo
Mastro's Steak
Matisse
Matsuhisa
McCormick/Schmick
McKenna's
Mélisse
Meson G
Michael's
Minibar
Monsoon Cafe
Moonshadows
Morels French Steak
Mr. Chow
Napa Valley
Nick & Stef's Steak
Nirvana
Nonya
Norman's
Oasis
Oceanfront
Off Vine
One Pico
Opus B&G
Ortolan
Pacific Dining Car
Palm
Parkway Grill
Patina
Pinot Bistro
Polo Lounge
Ritz Huntington

Röckenwagner
R23
Ruth's Chris
Smitty's Grill
Sona
Sonora Cafe
Spago
Sterling Steak
Table 8
Tanino
Tantra
Thousand Cranes
Tower Bar
Urasawa
Valentino
Vibrato
Villa Sorriso
Whist
Windows
Woo Lae Oak
Xiomara
Yamashiro
Yi Cuisine
Yujean Kang's
Zucca

Romantic Places

Arnie Morton's
Bastide
Beacon
Beau Rivage
Belvedere
Bistro 45
Blvd
Brandywine
Brentwood
Buffalo Club
Cafe Del Rey
Cafe des Artistes
Café Mundial
Capo
Casa Vega
Cézanne
Chateau Marmont
Checkers
Chez Mimi
Chocolat
Cliff's Edge
Courtyard
Cucina Paradiso
Dakota
Derek's
Diaghilev
Dominick's
EM Bistro
E's Wine Bar
Four Oaks

Gardens
Geoffrey's
Grace
Green Patio Cafe
Harbor Drive
Hotel Bel-Air
Il Cielo
Il Grano
Il Sole
Inn of Seventh Ray
Ivy
Ivy at the Shore
Jaan
Jer-ne
JJ Steak
Joe's
Josie
La Boheme
La Cachette
L.A. Farm
La Finestra
La Fondue
La Parisienne
La Sosta Enoteca
Le Chêne
Le Dome
Little Door
L'Orangerie
Lucques
Madre's
Maximilians
Mélisse
Meson G
Michael's
Mimosa
Mistral
Mix
Moonshadows
Noé
Norman's
Oasis
Oceanfront
Off Vine
One Pico
Ortolan
Patina
Piccolo
Pinot Bistro
Providence
Rambutan Thai
Raymond
Ritz Huntington
Saddle Peak
Sir Winston's
Sky Room
Sona
Sterling Steak

Taste
Tower Bar
Valentino
Vito
Xiomara
Yamashiro

Singles Scenes

Abbey
Beechwood
BJ's
Boa
Bono's
Border Grill
Broadway Deli
Buddha's Belly
Café Santorini
Café Tu Tu Tango
Canal Club
Canter's
Chaya Brasserie
Chaya Venice
Cheebo
Chez Jay
Chez Melange
Chocolat
Cinch
Ciudad
Cobra Lily
Dominick's
Edendale Grill
El Coyote
Electric Lotus
E's Wine Bar
Father's Office
Formosa Cafe
Geisha House
Gordon Biersch
Gozar
Grace
Hal's B&G
Hama Sushi
Harbor Drive
i Cugini
Ivy at the Shore
James' Beach
Jones Hollywood
Koi
La Boheme
Le Dome
Lola's
Ma'kai
Mäni's Bakery
Maple Drive
Mastro's Steak
McCormick/Schmick
Mediterraneo

Mel's Drive-In
Miyagi's
Moonshadows
Morton's
Nick & Stef's Steak
Ocean Ave.
Ole!
Opus B&G
Outlaws B&G
Paladar
Palm
Parkway Grill
Primitivo
Rock 'N Fish
Standard
Stanley's
Sterling Steak
Sushi Roku
Swingers
Tengu
Teru Sushi
Twin Palms
Typhoon
Urth Caffé
Wabi-Sabi
White Lotus
Ye Olde King's Head

Special Occasions

Bastide
Belvedere
Bistro 45
Blvd
Ca' del Sole
Cafe Del Rey
Chinois on Main
Cicada
Diaghilev
Drago
Grace
Harbor Drive
Hotel Bel-Air
Jaan
JAR
Jer-ne
JJ Steak
Joe's
Kendall's Brasserie
La Boheme
La Cachette
Le Dome
Maple Drive
Marino
Mastro's Steak
Matsuhisa
Nick & Stef's Steak
Noé

Norman's
Ocean & Vine
One Pico
Ortolan
Palm
Patina
Providence
R23
Saddle Peak
Sona
Spago
Sterling Steak
Tower Bar
Tuscany
Valentino
Xiomara

Trendy

Ago
Akwa
Allegria
Ammo
Asia de Cuba
Bar Celona
Beacon
Beechwood
Blair's
Blowfish Sushi
blue on blue
Boa
Buddha's Belly
Cafe Stella
Chameau
Chateau Marmont
Chaya Venice
Cinch
Cliff's Edge
Cobra Lily
Cobras & Matadors
Dakota
Dan Tana's
Dolce Enoteca
Edendale Grill
Electric Lotus
Firefly
Geisha House
Giorgio Baldi
Gozar
Gyu-Kaku
Hama Sushi
Hump
Jones Hollywood
Katana
Katsu-ya
Koi
Kokomo Cafe
La Boheme

La Velvet Margarita
Le Dome
Lincoln
Little Door
Lodge Steak
Madre's
Ma'kai
Malo
Mastro's Steak
M Cafe de Chaya
Meson G
Minibar
Nine Thirty
Nobu Malibu
Norman's
Oasis
Ocean & Vine
Ole!
Opus B&G
Ortolan
Paladar
Pastis
Primitivo
Rock 'N Fish
R23
Sona
Spanish Kitchen
Standard
Sterling Steak
Sushi Roku
Table 8
Tantra
310 Lounge
Tower Bar
Urth Caffé
Venice Cantina
Villa Sorriso
Wabi-Sabi
White Lotus
Yi Cuisine
Yu Rest./Lounge
Zen Grill
Zip Fusion

Views

Asia de Cuba
Back on the Beach
Beau Rivage
Belmont Brewing
Bluewater Grill
Bob Morris'
Bono's
Cafe Del Rey
Chart House
Duke's
Encounter
Geoffrey's

Getty Center
Gladstone's Malibu
Hump
Inn of Seventh Ray
Ivy at the Shore
Khoury's
Kincaid's
Lobster
Malibu Seafood
Martha's 22nd St.
Moonshadows
Oceanfront
One Pico
Parker's Lighthouse
Reel Inn
Rock 'N Fish
Saddle Peak
Samba
Sapori
Sir Winston's
Sky Room
Sushi Roku
Taverna Tony
Tony P's Dockside
Torafuku
Tower Bar
Towne
22nd St. Landing
Windows
Yamashiro

Visitors on Expense Account

Ago
A.O.C.
Arnie Morton's
Arroyo Chop Hse.
Bastide
Belvedere
Blvd
Boa
Brass.-Cap.
Buffalo Club
Campanile
Capo
Celestino
Chaya Brasserie
Chaya Venice
Checkers
Chinois on Main
Cicada
Crustacean
Dakota
Devon
Diaghilev
Dominick's
Drago

Fogo de Chão
Four Oaks
Gardens
Geisha House
Geoffrey's
Grace
Grill on Hollywood
Harbor Drive
Hump
Ivy
Ivy at the Shore
Jaan
JAR
Jer-ne
JiRaffe
Joe's
Josie
La Boheme
La Cachette
Lincoln
Little Door
Lobster
L'Opera
L'Orangerie
Lucques
Mako
Mastro's Steak
Matsuhisa
Mélisse
Meson G
Michael's
Morton's
Mr. Chow
Nick & Stef's Steak
Nic's
Nobu Malibu
Norman's
Oceanfront
One Pico
Opus B&G
Ortolan
Pacific Dining Car
Palm
Parkway Grill
Patina
Polo Lounge
Porterhouse Bistro
Providence
Raymond
Ritz Huntington
Röckenwagner
Saddle Peak
Shiro
Sona
Sterling Steak
Sushi Nozawa
Sushi Roku
Takao
Valentino
Vincenti
Water Grill
White Lotus
Yujean Kang's

Waterside

Back on the Beach
Belmont Brewing
Blue Pacific
Bluewater Grill
Boa
Bob Morris'
Cafe Del Rey
Chart House
Cheesecake Factory
Daily Grill
Duke's
Ebizo's Skewer
El Torito
Geoffrey's
Gladstone's Malibu
Guido's
Il Boccaccio
Inn of Seventh Ray
Ivy at the Shore
Jody Maroni's
Joe's Crab
Khoury's
Kincaid's
Lobster
Malibu Seafood
Martha's 22nd St.
Moonshadows
Oceanfront
One Pico
Parker's Lighthouse
Patrick's
Pedals
Ruby's
Samba
Sapori
Sir Winston's
Sky Room
Tony P's Dockside
22nd St. Landing
Uncle Bill's Pancake
Venice Cantina

Winning Wine Lists

Admiral Risty
Ago
A.O.C.
Arroyo Chop Hse.
Avenue
Bastide
Beacon

Beechwood
Bistro 45
Blvd
Boa
Brass.-Cap.
Ca'Brea
Cafe Del Rey
Cafe Pinot
Campanile
Chaya Brasserie
Checkers
Chez Melange
Chinois on Main
Crustacean
Dakota
Devon
Drago
E's Wine Bar
555 East
Grace
Grill on the Alley
Harbor Drive
Hotel Bel-Air
Il Moro
Ivy
Jer-ne
JiRaffe
Kendall's Brasserie
King's Fish Hse.
La Cachette
La Sosta Enoteca
L'Orangerie
Lucques
Maple Drive
Mélisse
Meson G
Michael's
Morton's
Napa Valley
Nick & Stef's Steak
Ocean Ave.
Opus B&G
Ortolan
Pacific Dining Car
Parkway Grill
Patina
Peppone
Petrossian
Pinot Bistro
Pizzicotto
Primitivo
Raymond
Sona
Spago
Sterling Steak
Taste
Valentino

Water Grill
Yujean Kang's

Worth a Trip
Arcadia
  Din Tai Fung
Calabasas
  Mi Piace
  Saddle Peak
Conejo Valley/Simi Valley
  Leila's
  Mandevilla
  Padri
  Tuscany
Long Beach
  555 East
  Frenchy's Bistro
  L'Opera
Malibu
  Beau Rivage
  Geoffrey's
  Nobu Malibu
Monrovia
  Amori
  Devon
San Gabriel Valley
  Babita
  Empress Harbor
  Golden Deli
  Hayakawa
  Lake Spring Shanghai
  NBC Seafood
  Ocean Star
  Tung Lai Shun
San Pedro
  Papadakis Taverna
Santa Monica
  Lobster
Saugus
  Le Chêne
South Bay
  Café Pierre
  Chez Melange
  Christine
  Fonz's
  Gina Lee's Bistro
  Il Boccaccio
  Kincaid's
  Michi
  Reed's
  Sea Empress
  Tsukiji
Venice
  Baby Blues BBQ
Woodland Hills
  Gorikee

Orange County
Restaurant Directory

Top Food

27 Ramos House Cafe	Pascal
Studio	Napa Rose
26 Black Sheep	Troquet
Basilic	Pavilion
Zov's Bistro	**25** Hobbit

Top Decor

28 Studio	Summit House
26 Pavilion	Chat Noir Bistro
Aqua	Hush
Splashes	Napa Rose
25 Ritz Rest./Gdn.	**24** Cat & Custard Cup

Top Service

27 Pavilion	Cellar
26 Hobbit	Mr. Stox
Basilic	Ritz Rest./Gdn.
Napa Rose	**24** Studio
25 Anaheim White Hse.	La Vie en Rose

Best Buys

1. In-N-Out Burger	6. Zankou Chicken
2. Baja Fresh Mexican	7. Gypsy Den
3. Jody Maroni's	8. Original Pancake
4. Taco Mesa	9. La Salsa
5. Sharky's Mexican	10. Johnny Rockets

Top Food by Location

Anaheim

26 Napa Rose
25 Rosine's
Mr. Stox
24 Zankou Chicken
Anaheim White Hse.

Irvine

25 Ruth's Chris
24 Bistango
Wasa
23 Opah
22 Taiko Japanese

Corona Del Mar

24 Five Crowns
23 Oysters
Bungalow
Rothschild's
Mayur

Laguna Beach

27 Studio
25 Cafe Zoolu
Hush
Five Feet
24 Picayo

Costa Mesa

26 Troquet
25 Golden Truffle
Pinot Provence
Plums Café
24 Taco Mesa

Newport Beach

26 Basilic
Pascal
Pavilion
25 Abe
Fleming Prime Steak

Abe 　　　　　　　　25 | 14 | 19 | $49
2900 Newport Blvd. (29th St.), Newport Beach, 949-675-1739;
www.aberestaurant.com
Disciples descend on Balboa Peninsula to experience chef
Takahashi Abe's "exceptional" sushi "masterpieces" made with
"immaculate precision" from "only the freshest" fish; overlook the
"sterile decor" and wash down the "perfectly balanced flavors"
with "premium sakes", and if you can't swing the "incredible
omakase", remember "lunch is a bargain"; P.S. a "premiere
Crystal Cove" branch is set to open fall 2005.

Accents 　　　　　　　　▽ 21 | 20 | 21 | $47
Fairmont Newport Beach, 4500 MacArthur Blvd. (bet. Birch St. &
Von Karman Ave.), Newport Beach, 949-476-2001;
www.suttonplace.com
"Lovely" for Cal-French fare, this "atrium setting" within the
Fairmont (fka Sutton Place Hotel) across from John Wayne
Airport earns kudos for one of "the best Sunday champagne
brunches around"; come dinnertime, the "wine cellar is heaven"
and "perfect for impressing" VIPs; if you have a pre-flight meal here,
count on "wearing a silly grin all the way to your destination";
N.B. menu changes are afoot.

Agave Mexican Grill 　　　　　　　　▽ 20 | 19 | 19 | $24
El Paseo Plaza, 22322 El Paseo (Rancho Santa Margarita Pkwy.),
Rancho Santa Margarita, 949-766-9033;
www.agavemexicanrestaurant.com
"They really did this one right" attest suburbanites who descend
on this "trendy" eatery in RSM owned by the same group behind
Opah and 230 Forest for "creative Mexican" with "California flair",
"tasty" faves like "guacamole made at your table" and "margaritas
that pack a punch"; salsa music on Tuesdays and Thursdays
adds appeal, plus the "patio is a must" for alfresco feasts.

Agora Churrascaria 　　　　　　　　– | – | – | E
1830 Main St. (Macarthur Blvd.), Irvine, 949-222-9910
Massive magnitudes of meat comprise the soul of this dapper new
all-you-can-eat Brazilian steakhouse in Irvine where a plethora
of animal protein is slow-roasted over flames and served rodizio-
style, which means waiters dressed in gaucho gear gallop by your
table to carve cuts to your liking; a colossal salad bar satisfies
non-carnivore desires, while the full bar and business zone location
ensures heavy traffic from executive beef fiends.

Alvarado's Kitchen 　　　　　　　　▽ 20 | 13 | 22 | $32
430 S. Anaheim Hills Rd. (Nohl Ranch Rd.), Anaheim Hills, 714-279-0550
Hiding in a hilltop strip center in Anaheim Hills, this "delightful
neighborhood spot" serves Californian fare "with a unique" touch
to a cadre of locals who also praise the "pleasant ambiance" that
includes "attention from the owner" and customized "specials for
regulars"; "seating is limited" in the shoebox space, so go early
or late to avoid a wait.

Amazon Churrascaria 　　　　　　　　▽ 17 | 13 | 15 | $26
1445 S. Lemon St. (bet. Frwy. 91 & Orangethorpe Ave.), Fullerton,
714-447-1200; www.amazonbbq.com
"Meat, meat and more tasty meat" entices hungry hordes eager to
"eat by the ton" at Fullerton's all-you-can-chew Brazilian buffet

where sabers stacked with just-fired beef and game are offered tableside; so what if the rainforest "decor could better", it's quantity and food with "real flavor" that count at this "carnivore's paradise."

ANAHEIM WHITE HOUSE   24 | 24 | 25 | $48
887 S. Anaheim Blvd. (Vermont Ave.), Anaheim, 714-772-1381;
www.anaheimwhitehouse.com
Owner Bruno Serato's "charming" restored manor house in an improbably "rough" Anaheim neighborhood next door to Mickey's place is "top of the heap" for "fantastic" Northern Italian cuisine backed by "impeccable service"; "gorgeous" rooms swathed in silk add "pizzazz plus" making this a "favorite for gatherings" from "prom nights" to "business meetings" and even spotting celebs like hometown girl "Gwen Stefani."

Antonello ⌧   25 | 24 | 24 | $48
South Coast Plaza, 3800 Plaza Dr. (Sunflower Ave.), Santa Ana,
714-751-7153; www.antonello.com
"Everything is magical" at South Coast Plaza's "perennial powerhouse" for "delectable" "handmade pastas and family recipes" boosted by an "extensive wine list" and "professional old-world" service; the "labyrinthine" palazzo interior "exudes romance" that's "great for a date" but also works for "power lunches and expense-account meals"; if a handful harrumph there's "too much snoot", most retort that Antonio Cagnolo's "special place" is "a must for lovers of serious Italian."

AQUA   25 | 26 | 23 | $65
St. Regis Monarch Beach Resort & Spa, 1 Monarch Beach Resort Dr.
(PCH), Monarch Beach, 949-234-3325; www.stregismb.com
"Panoramic views of the Pacific" supply a "wowie kazowie" backdrop at sunset for "amazing seafood" at this "classy" setting in the St. Regis Monarch Beach Resort where "astronomical prices" are "probably appropriate" for "extra-special" meals "served with just enough élan"; if wavemakers squawk "the price is so lofty the food can't live up to it", aquanuts advise "don't leave this place to the hotel guests alone."

Arches ◗   21 | 17 | 23 | $48
3334 W. PCH (Newport Blvd.), Newport Beach, 949-645-7077;
www.thearchesrestaurant.com
"Step back in time" at PCH's "bit of Newport history" where "waiters in tuxes" serve "old-style" Continental classics and "make fantastic Caesar salads tableside"; the "quiet, dark" decor evokes "old mobster movies", though "prices are in the present" at this "steak boutique" "packed with locals any night of the week"; sure, a jaded few feel this "icon is becoming long in the tooth", nevertheless, most enjoy visiting "nostalgia city."

Baja Fresh Mexican Grill   19 | 10 | 15 | $10
2445 Imperial Hwy. (Kraemer Blvd.), Brea, 714-671-9992
171 E. 17th St. (bet. Fullerton & Orange Aves.), Costa Mesa,
949-722-2994
2540 Main St. (Jamboree Rd.), Irvine, 949-261-2214
26548 Moulton Pkwy. (La Paz Rd.), Laguna Hills, 949-360-4222
2220 E. 17th St. (Tustin Ave.), Santa Ana, 714-973-1943
www.bajafresh.com
Additional locations throughout Southern California
See review in Los Angeles Directory.

Bandera   21 | 20 | 20 | $32
3201 E. PCH (Marguerite Ave.), Corona del Mar, 949-673-3524;
www.houstons.com
See review in Los Angeles Directory.

Bangkok Four   22 | 18 | 19 | $29
South Coast Plaza, 3333 S. Bear St. (Sunflower Ave.), Costa Mesa,
714-540-7661
For "Thai done right", browsers head to this "modern" spot on the
top floor of a South Coast Plaza annex and fuel up on fare that
"surpasses" others in "presentation and subtlety of flavor"; despite
"glass walls", you can hold "quiet conversations" here, making it a
place to take "dates" "or clients" –"even if you're not shopping."

BASILIC ⑤Ⓜ   26 | 19 | 26 | $51
217 Marine Ave. (Park Ave.), Newport Beach, 949-673-0570
You "can't beat the excellent staff and intimate atmosphere" at this
"matchbox-sized bistro" on Balboa Island where "unassuming
genius" chef-owner Bernard Althaus turns out "sophisticated"
French-Swiss dinners from a "limited", but "surprising menu";
"every bite is worth every dollar", prompting acolytes to crow "tiny
space, big delight"; P.S. "don't miss the monthly raclette night."

Bayside   24 | 23 | 22 | $47
900 Bayside Dr. (Jamboree Rd.), Newport Beach, 949-721-1222;
www.baysiderestaurant.com
The "be-seen place to go" in the heart of "Newport's action", this
"stylish" "favorite" lures "old-timers and the young women who
love them" with New American fare "full of flavor"; whether you
"eat at the bar while checking out" the "great live music", on the
"patio with views of the boats" or come for the "excellent Sunday
jazz brunch", the staff "lets you relax", making it a real "treat."

BCD Tofu House   20 | 10 | 13 | $14
9520 Garden Grove Blvd. (Gilbert St.), Garden Grove, 714-636-5599;
www.bcdtofu.com
See review in Los Angeles Directory.

BeachFire   19 | 18 | 17 | $30
204 Avenida Del Mar (N. Ola Vista St.), San Clemente, 949-366-3232;
www.beachfire.com
Downtown San Clemente's "trendy hot spot" is really a "casual
hangout" chockablock with "nice artwork" and a "lively crowd"
noshing on "delicious" Californian dishes; never mind the "laid-
back" "staff of surfers", it's the hippest "thing going for the area",
so blaze a trail for the "music, adult beverages and single chicks."

Benihana   19 | 17 | 19 | $32
2100 E. Ball Rd. (State College Blvd.), Anaheim, 714-774-4940
4250 Birch St. (bet. Corinthian Way & Dove St.), Newport Beach,
949-955-0822
www.benihana.com
See review in Los Angeles Directory.

Bistango   24 | 24 | 22 | $42
19100 Von Karman Ave. (bet. Campus Dr. & DuPont Ave.), Irvine,
949-752-5222; www.bistango.com
A "jewel that never disappoints in any facet", corporate Irvine's
"hip" "atrium space" "explodes with color" from "rotating art

exhibits", setting an "eclectic Manhattan" gallery–type backdrop for "brilliantly executed" New American meals; while there are "lots of suits at lunch" and it's a "bit of a meat market" during "after-work martini" time, it's also "a great romantic destination on date night" with live jazz "enhancing the wonderful environment."

BJ's   17 | 15 | 16 | $18

600 Brea Mall Dr. (Imperial Hwy.), Brea, 714-990-2095
200 Main St. (Walnut Ave.), Huntington Beach, 714-374-2224
280 PCH (bet. Forest & Ocean Aves.), Laguna Beach, 949-494-3802
106 Main St. (Balboa Blvd.), Newport Beach, 949-675-7560
461 W. Esplanade Dr. (bet. Oxnard Blvd. & Vineyard Rd.), Oxnard, 805-485-1124
www.bjsbrewhouse.com
Additional locations throughout Southern California
See review in Los Angeles Directory.

BLACK SHEEP, THE 🖂 Ⓜ   26 | 15 | 24 | $41

303 El Camino Real (3rd St.), Tustin, 714-544-6060;
www.blacksheepbistro.com
An "incredible blend" of "savory, sensual" French and Spanish "delights" from the Mediterranean and "great wines for cheap" keep followers coming baa-ack to chef/co-owner Rick Bouffard's "hidden gem" in Old Towne Tustin "year after year"; the "really unique meals", including "awesome paella" and "wonderful bouillabaisse", are served with "loving customer care", providing a "unique" "break from the chains."

Blue Beet ❶   – | – | – | M

107 21st Pl. (Newport Pier), Newport Beach, 949-675-2338;
www.thebluebeet.com
Said to be the oldest eatery and saloon in the area, this funky joint near the Newport Pier lures an eclectic beach party crowd with high-value American faves like burgers, steaks and fish and an ocean view, if you pick the right table; specials are low-priced, freeing up cash to blow in the lively bar with nightly live music.

Bluewater Grill   19 | 17 | 18 | $31

630 Lido Park Dr. (Lafayette St.), Newport Beach, 949-675-3474
South Coast Plaza, 1621 W. Sunflower Ave. (bet. Bear & Bristol Sts.), Santa Ana, 714-546-3474
www.bluewatergrill.com
See review in Los Angeles Directory.

Britta's Café   21 | 19 | 18 | $31

4237 Campus Dr. (Stanford Ct.), Irvine, 949-509-1211;
www.brittascafe.com
This "cozy place" "tucked away in a strip mall across from UCI" "puts its wood-burning oven to good use", offering "wonderful" meals from an "affordable" "seasonal" American menu that incorporates "the freshest ingredients"; not everyone agrees that it's "a bright spot in Irvine", though, with critics calling the kitchen "hit-or-miss" and certain staffers "ill trained."

Brussels Bistro   ▽ 20 | 18 | 18 | $29

222 Forest Ave. (S. PCH), Laguna Beach, 949-376-7955;
www.brusselsbistro.com
Lagunatics laud this "unpretentious" "sub-street-level" boîte Downtown as "an absolute treat" for "authentic Belgian" noshes

such as "big ol' pots of mussels" and "sinfully good" pommes frites, all sluiced down with "an amazing assortment of beers and ales"; it's "perfect on a chilly night for comfort food" – but "if you're in a rush" remember "the place runs on European time."

Bungalow, The　　23　20　21　$48

2441 E. PCH (MacArthur Blvd.), Corona del Mar, 949-673-6585; www.thebungalowrestaurant.com

"A beautiful Arts and Crafts"–style "locals' hangout" "smack dab in the heart" of Corona del Mar, this surf 'n' turfer is "always crowded" with fans of its "dry-aged steaks", "excellent seafood" and "*magnifique* martinis"; detractors insist "there are better" places, but a majority maintains it "strikes the perfect balance of trendy and homey" and suggests sitting on the "relaxing patio" if the "throngs" inside get "too loud."

Cafe El Cholo　　17　16　17　$22

840 E. Whittier Blvd. (Harbor Blvd.), La Habra, 562-691-4618; www.elcholo.com

"An institution" for "old-fashioned Mexican", this tile-roofed La Habra spot is "still one of the best" of its kind according to fans of its "consistently good" food ("don't miss the green corn tamales" "when in season", May–October) with "amazing margaritas" and served in faux-adobe rooms or in the large patio courtyards; still, the "disappointed" dismiss the "middlin'" fare as "gringo" grub, wondering "what happened to this once great place?"

Café Hidalgo　　▽ 19　18　19　$27

Villa del Sol, 305 N. Harbor Blvd. (Commonwealth Ave.), Fullerton, 714-447-3202

"Totally unpretentious", this "cute little place" in a "historic building" in the heart of revitalized Downtown Fullerton earns praise for Southwestern fare like the "incredible chimichurri steak", "very good seviche" and "great sangria"; the "friendly staff" and "lovely setting", including an "attractive patio", add "just the right touch of old-world ambiance."

Café R&D　　19　21　19　$28

555 Newport Center Dr. (San Miguel Dr.), Newport Beach, 949-219-0555

"The Houston's guys have done it again" say supporters of this "hip eatery" in a "great Fashion Island location" that beckons shoppers in need of a "quick bite" with "mighty tasty" American sandwiches and salads and "good people-watching"; still, the "simple menu" may need more R&D "to work out the kinks" as some find it "too limited" and "pricey."

Café Tu Tu Tango ●　　18　20　16　$23

The Block at Orange, 20 City Blvd. W. (City Dr.), Orange, 714-769-2222; www.cafetututango.com

See review in Los Angeles Directory.

Cafe Zoolu Ⓜ　　25　13　19　$39

860 Glenneyre St. (bet. St. Anne's Dr. & Thalia St.), Laguna Beach, 949-494-6825

Laguna "locals" descend on this "funky", "retro" Californian "shanty of gastronomy" to tackle "some of the best seafood in Orange County" served in "come-hungry" portions – including "baseball-cut swordfish" "the size of George Foreman's fist"; sure, "you don't go for" the "cramped" "hole-in-the-wall" setting or occasionally "slow service", but the drawbacks are "worth" it since "the food is unbelievable" ("reservations are a must").

Californian, The
∇ 20 | 22 | 22 | $43 |

Hyatt Regency Huntington Beach, 21500 PCH (Beach Blvd.), Huntington Beach, 714-845-4776; www.huntingtonbeach.hyatt.com
"What a pleasant" Californian "surprise" exclaim enthusiasts of this "upscale" destination for all-day dining in Surf City's Hyatt Regency Huntington Beach resort, where a palm-lined courtyard with reflecting pool and Pacific views create a "beautiful setting"; hotel guests appreciate the "wonderful breakfasts", but locals confide this sleeper is "never crowded" for other meals.

California Pizza Kitchen
18 | 14 | 17 | $19 |

Brea Mall, 1065 Brea Mall (Imperial Hwy.), Brea, 714-672-0407
Park Pl., 2957 Michelson Dr. (Jamboree Rd.), Irvine, 949-975-1585
25513 Marguerite Pkwy. (La Paz Rd.), Mission Viejo, 949-951-5026
Santa Ana Main Pl., 2800 N. Main St. (Town & Country Rd.), Santa Ana, 714-479-0604
Market Pl., 3001 El Camino Real (Jamboree Rd.), Tustin, 714-838-5083
www.cpk.com
Additional locations throughout Southern California
See review in Los Angeles Directory.

California Wok ⊘
17 | 7 | 16 | $15 |

3033 S. Bristol St. (Paularino Ave.), Costa Mesa, 714-751-0673;
www.california-wok.com
See review in Los Angeles Directory.

Cannery Seafood of the Pacific
22 | 22 | 20 | $40 |

3010 Lafayette Ave. (30th St.), Newport Beach, 949-566-0060;
www.cannerynewport.com
"Valet your car or your boat" at this waterside classic where "superb" seafood is served with "astounding views of Newport Harbor" as "fancy yachts come and go"; the "fun scene" upstairs is "recommended" for its "great sushi", cocktails and "lounge atmosphere", while downstairs offers the appeal of "restful" "sit-down dinners" lit by suspended "glowing glass jellyfish" – even if a few carp that you get a side of "snooty thrown in for free."

Capriccio
∇ 23 | 15 | 18 | $25 |

Village Center Shopping Ctr., 25380 Marguerite Pkwy. (La Paz Rd.), Mission Viejo, 949-855-6866
"Don't walk – run" to this "longtime favorite", a "hidden gem" in "restaurant-poor Mission Viejo", where the "tasty", "authentic" "Italian basics" are "consistently good" and "reasonably priced" (don't miss the annual pasta festival in April); those who find the "small" space a tad "cramped" suggest you "try lunchtime when they're not so busy."

Catal Restaurant & Uva Bar
21 | 20 | 18 | $38 |

Downtown Disney, 1580 S. Disneyland Dr. (Ball Rd.), Anaheim, 714-774-4442; www.patinagroup.com
This "grown-ups' oasis in the Land of the Mouse" from the Patina Group is a "great escape" for "solid", "upscale" Med meals amid "atmosphere that's unmatchable" – at least "in Downtown Disney"; some find it "a bit lacking" due to "hit-or-miss service", but it beguiles most with "balcony views" and a "handy" "outdoor" bar for sitting "under the stars."

CAT & THE CUSTARD CUP, THE   24 | 24 | 24 | $45

800 E. Whittier Blvd. (Harbor Blvd.), La Habra, 562-694-3812; www.catandcustardcup.com

"Only true foodies know" of this "classy" "little secret" in La Habra with a "funny name", owned by the El Cholo folks, where "superb" Californian–New American fare and "fantastic service" ensure diners "leave with a smile"; add in "dark, clubby" "English pub atmosphere" and a "nice piano bar" and you have a "homey" "jewel" that's "good for a date" or "special occasion."

Catch, The   22 | 20 | 21 | $36

1929 S. State College Blvd. (Katella Ave.), Anaheim, 714-935-0101; www.catchanaheim.com

There's no catch when it comes to the "great location" of this "classy" but "not stuffy" surf 'n' turf canteen: it's adjacent to both Anaheim's stadium and arena, attracting spectators and players alike with its "interesting appetizers", "fine" steaks and "excellent seafood", all bolstered by "courteous service"; with "Dom Perignon, oysters and the Angels", no wonder some smitten supporters sigh "it's awfully close to heaven."

Cedar Creek Inn   19 | 20 | 19 | $29

20 Pointe Dr. (Lambert Rd.), Brea, 714-255-5600
384 Forest Ave. (3rd St.), Laguna Beach, 949-497-8696
26860 Ortega Hwy. (El Camino Real), San Juan Capistrano, 949-240-2229
www.cedarcreekinn.com

"A varied menu" of "always-dependable" American "basics" "to fit all tastes" lures all ages to this chainlet known for "pretty, flower-filled patio" courtyards, "good cocktails" and "great entertainment"; if cynics carp the "cozy surroundings" can't offset "boring" eats, plenty praise it for "a nice lunch or casual evening out"; N.B. the Palm Springs outpost is not related.

CELLAR, THE ⌧ Ⓜ   25 | 22 | 25 | $52

Villa del Sol, 305 N. Harbor Blvd. (Wilshire Ave.), Fullerton, 714-525-5682

"New ownership" "hasn't changed" this "classic" cradled beneath Fullerton's historic Villa del Sol, where "impeccable" "traditional" French cuisine is "beautifully presented" by a "professional" "black-tie staff" within the "genteel" setting of an "old wine cellar"; add in an "excellent" selection of *vins* and it's no wonder this "charming little spot" remains a "stalwart standby" for "romantic, special evenings."

Chakra   – | – | – | E

University Ctr., 4143 Campus Dr. (Berkeley Ave.), Irvine, 949-854-0009; www.chakracuisine.com

Indian cuisine reinvented is the daring domain of this UCI-adjacent hot spot where the upscale digs are as creative as the exotic drinks and sultry fare; the stylish patio and frequent lounge entertainment attract the post-dinner crowd (of course, there's a VIP room), creating a hip vibe rarely attempted in these parts.

Chanteclair   18 | 20 | 20 | $47

18912 MacArthur Blvd. (Douglass St.), Irvine, 949-752-8001; www.chanteclair.org

Supporters praise this country French venue near SNA (John Wayne Airport) as a "classy" choice thanks to a "romantic" setting, "very good food" and a staff that's "able to read [your] mind"; still, critics find the proceedings at the "once-proud" institution "somewhat pretentious" and complain that the "nostalgia" comes "at a high price."

Chart House | 19 | 21 | 19 | $37 |
34442 St. of the Green Lantern (PCH), Dana Point, 949-493-1183
2801 W. PCH (Riverside Dr.), Newport Beach, 949-548-5889
www.chart-house.com
See review in Los Angeles Directory.

CHAT NOIR BISTRO & JAZZ LOUNGE | 22 | 25 | 22 | $50 |
655 Anton Blvd. (Bristol St.), Costa Mesa, 714-557-6647;
www.culinaryadventures.com
"Ooh-la-la" purr "hip" cats who "love" the "eye-popping decor" and "excellent" French bistro fare at this "sultry" South Coast Plaza–adjacent "Parisian lounge"; some howl that its "overly red, overly themed" digs get "noisier than an airport tarmac", but for most it's a "great spot" for "live jazz" after a show at OCPAC; N.B. a post-*Survey* chef change may impact the Food rating.

CHEESECAKE FACTORY | 20 | 18 | 18 | $24 |
Brea Mall, 120 Brea Mall (Imperial Hwy.), Brea, 714-255-0115 ●
Irvine Spectrum Ctr., 71 Fortune Dr. (Pacifica St.), Irvine, 949-788-9998
42 The Shops at Mission Viejo (I-5), Mission Viejo, 949-364-6200
Fashion Island, 1141 Newport Center Dr. (Santa Barbara Dr.),
Newport Beach, 949-720-8333
www.thecheesecakefactory.com
See review in Los Angeles Directory.

Chimayo at the Beach | 18 | 21 | 17 | $31 |
315 PCH (Main St.), Huntington Beach, 714-374-7273;
www.culinaryadventures.com
The "fun vibe" lasts all day at this "oceanfront location" "on the boardwalk" in Huntington Beach that puts sol-seekers "right on the sand" for "delish mango martinis" and "fish tacos while watching surfers" and other "eye candy" or "relaxing" near the "wonderful fire pit"; "exceptional setting" aside, though, most report that the Pacific Rim menu "tries too hard" but just "can't beat" the "fantastic view", especially "at sunset."

Citrus Cafe | 19 | 18 | 19 | $29 |
1481 Edinger Ave. (Red Hill Ave.), Tustin, 714-258-2404;
www.citruscafe.com
Citrus City Grille ⌧
122 N. Glassell St. (Chapman Ave.), Orange, 714-639-9600;
www.citruscitygrille.com
"Cheerful in every aspect", this "funky" joint in Old Towne Orange is "not to be missed" according to fans of its "creative" Californian fare and "excellent martinis"; some sensitive sorts bemoan the "deafening noise level", but most maintain it's a "refreshing" stop for "lunch on the patio while out antique shopping"; P.S. in addition to the unrated Tustin cousin, there's a new sibling "in Riverside."

Claes | 22 | 22 | 21 | $43 |
Hotel Laguna, 425 S. PCH (Laguna Ave.), Laguna Beach, 949-376-9283;
www.claesrestaurant.com
Smack dab on Main Beach, this "all-around" winner in the storied Hotel Laguna beguiles admirers with "fresh, well-prepared" seafood that's "better than people expect" (if somewhat "pricey");

the main dining room offers "a magnificent ocean view" from "windows that open" "right onto the Pacific", but for "privacy and romance, ask for a table in the wine cellar"; P.S. the brunch "prix fixe is unbelievable."

Claim Jumper Restaurant   18 | 17 | 18 | $22

190 S. State College Blvd. (Birch St.), Brea, 714-529-9061
3333 Bristol St. (Town Center Dr.), Costa Mesa, 714-434-8479
3935 Alton Pkwy. (Culver Dr.), Irvine, 949-851-5085
25322 McIntyre St. (La Paz Rd.), Laguna Hills, 949-768-0662
2250 E. 17th St. (Tustin Ave.), Santa Ana, 714-836-6658
www.claimjumper.com
Additional locations throughout Southern California
See review in Los Angeles Directory.

Cottage, The   17 | 16 | 16 | $21

308 N. PCH (Aster St.), Laguna Beach, 949-494-3023;
www.thecottagerestaurant.com
There may be "very little atmosphere" on offer at this "old-fashioned" Downtown Laguna "institution", but it still attracts a "mix of locals and tourists" with its "homestyle" American meals; naysayers decry the fare as "just average" and "not worth the long wait", but others ask "who doesn't like a patio breakfast overlooking the Pacific on a sunny California day?"

Coyote Grill   – | – | – | I

31621 S. PCH (bet. Eagle Rock Way & Sea Bluff Ln.), Laguna Beach,
949-499-4033; www.coyotegrill-lagunabeach.com
Affordable Baja-style Mexican chow fit for surfers and even intrepid tourists keeps this joint jumping, though it's also a longtime fave for laid-back mega-breakfasts of *chilaquiles* and *huevos rancheros*; the weathered venue has a beach shack aura and the patio boasts a Catalina view by day and fire pit action by night.

Crab Cooker, The   22 | 11 | 16 | $24

2200 Newport Blvd. (22nd St.), Newport Beach, 949-673-0100
Enderle Ctr., 17260 E. 17th St. (Yorba St.), Tustin, 714-573-1077
www.crabcooker.com
"A hoot" is how crustacean-coveters classify this "kitschy" "classic" on Balboa Peninsula that "doesn't yield to trends" and is "always crowded" with folks "dining in flip-flops" as "charmingly rude waitresses" shuttle "paper plates" heaping with "reasonably priced", "no-frills seafood"; P.S. the less-crowded Tustin branch is "a great stop on the way to an Angels game."

Crab Cove   ▽ 22 | 22 | 21 | $44

Monarch Bay Plaza, 8 Monarch Bay Plaza (Crown Valley Pkwy.),
Monarch Beach, 949-240-4401; www.crabcoverestaurant.com
Supporters say the "whole Dungeness crab is a winner" at this Monarch Beach Euro-Asian seafooder where "well-prepared" fare is offered in a strip-mall space dressed up with gold walls and a koi-pond walkway; nixxers note "small portions" at "hefty prices", but optimists opine that "fine tuning could turn it into a gem."

Crescent City   ▽ 15 | 12 | 15 | $16

The Market Place in Tustin, 2933 El Camino Real (East Dr.), Tustin,
714-453-3555; www.crescentcitybeignets.com
City folk settle into this "cafe-style environment" for "good comfort food" of the Cajun-Creole variety ("great beignets and café au

lait") at this Tustin tyro, the sole California outpost of a Houston-based chain; but the less moonstruck consider the "hit-or-miss menu" "undistinguished" and the modest digs "pretty weak" decorwise, advising it's "better to take out than sit down."

Daily Grill
18 16 18 $27

Jamboree Promenade, 2636 Dupont Dr. (Via Nicola), Irvine, 949-474-2223
Fashion Island, 957 Newport Center Dr. (Santa Barbara Dr.), Newport Beach, 949-644-2223
www.dailygrill.com
See review in Los Angeles Directory.

Darya
23 21 22 $28

South Coast Plaza Vlg., 1611 W. Sunflower Ave. (bet. Bear & Bristol Sts.), Santa Ana, 714-557-6600; www.daryasouthcoastplaza.com
"Try it, you'll like it" suggest followers who flock to this "hangout for Iranian expats" "tucked away" in the "foodie mall" of South Coast Plaza for "generous portions" of "fragrant" "authentic" fare, perhaps "the best Persian food in OC, hands down"; the "nondescript entrance hides" an "elegant" setting worthy of a "grand" "Istanbul hotel", complete with "waiters in tuxes", making it a "great place to entertain associates or family."

Dizz's as Is Ⓜ
23 18 22 $42

2794 S. PCH (Victoria Dr.), Laguna Beach, 949-494-5250
"Off the beaten path, unknown to tourists", this "totally funky, totally fun" "art deco" south Laguna "institution" with "mismatched eclectic decor" is "full of loco locals" eager to "step back in time", "grab a favorite cocktail" and "peruse the descriptive menu" of "to-die-for" Eclectic fare; "friendly", "professional service" helps ease the sting of "difficult parking" and a "no-reservations" policy.

Dolce Ristorante
20 18 18 $44

800 W. PCH (Dover Dr.), Newport Beach, 949-631-4334
Surveyors clash on this upscale Newport Italian noted to be "popular with the Ferrari/mistress set"; sweet talkers say it's "expensive but worth it" for "delicious", "really romantic meals by the fire pit" while detractors who dispense with the sugarcoating snipe it's "overpriced" for "adequate" food, plus service "might just depend on if you arrived by Rolls-Royce or Ford."

Duke's Malibu/Huntington Beach
18 21 18 $30

317 PCH (Main St.), Huntington Beach, 714-374-6446; www.hulapie.com
See review in Los Angeles Directory.

El Cholo
18 18 18 $22

Alton Sq., 5465 Alton Pkwy. (Jeffrey Rd.), Irvine, 949-451-0044; www.elcholo.com
See review in Los Angeles Directory.

El Torito
15 15 16 $19

2020 E. Ball Rd. (State College Blvd.), Anaheim, 714-956-4880
5980 Orangethorpe Ave. (Valley View St.), Buena Park, 714-521-8338
3520 The City Way E. (The City Dr. S.), Orange, 714-939-6711
17420 17th St. (Yorba St.), Tustin, 714-838-6630
22699 Oakcrest Circle (Yorba Linda Blvd.), Yorba Linda, 714-921-2335
www.eltorito.com
Additional locations throughout Southern California
See review in Los Angeles Directory.

El Torito Grill
18 | 16 | 17 | $23

555 Pointe Dr. (Lambert Rd.), Brea, 714-990-2411
1910 Main St. (MacArthur Blvd.), Irvine, 949-975-1220
Kaleidoscope, 27741 Crown Valley Pkwy. (I-5), Mission Viejo,
949-367-1567
Fashion Island, 951 Newport Center Dr. (Santa Barbara Dr.),
Newport Beach, 949-640-2875
www.eltorito.com
See review in Los Angeles Directory.

Filling Station
▽ 19 | 15 | 21 | $15

201 N. Glassell St. (W. Maple Ave.), Orange, 714-289-9714
Refuel with "homemade" American fare at this "historical" Old
Towne Orange pit stop that "used to be a gas station back in the
day"; park yourself on the "funky patio", signal for "neighborly
service" and start your engines with one of the "best" breakfasts
"for miles" or a burger that'll make you "salivate"; add a "great
dessert" and you may dub it the "overfilling station."

Fish Market, The
18 | 15 | 16 | $27

Irvine Spectrum Ctr., 85 Fortune Dr. (Pacifica St.), Irvine, 949-727-3474;
www.thefishmarket.com
This "different for Irvine" eatery may be a chain offshoot, but it's
also Spectrum's sole seafooder, and some finatics feel it offers the
"best" fish "selection around", complete with an oyster bar in a
"bright" (some say "cafeteria-type") setting; still, cynics snipe it
"lacks the wow factor" and toss it back as "nothing spectacular."

Fitness Pizza/Grill
▽ 20 | 17 | 19 | $20

103 W. Imperial Hwy. (Brea Blvd.), Brea, 714-672-0911
Yorba Linda Station, 18246 Imperial Hwy. (bet. Lemon Dr. &
Yorba Linda Blvd.), Yorba Linda, 714-993-5421
www.fitnessgrill.com
"Don't let the name mislead you", these north county Med siblings
"easily prove healthy doesn't have to mean tasteless", offering a
"tasty menu" of "eclectic pizzas and salads" offset by a "fun wine
list"; "just because" it's good for you "doesn't mean you can eat
twice as much" counsel calorie counters who confide that the
"nicely presented" dishes come with "nutritional breakdowns."

Five Crowns
24 | 24 | 24 | $46

3801 E. PCH (Poppy St.), Corona del Mar, 949-760-0331;
www.lawrysonline.com
"Pleasing crowds for years", CdM's Tudor "landmark" "upholds
the fine Lawry's tradition", offering a "touch of England" with
"scrumptious" "prime rib and all the trimmings" served by a
"fantastic" staff in "period" "wench" costumes; some dethrone it
as a "boring" "trip down memory lane", but loyalists enjoy "the
extra something" for "special occasions", especially "during the
holidays" when "carolers" "transport" you to "Dickens' London."

Five Feet
25 | 18 | 20 | $44

Anaheim Marriott Suites, 12015 Harbor Blvd. (Chapman Ave.),
Garden Grove, 714-383-6000
328 Glenneyre St. (bet. Forest Ave. & Mermaid St.), Laguna Beach,
949-497-4955
"Eclectic, fun and funky", Laguna's "secluded" "cool spot" remains
"an old standard" for "wildly creative, expertly executed" Chinese–

New French with such "explosive flavors" some say it's "only for the daring"; the "postmodernist" digs are "crowded but tolerable", packed with a "wonderful mix of locals and tourists"; P.S. during the summer it's "a standby for the Pageant of the Masters" while the more tranquil Garden Grove branch is convention-center close.

Fleming's Prime Steakhouse & Wine Bar   25 23 23 $53
Fashion Island, 455 Newport Center Dr. (San Miguel Dr.), Newport Beach, 949-720-9633; www.flemingssteakhouse.com
See review in Los Angeles Directory.

Fox Sports Grill   16 20 16 $25
Irvine Spectrum Ctr., 31 Fortune Dr. (Pacifica St.), Irvine, 949-753-1369; www.foxsportsgrill.com
"The mother of all sports bars" with an "unbeatable cool factor" cheer supporters who "go for the food and beer but stay for the game" on the "wall-to-wall TVs", billiards and the bowling alley at this "entertaining" chain offshoot in the Spectrum Center; "mingle with friends" over brewskis or "take a date" to the "intimate dining room" for "good" American fare that's "not your typical bar" grub.

French 75   23 24 21 $55
1464 S. PCH (bet. Calliope & Mountyain Sts.), Laguna Beach, 949-494-8444; www.culinaryadventures.com
"Truly stunning" sigh the starry-eyed smitten by the "lovely" decor that evokes Paris in the "1940s" at Laguna's "longtime favorite" where diners "sip champagne" and indulge in "French delights" to a soundtrack of live piano or jazz; if a few are galled by "snobbish" service and "middle-of-the-road" fare, they're drowned out by love birds who gush it may be "the best date restaurant in OC."

Gaucho Grill   18 15 17 $23
210 W. Birch St. (Brea Blvd.), Brea, 714-990-9140
See review in Los Angeles Directory.

Gemmell's   ▽ 23 15 20 $39
34471 Golden Lantern St. (Dana Point Harbor Dr.), Dana Point, 949-234-0064; www.gemmellsrestaurant.com
OC veteran chef-owner Byron Gemell turns out "solid" French-Continental dishes while his staff "makes you feel like part of the family" at this "delightful" "sleeper" "in an unlikely" yet "enticing" Dana Point Harbor location; if a few frown that the "rich sauces" recall "the Reagan years" and dis the "unimaginative" decor, more insist it's "one of the best-kept secrets" around.

Golden Truffle, The ⒮Ⓜ   25 14 20 $44
1767 Newport Blvd. (bet. 17th & 18th Sts.), Costa Mesa, 949-645-9858
"Eccentric" chef-owner Alan Greeley's cult following worships at this "oddball outpost" where the "eclectic" French-Caribbean menu is an "adventurous mix" of "classics" and "culinary experiments"; the "crazy" strip-mall location can't diminish the glow of meals that "wow your palate"; all said, this "great find" is "very un-Orange County – in a good way."

Gordon James Grill   ▽ 22 20 21 $34
110 N. El Camino Real (Avenida Del Mar), San Clemente, 949-498-9100; www.gordonjamesgrill.com
"Finally, San Clemente has come of age" with this "diamond in a rough food town" agree south county admirers who applaud the

"interesting" New American at this "stylish" bistro in a carefully restored historic Downtown building; if a few find the fare "well prepared, but never outstanding", there are "enjoyable" pluses to compensate, from "giant martinis" to a "nice fireplace in the fall."

Green Parrot Cafe ⊠　　　　　▽ 22 | 13 | 19 | $24

2035 N. Main St. (north of 17th St.), Santa Ana, 714-550-6040; www.greenparrotcafe.net

On weekdays "when you want something different" wing your way over to this "hard to find" Spanish courtyard "across the street from OC's wonderful Bowers Museum" where "consistently good" Californian is served in a dining space that's all "great patio seating" adjoining an art gallery; P.S. "check out the wine nights", which aren't "common in this neck of the woods."

Gulfstream　　　　　20 | 19 | 20 | $33

850 Avocado Ave. (PCH), Newport Beach, 949-718-0187; www.houstons.com

See review in Los Angeles Directory.

Gulliver's　　　　　21 | 19 | 20 | $36

18482 MacArthur Blvd. (bet. Frwy. 405 & Michelson Dr.), Irvine, 949-833-8411; www.gulliversrestaurant.com

"The closest thing in SoCal to England" is located across from the John Wayne Airport in Irvine at this "trip back in time" steakhouse where "older patrons" and "business travelers" flock for "hearty" British fare served by waitresses in "period costumes"; Anglophiles agree there's nothing Lilliputian about the "Brobdingnagian portions" of "thick-cut prime rib with all the trimmings" and never fail to appreciate how "lovely it is at Christmastime."

Gypsy Den　　　　　19 | 17 | 15 | $13

The LAB, 2930 Bristol St. (bet. Baker St. & Randolph Ave.), Costa Mesa, 714-549-7012
125 N. Broadway (2nd St.), Santa Ana, 714-835-8840
www.gypsyden.com

"Pretend you're an artist, not a suit" at these coffeehouses serving "surprisingly good" desserts plus "mix 'n' match" soups, salads and sandwiches; "vintage decor" and "off-the-beaten-path" locations amp up the "alternative" aura, prompting patrons to quip it's "as anti-establishment as you can get in cookie-cutter OC"; P.S. the Costa Mesa original is alcohol free while the Santa Ana offshoot has "cool music" and serves beer and wine.

Habana　　　　　21 | 19 | 18 | $27

The LAB, 2930 Bristol St. (bet. Baker St. & Randolph Ave.), Costa Mesa, 714-556-0176; www.restauranthabana.com

Costa Mesa's "funky" LAB is home to this "truly unique" choice for Cuban standards from some of the "best roasted chicken" to "excellent" mojitos; whether you're hanging out in the "hip", "dark" space with "tons of" "dripping candles" enjoying the "flamenco dancers" or indulging in a "hopelessly romantic" "alfresco" meal on the "lovely patio" during "balmy summer evenings", it's a "nice break from the usual."

Heroes Bar & Grill ◐　　　　　19 | 16 | 16 | $17

125 W. Santa Fe Ave. (N. Harbor Blvd.), Fullerton, 714-738-4356; www.heroesrestaurant.net

See review in Los Angeles Directory.

Hibachi Steak House
▽ 22 | 15 | 20 | $30

*Rancho Plaza, 108 S. Fairmont Blvd. (Santa Ana Canyon Rd.),
Anaheim, 714-998-4110*
Sure, "there aren't many choices for Japanese in Anaheim Hills",
but this "popular teppan-style" joint is said to be "better than" its
widely known "brand-name competitor" for what may be "the
tenderest filet and seafood" "cooked in front of you" by knife-
twirling chefs; the "pleasant staff" keeps things moving, so no
matter how you slice it, it's always an "entertaining evening."

HOBBIT, THE Ⓜ
25 | 23 | 26 | $74

*2932 E. Chapman Ave. (Malena St.), Orange, 714-997-1972;
www.hobbitrestaurant.com*
"Dining the way it should be" rejoice foodies who journey to
Orange's "quaint" "old house" for "memorable" French-Continental
repasts with "remarkable service" that feels like "great theater";
the "divine", single seating "experience" can last for three and a
half hours, beginning in the "wondrous wine cellar" and proceeding
though seven courses in the "main part" of the establishment; in
short, this "prix fixe throwback" is "unlike any other."

House of Blues ◗
15 | 21 | 15 | $30

*Downtown Disney, 1530 S. Disneyland Dr. (off Harbor Blvd.),
Anaheim, 714-778-2583; www.hob.com*
See review in Los Angeles Directory.

HOUSTON'S
21 | 20 | 20 | $31

*Park Pl., 2991 Michelson Dr. (Jamboree Rd.), Irvine, 949-833-0977;
www.houstons.com*
See review in Los Angeles Directory.

HUSH
25 | 25 | 21 | $55

*858 S. PCH (bet. Cleo & Thalia Sts.), Laguna Beach, 949-497-3616;
www.hushrestaurant.com*
"There's nothing quiet" about Laguna's "very swanky", "high-
energy" "hot scene" that feels "like a W Hotel lobby" with a "great
glam crowd" "drinking at the community table" or tucking into
"inventive" New American creations complemented by an "out
of this world", though "astronomically priced wine list"; "get a
fireplace table", a "chichi" vantage point for "watching celebs"
or "choose the outside patio" "to hear oneself think" at what "may
be the loudest restaurant in the county."

Ichibiri
19 | 13 | 16 | $28

*16 Monarch Bay Plaza (Crown Valley Pkwy.), Dana Point, 949-661-1544
Rancho Niguel Shopping Ctr., 27981 Greenfield Dr. (Crown Valley Pkwy.),
Laguna Niguel, 949-362-8048
1814 N. El Camino Real (Pico Ave.), San Clemente, 949-361-0137*
These "always busy" south county Japanese triplets supply "solid
sushi" and "upbeat" "teppan corny fun" for a "mixed clientele"
that can biri well include everyone from "well-heeled high
schoolers" to families with kids itching to "watch the show"; if a
few frown it's "overpriced", they're drowned out by supporters
that insist it's "reasonable" for "food that sparkles."

IL FORNAIO
20 | 19 | 19 | $31

*Lakeshore Tower, 18051 Von Karman Ave. (bet. Main St. &
Michelson Dr.), Irvine, 949-261-1444; www.ilfornaio.com*
See review in Los Angeles Directory.

Inka Grill
18 | 14 | 16 | $20

260 Bristol St. (Red Hill Ave.), Costa Mesa, 714-444-4652
301 Main St. (Olive Ave.), Huntington Beach, 714-374-3399
23600 Rockfield Blvd. (Lake Forest Dr.), Lake Forest, 949-587-9008
www.inkagrill.com

"The green sauce is exceptional" – "put it on everything and all is right in the world" concur conquistadors who've discovered this "friendly" trio of "simple, sweet" Peruvians specializing in "tasty food with vibrant spices"; join the "fun mix of people" and dig into the "big portions" and "you'll be glad you sought out" these "hidden gems" assert seekers of "something different."

IN-N-OUT BURGER ●⍤
24 | 11 | 19 | $7

594 W. 19th St. (Anaheim Ave.), Costa Mesa
18062 Beach Blvd. (Talbert Ave.), Huntington Beach
4115 Campus Dr. (Bridge Rd.), Irvine
27380 La Paz Rd. (Avenida Breve), Laguna Niguel
Tustin Mktpl., 3020 El Camino Real (Jamboree Rd.), Tustin
www.in-n-out.com
Additional locations throughout Southern California
See review in Los Angeles Directory.

Islands
16 | 16 | 16 | $15

250 S. State College Blvd. (E. Birch St.), Brea, 714-256-1666
18621 Brookhurst St. (Ellis Ave.), Fountain Valley, 714-962-0966
2201 W. Malvern Ave. (N. Gilbert St.), Fullerton, 714-992-6685
4020 Barranca Pkwy. (Culver Dr.), Irvine, 949-552-1888
1380 Bison Ave. (Macarthur Blvd.), Newport Beach, 949-219-0445
www.islandsrestaurants.com
Additional locations throughout Southern California
See review in Los Angeles Directory.

Iva Lee's
▽ 24 | 22 | 23 | $34

DeNaults Plaza, 555 N. El Camino Real (Avenida Palizada), San Clemente, 949-361-2855; www.ivalees.com

South county goes Deep South at San Clemente's "beautiful" spot for "superlative" Creole-Cajun dishes "with a California touch"; saunter into the teensy bar for "delicious drinks" and live blues music then sink into the "cozy" room offering all the "charm" of "a small New Orleans bistro"; it's "packed", but "service doesn't suffer" – no wonder a "lively crowd" returns "again and again."

JackShrimp
19 | 11 | 15 | $22

26705 Aliso Creek Rd. (Pacific Park Dr.), Aliso Viejo, 949-448-0085
Park Pl., 3041 Michelson Dr. (Jamboree Rd.), Irvine, 949-252-1023
2400 W. PCH (Tustin Ave.), Newport Beach, 949-650-5577
www.jackshrimp.com

"Succulent" shrimp in an "unsurpassable" "spicy sauce" is the lure at these "down-home" sibs with a "tasty but not very diverse" menu of Big Easy basics; while detractors knock the "tiny" digs and "slow" service, hooked hordes retort "if you think you can find better Cajun"-style crustaceans, "you don't know Jack."

Javier's Cantina & Grill
22 | 19 | 18 | $26

Irvine Spectrum Ctr., 45 Fortune Dr. (Pacifica St.), Irvine, 949-872-2101
480 S. PCH (Laguna Ave.), Laguna Beach, 949-494-1239

"Always jammed with fun-loving beautiful people", these "festive" twin cantinas are a "delicious but deafening" "cut above" for "creative" "high-end" Mexican seafood coupled with "potent margaritas" made from a "killer list of tequilas"; the original "laid-back" Laguna site offers "great people-watching" while the new Irvine outpost boasts "architecturally interesting" digs, and since both are *mucho* "boisterous", "long waits are standard."

Jody Maroni's Sausage Kingdom 20 | 6 | 13 | $9 |
The Block at Orange, 20 City Blvd. W. (City Dr.), Orange, 714-769-3754; www.jodymaroni.com
See review in Los Angeles Directory.

Joe's Crab Shack 14 | 14 | 15 | $24 |
12011 Harbor Blvd. (Chapman Ave.), Garden Grove, 714-703-0505
2607 W. PCH (Tustin Ave.), Newport Beach, 949-650-1818
www.joescrabshack.com
See review in Los Angeles Directory.

Johnny Rebs' 22 | 18 | 21 | $20 |
2940 E. Chapman Ave. (bet. Malena Dr. & Prospect St.), Orange, 714-633-3369; www.johnnyrebs.com
See review in Los Angeles Directory.

Johnny Rockets 16 | 14 | 16 | $12 |
The Spectrum, 71 Fortune Dr. (Pacifica), Irvine, 949-753-8144
188 PCH (Ocean Ave.), Laguna Beach, 949-497-7252
20 City Blvd. (Justice Ctr.), Orange, 714-769-4500
www.johnnyrockets.com
Additional locations throughout Southern California
See review in Los Angeles Directory.

King's Fish House/King Crab Lounge 21 | 19 | 20 | $30 |
24001 Avenida de la Carlota (El Toro Rd.), Laguna Hills, 949-586-1515
1521 W. Katella Ave. (Main St.), Orange, 714-771-6655
www.kingsfishhouse.com
See review in Los Angeles Directory.

La Cave ☒ 22 | 17 | 19 | $41 |
1695 Irvine Ave., downstairs (17th St.), Costa Mesa, 949-646-7944; www.lacaverestaurant.com
Costa Mesa's "subterranean hideaway" is a "real blast from the past" reminiscent of "old lounge days" where Cave dwellers order "signature steaks" and seafood from a "visible menu" on a "rolling trolley"; while some diners liken the "dark" den to a "*Dracula* movie set", it's "caught on with a younger" group that revels in the "retro digs", and often packs 'em in for "consistently great live jazz."

La Salsa 16 | 9 | 13 | $10 |
3850 Barranca Pkwy. (Culver Dr.), Irvine, 949-786-7692
Fashion Island, 401 Newport Center Dr. (San Miguel Dr.), Newport Beach, 949-640-4289
www.lasalsa.com
See review in Los Angeles Directory.

Las Brisas 16 | 22 | 17 | $34 |
361 Cliff Dr. (PCH), Laguna Beach, 949-497-5434; www.lasbrisaslagunabeach.com
"Pretty people" and "tourists" galore skip the "Liberace decor" in this Laguna Beach classic's "stuffy" dining room and "race for a table" on the "lovely patio" to soak up "spectacular views of the

Pacific"; while the Mexican seafood gets mixed reviews from "divine" to "mediocre", the "breathtaking scenery" is "worth anything else this place lacks", making it "lovely for Sunday brunch" or "watching the sunset with a tall cool one."

La Vie en Rose ⌧　　24 | 24 | 24 | $45

240 S. State College Blvd. (Imperial Hwy.), Brea, 714-529-8333; www.lavnrose.com

"*Vive la France!*" declare "devotees" who "make a beeline" to Brea's "lovely old favorite" for "very gourmet" "classic French fare" served amid "a great deal of ambiance"; the "elegant but cozy" "countryside" surroundings feel Gallic "in every sense of the word", abetted by "understated" service that "exceeds your expectations"; all said, this "nice-for-suburbia" "touch of class" is the place "when you want to impress or be impressed."

Lawry's Carvery　　19 | 12 | 13 | $19

South Coast Plaza, 3333 Bristol St. (Sunflower Ave.), Costa Mesa, 714-434-7788

Carnivores "dying for a Lawry's fix" hunt down this "fast-food version" in a far-flung nook in South Coast Plaza where the "famous" "succulent, carved" roasts are served "counter-style" to the "sandwich market" with "crispy" "homemade potato chips"; while an insatiable few find the fare "too spare for the price", most opine it's like "heaven on a bun for the weary shopper", making this "meat-licious" stop a "step above" "standard mall food."

Lazy Dog Cafe, The　　▽ 19 | 17 | 18 | $21

Target Pavillions Shopping Ctr., 16310 Beach Blvd. (MacDonald Ave.), Westminster, 714-500-1140

Tails wag over Westminster's "cute", "casual" Traditional American–Eclectic eatery boasting the "longest menu ever seen"; pet dishes include "solid" renditions of "everything from pizza to stir-fries" and even four-legged friends are "accommodated on the long, thin outside porch" with a "water bowl"; throw in "sincere" service and know why this "noisy, crowded" "retreat" fetches "long waits on weekends."

L'Hirondelle Ⓜ　　23 | 19 | 22 | $35

31631 Camino Capistrano (Ortega Hwy.), San Juan Capistrano, 949-661-0425

Veteran voters report "even under new ownership" this "true Belgian" "jewel" "hidden in the rail station's shadow" across the street from the Mission in San Juan Capistrano is "a delight", so "bring your passport" for a "friendly" "European experience"; *amis* agree that the "cozy" "old-world" dining room and "ample menu" of "reliable dishes" make it "worth a visit" for dinner, adding "it's a real treat to dine in the outdoor garden at lunch."

Lodge, The　　▽ 17 | 16 | 16 | $33

The Camp, 2937 Bristol St. (bet. Baker & Bear Sts.), Costa Mesa, 714-751-1700

Respondents spar over Tim Goodell's "interesting" Costa Mesa destination for American comfort food and lounge action; critics say the "menu needs work", the "service is snooty" and the "weird" decor "won't win any awards", but Lodge lizards insist the "rustic *Brady Bunch*" "linoleum" setting where "the bar is the star" "sends you back a few decades", offering a "cool vibe" for "great basic fare."

Loft, The ⓩ   18 │ 15 │ 17 │ $15
7862-B Warner Ave. (Beach Blvd.), Huntington Beach, 714-842-2911;
www.loft.d2g.com
See review in Los Angeles Directory.

Luciana's   ▽ 20 │ 18 │ 20 │ $37
24312 Del Prado Ave. (bet. Blue Lantern & Ruby Lantern Sts.),
Dana Point, 949-661-6500; www.lucianas.com
Coast dwellers in search of an "intimate" evening head to Dana
Point's "reliable", "retro", "romantic setting" that's "cozy, warm
and Italian all the way"; the fare has a "down-home" feel, and
while it may "not be innovative", the "shirt-staining wine list",
"friendly" hospitality, "happy clientele" and "great ambiance in
winter" (fueled by multiple fireplaces) more than "make up for" it.

Lucille's Smokehouse Bar-B-Que   22 │ 18 │ 19 │ $24
1639 E. Imperial Hwy. (Rte. 57), Brea, 714-990-4944; www.lucillesbbq.com
See review in Los Angeles Directory.

Maggiano's Little Italy   19 │ 19 │ 19 │ $27
South Coast Plaza, 3333 Bristol St. (Anton Blvd.), Costa Mesa,
714-546-9550; www.maggianos.com
See review in Los Angeles Directory.

Market City Caffe   17 │ 18 │ 16 │ $22
110 Birch St. (Imperial Hwy), Brea, 714-529-7005;
www.marketcitycaffe.com
See review in Los Angeles Directory.

Mascarpone's Ⓜ   ▽ 25 │ 14 │ 22 │ $34
1446 E. Katella Ave. (bet. N. California & N. Tustin Sts.), Orange,
714-633-0101
The owners are "sticklers for high-quality ingredients" – you
"notice the difference the moment" your "marvelous food" arrives
assert amici of this "outstanding family-run Italian" set in a
"rather secluded" Orange strip mall; sure, the "decor needs
work, but nothing can stop" loyalists who laud the "marvelous"
dishes and the "best cheesecake on earth" delivered by a staff
that makes you "feel like a VIP regular."

Mayur   23 │ 14 │ 19 │ $34
2931 E. PCH (bet. Heliotrope & Iris Aves.), Corona del Mar, 949-675-6622
Villagers seek out CdM's "little jewel" for "sensitively prepared"
Indian "done right" and "outside the Americanized norm" in an
"area not known for ethnic"; yes, it's a "little pricey", but the
service is "polite" and it's hard to resist those "terrific" aromas
wafting "inside and out" the "peaceful environs"; P.S. "it's a
wonderful lunch retreat as well."

McCormick & Schmick's   19 │ 19 │ 19 │ $35
2000 Main St. (Gillette Ave.), Irvine, 949-756-0505;
www.mccormickandschmick.com
See review in Los Angeles Directory.

Melting Pot, The   20 │ 20 │ 20 │ $43
Jamboree Promenade, 2646 Dupont Dr. (Jamboree Rd.), Irvine,
949-955-3242; www.meltingpot.com
For a "dipping good time" that's "great for a date" or "interactive"
"group festivities" head to this "clever fondue concept", a national

chain outpost in Irvine where prix fixe "dining becomes a leisure activity"; there are "oodles of choices" from "fabulous cheeses" to "decadent chocolate" finales – add a "nice bottle of wine and that's all you need"; still, not everyone is willing to fork over for tabs that seem "expensive" "once the novelty has worn off."

Memphis 21 | 13 | 17 | $26
2920 Bristol St. (Randolph Ave.), Costa Mesa, 714-432-7685
Artists Vlg., 201 N. Broadway (2nd St.), Santa Ana, 714-564-1064
www.memphiscafe.com
"Campy and fun", these "funky" "hole-in-the-wall" "roadhouse settings" offer "a fantastic spin" on Southern "recipes" ("soul food" in Costa Mesa and Santa Ana, "who knew?"); "you're sure to be impressed" by the "spicy" "down-home" victuals and the "delightful, friendly staff", especially if you're looking for "a refreshing change from the OC scene."

Mimi's Cafe 17 | 17 | 17 | $18
1240 N. Euclid St. (W. Romneya Dr.), Anaheim, 714-535-1552
18461 Brookhurst St. (Ellis Ave.), Fountain Valley, 714-964-2533
27430 La Paz Rd. (Avila Rd.), Laguna Niguel, 949-643-0206
22651 Lake Forest Dr. (Muirlands Blvd.), Lake Forest, 949-457-1052
17231 E. 17th St. (I-55), Tustin, 714-544-5522
www.mimiscafe.com
Additional locations throughout Southern California
See review in Los Angeles Directory.

Mirabeau ●Ⓜ 25 | 20 | 21 | $42
17 Monarch Bay Plaza (Crown Valley Pkwy.), Monarch Beach,
949-234-1679; www.mirabeaubistro.com
Offering a "piece of Provence in Monarch Beach", this "cozy" "find" "gets an A for effort", luring locals with its "authentically French", "unpretentious", "well-prepared" bistro fare backed by a "balanced wine list" and "Johnny-on-the-spot" service; "brave the strip-mall parking lot" and you'll be rewarded with a "romantic" dinner "by the fireplace" or a "view of the ocean" from the "inviting outside patio" – and "be sure to leave room for dessert."

Modo Mio Cucina Rustica Italiana – | – | – | E
Crystal Cove Promenade, 7946 E. PCH (Crystal Heights Dr.),
Newport Beach, 949-497-9770; www.modomiocucinarustica.com
See review in Los Angeles Directory.

Morton's, The Steakhouse 24 | 22 | 23 | $58
South Coast Plaza, 1641 W. Sunflower Ave. (bet. Bear & Bristol Sts.),
Santa Ana, 714-444-4834; www.mortons.com
"It's all about" the "mouthwatering", "massive portions of prime beef" at this "classy" South Coast Plaza chain outpost that feels like a "real man's steakhouse", replete with "unparalleled" service, "exceptional martinis" and a noise level "so loud nobody will hear you gasp when the check arrives"; bashers bray it's "pretentious", but hordes of carnivores are eager to tap their "home-equity line" for "a whole new cholesterol reading."

Motif ▽ 24 | 22 | 21 | $50
St. Regis Monarch Beach Resort & Spa, 1 Monarch Beach Resort Dr.
(PCH), Monarch Beach, 949-234-3200; www.stregismb.com
The "quiet" "un-hip feel" at the St. Regis Monarch Beach Resort belies its "adventurous" Eclectic-International offerings; the

"savory" small plates add up to a "truly fun experience" for a "moneyed OC crowd" that falls into the pattern of "trying many things without filling up", while soaking up the ocean view from the posh playground's terrace; tipsters whisper "two words: Sunday brunch", it's "great" and "well worth the $$$."

Mrs. Knott's Chicken Dinner   22 | 14 | 18 | $18

California Market Pl., 8039 Beach Blvd. (La Palma Ave.), Buena Park, 714-220-5080

"Colonel, watch out – the Mrs. sure knows how to cook" cackle loyalists who flock to Berry Farm's "old-fashioned" "family favorite" dining hall for the "guilty pleasure" of "crispy chicken joy" with all the American "fixin's" like "fresh, buttery biscuits that are the gold standard" and "trademark boysenberry pie"; the devoted "don't care if they have to wait in line for an hour" because even "the memories make it special."

MR. STOX ◐   25 | 23 | 25 | $48

1105 E. Katella Ave. (bet. Lewis St. & State College Blvd.), Anaheim, 714-634-2994; www.mrstox.com

"Don't be fooled by its low-rent locale", Anaheim's "longtime winner" "meets all the requirements for a fine-dining experience", from its "plush" "clubby" digs to its "exceptional" New American–Continental standards; "elegant" "power lunches and romantic dinners" "continue to delight", enhanced by "unusual breads" and a "world-class wine list" ("ask to see the cellar"), while the service proves "this place knows the customer is the reason it lives."

Mulberry Street Ristorante   ▽ 20 | 15 | 19 | $29

114 W. Wilshire Ave. (Harbor Blvd.), Fullerton, 714-525-1056

Perhaps "the closet thing to NYC's Little Italy we have in OC", this "perfect place for a casual meal" of "consistently good" "basic" Italian fare is "helping to revamp Old Town Fullerton"; the "quaint", "minimalist" digs feel like a "good, old-fashioned neighborhood bar", "a dying breed" this "favorite" calls to mind – little wonder it draws a "mix of locals" from "college students to doctors."

Muldoon's Dublin Pub & Celtic Bar Ⓜ   18 | 20 | 20 | $26

202 Newport Center Dr. (Anacapa Dr.), Newport Beach, 949-640-4110; www.muldoonspub.com

"Very serviceable" Irish "pub grub" "isn't the main attraction" at this "hangout" outside of the Fashion Island mall where folks "eat when they go to drink" from a "nice beer selection"; still, you'll find "arguably the best hamburgers in OC" at this Celtic bar that has "something for everyone", from "great bands" and a "delightful patio" to a "blazing fireplace" that's "welcoming" in the winter.

NAPA ROSE   26 | 25 | 26 | $56

Grand Californian Hotel, 1600 S. Disneyland Dr. (Katella Ave.), Anaheim, 714-300-7170

"The Rose has no thorns" at this "un-Disney", "beautiful Craftsman-style" Californian set "amid the hubbub" of Anaheim's "Mouse empire" in the Grand Californian Hotel; "master" chef Andrew Sutton's "kitchen shines", turning out "Napa Valley–quality" "culinary creations", while "charming" GM-sommelier Michael Jordan offers "remarkable assistance selecting wine" from the "outstanding list"; sure, you "may sit next to the ubiquitous tourist family", but few mind because "this place rocks" ("ears to you" is the decisive kudo) for "special evenings."

Naples Ristorante e Pizzeria   17 | 16 | 16 | $24
1550 S. Disneyland Dr. (Ball Rd.), Anaheim, 714-776-6200;
www.patinagroup.com
Joachim "Splichal goes Neapolitan" at this Patina Group Italian,
a "lighthearted, family-friendly" affair serving "above-standard
pizza and pastas" that are "just good enough" to be "satisfying"
and "reasonably priced" to boot; still, the "excruciating waits" and
"rude service" "by the walking dead" turn some visitors sour, while
more complacent types shrug "it's Disneyland, whadya expect?"

Native Foods   ▽ 22 | 17 | 16 | $15
The Camp, 2937 Bristol St. (bet. Baker & Bear Sts.), Costa Mesa,
714-751-2151; www.nativefoods.com
See review in Los Angeles Directory.

Natraj   19 | 12 | 16 | $16
Food Festival Ct., 26612 Towne Center Dr. (bet. Alton & Bake Pkwys.),
Foothill Ranch, 949-830-2015
13246 Jamboree Rd. (Irvine Blvd.), Irvine, 714-665-0040
24861 Alicia Pkwy. (Hon Ave.), Laguna Hills, 949-581-4200
www.natrajusa.com
"Exotic scents and flavors draw you in" to this trio of "consistently
good" "authentic" Indians deemed "one of the better" choices "by
OC standards" and "reasonably priced" to boot; the "incredible
lunch buffet is the play" that "can't be beat" (though "Sunday
brunch is a huge value"), while "absolutely no atmosphere" makes
it "great for takeout"; N.B. the Foothill Ranch location is a fast-
food spin-off, so natch, no table service.

Nello Cucina   ▽ 20 | 13 | 19 | $30
South Coast Plaza, 3333 Bear St. (Sunflower Ave.), Costa Mesa,
714-640-3365; www.nellocucina.com
"Pretty darn good for being in the middle of South Coast Plaza"
concur customers who congregate for "old-fashioned Italian in a
new-fangled mall"; the "light, fresh fare", conceived by the minds
behind neighboring deluxe Antonello, is more "reasonably priced"
than its "older sibling's" menu, making it a "great place for lunch
after a hard day of shopping."

Nieuport 17   20 | 22 | 21 | $43
13051 Newport Ave. (Irvine Blvd.), Tustin, 714-731-5130
Tustin's "underappreciated gem" is "hidden from the coastal
limelight" but flies high with an "older set" out for "fine" "classically
prepared" Continental boosted by "very good" service from
"experienced waitresses"; the "elegant room" showcases
"unique" vintage aviation mementos, adding appeal a "younger
group is now discovering" and regulars liken to "an old friend."

Oceans 33°   20 | 19 | 16 | $31
799 The Shops at Mission Viejo (Crown Valley Pkwy.), Mission Viejo,
949-365-0200; www.oceans33.com
Opinions ebb and flow over Mission Viejo's "beautifully decorated"
Californian seafooder; fans feel "what's not to love?" – it's got
"some originality", "great appetizers and martinis", "fresh" fin fare
and "warm" hospitality – "the only missing element is an ocean
view"; wavemakers wail it's "overpriced" and dis the "poor
service" from "mall brats", but even they allow it's a "place to
go" when adjacent chains "have a wait."

Olde Ship, The
19 | 19 | 19 | $20

709 N. Harbor Blvd. (bet. Chapman & Union Aves.), Fullerton, 714-871-7447
1120 W. 17th St. (bet. Bristol St. & Flower Ave.), Santa Ana, 714-550-6700
www.theoldeship.com

"It's not hard to imagine the rain" at these "cozy", "atmospheric" British twin pubs in Fullerton and Santa Ana that are "limey heaven" for "expats and Anglophiles" longing for "fish 'n' chips that will spoil you for all others", washed down "with a pint" from the "best selection" of "good draft ales"; expect "long waits on weekends" for "food better than most served on the Isle."

Old Spaghetti Factory, The
14 | 17 | 16 | $17

110 E. Santa Fe Ave. (S. Harbor Blvd.), Fullerton, 714-526-6801
2110 Newport Blvd. (21st St.), Newport Beach, 949-675-8654
www.osf.com

See review in Los Angeles Directory.

O-Nami
18 | 13 | 13 | $24

Laguna Hills Mall, 24155 Laguna Hills Mall (El Toro Rd.), Laguna Hills, 949-768-0500; www.o-nami.com

See review in Los Angeles Directory.

Opah
23 | 20 | 19 | $33

Aliso Viejo Town Ctr., 26851 Aliso Creek Rd. (Enterprise St.), Aliso Viejo, 949-360-8822
The Marketplace, 13122 Jamboree Rd. (Irvine Blvd.), Irvine, 714-508 8055
22332 El Paseo (El Corazon), Rancho Santa Margarita, 949-766-9988
www.opahrestaurant.com

"A splash of trendy" in "ultrasuburban" "SUV land", this "very modern" native OC chainlet hooks an "energetic adult crowd" with "truly original" seafood-centric Californian dishes that look like "works of art"; while a few opah-ine that service is "indifferent" and the "acoustics horrible" ("practice your lip-reading"), it doesn't deter the "lively" "second-time-around social scene" fueled by "fantastic cocktails" and the promise of a "hip", "kid-free zone."

Original Fish Co.
23 | 17 | 22 | $29

11061 Los Alamitos Blvd. (Katella Ave.), Los Alamitos, 562-594-4553; www.originalfishcompany.com

"One of the few in OC" for "ultrafresh fish", Los Alamitos' enduring "throwback" ladles out "fantastic clam chowder" and "delicious" "mesquite-grilled seafood"; the "old-school" Victorian decor may look like "my grandmother's living room", but the "patio is nice" and the staff "couldn't be friendlier", so don't be surprised by "long lines"; N.B. there's a retail market inside.

Original Pancake House, The
23 | 9 | 17 | $13

1418 E. Lincoln Ave. (bet. East St. & State College Blvd.), Anaheim, 714-535-9815 Ⓜ ⌁
18453 Yorba Linda Blvd. (bet. Imperial Hwy. & Lakeview Ave.), Yorba Linda, 714-693-1390
www.originalpancakehouse.com

The "awesome" "pancakes made every way imaginable" are "bar-none the best" say late-sleepers and early-risers of this franchised "monument to American breakfasts" built on "exotic", "high-carb" flapjacks; if a few spirits are flattened by "the dated decor", "tired staff" and long wait "to be seated", it stacks up for most – "how could you not love a Belgian waffle for lunch?"

Outback Steakhouse 18 | 15 | 18 | $25
402 Pointe Dr. (Lambert Rd.), Brea, 714-990-8100
7575 Beach Blvd. (Frwy. 91), Buena Park, 714-523-5788
1670 Newport Blvd. (17th St.), Costa Mesa, 949-631-8377
12001 Harbor Blvd. (Chapman Ave.), Garden Grove, 714-663-1107
2341 Lockwood St. (Solar Dr.), Oxnard, 805-988-4329
www.outback.com
Additional locations throughout Southern California
See review in Los Angeles Directory.

Oysters 23 | 18 | 20 | $42
2515 E. PCH (Bayside Dr.), Corona del Mar, 949-675-7411;
www.oystersrestaurant.com
"Chef Scott Brandon always mixes up the menu" of "imaginative" Cal-Asian fare at this "pearl" nestled in CdM that lures a "see-and-be-seen thirtysomething crowd" with "fabulous jazz", "great cocktails" and a "city feel"; "rich" "locals even get out of their shorts" to enjoy the "grand experience" of this "social mecca", delighting in "delicious mollusks and fin fare" that "surpasses expectations"; regulars suggest retreating to the "garden room if you don't care for noise" and hint that "happy hour is a bargain."

Ozumo ∇ 21 | 24 | 19 | $47
Fashion Island, 849 Newport Center Dr. (Santa Barbara Dr.), Newport Beach, 949-721-0077; www.ozumo.com
Offering a "tasty menu with great variations of Japanese cuisine", this "San Francisco favorite" brings its trademark combo concept of sushi bar, robata grill and sake lounge to Fashion Island, wrapping visitors in an "incredible atmosphere" of "beautiful" Zen high-design; if critics pan the "outrageously priced" "so-so food" and say it's "lacking the vibe" of its SF sis, others declare this newbie is "still working out the kinks."

Pane e Vino 20 | 19 | 19 | $34
240 S. Brea Blvd. (Imperial Hwy.), Brea, 714-256-7779; www.panevino.biz
See review in Los Angeles Directory.

Paolo's Ristorante 🅼 – | – | – | M
Old World Vlg., 7561 Center Ave. (Huntington Village Ln.), Huntington Beach, 714-373-5399
Insiders whisper this indie Italian trattoria "is one of the best-kept secrets in SoCal", "if you can find it", curiously located in the creaky German-themed Old World Village shopping center in Huntington Beach; "locals frequent" this "cute" "little spot" where chef-owner Paolo Pestarino "seems to live and loves to visit his guests" as they devour his Roman classics made with mostly organic ingredients.

PASCAL 🆇 26 | 19 | 24 | $54
1000 N. Bristol St. (Jamboree Rd.), Newport Beach, 949-752-0107; www.pascalnewportbeach.com
"Forever wonderful" sigh smitten Francophiles of "gracious magician" chef-owner Pascal Olhats' "rock solid performer" in Newport Beach that's "not flashy or fussy, just one of the best" for "perfectly authentic" French cooking; the "so-so strip-mall" "impression fades once you step inside" the "white-washed brick room" adorned with "gorgeous roses" and fixate on the "mouthwatering" "comfort food" served by a "knowledgeable staff"; N.B. wine and cheese are sold next door at the Epicerie.

PAVILION　　　　　　　　　　　26 │ 26 │ 27 │ $60

Four Seasons Hotel, 690 Newport Center Dr. (Santa Cruz Dr.),
Newport Beach, 949-760-4920; www.fourseasons.com
"Hotel dining at its best" – yes, "everything is first class" at this
"celebration kind of place" near the Fashion Island mall, from
"personalized" "service that sets the standard" (and ranks No.1
in OC) to the "beautiful room" with "well-spaced tables that permit
conversation"; "expertly prepared" Cal-Med dishes boast "the
finest ingredients", adding to an "experience" that's "memorable in
all respects" (really, "how can you go wrong at a Four Seasons?").

Pei Wei Asian Diner　　　　　　　16 │ 13 │ 14 │ $15

Oak Creek Vlg., 5781 Alton Pkwy. (bet. Jeffrey Rd. & Royal Oak),
Irvine, 949-857-8700
The Bluffs, 1302 Bison Ave. (MacArthur Blvd.), Newport Beach,
949-629-1000
www.peiwei.com
See review in Los Angeles Directory.

Peppino's　　　　　　　　　　　17 │ 12 │ 17 │ $20

26952 La Paz Rd. (Pacific Park Dr.), Aliso Viejo, 949-643-1355
31371 Niguel Rd. (Clubhouse Dr.), Laguna Niguel, 949-661-1250
23600 Rockfield Blvd. (Lake Forest Dr.), Lake Forest, 949-951-2611
27782 Vista del Lago (Marguerite Pkwy.), Mission Viejo,
949-859-9556
651 E. First St. (Newport Ave.), Tustin, 714-573-9904
www.peppinosonline.com
Additional locations throughout Southern California
A "no-frills" choice for "noisy, family-oriented" feasts of "everyday
Italian", this homegrown tribe of "red-sauce houses" offers "large
portions" of "surprisingly addictive" "pizza and beyond", all at
"reasonable prices"; ask them to go "easy on the garlic unless
you plan to sleep in a graveyard" advise the vampire-wary.

Pescadou Bistro Ⓜ　　　　　▽ 20 │ 14 │ 17 │ $32

3325 Newport Blvd. (bet. Finley Ave. & 32nd St.), Newport Beach,
949-675-6990; www.pescadoubistro.com
Hiding in plain sight on the Newport Peninsula, this "locals' place"
charms with "home-cooked" Gallic fare and a "welcoming" aura
that "recalls Provence"; bistro buffs believe it's the "best value" of
its ilk (the "prix fixe is a great deal") and conclude it's a "wonderful"
spot where you can "feel French and eat that way too."

P.F. CHANG'S CHINA BISTRO　　20 │ 19 │ 18 │ $26

Irvine Spectrum Ctr., 61 Fortune Dr. (Irvine Center Dr.), Irvine,
949-453-1211
The Shops at Mission Viejo, 800 The Shops at Mission Viejo
(Crown Valley Pkwy.), Mission Viejo, 949-364-6661
Fashion Island, 1145 Newport Center Dr. (Santa Barbara Dr.),
Newport Beach, 949-759-9007
www.pfchangs.com
See review in Los Angeles Directory.

Pho 79 ⌷　　　　　　　　　　21 │ 6 │ 13 │ $11

9941 Hazard Ave. (Brookhurst St.), Garden Grove, 714-531-2490
Asian Garden Mall, 9200 Bolsa Ave. (bet. Bushard & Magnolia Sts.),
Westminster, 714-893-1883
See review in Los Angeles Directory.

Picayo | 24 | 19 | 23 | $45 |

610 N. PCH (Boat Canyon Dr.), Laguna Beach, 949-497-5051; www.picayorestaurant.com

"Beyond excellent" despite a "less than scenic" "strip-mall" site, Laguna's "hidden gem" "does everything right", "delighting" diners with "intimate" dinners of "inspired" Med fare, "sauces that dazzle" and "friendly" hospitality; if a few feel the "food has declined under new ownership" (Laurent Brazier is no longer a partner, but still a consulting chef) and "don't know what the hype is about", for most it's still a "memorable experience."

Pinot Provence | 25 | 24 | 24 | $51 |

The Westin South Coast Plaza Hotel, 686 Anton Blvd. (Bristol St.), Costa Mesa, 714-444-5900; www.patinagroup.com

"*Magnifique!*" is the word on this "top-tier" choice in the Patina Group empire (some say the "best Pinot" of the bunch) set in Costa Mesa's Westin South Coast Plaza where chef Florent Marneau devises "innovative" "sooo French" "seasonal specialties"; service is "flawless" and the "dreamy" room lends a "serene" quality to "romantic evenings"; proximity to OCPAC means guests can "park, dine, walk to the theater" then return for "dessert after the show."

Plums Café & Catering | 25 | 16 | 19 | $19 |

Westport Square Shopping Ctr., 369 E. 17th St. (Tustin Ave.), Costa Mesa, 949-722-7586; www.plumscafe.com

The "Pacific Northwest comes to SoCal" via Costa Mesa's "adorable" eatery serving "treats" "you won't find elsewhere" like pan-fried trout and wild berry tarts; "hats off to the owners" cheer customers "hooked" on the "incredibly good", "well-priced" "breakfast/brunch/lunch" options; most shrug off "hit-or-miss service" and the "simple strip-mall" location, because this Plum provides a "great way to while away a weekend morning."

Pomodoro Cucina Italiana | 18 | 14 | 17 | $19 |

26611 Aliso Creek Rd. (Enterprise St.), Aliso Viejo, 949-831-1400
5789 Alton Pkwy. (Royal Oak), Irvine, 949-654-1100
234 Forest Ave. (S. PCH), Laguna Beach, 949-497-8222
Newport Coast Shopping Ctr., 21133 Newport Coast Dr. (N. PCH), Newport Beach, 949-759-1303
2214 N. Tustin St. (off E. Meats Ave.), Orange, 714-998-3333
www.pastapomodoro.com

See review in Los Angeles Directory.

Prego | 20 | 19 | 20 | $39 |

18420 Von Karman Ave. (Michelson Dr.), Irvine, 949-553-1333; www.spectrumfoods.com

See review in Los Angeles Directory.

Rainforest Cafe | 15 | 23 | 16 | $23 |

1515 S. Disneyland Dr. (Katella Ave.), Anaheim, 714-772-0413; www.rainforestcafe.com

"Fun for the li'l 'uns" and "usually crowded" with "tourists", this "cheesy", "veritable theme park" chain replicates "eating in a jungle", complete with "animatronic gorillas and sudden rain showers"; predictably, the "overpriced" New American food is "more adventure than meal" and "subpar" by grown-up standards while the "random" service is also drubbed ("is the waitperson an extra from *Lost*?"), but at least "they do have cocktails."

Ralph Brennan's Jazz Kitchen 19 22 19 $32

*Downtown Disney, 1590 S. Disneyland Dr. (Magic Way), Anaheim,
714-776-5200; www.rbjazzkitchen.com*

As brought to you by the "first family of New Orleans restaurants",
Downtown Disney's "little piece of the Big Easy" offers "loud
jazz", "spot-on decor" and a "balcony for watching the passing
parade of happy people"; confederates consider the Creole fare
"as authentic as you can get locally", but critics judge it "priced
too high" for "Californized" "N'Awlins" food.

RAMOS HOUSE CAFE Ⓜ 27 22 23 $26

*31752 Los Rios St. (Ramos St.), San Juan Capistrano, 949-443-1342;
www.ramoshouse.com*

"Bring your GPS" to find San Juan Capistrano's "hideaway" lodged
in a historic adobe hugging the train tracks where "culinary
genius" chef-owner John Q. Humphreys turns out "magical" New
American cuisine "with Southern flair" that ranks No.1 for Food in
OC; the "tranquil patio" seating flanking the herb garden provides a
"delightful respite from high-powered" options, while "enthusiastic
service" and "killer Bloody Marys" only swell the popularity of
this "unique" choice for breakfast and lunch, prompting fans to
ask "when will they add dinner?"

Red Pearl Kitchen 17 18 15 $33

*412 Walnut Ave. (bet. 5th & Main Sts.), Huntington Beach, 714-969-0224;
www.domainerestaurants.com*

It's a "diamond in the rough" say acolytes who turn to Tim and Liza
Goodell's "crowded" Huntington Beach Pan-Asian for "flavorful"
small and large plates and "fun drinks" in a "1940s Shanghai
den"–type atmosphere; but cynics sniff it's "not up to the owners'
standard", and snipe the staff's in "need of an attitude adjustment."

Ristorante Mamma Gina 20 18 20 $43

*251 PCH (Bayside Dr.), Newport Beach, 949-673-9500;
www.mammagina.com*

"Mama Mia itsa good" laud "loyalists" who "keep coming back"
to these "old-world" twins in Newport Beach and Palm Desert
for "Northern Italian favorites" "comparable to its mother ship in
Florence"; the "problem is choosing" from the "wide variety", so
rely on the "career" staff that "tries hard to please"; if some shrug
"not bad, not spectacular", for most it's "always a pleasure."

RITZ RESTAURANT & GARDEN, THE 25 25 25 $54

*880 Newport Center Dr. (Santa Barbara Dr.), Newport Beach,
949-720-1800; www.ritzrestaurant.com*

A "venerable" "favorite under new ownership", Newport Beach's
"rejuvenated" "classy clubhouse" near the Fashion Island mall is
"still going strong"; "excellent" Continental cuisine "executed
with aplomb" in "glowingly beautiful" surroundings coupled with
"service that shines" make it a "memorable experience"; P.S. the
"rarified air" also yields "fun people-watching" when "elder
statesmen" "crowd the bar" to chat up "the young and beautiful."

Riviera at the Fireside Ⓢ ▽ 23 18 25 $45

*13950 Springdale St. (Frwy. 405), Westminster, 714-897-0477;
www.rivierarestaurant.net*

Westminster's "throwback to a time long gone" lures OC's "old
guard" to its "huge booths" for "rare" Continental dishes prepared

"tableside" by "tuxedoed waiters" delivering "stellar" service with "a personal touch" "the in-laws really like"; sure, the "clubby, dark" dining room is "dated", but the "warm" vibe leads supporters to suggest this "old-school" "landmark" is "so retro it's back again."

Rosine's
25 | 16 | 20 | $22

Ralph's Mkt., 721 S. Weir Canyon Rd. (E. Santa Ana Canyon Rd.), Anaheim, 714-283-5141; www.rosines.com

Anaheim Hills' "family-run" "hidden wonder" is hardly a secret as revealed by "loyal locals" awaiting their turn for "astoundingly" "excellent" Mediterranean-Armenian "comfort food", especially the "addictive" rotisserie chicken; "friendly" service, "super-value" pricing and an "extensive" list of "bargain wines" "that would make Bacchus proud" keep this "strip-mall storefront" "crowded all week"; P.S. "they do takeout" if you're in a hurry.

Rothschild's
23 | 21 | 22 | $44

2407 E. PCH (MacArthur Blvd.), Corona del Mar, 949-673-3750; www.rothschildscdm.com

Corona del Mar's "charming", "comfy" bistro is a "neighborly" choice for "imaginative" Continental–Northern Italian cuisine; the "knowledgeable staff" is adept at "matching food" with their "fine wines", plus there's "never a rush to turn the table", making it a natural for "romantic" encounters for two.

Rouge Bistro & Bar
21 | 24 | 21 | $45

Fashion Island, 327 Newport Center Dr. (Atrium Ct.), Newport Beach, 949-640-2700; www.culinaryadventures.com

"Another David Wilhelm classic" leaves its lipstick imprint on Fashion Island's "fun, flirty" nod to bistro life with a "lush" yet "relaxed" setting saturated in "shades of red and black"; "top-notch" Gallic fare, "great champagne by the glass" and a "pretty", "happening" bar keep it "brasserie noisy" and "hopping with Newport Beach types"; still, a few kiss it off as "faux French", harrumphing "not a destination for foodies."

Royal Khyber
∇ 21 | 21 | 21 | $36

South Coast Plaza, 1621 W. Sunflower Ave. (bet. Bear & Bristol Sts.), Santa Ana, 714-436-1010; www.royalkhyber.com

For "flavors that never disappoint" head to what may be "the nicest" Indian "in OC" right next door to South Coast Plaza; "ample quantities" of "delicious" standards like "perfect tandoori" and naan and samosas that "couldn't be better" are served by a "knowledgeable staff" in a "quietly sophisticated" space where "some thought is paid to decor"; the "smallish wine list" boasting "some nice finds" only gilds this "real" deal for "high-quality" fare.

Royal Thai Cuisine
21 | 15 | 19 | $26

1750 S. PCH (bet. Agate & Pearl Sts.), Laguna Beach, 949-494-8424
4001 W. PCH (bet. Newport Blvd. & Superior Ave.), Newport Beach, 949-645-8424
www.royalthaicuisine.com

The "spartan" surroundings may be "very unassuming" but that doesn't deter adherents from seeking out these "casual", "pleasant", family-run coastal twins in Newport and Laguna for "reliably fresh and tasty" "Thai by the sea" offering "excellent value for the money"; "friendly service" and "great drink prices" prompt promises to "definitely return."

Roy's   24 | 22 | 22 | $45

Fashion Island, 453 Newport Center Dr. (San Miguel Dr.), Newport Beach, 949-640-7697; www.roysrestaurant.com
See review in Los Angeles Directory.

Ruby's   15 | 16 | 17 | $14

1 Balboa Pier (Palm Ave.), Balboa, 949-675-7829
4602 Barranca Pkwy. (Lake Rd.), Irvine, 949-552-7829
30622 S. PCH (Wesley Dr.), Laguna Beach, 949-497-7829
Seal Beach Pier (Ocean Ave.), Seal Beach, 562-431-7829
13102 Newport Ave. (Irvine Blvd.), Tustin, 714-838-7829
www.rubys.com
Additional locations throughout Southern California
See review in Los Angeles Directory.

Rusty Pelican   19 | 19 | 20 | $34

2735 W. PCH (bet. Riverside & Tustin Aves.), Newport Beach, 949-642-3431; www.rustypelican.com
Loyalists drop anchor at Newport Harbor's "perennial favorite" for "very tasty" (if "ordinary") fin fare served by a crew that "goes well beyond the call of duty" with a "view of the bay" that's "perfect around sunset" as a backdrop; if a handful crab that it "needs a major face-lift", most admit it's "nice to see this old-timer hang on."

RUTH'S CHRIS STEAK HOUSE   25 | 21 | 23 | $54

2961 Michaelson Dr. (Jamboree Rd.), Irvine, 949-252-8848; www.ruthschris.com
See review in Los Angeles Directory.

Sabatino's Lido Shipyard   – | – | – | I
Sausage Company

251 Shipyard Way (Lido Park Dr.), Newport Beach, 949-723-0621
Low-key dockside charm, robust Italian fare and a Sicilian family recipe for exceptional sausage are all reasons why locals crowd this Newport Beach spot so hidden within quays and channels, tourists can't find it; snappy service and comfy seating on the patio or in the mural-splashed dining rooms make it a popular choice for dates or casual feasts with family or friends.

Sage   25 | 19 | 22 | $41

Eastbluff Shopping Ctr., 2531 Eastbluff Dr. (Vista del Sol), Newport Beach, 949-718-9650; www.sagerestaurant.com
Sage on the Coast
Crystal Cove Promenade, 7862 East Coast Hwy., Newport Beach, 949-715-7243; www.sagerestaurant.com
"Culinary paradise" rave disciples of "food genius" chef-owner Rich Mead's "charmers", enraptured by the "picture-perfect plates" of New American fare that "cannot be commended enough", ferried to table by an "enthusiastic staff"; "when you want something special without making a big event out of it", the "Eastbluff favorite" is a "gem"; the new Crystal Cove "baby" "may be prettier" and "more of a scene", but it's "equally tasty" and also features "seasonal" organic produce.

Salt Creek Grille   20 | 20 | 18 | $32

32802 PCH (Crown Valley Pkwy.), Dana Point, 949-661-7799; www.saltcreekgrille.com
See review in Los Angeles Directory.

Sam Woo's   21 | 11 | 14 | $19

Metro Pointe Shopping Ctr., 901-C S. Coast Dr. Ste. 180 (bet. Bear St. & Fairview Ave.), Costa Mesa, 714-668-0800

15333 Culver Dr. (Irvine Center Dr.), Irvine, 949-262-0688

Orange Tree Sq., 54068 Walnut Ave. (Jeffrey Rd.), Irvine, 949-262-0128

"Always busy with an ethnic crowd", this "authentic" chain of "bright" Hong Kong–style "no-frills" dining halls churns out "fresh" dim sum and an "exceptional variety" of Chinese dishes; the "incredibly cheap" prices ease the pain of service from "servers snappy as turtles", nonetheless, the "lines out the door" are the ultimate verdict: it's "worth the wait" (and "great for takeout").

Savannah Steak & Chop House   22 | 22 | 21 | $41

Ocean Ranch Shopping Ctr., 32441 Golden Lantern St. (Camino Del Avion), Laguna Niguel, 949-493-7107; www.culinaryadventures.com

"Reminiscent of old steakhouses", David Wilhelm's "clubby" Laguna Niguel "favorite" for surf 'n' turf wins over fans with "huge" "booths that makes you feel like you're dining with just your group", stone fireplaces and an "enjoyable" patio with an ocean view; if a few beef "preparations can be erratic", most enthuse they do an "excellent job on basic meat, potatoes and booze."

Savoury's   ▽ 21 | 22 | 22 | $45

Hotel La Casa Del Camino, 1287 S. PCH (Cress St.), Laguna Beach, 949-376-9718; www.savourys.com

Fans of Laguna's shore-hugging dining room in the vintage Hotel La Casa Del Camino contend it's "underappreciated", though "superb in every way" from the "decent wine list" to the "attentive staff"; if skeptics note the French-Med fare with Pac-Rim accents "can be inconsistent", adventurers insist it's "worth chancing" for the "pleasant ambiance" including a shoreline view from the deck.

Scott's Seafood   23 | 22 | 21 | $43

3300 Bristol St. (Anton Blvd.), Costa Mesa, 714-979-2400; www.scottsseafood.com

"Rub shoulders with the arty crowd" at Costa Mesa's "sure-thing" seafooder "ideally located" for "pre- or post-theater" dining; the "upscale" ambiance is "serene" with "windows all around", yet it "exudes a gracious warmth", and what's more, the menu "manages to stay current", boasting "expertly prepared" fish and "outstanding" "fine steaks" too; still, a handful huff it's "somewhat pricey" and "wonder why it's so busy."

Seafood Paradise   22 | 10 | 16 | $21

8602 Westminster Blvd. (bet. Magnolia & Newland Sts.), Westminster, 714-893-6066

"Mega dim sum" offered "daily" plus a "voluminous" menu of "fabulous" Chinese seafood "bring in" droves of diners and "warrants" "the long wait" at Westminster's "impersonal", "cavernous" "palace"; "weekends are packed" due to "lots of wedding receptions", plus they offer what may be "the best prices in the area" for "live lobster, cooked any way you want it."

Selma's Chicago Pizzeria   – | – | – | I

30461 Avenida de las Flores (Sarracenia), Rancho Santa Margarita, 949-709-8165; www.selmaspizza.com

It's all about the deep-dish pie that pays homage to Chicago at RSM's unpretentious brick walled joint with a Windy City edge; of course there are pastas and calzones, all, like the pizzas, made from scratch using Grandma Selma's recipes.

Shabu Shabu Ⓜ   – | – | – | M
28715 Los Alisos Blvd., Mission Viejo, 949-588-3225
Improbably located on the distant edge of Mission Viejo, this Japanese cafe specializes in shabu-shabu meals diners cook by swish-swishing thinly sliced meats and vegetables in a boiling broth pot; the U-shaped counter includes individual vessels, allowing lively owner Kumi Hirokawa to supply lessons to patrons.

Sharky's Mexican Grill   18 | 11 | 15 | $11
26811 Aliso Creek Rd. (Park Pl.), Aliso Viejo, 949-643-0900
6725 Quail Hill Pkwy. (Passage), Irvine, 949-856-1300
21119 Newport Coast Dr., Newport Beach, 949-729-1000
www.sharkys.com
Additional locations throughout Southern California
See review in Los Angeles Directory.

Shenandoah at the Arbor   ∇ 21 | 23 | 23 | $24
10631 Los Alamitos Blvd. (Sausalito St.), Los Alamitos, 562-431-1990
The "beautiful" "garden setting" sheltered by a "huge mulberry tree draped in lights" distinguishes this "quaint" Los Alamitos cottage-style cafe praised for its "great" hospitality and SoCal "interpretations" of down-South–Cajun cooking from the now-defunct "original" in Long Beach; the "neat setting" sets the scene for a "great lunch" "by the koi pond" or dinner on "chilly nights" with "heat lamps to make it comfortable."

Side Street Cafe ♯   ∇ 22 | 10 | 17 | $14
1799 Newport Blvd. (18th St.), Costa Mesa, 949-650-1986
On a "lazy weekend" relax over "deeelicious" "mongo breakfasts" at this "family-run" American "favorite" in Costa Mesa where the "homemade" fare is "reminiscent of the" "cooking at grandma's" right down to "fresh-squeezed OJ in Mason jars" and the "cute photos" on the wall; yes, the strip-mall site is "cramped" and it's "cash only", but when you're "craving pancakes, this is the place."

6ix Park Grill   ∇ 21 | 18 | 22 | $39
Hyatt Regency Irvine, 17900 Jamboree Rd. (San Diego Frwy.), Irvine, 949-225-6666
"Surprise, surprise, what a delight to find" that this newly refashioned restaurant in the Hyatt Regency in corporate Irvine "exceeds expectations" assert enthusiasts who give the "attentive staff" and "visually enticing" Californian dishes, many made on a wood-fire grill with local ingredients and a French twist, two thumbs-up; new walls of windows bring the patio indoors to airy effect, making it a "good location for a company party."

Sorrento Grille   21 | 20 | 19 | $44
370 Glenneyre St. (Mermaid St.), Laguna Beach, 949-494-8686; www.culinaryadventures.com
Plenty of "beautiful" village people pack this "cramped" "classic Laguna spot" where the "inventive", "crowd-pleasing fare" is Cal-Mediterranean, the "fabulous martinis" are "even better" and the "vibe is nice", especially the upstairs mezzanine where it's "dark and romantic"; if a few rake it over the grille for its "deafening decibel level", scoffing it's "mistaken for high energy", most shrug "otherwise it's a delight", in fact, it "feels just right."

Souplantation   16 | 11 | 12 | $12
1555 Adams Ave. (Royal Palm Dr.), Costa Mesa, 714-556-1903
26572 Towne Centre Dr. (Market Pl.), Foothill Ranch, 949-472-1044
11179 Talbert Ave. (Newhope St.), Fountain Valley, 714-434-1814
2825 Main St. (Jamboree Rd.), Irvine, 949-474-8682
26420 Ynez Rd. (Winchester Rd.), Temecula, 951-296-3922
www.souplantation.com
Additional locations throughout Southern California
See review in Los Angeles Directory.

Spaghettini   21 | 19 | 20 | $35
3005 Old Ranch Pkwy. (bet. Frwy. 405 & Seal Beach Blvd.), Seal Beach,
562-596-2199; www.spaghettini.com
The "interesting" Northern Italian fare is "consistently good" at
this "hip joint" in freeway-close Seal Beach, but it's the "awesome"
"live jazz that definitely attracts" the crowds for "Sunday brunch"
and every night except Monday; while a few cynics sing a different
tune, opining it's "overpriced" for "average" food, plenty more
consider it a "destination" in "a sea of chains and strip malls."

Spark Woodfire Grill   19 | 18 | 18 | $29
300 PCH (Main St.), Huntington Beach, 714-960-0996;
www.sparkwoodfiregrill.com
See review in Los Angeles Directory.

SPLASHES   20 | 26 | 20 | $44
Surf & Sand Resort, 1555 S. PCH (bet. Blue Bird Canyon Dr. & Calliope St.),
Laguna Beach, 949-497-4477; www.surfandsandresort.com
The "scrumptious" Cal-Med dishes are "secondary to the gorgeous
setting" "decorated by Mother Nature" reveal waterbuffs who
believe that "the California lifestyle doesn't get any better" than
sitting on the beach at the Surf & Sand; the "tiered patio niches"
allow diners to "see, hear and feel" the "Pacific rushing in", making
it "romantic at sunset", while "the waves splashing against the
windows" of the lounge "make early arrival for dinner a must."

Steelhead Brewing Co.   14 | 14 | 14 | $21
University Mktpl., 4175 Campus Dr. (Bridge Rd.), Irvine, 949-856-2227;
www.steelheadbrewing.com
"College profs and frat bros" predictably populate UCI's "cheap,
friendly" "place to chill and relax"; a "surprisingly sophisticated"
American menu offers "a little bit of everything", "nevertheless",
there's no mistaking that this offshoot of a Eugene, Oregon, outfit
"is a microbrewery so be prepared for inconsistent service and a
barlike" vibe; in short, it's "just what you would expect across
from a college campus": "average" on all counts."

STUDIO Ⓜ   27 | 28 | 24 | $78
Montage Resort & Spa, 30801 S. PCH (Montage Dr.), Laguna Beach,
949-715-6420; www.montagelagunabeach.com
Though the "kitchen aspires to be the best" at Laguna's "stellar
oceanside offering" "on the cliffs", it's the "enchanting" vistas
of "the turquoise Pacific" seen from the "elegant comfort" of the
"ultradeluxe" Montage Resort that nabs the No. 1 Decor ranking in
OC; when not hypnotized by the "drop-dead" scenery, acolytes
coo over chef James Boyce's "superb" Cal–New French cuisine,
the "endless wine list" and the "polished service", asserting it's
a "special experience."

SUMMIT HOUSE 23 | 25 | 23 | $43
2000 E. Bastanchury Rd. (State College Blvd.), Fullerton, 714-671-4111;
www.summithouse.net
Suitable for "large groups or smaller dinners", North Fullerton's
"top of the hill" ersatz Tudor manse offers "great grounds" and
"awesome views", a "lovely setting" for "elegant meals" of
"traditional" Continental fare like "dreamy prime rib"; "attentive
service" and three fireplaces make it "warm and cozy on cold,
rainy nights" and truly "super duper" during the "holidays when
everything is decorated so festively"; if a scenery seat is imperative,
reserve ahead since "they tend to ration the view tables."

Sundried Tomato Cafe 22 | 17 | 21 | $32
361 Forest Ave. (bet. Beach & Glenneyre Sts.), Laguna Beach,
949-494-3312
Franciscan Plaza, 31781 Camino Capistrano (Ortega Hwy.),
San Juan Capistrano, 949-661-1167
www.thesundriedtomatocafe.com
"A welcome" choice in a "region that favors surf 'n' turf over
adventuresome" fare, these "unassuming" south county beach
burg twins win over locals with "creative", "delectable" Californian
dishes and a "great wine selection", all toted to table by a "cute,
flirtatious staff"; the "intimate" "heart of town" locations boast
"lots of outdoor seating", making this "cute" Tomato a "find" for
a "nice lunch" or "leisurely meal."

Sutra Lounge ⊠ ∇ 19 | 25 | 19 | $38
Triangle Sq., 1870 Harbor Blvd. (bet. Newport Blvd. & 19th St.),
Costa Mesa, 949-722-7103; www.sutrabar.com
"For the very hip and very trendy", Costa Mesa's "exotic"
"Downtown club in a small town" is "very hot right now",
rounding up "good looking people" with a velvet rope for late-
night hanging in a "sexy" setup ("love the opium bed" and
Moroccan-inspired patio); tantric types "into the food scene"
confide "don't put it aside as just a dance place" because the
Eclectic small plates of aphrodisiac eats are way "creative" – but
do "go early" "before the hoochie mamas arrive."

Svelte ●⊠ ∇ 18 | 18 | 16 | $50
440 Heliotrope Ave. (bet. 1st & 2nd Aves.), Corona del Mar, 949-723-9685;
www.svelte.cc
CdM's "very hip neighborhood" destination with an "interesting
communal table" and "St. Tropez–meets–South Beach" setting
dishes out "nice, not spectacular" New American–Asian cuisine
"worth coming for" as long as you "bring a fat wallet"; still, the tea
light–lit ambiance strikes some as "more club than restaurant",
that perhaps best satisfies a "faux Euro-trash crowd" and "singles
searching" for a "little social intercourse."

Sweet Divas Cottage Bistro Ⓜ – | – | – | M
518 E. Imperial Hwy. (Laurel Ave.), Brea, 714-990-4832;
www.sweetdivascakes.com
By day, this charming restored 1920s Craftsman bungalow in
Brea lures ladies for civilized afternoon teas and refined lunches
featuring Cal-French creations by chef-baker/owner Adrianna
Hyman (who also turns out extravagant special-occasion cakes);
weekend evenings and Sunday brunch bring on the men enticed
by the likes of braised short ribs and crab cakes Benedict.

Tabu Grill
▽ 26 | 22 | 24 | $46

2892 S. PCH (Nyes Pl.), Laguna Beach, 949-494-7743;
www.tabugrill.com

"Date worthy, for sure" assert admirers who find nothing taboo about South Laguna's "intimate", "dark, romantic" matchbox, an "exotic setting" for dining on "excellent" steaks and seafood with a Pac-Rim spin bolstered by a "great by-the-glass" wine selection; sure, it's "tiny and often crowded", but for most "it's worth it" for a "great meal."

Taco Loco ◗
22 | 8 | 12 | $11

640 S. PCH (bet. Cleo & Legion Sts.), Laguna Beach, 949-497-1635

"Get your hippie groove on" as you "find your own table, dress your own" Cal-Mexican order, "grab a cerveza and watch the world go by" at Laguna's "classic" "reggae slack-shack" renowned for "innovative" tacos and vegan choices; so what if it's "short on style and service", the "great vibe", "amazing" chow and "late-night" hours make this "local" "Loco" a "favorite."

Taco Mesa ⌂
24 | 9 | 15 | $11

647 W. 19th St. (bet. Harbor Blvd. & Placentia Ave.), Costa Mesa,
949-642-0629
Bridgepark Plaza, 27702 Crown Valley Pkwy. (Marguerite Pkwy.),
Ladera Ranch, 949-364-1957
Los Alisos Vlg., 22922 Los Alisos Blvd. (Trabuco Rd.), Mission Viejo,
949-472-3144
Saddleback Shopping Ctr., 3533 E. Chapman Ave. (Prospect St.),
Orange, 714-633-3922
www.tacomesa.net

"Don't let the lack of atmosphere fool you", this OC family of "cash-only" "dives" earns kudos for "ultratasty" "unique" south-of-the-border creations "with a seafood slant" "made to order" and washed down with "refreshing agua frescas"; "the specials are really special", especially for "gourmet" "Mexi-Californian on a budget", allowing you to "fill your tummy on incredible carnitas with the change in your pocket" – in a word, "¡Fabuloso!"

Taco Rosa
22 | 15 | 19 | $23

Newport Hills Shopping Ctr., 2632 San Miguel Dr. (Bonita Canyon Dr.),
Newport Beach, 949-720-0980

"Inspired" "regional Mexican" with "thoughtful" "variations on favorites" that "leave your mouth zinging for more" draw "foodies" to Newport Beach's "lively, hip" yearling aka the "fancier sister" of the Taco Mesa joints; the more "upscale" digs, "accommodating staff" plus a "full bar" (try the "delicious prickly pear margaritas") lend a "free spirit" vibe for "dates and families alike to enjoy a night out"; leave room for "homemade churros" and "don't miss" the "eye-catching chocolate fountain."

Taiko Japanese Restaurant
22 | 13 | 15 | $25

14775 Jeffrey Rd. (Walnut Ave.), Irvine, 949-559-7190

"Everything's good except the line" to get a seat at Irvine's "amazing" sushi bar revered for "the best and freshest" prepared with "skill and artistry" served in "huge portions" for a "reasonable price"; regulars advise "stick to sushi or sashimi" because "food from the kitchen is just ok"; "little to no ambiance" doesn't deter fin fans from joining the "daunting line outside" to get their fill of "simply the finest sushi ever."

Taleo Mexican Grill
∇ 23 | 22 | 23 | $29

Park Pl., 3309 Michelson Dr. (Jamboree Rd.), Irvine, 949-553-9002; www.taleomexicangrill.com

"Not your standard Mexican", this "welcome addition" to Irvine dares diners to "be adventurous", tempting taste buds with "original" dishes spiked with a "roller-coaster ride of flavors" and seducing the senses with surroundings "full of style" and "vivid colors"; "flawless" service imparts a "positive energy" at this "new venture" that "has it all", particularly for "chatty business lunches" or "semi-romantic meals."

Tangata ⊠ Ⓜ
∇ 22 | 21 | 17 | $30

Bowers Museum of Cultural Art, 2002 N. Main St. (20th St.), Santa Ana, 714-550-0906; www.patinagroup.com

The "artful food" at this convenient cafe "fits its wonderful" Bowers Museum location nestled in the "pretty, peaceful" Old California courtyard; sure, this Patina Group lunch-only outpost "has had its ups and downs", but the "interesting" Californian food is "much improved", prompting perusers to declare "there's no better" for a bite "before, during or after visiting the collections."

Tannins
∇ 17 | 15 | 17 | $29

Rancho Ortega Plaza, 27211 Ortega Hwy. (Rancho Viejo Rd.), San Juan Capistrano, 949-218-3560; www.tanninsrestaurant.com

Grape expectations are fulfilled at San Juan Capistrano's "nice surprise" in a "strip mall" that pairs "very good (or better)" Southern Italian dishes with an "extensive" vino selection; "fun flights" of small pours from many bottles "complement each other in some way", plus the by-the-glass options are "equally solid" making dinner at this "local watering hole" a "wine-tasting experience."

TAPS Fish House & Brewery
22 | 21 | 19 | $32

101 E. Imperial Hwy. (Brea Blvd.), Brea, 714-257-0101; www.tapsbrea.com

This "lively" American microbrewery in Brea wins suds fans over with "uniquely prepared fresh seafood" and "wonderful meat dishes"; the warehouse-style space offers choices beyond the "classic" dining room, including a "good oyster bar", a "dead-on happy hour" and even a patio "where you can enjoy a fine cigar"; P.S. "Sunday bunch is a great value" complete with "champagne and live Dixieland jazz."

Ten Asian Bistro
∇ 20 | 22 | 18 | $32

4647 MacArthur Blvd. (bet. Birch St. & Campus Dr.), Newport Beach, 949-660-1010; www.tenrestaurantgroup.com

"Very with-it and uptempo", this Japanese newcomer near John Wayne Airport "is what OC has been waiting for"; sure, there's "innovative" sushi plus a "jumble of different" dishes, but the "palates" of the "twenty- and thirtysomething" clientele "are tempted by more than the food" what with the "interesting" Asian ambiance and waterfall, "happening" "adjacent night club" and "hot" "staff that looks better than anything on the menu."

Thai Dishes
18 | 11 | 17 | $17

10065 Garfield Ave. (Brookhurst St.), Fountain Valley, 714-962-1312
Additional locations throughout Southern California
See review in Los Angeles Directory.

Thaifoon 18 | 21 | 18 | $29

Irvine Spectrum Ctr., 85 Fortune Dr. (Pacifica St.), Irvine,
949-585-0022
Fashion Island, 857 Newport Center Dr. (bet. Corporate Plaza &
Farallon Drs.), Newport Beach, 949-644-0133
www.thaifoon.com
Surveyors stir up a storm of conflicting opinions over these
"upscale", "trendy" twins in Irvine and Newport Beach boasting
"chichi" ambiance and a "nice" waterfall wall; fans find it "fun
with a group", agreeing it's "not your father's" Thai–Pan-Asian
place, thanks to "exotic" fare and "great cocktails"; but the menu is
a bowl of "confusing" to detractors who swear it "feels, looks and
smells like a chain" with "Americanized food for the faint-hearted."

Thai This ▽ 25 | 16 | 19 | $24

24501 Del Prado (Amber Lantern St.), Dana Point, 949-240-7944;
www.thaithis.com
"Never mind the silly menu puns" assert shore dwellers, this
"little sleeper" in Dana Point surprises" with "light, fresh takes"
on "delicious, cheap Thai" chased with "great cocktails"; despite
the "bizarre" setting in a "garden-office" complex, the "nice,
pleasant" Indonesian-style space is "always hopping", but for
others, takeout is a more appealing option.

Thanh My ● ▽ 22 | 10 | 14 | $14

9553 Bolsa Ave. (Bushard St.), Westminster, 714-531-9540
Who cares if "not every waiter can speak our language" when
"good, cheap eats" await till 1 AM at Westminster's modest,
"quick"-service eatery in the "heart" of "Little Saigon"; the "diverse
menu" of "excellent Vietnamese" dishes outshines "most others
in the area" and "you get your money's worth" too – it "doesn't
get better than that."

3Thirty3 Waterfront ● ▽ 19 | 22 | 17 | $36

333 Bayside Dr. (PCH), Newport Beach, 949-673-8464;
www.3thirty3nb.com
Early chatter on this "welcome addition to the Newport Coast
scene" is all about the "sexy, sophisticated" remodel of the old
Yankee Tavern site and the "upscale" "singles scene" complete
with "lines outside", "romantic windows on the water" and
"tapas-style dining" on New American fare; but others are left
afloat by an "eclectic, even goofy" menu, and feel the "trendy"
setting is "designed more with drinkers in mind."

Ti Amo 20 | 19 | 20 | $39

31727 S. PCH (3rd St.), South Laguna Beach, 949-499-5350
"Always romantic", "like a visit to Tuscany" say lovers of Laguna's
"sure-thing" Italian-Med where "locals galore" head when they
want to "woo the mate" or a "date" with "gourmet food" and an
ambiance awash in "funky" "old-world charm"; canoodlers can
"cozy" up in "intimate" "booths hidden in every nook" and even
take in the "ocean view from certain rooms"; still, the less-
enchanted feel a "bit disappointed" and find "service rude."

Todai 13 | 11 | 12 | $24

Mall of Orange, 2203 N. Orange Mall (bet. Heim & Meats Aves.),
Orange, 714-974-0763; www.todai.com
See review in Los Angeles Directory.

Tommy Bahama Tropical Café   20 | 22 | 19 | $35

Corona Del Mar Plaza, 854 Avocado Ave. (bet. MacArthur Blvd. & PCH), Newport Beach, 949-760-8686; www.tommybahama.com

"Wear your linen shirt and sandals" to this "novel" boutique-cum-cafe in Newport Beach (and Palm Desert) that evokes an "island paradise" so "welcoming", it "feels like Jimmy Buffet will walk in at any moment"; are we "in the Bahamas"?, no, we're in "kitschy" "Tommy" territory, so "browse the store while waiting", then sit down to "pricey" though "perfectly good" Caribbean creations and "tropical drinks" and "enjoy the steel drum music."

Tony Roma's   16 | 13 | 15 | $22

1640 S. Harbor Blvd. (bet. I-5 & Katella Ave.), Anaheim, 714-520-0200
1300 S. Harbor Blvd. (Puente St.), Fullerton, 714-871-4000
7862 Warner Ave. (Beach Blvd.), Huntington Beach, 714-841-7427
3642 Katella Ave. (Los Alamitos Blvd.), Los Alamitos, 562-598-0401
27464 Jefferson Ave. (Winchester Rd.), Temecula, 951-676-7662
www.tonyromas.com
Additional locations throughout Southern California
See review in Los Angeles Directory.

Tortilla Flats   ∇ 15 | 19 | 15 | $23

27792 Vista del Lago (Marguerite Pkwy.), Mission Viejo, 949-830-9980; www.tacotuesday.com

"Taco Tuesday is the night" to hit this Mission Viejo veteran villa vow vaunters who also vie for seats on the "terrace on a sunny afternoon" to soak up "great vistas of the lake"; but it falls flat for foes who deride the fare as "bland" "Americanized Mexican" that's just "not as good as the setting."

Tortilla Jo's   ∇ 20 | 20 | 20 | $21

Downtown Disney, 1510 S. Disneyland Dr. (bet. Katella Ave. & Magic Way), Anaheim, 714-535-5000; www.patinagroup.com

"Well-made" "imaginative" "flavor combinations" fuel Downtown Disney sightseers at this "touristy" Patina Group culinary foray to south of the border complete with "strolling mariachis", "mind-numbing margaritas" and "great outside seating"; if a few grumblers gripe "something's missing" at this "terribly ordinary faux Mexican place", most consider it "surprisingly good" for "the house of mouse."

Trabuco Oaks Steak House   20 | 15 | 18 | $33

20782 Trabuco Oaks Dr. (Trabuco Canyon Rd.), Trabuco Canyon, 949-586-0722; www.trabucooakssteakhouse.com

"Tasty" meat "priced right" is the lure at this "rustic" steakhouse "tucked" "in the woods" of Trabuco Canyon; most don't mind the "funky decor" in need of a "remodel", after all, the "excellent" wines are "reasonable" and the vibe "casual" ("they cut your tie if you wear one") making it "an oasis in this era of overpriced" beef joints; P.S. it's "hard to find", though the "drive is gorgeous."

TROQUET   26 | 23 | 23 | $53

South Coast Plaza, 3333 Bristol St. (Anton Blvd.), Costa Mesa, 714-708-6865; www.troquetrestaurant.com

"Not what you'd expect to find" "perched atop South Coast Plaza", Tim and Liza Goodell's "smart" "hideway" is "absolutely stellar" for "divine", "pricey" French bistro fare backed by a "first-rate wine program"; when "you grow up", this is where "you want to go", especially for the "transcendent mall experience" of "unbelievable foie gras" on the back patio; *oui,* a few dis "hit-or-miss" service, but for most, it's "never a disappointment", "after you've survived the expense of the stores downstairs."

Turner New Zealand 23 | 20 | 23 | $52
650 Anton Blvd. (Park Center Dr.), Costa Mesa, 714-668-0880; www.turnernewzealand.com
"All New Zealand, all the time" makes for a "unique dining experience" at Costa Mesa's "expensive" showcase for "top-quality, hormone-free" steaks and seafood imported by impresario/owner-purveyor Noel Turner; "farm"-"fresh" ingredients, a "good-value wine list" and "attentive service" are enough to make you think you're "Down Under"; still, Kiwi quibblers cry the fare "can be astonishingly good" or "a disappointment" and find the 'tude "self-important."

Tutto Fresco ∇ 17 | 15 | 18 | $23
30642 Santa Margarita Pkwy. (bet. Avenido De Las Flores & El Paseo), Rancho Santa Margarita, 949-858-3360
Not surprisingly, there's "a lot of kid noise and activity" at this Italian wedged beside the cinemas in a busy Rancho Santa Margarita shopping center; still, "creative specials", "great" food and 18 by-the-glass wine options make it a *fresco* choice for locals.

Tutto Mare 18 | 19 | 19 | $39
Fashion Island, 545 Newport Center Dr. (Santa Rosa Dr.), Newport Beach, 949-640-6333; www.tuttomare.com
Fashion Island habitués head here for "good people-watching" and "expense-account lunches" of "very reliable" "fresh seafood specials" and "tasty" pasta in an "elegant" space prettified with "warm woods" and "white tablecloths"; but detractors drub the "not so memorable" cuisine and declare it's "lost its heat" – "what happened to the Italian restaurant that used to rock in the '90s?"

21 Oceanfront 24 | 23 | 24 | $51
2100 W. Oceanfront (Balboa Blvd.), Newport Beach, 949-673-2100; www.21oceanfront.com
"Old as the sea and also as reliable", this "dressed-up" "event restaurant" across from Newport Beach Pier attracts a "local crowd" with its "splurge"-worthy seafood and steak, "great sunset views" and "friendly service"; "dark and romantic", with red leather booths, a retro ambiance offering a "fun flashback to the past" and nightly entertainment, it's "perfect for a first date" or when "the ex-boyfriend is in town and wants to pay."

230 Forest Avenue 23 | 17 | 19 | $39
230 Forest Ave. (PCH), Laguna Beach, 949-494-2545; www.230forestavenue.com
"Beautiful people" sipping "dynamite martinis" and "dining elbow to elbow" in "high-energy surroundings" make this "welcoming" "indoor/outdoor" room a "hot spot" in the "heart of Laguna" for "creative" Californian "fusion controlled to perfection"; sure, the "skinny" "little storefront" digs are "always packed" and "louder than a Who concert", but "well-executed fish dishes", "nice little patio" and "great people-watching" more than compensate.

Vessia Ristorante   21 | 17 | 20 | $32

Crossroads Shopping Ctr., 3966 Barranca Pkwy. (Culver Dr.),
Irvine, 949-654-1155; www.vessia.com

"Here, I'm a happy eater" agree admirers of Irvine's "convenient", "businessy" family-owned trattoria where "local politicos" gather for "delicious Southern Italian" "just like nana made" matched with a "surprisingly good" wine list; "part of the pleasure is going in, and being treated like they are truly glad you chose their restaurant – that is" "warm service."

Villa Nova ●   20 | 20 | 21 | $40

3131 W. PCH (Newport Blvd.), Newport Beach, 949-642-7880;
www.villanovarestaurant.com

"Practically a Newport institution", this "late-night" "standby" with an "incredible harbor view" draws droves for "sooo romantic" meals ferried by a "well-trained staff"; foodies may judge the Italian "red-sauce" fare "forgettable", but regulars can't resist the "classic piano bar" crowded with "60-year-old groupies" or "water's edge" seating for the "boat parade every December."

Vine, The ⊠Ⓜ   ∇ 23 | 19 | 20 | $46

211 N. El Camino Real (Avenida Cabrillo), San Clemente, 949-361-2079;
www.vinesanclemente.com

An only-in-San-Clemente mix of oenophiles and "yummy pro surfers" (compadres of chef-owner Justin Monson) frequents this "intimate" Cal-Med eatery offering "super-delicious" dishes and wine pairing dinners; if nitpickers wonder why the vino list is "so hodge-podgy", for most it's a "wonderful new addition" to an "area that could use a few upscale" options.

Walt's Wharf   25 | 17 | 21 | $32

201 Main St. (Central St.), Seal Beach, 562-598-4433;
www.waltswharf.com

"The aromatic scent of mesquite" perfumes "long waits" at Seal Beach's "lively" "fish joint" "with a heart" that "makes the effort to be excellent" with "nicely plated" "awesome quality seafood" boosted by a "very, very good" vino list ("the owner's son is a top winemaker"); sure, the dockside interior is a bit "campy", but "who cares about decor" with "food this top-notch", prices this "reasonable" and a "small town vibe" this "friendly"?

Wasa   24 | 17 | 20 | $32

Market Pl., 13124 Jamboree Rd. (Irvine Blvd.), Irvine, 714-665-3338
Bluffs Shopping Ctr., 1346 Bison Ave. (MacArthur Blvd.), Newport Beach,
949-760-1511
www.wasasushi.com

"Almost as good as it gets in OC" agree ahi-addicts who flip for the "wonderfully unique sushi" at these sibling storefronts with a "datelike atmosphere" in Irvine and Newport Beach; the "creations" are "definitely 'not from Japan'", rather from a strip mall, but "amazing" all the same; if a few snap "service is spotty", "bargain lunches" help compensate.

White Horses Ⓜ   – | – | – | E

610 Avenida Victoria (Monterey Ln.), San Clemente, 949-429-1800;
www.whitehorses.us

Its name is a Scottish term for foaming waves and the ocean is undeniably the muse for this Eclectic newbie opposite San

Clemente's pier; the menu and locally produced artwork change in tandem every several weeks, but the huge salt water coral tank and closed-circuit images of the surf and beach are constants.

Wingnuts   15 | 13 | 17 | $15

26711 Aliso Creek Rd. (Rte. 73), Aliso Viejo, 949-305-7700
Target Great Lands, 3030 Harbor Blvd. (Baker St.), Costa Mesa, 714-434-7700
www.wingnuts.biz

When it comes to "addictive wings" and BBQ ribs with a "large variety of sauces", "no one does it better" than these "fun" Aliso Viejo and Costa Mesa "hangouts" – "you can never be bored" with the "interesting menu" or "unusual" aviation-themed decor; if a few shrug "not much appeals", most deem it "heaven" for "game night", with "prices easy on the pocketbook, unless you're a drinking pilot."

Wolfgang Puck Cafe   17 | 15 | 17 | $24

South Coast Plaza, 3333 Bristol St. (Anton Blvd.), Costa Mesa, 714-546-9653; www.wolfgangpuck.com
Wolfgang Puck Grand Cafe
The Block at Orange, 20 City Blvd. W. (City Dr.), Orange, 714-634-9653; www.wolfgangpuck.com
See review in Los Angeles Directory.

Wood Ranch BBQ & Grill   20 | 16 | 18 | $24

8022 E. Santa Ana Canyon Rd. (Weir Canyon Rd.), Anaheim Hills, 714-974-6660; www.woodranch.com
See review in Los Angeles Directory.

Woody's at the Beach   21 | 18 | 20 | $34

1305 S. PCH (Cress St.), Laguna Beach, 949-376-8809; www.woodysatthebeach.com
"Sure, the gay scene is hopping in the open bar and patio areas", but the "imaginative" Cal cuisine "is serious business", perhaps "better than it needs to be", at this "tasteful space" that's also "straight-friendly"; this is Laguna "at its best": men (and women) mixing over "delightful food" bolstered by a "well-chosen wine list" with a "peekaboo ocean view" yards from the dining room.

Yard House   19 | 17 | 17 | $25

Triangle Square Shopping Mall, 1875 Newport Blvd. (bet. Harbor Blvd. & 19th St.), Costa Mesa, 949-642-0090
Irvine Spectrum Ctr., 71 Fortune Dr. (Pacifica St.), Irvine, 949-753-9373
www.yardhouse.com
See review in Los Angeles Directory.

Yi Dynasty Restaurant ⌷   ▽ 21 | 15 | 20 | $30

1701 Corinthian Way (Martingale Way), Newport Beach, 949-797-9292
"High-quality, authentic Korean BBQ" plus "more than friendly" service add up to "customer loyalty" and lots of "repeat business" for this Newport Beach establishment; regulars recommend "be sure to reserve" to ensure that you "get a good-sized table for handling your own" 'cue, since you cook it yourself.

Yves' Bistro   ▽ 23 | 17 | 20 | $32

Canyon Plaza, 5753 E. Santa Ana Canyon Rd. (bet. Imperial Hwy. & Via Cortez), Anaheim Hills, 714-637-3733; www.yvesbistro.com
"Lots of regulars" frequent Anaheim Hills' shopping-center choice for "casual" French-Italian meals prepared with "consistent

quality" and fortified by a "friendly wine list"; add an owner "who welcomes you like a houseguest" and a "nice patio area" and you have all the makings of a "romantic evening."

Zankou Chicken ⊄   24   4   12 $10
2424 W. Ball Rd. (bet. Brookhurst Ave. & Magnolia Ave.), Anaheim, 714-229-2060; www.zankouchicken.com
See review in Los Angeles Directory.

Zinc Cafe & Market   21   16   13 $17
3222 E. PCH (Marguerite Ave.), Corona del Mar, 949-719-9462
350 Ocean Ave. (Beach St.), Laguna Beach, 949-494-6302
www.zinccafe.com
"You'll want to hug a tree" after bellying up to the counter at these "bright" sidewalk siblings in CdM and Laguna serving Californian vegetarian food "so tasty you won't miss the meat"; "fresh" breakfasts, "gourmet" sandwiches and salads make it a "favorite" for a "laid-back" beach crowd willing to overlook "harried" service just to sit on the "sunny patio"; P.S. the market has "interesting finds" for "picnics and takeout."

Zipangu ◐   ▽ 26   22   23 $36
The LAB, 2930 Bristol St. (Randolph Ave.), Costa Mesa, 714-545-2800;
www.zipanguoc.com
"The most flavorful", "fresh" fish along with "tasty" Japanese-French fusion dishes that "melt in your mouth" lure the "younger crowd" to this "hot" LAB newcomer with "more atmosphere than most sushi houses"; service is "wonderful" provided you "brush up on" your language skills while tables set "close together" lend an "intimate vibe", making it a "great date place."

ZOV'S BISTRO   26   20   22 $34
Enderle Ctr., 17440 E. 17th St. (Yorba St.), Tustin, 714-838-8855;
www.zovs.com
"Unique in a land of sameness" swoon admirers of "acclaimed" chef-owner Zov Karamardian's "delectable", "original" take on "perfectly prepared" Med dishes "served with flair"; the "elegant yet homey" Tustin bistro is favored for "perfect dinners" with "attentive service" on the "restful patio", while the attached bakery is an "oasis" for "excellent" sandwiches or breakfast while "soaking up the sun"; "always leave room" for the "out-of-this-world" pastries that "taste even better than they look."

Z'tejas   19   18   18 $24
South Coast Plaza, 3333 Bristol St. (Anton Blvd.), Costa Mesa, 714-979-7469; www.ztejas.com
"Surprisingly good" "mall-spree" Southwestern eats and "awesome margaritas" made with "the best tequila selection" lasso lotsa locals to this South Coast Plaza outpost of a "casual", "reasonably priced" chain; if some find the bar atmosphere more "bright and cheerful" than the main dining room (feels "a little 1990"), others suggest "eating on the patio", adding it's "worth a visit on your next shopping" trip.

Palm Springs/ Santa Barbara Restaurant Directory

Palm Springs & Environs*

Top Food

27 Le Vallauris
26 Cuistot
25 Johannes
   Ruth's Chris
   Wally's Desert

Top Decor

26 Cuistot
25 Jillian's
   Wally's Desert
   Le Vallauris
   Lodge/Rancho Mirage

Top Service

25 Le Vallauris
   Cuistot
24 Wally's Desert
23 Ruth's Chris
   Azur

Best Buys

1. In-N-Out Burger
2. Johnny Rockets
3. Ruby's
4. Souplantation
5. Islands

	F	D	S	C

AZUR 🗷 Ⓜ

	24	22	23	$71

(fka Azur by Le Bernardin)
La Quinta Resort & Club, 49-499 Eisenhower Dr. (Washington St.), La Quinta, 760-777-4835; www.laquintaresort.com

A post-*Survey* split with Le Bernardin, the famed NYC French seafooder, may put the Food rating in question, nevertheless, this "absolutely delightful" signature restaurant set in the historic lobby of the La Quinta Resort & Club remains an "exceptional" "oasis" for a "romantic" rendezvous; chef Eric Wadlund mans the stove, turning out Gallic fare, with an emphasis *bien sûr,* on *poisson,* and local, seasonal ingredients.

Bellini 🗷

	▽ 23	20	23	$49

73-111 El Paseo (Hwy. 111), Palm Desert, 760-341-2626

"Always busy and always good", this "charming, sophisticated" bit of Italy in Palm Desert offers "an excellent dining experience" thanks to "flavorful and well-presented" cuisine ("the cannelloni was the best I've ever had") served along with "creative drinks" by "friendly, attentive" staffers "in a gracious setting"; no wonder "first-time" visitors report they "will go back" – even if it is "a bit pricey."

Billy Reed's

	15	14	16	$23

1800 N. Palm Canyon Dr. (Vista Chino), Palm Springs, 760-325-1946

In a town full of golf-crazed retirees, this Palms Springs "coffee shop with ideas of grandeur" gives loyalists their green's worth with "copious" portions of American "comfort food" served by "waitresses with beehives" in a "Victorian" atmosphere; though the "excellent desserts" are beatified as "a religious experience", a handful of scoffers say Reed our lips: "it's seen better days."

---

* Environs include Riverside and San Bernardino counties.

BJ's
17 | 15 | 16 | $18

2520 Tuscany Rd. (Grand Oaks Dr.), Corona, 951-271-3610
1045 E. Harriman Pl. (Tippecanoe Ave.), San Bernardino, 909-380-7100
www.bjsbrewhouse.com
Additional locations throughout Southern California
See review in Los Angeles Directory.

Café des Beaux-Arts
18 | 16 | 18 | $30

73-640 El Paseo (Larkspur Ln.), Palm Desert, 760-346-0669;
www.cafedesbeauxarts.com
"A bit of Paris in" Palm Desert, this shopping-strip sidewalk cafe is
"a solid contender" thanks to its "well-prepared" French bistro
classics; it's popular for a "pleasant" lunch (and Sunday brunch "is
not to be missed"), so even Beaux-zos who call it "so-so" admit
that the "people-watching is worth the price of admission."

California Pizza Kitchen
18 | 14 | 17 | $19

73-080 El Paseo (bet. Hwy. 74 & Ocotillo Dr.), Palm Desert, 760-776-5036
123 N. Palm Canyon Dr. (bet. Amado Rd. & Tahquitz Canyon Way),
Palm Springs, 760-322-6075
www.cpk.com
Additional locations throughout Southern California
See review in Los Angeles Directory.

Castelli's
▽ 23 | 16 | 22 | $42

73-098 Hwy. 111 (Monterey Ave.), Palm Desert, 760-773-3365;
www.castellis.cc
You'd almost expect to find "Tony Soprano at the next table" at
this "local standout" in Palm Desert that oozes "Rat Pack–retro"
ambiance and wows with its "classic" Italian cuisine (don't miss the
"signature fettuccini Alfredo"); the "fantastic" staff and "friendly"
bartenders add a "homey" feel, so even when it's "crowded", you
still get "a wonderful meal"; N.B. closed July and August.

Cedar Creek Inn
19 | 20 | 19 | $29

1555 S. Palm Canyon Dr. (Sonora Rd.), Palm Springs, 760-325-7300
See review in Orange County Directory.

Cheesecake Factory
20 | 18 | 18 | $24

The River, 71-800 Hwy. 111 (bet. Rancho Las Palmas Dr. &
Rancho Mirage Ln.), Rancho Mirage, 760-404-1400;
www.cheesecakefactory.com
See review in Los Angeles Directory.

Chop House
22 | 20 | 21 | $45

74-040 Hwy. 111 (Portola St.), Palm Desert, 760-779-9888
262 S. Palm Canyon Dr. (bet. Arenas & Baristo Rds.), Palm Springs,
760-320-4500
Slicing up meat that "can't be beat" (in the Coachella Valley, at
least), this desert duo babies beef eaters with "terrific" steaks,
"great sides" and "strong drinks"; the "enthusiastic" servers "carry
flashlights to help you see the menu in the dimly lit room", and if
a few fret that this "uneven" pair is "resting on past laurels", the
contented contend it's still an "above-average" experience.

Citrus City Grille
19 | 18 | 19 | $29

Riverside Plaza, 3555 Riverside Plaza Dr. (bet. Central & Merrill Aves.),
Riverside, 951-274-9099
See review in Orange County Directory.

Claim Jumper Restaurant   18 | 17 | 18 | $22
380 McKinley St. (Frwy. 91), Corona, 951-735-6567
12499 Foothill Blvd. (Frwy. 15), Rancho Cucamonga, 909-899-8022
1905 S. Commercenter E. (bet. Hospitality Ln. & Waterman St. N.),
San Bernardino, 909-383-1818
www.claimjumper.com
Additional locations throughout Southern California
See review in Los Angeles Directory.

CUISTOT Ⓜ   26 | 26 | 25 | $61
72-595 El Paseo (Hwy. 111), Palm Desert, 760-340-1000
Its name is French slang for 'cook', and Bernard Dervieux, the
top toque at this Palm Desert "diamond", cooks up "fabulous",
"imaginative" French-Cal cuisine paired with a "tremendous"
wine list; even though you must "bring the bucks", "special events"
simply "belong here" in this "gorgeous room" rated No. 1 for Decor
in Palm Springs, and with mountain views and "attentive service",
worshipers vow "this isn't dining – it's an experience."

Daily Grill   18 | 16 | 18 | $27
73-061 El Paseo (Monterey Ave.), Palm Desert, 760-779-9911;
www.dailygrill.com
See review in Los Angeles Directory.

Falls Prime Steakhouse   20 | 23 | 19 | $48
78-430 Hwy. 111 (Washington St.), La Quinta, 760-777-9999
The Mercado Plaza, 155 S. Palm Canyon Dr., 2nd fl. (Arenas Rd.),
Palm Springs, 760-416-8664
www.thefallsprimesteakhouse.com
For "irresistible smoking martinis" (made with dry ice) and "tasty
steak", beef eaters canter over to this desert steakhouse duo; the La
Quinta locale boasts an "unusual" red velvet room and waterfall-
graced garden, while the Palm Springs site is more "visually
stimulating" with "intimate balcony tables" "overlooking the plaza"
where you can watch "the world pass below"; still, the put-off pout
it's Prime-arily "like Disneyland – all looks, little substance."

IN-N-OUT BURGER ⦿⌀   24 | 11 | 19 | $7
450 Auto Center Dr. (Frwy. 91), Corona
2305 Compton Ave. (Ontario Ave.), Corona
6634 Clay St. (Van Buren Blvd.), Riverside
7467 Indiana Ave. (Madison Ave.), Riverside
72265 Varner Rd. (Ramon Rd.), Riverside
www.in-n-out.com
Additional locations throughout Southern California
See review in Los Angeles Directory.

Islands   16 | 16 | 16 | $15
72-353 Hwy. 111 (Desert Crossing), Palm Desert, 760-346-4007;
www.islandsrestaurants.com
Additional locations throughout Southern California
See review in Los Angeles Directory.

JILLIAN'S Ⓢ   25 | 25 | 23 | $58
74-155 El Paseo (Hwy. 111), Palm Desert, 760-776-8242
A somewhat "older upper-crust set" graces the "lovely enclosed
patio" at this "elegant" Continental where locals flock for "outdoor
fine dining at its best", an experience abetted by "stellar" service, a
"great" pianist and "charming" decor; it all adds up to "a special

evening" in the "most romantic atmosphere" in Palm Desert with the bonus of "nice people running the show."

JOHANNES Ⓜ   25 | 16 | 21 | $53
196 S. Indian Canyon Dr. (E. Arenas Rd.), Palm Springs, 760-778-0017;
www.johannesrestaurant.com
The bravos echo across the Coachella Valley for chef-owner Johannes Bacher's "perfectly executed" Pan-Asian–Austrian cuisine and "excellent wine selection" at this "great" "minimalist" "find" in Palm Springs; if a handful find the "ultracontemporary setting" "austere" and the "service lackluster", for most the "exceptional food", like the "Wiener schnitzel", compensates.

John Henry's Ⓢ   21 | 14 | 20 | $32
1785 E. Tahquitz Canyon Way (Sunrise Way), Palm Springs, 760-327-7667
"Crowded with Palm Springs locals", this "delightfully reliable", "tiny, little" French-Eclectic "wows" "aficionados" "with big flavors", from the "best rack of lamb west of the Colorado river" to "fabulous desserts", preferably "enjoyed sitting under the stars on the patio"; "call ahead for a reservation" during season when it's "extremely busy" and you'll be rewarded with "lotsa food and lotsa fun" "for your money"; N.B. closed during the summer.

Johnny Rebs'   22 | 18 | 21 | $20
15051 Seventh St. (bet. La Paz & Mojave Drs.), Victorville, 760-955-3700;
www.johnnyrebs.com
See review in Los Angeles Directory.

Johnny Rockets   16 | 14 | 16 | $12
The River, 71-800 Hwy. 111 (W. Veldt St.), Rancho Mirage, 760-674-2064;
www.johnnyrockets.com
Additional locations throughout Southern California
See review in Los Angeles Directory.

Kaiser Grille   17 | 17 | 17 | $32
205 S. Palm Canyon Dr. (Arenas Rd.), Palm Springs, 760-323-1003
Coachella Valley denizens are divided on this Palm Springs American; supporters relish the "friendly" service, "great" salads and "super people-watching patio" and insist they "take care of their regulars", but cross critics carp it "used to be one of my favorites", but these days it's "not as impressive as expected"; N.B. the former Palm Desert branch is now called The Big Fish.

La Quinta Cliffhouse   15 | 20 | 18 | $34
78-250 Hwy. 111 (Washington St.), La Quinta, 760-360-5991;
www.laquintacliffhouse.com
"Tourists" and "locals" alike flock to the "great deck" "built around a fire" at this "historic property" "perched on the side" of Point Happy in La Quinta to watch "spectacular sunsets" over "solid" New American fare; you'll find "loads of atmosphere", but fence-sitters say the "rest is on the ordinary side", suggesting dive into the "bar chow" and skip the "iffy food" in the "upscale dining area."

Las Casuelas   17 | 19 | 17 | $24
78-480 Hwy. 111 (Washington St.), La Quinta, 760-777-7715
368 N. Palm Canyon Dr. (Alejo Rd.), Palm Springs, 760-325-3213
222 S. Palm Canyon Dr. (W. Arenas Rd.), Palm Springs, 760-325-2794;
www.lascasuelas.com

(continued)

(continued)

Las Casuelas

70-050 Hwy. 111 (Via Florencio), Rancho Mirage, 760-328-8844;
www.lascasuelasnuevas.com

It's a fiesta every night at this "home-grown" Mexican chain that's "a mainstay in the desert" towns; "stuff your face" with "enormous" combo plates and "birdbath-size margaritas", while enjoying the same "strolling" mariachis that have been playing here forever (it's "fun" "for families"); still, critics contend that the "mass-produced" food is dumbed down for "gringo tourists."

Le St. Germain ❶   24 | 23 | 21 | $58 |

74-985 Hwy. 111 (Cook St.), Indian Wells, 760-773-6511;
www.lestgermain.com

"Now that's what I call authentic French"-Med cuisine coo customers who cozy up to this "sister to Le Vallauris", an Indian Wells "dining experience to be remembered" staffed with an "exceptionally capable" crew; the "dazzling dishes" and the "astounding wine list" add to Le "loverly, loverly" evenings while the "patio with a fireplace" and "soft piano" music enhance the "special-occasion" vibe.

LE VALLAURIS   27 | 25 | 25 | $59 |

385 W. Tahquitz Canyon Way (N. Museum Dr.), Palm Springs,
760-325-5059; www.levallauris.com

"Tucked away near the hills in the center" of town, this "fantastic" "white-glove" French-Med destination ranks No. 1 in Palm Springs for Food and Service, making it a "desert must-go"; whether you relax with a "leisurely" champagne lunch in the "enchantingly" "beautiful garden patio", "dine under the stars or in the gorgeous dining room", it's "romantic", European and "nonstop wonderful"; the "expensive prices" are "not in your everyday budget, but who cares when it's" this "close to perfection."

LG's Prime Steakhouse   22 | 19 | 20 | $54 |

78-525 Hwy. 111 (Washington St.), La Quinta, 760-771-9911
74-225 Hwy. 111 (El Paseo), Palm Desert, 760-779-9799
255 S. Palm Canyon Dr. (bet. Arenas & Baristo Rds.), Palm Springs,
760-416-1779
www.lgsprimesteakhouse.com

This "retro" meatery "withstands the test of time", serving what legions of followers swear may be "the best steaks in the desert" accompanied by "fresh, light, Caesar salads" prepared tableside and offset by a "spendy wine list"; the "tender, juicy" slabs of beef are "full of flavor", and though "expensive, worth the price of admission in spades"; nevertheless, the sticker-shocked would rather have "some money left over for a round of golf."

LODGE AT RANCHO MIRAGE, THE   21 | 25 | 21 | $54 |

The Lodge at Rancho Mirage, 68900 Frank Sinatra Dr. (Hwy. 111),
Rancho Mirage, 760-321-8987;
www.ranchomirage.rockresorts.com

The "food and service still live up to the days when it was owned by the Ritz-Carlton", but the "lovely" patio "overlooking the pool with fire pits" and "breathtaking views" of the Coachella Valley is what sets admirers ablaze; but this Rancho doesn't rate-o for others who spurn the "disappointing" New American fare adding "if you're not staying here, it's not worth going out of your way" for.

Lord Fletcher's 🅂🅼   ▽ 17 | 17 | 20 | $39

70-385 Hwy. 111 (Country Club Rd.), Rancho Mirage, 760-328-1161

When you long for the "comfort" of British pub fare "washed down with cocktails", "dig out your white shoes" and hop over to this "hokey" "time warp" with a "cozy English atmosphere" and "lots of history in Rancho Mirage"; if a few unruly subjects snipe this Lord "needs to retire", others counter it's "long past its prime, but it has a loyal following."

Lucille's Smokehouse Bar-B-Que   22 | 18 | 19 | $24

12624 N. Main St. (Foothill Blvd.), Rancho Cucamonga, 909-463-7427; www.lucillesbbq.com

See review in Los Angeles Directory.

Native Foods 🅂   ▽ 22 | 17 | 16 | $15

73-890 El Paseo (Portola Ave.), Palm Desert, 760-836-9396
1775 E. Palm Canyon Dr. (S. Sunrise Way), Palm Springs, 760-416-0070
www.nativefoods.com

See review in Los Angeles Directory.

Old Spaghetti Factory, The   14 | 17 | 16 | $17

3191 Mission Inn Ave. (Vine St.), Riverside, 951-784-4417; www.osf.com

See review in Los Angeles Directory.

Outback Steakhouse   18 | 15 | 18 | $25

Waring Plaza, 72-220 Hwy. 111 (Fred Waring Dr.), Palm Desert, 760-779-9068
620 E. Hospitality Ln. (Waterman Ave.), San Bernardino, 909-890-0061
530 N. Mountain Ave. (Arrow Hwy.), Upland, 909-931-1050
www.outback.com
Additional locations throughout Southern California

See review in Los Angeles Directory.

Picanha Churrascaria   18 | 13 | 18 | $34

73-399 El Paseo (San Pablo Ave.), Palm Desert, 760-674-3434; www.picanharestaurant.com

See review in Los Angeles Directory.

Pomodoro Cucina Italiana   18 | 14 | 17 | $19

510 Hidden Valley Pkwy. (off Rte. 15), Corona, 951-808-1700; www.pastapomodoro.com

See review in Los Angeles Directory.

Ristorante Mamma Gina   20 | 18 | 20 | $43

73-705 El Paseo (bet. Larkspur Ln. & San Luis Rey Ave.), Palm Desert, 760-568-9898; www.mammagina.com

See review in Orange County Directory.

Ristorante Tuscany   ▽ 23 | 23 | 23 | $51

JW Marriott Desert Springs Resort & Spa, 74855 Country Club Dr. (Cook St.), Palm Desert, 760-341-1725; www.ristorantetuscany.com

"Hooray", finally a Northern Italian in Palm Desert that "really feels like Italy"; with 800 wines to choose from and a "terrific" tasting menu "it's a wonderful place to entertain guests" and an "outstanding must every time" you're in town; take the "wonderful gondola ride" from the lobby and "arrive via the scenic route" – you'll "forget that you're in the JW Marriott Resort."

Romano's Macaroni Grill　　17 | 17 | 18 | $22
72-920 Hwy. 111 (bet. Monterey Ave. & Town Center Way), Palm Desert,
760-837-1333
Terra Vista Town Ctr., 10742 Foothill Blvd. (Aspen St.),
Rancho Cucamonga, 909-484-3200
www.macaronigrill.com
See review in Los Angeles Directory.

Roy's　　24 | 22 | 22 | $45
71-959 Hwy. 111 (Magnesia Falls Dr.), Rancho Mirage, 760-340-9044;
www.roysrestaurant.com
See review in Los Angeles Directory.

Ruby's　　15 | 16 | 17 | $14
Tyler Galleria, 1298 Tyler St. (Magnolia Ave.), Riverside, 909-359-7829;
www.rubys.com
Additional locations throughout Southern California
See review in Los Angeles Directory.

RUTH'S CHRIS STEAK HOUSE　　25 | 21 | 23 | $54
74-740 Hwy. 111 (Portola Ave.), Palm Desert, 760-779-1998;
www.ruthschris.com
See review in Los Angeles Directory.

Sirocco　　∇ 24 | 26 | 22 | $53
Renaissance Esmeralda Resort & Spa, 44-400 Indian Wells Ln. (Hwy. 111),
Indian Wells, 760-773-4444; www.renaissanceesmeralda.com
"Much better than most hotel restaurants", this Italian housed in the
Renaissance Esmeralda in Indian Wells offers a "varied" menu of
"homemade pastas" and other "fresh" fare, dished out in huge
portions that excuse the "sky-high" prices; "lovely" decor, a "quiet"
ambiance and "responsive" service make it a "real winner."

Souplantation　　16 | 11 | 12 | $12
8966 Foothill Blvd. (Vineyard Ave.), Rancho Cucamonga, 909-980-9690
228 W. Hospitality Ln. (Hunts Ln.), San Bernardino, 909-381-4772
www.souplantation.com
Additional locations throughout Southern California
See review in Los Angeles Directory.

Tommy Bahama Tropical Café　　20 | 22 | 19 | $35
Shops at El Paseo, 73-595 El Paseo (bet. Larkspur Ln. & San Pablo Ave.),
Palm Desert, 760-836-0188; www.tommybahama.com
See review in Orange County Directory.

Tony Roma's　　16 | 13 | 15 | $22
73-155 Hwy. 111 (bet. Monterey Ave. & San Pablo St.), Palm Desert,
760-568-9911; www.tonyromas.com
Additional locations throughout Southern California
See review in Los Angeles Directory.

WALLY'S DESERT TURTLE　　25 | 25 | 24 | $64
71-775 Hwy. 111 (Rancho Las Palmas Dr.), Rancho Mirage, 760-568-9321
"As good as it gets" in Rancho Mirage say fans of this "fine-dining"
French classic that serves "excellent food" with a side of "people-
watching" to an "over-40 crowd" "dripping with diamonds"; the
"decor is divine" and "service impeccable", and "although it's
expensive", it's "comfy" and "you don't feel like you've overspent";
if a few sniff it's "stuffy", for most its "elegance" endures.

Santa Barbara & Environs

Top Food
28 Downey's
26 Suzanne's
    Arigato Sushi
25 Olio e Limone
    Wine Cask

Top Decor
27 Four Seasons
26 Miró
25 Cafe Fiore
24 El Encanto
    El Paseo

Top Service
26 Downey's
25 Four Seasons
24 Suzanne's
    Palace Grill
    Wine Cask

Best Buys
1. In-N-Out Burger
2. Noah's NY Bagels
3. Baja Fresh Mexican
4. Sharky's Mexican
5. La Salsa

F	D	S	C

ARIGATO SUSHI

26	20	21	$38

1225 State St. (bet. Anapamu & Victoria Sts.), Santa Barbara, 805-965-6074

"If the fish were any fresher, they would still be alive" assert admirers of this "top-notch" Santa Barbara Japanese with "to-die-for", "inventive" sushi (particularly the chef's specials) as well as "creative" cooked dishes; just note that the "penalty" for choosing such a "popular", "hip and happening" spot is a "crowded and noisy" experience.

Baja Fresh Mexican Grill

19	10	15	$10

4726-2 Telephone Rd. (Westinghouse St.), Ventura, 805-650-3535; www.bajafresh.com
Additional locations throughout Southern California
See review in Los Angeles Directory.

Ballard Inn Restaurant Ⓜ

▽ 24	23	23	$50

2436 Baseline Ave. (bet. Alamo Pintado & Refugio Rds.), Ballard, 805-688-7770; www.ballardinn.com

"A quaint dining experience in a quaint town" exclaim those who've discovered this "great little" restaurant in the Ballard Inn, northwest of Santa Barbara; the "new chef has vastly improved the menu", a New French affair with Asian accents, plus the "cozy" setting has a "wonderful" three-sided fireplace, making for a "perfect meal and feel" amid the surroundings of Santa Ynez wine country.

Bay Café

19	15	17	$27

(fka Bay Café & Fish Market)
131 Anacapa St. (Yanonali St.), Santa Barbara, 805-963-2215
"Worth the hunt", this "hidden gem" of Santa Barbara lures fin-addicts with "simply prepared", "interesting seafood dishes" served in a recently refurbished, "unpretentious setting"; if a few feel that it's hard to reel in the "nonexistent service", most deem it a local "favorite."

Bouchon
23 | 21 | 23 | $50

9 W. Victoria St. (bet. Chapala & State Sts.), Santa Barbara, 805-730-1160;
www.bouchonsantabarbara.com

A "quintessential California" dining experience opine oenophiles who admire the "wine country cuisine" and "excellent" "Santa Barbara–centric" vino selection at this "relaxed" yet "refined" Cal-French eatery staffed by "incredibly knowledgeable" servers; thanks to a "farmer's market philosophy", the "inspired menu" always offers "wonderful little surprises", so nab a seat in the "intimate courtyard" and enjoy a "romantic evening"; N.B. no relation to Thomas Keller's Bouchon in Napa.

Brophy Bros. Clam Bar & Restaurant
21 | 17 | 18 | $25

119 Harbor Way (Shoreline Dr.), Santa Barbara, 805-966-4418;
www.brophybros.com

With seafood so "ultrafresh" it's "like eating off the back end of a fishing trawler", this Santa Barbara "institution" "nestled in a wharf-front building" with "ocean vistas" is "bound to be full of tourists", but "locals" line up too for boatloads of "delicious" fin fare and "made-from-scratch cioppino"; the scene is "lively" (as in "jammed and noisy"), plus it's so "reasonable" "even a college student can afford to take a date."

Brown Pelican
15 | 20 | 15 | $24

2981½ Cliff Dr. (Las Positas Rd.), Santa Barbara, 805-563-4960

"Nothing like watching dolphins and surfers" over a "hearty" Californian breakfast or lunch and a "good Bloody Mary" agree supporters of this casual spot "perched on Hendry's Beach" in Santa Barbara; but while "everyone wants to" get "up-close and personal with the beautiful coastline" by sitting "on the patio", for most, the "spectacular location" "overshadows" the "so-so food" and service, a "crying shame" since it has "such potential."

Bucatini
21 | 16 | 18 | $28

436 State St. (Haley St.), Santa Barbara, 805-957-4177;
www.bucatini.com

Pasta purists urge "don't be fooled by the appearance" of this "little" Santa Barbara trattoria (the "less hectic" sibling of Ca' Dario) – it's a "reliable" option for "well-prepared" Northern Italian fare and "tasty" wood-fired pizza; while some agoraphobics call the "alfresco dining" "noisy", others insist "you don't even notice that bustling State Street is on the other side" of the patio wall.

Ca' Dario
25 | 19 | 21 | $38

37 E. Victoria St. (Anacapa St.), Santa Barbara, 805-884-9419;
www.cadario.net

Real "passion shows" in the "exceptional food" and "excellent service" at this "superb" Santa Barbara trattoria, big brother of Enoteca Primo; the "convivial, warm" ambiance of the "cozy dark-wood" furnishings sets the stage for "authentic" Italian cuisine that includes "divine" ravioli and "on-the-money" osso buco; just note that on busy nights the "special" space can "get really cramped" and "noisy."

Cafe Buenos Aires
17 | 23 | 20 | $36

1316 State St. (E. Victoria St.), Santa Barbara, 805-963-0242

"On a beautiful afternoon in Santa Barbara", "lunch on the sun-filled courtyard" of this "all-time favorite" South American cafe is a "treat" agree admirers who also hotfoot it here after dark, particularly on Wednesday nights for tango dancing "under the stars"; but "unbelievable ambiance" aside, few dance a jig about the food, sighing it's indicative of "Buenos Aires only in name."

Cafe del Sol   18 | 17 | 19 | $28 |
30 Los Patos Way (Cabrillo Blvd.), Montecito, 805-969-0448
"Underrated", perhaps, "because of its eclectic menu" that rambles from steaks and lamb shanks to "excellent" salads to flan, this Montecito Californian still ranks as "above average"; while the food may "not leave one craving to go back", the "nice patio" is "one of the best spots in" the Santa Barbara area "for a sunset drink."

CAFE FIORE   21 | 25 | 20 | $29 |
66 S. California St. (Main St.), Ventura, 805-653-1266; www.fiorerestaurant.net
With its "beautiful" rustic decor and "attention to detail", this Southern Italian is right in line with "gentrified Ventura", pleasing local gentry with a "varied menu of well-prepared dishes", including "tasty" pasta and pizza made "just like in Rome"; the "to-die-for martinis" and the "helpful" service make even the most standoffish patroon feel "part of the Cafe Fiore family."

California Pizza Kitchen   18 | 14 | 17 | $19 |
719 Paseo Nuevo Mall (bet. Chapala & De La Guerra Sts.), Santa Barbara, 805-962-4648; www.cpk.com
Additional locations throughout Southern California
See review in Los Angeles Directory.

Carlitos Cafe Y Cantina   21 | 18 | 18 | $27 |
1324 State St. (Arlington Ave.), Santa Barbara, 805-962-7117
"Enjoy margaritas on the sunny patio before catching a film at the Arlington Theater across the street", suggest amigos of Cava's older sibling, an "upscale" Santa Barbara cantina that earns *olés* for its "innovative" Mexican cuisine; while some tamales simply love "to sit by the fountain and listen to live music", prickly sorts snipe the fare is "too pricey."

Cava   20 | 21 | 19 | $34 |
1212 Coast Village Rd. (Olive Mill Rd.), Montecito, 805-969-8500; www.cavarestaurant.com
"A favorite of Montecito locals", Carlitos Cafe's younger sister is a "lively" spot that does Pan-Latin/"Nuevo Latino food as it should be: colorful, creative and *sabroso*"; the "tasty" creations go down nicely, while the "pretty" patio, "cute atmosphere" and nightly live music "set the mood"; if a couple of Cava dwellers kvetch "it's overpriced", even they assert "service is pleasant" and the food "does not disappoint."

Chuck's Waterfront Grill   19 | 20 | 20 | $37 |
(fka Waterfront Grill)
Waterfront Ctr., 113 Harbor Way (Shoreline Dr.), Santa Barbara, 805-564-1200; www.chuckswaterfrontgrill.com
The "spectacular" "beauty of the Santa Barbara" harbor is "in full view" at this "solid" surf 'n' turfer that's "greatly improved" since tweaking its name and adding more beef to the menu; but while a handful are hooked on the "fresh, tasty" fish, critics knock this docksider, carping it "isn't the catch it used to be."

Citronelle 24 | 21 | 21 | $54
Santa Barbara Inn, 901 E. Cabrillo Blvd. (Milpas St.), Santa Barbara,
805-963-0111; www.santabarbarainn.com
"Eat your way into another dimension" at this "imaginative" Cal-
French atop the Santa Barbara Inn blessed with "stunning" views
of "Palm Park and the ocean", plus an "eclectic" menu that
"capitalizes on seasonal offerings"; service is "seamless", and
the wine list "spectacular", so if a few can't get past the "cheesy"
"motel" feel, most maintain it's "one of SB's finest."

Cold Spring Tavern 19 | 23 | 19 | $34
5995 Stagecoach Rd. (Hwy. 154), Santa Barbara, 805-967-0066;
www.coldspringtavern.com
"Go hungry, wear boots and" "get wild (game, that is)" at this
"Old West" tavern and former stagecoach stop where "foodies
join the Harley crowd for American" grilled fare; set "high in
the hills above Santa Barbara", it feels like a "romantic, rustic"
"nook in a cranny", but it's the "unique" food that really hits the
spot "after a day of wine tasting"; N.B. live country and blues
music on weekends.

Deco ▽ 22 | 21 | 19 | $39
394 E. Main St. (Oak St.), Ventura, 805-667-2120;
www.decorestaurant.com
Owner Norbert Furnee "is happy to share his vast knowledge of
local wines with you" at this oenophilic Ventura Californian that, as
the name suggests, is outfitted in sleek art deco style; the handful
of surveyors who've dined here speak well of the "excellent"
service and consider it "a special-occasion place" – or "an anytime
place, if you have the means."

Dish ⊠ 21 | 15 | 19 | $44
138 E. Cañon Perdido St. (Santa Barbara St.), Santa Barbara,
805-966-5365; www.eatdish.com
"You'll find things that you won't find anywhere else" – in Santa
Barbara, anyway – at this "super-chic" Pan-Asian–French hot
spot that cooks up all sorts of "creative and delicious" fare; it's
"trendy" and rather "elegant", bringing in plenty of "beautiful
young people", but the "densely packed" dining room can be
"way too noisy."

DOWNEY'S Ⓜ 28 | 21 | 26 | $56
1305 State St. (Victoria St.), Santa Barbara, 805-966-5006;
www.downeyssb.com
Rated No. 1 in Santa Barbara time and again for both Food and
Service, this New American sets the "gold standard"; chef "John
Downey creates a perfect feast", offering "unbelievably fabulous"
cuisine that brims with "subtle flavors", while the "attentive" staff's
"careful" stewardship makes this "sophisticated restaurant" "well
worth" both the "lighter wallet" and "the drive from LA"; co-owner
Liz Downey's paintings "dress the place up", adding more of the
"ooh-la-la" factor to this "artistic experience."

Eladio's 22 | 20 | 19 | $39
Harbor View Inn, 1 State St. (Cabrillo Blvd.), Santa Barbara, 805-963-4466;
www.harborviewinnsb.com
"Chef Nathan Simandle" is "changing the menu" for the better at
this "enticing" Italian eatery in Santa Barbara's Harbor View Inn,

which is already admired for a beach-adjacent location that "can't be beat"; it's a "great spot for" "weekend brunch" — now if they'd just spruce up the "conference-room-boring" interior.

El Encanto   22 ┃ 24 ┃ 22 ┃ $50 ┃
El Encanto Hotel & Garden Villas, 1900 Lasuen Rd. (Moreno Rd.),
Santa Barbara, 805-687-5000; www.elencantohotel.com
Boasting "drop-dead" "views of paradise" and "'yes sir, right away sir' service", this "enduring" restaurant at the same-named Santa Barbara hotel "never fails to impress" those in search of a "romantic getaway"; you can "start the day" with a "heavenly breakfast" or top it off with an "evening drink" at the piano bar, though not all are enchanted with the "refined" Cal-French cuisine; N.B. a recent change of ownership and chef may impact the ratings.

El Paseo ⓜ   16 ┃ 24 ┃ 19 ┃ $23 ┃
10 El Paseo (Anacapa St.), Santa Barbara, 805-962-6050
Count on a "fun atmosphere" at this 1921 SB landmark, where you "feel like you're in a Spanish plaza" as you devour "handmade tortillas", guacamole made tableside and other Mexican dishes with "killer margaritas" or any of the 100 varieties of tequila; though some are impressed with the "great happy hour" and weekend brunch, el passersby opine that the fare is "just ordinary."

El Torito   15 ┃ 15 ┃ 16 ┃ $19 ┃
29 E. Cabrillo Blvd. (Anacapa St.), Santa Barbara, 805-963-1968;
www.eltorito.com
Additional locations throughout Southern California
See review in Los Angeles Directory.

Emilio's   23 ┃ 21 ┃ 22 ┃ $40 ┃
324 W. Cabrillo Blvd. (Bath St.), Santa Barbara, 805-966-4426;
www.emilios-restaurant.com
Boasting a "great location near the water with food to match", this "cozy" Northern Italian–Mediterranean has been a "consistent" "favorite" "over the years" for its "well-prepared dishes" paired with a "good selection of wines"; factor in a "knowledgeable staff" and owners who "make you feel at home" in the Tuscan-style space, and you have "one of Santa Barbara's gems."

Enoteca Primo ⓜ   – ┃ – ┃ – ┃ M ┃
11 W. Victoria St. (State St.), Santa Barbara, 805-884-0828
With a "creative" kitchen turning out "satisfying" Italian food, this casual offshoot of Ca' Dario in Santa Barbara is a "great little hideaway" for a bite and a glass of wine; there are only 30 seats (and the staff "can get overwhelmed when it's crowded"), but that's all right with locals looking for "a break from the big restaurants."

Enterprise Fish Co.   17 ┃ 16 ┃ 17 ┃ $29 ┃
225 State St. (Frwy. 101), Santa Barbara, 805-962-3313;
www.enterprisefishco.com
See review in Los Angeles Directory.

Epiphany   22 ┃ 21 ┃ 20 ┃ $47 ┃
21 W. Victoria St. (State St.), Santa Barbara, 805-564-7100;
www.epiphanysb.com
It's a "treasure awaiting discovery", reveal reviewers who revel in the "innovative" cuisine at this Santa Barbara New American tucked into a 19th-century house that's been transformed into a

"stylish", "intimate" dining space with a "beautiful red bar"; those who haven't seen the light criticize the "inconsistent" food and pure "Hollywood attitude" – perhaps they're too aware that actor "Kevin Costner is a partner here."

Eric Ericson's
▽ 16 | 19 | 15 | $29

668 E. Harbor Blvd. (California St.), Ventura, 805-643-4783
The "nice ocean view" "far exceeds anything served for lunch or dinner" at this Ventura seafooder, whose "convenient location" on the pier and "good beer selection" nonetheless make it a handy haven for "meeting friends from out of town"; unfortunately, scalawags scoff at the decor that seems out of "the 1950s" and the basic food that's mighty "mediocre."

FOUR SEASONS RESORT SANTA BARBARA Ⓜ
25 | 27 | 25 | $54

(aka La Marina)
Four Seasons Resort, 1260 Channel Dr. (Hill Rd.), Santa Barbara, 805-969-2261; www.fourseasons.com
Rated No. 1 for Decor in Santa Barbara, the "classy" Four Seasons "grande dame" resort creates a "spectacular", "sublime" setting for an "outrageously opulent" Sunday buffet brunch on the patio "that's not to be missed", or a "fab" Californian prix fixe dinner in the "elegant" La Marina dining room "for your special night"; while it's certainly "no bargain", it's "worth every dollar" – after all, "where else can you have high tea with a harpist?"

Hitching Post
23 | 15 | 21 | $38

406 E. Hwy. 246 (½ mi. east of Hwy. 101), Buellton, 805-688-0676; www.hitchingpost2.com
3325 Point Sal Rd. (Santos Rd.), Casmalia, 805-937-6151; www.hitchingpost1.com
Thanks to "its starring role in *Sideways*", the Buellton half of this BBQ duo "has been discovered", so "be prepared to wait" – or hoof it to the "not-to-be-missed Casmalia" site; either way, you'll have a "hell of a good time" chowing down on "to-die-for filet mignon" or "heavenly grilled artichokes" with the "house Pinot"; sure, the movie helped put it "on the map", but longtime hitchers find its "popularity no surprise" – "it's the meat, man."

IN-N-OUT BURGER ●⊘
24 | 11 | 19 | $7

4865 Calle Real (Turnpike Rd.), Goleta
1330 S. Bradley Rd. (Stowell Rd.), Santa Barbara
www.in-n-out.com
Additional locations throughout Southern California
See review in Los Angeles Directory.

Joe's Crab Shack ⊠Ⓜ
14 | 14 | 15 | $24

567 San Jon Rd. (Vista Del Mar Pl.), Ventura, 805-643-3725; www.joescrabshack.com
See review in Los Angeles Directory.

Kai
▽ 18 | 19 | 17 | $35

738 State St. (bet. De La Guerra & Ortega Sts.), Santa Barbara, 805-560-8777; www.kaisushishabushabu.com
It's "the only place in town for shabu-shabu" insist Kai-stomers who swish-swish meat or veggies in boiling pots at chef-owner Kaz Sato's "fun" Santa Barbara spot; traditionalists talk up the "high-quality sushi" and a selection of "good" Japanese offerings, from

sukiyaki, tempura and teriyaki dishes to donburi and noodle selections worth the slurp.

La Salsa　　16 │ 9 │ 13 │ $10

1131 State St. (bet. Anapamu & Victoria Sts.), Santa Barbara, 805-963-1001
3987 State St. (La Cumbre Rd.), Santa Barbara, 805-964-1146
www.lasalsa.com
See review in Los Angeles Directory.

La Super-Rica ⌷　　25 │ 5 │ 13 │ $13

622 N. Milpas St. (Alphonse St.), Santa Barbara, 805-963-4940
"Don't even think about driving through Santa Barbara without stopping at this Mexican mecca" aver amigos of the "super-authentic" "street food" at this "famous" "homestyle" taqueria; "expect to stand" in a "ridiculously long" line before nabbing a "plastic chair" in the "dumpy seating area" (the "staff treats customers like cattle"), and if some gauchos groucho that the "buzz is undeserved", loyalists insist that even "with gas at $3 a gallon", it would "be worth the" trip for such "*delicioso*" treats.

L'Auberge　　– │ – │ – │ E

314 El Paseo Rd. (Rincon Rd.), Ojai, 805-646-2288; www.laubergeojai.com
"What more could one ask" for in Ojai than to savor "sublime" mountain views while enjoying rabbit, frogs' legs, sweetbreads or other French-Belgian classics?; this long-standing restaurant may be "pricey", but Francophiles suggest a meal here makes a pleasant stop for weekend brunch or for "a lovely finish to the day."

Louie's　　▽ 22 │ 17 │ 19 │ $42

Upham Hotel, 1404 De La Vina St. (Sola St.), Santa Barbara, 805-963-7003; www.louiessb.com
"Locals in-the-know" "love" "sitting on the porch" and dining on "consistently good" Californian food at this "charming" "favorite" "tucked away" in the "historic", "restored" Upham Hotel; "don't expect culinary fireworks, but" do expect "solid classic fare" and a "creative wine list" with "unusual" local choices.

Lucky's　　24 │ 22 │ 21 │ $60

1279 Coast Village Rd. (Olive Mill Rd.), Montecito, 805-565-7540
"Money, power and fame" collide at Lucky Jeans imresario Gene Montesano's "old-school" Montecito steakhouse, big brother of Tre Lune, a "laid-back" yet "big-night-out" place for "bling-bling" and denim-clad "celebrities to mingle" over "terrific" meat and "trimmings"; still, after "you realize that, yes, that's Oprah" at the next table, and yes, "your bank account is now empty", remember that with a "burger in the bar you can still enjoy the best people-watching in town."

Maravilla　　– │ – │ – │ E

Ojai Valley Inn & Spa, 705 Country Club Dr. (Old Coast Hwy.), Santa Barbara, 805-646-5511; www.ojai-valley-inn.com
Following a $70-million renovation at the historic Ojai Valley Inn, the new signature restaurant has been revamped into a sophisticated Californian featuring locally grown, healthy ingredients and a hint of Vietnamese flavor, offset by a 700-strong wine list; the three intimate dining areas boast cozy fireplaces and banquettes covered in Moroccan pillows, while the outdoor patio provides a view of the golf course.

Mattei's Tavern   25 | 21 | 21 | $43
(aka Brothers Restaurant at Mattei's Tavern)
2350 Railway Ave. (Foxen Canyon Rd.), Los Olivos,
805-688-4820
A "perfect place after a hard day's wine tasting", this "cozy,
down-home" eatery in an "old stagecoach stop" "provides one
of the Santa Ynez Valley's best dining experiences", thanks to
fraternal chef-owners Matt and Jeff Nichols; their "superb"
seasonal American fare features the bounty of the region, as
does the "great" wine cellar; after dinner, unwind by the fire and
soak up the "historic atmosphere."

Mimosa   20 | 16 | 22 | $32
2700 De La Vina St. (Alamar Ave.), Santa Barbara,
805-682-2272
Truly "a local's fave", this "friendly" French bistro has "carved out"
a spot in Santa Barbara over the past twentysomething years and
still puts on a "decent show", offering a "true taste" of "country
cooking" without a drop of "pretentiousness"; nevertheless,
naysayers nip it in the bud, deeming the decor "drab" and the fare
and "service nothing special."

MIRÓ 🖼 Ⓜ   23 | 26 | 23 | $63
Bacara Resort, 8301 Hollister Ave. (south of Hwy. 101), Santa Barbara,
805-968-0100; www.bacararesort.com
"Just wish it was closer to town" sigh the few surveyors who've
ventured to this "out-of-the-way" "lovely setting" in the Bacara
Resort, named after artist Joan Miró and perched "on a bluff
overlooking" the Pacific outside of Santa Barbara; aesthetes adore
the "beautiful" Basque-Catalan cuisine, "polished, professional
service" and the "sumptuous" dining room that looks like it "cost
an arm and a leg"; but a handful paint another picture, deeming it
"overpriced" and "disappointing."

Montecito Cafe   23 | 19 | 22 | $33
Montecito Inn, 1295 Coast Village Rd. (Olive Mill Ln.), Santa Barbara,
805-969-3392; www.montecitoinn.com
The "ultimate gourmand's dream of outstanding food" at
"unbelievable prices" can be found at this Californian "mainstay"
in the "darling" Montecito Inn; "homestyle" "inventive food
prepared with the freshest ingredients" and "mouthwatering
coconut cake" make it a "favorite" with "lunching ladies" and
other "locals" "year in and year out" "for good reason"; "get there
early" or "be prepared to wait in the adorable bar."

Noah's New York Bagels   17 | 10 | 14 | $8
1413 S. Victoria Ave. (bet. Ralston & Telephone Sts.), Ventura,
805-650-1413; www.noahs.com
See review in Los Angeles Directory.

Nu Ⓜ   23 | 22 | 20 | $45
1129 State St. (W. Figueroa St.), Santa Barbara, 805-965-1500
Chef/co-proprietor "David Cecchini is a master at stacking his"
"delicious Californian cuisine" as "high as the restaurant's
ceilings" at this "serene", "pretty" "very Santa Barbara-ish" spot
with a "beautiful courtyard" "hidden" from the State Street hustle
bustle; if a handful shrug it's "nothing nu, but good", for most it's
one of the "best in SB."

OLIO E LIMONE
25 | 18 | 20 | $48

11 W. Victoria St. (bet. Chapala & State Sts.), Santa Barbara, 805-899-2699; www.olioelimone.com

There are "too many" "innovative" dishes on the chef/co-owner Alberto Morello's menu "to order in just one visit" say regulars of this Santa Barbara Italian, with some of "the warmest hosts in town"; the "cool, low-key space" has "been discovered", and little wonder, what with "earthy pastas" (try the spaghetti à la bottarga) and an "impressive wine list"; still, a squished few whine "the tables are crammed so close together."

Opal
22 | 19 | 21 | $34

(fka Brigitte's)

1325 State St. (Arlington Ave.), Santa Barbara, 805-966-9676; www.opalrestaurantandbar.com

Set in a historic building "convenient to the Arlington Theater", this "noisy", "informal" bistro (formerly Brigitte's) is "not as pretentious as the other places in Santa Barbara"; they "make you feel at home" with "reliable" (if sometimes "unexciting") New American–Californian fare at "reasonable prices", coupled with an "inspired wine list."

Outback Steakhouse
18 | 15 | 18 | $25

5690 Calle Real (bet. Fairview & Patterson Aves.), Goleta, 805-964-0599; www.outback.com

Additional locations throughout Southern California

See review in Los Angeles Directory.

Palace Grill
24 | 20 | 24 | $33

8 E. Cota St. (State St.), Santa Barbara, 805-963-5000; www.palacegrill.com

This "little slice of the Big Easy in the California Riviera" sure "isn't the quietest place in Santa Barbara", but fans aren't coming for subdued conversation; instead, "real deal" Cajun-Creole cuisine (including "to-die-for bread pudding soufflé"), "friendly, knowledgeable" service, live jazz and a "partylike" atmosphere are the reasons for the "long lines"; P.S. there's "nothing like a martini in a mason jar."

Palazzio
19 | 16 | 17 | $24

1026 State St. (bet. Carillo & Figueroa Sts.), Santa Barbara, 805-564-1985; www.palazzio.com

"You can be as loud as you like" at this family-style Italian, a Santa Barbara "standby" where the "friendly" staff "sings Dean Martin's 'That's Amore'"; it's a "good value for the college crowd" or wallet-watchers "on an extreme budget", offering "huge portions" at "fair prices" and "self-serve wine"; but detractors demur, citing an "emphasis on quantity, not quality" and "too much garlic on everything."

Pane e Vino 🅂
20 | 19 | 19 | $34

Upper Montecito Vlg., 1482 E. Valley Rd. (bet. Santa Angela Ln. & San Ysidro Rd.), Santa Barbara, 805-969-9274

See review in Los Angeles Directory.

Piatti
20 | 20 | 18 | $30

516 San Ysidro Rd. (E. Balley Rd.), Santa Barbara, 805-969-7520; www.piatti.com

See review in Los Angeles Directory.

Piranha Restaurant & Sushi Ⓜ 25 | 22 | 22 | $33

714 State St. (W. Ortega St.), Santa Barbara, 805-965-2980
The "knowledgeable" chefs will "whip up whatever you ask for" at this small, "chic" Japanese eatery in Santa Barbara praised for its "imaginative" sushi rolls that are among the "best" in the area; word on the street is that the sake-tinis are "amazing."

Ranch House Ⓜ ▽ 23 | 27 | 23 | $50

500 S. Lomita Ave. (Tico Rd.), Ojai, 805-646-2360; www.theranchhouse.com
It's "worth the drive from wherever for a truly fine" meal of "inventive" Californian cuisine at this "lovely" ranch house in a "pristine, soothing" Ojai Valley setting agree admirers; with the "romantic hillside" and "wonderful garden" patio as a great backdrop", you "feel like you're in paradise", making it "the perfect ending to a weekend in Santa Barbara."

Rodney's Steakhouse Ⓢ Ⓜ – | – | – | E

Fess Parker Doubletree Resort, 633 E. Cabrillo Blvd. (S. Salispuedes St.), Santa Barbara, 805-884-8554; www.rodneyssteakhouse.com
Check the balance of your "expense account" then order a double martini from a "cocktail list that doesn't stop" at "one of the nicest bars in town", before digging into the "great steak and all the trimmings" at this classic art deco–style American steakhouse inside the Doubletree hotel owned by Davy Crockett, er, Fess Parker.

Sage & Onion 24 | 20 | 22 | $51

34 E. Ortega St. (Anacapa St.), Santa Barbara, 805-963-1012; www.sageandonion.com
"Always on the short list" for a "great date place" reveal admirers captivated by the "comfortable, romantic" setting and "heavenly" Euro-American fare at this "favorite"; the "creative menu and patio dining are what bring customers back", so "grab a table outside" – it's a "nice place to end a day in Santa Barbara"; N.B. a recent expansion may impact the Decor rating.

Sevilla ◗ – | – | – | E

428 Chapala St. (State St.), Santa Barbara, 805-564-8446
Contrary to its name (an homage to previous occupant Casa de Sevilla), the food at this atmospheric Santa Barbara building dating back to 1926 is Brazilian, which explains why there's a sense of Carnival in the air; the updated offerings include a feijoada made with Niman Ranch pork shank, and while pricey, it's still cheaper than a ticket to Rio.

Sharky's Mexican Grill 18 | 11 | 15 | $11

Gateway Ctr., 4960 Telephone Rd. (bet. Portola Rd. & Saratoga Ave.), Ventura, 805-339-9600; www.sharkys.com
Additional locations throughout Southern California
See review in Los Angeles Directory.

Spice Avenue ▽ 19 | 12 | 16 | $22

1027 State St. (Figueroa St.), Santa Barbara, 805-965-6004; www.spiceavenuesb.com
Get "good-quality" Indian fare in Downtown Santa Barbara at this "unassuming" BYO currying favor with an "excellent lunch buffet" that, at $7.95–$8.95, is "a steal"; if the food's "unadventurous" to a few, others consider the eatery "a step up" from its competitors.

Stella Mare's Ⓜ   20 | 24 | 21 | $39 |
50 Los Patos Way (Cabrio Blvd.), Santa Barbara, 805-969-6705;
www.stellamares.com
Ornithologists and oenophiles alike flock to this "friendly" eatery
set in an "adorable", renovated Victorian, where patrons partake
in "well-prepared" Californian fare paired with Santa Barbara
wines; you'll dine in one of the "beautiful rooms" including a
"lovely greenhouse" overlooking a bird refuge, making this
"welcome retreat" a "delight on all counts."

SUZANNE'S CUISINE   26 | 23 | 24 | $43 |
502 W. Ojai Ave. (Bristol Ave.), Ojai, 805-640-1961;
www.suzannescuisine.com
"SoCal's answer to Chez Panisse" is this mother-daughter-owned
"hideaway" in Ojai that shines with "incredibly fresh" French-
Italian fare prepared with "imagination" and served by an "attentive
staff"; P.S. the garden seating is ideal for a "leisurely lunch"
or "romantic dinner."

Taiko   21 | 16 | 18 | $24 |
511 State St. (bet. Cota & Haley Sts.), Santa Barbara, 805-564-8875
See review in Los Angeles Directory.

Trattoria Grappolo   ▽ 26 | 15 | 21 | $36 |
3687 Sagunto St. (Meadowvale Rd.), Santa Ynez, 805-688-6899;
www.trattoriagrappolo.com
"Skip the *Sideways* tour and head to this "quaint", "fabulous
little" trattoria "nestled in Santa Ynez", the "perfect" destination
"after a day of tasting at the local" vineyards in Santa Barbara
wine country; the "awesome" "real Italian" food, straight from the
wood-burning oven, ensures it's "always popular and crowded",
plus the staff is "cute and attentive."

Trattoria Mollie Ⓜ   21 | 21 | 18 | $45 |
1250 Coast Village Rd. (Olive Mill Rd.), Montecito, 805-565-9381;
www.tmollie.com
"Mollie was an institution even before she was featured on
Oprah" because her "handmade" "fresh pastas", "especially
good thin-crust pizzas" and other Tuscan "standards with an
unusual twist" are "served with cheer" and "made with so
much love"; but while some consider this trattoria the "jewel of
Montecito", a few feel "there's still room for improvement", citing
"small portions", "expensive" tabs and a bit of an "attitude."

Tre Lune   19 | 20 | 18 | $43 |
1151 Coast Village Rd. (bet. Butterfly Ln. & Middle Rd.), Montecito,
805-969-2646
Like "sibling Lucky's", this venture from Lucky Jeans tycoon Gene
Montesano is the "place to be" for "very fresh, well-prepared"
Italian; but while fans "enthuse about" "great pasta dishes" and
"meat sauce that constantly stays in your mind", others are less
over the moon, citing food that's "ok, but lacking in distinction" and
"a touch too expensive, even for Montecito."

Tupelo Junction Ⓜ   25 | 17 | 22 | $30 |
1218 State St. (bet. Anapamu & Victoria Sts.), Santa Barbara,
805-899-3100; www.tupelojunction.com
"Charming in character", this "funky" SB "gem" moved two doors
up to a bricks-and-beams space twice as big as the original, but

it still feels like sweet salvation to locals who come for "creative" "Southern-style" fare made in a wood-burning oven; it's "a great place to hang over a lazy breakfast" or on weekends during jazz and blues performances – little wonder customers keep "running back"; N.B. the relocation may not be reflected in the Decor score.

Via Vai 20 17 19 $29
Upper Vlg., 1483 E. Valley Rd. (San Ysidro Rd.), Montecito, 805-565-9393

Pane e Vino's "affordable" baby sister is also a "fun little Italian joint" in Montecito with "lots of choices", ranging from "cracker-thin pizzas perfectly cooked in the wood-burning oven" to "tasty pasta" and "wonderful" Venetian specials; you can "go every week" and never "go wrong with anything you order", plus the "view of the mountains" from the "pleasant patio" "can't be beat."

WINE CASK 25 24 24 $53
813 Anacapa St. (Canon Perdido St.), Santa Barbara, 805-966-9463; www.winecask.com

"Try to snag an outside table even if it's cool, because it's magical" on the "beautiful" courtyard "heated by torchieres" proclaim "romantics" equally smitten by Santa Barbara's "gorgeous" 19th-century "El Paseo home"; owner "Doug Margerum knows his food and his wine, and they both shine" at this "winner" that sets the "gold standard" with "exquisite" Californian cuisine matched by an "oenophile's dream" of a wine list, served by a staff that "never misses a beat."

Orange County/ Palm Springs/ Santa Barbara Indexes

CUISINES
LOCATIONS
SPECIAL FEATURES

Restaurant locations are indicated by the following abbreviations: Orange County=OC; Palm Springs & Environs=PS; and Santa Barbara & Environs=SB.

† Multiple locations in the Outlying Areas.

CUISINES

American (New)
Bayside/OC
Bistango/OC
Cat & Custard Cup/OC
Downey's/SB
Epiphany/SB
Gordon James/OC
Hush/OC
La Quinta Cliffhse./PS
Lodge/Rancho Mirage/PS
Mr. Stox/OC
Opal/SB
Rainforest Cafe/OC
Ramos House Cafe/OC
Sage/OC
Svelte/OC
3Thirty3/OC

American (Traditional)
Bandera/OC
Billy Reed's/PS
BJ's†
Blue Beet/OC
Bluewater Grill/OC
Britta's Café/OC
Café R&D/OC
Cedar Creek Inn†
Cheesecake Factory†
Claim Jumper†
Cold Spring/SB
Cottage/OC
Daily Grill†
Filling Station/OC
Fox Sports/OC
Gulfstream/OC
Heroes B&G/OC
Houston's/OC
Islands†
Johnny Rockets†
Kaiser Grille/PS
Lazy Dog/OC
Lodge/OC
Mattei's Tavern/SB
Mimi's Cafe/OC
Mrs. Knott's/OC
Original Pancake/OC
Rodney's Steak/SB
Ruby's†
Sage & Onion/SB

Salt Creek/OC
Side Street Cafe/OC
Souplantation†
Steelhead Brewing/OC
TAPS Fish/OC
Wood Ranch BBQ/OC
Yard House/OC

Argentinean
Gaucho Grill/OC

Armenian
Rosine's/OC
Zankou Chicken/OC

Asian
Crab Cove/OC
Oysters/OC
Svelte/OC

Austrian
Johannes/PS

Bakeries
Sweet Divas/OC

Barbecue
Hitching Post/SB
Johnny Rebs'†
Lucille's BBQ†
Tony Roma's†
Wingnuts/OC
Wood Ranch BBQ/OC

Belgian
Brussels Bistro/OC
L'Auberge/SB
L'Hirondelle/OC

Brazilian
Agora Churrascaria/OC
Amazon Churrascaria/OC
Picanha Churrascaria/PS
Sevilla/SB

Cajun
Crescent City/OC
Iva Lee's/OC
JackShrimp/OC
Palace Grill/SB
Shenandoah/Arbor/OC

55555666

Californian
Accents/OC
Alvarado's Kitchen/OC
BeachFire/OC
Bouchon/SB
Brown Pelican/SB
Cafe del Sol/SB
Cafe Zoolu/OC
Californian/OC
Cat & Custard Cup/OC
Citronelle/SB
Citrus†
Cuistot/PS
Deco/SB
El Encanto/SB
Four Seasons/SB
Green Parrot Cafe/OC
Louie's/SB
Maravilla/SB
Market City/OC
Montecito Cafe/SB
Napa Rose/OC
Nu/SB
Oceans 33°/OC
Opah/OC
Opal/SB
Oysters/OC
Pavilion/OC
Ranch House/SB
6ix Park Grill/OC
Sorrento Grille/OC
Splashes/OC
Stella Mare's/SB
Studio/OC
Sundried Tomato/OC
Sweet Divas/OC
Taco Mesa/OC
Tangata/OC
230 Forest Ave./OC
Vine/OC
Wine Cask/SB
Wolfgang Puck/OC
Woody's at Beach/OC
Zinc Cafe/OC

Caribbean
Golden Truffle/OC
Tommy Bahama†

Chinese
(* dim sum specialist)
California Wok/OC
Five Feet/OC
P.F. Chang's/OC
Sam Woo's/OC*
Seafood Paradise/OC*

Coffeehouses
Gypsy Den/OC

Coffee Shops/Diners
Johnny Rockets†
Mimi's Cafe/OC
Ruby's†

Continental
Arches/OC
Gemmell's/OC
Hobbit/OC
Jillian's/PS
Mr. Stox/OC
Nieuport 17/OC
Ritz Rest./Gdn./OC
Riviera at Fireside/OC
Rothschild's/OC
Summit House/OC

Creole
Crescent City/OC
Iva Lee's/OC
Palace Grill/SB
Ralph Brennan's/OC

Cuban
Habana/OC

Dessert
Cheesecake Factory†
Mascarpone's/OC
Zov's Bistro/OC

Eclectic
Café Tu Tu Tango/OC
Dizz's as Is/OC
John Henry's/PS
Lazy Dog/OC
Motif/OC
Sutra Lounge/OC
White Horses/OC
Yard House/OC

English
Five Crowns/OC
Gulliver's/OC
Lord Fletcher's/PS
Olde Ship/OC

European
Crab Cove/OC
Sage & Onion/SB

Fondue
Melting Pot/OC

French
Accents/OC
Azur/PS
Basilic/OC
Black Sheep/OC
Bouchon/SB
Cellar/OC
Chanteclair/OC
Citronelle/SB
Cuistot/PS
Dish/SB
El Encanto/SB
French 75/OC
Gemmell's/OC
Golden Truffle/OC
Hobbit/OC
John Henry's/PS
L'Auberge/SB
La Vie en Rose/OC
Le St. Germain/PS
Le Vallauris/PS
Pascal/OC
Pinot Provence/OC
Savoury's/OC
Suzanne's/SB
Wally's Desert/PS
Yves' Bistro/OC
Zipangu/OC

French (Bistro)
Café des Beaux-Arts/PS
Chat Noir Bistro/OC
Mimosa/SB
Mirabeau/OC
Pescadou/OC
Rouge Bistro/OC
Sweet Divas/OC
Troquet/OC

French (New)
Ballard Inn/SB
Five Feet/OC
Studio/OC

Hamburgers
In-N-Out Burger†
Islands†

Johnny Rockets†
Muldoon's Dublin/OC
Ruby's†

Hawaiian
Loft/OC

Hawaii Regional
Roy's†

Hot Dogs
Jody Maroni's/OC

Indian
Chakra/OC
Mayur/OC
Natraj/OC
Royal Khyber/OC
Spice Avenue/SB

Irish
Muldoon's Dublin/OC

Italian
(N=Northern; S=Southern)
Anaheim White Hse./OC (N)
Antonello/OC
Bellini/PS
Bucatini/SB (N)
Ca' Dario/SB
Cafe Fiore/SB (S)
Capriccio/OC
Castelli's/PS
Dolce Ristorante/OC
Eladio's/SB
Emilio's/SB (N)
Enoteca Primo/SB
Il Fornaio/OC
Luciana's/OC
Maggiano's/OC
Market City/OC
Mascarpone's/OC
Modo Mio Cucina/OC (N)
Mulberry St. Rist./OC
Naples/OC (S)
Nello Cucina/OC
Old Spaghetti Factory†
Olio e Limone/SB
Palazzio/SB
Pane e Vino†
Paolo's/OC (N)
Peppino's/OC
Piatti/SB

Pomodoro†
Prego/OC
Rist. Mamma Gina† (N)
Rist. Tuscany/PS (N)
Romano's Macaroni/PS
Rothschild's/OC (N)
Sabatino's Sausage/OC (S)
Selma's Pizzeria/OC
Sirocco/PS
Spaghettini/OC (N)
Spark Woodfire Grill/OC
Suzanne's/SB
Tannins/OC (S)
Ti Amo/OC
Trattoria Grappolo/SB
Trattoria Mollie/SB (N)
Tre Lune/SB
Tutto Fresco/OC
Tutto Mare/OC
Vessia/OC (S)
Via Vai/SB
Villa Nova/OC
Yves' Bistro/OC

Japanese
(* sushi specialist)
Abe/OC*
Arigato Sushi/SB*
Benihana/OC*
Cannery Seafood/OC*
Hibachi Steak/OC
Ichibiri/OC*
Kai/SB*
O-Nami/OC*
Ozumo/OC
Piranha/SB*
Shabu Shabu/OC
Taiko/SB*
Taiko Japanese/OC*
Ten/OC*
Todai/OC*
Wasa/OC*
Zipangu/OC

Korean
(* barbecue specialist)
BCD Tofu/OC
Yi Dynasty/OC*

Mediterranean
Catal/Uva Bar/OC
Emilio's/SB

Fitness Pizza/OC
Le St. Germain/PS
Le Vallauris/PS
Pavilion/OC
Picayo/OC
Rosine's/OC
Savoury's/OC
Sorrento Grille/OC
Splashes/OC
Ti Amo/OC
Vine/OC
Zov's Bistro/OC

Mexican
Agave Mex. Grill/OC
Baja Fresh Mexican†
Cafe El Cholo/OC
Carlitos Cafe/SB
Coyote Grill/OC
El Cholo/OC
El Paseo/SB
El Torito†
El Torito Grill/OC
Javier's Cantina/OC
La Salsa†
Las Brisas/OC
Las Casuelas/PS
La Super-Rica/SB
Sharky's Mexican†
Taco Loco/OC
Taco Mesa/OC
Taco Rosa/OC
Taleo Mexican/OC
Tortilla Flats/OC
Tortilla Jo's/OC

New Zealand
Turner New Zealand/OC

Noodle Shops
Pho 79/OC

Nuevo Latino
Cava/SB

Pacific Northwest
Plums Café/OC

Pacific Rim
Chimayo at Beach/OC
Duke's/OC

Pan-Asian
Dish/SB
Johannes/PS

Pei Wei Diner/OC
Red Pearl Kitchen/OC
Thaifoon/OC

Pan-Latin
Cava/SB

Persian/Iranian
Darya/OC

Peruvian
Inka Grill/OC

Pizza
BJ's†
California Pizza Kitchen†
Fitness Pizza/OC
Naples/OC
Peppino's/OC
Selma's Pizzeria/OC
Spark Woodfire Grill/OC
Trattoria Mollie/SB
Via Vai/SB
Wolfgang Puck/OC

Pub Food
Heroes B&G/OC
Lord Fletcher's/PS
Muldoon's Dublin/OC
Olde Ship/OC
Steelhead Brewing/OC

Sandwiches
Lawry's Carvery/OC
Noah's NY Bagels/SB

Seafood
Aqua/OC
Azur/PS
Bay Café/SB
Bluewater Grill/OC
Brophy Bros./SB
Bungalow/OC
Cannery Seafood/OC
Catch/OC
Chart House/OC
Chuck's Waterfront/SB
Claes/OC
Crab Cooker/OC
Crab Cove/OC
Duke's/OC
Enterprise Fish/SB
Eric Ericson's/SB
Fish Market/OC

Gulfstream/OC
JackShrimp/OC
Javier's Cantina/OC
Joe's Crab†
King's Fish Hse./OC
La Cave/OC
Las Brisas/OC
McCormick/Schmick/OC
Oceans 33°/OC
Opah/OC
Original Fish Co./OC
Rusty Pelican/OC
Savannah Steak/OC
Scott's Seafood/OC
Seafood Paradise/OC
Tabu Grill/OC
TAPS Fish/OC
Tutto Mare/OC
21 Oceanfront/OC
230 Forest Ave./OC
Walt's Wharf/OC
Zipangu/OC

Small Plates
Café Tu Tu Tango/OC
Motif/OC
Red Pearl Kitchen/OC
Sutra Lounge/OC
3Thirty3/OC

South American
Cafe Buenos Aires/SB

Southern
House of Blues/OC
Johnny Rebs'†
Lucille's BBQ/OC
Memphis/OC
Shenandoah/Arbor/OC
Tupelo Junction/SB

Southwestern
Bandera/OC
Café Hidalgo/OC
Z'tejas/OC

Spanish
Black Sheep/OC
Miró/SB

Steakhouses
Benihana/OC
Bungalow/OC

Catch/OC
Chart House/OC
Chop House/PS
Chuck's Waterfront/SB
Falls Prime Steak/PS
Fleming Prime Steak/OC
Gaucho Grill/OC
Gulliver's/OC
Hibachi Steak/OC
La Cave/OC
LG's Prime Steak/PS
Lucky's/SB
Morton's Steak/OC
Outback Steak†
Rodney's Steak/SB
Ruth's Chris†
Salt Creek/OC
Savannah Steak/OC
Tabu Grill/OC
Trabuco Oaks Steak/OC
21 Oceanfront/OC

Swiss
Basilic/OC

Thai
Bangkok Four/OC
Royal Thai/OC
Thai Dishes/OC
Thaifoon/OC
Thai This/OC

Vegetarian
(* vegan)
Native Foods†*
Zinc Cafe/OC

Vietnamese
Pho 79/OC
Thanh My/OC

LOCATIONS

ORANGE COUNTY

Aliso Viejo
JackShrimp
Opah
Peppino's
Pomodoro
Sharky's Mexican
Wingnuts

Anaheim/Anaheim Hills
Alvarado's Kitchen
Anaheim White Hse.
Benihana
Catal/Uva Bar
Catch
El Torito
Hibachi Steak
House of Blues
Mimi's Cafe
Mr. Stox
Napa Rose
Naples
Original Pancake
Rainforest Cafe
Ralph Brennan's
Rosine's
Tony Roma's
Tortilla Jo's
Wood Ranch BBQ
Yves' Bistro
Zankou Chicken

Balboa
Ruby's

Brea
Baja Fresh Mexican
BJ's
California Pizza Kitchen
Cedar Creek Inn
Cheesecake Factory
Claim Jumper
El Torito Grill
Fitness Pizza
Gaucho Grill
Islands
La Vie en Rose
Lucille's BBQ
Market City

Outback Steak
Pane e Vino
Sweet Divas
TAPS Fish

Buena Park
El Torito
Mrs. Knott's
Outback Steak

Corona Del Mar
Bandera
Bungalow
Five Crowns
Mayur
Oysters
Rothschild's
Svelte
Zinc Cafe

Costa Mesa
Baja Fresh Mexican
Bangkok Four
California Wok
Chat Noir Bistro
Claim Jumper
Golden Truffle
Gypsy Den
Habana
Inka Grill
In-N-Out Burger
La Cave
Lawry's Carvery
Lodge
Maggiano's
Memphis
Native Foods
Nello Cucina
Outback Steak
Pinot Provence
Plums Café
Sam Woo's
Scott's Seafood
Side Street Cafe
Souplantation
Sutra Lounge
Taco Mesa
Troquet

Turner New Zealand
Wingnuts
Wolfgang Puck
Yard House
Zipangu
Z'tejas

Dana Point
Chart House
Gemmell's
Ichibiri
Luciana's
Salt Creek
Thai This

Foothill Ranch
Natraj
Souplantation

Fountain Valley
Islands
Mimi's Cafe
Souplantation
Thai Dishes

Fullerton
Amazon Churrascaria
Café Hidalgo
Cellar
Heroes B&G
Islands
Mulberry St. Rist.
Olde Ship
Old Spaghetti Factory
Summit House
Tony Roma's

Garden Grove
BCD Tofu
Five Feet
Joe's Crab
Outback Steak
Pho 79

Huntington Beach
BJ's
Californian
Chimayo at Beach
Duke's
Inka Grill
In-N-Out Burger
Loft
Paolo's

Red Pearl Kitchen
Spark Woodfire Grill
Tony Roma's

Irvine
Agora Churrascaria
Baja Fresh Mexican
Bistango
Britta's Café
California Pizza Kitchen
Chakra
Chanteclair
Cheesecake Factory
Claim Jumper
Daily Grill
El Cholo
El Torito Grill
Fish Market
Fox Sports
Gulliver's
Houston's
Il Fornaio
In-N-Out Burger
Islands
JackShrimp
Javier's Cantina
Johnny Rockets
La Salsa
McCormick/Schmick
Melting Pot
Natraj
Opah
Pei Wei Diner
P.F. Chang's
Pomodoro
Prego
Ruby's
Ruth's Chris
Sam Woo's
Sharky's Mexican
6ix Park Grill
Souplantation
Steelhead Brewing
Taiko Japanese
Taleo Mexican
Thaifoon
Vessia
Wasa
Yard House

Ladera Ranch
Taco Mesa

Laguna Beach/
S. Laguna Beach
BJ's
Brussels Bistro
Cafe Zoolu
Cedar Creek Inn
Claes
Cottage
Coyote Grill
Dizz's as Is
Five Feet
French 75
Hush
Javier's Cantina
Johnny Rockets
Las Brisas
Picayo
Pomodoro
Royal Thai
Ruby's
Savoury's
Sorrento Grille
Splashes
Studio
Sundried Tomato
Tabu Grill
Taco Loco
Ti Amo
230 Forest Ave.
Woody's at Beach
Zinc Cafe

Laguna Hills
Baja Fresh Mexican
Claim Jumper
King's Fish Hse.
Natraj
O-Nami

Laguna Niguel
Ichibiri
In-N-Out Burger
Mimi's Cafe
Peppino's
Savannah Steak

La Habra
Cafe El Cholo
Cat & Custard Cup

Lake Forest
Inka Grill
Mimi's Cafe
Peppino's

Los Alamitos
Original Fish Co.
Shenandoah/Arbor
Tony Roma's

Mission Viejo
California Pizza Kitchen
Capriccio
Cheesecake Factory
El Torito Grill
Oceans 33°
Peppino's
P.F. Chang's
Shabu Shabu
Taco Mesa
Tortilla Flats

Monarch Beach
Aqua
Crab Cove
Mirabeau
Motif

Newport Beach
Abe
Accents
Arches
Basilic
Bayside
Benihana
BJ's
Blue Beet
Bluewater Grill
Café R&D
Cannery Seafood
Chart House
Cheesecake Factory
Crab Cooker
Daily Grill
Dolce Ristorante
El Torito Grill
Fleming Prime Steak
Gulfstream
Islands
JackShrimp
Joe's Crab
La Salsa
Modo Mio Cucina
Muldoon's Dublin
Old Spaghetti Factory
Ozumo
Pascal

Pavilion
Pei Wei Diner
Pescadou
P.F. Chang's
Pomodoro
Rist. Mamma Gina
Ritz Rest./Gdn.
Rouge Bistro
Royal Thai
Roy's
Rusty Pelican
Sabatino's Sausage
Sage
Sharky's Mexican
Taco Rosa
Ten
Thaifoon
3Thirty3
Tommy Bahama
Tutto Mare
21 Oceanfront
Villa Nova
Wasa
Yi Dynasty

Orange
Café Tu Tu Tango
Citrus
El Torito
Filling Station
Hobbit
Jody Maroni's
Johnny Rebs'
Johnny Rockets
King's Fish Hse.
Mascarpone's
Pomodoro
Taco Mesa
Todai
Wolfgang Puck

Oxnard
BJ's
Outback Steak

Rancho Santa Margarita
Agave Mex. Grill
Opah
Selma's Pizzeria
Tutto Fresco

San Clemente
BeachFire
Gordon James

Ichibiri
Iva Lee's
Vine
White Horses

San Juan Capistrano
Cedar Creek Inn
L'Hirondelle
Ramos House Cafe
Sundried Tomato
Tannins

Santa Ana
Antonello
Baja Fresh Mexican
Bluewater Grill
California Pizza Kitchen
Claim Jumper
Darya
Green Parrot Cafe
Gypsy Den
Memphis
Morton's Steak
Olde Ship
Royal Khyber
Tangata

Seal Beach
Ruby's
Spaghettini
Walt's Wharf

Temecula
Souplantation
Tony Roma's

Trabuco Canyon
Trabuco Oaks Steak

Tustin
Black Sheep
California Pizza Kitchen
Citrus
Crab Cooker
Crescent City
El Torito
In-N-Out Burger
Mimi's Cafe
Nieuport 17
Peppino's
Ruby's
Zov's Bistro

Westminster
Lazy Dog
Pho 79
Riviera at Fireside
Seafood Paradise
Thanh My

Yorba Linda
El Torito
Fitness Pizza
Original Pancake

PALM SPRINGS & ENVIRONS

Corona
BJ's
Claim Jumper
In-N-Out Burger
Pomodoro

Indian Wells
Le St. Germain
Sirocco

La Quinta
Azur
Falls Prime Steak
La Quinta Cliffhse.
Las Casuelas
LG's Prime Steak

Palm Desert
Bellini
Café des Beaux-Arts
California Pizza Kitchen
Castelli's
Chop House
Cuistot
Daily Grill
Islands
Jillian's
LG's Prime Steak
Native Foods
Outback Steak
Picanha Churrascaria
Rist. Mamma Gina
Rist. Tuscany
Romano's Macaroni
Ruth's Chris
Tommy Bahama
Tony Roma's

Palm Springs
Billy Reed's
California Pizza Kitchen
Cedar Creek Inn

Chop House
Falls Prime Steak
Johannes
John Henry's
Kaiser Grille
Las Casuelas
Le Vallauris
LG's Prime Steak
Native Foods

Rancho Cucamonga
Claim Jumper
Lucille's BBQ
Romano's Macaroni
Souplantation

Rancho Mirage
Cheesecake Factory
Johnny Rockets
Las Casuelas
Lodge/Rancho Mirage
Lord Fletcher's
Roy's
Wally's Desert

Riverside
Citrus
In-N-Out Burger
Old Spaghetti Factory
Ruby's

San Bernardino
BJ's
Claim Jumper
Outback Steak
Souplantation

Upland
Outback Steak

Victorville
Johnny Rebs'

SANTA BARBARA & ENVIRONS

Ballard
Ballard Inn

Buellton
Hitching Post

Casmalia
Hitching Post

Goleta
In-N-Out Burger
Outback Steak

Los Olivos
Mattei's Tavern

Montecito
Cafe del Sol
Cava
Lucky's
Trattoria Mollie
Tre Lune
Via Vai

Ojai
L'Auberge
Ranch House
Suzanne's

Santa Barbara
Arigato Sushi
Bay Café
Bouchon
Brophy Bros.
Brown Pelican
Bucatini
Ca' Dario
Cafe Buenos Aires
California Pizza Kitchen
Carlitos Cafe
Chuck's Waterfront
Citronelle
Cold Spring
Dish
Downey's
Eladio's
El Encanto

El Paseo
El Torito
Emilio's
Enoteca Primo
Enterprise Fish
Epiphany
Four Seasons
In-N-Out Burger
Kai
La Salsa
La Super-Rica
Louie's
Maravilla
Mimosa
Miró
Montecito Cafe
Nu
Olio e Limone
Opal
Palace Grill
Palazzio
Pane e Vino
Piatti
Piranha
Rodney's Steak
Sage & Onion
Sevilla
Spice Avenue
Stella Mare's
Taiko
Tupelo Junction
Wine Cask

Santa Ynez
Trattoria Grappolo

Ventura
Baja Fresh Mexican
Cafe Fiore
Deco
Eric Ericson's
Joe's Crab
Noah's NY Bagels
Sharky's Mexican

SPECIAL FEATURES

(Indexes list the best in each category. Multi-location restaurants' features may vary by branch.)

Breakfast
(See also Hotel Dining)
Britta's Café/OC
Cottage/OC
Crescent City/OC
Filling Station/OC
Original Pancake/OC
Plums Café/OC
Ramos House Cafe/OC
Ruby's†
Side Street Cafe/OC
Zinc Cafe/OC
Zov's Bistro/OC

Brunch
Accents/OC
Bayside/OC
Cannery Seafood/OC
L'Hirondelle/OC
Mirabeau/OC
Pinot Provence/OC
Plums Café/OC
Ralph Brennan's/OC
Ramos House Cafe/OC
Rist. Mamma Gina/OC
Rouge Bistro/OC
6ix Park Grill/OC
TAPS Fish/OC

Business Dining
Accents/OC
Anaheim White Hse./OC
Antonello/OC
Aqua/OC
Arches/OC
Bayside/OC
Bistango/OC
Bucatini/SB
Californian/OC
Cat & Custard Cup/OC
Catch/OC
Cellar/OC
Chanteclair/OC
Claes/OC
Daily Grill/OC
Fleming Prime Steak/OC

Green Parrot Cafe/OC
Gulliver's/OC
Houston's/OC
Il Fornaio/OC
La Vie en Rose/OC
McCormick/Schmick/OC
Morton's Steak/OC
Mr. Stox/OC
Mulberry St. Rist./OC
Nieuport 17/OC
Opah/OC
Oysters/OC
Ozumo/OC
Pascal/OC
Pavilion/OC
Pinot Provence/OC
Prego/OC
Ritz Rest./Gdn./OC
Riviera at Fireside/OC
Roy's/OC
Ruth's Chris/OC
Salt Creek/OC
Sevilla/SB
6ix Park Grill/OC
Spaghettini/OC
Summit House/OC
Taleo Mexican/OC
Tangata/OC
Turner New Zealand/OC
Tutto Mare/OC
21 Oceanfront/OC
Vessia/OC
Villa Nova/OC
Zov's Bistro/OC

Child-Friendly
(Alternatives to the usual fast-food places; * children's menu available)
Accents/OC*
Bandera/OC*
Bay Café/SB
BeachFire/OC*
Benihana/OC*
Billy Reed's/PS*
Bluewater Grill/OC*

Britta's Café/OC
Brophy Bros./SB
Cafe El Cholo/OC*
Café Tu Tu Tango/OC*
Californian/OC*
California Pizza Kitchen/OC*
Carlitos Cafe/SB*
Cedar Creek Inn†*
Cheesecake Factory/OC
Chimayo at Beach/OC*
Claim Jumper/OC*
Cold Spring/SB*
Duke's/OC*
El Torito Grill/OC*
Filling Station/OC*
Fish Market/OC*
Hibachi Steak/OC*
Ichibiri/OC
In-N-Out Burger†
Islands/OC*
Jody Maroni's/OC*
Joe's Crab/OC*
King's Fish Hse./OC*
Las Casuelas/PS*
Louie's/SB
Maggiano's/OC*
Mimosa/SB
Mrs. Knott's/OC*
Naples/OC*
Old Spaghetti Factory/OC*
Original Fish Co./OC*
Original Pancake/OC
Palazzio/SB*
Peppino's/OC*
P.F. Chang's/OC
Romano's Macaroni/PS*
Ruby's†*
Souplantation†*
Taco Rosa/OC*
TAPS Fish/OC*
Thai Dishes/OC
Todai/OC
Tortilla Jo's/OC*
Trabuco Oaks Steak/OC*
Trattoria Mollie/SB
Wingnuts/OC*
Zankou Chicken/OC

Dancing
Bistango/OC
Blue Beet/OC
Cafe Buenos Aires/SB
Las Casuelas/PS
Sutra Lounge/OC
Ten/OC

Entertainment
(Call for days and times of performances)
Bayside/OC (piano)
Benihana/OC (chefs)
Café Tu Tu Tango/OC (varies)
Cat & Custard Cup/OC (piano)
Cedar Creek Inn/OC (varies)
Chat Noir Bistro/OC (jazz)
Duke's/OC (varies)
House of Blues/OC (varies)
La Cave/OC (jazz)
Lodge/OC (piano/DJs)
Lucille's BBQ† (blues)
Market City/OC (strings)
Mulberry St. Rist./OC (varies)
Nieuport 17/OC (piano)
Oysters/OC (jazz)
Ralph Brennan's/OC (jazz)
Rist. Mamma Gina/OC (band)
Romano's Macaroni/PS (opera)
Salt Creek/OC (varies)
Spaghettini/OC (jazz)
Sutra Lounge/OC (DJ/jazz)
Ten/OC (DJ)
Villa Nova/OC (piano)

Historic Places
(Year opened; * building)
1800 Tupelo Junction/SB*
1881 Ramos House Cafe/OC*
1886 Cold Spring/SB*
1890 Wine Cask/SB*
1900 Five Crowns/OC*
1900 Hobbit/OC*
1909 Anaheim White Hse./OC*
1912 Blue Beet/OC*
1915 El Encanto/SB*
1917 Cottage/OC*
1920 El Paseo/SB*
1920 Old Spaghetti Factory/OC*
1920 Sweet Divas/OC*
1922 Arches/OC
1922 Cellar/OC*
1923 Maravilla/SB
1923 Woody's at Beach/OC*
1926 Gordon James/OC*
1927 Four Seasons/SB*

1928 Ti Amo/OC*
1930 Dizz's as Is/OC*
1930 Las Casuelas/PS*
1930 Luciana's/OC*
1933 Villa Nova/OC
1940 Mrs. Knott's/OC
1949 Tortilla Flats/OC
1951 Crab Cooker/OC
1952 Hitching Post/SB
1953 Ranch House/SB*

Hotel Dining

Anaheim Marriott Suites
  Five Feet/OC
Bacara Resort
  Miró/SB
El Encanto Hotel
  El Encanto/SB
Fairmont Newport Beach
  Accents/OC
Fess Parker Doubletree Resort
  Rodney's Steak/SB
Four Seasons Hotel
  Pavilion/OC
Four Seasons Resort
  Four Seasons/SB
Grand Californian Hotel
  Napa Rose/OC
Harbor View Inn
  Eladio's/SB
Hyatt Regency Huntington
  Californian/OC
Hyatt Regency Irvine
  6ix Park Grill/OC
JW Marriott Desert Springs
  Rist. Tuscany/PS
La Casa Del Camino, Hotel
  Savoury's/OC
Laguna, Hotel
  Claes/OC
La Quinta Resort & Club
  Azur/PS
Lodge at Rancho Mirage
  Lodge/Rancho Mirage/PS
Montage Resort & Spa
  Studio/OC
Montecito Inn
  Montecito Cafe/SB
Ojai Valley Inn & Spa
  Maravilla/SB
Renaissance Esmeralda Resort
  Sirocco/PS

Santa Barbara Inn
  Citronelle/SB
St. Regis Monarch Beach
  Aqua/OC
  Motif/OC
Surf & Sand Resort
  Splashes/OC
Upham Hotel
  Louie's/SB
Villa del Sol
  Café Hidalgo/OC
Westin South Coast Plaza
  Pinot Provence/OC

Late Dining

(Weekday closing hour)
Arches/OC (1 AM)
Blue Beet/OC (2 AM)
Café Tu Tu Tango/OC (12 AM)
In-N-Out Burger† (1 AM)
Le St. Germain/PS (12 AM)
Mirabeau/OC (1:30 AM)
Mr. Stox/OC (12 AM)
Sevilla/SB (2 AM)
Svelte/OC (12 AM)
Taco Loco/OC (12 AM)
Thanh My/OC (1 AM)
3Thirty3/OC (2 AM)
Villa Nova/OC (12 AM)
Zipangu/OC (varies)

Meet for a Drink

Antonello/OC
Arches/OC
Bayside/OC
Bistango/OC
BJ's/OC
Brown Pelican/SB
Bungalow/OC
Cafe Buenos Aires/SB
Cafe Fiore/SB
Café Tu Tu Tango/OC
Cannery Seafood/OC
Catal/Uva Bar/OC
Catch/OC
Cedar Creek Inn/OC
Chakra/OC
Chat Noir Bistro/OC
Dolce Ristorante/OC
El Paseo/SB
Epiphany/SB

Fleming Prime Steak/OC
Fox Sports/OC
Gulfstream/OC
Habana/OC
Il Fornaio/OC
Javier's Cantina/OC
McCormick/Schmick/OC
Memphis/OC
Mr. Stox/OC
Mulberry St. Rist./OC
Muldoon's Dublin/OC
Napa Rose/OC
Nieuport 17/OC
Olde Ship/OC
Opah/OC
Oysters/OC
Prego/OC
Red Pearl Kitchen/OC
Ritz Rest./Gdn./OC
Sevilla/SB
Sorrento Grille/OC
Spaghettini/OC
Steelhead Brewing/OC
Tannins/OC
TAPS Fish/OC
3Thirty3/OC
Tutto Mare/OC
Villa Nova/OC
Woody's at Beach/OC
Yard House/OC

Noteworthy Newcomers
Ballard Inn/SB
Cafe Fiore/SB
Café R&D/OC
Dish/SB
Green Parrot Cafe/OC
Javier's Cantina/OC
Modo Mio Cucina/OC
Ozumo/OC
6ix Park Grill/OC
Sundried Tomato/OC
Taleo Mexican/OC
Ten/OC
3Thirty3/OC
Zipangu/OC

Offbeat
Benihana/OC
Cafe Zoolu/OC
Crab Cooker/OC
Dizz's as Is/OC

Filling Station/OC
Gypsy Den/OC
Habana/OC
La Cave/OC
Memphis/OC
Pescadou/OC
Ramos House Cafe/OC
Red Pearl Kitchen/OC
Side Street Cafe/OC
Taco Loco/OC
Trabuco Oaks Steak/OC
Walt's Wharf/OC

Outdoor Dining
(G=garden; P=patio;
S=sidewalk; T=terrace)
Bistango/OC (P)
Bluewater Grill/OC (G,T)
Bungalow/OC (G,P)
Café Tu Tu Tango/OC (P)
Cannery Seafood/OC (P)
Catal/Uva Bar/OC (T)
Cedar Creek Inn/OC (P)
Chakra/OC (P)
Chat Noir Bistro/OC (P)
Dolce Ristorante/OC (P)
Filling Station/OC (P)
Green Parrot Cafe/OC (P)
Gulfstream/OC (P)
Habana/OC (P)
Javier's Cantina/OC (P)
L'Hirondelle/OC (P)
Mirabeau/OC (P)
Motif/OC (T)
Muldoon's Dublin/OC (P)
Pinot Provence/OC (P)
Plums Café/OC (P)
Prego/OC (P)
Ramos House Cafe/OC (P)
Ritz Rest./Gdn./OC (G)
Sage/OC (G,P)
Shenandoah/Arbor/OC (P)
Splashes/OC (P,T)
Sundried Tomato/OC (P,T)
Svelte/OC (P)
Tangata/OC (P)
TAPS Fish/OC (P)
Thaifoon/OC (P)
Tommy Bahama/OC (P)
Zinc Cafe/OC (G,P)
Zov's Bistro/OC (P,T)

People-Watching
Antonello/OC
Arigato Sushi/SB
Bayside/OC
Bistango/OC
Brown Pelican/SB
Bungalow/OC
Catal/Uva Bar/OC
Chat Noir Bistro/OC
Chimayo at Beach/OC
Duke's/OC
El Paseo/SB
Epiphany/SB
Gulfstream/OC
Habana/OC
Javier's Cantina/OC
Las Brisas/OC
Memphis/OC
Oysters/OC
Red Pearl Kitchen/OC
Sorrento Grille/OC
Studio/OC
Ten/OC
Tutto Mare/OC
230 Forest Ave./OC
Woody's at Beach/OC
Yard House/OC
Zinc Cafe/OC

Power Scenes
Anaheim White Hse./OC
Antonello/OC
Aqua/OC
Arches/OC
Bayside/OC
Bistango/OC
Cellar/OC
Chanteclair/OC
Five Crowns/OC
Fleming Prime Steak/OC
Morton's Steak/OC
Mr. Stox/OC
Pascal/OC
Pavilion/OC
Pinot Provence/OC
Ritz Rest./Gdn./OC
Roy's/OC
Ruth's Chris/OC
Studio/OC
Troquet/OC
21 Oceanfront/OC

Private Rooms
(Restaurants charge less at
off times; call for capacity)
Anaheim White Hse./OC
Antonello/OC
Arches/OC
Bayside/OC
Bistango/OC
Cat & Custard Cup/OC
Chanteclair/OC
Claes/OC
Five Crowns/OC
Fleming Prime Steak/OC
Green Parrot Cafe/OC
Hobbit/OC
La Vie en Rose/OC
Maggiano's/OC
Melting Pot/OC
Motif/OC
Mr. Stox/OC
Napa Rose/OC
Nieuport 17/OC
Pinot Provence/OC
Prego/OC
Ritz Rest./Gdn./OC
Rouge Bistro/OC
Roy's/OC
Salt Creek/OC
Scott's Seafood/OC
6ix Park Grill/OC
Studio/OC
Summit House/OC
Sutra Lounge/OC
Svelte/OC
TAPS Fish/OC
21 Oceanfront/OC
Zov's Bistro/OC

Romantic Places
Anaheim White Hse./OC
Antonello/OC
Ballard Inn/SB
Basilic/OC
Black Sheep/OC
Brown Pelican/SB
Bucatini/SB
Cafe Fiore/SB
Californian/OC
Cat & Custard Cup/OC
Cellar/OC
Chakra/OC

Chanteclair/OC
Chat Noir Bistro/OC
Claes/OC
Dizz's as Is/OC
French 75/OC
Green Parrot Cafe/OC
Hobbit/OC
La Cave/OC
La Vie en Rose/OC
Luciana's/OC
Maggiano's/OC
Melting Pot/OC
Mirabeau/OC
Mr. Stox/OC
Nieuport 17/OC
Pascal/OC
Pavilion/OC
Picayo/OC
Pinot Provence/OC
Ritz Rest./Gdn./OC
Rothschild's/OC
Savoury's/OC
Sevilla/SB
Splashes/OC
Studio/OC
Ti Amo/OC
21 Oceanfront/OC
Villa Nova/OC

Singles Scenes
Bayside/OC
BeachFire/OC
Bistango/OC
Bungalow/OC
Chat Noir Bistro/OC
El Paseo/SB
Gulfstream/OC
Habana/OC
Heroes B&G/OC
Houston's/OC
Javier's Cantina/OC
Las Brisas/OC
Lodge/OC
Memphis/OC
Muldoon's Dublin/OC
Opah/OC
Oysters/OC
Red Pearl Kitchen/OC
Rusty Pelican/OC
Salt Creek/OC
Sorrento Grille/OC

Spaghettini/OC
Sutra Lounge/OC
3Thirty3/OC
Tutto Mare/OC
230 Forest Ave./OC
Woody's at Beach/OC
Yard House/OC

Special Occasions
Anaheim White Hse./OC
Antonello/OC
Aqua/OC
Arches/OC
Bayside/OC
Bistango/OC
Bungalow/OC
Californian/OC
Cellar/OC
Chanteclair/OC
Dizz's as Is/OC
Five Crowns/OC
Fleming Prime Steak/OC
French 75/OC
Hobbit/OC
Las Brisas/OC
La Vie en Rose/OC
Melting Pot/OC
Morton's Steak/OC
Napa Rose/OC
Nieuport 17/OC
Pascal/OC
Pavilion/OC
Picayo/OC
Pinot Provence/OC
Riviera at Fireside/OC
Splashes/OC
Studio/OC
Ti Amo/OC
21 Oceanfront/OC

Trendy
Abe/OC
Anaheim White Hse./OC
Bayside/OC
Bistango/OC
Café R&D/OC
Chat Noir Bistro/OC
Epiphany/SB
Five Feet/OC
Fleming Prime Steak/OC
Fox Sports/OC
French 75/OC

Gulfstream/OC
Gypsy Den/OC
Hush/OC
La Cave/OC
Morton's Steak/OC
Napa Rose/OC
Opah/OC
Oysters/OC
Ozumo/OC
Pinot Provence/OC
Red Pearl Kitchen/OC
Rouge Bistro/OC
Roy's/OC
Sorrento Grille/OC
Studio/OC
Sutra Lounge/OC
Svelte/OC
Taleo Mexican/OC
Ten/OC
3Thirty3/OC
230 Forest Ave./OC
Yard House/OC
Zipangu/OC

Views

Aqua/OC
Bellini/PS
Bluewater Grill/OC
Brown Pelican/SB
Cafe del Sol/SB
Californian/OC
Cannery Seafood/OC
Chart House/OC
Cheesecake Factory/OC
Chimayo at Beach/OC
Citronelle/SB
Claes/OC
Coyote Grill/OC
Cuistot/PS
Duke's/OC
Eladio's/SB
Emilio's/SB
Falls Prime Steak/PS
Four Seasons/SB
Las Brisas/OC
L'Auberge/SB
Lodge/Rancho Mirage/PS
Miró/SB
Motif/OC
Rist. Tuscany/PS

Rodney's Steak/SB
Ruby's/OC
Rusty Pelican/OC
Splashes/OC
Stella Mare's/SB
Studio/OC
Summit House/OC
Tortilla Flats/OC
21 Oceanfront/OC
Villa Nova/OC
White Horses/OC

Visitors on Expense Account

Abe/OC
Anaheim White Hse./OC
Antonello/OC
Aqua/OC
Arches/OC
Bayside/OC
Bistango/OC
Californian/OC
Cellar/OC
Five Crowns/OC
Five Feet/OC
Fleming Prime Steak/OC
French 75/OC
Hobbit/OC
La Vie en Rose/OC
Mirabeau/OC
Morton's Steak/OC
Motif/OC
Mr. Stox/OC
Napa Rose/OC
Pascal/OC
Pavilion/OC
Pinot Provence/OC
Ritz Rest./Gdn./OC
Riviera at Fireside/OC
Roy's/OC
Ruth's Chris/OC
Savoury's/OC
Splashes/OC
Studio/OC
Summit House/OC
Troquet/OC
Turner New Zealand/OC
21 Oceanfront/OC
Villa Nova/OC
Zov's Bistro/OC

Waterside
Bluewater Grill/OC
Brown Pelican/SB
Cannery Seafood/OC
Chart House/OC
Cheesecake Factory/PS
Chimayo at Beach/OC
Chuck's Waterfront/SB
Claes/OC
Coyote Grill/OC
Duke's/OC
Eladio's/SB
Emilio's/SB
Joe's Crab/OC
Las Brisas/OC
Motif/OC
Rist. Mamma Gina/OC
Ruby's/OC
Rusty Pelican/OC
Spark Woodfire Grill/OC
Splashes/OC
Stella Mare's/SB
Studio/OC
3Thirty3/OC
Tortilla Flats/OC
21 Oceanfront/OC
Villa Nova/OC
White Horses/OC

Winning Wine Lists
Accents/OC
Anaheim White Hse./OC
Antonello/OC
Aqua/OC
Arches/OC
Bayside/OC
Bistango/OC
Black Sheep/OC
Cellar/OC
Claes/OC
Deco/SB
Dish/SB

Five Crowns/OC
Fleming Prime Steak/OC
Golden Truffle/OC
Hobbit/OC
Mr. Stox/OC
Napa Rose/OC
Oysters/OC
Pascal/OC
Pavilion/OC
Pinot Provence/OC
Ritz Rest./Gdn./OC
Rosine's/OC
Roy's/OC
Studio/OC
Troquet/OC
Walt's Wharf/OC

Worth a Trip
Anaheim
　　Napa Rose/OC
Costa Mesa
　　Chat Noir Bistro/OC
　　Pinot Provence/OC
　　Troquet/OC
Fullerton
　　Cellar/OC
Laguna Beach
　　Five Feet/OC
　　French 75/OC
　　Studio/OC
Monarch Beach
　　Aqua/OC
Newport Beach
　　Abe/OC
　　Pascal/OC
　　Pavilion/OC
　　Ritz Rest./Gdn./OC
Santa Ana
　　Antonello/OC
Tustin
　　Zov's Bistro/OC

Wine Vintage Chart

This chart is designed to help you select wine to go with your meal. It is based on the same 0 to 30 scale used throughout this *Survey*. The ratings (prepared by our friend **Howard Stravitz**, a law professor at the University of South Carolina) reflect both the quality of the vintage and the wine's readiness for present consumption. Thus, if a wine is not fully mature or is over the hill, its rating has been reduced. We do not include 1987, 1991–1993 vintages because they are not especially recommended for most areas. A dash indicates that a wine is either past its peak or too young to rate.

	'85	'86	'88	'89	'90	'94	'95	'96	'97	'98	'99	'00	'01	'02	'03
WHITES															
French:															
Alsace	24	–	22	28	28	27	26	25	25	26	25	26	27	25	–
Burgundy	26	25	–	24	22	–	28	29	24	23	26	25	23	27	24
Loire Valley	–	–	–	–	24	–	20	23	22	–	24	25	23	27	26
Champagne	28	25	24	26	29	–	26	27	24	24	25	25	26	–	–
Sauternes	21	28	29	25	27	–	21	23	26	24	24	24	28	25	26
Germany	25	–	25	26	27	25	24	27	24	23	25	24	29	27	–
California (Napa, Sonoma, Mendocino):															
Chardonnay	–	–	–	–	–	–	–	24	26	25	25	24	27	29	–
Sauvignon Blanc/Semillon	–	–	–	–	–	–	–	–	–	25	25	23	27	28	26
REDS															
French:															
Bordeaux	24	25	24	26	29	22	26	25	23	25	24	28	26	23	24
Burgundy	23	–	21	24	26	–	26	28	25	22	28	22	24	27	–
Rhône	25	19	27	29	29	24	25	23	24	28	27	27	26	–	25
Beaujolais	–	–	–	–	–	–	–	–	–	–	23	24	–	25	28
California (Napa, Sonoma, Mendocino):															
Cab./Merlot	27	26	–	21	28	29	27	25	28	23	26	23	27	25	–
Pinot Noir	–	–	–	–	–	–	–	–	24	24	25	24	26	29	–
Zinfandel	–	–	–	–	–	–	–	–	–	–	–	–	26	26	–
Italian:															
Tuscany	–	–	–	–	25	22	25	20	29	24	28	26	25	–	–
Piedmont	–	–	–	27	28	–	23	27	27	25	25	28	23	–	–

subscribe to zagat.com